THE LAW OF
INTERNATIONAL
TRADE

AUSTRALIA
Law Book Co.
Sydney

CANADA AND USA
Carswell
Toronto

HONG KONG
Sweet & Maxwell Asia

NEW ZEALAND
Brookers
Wellington

SINGAPORE AND MALAYSIA
Sweet & Maxwell Asia
Singapore and Kuala Lumpur

THE LAW
OF
INTERNATIONAL
TRADE

SECOND EDITION

By

HANS van HOUTTE, FCIArb.

**Professor of Law at the University
of Leuven, Belgium
Avocat**

LONDON
Sweet & Maxwell
2002

Published in 2002 by
Sweet & Maxwell Limited of
100 Avenue Road London NW3 3PF
http://www/sweetandmaxwell.co.uk
Typeset by Interactive Sciences Ltd,
Gloucester
Printed in Great Britain
by MPG Books Ltd, Bodmin, Cornwall

A CIP catalogue record for this book
is available from the British Library.

ISBN (hardback) 0421 764 805

First published 1995
Second edition 2002

No natural forests were destroyed to make this product,
only farmed timber was used and re-planted.

ISBN 0-421-76480-5

9 780421 764804

To my wife Vera, also my companion in the law
To Anne who studied the law
To Thomas who found the law
To Jan, who still thinks law is not important

PREFACE

Writing a handbook on international trade law is a bold undertaking: the subjects to be explored are immense and extremely varied; many areas have not yet been examined in depth. Moreover the legal landscape changes quickly and new phenomena have to be mapped constantly.

The international trade scene has changed substantially since the first edition of this book was published in 1995. The start of the WTO, the privatisation of state-run economies, a host of new instruments and conventions, the introduction of new actors on the international scene, all illustrate how much has changed in the last six years.

Precisely because of the complexity of the subject-matter and the need for updated information a comprehensive handbook on international trade law may be most useful for practitioners and students, lawyers and non-lawyers.

Unlike other handbooks on international trade, this handbook does not approach trade from a national (*e.g.* English or American) perspective but tries to reflect a more transnational view—with, this has to be admitted, some emphasis on the European markets. Moreover, it covers business transactions as well as trade regulations, and considers private law as well as conflict of laws and international public law.

Compared to the previous edition, the present edition is not only an update, but also reflects a change in my appraisal of different phenomena: some issues considered important six years ago receive less attention; others receive more focus than in the previous edition. The reader who wants to explore matters in more depth can find references for further reading and research in the footnotes. However, in tune with the times, many references to websites will allow the reader without an extensive library at his disposal to discover, as a present day Alibaba in the internet grotto, a treasure of conventions, decisions, resolutions and reports on international trade.

I would like to thank the team of the Institute of International Trade Law, who helped me with this second edition. Dr Melaku Geboye Desta, Karen Vandekerckhove, Dr Marta Pertegas Sender and Thalia Kruger updated respectively Chapters 3, 5, 6 and 10. Thalia Kruger, Jos Decoker, Johan Verlinden and the LL.M. graduates Teresa Basile, Luis Moscoso del Prado and Geoffrey Deasy helped with the final editing. My Secretary, Viviane Verbist, took care of the logistics. Special thanks also to Dr Christian Vincke, Director of the Belgian Office National du Ducroire, for the insight he gave me into the world of export insurance and financing.

Finally I wish to thank students, parties in arbitrations, fellow-arbitrators and colleagues from the academic world for all that I am learning from them. Remarks and suggestions for a next edition are most welcome. I was grateful for

the suggestions on the first edition I received from different parts of the world
and I hope to have the same interaction with this second edition.

Hans van Houtte
Institute for International Trade Law
Tiensestraat 41, 3000 Leuven, Belgium
e-mail: hans.vanhoutte@law.kuleuven.ac.be

CONTENTS

CHAPTER 1
COMPONENTS OF THE LAW OF INTERNATIONAL TRADE

CHAPTER 2
THE ROLE OF STATES AND INTERNATIONAL
ORGANISATIONS IN INTERNATIONAL TRADE

CHAPTER 3
THE REGULATION OF INTERNATIONAL TRADE

CHAPTER 4
INTERNATIONAL SALES

CHAPTER 5
DISTRIBUTION AGREEMENTS

CHAPTER 6
INTERNATIONAL TRANSFER OF TECHNOLOGY

CHAPTER 7
FOREIGN INVESTMENT

CHAPTER 8
FINANCE OF INTERNATIONAL TRADE

CHAPTER 9
INTERNATIONAL PAYMENT

CHAPTER 10
INTERNATIONAL PROCEDURE

CHAPTER 11
INTERNATIONAL COMMERCIAL ARBITRATION

TABLE OF CASES

ALPHABETICAL LIST OF CASES BEFORE THE EUROPEAN COURT OF JUSTICE AND OF FIRST INSTANCE

xvii

EUROPEAN COURT OF JUSTICE (CHRONOLOGICAL ORDER)

E.C. COMMISSION DECISIONS

NATIONAL CASES

INTERNATIONAL COURT OF JUSTICE

TABLE OF LEGISLATION

E.C. REGULATIONS

E.C. DIRECTIVES

E.C. COUNCIL DECISIONS

NATIONAL AND INTERNATIONAL LEGISLATION

TABLE OF INTERNATIONAL AND EUROPEAN CONVENTIONS, TREATIES AND OTHER FORMULATIONS OF INTERNATIONAL TRADE LAW

TABLE OF ABBREVIATIONS

A.C.	Arrêts de la Cour de Cassation
AcP	Archiv für die civilistiche Praxis
AFDI	Annuaire Français de Droit International
Arb.Int.	Arbitration International
AIDI	Annuaire de l'Institut de Droit International
A.J.I.C.L.	African Journal of International and Comparative Law
Am.J.Comp.L.	American Journal of Comparative Law
Am.J.Int'l.L.	American Journal of International Law
AmRIA	The American Review of International Arbitration
Ann.Dr.Liège	Annales de Droit de Liège
ASDI	Annuaire Suisse de Droit International
AVR	Archiv des Völkerrechts
Banking L.J.	Banking Law Journal
BB	Der Betriebsberater
Bost.I.L.J.	Boston University International Law Journal
Bus.Law.	Business Lawyer
Butt.J.Int'l.Banking & Fin.L.	Butterworths Journal of International Banking and Financial Law
B.Y.I.L.	British Yearbook International Law
Cah.Dr.Eur.	Cahiers de droit européen
C.L.J.	Cambridge Law Journal
C. de D.	Cahiers de droit
C.L.Y.I.B.	Comparative Law Yearbook of International Business
C.M.L.R.	Common Market Law Reports
C.M.L.Rev.	Common Market Law Review
Colum.J.Transnat.L.	Columbia Journal of Transnational Law
Colum.L.Rev.	Columbia Law Review
Cop.	Copyright (Monthly review of the World Intellectual Property Organization)
Cornell.Int'l.L.J.	Cornell International Law Journal
C.Y.I.L.	Canadian Yearbook of International Law
D	Receuil Dalloz Sirey
D.P.C.I.	Droit et Pratique du Commerce International
Dalloz	Dalloz recueil périodique.
Dr.Mar.Fr.	Droit Maritime Français
DukeJCIL	Duke Journal of Comparative and International Law
E.B.L.R.	European Business Law Review
E.C.L.R.	European Competition Law Review
E.C.R.	European Court Reports
EIDer	El Derecho
E.I.P.R.	European Intellectual Property Review
E.J.I.L.	European Journal of International Law
E.L.Rev.	European Law Review
ELSA L.R.	Elsa Law Review
Env.Pol. & L.	Environmental Policy and Law
E.T.S.	European Treaty Series
EuZW	Europäische Zeitschrif für Wirtschaftsrecht
EwiR	Entscheidungen zum Wirtschaftsrecht

Fed.Supp.	Federal Supplement
Fordham.Int'l.L.J.	Fordham International Law Journal
Geo.Wash.J.Int'l.L. & Econ.	George Washington Journal of International Law and Economics
GP	Gazette du palais
G.Y.I.L.	German Yearbook of International Law
Harv.Int'l.L.J.	Harvard International Law Journal
Harv.L.Rev.	Harvard Law Review
IBLJ	International Business Law Journal
I.C.J.Rep.	International Court of Justice Reports
I.C.L.Q.	International and Comparative Law Quarterly
I.C.L.R.	International Construction Law Review
ICSID Rev.	ICSID Review — Foreign Investment Law Journal
I.F.L.R.	International Financial Law Review
I.I.C.	International Review of Industrial Property and Copyright Law
I.L.M.	International Legal Materials
ILR	International Law Report
Indian J.Int'l.L.	Indian Journal of International Law
IntL	The International Lawyer
Int'l Bus.Law.	International Business Lawyer
Int'l Tax & Bus.Law.	International Tax & Business Lawyer
IPRax	Internationales Privatrecht Praxis
I.R.	Informations Rapides
I.Y.I.L.	Italian Yearbook of International Law
J.Int'l Bus.L.	Journal of International Business Law
J.Int'l Econ.L.	Journal of International and Economic Law
J.Int'l L.S.	Journal of International Legal Study
J.B.L.	Journal of Business Law
JCP	Jurisclasseur Périodique
J.D.I.	Journal de Droit International
J.E.N.R.L.	Journal of Energy and Natural Resources Law
J.I.A.	Journal of International Arbitration
J.I.B.L.	Journal of International Banking Law
J.I.L.	Journal of International Law
J.L.T.	Journal of Law and Technology
J.L.C.	Journal of Law and Commerce
J.T.	Journal des Tribunaux
J.W.T.	Journal of World Trade
JZ	Juristenzeitung
Leiden J.Int'l.L.	Leiden Journal of International Law
LIEI	Legal Issues of European Integration
Ll.L.R.	Lloyds Law Rep.
Ll.Mar.&Com.L.Q.	Lloyd's Maritime and Commercial Law Quarterly
L. & Pol.Int'l.Bus.	Law and Policy in International Business
L.Q.R.	Law Quarterly review
M.B.	Moniteur belge
Med.Ned.Ver.Int.R.	Mededelingen Nederlandse Vereniging Internationaal Recht
MichJIL	Michigan Journal of International Law
Mich.L.Rev.	Michigan Law Review
Min.J.Gl.Tr.	Minnesota Journal of Global Trade
N.I.L.R.	Netherlands International Law Review
N.I.P.R.	Nederlands Internationaal Privaatrecht
N.J.	Nederlandse Jurisprudentie
N.J.B.	Nederlands Juristenblad

N.J.W.	Neue juristische Wochenschrift
NJW-RR	Neue juristische Wochenschrift-Rectsprechungs Report
Nord.J.I.L.	Nordic Journal of International Law
NW.J.Int'l.L. & Bus.	Northwestern Journal of International Law & Business
N.Y.I.L.	Netherlands Yearbook of International Law
N.Y.U. J.Int'l.L. & Pol.	New York University Journal of International Law and Policy
O.J.	Official Journal
P.	Pasicrisie
Pace Int'l L.Rev.	Pace International Law Review
Pat.World	Patent World
P.C.I.J.	Permanent Court of International Justice
P.P.L.R.	Public Procurement Law Review
RAE	Revue des affaires européennes
RabelsZ	Rabelszeitschrift
R.B.D.C.	Revue belge de droit commercial
R.B.D.I.	Revue belge de droit international
RCDIP	Revue critique de droit international privé
R.C.J.B.	Revue critique de jurisprudence belge
RDAI	Revue de droit des affaires internationales (see also IBLJ)
RDBB	Revue de droit bancaire et de la bourse
R.D.I.D.C.	Revue de droit international et de droit comparé
RDU	Revue de droit uniforme
Rec.Cours	Recueil des Cours
Rev. Arb.	Revue de l'arbitrage
Rev. Banque.	Revue de la banque
Rev. gen. dr. int. pub.	Revue générale de droit international public
Rev. hellénique. dr. int.	Revue hellénique de droit internationale
Rev. Marché. Comm.	Revue du Marché Commun et de l'Union Européenne
R.I.D.C.	Revue internationale de droit comparé
R.I.D.E.	Revue internationale de droit économique
Riv. dir. int. civ. & proc.	Rivista de diritto internazionale privato e processuale
RIW	Recht der Internationalen Wirtschaft
R.P.D.B.	Répertoire pratique de droit belge
RSDIE	Revue suisse de droit international et de droit européen
RTD com.	Revue trimestrielle de droit commercial
RTDE	Revue trimestrielle de droit européen
S.E.W.	Sociaal-Economische Wetgeving
SJ	Semaine Juridique
Stan.J.Int'l.L.	Stanford Journal of International Law
Tex.Int'l.L.J.	Texas International Law Journal
T.P.R.	Tijdschrift voor Privaatrecht
Transn.L.	Transnational Law
Trav.Com.Fr.Dr.Int.Privé	Travaux du Comité français de droit international privé
U.L.Rev.	Uniform Law Review
Univ. Pittsb. L.Rev.	University of Pittsburg Law Review
U.Pa.J.Int'l.Bus.L.	University of Pennsylvania Journal of International Business Law
Va.J.Int'l.L	Virginia Journal of International Law

Vand.J.Transnat.L.	Vanderbilt Journal Transnational Law
Wash.L.Rev.	Washington Law Review
WiB	Wirtschaftsrechtliche Beratung
W.L.R.	Weekly Law Reports
WLY	World Leasing Yearbook
World Comp.	World Competition
World Developm.	World Development
World Ec.	World Economy
Yale J.Int'l.L.	Yale Journal International Law
Yale.L.J.	Yale Law Journal
Y.Com.Arb.	Yearbook of Commercial Arbitration
YEL	Yearbook of European Law
Y.I.T.L.	Yearbook of international trade law
ZaöRV	Zeitschrift für ausländisches öffentliches Recht und Völkerrecht
ZeuP	Zeitschrift für euröpaisches Privatrecht
ZfRV	Zeitschrift für Rechtsvergleichung Internationales Privatrecht und Europarecht
ZRV	Zeitschrift für Rechtsvergleichung
ZHW	Zeitschrift für das gesamte Handelsrecht und Wirtschaftsrecht
ZVgIRWiss.	Zeitschrift für vergleichende Rechtswissenschaft

CHAPTER 1

COMPONENTS OF THE LAW OF INTERNATIONAL TRADE

Overview   The law of international trade draws from both international law   **1.01**
as well as from the domestic law of the states concerned.[1]
General international law governs the relationship between states and international organisations. Treaties (bilateral or multilateral) concluded between states are, however, sources of a substantial part of the law of international trade. Moreover, other sources of general international law, like resolutions of international organisations and international custom, also shape the law of international trade. Furthermore, the domestic laws of the states concerned also affect international trade. Consequently the law of international trade is partly international law, partly national law.

Within the parameters of this textbook only the aspects of international law (Part I) and national law (Part II), which are most relevant to international trade, can be highlighted. The growing role of *lex mercatoria* as an independent source of the law of international trade will be taken up in Part III of this chapter.

PART I: INTERNATIONAL LAW

Treaties

Categories

Bilateral and multilateral treaties   Bilateral and multilateral treaties play an   **1.02**
important part in international trade law. The objectives pursued, and the subject matters covered, are wide and varied. A treaty is bilateral when it is in force between only two subjects of international law (states or international organisations). A treaty is multilateral when it is in force between more than two parties—some are in fact binding on a large number of states. Sometimes a state can make a "reservation" in respect of a particular treaty provision when it enters into a multilateral treaty. If this reservation is valid, the treaty provision for which the reservation is made will not apply to that state.

---

[1] See *e.g.* D. Carreau and J. Juillard, *Droit international économiques* (LGDJ, Paris, 1998), pp. 11–16; D. M. McRae, "The contribution of international trade law to the development of international law" (1996) Rec. Cours. 260, p. 99.

Bilateral treaties are concluded, for example, to avoid double taxation. Bilateral friendship treaties ("FNC treaties": friendship, navigation and commerce) involve states granting each advantages in relation to imports and exports, rights of establishment and free movement of services, trade in general and rights of carriage of goods by sea. Bilateral investment treaties ("BIT": see paragraph 7.15) are increasingly negotiated between industrialised nations and developing countries. Some bilateral treaties may frame specific transactions, such as loans from state to state.

Some multilateral treaties regulate trade between the contracting states in a more general way. Many multilateral treaties grant trade regulatory powers to particular international organisations.[2] Other multilateral treaties seek to unify the law in order to facilitate international trade and financing.[3]

1.03   **Subject matter: liberalisation of trade or unification of law**   The purpose of some treaties (for instance, those creating the IMF, the OECD, etc.) is to liberalise trade between the contracting states. Generally their further implementation has to be agreed unanimously by the Member States; majority voting is an exception.

Other treaties are aimed at economic integration by way of a customs union, a free trade zone or an economic union (see paragraph 3.11). Such treaties generally also establish an international organisation to implement the treaty programme.

Another group of treaties aims at unification of law.[4] They introduce common substantive rules for legal relationships between private persons and companies. Many of these treaties are not yet in force, or are at present only applied by a limited number of countries. For that reason, many such treaties achieve only a limited or a regional unification.

Some law unifying treaties only introduce rules for situations with an international dimension (*e.g.* international transport); besides the unified rules for international situations, domestic law continues to apply to internal matters. Some treaties, however, introduce rules for situations that do not necessarily have an international dimension (*e.g.* the treaties introducing uniform laws on bills of exchange and promissory notes, cheques, trade marks, drawings and models).

The provisions of a treaty or uniform law become part of the national law of the contracting states concerned. However, treaties and uniform laws are often interpreted differently in each country. Usually, there is no common forum that can give a consistent interpretation. It is only exceptionally that treaty provisions

---

[2] *e.g.* The United Nations (see paras 2.19–2.27), World Bank (para. 7.03), European Bank for Reconstruction and Development (para. 7.05), OECD (para. 2.32), OPEC (para. 2.70).

[3] *e.g.* concerning intellectual property (see paras 3.98–3.105), bills of exchange (paras 9.27–9.31), international sale (paras 2.23, 4.05). See, *e.g.* I. Cass and R. Kidner, *Statutes and Conventions on International Trade Law* (Cavendish, London, 1999); C. J. Cheng, *Basic Documents on International Trade Law* (Kluwer, The Hague, 1999).

[4] See in the different paths towards uniform law, H. van Houtte, "La modalisation substantielle", in E. Loquin, ed., *La Mondialisation du Droit* (Litec, Paris, 2000), pp. 207–236.

empower certain bodies to give binding and uniform interpretations for all the parties to such treaties. The 1971 Protocol on the interpretation by the Court of Justice of the Brussels Convention on Jurisdiction and Enforcement of Foreign Judgments was a good example thereof.[5] The uniform laws adopted by the Benelux counties on trade marks, on drawings and models and on punitive damages are similarly subject to uniform interpretation by the Benelux Court of Justice on a prejudicial question from a national court of a Benelux Member State.

Some treaties which introduce uniform law (*e.g.* on international carriage of goods by sea) are frequently adapted to developments in international trade. This can lead to confusing situations when some states have not yet adopted all of the changes. For example, there are three different agreements in existence governing carriage of goods by sea: the Hague Rules (1924), the Hague-Visby Rules (1968), and the Hamburg Rules (1978). This is because all parties to the previous agreement did not accept some specific changes introduced by subsequent amendments. While most developed countries which were parties to the 1924 Hague Rules accepted the Visby amendments of 1968, the Hamburg Rules have been accepted predominantly by developing countries.[6] The practitioner always has to verify which states are bound by (the latest version of) a particular treaty.

Direct effect   A treaty binds the contracting states. However, taking into account the wording and the objectives of the treaty, certain treaty provisions may also be self-executing, *i.e.* give rights and duties to private parties *vis-à-vis* a contracting state. The national court must then enforce those treaty obligations.[7] The particular treaty provisions are in this case directly applicable: they have direct effect. Many provisions in the E.C. Treaty have direct effect.[8] Article VIII (2) (b) of the IMF treaty (see paragraph 9.03) also attributes enforceable rights to individuals and is therefore directly applicable.[9] The GATT provisions, on the contrary, are deemed to have no direct effect (see paragraph 3.05).   **1.04**

---

[5] Under this Protocol, the courts of the E.U. Member States could refer a question for a preliminary ruling on the interpretation of the Convention to the European Court of Justice; a judgment of the Court of Justice not only bound the national court that had referred the question, but also served as a guideline for later interpretations. However, as the Brussels Convention has been replaced by a Regulation, the possibility of a preliminary ruling has become part of general E.U. law (see para. 10.02).

[6] See, for a recent list of the respective contracting states, *e.g.* C.J. Cheng, *op.cit.*, 415–458. For practical problems which can arise in such situations, see for example the English judgment in the *Hollandia* case, [1982] 2 W.L.R. 556.

[7] See, *e.g.* T. Buergenthal, "Self-executing and non-self-executing treaties in national and international law" (1992) IV Rec. Cours 303; R. A. Brand, "Direct effect of international economic law in the United States and the European Union" (1996–97) NW.J.Int'l.L. & Bus. 17, pp. 556–608.

[8] See, *inter alia*, P. Kapteyn and P. Verloren van Themaat, *Introduction to the law of the European Communities* (Kluwer, The Hague, 1998), pp. 82–89 ; K. Lenaerts and P. van Nuffel, *Constitutional Law of the European Union* (Sweet and Maxwell, London, 1999).

[9] However, the rights referred to do not apply against a state that does not observe the IMF treaty, but against other individuals within the framework of a contractual relationship. See para. 9.03.

International standards of treatment

1.05 **Description** Treaty provisions often refer to specific standards of treatment, which play an essential role on the international economic regulatory scene.[10] These standards, however, only apply in so far as a treaty imposes them (with the exception of the "minimum standard", which is always applicable even in the absence of treaty provisions (see paragraph 1.06). Unless stated to the contrary in the treaty, the standards are interpreted in a way consistent with general treaty practice and jurisprudence. In general, the following standards are applied.

1.06 **Minimum standard or equitable treatment** The "minimum standard" is the traditional standard of treatment in international law. It is the minimum norm with which all states have to comply.[11] Even if the treatment of its own citizens does not comply with the minimum standard, it must in all events be applied to foreigners.

Somewhat related to the minimum standard is the more recent "standard of equitable treatment", which requires a state to apply its law to all individuals in a fair, reasonable, equitable and adequate manner.[12] Moreover, equitable treatment applies not only to individuals, but also to states (more specifically to developing states), which are entitled to fair and equitable treatment from the other states.[13]

1.07 **National treatment** Other treaty provisions aim at achieving some standard of national treatment.

The standard of national treatment demands that subjects of other contracting state(s) be treated in the same way as nationals. This accords with the prohibition of discrimination on grounds of nationality. Article 12 of the E.U. Treaty is a typical example of this principle.

---

[10] G. Schwarzenberger, "The principles and standards of international economic law" (1966) I Rec. Cours 66; P. Verloren van Themaat, *The Changing Structure of International Economic Law* (Nijhoff, The Hague, 1981) pp. 16–18.

[11] P. Verloren van Themaat, *op. cit.* pp. 16–18. This so-called international standard of civilisation is now expressed in the Universal Declaration of Human Rights (UN, General Assembly, December 10, 1948). See, *e.g.* A. Enders, "The role of the WTO in minimum standards", in P. van Dyck, *Challenges to the New World Trade Organization* (Kluwer Law International, The Hague,1996), pp. 61–75; and P. De Waart, "Minimum Labour standards in international trade from a legal perspective" in ibid, pp. 245–264.

[12] *cf., e.g.* K. Hossain and M. Bulajic, "Legal aspects of the new international economic order" (International Law Association, Report of the 61st conference 1984, Paris), p.125.

[13] The Seoul Declaration of the International Law Association (1986) expresses this as follows:
"Without ensuring the principle of equity there is no true equality of nations and states in the world community consisting of countries of different levels of development. A new international economic order should therefore be developed by the United Nations and international organizations, by treaties and by State practice in conformity with the principle of equity, which means that this development should aim at a just balance between converging and diverging interests and in particular between the interest of developed and developing countries. The principle is also an integral element in the interpretation of the law by international courts or arbitration tribunals and may be applied by them to supplement the law", (1986) N.I.L.R. 326. Although the principle of formal equality is generally recognized in international law, it is difficult to enforce: see O. Chinn, P.C.I.J., Ser. A/B, No. 63, 87 (December 12, 1934).

However, the national treatment is not allowed to fall below the minimum standard.[14] If this should be the case, the minimum standard (see paragraph 7.23) will apply to foreigners, conferring a better standard of treatment than that applying to nationals.[15]

Most favoured nation ("MFN") clause   Under the standard of most **1.08** favoured nation treatment, any advantages or favours a country grants to another country, or to the subjects, products or services of any other country have also to be granted to other states or to subjects, like products and like services of all the other parties who enjoy MFN status.[16]

The actual impact of the MFN clause upon its beneficiaries is determined by the advantages granted to third parties. The MFN clause is thus a catalyst that extents benefits granted to some states, subjects, products or services to all the beneficiaries of the MFN clause. It thus introduces a certain degree of equal treatment in international economic relations. The operation of the MFN clause, adds to the specific content of treaties whatever has to be added from other treaties.

The MFN clause is usually:

- reciprocal (both parties promise each other most favoured status);

- unconditional (the other contracting state is by right entitled to the same preferences as are granted to a third state).

This clause is found in many bilateral treaties.[17] It can also be found in multi-lateral treaties, for instance, under the GATT and the GATS, the most favoured nation clause operates on a multilateral basis to liberalise international trade (see paragraph 3.11); in the draft Multilateral Agreement in Investments (MAI), an MFN clause multilateralised bilateral investment treaties (see paragraph 7.15).

Preferential treatment   The possibility of preferential treatment forms an **1.09** exception to the most favoured nation standard. It means that more preferences are granted to another contracting state (or its subjects) than to third states (or

---

[14] I. Seidl-Hohenveldern, *International Economic Law* (Nijhaff, Dordrecht, 1992) *op. cit.* p. 135.

[15] Art. 2 of the Paris Convention on the International Protection of Intellectual Property Rights (1883) formulates, besides the principle of national treatment, a similar minimum standard: "Nationals of any country to the Union shall, as regards the protection of industrial property, enjoy in all the other countries of the Union the advantages that their respective laws now grant, or may hereafter grant, to nationals; all without prejudice to the rights specially provided for by this Convention."

[16] See the definition of the International Law Commission: (1978) I.L.M. 1518; *cf.* also E. Sauvignon, *La clause de la nation la plus favorisée* (Presses Universetaires de Grenoble, 1972); P. Pescatore "La clause de la nation la plus favorisée dans les conventions multilaterales" (Institut de droit international 1969, Annuaire) 53, I; D. Vignes, "La clause de la nation la plus favorisée et sa pratique contemporaine" (1970) II Rec. Cours 207; S. Kramer, "Die Meistbegünstigung" (1989) R.I.W. 473.

[17] *e.g.* in recent bilateral investment treaties (see para. 7.15); C.G. Buys, "United States economic sanctions: the fairness of targeting persons from third countries" (1999) Bost.I.L.J. 17 No. 2, pp. 241–267.

their subjects). Preferential treatment usually applies between states, which are closely linked politically or economically.

The standard of preferential treatment is at present applied to trade agreements with developing countries (see paragraph 2.46) and within customs unions or free trade areas (paragraph 3.11). The GATT allows for the possibility of granting such preferential treatment.[18]

Preferential treatment is also adopted in some areas of national legislation, for example where particular geographic zones are allocated more favourable economic and fiscal regimes for foreign enterprises, in order to attract foreign investment.[19]

Customary law

1.10 **Description** International customary law is created when a general practice, followed by a number of states (state practice), has been accepted as law *(opinio iuris)*. The right of a state to issue its own currency rules, and its obligation to punish counterfeiters of foreign currency, are for instance, based upon international customary law.[20]

However, it is not always easy to assess whether a rule of customary international economic law exists and what its specific content is.[21] For instance, what is the international custom with regard to evaluating the amount of compensation to be paid in the event of nationalisation of certain assets?[22] Opinion on this matter differs considerably between states.[23] Moreover, many states, having declared that damages may only be paid in exceptional circumstances, agree in bilateral investment treaties (see paragraph 7.15) to pay at all times a reasonable level of compensation. Such clauses appear so regularly in investment treaties that it may be argued that these treaty provisions in themselves create a rule of international customary law for reasonable damages.[24]

To take another example, there is an international custom that a state should not to sit in judgment of a foreign state, and should not enforce a judgment against this foreign state (see paragraphs 2.06–2.07). However, how far this immunity extends, and what exceptions are permitted, differs from state to state.

---

[18] M. Broszkamp, *Meistbegünstigung und Gegenseitigkeit in GATT* (Carl Heymans, Cologne, 1990).

[19] For the statute of the "free zones", see para. 3.11.

[20] S. Zamora, "Is there customary international economic law?" (1989) 32 G.Y.I.L. 28–30.

[21] S. Zamora, *op. cit.*, 34–42.

[22] See, *e.g.* Arbitrator J. Dupuy in *Texaco Overseas Petroleum Co. v. Libyan Arab Republic* (1978) I.L.M. 21:" The Right of a State to nationalize is unquestionable today. It results from international customary law, established as the result of general practices considered by the international community as being law."

[23] See para. 1.35.

[24] See R. Dolzer, "New foundations of the law of expropriation of alien property" (1981) Am. J. Int'l. L., p. 566; D. Verwey and N.J. Schrijver, "The taking of foreign property under international law"(1984) N.Y.I.L., pp. 60–75.

Other sources

Resolutions of international organisations

Binding resolutions Most resolutions passed by international organisations **1.11** are not binding on their Member States.[25] In exceptional cases, however, they may have this binding character.[26]

For example, the resolutions adopted by an organisation for its internal operation (*e.g.* concerning the structure of activities, procedure of decision-making, admission of members) are always binding. The charter of an organisation may also determine that the members (and possibly their subjects) are bound by other resolutions.

Member States may also be obliged by treaty to give effect to the resolutions of the organisation. Even the so-called "Resolutions" and "Recommendations" of organisations such as, for example, the ILO or the FAO (see paragraph 2.27), are in fact binding on the Member States who must give effect to these resolutions and recommendations in their national legislation.[27] Sometimes regulations issued by international organisations may be binding on those members who did not make any reservation against them. Even non-members are, in exceptional circumstances, bound by the resolutions of an organisation. This is the case, for instance, with resolutions of organisations (*e.g.* The Rhine Commission, the International Civil Aviation Organisation) that have authority over a geographic area (*e.g.* a river, or air space). Everyone within that area has to abide by the rules of the competent authority.[28]

Some international organisations may adopt a text unanimously (a so-called "accord resolution"), that can be considered as a treaty in a simplified form. The text of such a resolution is then sometimes transposed into a treaty afterwards and presented to the Member States for signature.[29]

After these general principles, two specific illustrations: the binding force of the resolutions of the E.U. and of the UN Security Council.

The E.U. Member States are bound by the Decisions, Regulations and Directives of the E.U. Regulations are also binding for private parties; Decisions are binding on the private parties to which they are expressly addressed.[30]

Resolutions of the UN General Assembly are not binding; they only can become a starting point for the development of an international custom (see paragraph 1.10) or of "soft law" (see paragraph 1.13). Resolutions of the Security Council are similarly not binding,[31] unless they are taken in the framework of Chapter VII of the UN Charter (actions with respect to threats to peace, breaches of peace and acts of aggression) and indicate by their terminology that

---

[25] See, *inter alia*, J. Frowein, "The internal and external effects of resolutions by international organizations" (1989) ZaÖRV, p.778.

[26] See *e.g.* J. Verhoeven, *Droit International Public* (Larcier, Brussels, 2000), pp. 355–363.

[27] See D. Carreau, *Droit International Public* (Pedone, Paris, 1999), para. 612.

[28] See D. Carreau, *op. cit.,* paras 620–626.

[29] See D. Carreau, *op. cit.,* paras 609–611; I. Seidl-Hohenveldern, *International Economic Law* (Nijhoff, Dordrecht, 1989), p. 42.

[30] E.C. Treaty, Art. 249.

[31] J.P. Cot and A. Pellet *et al., La Charte des Nations Unies* (Economica, Paris, 1999), p. 252.

they are binding.[32] In this last hypothesis, all members of the UN are bound by these resolutions of the Security Council: all UN Member States must comply with these resolutions. However, it has been argued that private persons are not bound by those resolutions unless there are implementing measures in the respective states.[33] To make such resolutions binding on citizens, *e.g.* in case of the implementation of economic sanctions, UN members must transpose them into their national laws—as was the case with the boycott resolutions of the Security Council against Iraq in 1990 following that country's invasion of Kuwait.[34]

Resolutions often precede established law. Since they are not binding, they provide an excellent base from which to launch new proposals. Thus their substance is often not a reflection of the present law (*de lege lata*), but a forerunner of future law (*de lege ferenda*). They offer a programme for the creation of new law (the so-called *droit programmatoire*).[35]

1.12   **Contribution to the creation of law**   Resolutions, which are not binding, are nevertheless often important: they are certainly of political significance (since they reflect the opinion of the majority of the members) and moreover, they contribute to the creation of law. Since they are not binding, they provide an excellent base from which to launch new proposals. They offer a programme for the creation of new law (the so-called *droit programmatoire*). Their substance is often not a reflection of the present law (*de lege lata*), but a forerunner of future law (*de lege ferenda*).

Resolutions may thus function as a catalyst for the two components of international customary law: *i.e.* established practice and *opinio iuris*.[36] The resolutions of the UN General Assembly have thus created international rules of law concerning the permanent sovereignty of states over their natural resources (see paragraph 7.29).

Soft law

1.13   **Definition**   It is true that some treaties are phrased in rather vague terms and contain many escape clauses. However, a state nevertheless can be held legally responsible if it fails to perform a treaty obligation, however loose it may be.

States sometimes avoid the mandatory character of treaty obligations through their resort to "soft law", *i.e.* to resolutions, recommendations, gentlemen's agreements, guidelines, codes of conduct. Soft law stands in fact midway

---

[32] UN Charter, Arts 48–49. However, it is not always clear whether a Resolution of the Security Council is a recommendation or a binding decision.

[33] See, *e.g.* High Court of Australia, *Bradley v. Post-Master General* (1974) J.D.I. 865.

[34] B. Campbell, *The Impact of the Freeze of Kuwaiti and Iraqi Assets on Financial Institutions and Financial Transactions* (Graham and Trotman, 1990); E. Lauterpacht (ed.), *The Kuwait Crisis, vol. I: Basic Documents; Vol. II: Sanctions and their economic consequences* (Grotius, Cambridge, 1991).

[35] See D. Carreau, *op. cit.*, pp. 639–642.

[36] See D. Carreau, *op. cit.*, pp. 630–638; I. Seidl-Hohenveldern, *op. cit.*, para. 37–42.

between so-called hard law (*e.g.* treaty, custom) and sheer political engagement.

Certain matters many not yet, for instance, be "ready" to be adopted in a binding treaty text. In that case states may negotiate a "gentlemen's agreement" or recommend a code of conduct. For instance, many states have negotiated gentlemen's agreements for export financing (see paragraph 8.30) or co-operation in the anti-trust area (see paragraph 1.22). They have also adopted many other codes of conduct for themselves and their citizens (see paragraph 3.63).[37]

Nevertheless, soft law has *certain* legal effects.[38] It often provides guidance for the conduct of states and individuals. Furthermore, it functions as a "laboratory test" for a certain idea or behavioural pattern. Soft law can offer the framework or even the draft text for later treaty negotiations, for national legislation.[39]

State contracts

Concepts States, state enterprises and state organisations frequently grant **1.14** exploitation contracts to foreign investors. These contracts (so-called state contracts), which establish the legal basis for the investment, are at least in part subject to international law. The role of international law for state contracts will be further discussed in Chapter 7 (see paragraph 7.09).

Economic sanctions[40]

Outline How international law may affect international trade can be best **1.15** illustrated by the international law on economic sanctions and boycott.

There is no general international obligation for states to trade with each other. However, trade agreements may oblige a state to trade with the contracting states. The E.C. Treaty, the GATT (see paragraph 3.26) and the numerous FNC treaties

---

[37] E. Decaux, "La forme et la force obligatoire des codes de bonnes conduites" (1983) A.F.D.I. 81.

[38] See, *e.g.*, incl. A. Aust, "The theory and practice of informal international instruments" (1986) I.C.L.Q. 787; D. Carreau, *op. cit.,* paras 505–539; C. Chinkin "The challenge of soft law: development and change in international law" (1989) I.C.L.Q. 850; C. Elias, "General principles of laws: soft law and the identification of international law", (1997) N.Y.I.L 28., pp. 3–49; H. Hilgenberg, "A fresh look at soft law" (1999) E.J.I.L., pp. 499–515; J. Klabbers, "The undesirability of soft law", (1999) Nord.J.I.L., pp. 381–391; I. Seidl-Hohenveldern, *op. cit.,* p. 42; M. Virally, *La Distinction entre Textes Internationaux de Portée Juridique et Textes Internationaux Dépourvus de Portée Juridique* (Institut de droit international, Annuaire, 1983) vols 60—1, p. 166 ; K. Zemanek, *Is the term "Soft Law" convenient ? (* Liber Amicorum I. Seidl-Hohenveldern, 1998,The Hague), pp. 843–862; E. Olufemi and C.Lim, "General principles of law, 'Soft' Law and the identification of International Law" (1997) N.Y.I.L. 28, pp. 3–49.

[39] A. Boyle, "Some reflections on the relationship of treaties and soft law" (1999) I.C.L.Q. 48, pp. 901–913.

[40] For an interesting discussion of the motives and effects of sanctions and boycott from a U.S. perspective, see Raj Bhala, "MRS. WATU and international trade sanctions", (Spring 1999) *International Lawyer* 33 (1), at 1–26.

(see paragraph 1.02), for example, prevent contracting states from prohibiting trade with other treaty parties.

Furthermore, international law prohibits so-called "economic aggression", for examples the use of a boycott against a foreign state or government. On the other hand, economic sanctions against a state may be permitted as form of reprisal against an unlawful act of that state. The United Nations Security Council can oblige the UN's Member States to take part in collective economic sanctions against a state that has breached international peace and security; the General Assembly sometimes recommends such sanctions. Legal doctrine deals extensively with the legal implications resulting from international customary law, treaty obligations and UN resolutions in relation to the application of economic sanctions and boycott.[41]

PART II: NATIONAL LAW

1.16   Significance   National law gives substance to the legal relationships between private parties and regulates their behaviour. Traditionally, national law is divided into two branches, public law and private law, both of which are relevant for commercial transactions.

A transnational transaction has, by definition, links with different states. Different legal systems thus may govern the transaction. This part will examine how national law affects transnational commercial transactions.

Public Law

Substance

1.17   Outline   Every state has the authority to regulate economic activity within its territory by means of public law. Public law is important for the economic order. For instance, the state has control over import and export to and from its territory through customs legislation, it has control over its currency through exchange

---

[41] See, *e.g.* J. Delbrück, "International economic sanctions and third states" (1992) A.V.R. 86; A. Giardina, *The Economic sanctions of the United States against Iran and Libya and the GATT security exception (* Liber Amicorum I. Seidl-Hohenveldern, The Hague, 1998), pp. 219–231; K. Hailbronner, "Sanctions and third parties and the concept of public international order" (1992) A.V.R. 2; C. Joyner, "The transnational boycott as economic coercion in international law" (1984) Vand. J. Transnat. L. 205; E. Klein, "Sanctions by international organizations and economic communities"(1992) A.V.R. 101; J. H. Moitry, "L'arbitre international et l'obligation de boycottage imposée par un Etat" (1991) J.D.I. 349; S. Neff, "Boycott and the law of nations: economic warfare and modern international law in historical perspective" (1988) B.Y.I.L. 113; P. Szasz, "The Law of economic sanctions", in M. Schmitt, ed., *The Law of Armed Conflict* (Newport, 1998), pp. 455–481 ; H. van Houtte, "Treaty protection against economic sanctions" (1984–85) R.B.D.I. 34 and the general theme issue on trade sanctions and international relations in (1987) N.Y. U. J. Int'l. L. & Pol., pp. 781 *et seq.*; W. Meng, "Economic sanctions and state jurisdiction: some grey areas under international law" (1997) ZaoRV 57(1), pp. 324–327; R. Paroni, "UN Sanctions in EU and national law: the centro-com case" (1994) I.C.L.Q. U.K. 48, pp. 582–612; S. Karagiannis, "Sanctions internationales et droit communautaire. A propos du règlement 1901/98 sur l'interdiction de vol des transporteurs yougoslaves" (1999) R.T.D.E. 35, pp. 363–394.

rate regulations and it can raise taxes through its fiscal law. Furthermore, the state may regulate specific sectors (*e.g.* banks, insurance companies) or products (*e.g.* shares, medicines). A state may decide to nationalise private enterprises. It may use legislation on patents, copyrights, trade marks and other intellectual property rights to give certain enterprises an exclusive advantage. To maintain fair competition it can introduce competition rules. States ensure the strict observance of their economic legislation through economic criminal law and through criminal courts.

Within the European Union, Community law has to a certain extent replaced national public law for the regulation of trade and the economy.

Extraterritorial application of public law

Territorial application   The state has authority to regulate economic life **1.18** within its own territory. Its public law therefore generally has a territorial application. Thus, Belgian social security law is concerned with employees in Belgium, employed by employers established in Belgium. The U.S. custom duties apply to goods imported into the United States. The E.U. competition rules apply to competition within the E.U. A state should not regulate issues which have an insufficient connection with that state.

Extraterritorial application   Sometimes, states introduce legislation of a **1.19** public law nature intended to regulate behaviour outside their territories.

This extraterritorial application is, for instance, quite common when the particular behaviour, such as unfair trade practices or environmental pollution, is committed abroad but affects the territory of that state. For example, the United States as well as the E.U. apply their antitrust laws to agreements between foreign enterprises as soon as they affect competition in respectively the United States or the E.U.[42]

Moreover, states may introduce extraterritorial legislation for foreign policy objectives. During the Cold War period, the United States thus forbade foreign companies under the control of American citizens or American firms to export technology to the Soviet Union, although it affected companies in Europe and

---

[42] See, *e.g.*: for the USA: *U.S. v. Aluminum Co. of America (Alcoa)* 148 F 2d 416 (2d Cir. 1945); *U.S. v. Imperial Chemical Industries (I.C.I)* 105 F Supp. 215 (SDNY 1952) (British reaction: *British Nylon Spinners Ltd v. I.C.I.* (1953 1 Ch. 19); *U.S. v. Watchmakers of Switzerland Info Center* 133 F Supp. 40 (SDNY 1962); *U.S. v. First National City Bank* 396 F 2d 897 (1968); *Laker v. Sabena*, 731 F 2d 909 (D.C. Cir.1984). For the E.U.: Court of Justice, *Woodpulp* Decision, Cases 89, 104, 116, 118 and 125/85, [1988] E.C.R. 5243. Also more generally: J. Castel, "The extraterritorial effect of antitrust laws" (1983) I. Rec. Cours. 9; K. Meessen, *Völkerrechtliche Grundsätze des internationalen Kartellrechts* (Nomos, Baden-Baden, 1975); R. C. Renland, "Extraterritorial reach of US antitrust laws" (1994) Tex.Int'l L.J. 29, pp. 159–210; M. A. A. Warner, "Restrictive trade practices and the extraterritorial application of U.S. antitrust and trade legislation" (1999) NW.J.Int'l L. & Bus. 19, pp. 330–363; J. Basedow, "Souveraineté territoriale et globalisation des marchés: le demande d'application des lois contre les restrictions de la concurrence" (1997) Rec. Cours. 264, p. 9; L. Idot, "Les conflicts de lois en droit de la concurrence" (1995) J.D.I. Clunet 122, pp. 321–341.

elsewhere in the world.[43] The highly contentious "Cuban Liberty and Democratic Solidarity Act" of 1996—the so-called Helms-Burton Act—is a more recent case in point.[44]

Finally, states may also regulate behaviour in a territory that is beyond the jurisdiction of any state. National regulations governing the deep seabed mining activities by their own nationals or companies on the high seas are a good example here.[45]

The extraterritorial application of legislation is a very delicate problem for international trade and has been covered extensively. Companies must be aware that they may be subject to foreign public law rules.[46]

1.20　**International law and extraterritoriality**　As early as 1927, in the *Lotus* case, the Permanent Court of International Justice decided that a state can declare

---

[43] The regulation applied to exports of goods produced by foreign subsidiaries of U.S. companies as well as exports by foreign firms that incorporated specific U.S. goods or that were made under licensing arrangements with U.S. companies. The U.S. measures were condemned by, *inter alia*, the E.C. as "unacceptable under international law because of their extraterritorial nature". See E.C., "Comments on the U.S. regulations concerning trade with the U.S.S.R.," reproduced in I.L.M. 891 (1982) and 855, 864 and 891, and I.L.M (1983), 353, Act of July 27, 1969, Art. 3.

[44] The Cuban Liberty and Democratic Solidarity Act, Pub. L. No. 104–114, 110 Stat. 785 (1996), hereafter the Helms-Burton Act. The Act aroused strong hostile reactions from all over the world. The E.U. in particular took two important measures in this regard. First, it brought an action under the dispute settlement rules of the WTO alleging, *inter alia*, that "U.S. restrictions on goods of Cuban origin as well as the possible refusal of visas and the exclusion of non-U.S. nationals from the U.S. territory are inconsistent with the U.S. obligations under the WTO Agreement." A Panel was established on November 20, 1996, but the case was suspended at the request of the E.C. made on April 22, 1997 and remained so until its expiry a year later. However, an understanding between the parties was reached on May 18, 1998. Secondly, the E.U. enacted a Regulation "protecting the effects of the extra-territorial application of legislation adopted by a third country, and actions based thereon or resulting therefrom" (Council Regulation 2271/96, [1996] O.J. L309/1) As stated under Art. 1, the regulation provides protection against and counteracts the effects of the extra-territorial application of the Helms-Burton law. For an interesting discussion of the Helms-Burton Act from an international law perspective, see R. Muse, "A public international law critique of extraterritorial jurisdiction of the Helms-Burton Act (Cuban Liberty and Solidarity (LIBERTAD)) Act of 1996"(1996–97) Geo.Wash. J.Int'l. L. & Econ. 30, at 207–270; M. Gebauer, "Kollisonsrechtliche Auswirkungen der U.S.– amerikanischen Helms-Burton Gesetzgebung" (1998) I.P.Rax No. 3, pp. 145–155; J. van den Brink, " Helms-Burton: extending the limits of US jurisdiction" (1997) N.I.L.R. XLIV, pp. 131–148; J. Anderson, "US Economic sanctions on Cuba, Iran & Libya: Helms-Burton and the Iran and Libya Sanctions Act" (1996) I.B.L.J., p. 1007; H. Lesguillons, "Helms-Burton and D'Amato Acts: Reactions of the European Union" (1997) I.B.L.J., pp. 95–111.

[45] See, *e.g.* (1980) I.L.M. 1003; (1981) I.L.M. 1228 and (1982) I.L.M. 867 (in respect of U.S.); (1981) I.L.M. 1218 (in respect of the U.K.); (1981) I.L.M. 393 and (1982) I.L.M. 832 (in respect of Germany); (1983) I.L.M. 102 (in respect of Japan); (1982) I.L.M. 551 (in respect of the U.S.S.R.); G. Jaenicke, "Joint ventures for deep seabed mining operations" (1995), ZaoRV 55, pp. 329–347.

[46] See, *inter alia*, M. Bazex *et al.*, *L'application extraterritoriale du droit économique* (Montchristian, Paris, 1986); J. Jacquet "La norme juridique extraterritoriale dans le commerce international" (1985) J.D.I. 327; J. Kaffanke, *Nationales Wirtschaftsrecht und internationale Wirtschaftsordnung* (Nomos, Baden-Baden, 1990); A.V. Lowe, *Extraterritorial Jurisdiction* (Grotius, Cambridge, 1983); P. Mavroidis, *Some reflexions on extraterritoriality in international economic law* (Mélanges M. Waelbroeck, Brussels, 1999), pp. 1297–1325 ; E.J. Mestmaecker, "Staatliche Souveranität und offene Märkte, Konflikte bei der extraterritorialen Anwendung von Wirtschaftsrecht" (1988) RabelsZ 205; A. Neale and M. Stephens, *International Business and National Jurisdiction* (Clarendon, Oxford, 1988) and the critical analysis hereof by J. Westbrook, "Extraterritoriality, conflict of laws and the regulation of transnational business" (1990) 25 *Texas International Law Journal* 71; F. Rigaux, "Droit économique et conflits de souveraConetés (1988) RabelsZ 104.

its laws applicable outside its own territory and exercise jurisdiction over actions, committed beyond its borders, as long as this is not prohibited by international law.[47]

It is not quite clear what limitations international law imposes. Often principles such as comity, co-operation between states, reasonableness or reciprocity are invoked to delimit the extraterritorial powers of a state. However, it remains difficult to extract clear (let alone generally accepted) criteria.[48]

Extraterritorial jurisdiction is often justified by the existence of some connection, which may generally be classified under one of the following four theories: the theory of active personality, the theory of passive personality, the protective theory, and the effects theory.

According to the theory of active personality, a state exercises jurisdiction on its nationals (whether natural persons or juridical entities) wherever they might be in the world. Nationality is for instance taken as a sufficient link for U.S. tax law to be enforced on American citizens residing outside the United States.

The theory of passive personality, on the other hand, may be invoked by a state to exercise its jurisdiction in respect of actions, which cause damage to its nationals outside its territory. The element of nationality is thus an important connecting factor for these two theories.

The protective theory allows a state to exercise its jurisdiction in respect of actions which take place outside its territory but which may threaten its security or political integrity.

Finally, the effects theory, which is very much akin to the protective theory, argues that a state may regulate actions outside its territory in so far as these actions have a "direct, foreseeable, and substantial effect" within its territory. As a result, the effects theory is often invoked as the basis for extraterritorial legislative jurisdiction on matters such as competition and environmental pollution.[49]

In any event, extraterritorial legislation can only be justified for as long as it does not conflict unreasonably with the interests of other states (principle of proportionality).[50]

---

[47] *The Lotus* (1927), P.C.I.J. ser. A No. 10. In this case the Turkish court was allowed to apply Turkish criminal law to the French helmsman of the French ship, the *Lotus*, which had collided with a Turkish ship on the high seas.

[48] See C. Engel, "Die Bedeutung des Völkerrechts für die Anwendung in– und ausländischen Wirtschaftsrecht" (1988) RabelsZ 271; J. Basedow, "Conflicts of economic regulation" (1994) A.J.I.C.L. 42, pp. 423–447.

[49] In its "Comments on the 1982 U.S. Regulations Concerning Trade with the U.S.S.R.", the E.C. characterised the territoriality and nationality (active and passive personality) principles as "generally accepted bases of jurisdiction in international law, while the protective and effects theories were termed possible bases of jurisdiction which have found "less than general acceptance under international law".

[50] The Restatement of the Foreign Relations Law of the United States (American Law Institute, 1987) restricts the possibility of extraterritorial legislation as follows:
"[s.] 402. Bases of Jurisdiction to Prescribe.
Subject to [s.] 403, a state may, under international law, exercise jurisdiction to prescribe and apply its law with respect to
  (1) (a) conduct a substantial part of which takes place within its territory;
        (b) the status of persons, or interests in things, present within its territory;
        (c) conduct outside its territory which has or is intended to have substantial effect within its territory;

Relevance of foreign public law

1.21   Application   A state shall not, in principle, apply the public law rules of another state, since states conventionally refuse to act as the "policeman" for foreign powers. Courts will not therefore generally entertain claims that are directly based on the public law of another state. However, a court may, if necessary, apply foreign public law when these legal rules are not so much an expression of the sovereign, regulating authority of the foreign state. Thus, a court may, for instance, award compensation to a foreign state on the basis of the latter's own public law on administrative contracts.

A foreign public law rule may also have an effect on a private law relationship. For instance, a foreign export prohibition may make the negotiated delivery of advanced technology impossible. A foreign competition authority may block a merger between two companies, etc. In such circumstances a judge may, when considering a breach of contract, take the foreign public law prohibition into account (see paragraph 1.26).[51]

1.22   Concurrence   It is not excluded that the public law of more than one state is applicable to one and the same situation. After all, public law rules define their

---

(2) the conduct, status, interest or relations of its nationals outside its territory; or
(3) certain conduct outside its territory by persons not its nationals which is directed against the security of the state or certain state interests.
[s.] 403. Limitations on Jurisdiction to Prescribe
(1) Although one of the bases for jurisdiction under [s.] 402 is present, a state may not apply law to the conduct, relations, status, or interests of persons or things having connections with another state or states when the exercise of such jurisdiction is unreasonable.
(2) Whether the exercise of jurisdiction is unreasonable is judged by evaluating all the relevant factors, including:
(a) the extent to which the activity (i) takes place within the regulating state, or (ii) has substantial direct, and foreseeable effect upon or in the regulating state;
(b) the links, such as nationality, residence, or economic activity, between the regulating state and the persons principally responsible for the activity to be regulated or between that state and those whom the law or the regulation is designed to protect;
(c) the character of the activity to be regulated, the importance of regulation to the regulating state, the extent to which other states regulate such activities, and the degree to which the desirability of such regulation is generally accepted;
(d) the existence of justified expectations that might be protected or hurt by the regulation in question;
(e) the importance of regulation to the international political, legal, or economic system;
(f) the extent to which such regulation is consistent with the traditions of the international system;
(g) the extent to which another state may have an interest in regulating the activity;
(h) the likelihood of conflict with regulation by other states.
(3) An exercise of jurisdiction which is not unreasonable according to the criteria indicated in Subsection (2) may nevertheless be unreasonable if it requires a person to take action that would violate a regulation of another state which is not unreasonable under those criteria. Preference between conflicting exercises of jurisdiction is determined by evaluating the respective interests of the regulating states in light of factors listed in Subsection (2).
(4) . . . "
[51] See P.B. Carter, "Transnational recognition and enforcement of foreign public laws" (1989) C.L.J. 417; H.W. Baade, "Operation of foreign public law" in *International Encyclopaedia of Comparative law*, Part III, Chapter 12 (Mohr, Tubingen, 1991); F.A. Mann, "Conflict of Laws and public law" (1971) I Rec. Cours, pp. 166–170; F. Rigaux, *Droit public et droit privé dans les relations internationales* (Pedone, Paris, 1977), pp. 171–173.

own scope of application. As states independently and without consultation decide the scope of application of their public law it often happens that the public law rules of two states are applicable to the same facts. Sometimes the rules complement each other: for example, an agreement can be covered by American competition law as well as by E.U. competition law and can be sanctioned in both territories. (For instance, IBM has had trouble with both the American and the E.U. competition authorities.) However, it may also occur that states have opposing regulations, which can create difficulties for a private company when it cannot possibly observe both regulations at the same time. The American authorities may, for example, require that a British company co-operate with an anti-trust prosecution in the United States, whereas English law prohibits British nationals to giving effect to such demands from a foreign state.[52]

At present, states attempt to bring the scope of application of their respective public law into line. To this end, tax treaties, modelled after the 1977 OECD Model Double Taxation Convention, for instance prevent an internationally operating company or person from suffering double taxation. Other examples are bilateral and multilateral treaties to harmonise social security systems.[53] In the area of anti trust law there are only a few arrangements to bring the scope of respective competition laws into line.[54] With regard to criminal law, states usually only have their own rules to avoid double convictions for the same crime.

Private law

Outline   Private law is crucial for a commercial transactions. Contract law, **1.23** for instance, is part of private law and determines whether there is a contract in existence, what the rights and obligations of the parties to the contract are and to what extent the parties are liable when the contract is not performed. Company law, which is also part of private law, lays down how a company is established, how it functions, how it is dissolved, etc.

---

[52] See, *e.g.*, *British Airways v. Laker Airways* [1985] A.C. 58, HL; *Midland Bank v. Laker Airways*, [1986] Q.B. 689, CA. See also J. Morris (ed.), Dicey and Morris, *Conflict of Laws*, Part I, (Sweet & Maxwell, London, 1993), p. 441; Canada: "Foreign extraterritorial measures act incorporating the amendments countering the U.S. Helms-Burton Act." (1997) I.L.M. 34, p. 111; European Union: "Council Regulation 2271/96, Protecting against the effects of the extra-territorial application of legislation adopted by a third Country." (1997) I.L.M. 34, p.125.

[53] See, *e.g.* B. Von Maydell, "Der Multilaterale Effect von Sozialversicherungsabkommen" (1983) I.P.Rax. 156.

[54] See, *inter alia*, the Agreement between the European Communities and the Government of Canada regarding the application of competition law, [1999] O.J.L. 175; moreover, the Agreement between the European Communities and the USA regarding the application of competition law, in [1995] O.J. L95/47 and [1995] O.J. L131/38; furthermore, the Agreement between the European Communities and the USA on the application of positive comity principles in the enforcement of their competition laws, in [1998] O.J. L173; A. Mattoo and A. Subramanian, "Multilateral rules on competition policy—a possible way forward" (1997) J.W.T. 31(5), pp. 95–115; F. Romano, "First assessment of the agreement between the European Union and the USA concerning the application of their competition rules" (1997) I.B.L.J., pp. 491–501; United States: "International antitrust enforcement assistance Act of 1994" (1995) I.L.M.34, p. 494; Canada-U.S.: "Agreement regarding the application of their competition and deceptive marketing practices laws" (1996) I.L.M.35, p. 309.

By definition, different states are involved in a transnational commercial relationship. Thus, the private law of various legal systems may have to be considered when dealing with transnational legal issues. However, private law differs from country to country. The selection of the applicable legal system is the subject of "private international law" (or "conflicts of laws", as it is also sometimes called).

States sometimes adopt uniform substantive law in respect of some issues. In that case it is less important whether the law of one or the other of those states is applicable, since their respective national laws then contain the same uniform rules for the same issue. We will look at private international law and uniform substantive law respectively.

Private international law

Method

1.24 **Conflict of law rules** Private international law seeks to "localise" a legal relationship, which touches upon more than one state within a specific national legal order. The law of this legal system will then be declared applicable to the case. Private international law chooses the applicable law by applying conflict of law rules. Each legal system has developed its own international private law. In spite of frequent similarities, there are sometimes substantial differences between the different systems.

First, it is important to know how a specific legal issue is to be classified in order to be brought under one or another category. Take for instance the conflict of law rule for corporations. This conflict of law rule concerns a specific category of legal issues: it only applies to questions concerning a company. Is the validity of the memorandum and articles of association of a company, however, "a question concerning a company", or "a question concerning a contract'? Each of these categories has their own conflict of law rule. In short, the legal issue must be characterised and assigned to a particular category. The classification into categories may be different from system to system.

Each category has a connecting factor (in exceptional situations, more than one). The connecting factor indicates in abstract terms the country, and consequently the law of that country, with which the legal issue has the closest connection.

Every country draws up its own conflict of law rules. Although these rules to a large extent run parallel from country to country, there may be differences. Within Europe, for instance, in some countries issues of company law are governed by the law of the country where that company has its seat ; in other countries by the law where the company is registered (see paragraph 1.28). Private international law is therefore not "international" and uniform in the same way as international law is international. The designation "international" only points to the fact that private international law is intended for legal relations involving more than one country.

16

Differences in national private international law and thus also in the choice of the applicable substantive law are hampering international trade. For many years the countries have worked towards the establishment of common conflict of law rules in treaties. Examples are the Convention of Rome of June 19, 1980 on the law applicable to contractual obligations (see paragraph 1.29), the Geneva Convention of June 7, 1930 on the regulation of certain legal conflicts concerning bills of exchange and promissory notes (see paragraph 9.28) and the Geneva Convention of March 19, 1931 on the regulation of certain conflicts of law concerning cheques. Many other treaties, which introduce substantive law for a specific legal issue , also sporadically contain conflict of law rules.

Exception of public order   It is conceivable that the foreign law, applicable   **1.25** according to the conflict of law rule, leads to results, which are unacceptable to society and its courts. The application of foreign law may in some situations indeed lead to an infringement of the fundamental principles of the ethical, political or economic order of society. Under these circumstances the exception of public order comes into force and the courts will not apply the foreign law otherwise applicable. When the court has thus decided not to apply the foreign law, it may instead apply its own law, if necessary.

Mandatory law   Some provisions, the so-called "mandatory laws" (*lois de*   **1.26** *police, lois d'application immédiate*), are considered to be of such vital importance to a country that courts of that country always apply them when there is some connection with the forum. Belgian courts, for instance, always apply the Belgian statute on the unilateral termination of an exclusive distributorship agreements when the agreement covers part of Belgian territory (see paragraph 5.07). However, the statute only concerns the termination of the concession. For other contractual disputes the conflict of law rule for contracts remains in force.[55]

Mandatory laws differ from the exception of public order rule in that they impose some substantive law, but do not otherwise prevent the application of the normal conflict of law rules.

It is traditionally accepted that courts may apply relevant rules of their own national laws when they are mandatory irrespective of the law otherwise applicable to the legal issue. Nowadays, it is also more and more being accepted that the court might also apply foreign mandatory laws when the case has a close connection with the foreign country.[56] This means for instance that when a dispute is brought before a non-Belgian court, the Statute of 1961 could be applied as Belgian mandatory law if that court decides that the concession agreement has close connections with Belgium.

---

[55] H. van Houtte, "La concession de vente: loi du contrat ou loi du 27 juillet 1961" (1980) R.B.D.C. 613; see para. 5.13.

[56] K. Anderegg, "Die Anwendung ausländischer Eingriffsnormen" (1988) RabelsZ 260; P. Mayer, "Les lois de police étrangères" (1988) J.D.I. 277; J. Schulsz, "Les lois de police étrangères" (1982–1983) *Comité français de droit international privé* 39; K. Siehr, "Ausländische Eingriffsnormen im inländischen Wirtschaftkollisionsrecht" (1988) Rabelsz 41. See also European Contracts Convention, Art. 7(1) (para. 1.29); Swiss Private International Law Statute, Art. 19.

However, in very exceptional cases a court may be obliged to apply the mandatory laws of another country. For instance, Article VIII(2)(b) of the Charter of the International Monetary Fund determines:

"Exchange contracts which involve the currency of any Member and which are contrary to the exchange regulations of that Member maintained or imposed consistently with this Agreement shall be unenforceable in the territories of any Member." (See paragraph 9.03.)

1.27 **Evasion of the law** The court may refuse to apply foreign law if it appears that the connection with a particular country, brought about by the parties, does not reflect reality. For instance, the memorandum and articles of association of a company may state that its head office is in Switzerland, because the parties want Swiss law to apply even if in reality the company operates exclusively from France. The court may then look at the real connection and apply the law of the real connection.[57]

Applications

1.28 **Companies** There are mainly two alternative connecting factors (see paragraph 1.24) to find the law applicable to issues of company law. These issues can be governed by the law of the principal seat of the company, *i.e.* the place where the most important decisions are taken and from where management operates (*siège réel*); they also can be governed by the law of the country where the company has been incorporated. In Austria, Belgium, France, Germany, Greece, Luxembourg, Portugal and Spain, for instance, the courts use as the connecting factor the principal seat of the company. The Netherlands, the United Kingdom, Ireland, Denmark, Finland, Sweden and Switzerland, on the other hand, have opted for the law of the state of incorporation. In Italy a combination of both connecting factors is in operation.

Legal questions covered by the law applicable to company issues, relate for instance, to:

(a) the incorporation of the company: *i.e.* the basic requirements (*e.g.* minimum capital, number of partners), formal requirements (a deed or a private instrument to create the company), conditions for publicity and sanctions for non-observance of those requirements (*e.g.* dissolution *ex nunc* or *ex tunc*);

(b) the functioning of the company: for instance, rights and duties of the shareholders, representation of the company;

(c) the dissolution of the company (*e.g.* grounds for and manner of dissolution).

---

[57] See, *inter alia*, B. Audit, *La fraude à la loi en droit international privé* (Dalloz, Paris, 1974).

Rome Convention on the Law Applicable to Contractual Obliga- **1.29**
tions State courts within the E.U. apply the Rome Convention on the Law
Applicable to Contractual Obligations (European Contracts Convention) to find
which law they have to apply to a contractual issue.[58]

The main principle is that of party autonomy, i.e. that the parties are free to
choose the law that will apply to their contract (Article 3). Their choice may be
express or implied. They can, for instance, include in the contract a clause that
clearly stipulates: "This agreement is subject to [Belgian] law." It is also
conceivable that the court deduces from terms of the contract or from the
circumstances of the case that there is an implied choice for a particular legal
system. Thus, it may infer the choice for a particular law from the stipulation that
declares a particular national court competent, from a clause for arbitration in a
particular country, from the use of standard contracts which are used in a
particular legal system (*e.g.* a Lloyd's insurance policy), from the reference to
sections of the law or terminology of a particular country or from the choice of
law made in former contracts by the same contracting parties.

However, parties are not entirely free in their choice of the applicable law.[59]
For instance, parties to a purely domestic case cannot exclude the application of
the mandatory laws[60] of the country with which all the other elements relevant
to the situation at the time of the choice are connected, by making a choice of the
law of another country.[61] This means that even when the parties have chosen the
tribunal of a country as well as its law to govern their contract, the mandatory
laws of the other country with which all relevant elements of the contract are
connected shall be given effect to. Other restrictions on the party autonomy
follow from other provisions of the Convention (see below).

Moreover, in all events, under Article 7(2) of the Convention, courts have to
apply the mandatory rules which apply in that jurisdiction, regardless what law
has been chosen by the parties. Article 7(1) of the Convention allows the court
also to give effect to the mandatory rules of a third country with which the

---

[58] Convention on the Law Applicable to Contractual Obligations of June 19, 1980, Rome [1980] O.J.
L266. Art. 28 of the Convention provides that it can be signed only by states party to the Treaty
establishing the European Economic Community. As a result, this Convention is applicable in
Belgium, Denmark, France, Germany, Greece, Italy, Luxembourg and the United Kingdom to
contracts concluded after April 1, 1991; in the Netherlands to contracts concluded after September
1, 1991; in Ireland to contracts concluded after January 1, 1992; in Spain and Portugal for contracts
concluded after September 1, 1993 and October 1, 1994 respectively. The latest to accede to this
Convention are the three newest Members of the E.U.—the Republic of Austria, the Republic of
Finland, and the Kingdom of Sweden—whose accession was adopted on November 29, 1996
[1997] O.J. C191/11. Belgium, Denmark, Germany and Luxembourg, had already incorporated the
text of the Convention into their domestic legislation so that they applied the rules of the
Convention concluded earlier (in Denmark by a Statute of May 9, 1984, in Luxembourg by a
Statute of March 27, 1986, in Germany by a Statute of July 25, 1986 and in Belgium by a Statute
of July 14, 1987).
As the 1988 interpretative protocols conferring powers on the ECJ to interpret the Convention have
not yet entered into force, the envisaged uniform interpretation of the Convention in all Members
States has yet to be realised.

[59] For a discussion of choice of law issues in relation to consumer and employment contracts, see
below.

[60] Mandatory laws are defined as rules which cannot be derogated from by contract. (See Art. 3(3)
of the Rome Convention.)

[61] See Art. 3(3) of the Rome Convention.

situation has a close connection, if and in so far as, under the law of the latter country, those rules must be applied whatever the law applicable to the contract.[62] Finally, under Article 16, a court may not apply a legal rule, otherwise applicable, if such application would manifestly be incompatible with the public policy ("*ordre public*") of the jurisdiction.[63]

When parties have neither expressly nor implicitly chosen a law, the contract is governed by the law of the country with which the contract has its closest connection (Article 4.1). This closest connection is, however, not always easy to determine. There is a presumption that the contract has the closest connection with the country in which the party, who has to effect the characteristic performance, habitually resides (or in the case of a company, the country where it has its seat), (Article 4.2).

In reciprocal contracts the characteristic performance is the performance in exchange of payment. Thus, the characteristic performance in a sales contract is the delivery of goods; in a service contract it is the performance of a service. In principle, when no law is chosen, it is the law of the habitual residence of the seller or of the contractor which thus governs the contract. Similarly, as the characteristic performance in a loan is the lending of capital, it is the law of the country where the lender of the capital habitually resides, which governs the loan agreement.

There are, however, three exceptions to the general presumption in favour of the residence of the characteristic performer. First, agreements concerning immovable property are presumed to be most closely connected with the country where the property is situated (Article 4.3). Secondly, the characteristic performance rule does not apply as such to contracts for the transport of goods. The country where the carrier has his principal seat shall be presumed to be most closely connected only if that country also happens to be either the place of loading or unloading of the goods, or the place of the principal place of business of the consignor (Article 4.4). For the transport of persons, though, the general presumption still applies: the law of country where the carrier is established applies. Thirdly, the criterion of the characteristic performance only creates a presumption. Sometimes it is impossible to determine what the characteristic performance is. There may also be situations where the agreement has closer ties with another country than the country where the party, who has to effect the characteristic performance, habitually resides. In that case the law of the country with which

---

[62] For curious observations on the wording of Arts 3 and 7 in the French and German versions of the Convention, see R. Plender, *The European Contracts Convention: The Rome Convention on the Choice of Law for Contracts* (Sweet & Maxwell, London, 1991), at 5.21. It has also been observed that mandatory rules in Art. 3(3) "are not necessarily mandatory in an international relationship foreseen by art. 7": Marielle Koppenol-Laforce (ed.), *International Contracts: Aspects of Jurisdiction, Arbitration and Private International Law*, (Sweet & Maxwell, London, 1996), at 145.

[63] Compare this with the following: Art. 7 "permits courts to give effect to the mandatory rules of a country with which the situation has a close connection, when those courts are applying the law of another country under the Convention. Thus, mandatory rules referred to under Article 7 survive, but do not frustrate, the choice of the applicable law. Subject to the effect of Article 7, therefore, it is thought that a legal system specified by the parties, without any element of error, as the governing law of their contract, will be applied as the chosen law, even if it was selected for the purpose of circumventing statutory provisions which would otherwise apply to the situation." Plender, *op. cit.*, 5.05.

the contract has in fact the closest connection applies (Article 4.5). For instance, a contract by a Dutch contractor to build a factory in Germany for a German client may be governed by German, rather than Dutch, law.

Consumer contracts have a specific regime under the Convention, which protects the presumed weaker party.[64] Under the Convention, a consumer contract is a contract the object of which is the supply of goods or services to a person for a purpose, which can be regarded as being outside his trade or profession (Article 5(1)). A consumer, as understood here, thus refers to "a private final consumer not engaged in trade or professional activities".[65] A choice of law made by the parties to a consumer contract does not have the effect of depriving the consumer of the protection afforded him by the mandatory rules of the law of the country of his habitual residence. The only necessary conditions are either that the consumer be solicited to enter into the contract by a specific invitation or simple advertising in his country, and that he took all the steps necessary for the conclusion of the contract in that country, or that the other party received the order in that country, or that the seller arranged a trip for the consumer to another country for the purpose of inducing him to buy and that he gave his order there.[66] This means that even if the parties have expressly chosen the law of, say, the country of the seller to be applicable to their contract, the mandatory rules of the country of residence of the consumer still apply. A consumer cannot contract out these rules. This is thus one area in which the freedom of parties to choose their governing law is limited. Moreover, even in case of absence of choice of law, the rule of Article 4 on closest connection and the presumption of characteristic performance does not hold. In furtherance of the objective of protecting the interests of the weaker party, such a contract is governed by the law of the country in which the consumer has his habitual residence.

The same principles apply to employment contracts. Driven by the same wish to protect the weaker party,[67] employment contracts are governed by the law of the place where the employee habitually carries out his or her work. Even if there is a chosen law, it cannot have the effect of depriving the employee of the protection afforded to him by the mandatory rules of the law of the country in which he habitually carries out his work in the performance of the contract (Articles 6.1 and 62). In the case of an employee who does not habitually carry out his work in a specific country, the law of the country where the place of business through which he was engaged is situated applies (Article 6). However, it should always be borne in mind that this is a rebuttable presumption; if it appears from the circumstances as a whole that the contract is more closely connected with another country, the law of that country governs the contract.

The Convention also provides that mandatory rules, which are not part of the proper law of the contract, apply. Article 7(2) orders the court to apply the

---

[64] See, *e.g.*, F. Leclerc, *La Protection de la Partie Faible dans les Contrats Internationaux* (Bruylant, Brussels, 1999) ; C. Joustra, *De Internationale Consumentenovereenkomst* (Kluwer, Deventer, 1997).

[65] See also ECJ with regard to the analogous notion in the Brussels Judgments Convention: Case C–269/95, *Francesco Benincasa v. Dentalkit Srl* [1997] E.C.R. I–3795.

[66] See Art. 5(2).

[67] G. Lagarde, "Report on the Rome Convention" [1980] O.J. C–282/25.

mandatory rules of its own legal system, regardless of what the proper law of the contract is and what it tells. Article 7(1) specifically addresses the issue of application of the mandatory rules of countries whose law is "neither the applicable law nor the law of the forum". Accordingly, a court, when applying the law of a country, may still give effect to the mandatory laws (*lois de police*) of another country with which the contract has a close connection if, under the law of this latter country, those rules must be applied whatever the law applicable to the contract. Thus, if a contract has close connections with Germany but French law governs it, then a Belgian court which has jurisdiction over the case, while applying French law, may have to give effect to the mandatory rules of Germany on certain matters.

Finally, the Convention allows the court to set aside foreign legal rules, applicable under the Convention if they are manifestly incompatible with the public policy (*ordre public*) of the forum (exception of public order) (Article 16) (see paragraph 1.25).

The law that applies to the contract according to the conflict of law rule, *i.e.* the proper law, governs the existence and the validity of the contract (Article 8). It thus covers, for example, questions such as whether there is an offer and an acceptance; or whether the agreement has a valid object. Nevertheless, the party who claims that it did not consent may sometimes rely on the law of its habitual residence (for instance, when it appears from the circumstances that it would be unreasonable to apply a different law in this respect) (Article 8.2). So it may argue that the question whether its silence implied consent should not be judged by the proper law of the contract, but by the law of the habitual residence of the party whose consent is questioned.

Whether the contract has formal validity is as a rule determined by the law governing the contract, or by the law of the country where the contract is concluded (or when the contract is concluded between persons who are in different countries, by the law of one of those countries) (Article 9). The formal validity is thus granted by the most favourable of these laws. However, the formal validity of consumer contracts must be in accordance with the law of the country where the consumer resides. Contracts in respect of immovable property likewise must follow the formal requirements of the country where the immovable property is situated.

The law governing the contract covers its substance and effect. This law determines, for instance, questions about interpretation, performance and breach of the contract. As an exception, the manner of the performance shall be judged by the law of the place of performance (Article 10): for instance, if a sale is subject to Belgian law but the goods are delivered in England, English law will determine the time within which the purchaser must examine the goods and, if necessary, put in a claim (Article 10).

1.30   **General contracts; private international law**   When the European Contracts Convention is not applicable (*e.g.* because the court seised of the case is in a country that is not a party to the Convention), the court shall use its own conflict of law rules in respect of such contracts.

The conflict of law rules on contracts of most countries run parallel to a great extent.[68] All systems recognise, for instance, the possibility of a choice of law by the parties. However, the implied choice of law is not everywhere readily accepted. In the absence of an express choice of law some countries stop short of applying the law with which the contract has objectively the closest connection. Instead, some countries weigh up all connecting factors which the contractual relationship has with various legal systems in order to locate the contract objectively; other countries prefer to opt for the law of the place where the characteristic performance has to be effected; yet again, other countries elect—as does the European Contracts Convention—the law of the habitual residence of the party that has to effect the characteristic performance. Lastly, there are also countries where the place where the contract is finalised, still determines the applicable law.

In sum, one has to consult the private international law of each individual country to discover which law the court of that country will apply to the contract.

Specific contracts The question of which law is applicable to international **1.31** sales (see paragraphs 4.02–4.05), distribution agreements (see paragraph 5.04), agencies (see paragraph 5.24), and licensing agreements (see paragraph 6.35) will be considered later.

Uniform substantive law

Significance Private international law indicates which national law is appli- **1.32** cable to a question of law that involves more than one legal system. The conflict of law rules , however, are not the same in every country. Furthermore, the law, which is referred to often differs substantially from country to country. Different rules of law may therefore be applicable to one transnational legal problem, depending on the private international law of the court seised and the substantive law to which it refers. The legal unpredictability and uncertainty that this creates, are a barrier to international trade. Indeed, businessmen generally prefer to see the same rules applied to their transactions, no matter which court decides on it.

For this reason many states have adopted uniform substantive laws in respect of matters where uniform rules were most welcome, such as international sales and international transport. Uniform laws can be introduced either by international treaty or by a model law. In the first hypothesis the treaty incorporates the uniform substantial rules which become binding as part of the treaty (if self-executing—see paragraph 1.04) or through implementation in the domestic law. In the second hypothesis, any interested country may adopt the text of the model

---

[68] O. Lando, "Contracts", *III International Encyclopedia of Comparative law*, (1976) Ch. 24.

law—if necessary with some amendments, as statutory text.[69] For instance, the Convention on the International Sale of Goods (see paragraph 4.07), the Warsaw Convention (1929) on the liability for air transport, the Inter-American Convention and the CMR Convention on road transport, and the CIM Convention are all successful illustrations of conventions that have introduced uniform rules for essential operations of international commerce.[70] The UNCITRAL Arbitration law (see paragraph 11.02) is another well-known example of a model law which became widely accepted.

Many treaties on the unification of international trade law have only a limited, often regional application. However, even if they are not widely in force, they are useful for the international business lawyer. Indeed, they often contain many interesting principles as they are drafted by experts from different legal systems in response to the needs of modern commercial life.

Uniform substantive law makes private international law largely superfluous. The very idea of uniformity excludes the question of choice of law. After all, the uniform law applies as soon as the transnational relationship falls within its scope. Nevertheless, private international law still remains important because, sometimes the uniform law is only applicable if it is part of a national law, which is applicable by virtue of conflict of law rules.[71] Moreover, uniform law still leaves many matters unregulated and private international law has to refer in such a case to the national law regulating these matters.

PART III: LEX MERCATORIA

1.33   **Concept**   Many authors claim that international commercial transactions are subject to their own rules, the *lex mercatoria*, or merchant law.[72]

---

[69] See, on the pros and cons of treaties, model laws etc. as tools for uniform law : Hans van Houtte, "La modelisation substantielle", in E. Loquin, *La Mondialisation du Droit* (Litec, Paris, 2000), pp. 207–236.

[70] For the text of the Inter-American Convention on Contracts for the International Carriage of Goods by Road, see (1990) I.L.M. 81.

[71] The Vienna Convention on the International Sale of Goods applies, *inter alia*, when it is part of the applicable law pursuant to private international law (see para. 4.09).

[72] See on this subject the excellent work of F.De Ly, *The Lex Mercatoria* (North Holland, Amsterdam, 1992) and its extensive bibliography. F. Dasser, *Internationale Schiedsgerichte und Lex Mercatoria* (Schulthess, Zurich, 1989); F. Osman, *Les Principes généraux de la Lex Mercatoria* (L.G.D.J., Paris, 1992); *Principes généraux de la Lex Mercatoria* (L.G.D.J., Paris, 1992); M. Mustill, "The new Lex Mercatoria; the first twenty five years" (1988) Arb. Int. 86; A. Spickhoff, "Internationales Handelsrecht vor Schiedsgerichten und staatlichen Gerichten" (1992) RabelsZ 116; K.P. Berger, *The creeping codification of the Lex Mercatoria* (Kluwer Law International, The Hague, 1999); E. Gaillard, "Thirty years of Lex Mercatoria: towards the selective application of transnational rules" (1995), I.C.S.I.D. Rev. 10, pp. 208–231; E. Gaillard, "Trente ans de *Lex Mercatoria*. Pour une application sélective de la méthode des principes généraux de droir" (1995) J.D.I. Clunet 122, pp. 5–30 ; K.P. Berger, ed., *The Practice of Transnational Law*, (Kluwer, The Hague, 2001), with I.A. M.J. Bonell, "The UNIDROIT principles and transnational law"; Y. Derains, "Transnational law in ICC arbitration"; E. Gaillard, "Transnational law: A legal system or a method of decision-making"; N. Horn, "The use of transnational law in the contract law of international law and finance".

The *lex mercatoria* is said to be created spontaneously by the participants in international trade and applied by arbitrators to settle international trade disputes.[73]

The rules of the *lex mercatoria* are founded on usages developed in international trade, on standard clauses, on uniform laws, on general principles of law and on the contract negotiated by parties.

- Trade usages are important in international trade.[74] Each branch of industry has developed its own practices and usages, adapted to the needs of the business sector: thus there are specific usages in the grain trade, the oil industry, the banking sector, etc. There are very few universal commercial practices. Usually, these practices only apply within a specific industrial sector and/or a specific region.

- Standard contracts or standard clauses, which often codify the usages of the trade, are usually drawn up by the commercial organisation of a business sector and are used by the members of that sector.[75] Many standard clauses are typical for a specific sector and have no general validity. (For that reason there exists probably a variety of *lex mercatoria* systems, depending on sector or region, and no universal *lex mercatoria* as such.[76])

- Uniform laws, model laws and conventions—even if they are not in force— are often developed in response to the needs of modern commercial life; as such, they are also important for the regulation of international trade.

- General principles of law complement the *lex mercatoria*. For example[77]:

---

[73] See T. Carbonneau, *Lex mercatoria and arbitration* (Juris Publ. Yonkers, 1998), p. 296 ; A. Lowenfeld, "Lex Mercatoria: An Arbitrator's View" (1990) Arb. Int. 133; IPRax 281; N. Jin, "The status of Lex mercatoria in international commercial arbitration", 1996 Am.R.I.A., pp. 163–198 ; J. Paulsson, "La Lex Mercatoria dans l'Arbitrage CCI" (1990) Rev. Arb. 55; "Arbitral award ICC", para. 3267, (1980) J.D.I. 961; See also the various peripeteia of the *Norsolor* case: Oberste Gerichtshof Wien, November 18, 1982, (1983) R.I.W. 868; (1983) Rev.Arb. 514; Tribunal de Grande Instance de Paris, December 9, 1981, (1982) J.D.I. 931; Cass. Fr. October 9, 1984, (1985) Dalloz 101; (1985) I.L.M. 363. Also, *Deutsche Schachtbau-und Tiefbaugesellschaft v. Ras Al Kaimah National Oil Company* (1987) 2 All E.R. 769; Obergericht Zurich, May 9, 1985: the international bank guarantee at first demand is controlled by a "supranational Lex Mercatoria" (cited by A. Kappus, "Conflict avoidance durch Lex Mercatoria und UN Kaufrecht 1980" (1990) R.I.W., pp. 791–792).

[74] E. Loquin, "La réalité des usages du commerce international" (1989) R.I.D.E. 163; A. Kassis, *Théorie générale des usages du commerce* (L.G.D.J., Paris, 1984). M. Goode, "Usage and its reception in transnational commercial law" (1997) I.C.L.Q. 46(1), pp. 1–36.

[75] *e.g.* the standard building contracts of FIDIC (Fédération Internationale des Ingénieurs-Conseils), the standard conditions of the London Corn Trade Association, of the Grain and Feed Trade Association (GAFTA), of the International Air Transport Association (IATA), as well as the Master Agreement of Factors Chain International.

[76] See in this respect the discerning article by P. Lagarde, "Approche critique de la lex mercatoria" *Le droit des relations économiques internationales, Etudes offertes à Berthold Goldman* (Litec, Paris, 1982), pp. 125–150.

[77] See, *e.g.* K.P. Berger,*op.cit.*; P. Kahn, "Les principes généraux du droit devant les arbitres du commerce international" (1989) J.D.I. 305 ; M. Mustill, "General principles of law in international commercial arbitration", (1988) Harv.L. Rev. 1816.

(a) the contract shall be enforced according to its terms (*pacta sunt servanda*)[78]; however, good faith may require that a change in circumstances be taken into account to alter the contract terms (*rebus sic stantibus*);

(b) the performance, as well as a possible renegotiation of the contract because of changed circumstances, shall be carried out in good faith[79];

(c) one party's conduct may, under certain conditions, be assumed to be an implied change of the terms of *a* contract if not opposed by the other party;

(d) the interpretation of the contract must be pragmatic (the doctrine of the so-called *effet utile*);

(e) if the legal terminology used by the parties does not reflect their intentions, the terminology must be adapted to the parties' intentions;

(f) use of goods by the buyer creates a presumption of acceptance of the goods;

(g) the onus of proof is on the plaintiff;

(h) *force majeure* may, under certain conditions, release the parties from their contractual obligations[80];

(i) a party that has suffered a breach of contract must take reasonable steps to mitigate its loss; damages have to be mitigated[81];

(j) the contractual liability is limited to foreseeable damages;

(k) a debtor may in certain circumstances set off his own counterclaims to diminish his liability to the creditor;

(l) the *exceptio non adimpleti contractus* is generally applicable;

(m) a contract is not enforceable when it is in conflict with the "international public order" (*e.g.* in relation to corruption) (see paragraph 1.25).[82]

1.34　　**The UNIDROIT Principles:** a step forward in the development of *lex mercatoria*?

UNIDROIT, after decades of research and deliberations, in 1994 came up with a form of "international restatement of general principles of contract law", called

---

[78] H. van Houtte, "Changed circumstances in pacta sunt servanda" in *Transnational Rules in International Commercial Arbitration* (ICC Dossiers, 1993) pp. 105 *et seq.*; F. Diesse, "The requirement of contractual cooperation in international trade" (1999) I.B.L.J. 7, pp. 737–782.

[79] G. Morin, "Le devoir de coopération dans les contrats internationaux" (1980) D.P.C.I., pp. 13 *et seq.*; P. Pinsolle, "Distinction entre le principe de l'estoppel et le principe de bonne foi dans le droit du commerce international" (1998) J.D.I. Clunet 125, pp. 905–931.

[80] *cf.* also M. Fontaine, "Les clauses de force majeure dans les contrats internationaux" (1979) D.P.C.I., pp. 469 *et seq.*; H. Lesguillons, "Frustration, force majeure, imprévision, Wegfall der Geschäftsgrundlage" (1979) D.P.C.I., p. 507; A. H. Puelinckx, "Frustration, hardship, force majeure" (1986/7) J.I.A. 47; U. Draetta, "*Force majeure* clauses in international practice" (1996) I.B.L.J. 547.

[81] Feduci, *L'obligation de Minimiser les Dommages en cas d'Inexécution des Contrats Internationaux* (L.G.D.J., Paris, 1986).

[82] P. Lalive, "Ordre public transnational (ou réellement international) et arbitrage international" (1986) Rev.Arb., pp. 329–373.

the UNIDROIT Principles of International Commercial Contracts (hereafter the "UNIDROIT Principles").[83] The object of the exercise was "merely to restate existing international contract law".[84] However, the existence of different and at times even conflicting rules often meant that choices had to be made. The criterion adopted for the purpose was this: "which of the rules under consideration had the most persuasive value and/or appeared to be particularly well-suited for cross-border transactions".[85] Consequently, it is specifically stated in the official text of the Principles that the objective is not simply to "codify" already developed rules of custom, but to "establish" a balanced set of rules designed for use the world over regardless of specific legal traditions and economic or political situations.[86]

The Principles set forth general rules for international commercial contracts. In furtherance of the principle of party autonomy, they apply whenever the parties to a transaction have expressly agreed to subject their agreement to them. Most importantly, the preamble states that they "may be applied when the parties have agreed that their contract be governed by 'general principles of law', the *lex mercatoria*' or the like."[87] The official commentary on this specific point provides that whenever parties agree to have their agreements governed by general principles of law, *lex mercatoria* and the like, and in view of the "vagueness" of such concepts, "it might be advisable to have recourse to a systematic and well defined set of rules such as the Principles."[88] The UNIDROIT Principles thus represent an important step forward in the development of the new international *lex mercatoria* as an autonomous body of law.

Legal status For some, the *lex mercatoria* is an autonomous legal system **1.35** that replaces national law (including private international law)—at least when the dispute is not decided by a national court but by commercial arbitration (see paragraph 11.26). In their view, international commercial contracts, submitted to arbitration, are no longer subject to some national law, which is inadequate for the needs of transnational transactions and only applicable by virtue of the whim

---

[83] UNIDROIT, Principles of International Commercial Contracts (Rome 1994).

[84] M.J. Bonnel, "The UNIDROIT Principles of International Commercial Contracts and the CISG— alternatives or complementary instruments?", 1996 R.D.U. 1, at 30; G. Baron, "Do the Unidroit Principles of International Commercial Contracts form a new *lex mercatoria?*" (2000) Arb.Int.15, pp. 115–130; C. Kessedjian, "Un exercise de rénovation des sources des droits des contracts du commerce international: Les Principes proposés par l'UNIDROIT" (1995) R.C.D.I.P. 84, pp. 641–670; M. J. Bonell, "The UNIDROIT Principles of International Commercial Contracts: towards a new *lex mercatoria*" (1997) I.B.L.J., pp. 145–161; M. Suchankova, "The UNIDROIT Principles of International Commercial Contracts and precontractual liability in the event of failed negotiations" (1997) I.B.L.J., pp. 691–702; A. Giardina, "Les Principes UNIDROIT sur les contracts internationaux" (1995) J.D.I. Clunet, Vol. 122, pp. 547–584; H. van Houtte, "The Unidroit Principles of International Commercial Contracts" (1995) Arb.Int.11, pp. 373–390.

[85] M.J. Bonnel, "The UNIDROIT Principles of International Commercial Contracts and the CISG— Alternatives or Complementary Instruments?", in R.D.U. 1996–1, at 30. Seer also K. Boele-Woelki, "Die Anwendung der UNIDROIT Principles auf internationale Handelsverträge", 1991 I.P.Rax. 161.

[86] UNIDROIT, Principles of International Commercial Contracts (Rome 1994) at viii.

[87] Para. 3 of the Preamble to the UNIDROIT Principles.

[88] *ibid.*, para 4. See K. P. Berger, "The Lex mercatoria doctrine and the UNIDROIT Principles" (1997) L.& Pol.Int'l. Bus.28, pp.943–990.

of some conflict of law rule. The *lex mercatoria* stands, as it were, substantively and procedurally apart from national laws.[89]

A few court decisions recognise the possibility for arbitrators to apply the *lex mercatoria*.[90] Others, however, doubt that the *lex mercatoria* can exist as a substantive and procedurally autonomous legal system.[91] Its components have their shortcomings: uniform laws have only a limited application as they regulate only a few matters and are adopted by only a few countries. The general principles of law are vague and often contradictory: for instance, when can *pacta sunt servanda* be set aside by *rebus sic stantibus*? In short, the *lex mercatoria* is not "self-sufficient". Its rules are insufficiently coherent or detailed to offer a solution to the legal issues, questions of law, which may come up in an international trade dispute.

Even those for whom the *lex mercatoria* is not an autonomous legal system have to recognise that there is substantial room for trade practices and usages in contract law. The Vienna Convention on International Sales of Goods (see paragraph 4.07) and the UNIDROIT Principles, for instance, expressly indicate that trade usages and practices established between the parties constitute implied obligations in a contract.[92] Parties moreover are bound not only by usages to which they have agreed, but also by the usages that are widely known and regularly observed by parties in a particular trade sector.[93] As such, there is also ample scope for regulation of trade usages within the respective national legal systems. Parties can expressly refer to trade usages in their contract. Moreover, numerous legal systems have accepted that the contract entered into by parties must be interpreted in the light of, and supplemented by, existing usages. In so far as trade usages are considered as *lex mercatoria*, the latter is also recognised as standard under national law.

---

[89] see, *inter alia*, B. Goldman," La lex mercatoria dans les contrats et l'arbitrage internationaux; réalité et perspectives" (1979) J.D.I., pp. 475–505; *ibid.*, *Lex Mercatoria*, Forum internationale no. 3 (Kluwer, Deventer, 1983); *ibid.*, "The applicable law: general principles of law—Lex Mercatoria" in J. Lew (ed.), *Contemporary problems in international arbitration* (London School of International Arbitration, Queen Mary College, 1986) pp. 113–125; *ibid.*, "Nouvelles réflexions sur la Lex Mercatoria" in *Etudes de droit international en l'honneur de P. Lalive* (Helbing & Lichtenhan, Basle, 1993), pp. 241–255; P.Kahn, "Droit international économique, droit du développement, Lex Mercatoria: concept unique ou pluralisme des ordres juridiques?" in *Le droit des relations économiques internationales, Etudes offertes à Berthold Goldman* (Litec, Paris, 1982), pp. 97–107; P. Lalive, "Ordre public transnational (ou réellement international) et arbitrage international" (1986) Rev.Arb., pp. 329–373.

[90] see, *e.g.* K. Berger, "Lex Mercatoria in der internationalen Wirtschaftsschiedsgerichtsbarkeit Der Fall Compania Valencian" (1993) IPRax 281; D. Rivkin, "Enforceability of arbitral awards based on lex mercatoria" (1993) Arb.Int.67.

[91] See A. Kappus, "Lex mercatoria als Geschäftsstatus vor staatlichen Gerichten im Deutschen internationalen Schuldrecht" (1993) IPRax, p.137. The Vienna Convention on the International Sale of Goods, Art. 9 (see para. 4.07) determines, *e.g.* that the parties, save other stipulations, are deemed to have incorporated existing practices into their legal relationship; this provision refers to "a usage of which the parties knew or ought to have known and which in international trade is widely known to, and regularly observed by, parties to contracts of the type involved in the particular trade concerned." See also in the French and Belgian civil code Art. 1135 and in English law, the doctrine of implied terms.

[92] Art. 5.2; see also Art. 4.3 on the role of such usages and customs in the interpretation of contractual obligations.

[93] Art. 1.8 of the Principles.

CHAPTER 2

THE ROLE OF STATES AND INTERNATIONAL ORGANISATIONS IN INTERNATIONAL TRADE

PART I: STATES

The state as regulating body

Overview Most regulations of international trade have emanated from states, or have been created with state assistance. International trade transactions are governed and regulated by national law introduced by the state (see paragraph 1.16). States also enter into treaties, which affect international trade. Treaties of friendship, navigation and commerce (see paragraph 1.02) or of investment (see paragraph 7.10) are only some examples. Moreover, the numerous treaties in which states establish international organisations for economic co-operation illustrate how states influence economic life indirectly, that is through organisations. GATT, and now the WTO (see paragraph 3.02), the OECD (paragraph 2.32), the World Bank (paragraph 7.03), the E.U. and many other economic organisations exist because they were established by states. The commodity agreements, through which states attempt to co-ordinate the production and marketing of commodities and to maintain stable commodity prices, deserve a special mention (see paragraph 2.65). The issue of commodities is closely linked to that of developing countries. As such, the plethora of measures introduced so far to accommodate the special interests of developing countries is addressed in this chapter. Furthermore, states also introduce through treaties uniform rules of international trade law, as with the Vienna Convention on the International Sale of Goods (see paragraph 4.05), several conventions on the carriage of goods (paragraph 1.32) and numerous other texts of great significance to international trade law. It is also through states that international customary law and the general principles of international trade law were created (see paragraph 1.10). **2.01**

The state as trader

Forms of trade States do not restrict themselves to the regulation of international trade; they often take an active part in international trade.[1] This participation can assume different forms. States purchase on the world market all that is needed for the administration, organisation and defence of a country. They commission the construction of roads to foreign private contractors; they award **2.02**

---

[1] J.M. Jacquet, "L'Etat, opérateur du commerce international" (1989) J.D.I. 621.

the construction of government buildings and technical installations to foreign companies; they buy weapons and ammunition abroad. Some states sell their natural resources (*e.g.* oil, ore, gas) on the world market. Furthermore, they procure goods abroad in order to secure supply of the country.

States occasionally participate directly in international trade. They themselves may enter into an investment agreement with a foreign company (see paragraph 7.09), for instance to order, say, a fleet of army helicopters.[2] Sometimes it is a state entity, *e.g.* a ministry, that conducts the business. Usually trade is conducted through a state company, which takes care of a particular sector of industry. Algeria, for instance, sells its oil through Sonatrach (*Société nationale pour la recherche, le transport et la commercialisation des hydrocarbures*); it orders turn-key factories abroad through Sonacome (*Société nationale de constructions mécaniques*). Iran exports its oil through NIOC (the *National Iranian Oil Company*). There are many more examples. States sometimes establish joint ventures with foreign companies to engage in production and trading with the benefit of foreign capital and/or know how.

The nature and characteristics of a state trading enterprise are determined by the purpose and objectives for which it is established. State trading enterprises tend to be more common in the agricultural sector than in manufacturing industry.[3] With respect to industrial goods, "state trading appears to arise either as a by-product of the nationalisation of an ailing industry or as a mechanism for pursuit of government policies pertaining to products/industries considered to have strategic importance."[4] The basic objectives for which state trading enterprises are established include income support for domestic producers, price stabilisation, expansion of domestic output, continuity in domestic food supply, increase in government revenue, decrease in government spending, rationalisation and control of foreign trade operations, protection of public health, and fulfilment of international commitments with respect to quantity and/or prices.[5]

The type of relationship between the state trading enterprise and the government covers a broad spectrum, ranging from enterprises that are fully integrated into the government administration to enterprises such as statutory and marketing boards that appear to be completely separate and distinct from the government administration.[6] State trading enterprises are generally called statutory marketing boards, export marketing boards, regulatory marketing boards, fiscal monopolies, canalising agencies, foreign trade enterprises, and boards or corporations with responsibility for nationalised industries.[7]

2.03   **Transnational procurement**   It can be tempting for states and state entities to pursue a policy of procuring supplies and services from within their country.

---

[2] See, *e.g. Westland Helicopters Ltd v. Arab Republic of Egypt* (1986) Y.Com.Arb. 127.
[3] WTO, *Operations of State Trading Enterprises as they Relate to International Trade: Background Paper by the Secretariat*, G/STR/226, October 1995.
[4] See WTO doc. G/STR/226, para. 5.
[5] See WTO doc. G/STR/226, para. 6.
[6] See WTO doc. G/STR/226, para. 9.
[7] See WTO doc. G/STR/226, para. 12.

Public funds would then benefit local businesses. This would improve employment. The state would even be able to recover part of the money spent through taxes. However, "buying national" does not always give the most competitive prices or the best quality. Moreover, if all states followed such a policy, international trade would be curbed dramatically. Consequently, international organisations which promote free trade, such as the WTO, NAFTA and the E.U., have limited the powers of their Member States to buy local (see paragraph 3.37).

Fighting against corruption   The post-Cold War era of liberalisation and **2.04** privatisation of formerly state-owned enterprises in many transition and developing countries has witnessed an unprecedented growth in the incidence and depth of corruption as means of influencing governmental decision-makers. Given the damaging nature of corruption to economic growth and social stability, there is a corresponding growing urgency for action in this vital area.[8] According to the World Bank, corruption in Eastern Europe and the former Soviet Union is "developing new dimensions, reaching new heights, and posing new challenges."[9]

Corruption is by no means limited to the developing countries and transition economies; it is also a serious problem in the developed world.[10] To address this global problem, a number of global initiatives are being taken at different levels. International financial institutions are increasingly linking financial assistance to the "recipient government's readiness and ability to control corruption"[11]; the UN has adopted a resolution calling for effective measures to combat corruption[12]; and international treaties are being concluded to address the problem.[13] Perhaps the most important development in this area has been the conclusion in

---

[8] For an in-depth analysis of the nature, forms and extent of corruption as well as a possible multi-pronged strategy to address the problem, see World Bank, *Anticorruption in Transition: A Contribution to the Policy Debate,* September 2000. See also S.R.Salbu, "The foreign corrupt practices act as a threat to global harmony" (1999) Mich.J.I.L. 20, pp. 419–449.

[9] See World Bank, *op.cit.*, p. xiii.

[10] See Transparency International, http://www.transparency.de.

[11] See, P. van den Bossche, "A 'normal' business practice becomes a criminal offence: the 1997 OECD Convention on Combating Bribery of Foreign Public Officials in International Business", in M. Bronckers and R. Quick, *New Directions in International Economic Law: Essays in Honour of John H. Jackson* (Kluwer, 2000) 441, p. 442. See also D. Gantz, "Globalizing sanctions against foreign bribery: the emergence of a new international legal consensus" (1998) NW.J.Int'l.L&Bus. 18, pp. 457 *et seq.*; P.M. Nichols, "Are extraterritorial restrictions on bribery a viable and desirable international policy goal under the global conditions of the late twentieth century? Increasing global security by controlling transnational bribery"(1999) Mich.J.I.L. 20, pp. 451–476; P.M. Nichols, "Regulating transnational bribery in times of globalization and fragmentation" (1999), YaleJ.Int'l.L. 24, pp. 257–304; P.M. Nichols, "Outlawing transnational bribery through the World Trade Organization" (1996–97) L.&Pol.Int'l.Bus. 28, pp. 305–381; W. Goossens, "National and international anti-bribery regulations: practical implications for multinational companies and compliance programs" (1999) I.B.L.J., vol.1, pp. 19–46; A. Posadas, "Combating corruption under international law" (2000) Duke.J.C.I.L., Vol. 10, pp. 345–414; S.R. Salbu, "Extraterritorial restriction on bribery: a premature evocation of the normative global village" (1999) YaleJ.Int'l.L. 24, pp. 223–256.

[12] See United Nations Declaration Against Corruption and Bribery in International Commercial Transactions, UN doc. G.A. Res. 51/191.

[13] The "world's first anti-corruption treaty" was concluded between Members of the Organisation of American States (OAS) in 1996; see "Inter-American Convention against Corruption" (1996) I.L.M. 35, p. 724. See also P. van den Bossche, *op cit.*; p. 442.

1997 of the Convention on Combating Bribery of Foreign Public Officials in International Business Transactions, under the auspices of the OECD.

The overall purpose of this Convention is to take effective measures

"to deter, prevent and combat the bribery of foreign public officials in connection with international business transactions, in particular the prompt criminalisation of such bribery in an effective and coordinated manner . . . ."[14]

To that end, Article 1.1 of the Convention provides that each party

"shall take such measures as may be necessary to establish that it is a criminal offence under its law for any person intentionally to offer, promise or give any undue pecuniary or other advantage, whether directly or through intermediaries, to a foreign public official, for that official or for a third party, in order that the official act or refrain from acting in relation to the performance of official duties, in order to obtain or retain business or other improper advantage in the conduct of international business."

Parties are also required to forbid the tax deductibility of private sector expenses made to bribe foreign public officials. The disciplines introduced by the Convention thus try to drain corruption from its source, *i.e.* the supply side of the problem—often called "active corruption". It does not address the so-called "passive corruption", *i.e.* the demand side of the problem. The Convention entered into force in 1999. As of June 2001, it had been signed[15] and ratified[16] by 33 countries.

---

[14] Para. 3 of the Preamble to the Convention. For a useful analysis of the Convention, see P. van den Bossche, *op.cit.*, pp. 441 453. See also R. D. Tronnes, "Ensuring uniformity in the implementation of the 1997 OECD Convention on combating bribery of foreign public officials in international business transactions" (2000) Geo.Wash.J.Int'l.L.&Econ. 33, pp. 97–130; P. Cavalerie, "La Convention OCDE du 17 Décembre 1997 sur la lutte contra la corruption d'agents publics étrangers dans les transactions commerciales" (1997) AFDI 609–632; G.Sacerdoti, "The 1997 OECD Convention on combating bribery of foreign public officials in international business transactions" (1999) I.B.L.J., vol.1, pp. 3–18; K.Loken, "The OECD Anti-Bribery Convention: coverage of foreign subsidiary" (2001) Geo.Wash.J.Int'l.L.&Econ. 33, pp. 325–340. The full text of the Convention is available at http://www.oecd.org/daf/nocorruption/20nov1e.htm.

[15] The 34 signatories to the Convention include all 29 OECD countries (Australia, Austria, Belgium, Canada, Czech Republic, Denmark, Finland, France, Germany, Greece, Hungary, Iceland, Italy, Japan, South Korea, Luxembourg, Mexico, the Netherlands, New Zealand, Norway, Poland, Portugal, Spain, Sweden, Switzerland, Turkey, United Kingdom, United States) as well as five non-OECD countries (Argentina, Brazil, Bulgaria, Chile, and Slovak Republic).

[16] The following have deposited instruments of ratification/acceptance of the Convention on the dates in parentheses: Iceland (August 17, 1998), Japan (October 13, 1998), Germany (November 10, 1998), Hungary (December 4, 1998), United States (December 8, 1998), Finland (December 10, 1998), United Kingdom (December 14, 1998), Canada (December 17, 1998), Norway (December 18, 1998), Bulgaria (December 22, 1998), Korea (January 4, 1999), Greece (February 5, 1999), Austria (May 20, 1999), Mexico (May 27, 1999), Sweden (June 8, 1999), Belgium (July 27, 1999), Slovak Republic (September 24, 1999), Australia (October 18, 1999), Spain (January 14, 2000), Czech Repulic (January 21, 2000), Switzerland (May 31, 2000), Turkey (July 26, 2000), France (July 31, 2000), Brazil (August 24, 2000), Denmark (September 5, 2000), Poland (September 8, 2000), Portugal (November 23, 2000), Italy (December 15, 2000), Netherlands (January 12, 2001), Argentina (February 8, 2001), Luxembourg (March 21, 2001), Chile (April 18, 2001), New Zealand (June 25, 2001).

State contracts Contracts concluded between, on the one hand, states or **2.05**
state entities or subdivisions, and on the other hand foreign companies, often
indicate that they are governed by the law of the state party thereto. This is
generally the law with the closest connection, as the contract most often has to
be performed on the territory of the state party. Besides, it would be politically
unacceptable for the state party to accept a contract governed by the law of
another state. However, as it may be easy for the state party to have its national
law changed, the terms of the contract may change to the detriment of the foreign
company. In order to protect the foreign company against changes in the national
law, state contracts therefore often indicate that they are governed by both the
national law as well as by international law or general principles of law. (See
further paragraph 7.09.)

Immunity from jurisdiction and enforcement

Concept of immunity from jurisdiction The problem of immunity some- **2.06**
times arises when states participate in international trade. Traditionally, the
sovereign equality of states meant that one country's court could have no
jurisdiction over the conduct of another state. A state thus enjoyed immunity
from jurisdiction before the courts of other states. When a state was summoned
before the court of another state, the court had to declare itself incompetent. This
immunity, which applied not only to states but also to its organs and other
entities,[17] still exists to some extent.[18] However, a foreign state that itself files a
claim before a court or arbitration tribunal is deemed to have waived its immunity of jurisdiction, so that it can be the subject of a counterclaim. Similarly, the
acceptance of an arbitration clause in a contract is considered a waiver of
immunity of jurisdiction.[19]

Restrictions In the past, the immunity from jurisdiction seldom led to **2.07**
difficulties; it was generally applied without restrictions. Nowadays, however,
this is no longer possible: states and private persons alike now often take part in
international trade. They buy and sell goods, charter ships and commission works
and services.

---

[17] See H. Schreuer, *State Immunity: Some Recent Developments* (Grotius, Cambridge, 1988) pp.
92–124; H. van Houtte, "Immunité de jurisdiction, in les Etats fédéraux dans les relations
internationales" (1983) R.B.D.I. 461–479.
[18] See H. Schreuer, *op.cit.*; the theme issue on immunity in (1979) N.Y.I.L.; M. Sornarajah, "Problems in applying the restrictive theory of sovereign immunity" (1982) I.C.L.Q. 661; *State
Immunity Cases*, 3 parts (Grotius Publications Llandysul, 1984). See also D. Nedjar, "Tendances
actuelles du droit international des immunités des Etats" (1997) J.D.I. 124, pp. 59–102.
[19] See, *e.g.* J. Langkeit, *Staatenimmunität und Schiedsgerichtsbarkeit* (Recht und Wirtschaft, Heidelberg, 1989). See also, *e.g.* G. Delaume, "Contractual waivers of sovereign immunity: some
practical considerations" (1990) *ICSID Review* 232.

It would be unreasonable with regard to its trading partners if the state enjoyed immunity in all these circumstances and could not be brought before a court for breach of contract. However, some countries still grant general immunity. Yet, most states restrict the possibility of immunity for a foreign state. In some countries, such as the United Kingdom,[20] the United States[21] Canada[22] and Australia,[23] statutes spell out the specific circumstances in which immunity will be granted. In other countries, courts have developed criteria for immunity of jurisdiction.

A convention on state immunity, which reflects general principles on this subject, is in force in some European countries.[24] Draft texts from international organisations,[25] which express more recent thinking, are not yet fully accepted.

Although the specific reasoning for granting or refusing immunity thus may differ from country to country, in most systems, transactions of public authority (acts *jure imperii*) have to be distinguished from commercial transactions (acts *jure gestionis*). The state maintains immunity for the first group of acts; no immunity is granted for the second group of acts. International law does not give a definition for what must be understood under acts of public authority. Many attempts have been made to provide an exhaustive list of transactions of public authority, but it turned out impossible to get agreement between the states. Each national court must give this concept substance. This inevitably leads to different opinions.[26]

Sometimes the purpose of the transaction determines whether it is an act of public authority or a commercial transaction. In this perspective the transaction, the purpose of which is to provide for the needs of the public service, is an act for which the state enjoys immunity. However, it is often the nature of the transaction that is examined: if the transaction can be characterised as one that may not only be carried out by the state, but also by a private person, then that transaction is commercial and therefore the state has no immunity; if, on the other hand, the transaction can only be performed by the state, then that

---

[20] See the State Immunity Act 1978, (1978) 17 I.L.M. 1123.
[21] See the Foreign Sovereign Immunities Act 1976, (1976) 15 I.L.M. 1388 and (1989) 28 I.L.M. 396. See, *e.g.*, S.R. Harjani, "Litigating claims over foreign government-owned corporations under the commercial activities exception to the foreign sovereign Immunities Act" (1999) NW.J. Int'l.L.&Bus. 20, pp. 181–201.
[22] State Immunity Act (1982), (1982) 21 I.L.M. 798.
[23] Foreign States Immunities Act (1985), (1986) 25 I.L.M. 715.
[24] The European Convention of May 16, 1972 on state immunity, in force between Austria, Belgium, Cyprus, Germany, Great Britain, Luxembourg, the Netherlands and Switzerland, (1972) 11 I.L.M. 470; C. Karczewski, "Das Europäische Übereinkommen über Staatenimmunität vom 16.5.1972" (1990) RabelsZ 533–550.
[25] See, *e.g.* with reference to the International Law Commission "Draft articles on jurisdictional immunities of states and their property" (1991) 30 I.L.M. 1566; D. Greig, "Forum state jurisdiction and sovereign immunity under the International Law Commission draft articles" (1989) I.C.L.Q. 560; C. Kessedjan and C. Schreuer, "Le project d'articles de la Commission du Droit International des Nations-Unies sur les Immunités des Etats" (1992) Rev.gen.dr.int.pub. 299; (1992) Yearbook Institute International Law, vol. 64–II, 214.
[26] See, *e.g.* I. Brownlie, "Contemporary problems concerning the jurisdictional immunity of states" (1989) A.I.D.I. 13; J. Crawford, "International law and foreign sovereigns: distinguishing immune transactions" (1983) B.Y.I.L. 75.

transaction is, as regards its character, an act of a public authority for which immunity is granted. Depending on which criterion is used, the objective or the nature of the transaction, it is either easier or more difficult to grant immunity. The purchase of cigarettes for the army by the state is, as regards its purpose, a government transaction (the objective being providing a public service need); as regards its nature, a commercial transaction (the purchase of cigarettes).[27]

Immunity from enforcement   The less the degree of immunity of jurisdiction enjoyed by states and state entities, the greater the possibility that they will be sanctioned by a foreign court. However, this does not necessarily mean that judgment can be enforced against them or that their assets can be seized. Indeed, under international law, states and state entities which do not enjoy immunity of jurisdiction for a specific claim, can still enjoy immunity of enforcement for assets used by the public service: a court is not allowed to seize foreign state property or to enforce judgments against foreign state property which is used for the public service. It is therefore not permitted to embargo foreign warships, which dock in port, or to seize the embassy building of a foreign state. Enforcement is only possible on the few assets that the state does not need for the functioning of its public service.[28] The borderline between assets required for the public service and other assets is not always clear. Therefore, whether, for instance, the bank account of a foreign embassy can be attached, is often open to question.[29] The European Convention on State Immunity (see paragraph 2.07) does not restrict immunity from enforcement. The Convention simply states that every state "has to give effect" to a judgment against it, but it accepts, nevertheless, that attachment measures and enforcement may be excluded.   **2.08**

When a foreign state has immunity from enforcement, a creditor may still attempt to achieve enforcement by means of diplomatic pressure from his own country.

Sovereign equality of states   One of the basic principles of international law is the "sovereign equality" of states[30]: every state is both sovereign and equal.   **2.09**

Sovereignty implies that each state can determine its own state structure and economic order. The Charter of Economic Rights and Duties of States (see paragraph 7.29) recognised that every state has "the sovereign and inalienable right to choose its economic system as well as its political, social and cultural systems in accordance with the will of the people, without outside interference,

---

[27] See, *e.g.* C. Schreuer, *op.cit.*, pp. 10–43; Paris, January 7, 1955 (1957) J.D.I. 408.
[28] C. Schreuer, *op.cit.*, pp. 125–167. Also P. Bourel, "Aspects récents de l'immunité d'exécution des Etats et services publics étrangers" (1983–1984) Comité français de droit international privé, 1983–84 133; Cass.Fr., June 28, 1989, (1990) J.D.I. 1004.
[29] See H. van Houtte, "Towards an attachment of embassy bank accounts" (1986) R.B.D.I. 70.
[30] See XXV G.A. Res. 2626(1970), Declaration on Principles of International Law concerning Friendly Relations and Co-operation among States in accordance with the Charter of the United Nations, sixth principle (accepted without a vote), as well as Charter of Economic Rights and Duties of States, Art. 10 (para. 7.29).

coercion or threat in any form whatsoever" (Article 1). This fundamental principle remains essential.

From a legal point of view, all states are equal, no matter what their political and social system. They are all equal members of the international community. They have the same rights and duties under international law. The Charter of Economic Rights and Duties of States specified what has to be understood under equality in economic terms: every state has the right to engage in international trade (Article 4). They have the right to participate fully and effectively in the international decision-making process in the solution of world economic, financial and monetary problems through the appropriate international organisations and to share equitably in the benefits resulting therefrom (Article 10). They have the right to benefit from the advances and developments in science and technology (Article 13). They have the right to enjoy fully the benefits of world "invisible trade" (transfer of technology, banking, insurances) and to engage in the expansion of such trade (Article 27).

The formal legal equality of states does not prevent factual inequality because of different political and economic structures.

2.10   **State-run economies and the international economic order**   Since the Second World War, but more especially during the past decade, the international economic order has seen the extension of the free market economy. Some countries have fared better in this free market than others. Those states which have, or had, a state-run economy (command economy) often have had some difficulty in adjusting to the free market structure. State controlled foreign trade, operating through a restricted number of enterprises, usually impedes or prevents free import and export of goods. State ownership of the means of production often discourages foreign investments. Nevertheless, those states with command economies are making efforts to integrate into the international economic order. Membership of the WTO, for instance, is open to countries with a state-run economy provided they respect the basic principles of international free trade.

2.11   **Developed and developing countries**   Differences in the development level of states have, in principle, no influence on their legal equality. All states, rich or poor, are equal under international law.

Nevertheless, those countries with less developed economies are often intended to benefit from certain advantageous arrangements that do not apply to more developed countries. Numerous organisations grant preferential treatment to developing countries. GATT has a special arrangement for developing countries (see paragraph 2.46), many UN organisations specifically care for developing countries (see paragraph 2.24), the World Bank gives them advantageous investment credits (see paragraph 7.03), MIGA insures the moneys invested in developing countries (see paragraph 7.44), and individual rich countries grant various preferences to developing countries (see paragraph 2.49). The purpose of these advantages must be to prevent the development gap between the richer and poorer nations growing any wider, and also to assist the developing countries on the road to economic development.

International development law   It has been argued that a specific part of   **2.12**
international law, *i.e.* international development law,[31] focuses on the position of
developing countries. Although this approach is no longer much discussed, it is
still worthwhile summarising the two basic principles of international development law:

1. developing countries have a "right to development";

2 developed and developing countries have a "duty of solidarity".

These principles are not yet recognised as fully fledged legal obligations. However, they may operate as guidelines for developed nations in their relations with
poorer nations.

The right to development   The right to development is mentioned in many   **2.13**
UN texts. The most extensive text in this respect is the Declaration on the Right
to Development, adopted by the General Assembly in 1986.[32]

The precise nature of the right to development, however, is not entirely
defined. Every state has, of course, complete liberty to develop through its own
efforts and its own economic means; but does the right to development also mean
that, when the poorer countries have insufficient means, the richer countries are
obliged to help them, for instance, with financial aid or trade preferences? Is the
right to development a kind of human right, given to a state instead of an
individual? Or is it an economic right?[33]

The richer countries have not yet accepted the right to development as a
binding norm of international law,[34] although they often do recognise a moral
duty to assist poorer countries. In many cases they are prepared to grant financial
aid or trade preferences to poorer countries on a voluntary basis. They do not
accept, however, that there is an international obligation to provide aid. This view
found some expression by the International Court of Justice, when it decided in

---

[31] See, *e.g.* G. Abi Saab, "Le droit au développement" (1988) A.S.D.I. 9; G. Blanc, "Peut-on encore
parler d'un droit du développement" (1991) J.D.I. 903; M. Flory, *Droit international du Développement* (Coll. Themis, Paris, 1977); G. Feuer and H. Cassan, *Droit international du Développement* (Dalloz, Paris, 1991); K. Mbaye, "Le droit au développement en droit international", *Essays
in International Law in Honour of Judge M. Lachs* (Nijhoff, Den Haag,1984) p. 163; H. Petersmann, "The right to development in the United Nations", in *Das Menschenrecht zwischen Freiheit
und Verantwortung, Festschrift K. Partsch* (Berlin, 1989); F. Snyder and P. Slinn (ed.), *International Law of Development, Comparative Perspectives* (Professional Books, Abingdon,
1987).

[32] G.A. Res. 41/128 of December 4, 1986, adopted with 146 votes for, 1 against (USA) and 8
abstentions (West Germany, Denmark, Finland, Iceland, Israel, Japan, Sweden, U.K.). See C.A.
Colliard, "L'adoption par l'Assemblée Générale de la Déclaration sur le droit au développement"
(1987) A.F.D.I. 614.

[33] See R. J. Dupuy (ed.), *The Right to Development at the International Level* (Academy of
International Law Workshop, Den Haag, 1979); P. De Waart, P. Peters and E. Denters, *Inter-
national Law and Development* (Nijhoff, Dordrecht, 1988); I. Seidl-Hohenveldern, *International
Economic Law* (Nijhoff, Dordrecht, 1989) p. 6.

[34] However, see N. Poulantzas, "Development aid as a legal obligation in process of formation"
(1982–3) Rev.hellenique.dr.int. 117.

the case between Nicaragua and the United States, that international aid is "rather unilateral and voluntary", so that this aid could be stopped unilaterally.[35]

2.14   Duty of solidarity   Richer states have to show solidarity with developing countries.[36] The Charter of Economic Rights and Duties dictated that states have to pursue a more just economic order, concerned with the needs and interests of developing countries (Art. 8). The richer countries have a duty to co-operate in the economic and social advancement of poorer countries (Arts 9 and 14). They should give tariff and other trade preferences to developing countries (Arts 18 and 19).

Article 17 summarises the duties of the developed countries in respect of the developing countries:

"International co-operation for development is the shared goal and common duty of all states. Every state should co-operate with the efforts of developing countries to accelerate their economic and social development by providing favourable external conditions and by extending active assistance to them, consistent with their development needs and objectives."

However, the Charter is rather soft law. It does not introduce binding rules or law, merely guidelines.

2.15   Qualification as a developing country   Developing countries enjoy some advantages. It is, therefore, important to know which countries belong to this group. Economists have developed criteria to distinguish developing and developed countries. These criteria are in principle of an economic nature (*e.g.* national product per capita) or social (*e.g.* degree of literacy). In the end, the states have to agree with the qualification. However, generally preferential treatment for developing countries depends on auto-selection: each country that wants a specific advantage granted to developing countries may present itself as a developing country to the richer countries and is usually accepted as such.

Developing countries are sometimes subdivided into three sub-groups: the least developed countries (LLDCs, such as Burundi), the less developed countries (LDCs, such as Morocco) and the newly industrialised countries (NICs, for example, in the Far East: Taiwan, Hong Kong, Singapore; and in Latin America: Argentina, Brazil and Mexico). The advantages are often adjusted to the needs of the three groups.

The E.U. grants the LLDCs unlimited general preferences; LDCs enjoy general preferences for a certain number of goods, while the normal import regime applies for the surplus of these goods. NICs can only import a certain number of goods with general preferences, while for the remainder an import stop applies

---

[35] ICJ, June 27, 1986, *Nicaragua v. United States-Merits*, (1986) I.C.J. Reports, 1986, 138, paras 245 and 276.
[36] U. Scheuner, "Solidarität unter der Nationen als Grundsatz in der gegenwärtigen internationalen Gemeinschaft" in J. Delbruck (ed.), *Festschrift E.Menzel* (Duncker & Humblot, Berlin, 1975) p. 274.

(see paragraph 3.25). The IBRD finances investments in LDCs, whereas the LLDCs are supported rather by the IDA (see paragraph 7.03).

PART II: INTERNATIONAL ORGANISATIONS

Outline International organisations are very important to international trade **2.16** law. We will focus successively on the multilateral trading system of the GATT/ WTO (paragraph 2.17), other organisations involving all countries in the world, such as the United Nations and some dependent bodies (paragraph 2.19), institutions dealing with the harmonisation of international law (paragraph 2.28), other restricted organisations (paragraph 2.31), regional economic organisations (paragraph 2.34), and the non-governmental organisations (NGOs) (paragraph 2.42).

GATT and WTO

GATT as an international organisation In the sense of being an inter- **2.17** national organisation, GATT never had any legal foundation. With its small Secretariat in Geneva, it was only a *de facto* international organisation, with neither regulatory nor jurisdictional powers. All regulatory and jurisdictional powers were vested in the contracting states themselves, who exercised their powers through the general conference of Contracting Parties held at regular intervals. This conference can be compared with a traditional international conference. Since 1960 the day-to-day administration was handled by a GATT Council composed of representatives of the Contracting Parties. All subsequent efforts to establish an international organisation administering the General Agreement, such as the 1954 proposed charter for an Organisation for Trade Co-operation (OTC), failed. The GATT had therefore to continue as the only organisation for such purpose until the Uruguay Round (1986–1994) succeeded in establishing a full-fledged successor, the World Trade Organisation (WTO).

The World Trade Organisation (WTO) The "constitution" establishing **2.18** the WTO as an organisation to provide the common institutional framework for the conduct of trade relations among its Members is contained in the Marrakesh Agreement of April 15, 1994 establishing the WTO. The WTO Ministerial Conference, composed of representatives of all Member States, convenes at least every two years; the General Council, likewise composed of representatives of the Member States, conducts the function of the Ministerial Conference in the period between two conferences; the WTO Secretariat renders administrative assistance. The Council for Trade in Goods oversees the functioning of GATT, the Council for Trade in Services oversees the GATS, and the Council for TRIPS oversees the TRIPS agreement. There are also separate bodies administering the dispute settlement system (the Dispute Settlement Body) and the trade policy review mechanism (the Trade Policy Review Body). The figure overleaf shows the organisational structure of the organisation.

WTO Structure[36a]

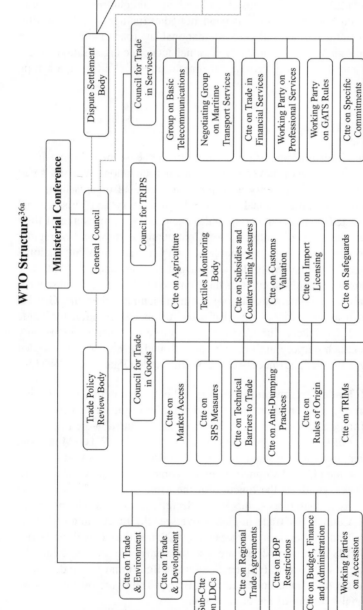

[36a] This diagram first appeared in *Dispute settlement in the World Trade Organization: practice and procedure*, by David Palmeter and Petros C. Mavroidis (Kluwer Law International, The Hague, 1999), p. 14 and is reproduced with kind permission of the publishers.

Currently,[37] the WTO has 141 member countries and 33 more have observer status. Thirty of the observers (including such big players as China and Russia) have already applied for accession and are negotiating their terms. Indeed, China's accession process has entered its last phase and could take place at any time. Observers (with the exception of the Holy See) are generally required to start accession negotiations within five years of acquiring observer status.

The status of the E.U. in the WTO is somewhat ambiguous. Formally, the Member States (but not the E.U.) were the contracting parties to GATT. However, both the E.U. and the Member States had a seat in the GATT Council and in the Conference of Contracting parties. Since the creation of the WTO as well, the E.U. has always represented the Member States, except on two occasions: when the budgetary matters are discussed, and when the E.U. has given its Member States permission to speak.

Other world organisations

Introduction The global organisations, which play an important role in the development of international economic law, belong to or are connected with the United Nations. The UN not only looks after international peace and security, but is also concerned with the more general economic and social situation in the world. A special chapter in the UN Charter (Chapter IX) is devoted to international economic and social co-operation organised under the auspices of the UN to improve living standards and economic and social development.[38]   **2.19**

The UN operates in the economic, social and technical field through its own bodies and specialised institutions. Some of these formulate resolutions; others initiate or finance development projects. Most give each member one vote, which means that the developing countries have a majority in numbers and can, therefore, influence decision-making; other, like the World Bank, give the Member States a vote weighted in accordance with their financial contribution, so that the richer countries have more power.

Main institutions of the United Nations

The General Assembly The General Assembly is one of the main institutions of the UN, holding its annual session in New York from the end of September until Christmas. Occasionally, special sessions are organised to discuss specific problems.[39] The General Assembly can discuss all issues that come   **2.20**

---

[37] As of May 2001.

[38] See Colloque Société française pour le droit international, *Les Nations Unies et le droit international économique* (Pedone, Paris, 1986); M. Belanger, *Institutions économiques internationales* (Economica, Paris, 1987) pp. 51–63; B. Colan (ed.), *Global Economic Co-operation—A guide to Agreements and Organizations* (Kluwer, Deventer, 1994).

[39] *e.g.* 6th special session (1974): Commodities and Development; 7th special session (1975): Development and international economic co-operation; 13th special session (1986): The critical economic situation in Africa; 18th special session (1990): International economic co-operation.

within the competence of the UN. All Member States of the UN have a seat in the General Assembly. Every state has one vote. Resolutions are adopted with ordinary or two-thirds majorities. The General Assembly is the forum *par excellence* for the developing countries, often acting as the so-called Group of 77. Because of their numerical superiority, the developing countries can influence the General Assembly.

The resolutions of the General Assembly are not binding. However, if they are accepted unanimously, they may crystallise customary law (see paragraph 1.10). For instance, in 1962 when the General Assembly unanimously adopted the resolutions on the Permanent Sovereignty over Natural Resources, this concept was introduced into international law (see paragraph 7.28). On the other hand, the Charter of Economic Rights and Duties, which it adopted in 1974 without sufficient consensus, did not become customary law.

The General Assembly occasionally gets involved in the negotiation of multi-lateral treaties. In this case, the General Assembly usually adopts the text of such a treaty in a resolution and urges the Member States to sign the treaty.

The General Assembly may request the Security Council to impose economic sanctions on states. Since resolutions of the General Assembly do not bind the Member States, the states are not obliged to give effect to such petitions. It is not clear to what extent a Member State, having complied with a request from the General Assembly for economic sanctions, may rely on the UN Charter.[40]

The General Assembly often refers discussions to one of the committees, also representing all Member States. The sixth committee, the Legal Affairs Committee, is particularly important for international trade law.

2.21   **Security Council**   The Security Council takes care of international peace and security. It consists of 15 members, of which five are permanent members (China, France, the United Kingdom, United States and Russia). The other 10 non-permanent members, coming from different regions, are appointed by the General Assembly. Procedural questions are decided by at least nine votes for; non-procedural questions are also decided with at least nine votes for, and no votes of the five permanent members against. Each permanent member has thus a right of veto.

The Security Council can impose economic measures against a state for the preservation of peace and security.[41] The Member States have to implement these economic measures.[42] The Security Council has imposed economic sanctions several times. Sanctions were imposed against Southern Rhodesia in the 1960s. In 1977, because of South Africa's policy of apartheid, the Security Council prohibited the supply of weapons, ammunition and military equipment and

---

[40] See, *inter alia*, P.M. Eisemann, "Article 41" in J.P. Cot and A. Pellet, *La Charte des Nations Unies* (Economica, Paris, 1991) pp. 691–704; H. van Houtte, "Treaty protection against economic sanctions" (1984–85) R.B.D.I. pp. 51–52.

[41] UN Charter, Art. 39. See *in casu* J.P. Cot and A. Pellet, *op.cit.*, pp. 645–666. The Security Council can also only recommend economic sanctions. See J.P. Cot and A. Pellet, *op.cit.*, p. 703.

[42] UN Charter, Arts 48 and 49; J.P. Cot and A. Pellet, *op.cit.*, pp. 749–762.

co-operation in the development of atomic weapons. In 1990 the Security Council prohibited trade with Iraq and Kuwait when Iraq illegally invaded Kuwait; the economic sanctions against Iraq remained in force after the military action against Iraq in 1991.[43] In 1991, the Security Council imposed sanctions on Yugoslavia because of its aggression in the Balkans, which have been lifted since.

The economic sanctions imposed by the Security Council have been effective only to a limited extent. Rhodesia succeeded in surviving the sanctions for 10 years because the boycott was not generally observed. The measures against South Africa were only limited in scope; the South African regime remained in power for a long time. And the boycott of Iraq did not remove Saddam Hussein from power.

ECOSOC   The Economic and Social Council (ECOSOC) is a UN body **2.22** active specifically in the social and economic area. Fifty-four UN Member States, all elected on the basis of a fair geographic distribution, have a seat in ECO-SOC.[44] The majority of members are therefore developing countries.

ECOSOC may commission studies on international economic problems. It may draft conventions and organise conferences on social or economic affairs. ECOSOC also functions as co-ordinator between various specialised institutions and the UN. It may co-ordinate the activities of the specialized institutions of the UN and it issues annually a report on their activities.[45] ECOSOC can only discuss; it has no actual power of decision. Moreover, it does not deal with economic issues, which are already covered by a specialised institution or another UN body.[46]

Several committees operate within ECOSOC.[47] The Regional Economic Committees deserve a special mention. The Economic Commission for Europe (ECE), for instance, has been very active in the field of international trade law. In the 1950s and 1960s it facilitated trade between Western Europe and of the state-run economies communist Eastern Europe. Arbitration rules,[48] an arbitration convention,[49] several standard contracts for turnkey projects, and many of its other documents are still relevant. At present, the ECE is involved in the simplification of international trade procedures, the standardisation of documents

---

[43] See, *inter alia*, M. Weller, "The Kuwait Crisis; a survey of some legal issues" (1991) A.J.I.C.L. 1; E. Lauterpacht, *The Kuwait crisis: sanctions and their economic consequences* (Grotius, Cambridge, 1991); T. Merow and B.H. Weston, "The Gulf crisis in international and foreign relations law" (1991) Am.J.Int'l.L. 63 *et seq.* and 506 *et seq.*; B. Grelon and C.E. Gudin, "Contrats et crise du Golfe" (1991) J.D.I. 633; B. Stern, *Les Aspects Juridiques de la Crise et de la Guerre du Golfe* (Montchrestien, Paris, 1991).

[44] Accordingly, the ECOSOC members are distributed as follows: Africa: 14; Asia: 11; Latin America: 10, eastern Europe: 6; western Europe and other countries: 13.

[45] UN Charter, and Arts 62–66.

[46] J. P. Cot and A. Pellet, *op.cit.*, pp. 691–704.

[47] *e.g.* in respect of natural resources, development planning, technology for development, transnational enterprises, transport of dangerous materials, international standards for accounting.

[48] The ECE Arbitration Rules have played an important role in East-West Trade dispute settlement, but have now been overtaken by the UNCITRAL Arbitration Rules (see para. 11.21).

[49] European Convention on International Commercial Arbitration of 1961.

and the promotion of harmonised practices through its recently created Centre for Trade Facilitation and Electronic Business (CEFACT).[50]

Other bodies and institutions of the United Nations

2.23   **UNCITRAL**   The United Nations Commission on International Trade Law (UNCITRAL) creates uniform law for international trade and co-ordinates the work of the various international institutions and private organisations active in this field. Located in Vienna, it is composed of delegates from 36 states, representative of the composition of the General Assembly.[51]

UNCITRAL has already drawn up conventions and model laws for *inter alia* the limitation period on the international sale of goods (New York Convention 1974),[52] the international sale of goods (Vienna Convention 1980) (see paragraph 4.05), the carriage of goods by sea (UN convention 1978, the so-called Hamburg Rules), international multi-modal transport (UN convention 1980), arbitration (UNCITRAL arbitration rules 1976 (see paragraph 11.21); UNCITRAL conciliation rules 1980; UNCITRAL arbitration model law 1985 (see paragraph 11.02)), international credit transfers (UNCITRAL model law 1989) (see paragraph 8.02), bills of exchange and promissory notes (UNCITRAL convention 1988) (see paragraph 9.27).

Within UNCITRAL there are several sub-committees working on drafts concerning, for instance, the establishment of an international monetary unit for international treaties, damages and penalty clauses for breach of contract, clauses safeguarding against price changes, contracts for industrial development, further codification of international commercial arbitration and counter-trade contracts.

2.24   **UNCTAD**   The UN first convened an UNCTAD conference on trade and development (United Nations Conference on Trade and Development) in 1964. With this conference the UN intended to increase the access of developing

---

[50] See K. Sahlgren, "Le rôle de la Commission économique pour l'Europe (CEE) dans l'élaboration du droit international économique" in *Les Nations Unies et le Droit International Économique* (Pedone, Paris, 1986) p. 185. More specifically about standard contracts: A. Tunc, "L'élaboration de conditions générale de vente sous les auspices de la Commission Economique pour l'Europe" (1960) R.I.D.C. 112 *et seq.*; P. Benjamin, "The ECE general conditions of sale and standard forms of contract" (1961) J.B.L. 131 *et seq.* For jurisprudence concerning ECE standard contracts see, for example, Bundesgerichtshof, October 22, 1969, (1970) N.J.W. 383; Cass.Fr., November 26, 1980, (1981) J.D.I. 355.

[51] G. Hermann, "The contribution of Uncitral to the development of international trade law" in N. Horn and C.M. Schmitthoff, *The Transnational Law of International Commercial Transactions* (Kluwer, Deventer, 1982) pp. 35 *et seq.*; J. Touscoz, Les National Unies et le droit international économique (Pedone, Paris, 1986) pp. 3, 32 *et seq.*; P. Volken, "Fünfundzwanzig Jahre UNCITRAL" (1992) RSDIE 133. UNCITRAL publishes a Yearbook of international trade law and a Bibliography of recent writings related to the work of UNCITRAL.

[52] T. Krapp, "The limitation Convention for international sales of goods" (1985) *Journal of World Trade Law* 343; H. Smit, "The convention on the limitation period in the international sale of goods" (1975) Am.J.Comp.L. 337.

countries to the world market. Since then, an UNCTAD conference has been convened every four years.[53]

UNCTAD's purpose is to give developing countries more access to the world's economy. UNCTAD is therefore working on, for instance, an Integrated Programme for Commodities, to regulate the price and the production of 18 commodities proposing multilateral commodity agreements (see paragraph 2.65). UNCTAD has also drawn up a code of conduct for the transfer of technology from developed to developing countries. Furthermore, it intends to increase the share of developing countries in international shipping and it therefore promotes bilateral shipping treaties (the so-called Shipping Conferences), which grant preference to shipping companies from developing countries for transport from those countries. UNCTAD also pays considerable attention to the financial and monetary situation of developing countries in respect of their burden of debts.

The Trade Development Board, on which all UNCTAD members have a seat, is responsible for the preparation of the conferences and the implementation of decisions of the conferences, as well as looking after the continuity of its work. The UNCTAD Secretariat in Geneva co-ordinates these activities.

In addition, there are numerous specialised committees within UNCTAD (*inter alia*, for commodities, shipping, technology, competition, trade preferences, etc.). UNCTAD also runs, together with WTO, the International Trade Centre.

UNDP   UNDP, the United Nations Development Programme, finances tech- **2.25** nical aid to developing countries from voluntary contributions. Running the projects is usually left to other bodies. However, UNDP decides the priorities and has, therefore, a great influence on development aid. Furthermore, it maintains supervision over projects through its own representative (resident co-ordinator), located in almost all developing countries (see paragraph 7.07).

UNIDO   UNIDO (United Nations Industrial Development Organisation) **2.26** promotes the industrialisation of developing countries. It makes studies and seeks advice from experts about the possibilities for fitting out new industrial plants in developing countries.[54] The model agreements for industrial projects, drawn up by UNIDO, assist developing countries in their negotiations with foreign investors.

Other organisations   Within the framework of the UN, a number of other **2.27** organisations play also a role in the international economic sphere.

• The International Labour Organisation (ILO) in Geneva is active in the international regulation of working conditions. It has drawn up a number of conventions in respect of minimum wage, working hours, safety at work, etc. It exercises pressure on governments to adopt these conventions.

---

[53] *e.g.* Geneva (1964); New Delhi (1968); Santiago de Chile (1972); Nairobi (1976); Manilla (1979); Belgrade (1983); Geneva (1987); Cartagena (1992); Midrand (1996); Bangkok (2000).
[54] A. Lewin, "Les services de promotion des investissements de l'O.N.U.D.I." (1987) AFDI 498.

- The Food and Agricultural Organisation (FAO) in Rome dispatches experts to developing countries and carries out development projects. Many agricultural projects are financed by the International Fund for Agricultural Development (IFAD), also established in Rome.

- The World Bank (see paragraph 7.03) will be discussed later. The International Maritime Organisation (IMO) in London,[55] the International Civil Aviation Organisation (ICAO) in Montreal, the World Health Organisation (WHO), the World Intellectual Property Organisation (WIPO) and the International Telecommunication Union (ITU) in Geneva ought also to be mentioned.

International institutions for the unification of law

2.28   **Outline**   The role of UNCITRAL (see paragraph 2.23) and the ECE (see paragraph 2.22) for the unification of law has already been highlighted. The significance of the International Chamber of Commerce will be illustrated when the non-governmental organisations are discussed (see paragraph 2.43). The following inter-governmental organisations should also be mentioned.

2.29   **UNIDROIT**   The *Institut international pour l'unification du droit privé* in Rome was established in 1926 within the framework of the League of Nations. This institution is still financed by just over 50 countries.[56] For more than 30 years UNIDROIT has carried out considerable preparatory work for the unification of law.

The UNIDROIT Principles of International Commercial Contracts have already been mentioned (see paragraph 1.34). UNIDROIT has also drawn up conventions in respect of international leasing (see paragraph 8.45), international factoring (paragraph 8.41), protection of cultural property, international agencies, etc .

Committees of experts are at present drafting rules on certain international aspects of security interests in mobile equipment. UNIDROIT runs a databank for uniform law as well as a programme of legal aid for developing countries.[57]

2.30   **The Hague Conference on Private International Law**   The Hague Conference has existed since 1893, but only in 1935 acquired the status of inter-governmental organisation. This institution provides, *inter alia*, the basis for the Hague Conventions on the law applicable to international contracts of sale (see paragraph 4.02) and on the law applicable to agency contracts (see paragraph

---

[55] The IMO prepares drafts for uniform law for carriage by sea.
[56] R. Dolzer, "International agencies for the formulation of transnational economic law" in N. Horn and C.M. Schmitthoff, *op.cit.*, pp. 71–72; M. Bonell, "The Unidroit initiative for the progressive codification of international trade law" (1978) I.C.L.Q. 413; R. Monaco, "L'activité scientifique d'UNIDROIT" (1976) R.D.C. 34. UNIDROIT publishes a quarterly News Bulletin.
[57] see UNIDROIT's website: http://www.unidroit.org

5.24). The Hague Conference is furthermore active in other areas of law, including family law, succession law and international procedural law. At present it is examining the possibility of a worldwide convention on judicial competence and enforcement of judgments (see paragraph 10.05).

Restricted organisations

Concept Although no international organisation has effectively all states as **2.31** actual members, some organisations have the ambition to regulate for the world. The organisations of the UN, for instance, have a universal objective and aim at universal membership.

Besides universal organisations there are restricted organisations that are only active in a certain geographic region (*e.g.* NAFTA, MERCOSUR or the E.U.) (see paragraph 2.34). Other restricted organisations regulate the economy or trade of states, which, although not located within the same geographic area, have a similar economic system (*e.g.* the OECD) (see paragraph 2.32).

In general, there is a greater solidarity between the members of restricted organisations than exists in world organisations. Usually, these organisations do not have extensive powers and leave the sovereignty of each member untouched. Their decisions, therefore, have to be taken unanimously.

OECD The Organisation for Economic Co-operation and Development **2.32** (OECD) in Paris is a good example of a restricted organisation. Its purpose is to streamline the economic policies of its members.[58] The OECD examines the economic situation in the Member States on an annual basis and issues recommendations. It encourages its members to develop sound energy policies and organises co-operation on energy matters (through the International Energy Agency). It has drafted many codes of conduct (see paragraph 1.13), (dealing with, *inter alia*, competition (paragraph 3.63), export subsidies (paragraph 8.31) and financial transactions, and publishes many studies.

OHBLA The Organisation for the Harmonisation of Business Law in Africa **2.33** (OHBLA), OHADA in French (*Organisation pour l'harmonisation en Afrique du Droit des Affaires*), was created by treaty in 1993. Today OHBLA is made up of 17 French-speaking African states.[59] The main objective of this organisation is "the harmonization of business laws in the Contracting States by the elaboration and adoption of simple modern common rules adapted to their economies, by setting up appropriate judicial procedures, and by encouraging arbitration for the settlement of contractual disputes".[60] OHBLA is served by a Council of Ministers, a Permanent Secretariat, a Common Court of Justice and Arbitration, and an

---

[58] The OECD is mainly a West European organisation of which Canada, the U.S., Japan, Australia and New Zealand are also members.
[59] Benin, Burkina Faso, Cameroon, the Central African Republic, Côte d'Ivoire, Congo, Comores, Gabon, Guinea, Guinea Bissau, Equatorial Guinea, Mali, Niger, Republic of Guinea (Conakry), Senegal, Chad and Togo.
[60] Art. 1 of the Treaty.

Advanced Regional School of Magistracy. Some of OHBLA's major achievements have been the adoption of Uniform Acts on business law, on company law, on economic interest groupings and on securities, as well as a uniform arbitration law and arbitration rules. The uniform acts are directly applicable and obligatory in contracting states, notwithstanding any contrary provisions of a previous or subsequent internal law.[61]

Free trade zones; customs unions; common markets

2.34 **Overview** Some organisations have a wider objective and aim at a more complete economic integration of their members. They further the creation of a larger market for their Member States to enable them to produce more efficiently and cost effectively. This integration can take place by means of a free trade zone, a customs union or a common market.

Members of a free trade zone agree to abolish customs duties between them so that they can import goods between them duty free or at reduced tariffs. For third countries, however, the customs duties of each participating state are maintained (otherwise, entrepreneurs from third countries, who wanted to export to a country in the free trade zone, could do so through the country with the lowest import tariff). Border controls are thus maintained within the free trade zone. To benefit from the free trade the importer has to prove that the goods do not originate from a third country but from a contracting state, for instance by a certificate of origin.

In a customs union, not only are customs duties between Member States abolished, but customs duties in respect of third countries are also equalised. Hence, an identical customs tariff is levied on a product imported from a third country into the customs union no matter in which country the import takes place. This means that products from third countries can circulate freely within the customs union, once tariffs have been paid.

A common market includes, besides the free movement of goods, free movement of persons, free movement of services and free movement of capital. The most important common market is the E.U. A common market needs continuous adjustment through a common economic policy. A common market could be undermined if, for instance, a state granted its enterprises state aid in order to drive competitors out of the market. The economic policies of the Member States have to be harmonised in order to avoid such distortions. The E.U. has, for this reason, not only a common market but also a common economic policy. With the

---

[61] T. M. Lauriol, "OHBLA law forces the pace" (2001) I.B.L.J., pp. 596. See also P. K. Agboyibor, "OHADA: new uniform company law" (1998) I.B.L.J., pp. 673–690; T. M. Lauriol, "The OHBLA Arbitration Centre: formation and effects of the Arbitration Agreement" (2000) I.B.L.J., pp. 999–1010; J. C. Otonmou, "The OHADA Letter of Guarantee" (1999) I.B.L.J., pp. 425–456; T. M. Lauriol, T. Gawel, "Legal aspects of creating security interests over mining titles in the states parties to the OHADA" (2001) I.B.L.J., pp. 175—187; R. Amoussou-Guenou, "Arbitration pursuant to the Treaty for the Harmonization for African Business Law (OHADA)" (1996) I.B.L.J., p. 321. For more on OHBLA, see the organisation's website: http://www.ohada.com. See also www2.lexum.umontreal.ca/ohada/ohada.html.

introduction of the euro (see paragraph 9.22), the E.U. is moving towards a more complete economic and monetary union.

Free trade areas and customs unions have a special status under the GATT as its members grant each other a more favourable treatment than they give third countries (see paragraph 3.11).

The European Free Trade Association (EFTA)   EFTA is an international **2.35** organisation currently comprising four states, Iceland, Liechtenstein, Norway and Switzerland, between which there are reduced customs duties and quantitative restrictions to trade. Originally, the EFTA arrangement also extended to Denmark, Portugal, the United Kingdom, Finland, Austria and Sweden.[62]

EFTA members also harmonised trade regulations and policies between themselves. Furthermore, the EFTA countries negotiated free trade agreements with the E.U. to extend their free trade zone to E.U. countries. EFTA members, with the exception of Switzerland, came to an even greater rapprochement with the E.U. with the creation of the European Economic Area. The Treaty for the European Economic Area (EEA) was signed on May 2, 1992 and entered into force on January 1, 1994, creating the world's largest free trade zone.[63] However, with the accession to the E.U. of Finland, Austria and Sweden in 1995, these countries now participate in the EEA only as members of the E.U. rather than as members of EFTA. The EEA Agreement unites the 15 E.U. Member States and three EFTA states into one single market governed by the same basic rules (*acquis communautaire*).[64]

North American Free Trade Area (NAFTA)   After more than a century **2.36** of attempts between Canada and the United States to achieve a bilateral liberalisation of trade, the first successful agreement between these two countries was signed in 1988 in the form of the U.S.–Canada Free Trade Agreement (USCFTA).[65] Subsequent negotiations with Mexico resulted in the creation of the North American Free Trade Agreement, which was concluded on August 12, 1992, largely extending the provisions of USCFTA to Mexico. On January 1, 1994, the North American Free Trade Agreement entered into force, creating the North American Free Trade Area (NAFTA).[66] NAFTA aims at the elimination of most tariffs between the three countries over a 10-year (exceptionally 15-year)

---

[62] Denmark and the U.K. relinquished their membership in 1972 when they joined the EEC, as did Portugal in 1985, and Finland, Austria, and Sweden, in 1994.

[63] The EEA brought together the (then) 12 members of the E.U. with five members of the EFTA (Austria, Finland, Iceland, Norway and Sweden). Switzerland rejected the EEA Agreement in a December 1992 referendum. For this reason Liechtenstein, forming a customs union with Switzerland, could not initially join the EEA. However, a referendum held on May 1995 confirmed Liechtenstein's entry into the EEA.

[64] For more on this, see http://secretariat.efta.int/euroeco (consulted March 15, 2001).

[65] USCFTA entered into force on January 1, 1989. For more on the evolution of U.S.–Canada bilateral trade relations, see Michael Trebilcock and Robert Howse, *The Regulation of International Trade* (2nd ed. Routledge, New York, 1999) pp. 38, 39.

[66] See Richard Schaffer, Beaverley Earle, and Filiberto Augusti, *International Business Law and Its Environment* (3rd ed., West Publishing Co., 1996), pp. 466–500.

phase-out period.[67] As a Free Trade Area, NAFTA explicitly states that it is "consistent with Article XXIV of the General Agreement on Tariffs and Trade".[68]

The NAFTA approach is set to expand southwards to Latin American countries. Immediately after the entry into force of NAFTA a summit of 34 countries of North and South America agreed in Miami on a schedule to complete negotiations for the creation of a single free trade area by 2005. This intercontinental free trade arrangement is to be called the "Free Trade Area of the Americas", or FTAA.[69]

2.37 **MERCOSUR** MERCOSUR, the emerging customs union composed of Argentina, Brazil, Paraguay and Uruguay is already a reality in Latin America.[70] Most intra-regional trade has been duty-free since January 1, 1995 and this is expected to be the case for practically all products with the expiration of the period for adaptation to the trade liberalisation programme (which was four years for Argentina and Brazil, and five years for Paraguay and Uruguay). Although the progress towards this end has been affected by different economic crises of its two big players, Brazil and Argentina, MERCOSUR works on the establishment of a common market with a common external tariff and common foreign trade policies.[71]

2.38 **Common Market for Eastern and Southern Africa (COMESA)** COMESA is a economic organisation made up of 22 eastern and southern African states.[72] COMESA is a continuation of a more transitional regional economic

---

[67] See *ibid*. See also A. de Mestral, "The North American Free Trade Agreement: A comparative analysis" (1998) *Rec.Cours.*, 275, p. 219; J.L. Gudofsky, "Shedding light on Article 1110 of the North American Free Trade Agreement (NAFTA) Concerning Expropriations: An environmental case study" (2000), NW.J.Int'l.L.&Bus. 21, pp. 243–316; C. O'Neal Taylor, "Dispute resolution as a catalyst for economic integration and an agent for deepening integration: NAFTA and MERCO-SUR" (1996–97) NW.J.Int'l.L.&Bus. 17, pp. 850–899; D. López, "Dispute resolution under NAFTA: Lessons from the early experience" (1997) Tex.Int'l.L.J. 32, pp. 164–208.

[68] See Art. 101 of the NAFTA Agreement.

[69] For further information on the FTAA negotiation process, see http://www.ftaa-alca.org/alca_e.asp.

[70] Brazil's President Cardoso is quoted to have said that MERCOSUR is "our destiny" while FTAA is "a mere 'policy option'". See "Some Realism for Mercosur", *The Economist*, March 31, 2001, p. 14. See the Treaty of Asunción of March 26, 1991. A look at the institutional provisions of the Additional Protocol to the Treaty of Asunción on the Institutional Structure of Mercosur Protocol of Ouro Preto shows that there is a close resemblance between MERCOSUR and the E.C. See also "Protocol of Buenos Aires on international jurisdiction in disputes relating to contracts" (1997) I.L.M. 34, p. 1263.

[71] For further information about MERCOSUR see, *e.g.*, V. J. Samtleben, "Das Internationale Prozeß- und Privatrecht des MERCOSUR" (1999) RabelsZ 63, pp. 1–69; M.C.A. del Prado, "The Formation of MERCOSUR and the harmonisation of rules in the field of industrial property" (1997) I.B.L.J., pp. 221–232; C. O'Neal Taylor, "Dispute resolution as a catalyst for economic integration and an agent for deepening integration: NAFTA and MERCOSUR" (1996–97) NW.J.Int'l.L.&Bus. 17, pp. 850–899. See also the organisation's website: http://www.mercosur-.org/english/.

[72] Angola, Burundi, Comoros, Djibouti, Eritrea, Ethiopia, Kenya, Lesotho, Madagascar, Malawi, Mauritius, Mozambique, Namibia, Rwanda, Seychelles, Somalia, Sudan, Swaziland, Uganda, Tanzania, Zambia, and Zimbabwe.

organisation introduced by the 1981 Treaty Establishing the Preferential Trade Area for Eastern and Southern Africa, commonly known as the Preferential Trade Area (or the PTA). The primary object of the PTA was to promote co-operation and integration covering diverse fields of economic activity including trade and industry and to prepare the ground for the formation of a much deeper economic integration in the form of a common market organisation. COMESA was created in 1994 largely as an embodiment of that long-term aspiration. In its drive toward the creation of a free trade area, COMESA had the target of complete removal of all internal trade barriers by the year 2000. COMESA further aims to create a kind of economic union by the adoption of a common external tariff by 2004. At the institutional level, COMESA has its headquarters in Lusaka, Zambia and a Court of Justice started operation in 1998.[73]

The Economic Community of West African States (ECOWAS) ECOWAS is a regional economic organisation of West African States headquartered in Lagos, Nigeria. Created in 1975, ECOWAS currently has 15 members.[74] Like most such regional economic organisations, the main mission of ECOWAS is to promote regional economic integration, with the ultimate object of creating the West African Economic Union. At the institutional level, ECOWAS has organs including a Council of Ministers, a Community Parliament, and a Community Court of Justice.[75]   **2.39**

Southern African Development Community (SADC) The Southern African Development Community (SADC) is a community of 14 nations.[76] SADC was created by the Declaration and Treaty establishing the Southern African Development Community which was signed at a Summit meeting held on July 17, 1992 in Windhoek, Namibia, replacing the Southern African Development Co-ordination Conference (SADCC), which had been in existence since 1980. SADC aims at the harmonisation and rationalisation of policies and strategies for sustainable development. The SADC Trade Protocol, which entered into force on September 1, 2000, calls for an 85 per cent reduction of internal trade barriers over eight years and constitutes the trade dimension of the organisation.[77]   **2.40**

The Association of South East Asian Nations (ASEAN) ASEAN is one of the most successful regional economic organisations consisting of a number of   **2.41**

---

[73] See http://www.comesa.int. For a useful survey of African regional economic arrangements, see T. Mulat, "Multilateralism and Africa's regional economic communities" (1998) J.W.T. 32(4), pp. 115–138.

[74] Benin, Burkina Faso, Cape Verde, Côte d'Ivoire, Gambia, Ghana, Guinea, Guinea Bissau, Liberia, Mali, Niger, Nigeria, Senegal, Sierra Leone, and Togo. See "Economic Community of West African States. Revised Treaty" (1996) I.L.M. 35 p. 660.

[75] http://www.ecowas.int/

[76] Angola, Botswana, Democratic Republic of Congo, Lesotho, Malawi, Mauritius, Mozambique, Namibia, Seychelles, South Africa, Swaziland, Tanzania, Zambia and Zimbabwe. Note that some countries are members of both SADC and COMESA.

[77] For more on SADC, see http://www.eia.doe.gov/cabs/sadc.html.

important competitive economies. Created by the signing of the ASEAN Declaration (also known as the Bangkok Declaration) of August 8, 1967 by five countries—Indonesia, Malaysia, the Philippines, Singapore and Thailand—ASEAN currently enjoys the membership of all 10 countries of South East Asia. The newly added members are Brunei Darussalam, Cambodia, Laos, Myanmar, and Vietnam. ASEAN has its headquarters in Jakarta, Indonesia. The economic co-operation aspect of ASEAN was initially limited to programmes for joint ventures and complementary schemes among ASEAN governments and/or companies. However, with the growing awareness of the importance of trade liberalisation as a tool of development, the Fourth ASEAN Summit of members in 1992 decided to open up members' economies, with the ultimate aim of full integration. To that end, an agreement has been reached to create the ASEAN Free Trade Area (AFTA) within 15 years (since reduced to 10 years), to eliminate all intra-regional trade barriers.[78]

International non-governmental organisations

2.42   **Overview** A number of international non-governmental organisations (NGOs) have an impact on international trade law. Indeed, many branches of business or profession have an international organisation with which the respective national professional association is connected. There is, for example, the Fédération Internationale du Commerce des Semences, which regulates amongst other things arbitration for that particular sector of industry, or FIDIC (Fédération internationale des ingénieurs-conseils) which draws up, *inter alia*, standard contracts for building projects.[79] Also well known is IATA (International Aviation Transport Association), which formulates, for instance, extensive air transport and tariff regulations.

As the name indicates, NGOs are not established by states; they exist by the initiative of private persons or associations. They are, as such, not governed by international law, but by national law. Nevertheless, they can be international in composition if they group together members from different countries. Sometimes, an international organisation involves NGOs in its activities. NGOs are frequently observers at international meetings and conferences and are often invited to submit position papers. The ultimate decisions, however, are taken by the international organisation itself or by its Member States, on the basis of the information received.

Some NGOs deserve a more detailed description.

2.43   **International Chamber of Commerce (ICC)** The (ICC), an association under French law and established in Paris, unites thousands of enterprises and business organizations from 110 countries.

---

[78] http://www.aseansec.org/
[79] See, *e.g.*, C.R. Seppala, "FIDIC's new standard forms of contract: Claims, resolution of disputes and the Dispute Adjudication Board" (2001) I.B.L.J., pp. 3–12; C.R. Seppala, "The new FIDIC provision for a Dispute Adjudication Board" (1997) I.B.L.J., pp. 967–984; C.R. Seppala, "The new FIDIC international civil engineering subcontract" (1995) I.B.L.J., pp. 659–683.

The ICC discusses the problems of international trade with its members. These members generally represent all sides interested in a particular problem, so that the outcome of the discussion is balanced and objective. The ICC then formulates the point of view of the business world at large. Businesses and organisations usually have little opportunity to be heard on an international level, where states and international organisations are in charge. Through the ICC they can make their viewpoint known.

The ICC has consultative status with the institutions of the UN. Moreover it can act through the national committees, which it has in about 60 countries, or through the direct members, which it has elsewhere.

The ICC also drafts standard contracts, guidelines, codes of conduct or other documents for specific trade issues with the co-operation of many practitioners and experts. The success of these private codifications depends on the business communities themselves. Thus, the "Uniform Customs and Practices for Documentary Credits" (UCP) (see paragraph 8.10) and the Incoterms (see paragraph 4.54) enjoy universal recognition. However, these uniform rules do not have the status of customary law. They have to be explicitly adopted by the parties.

The ICC has enjoyed less success with some of its other uniform rules. Its text on contractual guarantees (1978), for instance, apparently did not sufficiently reflect the international practice of bankers or of applicants for guarantees. The success of the Uniform Rules for Demand Guarantees (1991) (see paragraph 8.57), of its codes of conduct for fair publicity and for environmental protection, or of its model contracts for sales,[80] agency,[81] distribution,[82] etc, is as yet unclear.

The ICC has also established Arbitration Rules and a Court of Arbitration which allows enterprises to settle their trade disputes efficiently by arbitration (see paragraph 11.16).

A number of other organisations are active on the fringes of the ICC, including the Institute of World Business Law (Paris), where present trends in international trade law are discussed, the International Maritime Organisation (London), which gathers information on maritime fraud, the Counterfeit Investigation Office (London), which obtains information on the forgery of proprietary brands and patents and provides the police and customs authorities with the relevant evidence, and the International Environmental Agency (Geneva), which exchanges information on environmental technology with businesses and states (particularly developing countries).

The World Economic Forum   The World Economic Forum is associated   **2.44** with the annual gathering in Davos, Switzerland, of top business and political leaders as well as academics to discuss all sorts of issues, ranging from regional politics to globalisation and the divide between the haves and the have-nots.

Having started in 1970 with the modest ambition of serving as a forum for Europe's chief executives to discuss a coherent strategy for European business,

---

[80] ICC, *The ICC Model International Sale Contract* (ICC publication, No. 556, Paris).

[81] ICC, *The ICC Model Commercial Agency Contract* (ICC publication, No. 496, Paris).

[82] ICC, *The ICC International Distributorship Contract (Sole importer-Distributor)* (ICC publication, No. 518, Paris).

the Forum currently serves as an occasion at which pressing global issues are debated, opinions are exchanged, consensus is built, and new policy proposals are aired. Despite its non-governmental nature, and owing to the involvement of high-level business and political decision-makers in the Forum, Davos plays an important role in shaping global economic policy trends, perhaps more so than a number of intergovernmental organisations and forums.[83]

2.45 **Other organisations** The Comité Maritime International (CMI) is a private association, established in 1896 for the unification of legal rules for the carriage of goods by sea. To this end, 26 conventions have since been drafted,[84] amongst which are the so-called Hague Rules on the unification of some provisions in relation to bills of lading (see paragraph 1.32).[85] For some time, there has been an increased co-operation between the CMI and the International Maritime Organisation, which operates in the same area.

Two other private organisations of a more academic nature contribute significantly, through their comparative law studies, to the unification of law: the Institut de Droit International (IDI) and the International Law Association (ILA), both established in 1873.

PART III: DEVELOPING COUNTRIES AND INTERNATIONAL TRADE REGULATION

2.46 **UNCTAD** Awareness of the specific problems of developing countries increased, particularly in the UN, after the 1955 Bandung Conference. In 1964, the UN General Assembly convened a United Nations Conference on Trade and Development (UNCTAD) in Geneva (see also paragraph 2.24). Besides industrialised countries, developing countries also took part. From one conference, UNCTAD has grown into an international organisation, whose aim is to promote economic growth in the developing countries through international trade, to formulate principles and policy options for international trade and economic development, and to make proposals to this effect.

A general meeting has usually been held every four years, as follows: UNCTAD I (Geneva, 1964), UNCTAD II (New Delhi, 1968), UNCTAD III (Santiago, 1972), UNCTAD IV (Nairobi, 1976), UNCTAD V (Manilla, 1979), UNCTAD VI (Belgrade, 1983), UNCTAD VII (Geneva, 1987), UNCTAD VIII (Cartagena, 1992), UNCTAD IX (Midrand, South Africa, 1996) and UNCTAD X (Bangkok, 2000).

Different UNCTAD conferences have laid the foundation for international treaties or UN General Assembly resolutions on international trade with developing countries. The following issues in particular have been discussed at the UNCTAD meetings: agreements on basic products (see paragraph 2.65), general

---

[83] See http://www.weforum.org.
[84] See Xerry, "The contribution of the Comité Maritime International to the movement for the unification of maritime law" (1977) R.D.C. 87.
[85] Convention of Brussels, of August 25, 1924. This convention was changed by a "Protocol" of February 23, 1968, better known as the Hague-Visby Rules.

tariff preferences (paragraphs 2.49 *et seq.*), financing of development co-operation (for instance, by the International Monetary Fund) discriminatory and competition-distorting practices in carriage at sea, participation in the decision-making process of the IMF, special measures for the least developed countries, 1 per cent (later 0.7 per cent) of GNP as target figure for development aid from the industrialised countries, participation in the negotiation rounds of GATT, mutual co-operation and preferential tariffs between developing countries, transfer of technology (paragraph 6.32); restrictive business practices (paragraph 3.63), repayment of foreign debt of developing countries, and using globalisation as an effective instrument of development for all peoples.

At present, some 190 countries are members of UNCTAD, which has its Secretariat at Geneva. UNCTAD is governed by a Trade and Development Board. At the 1964 conference, besides the industrialised countries, 77 developing nations took part. Although the number of developing countries has since increased, the "Group of 77" is still used to designate the developing countries.

In 1964, GATT created the International Trade Centre (ITC), whose purpose is assisting developing countries in their efforts to promote their exports. Since 1968, the ITC has been jointly operated by the United Nations acting through UNCTAD and the GATT (now WTO) and has become a joint subsidiary organ of the WTO and the United Nations. As the focal point for technical co-operation with developing countries in trade promotion, the ITC works in such areas as product and market development, trade information, human resource development, international purchasing and supply management, as well as needs assessment and programme design for trade promotion.[86]

GATT Part IV   Largely as a result of the opposition of the United States, the   **2.47** original version of GATT did not go very far in addressing the specific problems of developing countries.[87] The 1955 Review Session of the contracting parties provided the first occasion for the concerns of developing countries to be considered.[88] However, mainly due to the influence of UNCTAD, more important changes have followed since the 1960s. Within months of the first session of UNCTAD, the GATT was supplemented on November 26, 1964, with a "Part IV" on trade and development (Articles XXXVI–XXXVIII). These provisions came into force on June 27, 1966.

Part IV recognises some fundamental needs of developing countries, including increased income from export of mainly agricultural products, increased share in

---

[86] For further information on the ITC, see http://www.intracen.org.

[87] As observed by Robert Hudec in connection with the negotiation of GATT 1947: "in spite of vigorous protests, the United States refused to agree to include the ITO provision permitting new trade preferences." Hudec, R. *Developing Countries in the GATT Legal System* (Gower for the Trade Policy Review Centre, London, 1987) at 14.

[88] It was during this session that, among others, the balance-of-payments exceptions of Art. XVIII(B) were introduced allowing developing countries to impose quantitative restrictions so as to safeguard their external financial position and to ensure a level of reserves adequate for the implementation of their programmes of economic development. See Hudec, R. *Developing Countries in the GATT Legal System* (Gower for the Trade Policy Review Centre, London, 1987) at 26–28. See also M. Flory, "Mondialisation et droit International de Development" (1997) Rev.gen.dr.int.pub. No. 101, Vol 2. pp. 609–633.

international trade, greater access to the world markets for their manufactured products; and financial participation from industrialised countries in the economic development of the developing countries.

Part IV moreover urges the developed countries to encourage participation either individually (Article XXXVII) or jointly (Article XXXVIII) in international trade by the developing countries. It is worth noting, however, that Part IV does not create concrete enforceable legal obligations on developed countries in favour of developing countries. In most cases, it provides only for a "best efforts" obligation. Article XXXVII, for example, although entitled "Commitments", commences as follows:

> "The developed contracting parties shall to the fullest extent possible—that is, except when compelling reasons, which may include legal reasons, make it impossible—give effect to the following . . . ." (emphasis supplied.)

The GATT provides no criteria for the determination of which countries must be considered as "developing countries". The UN refers, *inter alia*, to: the GNP per capita, the share of industry in the GNP, and the level of literacy. However, no strict criteria have been established for qualification as a developing country.[89]

2.48   **No reciprocity**   Reciprocity has always been a leading principle of trade negotiations under the GATT. However, Part IV of the General Agreement stipulates:

> "The developed contracting parties do not expect reciprocity for commitments made by them in trade negotiations to reduce or remove tariffs and other barriers to the trade of less developed contracting parties."[90]

The relationship between developed countries and developing countries ought not therefore to be based on the principle of reciprocity. In other words, the trade concessions granted to the developing countries by the developed countries (lower customs duties, fewer quantitative and other trade restrictions) must not be linked with the granting of similar advantages by the developing countries to the developed countries.

---

[89] The classification of countries on the basis of their levels of social and economic development has not been an easy task. Different organisations still use different criteria for their classification. By far the most common classification is that prepared by the Development Assistance Committee (DAC) of the OECD. According to the latest OECD listing, the category of "developing counties and territories" covers a wide range of countries and territories falling in about five sub-categories: 48 "Least-Developed Countries"; 24 "Low Income Countries" (per capita GNP <$760 in 1998); 45 "Lower Middle Income Countries and Territories" (per capita GNP $761–$3 030 in 1998); 32 "Upper Middle Income Countries and Territories" (per capita GNP $3 031–$9 360 in 1998); and two "High Income Countries and Territories" (per capita GNP >$9 360). This list is normally reviewed every three years. For further details, see http://www.oecd.org/dac/htm/daclist3.htm. See also, *e.g.*, G. Verdirame, "The definition of Developing Countries under GATT and other international law" (1996) G.Y.I.L. 39, pp. 164–197.

[90] Art. XXXVI(8) of the General Agreement.

Tariff preferences for developing countries

General In 1968 UNCTAD promoted the principle of a system of general, **2.49** non-reciprocal and non-discriminatory tariff preferences for the exportation of manufactured products and semi-finished products from developing countries. It gave further substance to this principle by an agreement of 1970. This agreement can be summarised as follows:

- all members of the OECD (see paragraph 2.27) or Comecon (see paragraph 3.50) are requested to give preferences to countries that have declared themselves to be developing countries;

- the preferences must concern processed or semi-processed industrial goods, or processed agricultural products (*e.g.* foodstuffs);

- the preference must consist of a reduced tariff or of the full removal of customs duties (so-called "zero rate").

In principle, however, preferential treatment is not allowed between contracting parties of the GATT because of the most favoured treatment rule (see paragraph 3.09). In order to introduce non-reciprocal preferential tariff treatment for products originating from developing countries, GATT contracting parties opted for a 10-year waiver of the provisions of Article I of the General Agreement, pursuant to Article XXV(5) thereof.[91] This temporary arrangement was later placed on a more permanent basis by a Tokyo Round Decision, "Differential and More Favourable Treatment, Reciprocity and Fuller Participation of Developing Countries", often called the "enabling clause".[92]

The "enabling clause" The enabling clause (*clause d'habilitation*) provides **2.50** expressly for a derogation from the most favoured nation treatment requirement of Article I of the GATT. It empowers the contracting states to accord "differential and more favourable treatment to developing countries without according such treatment to other contracting parties".

The enabling clause forms the legal basis for the preferential treatment of developing countries with regard to tariff and non-tariff barriers in developed countries; it also allows the establishment of reciprocal tariff and non-tariff preferences as between the developing countries themselves, and special preferences in favour of the least developed countries.

Conditions for preferential treatment Preferential treatment is permitted, **2.51** provided it satisfies substantive and formal requirements. Preferences granted to a developing country may not constitute new trade restrictions *vis-à-vis* other contracting states. Moreover, the preferences must be in response to real needs of developing countries. Each system of preferential treatment must be notified to

---

[91] See "Generalised system of Preferences, Decision of 25 June 1971" (L/3545), *BISD* 18S/24–26.

[92] See Decision, of November 28, 979, (L/4903), *BISD* 26S/203–205.

the GATT. Each contracting state may request consultation on specific preferential systems.

The combined effect of the clause of non-reciprocity and the enabling clause is that an industrialised country may grant tariff and non-tariff preferences to a developing country:

- without receiving reciprocal trade preferences from this country;

- without being compelled to give the same preferences to other contracting parties which are not developing countries.

2.52   **The "graduation rule"**   In addition to the formal recognition of the preferential treatment the "enabling clause" declaration also established the rule that developing countries must gradually submit to the common GATT rules as their economic development improves (the so-called graduation rule). The graduation rule is based on the fact that not all developing countries are at the same level of economic (under-) development. Usually the distinction is made between least developed countries (LLDCs), less developed countries (LDCs) and newly industrialised countries (NICs) (see paragraph 2.15). However, there are no multilaterally agreed guidelines on how to determine which country falls into which category and whether a country has graduated from one category to another.

For purposes of preferential treatment provisions, often the only meaningful distinctions are those between least developed countries (currently the 48 countries that are so designated by the Economic and Social Council of the United Nations[93]) and other developing countries.[94] It is not, however, difficult to find cases where certain developing countries outside the LLDC list are singled out and treated in the same way as the latter.[95]

2.53   **Evaluation**   Although the General System of Preferences (GSP) originated from UNCTAD, its management rests with the GATT. The practical impact of the GSP in helping the economic development of developing countries is often very doubtful, mainly because the GSP largely excludes agricultural products from its coverage. Moreover, even with regard to manufactured products, it "excludes product groups of principal interest to the developing countries, such as steel,

---

[93] See WTO doc. G/AG/3, 24 Nov. 1995.

[94] See, *inter alia,* Art. 12.2 of the Uruguay Round Agreement on Agriculture; Art. 27.3 of the SCM Agreement; Art. 14 of the SPS Agreement; Art. 66 of TRIPS; Art. 24 of the DSU; and the Uruguay Round Decision on Measures in Favour of Least Developed Countries.

[95] For example, in the area of export subsidies, Art. 27.2(a) of the SCM Agreement uses a GNP per capita of $1,000 per annum as the borderline dividing developing countries into two categories—those below the benchmark are treated more favourably than those above it. In the area of local content subsidies under Art. 3.1(b), instead of the $1,000 benchmark the Agreement uses the general categorisation of least developed countries and other developing countries (see Art. 27.3). Likewise, Art. 15.2 of the Agreement on Agriculture talks in terms of developing countries on the one hand, and LLDCs on the other. Art. 16 of the Agriculture Agreement, however, goes further and brings non-LLDC developing countries that are net food importers and treats them on almost the same terms as LLDCs.

textiles, clothing and shoes."[96] From studies on the application of the general tariff preferences between 1971 and 1980, it has appeared that the system has particularly favoured the "newly industrialised countries" (see paragraph 2.52).[97] This is not surprising, since the preferences apply mainly to industrial products.[98] By virtue of the "graduation rule" (see paragraph 2.52) the tariff preferences which favoured those countries were, however, gradually reduced. For example, Japan, the United States as well as the E.U. have already excluded Hong Kong, South Korea and Singapore from their list of beneficiary countries.[99] Additionally, more extensive preferences have been awarded in favour of least developed countries. The Uruguay Round decision on measures in favour of least developed countries specifically referred to the enabling clauses provisions on LLDCs and stated that consideration shall be given to further improve GSP and other schemes for products of particular export interest to least developed countries. There is thus a noticeable shift in approach from a more or less uniform treatment of all developing countries as a group, to a more differentiated one of paying special emphasis to the poorest among them.

Application of the general tariff preferences The E.U. was the first trading   **2.54**
partner to offer general tariff preferences in July 1970 (see paragraph 2.56). The United States has participated in the system since January 1976. The following countries also offer general tariff preferences: Japan, Norway, Australia, New Zealand, Switzerland, Canada, Poland, and Slovakia.[1]

Not all countries grant the same tariff preferences, however, and different countries attach different conditions to their preferences.

General tariff preferences in the United States The GSP system of the   **2.55**
United States, first enacted as part of the Trade Act of 1974, entered into effect in 1976. The law has been renewed and/or amended several times since.[2] Under this system, a product qualifies for GSP treatment at importation if (1) it is identified as an eligible product; (2) it comes from a country that is designated as a beneficiary country; and (3) the link between the two (*i.e.* the product and the country) satisfies the prescribed rules-of-origin criteria.[3] The Trade Act lists a

---

[96] See Belassa, B. and C. Michalopoulos, "Liberalising trade between developed and developing countries", (1986) 20 J.W.T. 7.

[97] A study on the application of GSP trade to the U.S. revealed that, in 1983, Taiwan, Korea and Hong Kong "captured 52 percent of the entire benefits of the program": Meltzer, R. "The U.S. renewal of the GSP: implications for North-South trade", (1986) 30, J.W.T. 510–511.

[98] See also Belassa and Michalopoulos, *op.cit.* at 9–10, and Weintraub, S. "Selective Trade Liberalization", paper presented at the Overseas Development Council Conference on U.S. Trade Policy and the Developing Countries, September 1984.

[99] The U.S. took this step as early as 1989, the E.U. in 1998, and Japan as of April 1, 2000. In each case, the GNP per capita of the countries as reported by the World Bank played a decisive role.

[1] See http://www.unctad.org/gsp/index.htm.

[2] The latest renewal was enacted in December 1999, expiring in September 2001.

[3] The rules of origin provide that in order to benefit from a GSP treatment, an eligible product must be shipped directly from an eligible country to the U.S. either without entering the territory of a third country at all, or if it has to do so, without entering the commerce of that third country. Moreover, the product is required to have at least 35% of its transaction value created in the beneficiary country.

number of conditions before a country becomes eligible for GSP benefits, and the level of economic development is only a necessary, and not sufficient, condition for country eligibility.

The President of the United States is authorised to designate any country, with the exception of a specified few,[4] as a beneficiary developing or least developed country. There are, however, some general exceptions. Historically, the United States' GSP system excluded most Communist countries, members of OPEC and some other similar commodity arrangements having a disruptive impact on the world economy, and countries that followed policies which were not in the interest of the United States regardless of their economic levels of development. Other grounds on which a country might be denied beneficiary status include granting other industrialised countries more preferences than they give to the United States, violation of the proprietary rights of United States citizens and companies contrary to international law, not acting in good faith when refusing to enforce arbitral awards in favour of United States subjects, and so forth.

Over time, some of the old conditions have been relaxed. For example, a number of formerly Communist states in Eastern Europe and the Baltic region, as well as several former republics of the Soviet Union, have been added to the list of GSP beneficiaries.[5] On the other hand, quite a number of new conditions have also been introduced progressively, an important one being the 1984 amendment introducing respect for "internationally recognised workers' rights" as a condition for eligibility to GSP benefits.[6] These rights have been defined to include the right of association, the right to organise and bargain collectively, prohibition of forced labour and child labour, and establishment of acceptable conditions of work. These conditions, together with the possibility of withdrawal of a benefit on several counts, makes the GSP system an important tool of U.S. foreign policy.[7]

Nevertheless, all products that are eligible for GSP treatment in the United States at this moment are imported duty free; however, the share of GSP imports has been rather limited.[8] The United States reserves the right to decide whether certain goods from the developing countries have to be kept outside the system or deserve less advantages because they are "sufficiently competitive". Applying the principle of graduation, the United States completely excludes a number of newly industrialised countries: Hong Kong, South Korea, Taiwan and Singapore in 1989, Israel in 1995, and Aruba, the Cayman Islands, Cyprus, Greenland, Malaysia, Macau, and the Netherlands Antilles in 1998.

---

[4] These are Australia, Canada, E.U. Member States, Iceland, Japan, Monaco, Norway, New Zealand and Switzerland. See s.2462(B) of the Trade Act of 1974 (as amended).

[5] At the time of writing, the only countries still subject to exclusion mainly on the ground of Communism are Cuba and North Korea.

[6] Trade Act of 1974 (as amended), s.2462(G).

[7] According to UNCTAD, the U.S. "has increasingly employed the GSP and other preferential trade programs as substitute form of enforcement authority." See *Handbook on the GSP Scheme of the United States of America* (2000).

[8] According to UNCTAD, only 1.3% of U.S. imports in 1999 entered duty-free under the GSP. See *Handbook on the GSP Scheme of the United States of America* (2000).

On May 18, 2000 the President of the United States signed into law the African Growth and Opportunity Act, which authorises a new trade and investment policy for sub-Saharan Africa.[9] The Act declares that free trade agreements should be negotiated, where feasible, with interested countries in sub-Saharan Africa. It requires the President to develop a plan to that effect.[10]

An important development brought about by the Act is its authorisation of duty-free and quota-free treatment for certain textiles and apparel products for eligible countries. Given that the exclusion of these products from the coverage of the United States' GSP scheme had been "one cause of African countries' less successful record of deriving benefit from the duty-free preferences of that scheme", the importance of this development cannot be doubted. At the same time, its potential benefit has been diminished by the fact that complete duty- and quota-free treatment is restricted almost exclusively to apparel products made using U.S. fabrics.[11] In line with the apparent shift to a more differentiated approach in the treatment of developing countries according to their levels of economic development, the so-called least developed sub-Saharan African countries (defined to mean countries that had a per capita gross national product of less than $1,500 a year in 1998) are exceptionally allowed to export apparel articles regardless of the country of origin of the fabric used to make them.[12]

The African Growth and Opportunity Act does not cover such sensitive commodities as coffee and sugar. At the level of products, the President can suspend duty-free treatment if the Secretary of Commerce determines that a surge in imports of a specific product, even within the quotas, injures or threatens competing U.S. industries.[13]

Under the terms of the Act, a "United States–Sub-Saharan Africa Trade and Economic Co-operation Forum", has been set up to foster closer economic ties between the two entities.

General tariff preferences under the E.U. The system of general tariff **2.56** preferences first introduced by the EEC in 1971 for an initial 10-year period

---

[9] The term "sub-Saharan Africa" has been defined to include the following 48 countries listed in s.107 of the Act: Angola, Benin, Botswana, Burkina Faso, Burundi, Cameroon, Cape Verde, Central African Republic, Chad, Comoros, D. R. Congo, Congo, Côte d'Ivoire, Djibouti, Equatorial Guinea, Eritrea, Ethiopia, Gabon, Gambia, Ghana, Guinea, Guinea-Bissau, Kenya, Lesotho, Liberia, Madagascar, Malawi, Mali, Mauritania, Mauritius, Mozambique, Namibia, Niger, Nigeria, Rwanda, São Tomé and Príncipe, Senegal, Seychelles, Sierra Leone, Somalia, South Africa, Sudan, Swaziland, Tanzania, Togo, Uganda, Zambia, and Zimbabwe. By a Presidential Proclamation of October 2, 2000, 34 of these countries were designated as eligible for purposes of the African Growth and Opportunities Act. Not included are the following: Angola, Burkina Faso, Burundi, Comoros, D. R. Congo, Côte d'Ivoire, Equatorial Guinea, Gambia, Liberia, Somalia, Sudan, Swaziland, Togo, and Zimbabwe.

[10] The African Growth and Opportunity Act, s.116.

[11] ibid., s.112.

[12] To be designated as an eligible sub-Saharan African country, a country must satisfy a set of general and specific conditions, including establishment of a market-based economy that protects private property rights, rule of law and political pluralism, the elimination of barriers to U.S. trade and investment, protection of internationally recognised workers rights, and distancing itself from activities that undermine U.S. national security or foreign policy interests. The President is authorised to terminate such status if an eligible country is not making continual progress in meeting those requirements.

[13] The African Growth and Opportunity Act, s.105

(1971–1981), has been modified and extended a number of times. Its second phase covered the decade 1981–1991. The overall revision that was due at the end of the second decade in 1991 had to be deferred, pending the outcome of the Uruguay Round in 1994.[14] The third major phase thus started on January 1, 1995 with the adoption of a scheme of generalised preferences for the 1995–2004 period.[15] In what has been termed a "radical departure" from the past, the 1995 revision "did away with the quantitative limitation of GSP imports".

Not all products qualify for the E.U.'s GSP scheme. For those that do, the applicable preferential margin depends on the degree of their import sensitivity, as so designated by the E.U. There are four classes of products with different applicable preferential margins over the corresponding MFN rate: very sensitive (15 per cent), sensitive (30 per cent), semi-sensitive (65 per cent), and non-sensitive (100 per cent). This classification broadly reflects their sensitivity on the Community market as established at the time of the Uruguay Round multi-lateral trade negotiations.[16]

The E.U. uses its GSP scheme to encourage countries to, *inter alia*, undertake effective programmes to combat drug production and trafficking. Such countries "continue to enjoy duty-free access for industrial and agricultural products provided they continue their efforts to combat drugs."[17] This treatment is extended to industrial products from the Central American Common Market countries and Panama. Since 1998, there have also been special incentive schemes designed to encourage countries towards compliance with labour standards and environmental norms set by relevant international organisations. More specifically, incentives are granted to countries that have adopted and applied in their national legislation the standards elaborated by the ILO concerning the right to organise and bargain collectively, as well as minimum age for employment, or the tropical forest protection standards of the International Tropical Timber Organisation (ITTO).

The E.U.'s GSP scheme provides for dual means to protect sectors or products that are sensitive to Community industry and agriculture against import surges— a mechanism involving a modulation of preferential tariff margins[18] and an emergency safeguard clause.[19] Finally, the E.U. applies the graduation principle and removes countries from the list of GSP beneficiaries in the event that their

---

[14] The previous scheme was thus kept in being until December 31, 1994.

[15] The basic legislative acts were Council Regulation 3281/94, concerning industrial products, which was extended until June 30, 1999, and Council Regulation 1256/96, concerning agricultural products. For the period from July 1, 1999 to December 31, 2001, the E.U. revised its GSP scheme on the basis of Council Regulation 2820/98. See UNCTAD, *Handbook on the GSP Scheme of the European Community,* http://www.unctad.org/gsp/eu.

[16] See [1999] O.J. C348/136.

[17] See para. 17 of the preamble to Council Regulation 2820/98 applying a multiannual scheme of generalised tariff preferences for the period July 1, 1999 to December 31, 2001, [1998] O.J.L357/1.

[18] Tariff modulation refers to the system under which individual "fixed duty-free amounts" and ceilings (concerning sensitive industrial products) and "fixed reduced duty" amounts (concerning agricultural products) are replaced by reduced rates of duty, classified according to four categories of product sensitivity. For a comprehensive and illustrated summary of the E.U.'s GSP system, see UNCTAD, *Handbook on the GSP Scheme of the European Community,* http://www.unctad.org/gsp/eu.

[19] See para. 8 of the preamble to Council Regulation [1998] 2820/98, [1998] O.J. L357/1.

per capita gross national product exceeds $8,210 (according to the most recent World Bank figures), and their development index (calculated in accordance with a given formula) is greater than 1.[20] Applying these criteria, the Council decided to withdraw Hong Kong, South Korea and Singapore from the list of preference-receiving countries as of May 1998.[21]

The recent shift of attention at the global level towards least developed countries has also been reflected in the preferential arrangements of the E.U. In fulfilment of a pledge made by WTO members to improve access to their markets for products originating in the least developed countries, Council Regulation 602/98 granted least developed countries not parties to the Lomé Convention preferences equivalent to those enjoyed by the parties to the Convention. Most recently, the E.U. has approved the Commission's proposal to eliminate quotas and duties on all products, except for arms, coming from the 48 LDCs[22]—hence often called the "everything but arms" market access principle, which entered into effect on March 5, 2001.[23] Although the move is quite exemplary, its actual impact is expected to be limited. First, largely due to pressure from the E.U. farming lobby, three "sensitive" products—bananas (until 2006), sugar (until 2009) and rice (until 2009)—have been excluded from immediate full liberalisation. And secondly, the impact of this move is likely to be modest because over 99 per cent of Community trade with the LDCs already carries zero import duty, either under the Lomé Convention or under the Generalised System of Preferences (GSP).

The general preferences of the E.U. do not affect the specific preferences granted by virtue of the Cotonou Partnership Agreement, to the so-called ACP countries, that is countries in Africa, the Caribbean and the Pacific associated with the E.U. (see paragraph 2.57). This is another expression of the E.U.'s use of the concept of "differentiation in preferences".

E.U. Preferences for ACP countries   The E.U. and its Member States have   **2.57** entered into successive association agreements, the so-called Lomé Agreements concluded in Lomé (Togo), with 78[24] countries in Africa, the Caribbean and the Pacific (the so-called ACP countries). The last Lomé Agreement (Lomé IV) was initially concluded in 1989 for a term of 10 years, but was revised in Port Louis (Mauritius) in 1995. Just before the expiry of Lomé IV on February 29, 2000, the E.U. and the ACP countries concluded a successor agreement, governing the future terms of co-operation between them. The new agreement, called the "ACP-EU Partnership Agreement" was signed in Cotonou (Benin) on June 23,

---

[20] See Art. 1.4 of Council Regulation 2820/98, [1998] O.J. L357/1.

[21] See Art. 3 of Regulation 2623/97, [1999] O.J. L354/9.

[22] Art. 37.9 of the Cotonou Agreement had in fact envisaged this to happen by 2005 at the latest.

[23] See press release by DG Trade entitled "EU approves 'Everything But Arms' trade access for least developed countries", Brussels, February 26, 2001, available on http://europa.eu.int/comm/trade/miti/devel/eba3.htm.

[24] In December 2000, the ACP Council of Ministers admitted Cuba as the 78th member of the ACP Group. For the latest list of members of the ACP, see http://www.acpsec.org. However, Cuba has yet to accede to the Cotonou Partnership Agreement. Moreover, the trade provisions of the Cotonou Agreement do not apply to South Africa, whose trade relations with the E.U. are regulated by a separate agreement.

2000. The Cotonou Agreement is intended to run for a term of 20 years with a five-yearly review clause.

2.58   **The Cotonou Agreement**   Cotonou, like Lomé, aims to provide a firm and solid foundation for economic and trade co-operation between the ACP states and the E.U. so as to foster the smooth and gradual integration of the ACP states into the world economy. The Cotonou Agreement explicitly provides that economic and trade co-operation "shall be implemented in full conformity with the provisions of the WTO, including special and differential treatment, taking account of the Parties' mutual interests and their respective levels of development."[25] In furtherance of the principle of "differentiation in preferences", the Agreement talks in terms of ensuring "special and differential treatment" for all ACP countries and of maintaining special treatment for ACP LLDCs.[26]

Cotonou has introduced important changes to the Lomé system. Notable, among others, are the following: (1) it has set strict deadlines for the transformation of the currently non-reciprocal preferential arrangement into a reciprocal free trade regime which would also require non-LDC ACP countries to progressively open their markets for E.U. products; (2) it has introduced new provisions on such new subjects as trade in services, competition policy, labour standards, intellectual property, and the environment; and (3) it has brought the different financial protocols and instruments, such as Stabex and Sysmin, operating under Lomé IV into a single instrument. These will be discussed in turn.

In trade matters, Cotonou is as much a concluded agreement as a programme for future negotiations designed eventually to phase out the traditional non-reciprocal preferential arrangement between the E.U. and ACP countries. In the short term, the Cotonou Agreement largely extends the life of Lomé IV for a preparatory period of eight years which expires on December 31, 2007. Accordingly, Annex V to the Cotonou Agreement provides that non-agricultural products originating in the ACP states shall be imported into the Community free of customs duties and charges having equivalent effect. As regards agricultural imports from the ACP states, the Community has "undertaken to adopt the necessary measures allowing more favourable treatment than that granted to third countries benefiting from the most-favoured nation clause".[27]

In the area of non-tariff barriers, too, Cotonou provides that the Community shall not apply any quantitative restrictions or measures having equivalent effect to imports of products originating in the ACP states.[28] This is, however, subject to a GATT–Article XX type of exception authorising import restrictions or prohibitions on grounds of health, security, public morals and others. Moreover,

---

[25] See Art. 34.4 of the Cotonou Agreement. See, *e.g.* F. Matambalya, S. Wolf, "The Cotonou Agreement and the challenges of making the New E.U.–ACP trade regime WTO compatible" (2001) J.W.T. 35, No. 1, pp. 123–144.

[26] See, *inter alia*, Art. 35:3 of the Cotonou Agreement.

[27] See Art. 1 of Annex V to the Cotonou Agreement. A "Joint Declaration" concerning agricultural products has been annexed to the Final Act which lists E.C. agricultural tariff lines with corresponding percentage reductions from generally applicable MFN rates. These rates generally range between exemption and a 15 per cent reduction in applicable *ad valorem* duties. See Declaration XXII for the details.

[28] See Arts 1 and 2 of Annex V to the Cotonou Agreement.

the Community is also free to introduce safeguard measures in cases where its domestic industries are threatened with serious injury due to increased quantities of imports from the ACP countries.

During the transitional period, no reciprocity is required from the ACP countries; they are required only to give the Community MFN treatment on the same level as their other developed trading partners. Indeed, a Declaration annexed to the Final Act even provides for an exception that ACP countries might discriminate in favour of other developed countries if those other developed countries grant them greater preferences than those granted by the Community.[29] As a result, since the Lomé IV waiver from the MFN principle of Article I of GATT 1994 expired on February 29, 2000, the E.U. and ACP member countries of the WTO have jointly submitted a new request under Article IX of the WTO Agreement "for the extension of the existing waiver in order to allow the maintenance of preferential trade between the parties."[30]

Rules of origin   In order to exclude countries that do not enjoy general or specific trade preferences from exporting their products under preferential conditions to the E.U., preferences are subject to strict rules for the origin of goods. Rules of origin are therefore an essential element of such an arrangement.

According to Protocol 1 attached to Annex V of the Cotonou Agreement, products incorporating materials which have not been wholly obtained in ACP states may still be considered as originating therefrom on condition that they have undergone "sufficient working or processing in the ACP States".[31] A detailed product-by-product description of about 120 pages has been attached to the Agreement in order to determine whether non-wholly obtained products are sufficiently worked or processed in the ACP states.[32] At a more general level, however, non-originating materials may be used if their total value does not exceed 15 per cent of the ex-works price of the product and if that does not take them beyond the limits set by the list regarding the allowable maximum value of non-originating materials for the specific product in question.[33] The combined territories of the ACP states are considered as being one territory for purposes of determination of origin. Moreover, applying the principle of cumulation, in determining the origin of finished goods coming directly from ACP countries, raw materials originating and works carried out on them in the Community are treated as materials and works of the ACP states.[34] Such products are also generally required to be transported directly without entering any other territory;

2.59

---

[29] See Declaration XXXI annexed to the Final Act of the Cotonou Agreement.
[30] See WTO doc. G/C/W/187, March 2, 2000. The request has so far been blocked by the five Latin American banana-exporting countries (Costa Rica, Ecuador, Guatemala, Honduras, and Panama) which demanded submission by the E.U. of an acceptable and WTO-consistent banana regime as a prior condition for consideration of the waiver request.
[31] Protocol 1 to Annex V of the Cotonou Agreement, Art. 2.
[32] *ibid.*, Annex II to Protocol 1.
[33] Cotonou Agreement, Protocol 1, *ibid.*, Art. 4.
[34] Protocol 1, *ibid.*, Art. 6.

this does not of course affect mere transit through non-ACP and non-E.U. territories.[35]

2.60   **Regional integration and Cotonou**   The Cotonou Agreement underlines that closer integration at the regional level is a key instrument for the gradual integration of ACP countries into the global economy. To that end, it sets detailed schedules for the conclusion of WTO-compatible free trade agreements—here termed "economic partnership agreements"—between the E.U. on the one hand and interested non-LDC ACP countries (alone or as a group), on the other. The new arrangements envisage the progressive removal of trade barriers between parties to the agreement after the eight-year preparatory period. Non-LDC ACP countries that would not be interested in entering into the envisaged economic partnership agreements will be provided with "a new framework for trade which is equivalent to their existing situation and in conformity with WTO rules."[36] The practical implementation of an undertaking to retain current privileges while at the same time being WTO-compatible will obviously be a daunting challenge. A realistic approach suggests that non-reciprocal preferences to these countries will be limited to whatever would be available under the GSP system of the E.U.—a less generous system covering fewer products, unilaterally granted and liable to a unilateral withdrawal at the discretion of the E.U.

For LDCs, however, the Community only undertakes to start a process which, at the latest by 2005, will allow "duty free access for essentially all products from all LDC building on the level of the existing trade provisions of the fourth ACP–E.C. Convention and which will simplify and review the rules of origin, including cumulation provisions, that apply to their exports."[37] The process in this respect has already entered an advanced level with the "everything but arms" proposal currently under debate before the E.C. Commission.

Non-Trade Aspects of Cotonou: An Overview

2.61   A strengthened political dimension, the involvement of new actors, and a more rationalised and performance-based aid management are some of the major innovations of the Cotonou Agreement.

2.62   **The political dimension**   In a clear departure from the past, the revised Lomé IV and the Cotonou Agreements have strengthened the political dimension of the relationship between the E.U. and the ACP countries. Issues such as human rights, good governance, rule of law, etc., which were traditionally taken as questions of sovereignty and internal affairs, beyond the purview of outside forces such as the Community, have progressively been brought to the centre of the new arrangements. The revised version of Lomé IV, for the first time, made respect for human rights, democratic principles and the rule of law, "essential

---

[35] *ibid.*, Art. 12.
[36] The Cotonou Agreement, Art. 37:6.
[37] *ibid.*, Cotonou Agreement Art. 37:9.

elements" of the Convention, whose violation could lead, as a last resort measure, to the partial or full suspension of application of the Convention to the concerned parties.[38] The revised Lomé IV made good governance "a particular aim of cooperation operations".

Cotonou repeated the "essential elements" of Lomé IV with the same consequences.[39] However, it advanced one step further in the case of good governance, defined to mean "the transparent and accountable management of human, natural, economic and financial resources for the purposes of equitable and sustainable development." Thus defined, good governance has been labelled as a "fundamental element" of the new agreement.[40] Unlike the "essential elements" mentioned above, it can be violated and can lead, as a last resort, to suspension, only in serious cases of corruption, including acts of bribery leading to such corruption.[41] Cotonou also enshrines a commitment to pursue an "active, comprehensive and integrated policy of peace-building and conflict prevention and resolution". The change of approach in aid allocation from "entitlement" for specific amounts, to amounts which vary depending on the performance of the receiving country, has given further leverage for the E.U. to control the political dimension of the relationship. An attempt by the E.U. to incorporate within the agreement powers following mandatory readmission and return of immigrants illegally present in the E.U. was defected at the insistence of the ACP countries.[42]

New actors For the first time in the history of E.U.–ACP co-operation, the **2.63** traditional government-to-government relationship has been extended to cover non-governmental as well as local governmental entities in the process. Article 6 of the Cotonou Agreement defines the "actors of co-operation" to include local, regional and national governmental bodies as well as non-state entities such as the private sector, trade union organisations, and civil society in all its forms. The involvement of these actors extends from the design and implementation of national development strategies to direct access to financial resources. Most attention is given to the private sector, whose role as an engine for development has been explicitly recognised. To that end, and for the first time, the private sector will have access to funding from the European Investment Bank (EIB), without the requirement of a state guarantee.

Performance-based aid management Unlike the previous system of fixed **2.64** allocations of aid regardless of performance, the new system allows the E.U. to allocate aid on the basis of each country's needs and performance. This flexibility enables the donor to spend money where it can be used most effectively. It also gives the E.U. more power than it had under the old system of fixed entitlements. Moreover, the Cotonou Agreement has reduced the many financing instruments

---

[38] The revised Lomé IV, Arts 5 and 366a.
[39] The Cotonou Agreement, Art. 9.2.
[40] *ibid.*, Art. 9.3.
[41] *ibid.*, Art. 97.
[42] For a readable description of the Cotonou Agreement, see ECDPM (2001), *Cotonou Infokit: Towards a Stronger Political Partnership (18),* Maastricht, the Netherlands.

operating previously to just two: an instrument for granting subsidies for long-term development support (a Grant Facility) and an investment facility to promote the private sector in the ACP countries (an Investment Facility).[43]

The Grant Facility is a single procedure for the granting of aid to ACP countries and regions on the basis of needs and performance. It will be possible to use these resources to finance a wide range of operations, such as macro economic support, sector policies, additional assistance in case of shortfall in export earnings, decentralised co-operation, debt relief, as well as traditional projects and programmes. Cotonou still recognises the particular problems of ACP countries arising from to the instability of their export earnings, particularly in the agricultural and mining sectors, and establishes a "system of additional support in order to mitigate the adverse effects of any instability in export earnings . . . within the financial envelope for support to long-term development."[44]

The Investment Facility focuses on fields of intervention and operations that cannot be financed sufficiently from private capital or by local financial institutions. It aims *inter alia*, to stimulate regional and international investment, particularly to strengthen the capacity of local financial institutions; help the development of the ACP private sector by financing projects and/or commercially viable enterprises and companies; and provide risk capital and loans on concessionary terms.

The Cotonou Agreement enters into force only after ratification by all the Member States of the E.U. and at least two-thirds of the ACP states, and a separate approval by the Community.[45] In the meantime, the provisions of the Lomé Convention, with some exceptions, continue to be applicable.[46]

Commodity agreements

2.65   **International agreements on basic products—general**   States have entered into agreements for the trade in commodities for many years. For instance, as early as 1902, nine Western European countries concluded, an agreement to reduce export subsidies for sugar. Later commodities agreements were aimed more directly at reducing production in order to keep prices sufficiently high and

---

[43] See statement by ACP Secretary-General Jean-Robert Guolongana in *The Courier: Special Issue* (September 2000), p. 5.

[44] The Cotonou Agreement, Art. 68.

[45] *ibid.*, Art. 93:3. In order to close any gaps resulting from the expiry of Lomé IV on February 29, 2000, transitional interim measures have been taken first by the ACP–E.U. Committee of Ambassadors (on February 28, 2000), and later by the ACP–E.U. Council of Ministers to cover the period between August 2, 2000 and the entry into force of the Cotonou Agreement. It is interesting to note here that this latter decision by the ACP–E.U. Council of Ministers enabled an early application of the final Agreement as from August 2, 2000 with the exception of provisions concerning the release and implementation of financial resources from the ninth European Development Fund (EDF). See Decision No. 1/2000 of the ACP–E.U. Council of Ministers of July 27, 2000 regarding transitional measures valid from August 2, 2000 until the entry into force of the ACP–E.U. Partnership Agreement ([2000] O.J. L195/46).

[46] See Decision No. 1/2000 ([2000] O.J. L195/46). See also Decision No. 1/2000 of the ACP–E.U. Committee of Ambassadors of February 28, 2000 on transitional measures valid from March 1, 2000 ([2000] O.J. L56/47).

stable. Before the Second World War, international arrangements thus restricted the production of tin, rubber, tea and sugar. Chapter VI of the Havana Charter (see paragraph 3.02), which never came into force, contained rules for the international trade in "basic products". Under this chapter, exporting and importing countries had to conclude multilateral agreements for, *inter alia*, stability in supply and price.

Basic products are produced and exported mainly by developing countries. Article 6 of the (not legally binding) Charter of Economic Rights and Duties of States (see paragraph 3.94) determines that it is the duty of all states to participate in multilateral agreements on basic products, for the purpose of, amongst other things, the establishment of fixed, compensatory and equitable prices.

International agreements The import and export restrictions that were thus **2.66** introduced by various agreements for basic products that have been concluded, particularly since the Second World War, were in principle contrary to Article XI of the GATT (see paragraph 3.26). However, Article XX(h) provides for an exception for import and export restrictions introduced by basic products agreements if these restrictions have been approved by the contracting parties (in practice the General Council). Moreover, Part IV of the GATT, on "trade and development" (see paragraph 2.47), imposes a duty on the contracting states, where appropriate, to enter into international trade agreements for basic products which are of particular importance to developing countries; measures for the stabilisation of market conditions and prices must be established in these agreements (Article XXXVIII [2][a]). However, Part IV does not provide for adequate rules for the negotiation of such agreements.

The existing agreements can be divided in to two groups:

- agreements on basic products limited to informal arrangements;

- agreements which bring about a market regulation, in which the producing and consuming countries both participate.

In view of the limited success in the past of agreements aimed at the introduction of extensive market regulation, a less far-reaching co-operation has been proposed in more recent negotiations for new commodities agreements.

Informal regulations For some basic products such as rubber, lead, zinc and **2.67** copper, there are intergovernmental consultative bodies consisting of representatives of producing and consuming countries. Within these groups consultations take place on the market development for the particular product.

The Food and Agricultural Organisation (FAO), a specialist institution of the UN, has created similar consultative bodies for, *inter alia*, tea, citrus fruits, cereals, rice, meat, bananas, skins and hides, oil-containing seeds, oils and fats, hard fibres and fish. Within UNCTAD there are consultative bodies for tungsten and copper.

Certain products (*e.g.* sugar, jute, hard fibres, tea, rice, bananas, oil-containing seeds) are covered by "gentlemen's agreements" which usually introduce price indications and/or export quotas. These arrangements are more readily accepted than strict agreements, since they do not impose legal duties and their execution is dependent on the willingness of the participant states.

2.68 **International market regulation** An international market regulation for a basic product can only be created through a multilateral convention in which the most important importing and exporting countries have agreed to comply with this regulation. These conventions have a "mixed" nature: producing as well as consuming countries are parties. Agreements between producing states only (*e.g.* OPEC; see paragraph 2.71) or consuming countries only lack this mixed nature.

At present, market regulation agreements have been concluded for, *inter alia*, cereal, cocoa, rubber, jute and timber. Some of these agreements (*e.g.* for rubber and timber) are currently being renegotiated. The international market regulation for tin suffered considerable financial problems, mainly as a result of speculation on the London Metal Exchange, and was abolished in 1985.

Each market regulation agreement requires an international institution, in which the producing and consuming countries are represented and which supervises the operation of the agreement. It also provides for sanctions and dispute regulation. Some market regulation agreements (*e.g.* for milk products and beef) refer to the GATT dispute settlement regulation (see paragraph 3.110).

The substantive rules of the market regulation agreements depend on the objectives (market mechanism or planning) set by the contracting parties. Some agreements only cover the removal of trade restrictions, others provide for direct intervention in supply and demand.

For instance, the agreement on olive oil regulates competition on the olive oil market, as well as overseeing the elimination of illicit practices, and quality control. Similar regulations are found with regard to other agreements (*e.g.* cocoa, milk products, natural rubber, jute and tropical timber), where they are supplemented by more interventionist measures. The agreements on jute and tropical timber provide, for instance, for research and production structures in the producing countries.

Other agreements are aimed at stabilising the market and the prices. To this end the following three systems are used:

(a) The agreement on milk products determines minimum export prices and provides for a mechanism for price adjustment.

(b) The coffee agreement (London, 1983) provided for a quota system for exports on the basis of the price level on the international market. Worldwide quota were fixed by the International Coffee Council and consisted of a fixed part (70 per cent) and a variable part (30 per cent). The fixed part was divided amongst the exporting countries in proportion to their export volumes; the variable part was divided in proportion to the existing stocks in the producing countries (Art. 35). The quotas came into effect when the market prices were below a minimum level; they were suspended when they were higher than the maximum level of the fixed reference prices. The dominant position of Brazil in the coffee market often complicated an efficient execution of the agreement. In 1989 the agreement was extended to September 30, 1991 after which date the existing quotas were to be abolished. However, negotiations on a new coffee agreement failed in 1993. The present agreement, which came into force September 30, 1994, does not provide for market regulation. As a reaction to the absence of a world-wide market regulation for coffee, Central American coffee producers, together with producers from Brazil and Colombia, concluded a separate agreement in 1993 to maintain control over the coffee market. This is achieved, for instance, by stockpiling 20 per cent of the coffee intended for export.

(c) The cocoa and natural rubber agreements provide for the establishment of a market regulation for buffer stocks, for the fixing of price scales and for a system for export control. When the market prices exceed the fixed maximum prices the institution must sell a given proportion of the buffer stock to stabilise the price within the agreed price scale. When, on the other hand, the market price slumps below the fixed minimum price this institution must buy (and replenish the buffer stock with) sufficient quantities to stabilise the price. When purchases are insufficient to bring the price within the agreed price range the institution may then impose temporary export restrictions on the producing countries. These agreements are at present being renegotiated. A similar, rather detailed, regulation operated under the now defunct international tin agreement. One of the consequences of the insolvency of the International Tin Council was that producing and consuming countries became reluctant to organise buffer stocks for other basic products. The buffer stocks are financed by the countries involved as well as through loans from the IMF.

The UNCTAD "integrated programme" Each of the various commodity **2.69** agreements concerns a specific product and has its own regulations. There is no common approach or harmonised implementation, although the UN has made efforts in this direction. As recently as 1976 an "integrated programme" for basic products agreements was established by UNCTAD. During the UNCTAD conference in Nairobi (1976) a global approach for the basic products agreements was accepted. This approach, the "integrated programme", rests on two principles:

(a) an international regulation, applicable to most basic products, should stabilise markets and prices;

(b) prices for basic products should be linked to prices for industrial goods.

The programme seeks to serve the interests of the exporting as well as the importing countries: the export income of the exporting countries must at least remain stable and if possible gradually increase; the importing countries must be assured of supplies.

The integrated programme applies during the first phase to 18 basic products, for each of which UNCTAD must convene an international conference in order to:

(a) establish a regulation for the composition of buffer stocks, possibly linked with production restrictions or export quotas;

(b) establish price mechanisms which take account of, amongst other things, price fluctuations for industrial products imported by producing countries, production costs, exchange rates, inflation and the volume of production and consumption. (This rule means index linked prices according to the price development for industrial products.)

The agreements concerning natural rubber, jute and tropical timber reflect these principles.

However, most of the integrated programme's commodity agreements are less ambitious and, for instance, set up market research and development programmes for production and distribution.

2.70 **The Common Fund** Extensive financing is needed for the realisation of the integrated programme and the storing of buffer supplies. In 1980 it was decided within UNCTAD to establish a "Common Fund" for this purpose.

The Common Fund consists of two accounts:

(a) the first account (needs estimated at $400 million) must serve for the financing of the buffer stocks which must be stockpiled in accordance with the respective agreements between the producing and consuming countries. The financial means are provided by the contracting states.

(b) The second account (needs estimated at $280 million) must serve for the financing of research and development, *inter alia* for improvement of market structures for basic products, for increased productivity and for diversification and marketing of basic products. The financial means are provided by the countries involved, on a partially voluntary basis.

One of the many obstacles in the difficult negotiations was the allocation of the votes in the Council, responsible for the management of the Fund. In the end the votes were allocated as follows: developing countries 45 per cent, industrialised countries 40.2 per cent, the former Eastern bloc 7.7 per cent, China 2.9 per cent and other countries 4.2 per cent.

Because the ratifications took some time, the Fund came into effect only in June 1989. By 1993, 105 countries (but not the United States and Canada) had acceded to the Common Fund. However, the financial means remain far below the proposed amounts: at present the first account has just over $137 million and the second account just over $22 million. The activities of the Fund are therefore rather restricted and concern mainly the second account. The Fund is managed from Amsterdam.

2.71 **Producer organisations** A number of countries that produce basic products or raw materials have set up producer organisations for the representation of their common interests.

Perhaps the best known producer organisation is OPEC (the Organisation of Petroleum Exporting Countries), founded by the Agreement of Bagdad (1960), to which, besides the Arab countries from the Middle East, Algeria, Libya, Iran, Venezuela, Indonesia, Nigeria, Ecuador and Gabon are also parties. Having initially restricted itself to consultation for the purpose of joint negotiations with the oil companies, OPEC introduced unilateral price fixing for oil in 1973. The industralised countries reacted to the increased oil price by developing alternative sources of energy and by buying oil increasingly from non-OPEC oil producers. In this way the influence of OPEC has been reduced. For some years the OPEC countries have been allotting export quotas among themselves, though, in the absence of sufficient solidarity, the quotas are not always observed.

There is a difference of opinion on the legitimacy of OPEC. The United States considers the organisation to be contrary to the spirit and objectives of the GATT. The developing countries, which are members of OPEC, are excluded from the general tariff preferences granted by the United States (see paragraph 2.55). The developing countries rely on Article 5 of the (non-binding) Charter of Economic Rights and Duties of States (see paragraph 7.29) for the legitimacy of producer organisations such as OPEC. According to most Western countries, a producer organisation is not as such illegitimate, though its actions can be.

There are also producer organisations representing countries which are also parties to international basic product agreements, for instance for cocoa, copper, natural rubber, coffee, bauxite, bananas, iron ore, tungsten, tea, sugar and tropical timber. These organisations do not intervene as such in the market. Rather they co-ordinate the viewpoints of producing countries on the existing agreements for basic products.

CHAPTER 3

THE REGULATION OF INTERNATIONAL TRADE

Overview The regulation of international trade is nearly as old as inter- **3.01**
national trade itself. For years, states regulated international trade through
national laws and international treaties. A multilateral approach in the regulation
of international trade is, however, a thing of the relatively recent past.

The multilateral approach, which started gradually after the Second World
War, promoted a market economy—a system, which allows the interplay of
market forces (such as the balance between supply and demand) to play a
primary role in shaping the overall direction of economic relations. A free market
requires, *inter alia,* liberalisation of the movement of goods and services as well
as the prohibition of restrictions on competition by the market participants.

However, beginning in the 1950s and early 1960s, there was a growing
consensus that the rules of the market could not fully serve the interests of
developing countries. Because of chronic balance-of-payments problems affecting these countries, trade liberalisation was believed only to worsen their trade
deficits.[1] UNCTAD (United Nations Conference on Trade and Development; see
paragraph 2.24) was established in 1964 to address the widening gap between
rich and poor countries, and soon came up with a policy of special and differential treatment in favour of developing countries.[2] The concept and actual
impact of special and differential treatment on the economic situation of its
intended beneficiaries might be a matter of debate. However, the principle
remains a central part of the trading system's attempts to improve the terms-
of-trade situation of the developing world.

---

[1] For an interesting discussion of how the multilateral trading system has been responding to the
perceived problems of developing countries, see Whalley, J. *Special and Differential Treatment in
the Millennium Round* (Blackwell Publishers, Oxford, 1999) pp. 1065–1093.

[2] As summarised by Hudec, the creation of UNCTAD was also a response to the Cold War situation
that prevailed at the time: " 'Cold war' competition for the loyalty of these emerging countries
intensified when the Soviet Union began to press for the creation of a global trade organization,
within the United Nations, that would provide an alternative to the Western-dominated GATT. The
prospect of a rival United Nations organisation grew more substantial each year and finally
materialised in the form of the United Nations Conference on Trade and Development
(UNCTAD)": R. Hudec, *Developing Countries in the GATT Legal System* (Trade Policy Research
Centre, London, 1987), at 39.

PART I: LIBERALISATION OF INTERNATIONAL TRADE

The GATT/WTO system: overview

3.02 **General** The acronym "GATT" (General Agreement on Tariffs and Trade) is often used in two senses: as an international agreement embodying the rules and principles governing cross-border trade, and as the international organisation overseeing the implementation of the agreement.[3] In the sense of an international agreement, GATT was negotiated as part of the endeavour to establish a world-wide regulation for trade and to found an international trade organisation to that end. However, the Havana Charter, which was to have created an international trade organisation, and which was signed in 1948, never came into effect due to lack of support from the United States. This lack of enthusiasm is surprising as the United States had taken the initiative for the diplomatic conference leading to the Charter of Havana.[4] The GATT was given "provisional" effect from January 1, 1948 by a Protocol of Provisional Application (the PPA).[5]

3.03 **"Codes"** The GATT has been amended on a number of occasions. Since the Tokyo Round (1973–1979), the contracting states have preferred not to amend the GATT, but to enter into supplementary treaties (side agreements) that are not always signed by all GATT members.[6] These side agreements are usually called Codes. They concern, amongst other things, dumping (see paragraph 3.64),

---

[3] The text of the GATT can be found in S. Zamora & R. A. Brand, *Basic documents of international economic law* (CCH, Chicago, 1990) I, pp. 9 *et seq.* C.J. Cheng, *Basic documents of international trade law* (2nd ed., M. Nijhoff Dordrecht, 1990) pp. 867 *et seq.* P. Kunig, N. Lau and W. Meng (eds.), *International economic law—Basic documents* (de Gruyter, Berlin, 1993) pp. 483 *et seq.* In the extensive literature on GATT, consult *inter alia* J. Barton and B. Fischer, *International Trade Regulation: Regulating International Business* (Boston, 1986); W. Benedek, *Die Rechtsordnung des GATT aus völkerrechtlicher Sicht* (Springer, Berlin, 1990); K.W. Dam, *Law and International Economic Organisation* (Chicago, 1970); D. Carreau, T. Flory and P. Juillard, *Droit international économique* (2nd ed., LGDJ, Paris, 1990) pp. 95 *et seq.*; R.E. Haddock, *The GATT Legal System and World Trade Diplomacy* (Butterworth, London, 1990); M. Hilf, F.G. Jacobs and E.U. Peters-mann (eds), *The European Community and GATT* (Kluwer Law & Taxation, Deventer, 1986); J. Jackson, *World Trade and the Law of GATT* (Bobbs—Merril, Indianapolis, 1969); O. Long, *Law and its Limitations in the GATT Multilateral Trade System* (M. Nijhoff, Dordrecht, 1985); E. McGovern, *International Trade Regulation: GATT, the United States and the European Community* (2nd ed., Exeter, 1986); P.J. Kuyper, "The law of GATT as a special field of international law— Ignorance, further refinement or self-contained system of international law?" (1994), 25 N.Y.I.L. 227–257; R. Silvestre J. Martha, "Precedent in world trade law" (1997) N.I.L.R. 346–377; F. Weiss, "The WTO and the progressive development of international trade law" (1998), 29 N.Y.I.L. 71–115; J.L. Dunoff, "The death of the trade regime" (1999) 10 E.J.I.L. 733–762; J.M. Jackson, "The perils of globalisation and the word trading system"(2000) 24 Ford I.L.J. 371–382; D. Palmeter, "The WTO as a Legal System" (2000) 24 Ford I.L.J. 444–480; E. Canal-Forgues, "Sur l'interprétation dans le droit de l'OMC" (2001) 105 R.G.D.I.P. 5–24.

[4] See J. Diebold, *The End of the ITO* (Princeton, 1952).

[5] On the relationship between the GATT and the Havana Charter, see Art. XXIX of the GATT. Pursuant to the Protocol, the participating countries were allowed to maintain certain restrictions (so-called "Grandfather" clause); see M. Hansen and E. Vermulst, "The GATT Protocol of provisional application: a dying grandfather?" (1989) Colum.J.Transnat.L. 263.

[6] One exception from the pre-Tokyo Round period was the Kennedy Round Anti-Dumping Code.

export subsidies (see paragraph 3.72), public procurement (see paragraph 3.34), customs value of goods (see paragraph 3.17) and technical standards (see paragraph 3.45).

The relationship between the GATT and the Codes was not always clear. Many assumed that the GATT took precedence over the Codes. Others argued that the Codes, as full-bodied treaties, had superiority over the GATT, which had only provisional application. Some also held that there was no hierarchy between treaties in international law, and that the GATT and the Codes were equivalent. In the event, the GATT and the Codes operated side by side and the Codes superseded the GATT only when the respective provisions were clearly incompatible.[7]

This problem came to an end with the conclusion of the Uruguay Round (1986–1994), which brought two important developments in this respect. First, all preceding side agreements (Codes) have been excluded from the GATT 1994 (see paragraph 3.7). Secondly, nearly all issues previously covered by the side agreements have been the subject of separate agreements annexed to the WTO Agreement which had to be accepted in their totality by all WTO members.[8]

"Understandings"   During the Uruguay Round negotiations the GATT con-   **3.04** tracting parties specified the interpretation of several GATT provisions in "Understandings". The original GATT and the respective Understandings are now together known as "GATT 1994". The Uruguay Round also led to other agreements applying to specific sectors and issues.[9] The GATT 1994 and these specific agreements are termed Multilateral Agreements on Trade in Goods and constitute Annex 1A to the Marrakesh Agreement establishing the World Trade Organisation (WTO).

The newly negotiated agreements on services (the General Agreement on Trade in Services, GATS) and on intellectual property rights (Agreement on Trade-Related Aspects of Intellectual Property Rights, TRIPs) form Annexes 1B and 1C to the Marrakesh Agreement, respectively.

Annex 2 to the Marrakesh Agreement provides for the Understanding on Rules and Procedures Governing the Settlement of Disputes (the DSU) and Annex 3 provides for the Trade Policy Review Mechanism (the TPRM). The agreements and associated legal instruments in Annexes 1, 2 and 3 are called the "Multilateral Trade Agreements"—agreements covered by the "package deal" principle and applying to all WTO Members. On the other hand, Annex 4 provides for

---

[7] See P.J. Kuyper, "Het GATT en het Volkenrecht" (1993) 107 Med.Ned.Ver.Int.R. 25.
[8] By virtue of the all-or-nothing approach of the package deal principle adopted by the Uruguay Round (see para. 3.108).
[9] They are the Agreement on Agriculture, the Agreement on Sanitary and Phytosanitary Measures, the Agreement on Textiles and Clothing, the Agreement on Technical Barriers to Trade, the Agreement on Trade-Related Investment Measures, the Agreement on Implementation of Article VI of the General Agreement on Tariffs and Trade 1994, the Agreement on Implementation of Article VII of the General Agreement on Tariffs and Trade 1994, the Agreement on Preshipment Inspection, the Agreement on Rules of Origin, the Agreement on Import Licensing Procedures, the Agreement on Subsidies and Countervailing Measures, and the Agreement on Safeguards.

the two (originally four) so-called Plurilateral Trade Agreements, falling outside the package deal principle and from which countries could pick and choose.[10]

The WTO administers both the Multilateral and the Plurilateral Agreements annexed to the Marrakesh Agreement.

3.05 **Direct effect** There is no clear answer to the question of whether the provisions of GATT have direct effect, *i.e.* whether they give rights to individual natural and legal persons and whether these rights can be invoked in the national courts by them (see paragraph 1.04).[11]

A number of authors have argued that the GATT should have direct effect to give it more legal significance; some earlier American judgments went in this direction.[12] However, most writers are of the opinion that the limited sanctions available in the event of the violation of GATT rules and, in particular, the vague wording of the GATT provisions, prevent those provisions from being self-executing. Indeed, in the United States the Uruguay Round Implementation Act expressly states that "No person other than the United States . . . shall have any cause of action or defence under any of the Uruguay Round Agreements or by virtue of Congressional approval of such an agreement."[13] The European Court of Justice has also clearly denied direct effect to GATT rules,[14] basing its decision on:

* the great flexibility of the GATT provisions;

* the many exceptions;

* the non-enforceable dispute regulation in the GATT.[15]

---

[10] At the beginning of the WTO, there were four such Plurilateral Agreements: the Agreement on Trade in Civil Aircraft, the Agreement on Government Procurement, the International Dairy Agreement, and the International Bovine Meat Agreement. However, the International Meat Council (administering the Bovine Meat Agreement) and the International Dairy Council (administering the Dairy Agreement), terminated their respective Agreements as of the end of 1997 (see WTO Press Release of September 30, 1997, PRESS/78.) As a result, only two Plurilateral Agreements remain in force today. The Arrangement Regarding Bovine Meat and the International Dairy Arrangement came into operation on January 1, 1980 after the Tokyo Round with the objective of expanding and liberalising world trade in their respective sectors. Both agreements—renamed the International Bovine Meat Agreement and the International Dairy Agreement—were annexed to the WTO Agreement.

[11] P. Eeckhout, "The domestic legal status of the WTO Agreement: interconnecting legal systems" (1997) 34 C.M.L.Rev. 11–58.

[12] See, *e.g.* J. Jackson, "The GATT in United States domestic Law" (1967) Mich.L.Rev. 249.

[13] s.102(c)(1)(A) of the Uruguay Round Agreements Act of 1994, Pub. L. No. 103–465. See also R. Brand, "Direct effect of international economic law in the United States and the European Union" (1997) 17 NW.J.Int'l.L.&Bus. 556.

[14] See, *inter alia*, Case 21–24/72, *International Fruit Company* [1972] E.C.R. 1219, Case 9/73, *Schluter* [1973] E.C.R. 1135, Case 38/75, *Douaneagent der Nederlandse Spoorwagen* [1976] E.C.R. 1439, and Case C–280/93, *Germany v. Council* [1994] E.C.R. I–4973. Consult M. Maresceau, "The GATT in the case law of the European Court of Justice", in M. Hilf, F.G. Jacobs and E.U. Petersmann (eds), *op.cit.* pp. 107 *et seq.* (with further commentaries on recent judgments of the Court); C. D. Ehlermann, "Application of GATT rules in the European Community", in *ibid.*, pp. 127 *et seq.*, and R. Brand, *op.cit.* n. 13.

[15] The recent substantive development of the GATT dispute regulation weakens this argument of the Court; see para. 3.108.

This means that neither an individual within the E.U. nor a Member State, can challenge a legal act on the grounds of incompatibility with a GATT provision.[16] The incorporation of the GATT into the WTO has strengthened the GATT decision mechanism and dispute regulation (see paragraph 3.106). However, the following summary of an ECJ case between Portugal and the Council indicates that the impact of this development on the question of direct effect seems to have been limited.

Portugal v. Council In this case,[17] Portugal challenged the legality of a   **3.06** Council decision, claiming that it constituted a breach of certain rules and principles of the WTO, *i.e.* those of GATT 1994. In response, the Council relied on what it called "the special characteristics of the WTO agreements" which, in its view, still necessitated denial of direct effect, just like GATT 1947. Portugal stressed the fact that "it is not GATT 1947 that is in issue in the present case but the WTO agreements" that are "significantly different from GATT 1947, in particular in so far as they radically alter the dispute settlement procedure."

The Court agreed with Portugal that the WTO agreements differed significantly from the provisions of GATT 1947, mainly on account of the strengthening of the dispute settlement system. However, it reiterated that "the system resulting from those agreements nevertheless accords considerable importance to negotiation between the parties". In a manner that magnifies the political aspect of its decision, the Court even went outside the confines of its system and observed that

> "some of the contracting parties, which are among the most important commercial partners of the Community, have concluded from the subject-matter and purpose of the WTO agreements that they are not among the rules applicable by their judicial organs when reviewing the legality of their rules of domestic law."

It thus concluded that the WTO agreements were not in principle among the rules in the light of which the Court would review the legality of measures adopted by the Community institutions.

GATT 1994 As pointed out, the expression "GATT 1994" is shorthand for   **3.07** the 1947 version of the General Agreement as amended over time, the tariff concession and accession protocols and other decisions taken under GATT 1947,

---

[16] How individuals somehow can rely on the GATT rules is described in the "new instrument for trade policy" of the E.U., which allows individuals to lodge a complaint with the Commission against "illicit commercial trade practices" from third countries, *i.e.* practices that are incompatible "with the international law or generally accepted rules" (see para. 3.54). In that event, individuals can rely on the GATT rules: Case 70/87, *Fediol* [1989] E.C.R. 1781. Moreover, the ECJ has admitted an action with respect to a Community act (Council Regulation 404/93), which is based *inter alia* on infringement of the GATT rules (Case C–280/93, *Federal Republic of Germany against the Council of the European Communities* [1993] O.J. C173/17). See however, J. Osterhond Berkey, "The European Court of Justice and direct effect for the GATT, a question worth revisiting" (1998) 8 E.J.I.L. 626–657.

[17] See *Portugal v. Council*, Case C–149/96, para. 25.

as well as the understandings reached on the interpretation of GATT provisions such as Articles II.1(b), XVII, XXIV, etc. The acronym "GATT" is used here in this wide sense.

3.08 **Substance of GATT** The GATT includes some important principles (*e.g.* non-discrimination and most favoured nation treatment in respect of other GATT members, see paragraph 3.09) and prohibitions. It also provides for procedures to advance the liberalisation of trade. The GATT thus counters:

- tariff restrictions (taxes, such as customs duties, which are charged when goods cross a border) (see paragraph 3.13);

- quantitative restrictions (quotas, import and export licences) (see paragraph 3.26);

- other non-tariff barriers (NTBs) (various protective measures which have the same effect as tariffs and quantitative restrictions) (see paragraph 3.32).

Most favoured nation treatment

3.09 **General** It is significant of the objectives of the GATT that its Article I provides for a general most favoured nation treatment (see paragraph 1.08):

" . . . any advantage, favour, privilege or immunity granted by any contracting party to any product originating in or destined for any other country shall be accorded immediately and unconditionally to the like product originating in or destined for the territories of all other contracting parties."

The various liberalisation measures which have been introduced pursuant to the GATT by members of the WTO must thus in principle be extended to all other WTO members. Although Article I applies mainly to customs and other duties, it is deemed that it is also applicable to other trade policy measures.[18] For instance, when identical instances of dumping (see paragraph 3.64) have been established in a contracting state on the occasion of imports from different contracting states, the country of importation must in principle enact the same anti-dumping measures against any such dumped imports.[19] Moreover, it appears from the words "any other country" that the most favoured treatment also applies when a contracting state gives preferences to a country that is not a contracting state of the GATT.[20]

---

[18] M. Broszkamp, *Meistbegünstigung und Gegenseitigkeit im GATT* (Carl Heymanns, Cologne, 1990); D. Carreau, T. Flory and P. Juillard, *op.cit.* pp. 105 *et seq.*; E. McGovern, *op.cit.* pp. 202 *et seq.*

[19] GATT, Basic Documents and Selected Instruments (1961) p. 198.

[20] The General Agreement on Trade in Services (GATS) also provides for an unconditional MFN in its Article II. For further discussion on this point, see para. 3.81.

Substance of the rule   The rule must be applied "unconditionally". This   **3.10**
means, for instance, that a state can invoke most favoured nation treatment
without granting in return some advantage. In other words, the rule is not based
on reciprocity.

Every "tariff concession" (see paragraph 3.15) granted by a Member State
thus has *erga omnes* effect for all other Member States. However, derogation
from the rule of most favoured nation treatment could be obtained on the basis
of a waiver adopted with a qualified majority by WTO members (see paragraph
3.56). Furthermore, the rule does not apply to customs unions and free trade areas
that satisfy the requirements set by pertinent GATT provisions (see paragraph
3.11). Neither does the rule apply to developing countries (see paragraph
3.49).

Customs unions and free trade areas   The MFN principle embodied in   **3.11**
Article I of the General Agreement testifies to the global approach adopted by
GATT in the liberalisation of international trade. GATT was not, however,
oblivious to the potential attractions of regional trade agreements (RTAs).
Indeed, recognition was given to "the desirability of increasing freedom of trade
by the development, through voluntary agreements, of closer integration between
the economies of the countries parties to such agreements."[21] To reconcile these
apparently contradictory approaches, GATT Article XXIV provided that "the
provisions of this Agreement shall not prevent, as between the territories of
contracting parties, the formation of a customs union or of a free-trade area."[22]
Article XXIV(5) of GATT thus provides for a general exception to the rule of
most favoured nation treatment for customs unions and free trade areas (see
paragraph 2.34), as does Article V of GATS from the MFN principle enshrined
under Article II thereof.

However, a number of conditions are attached to this recognition of the use of
free trade areas and customs unions. Article XXIV(8) of GATT gives a description of free trade areas and customs unions:

- A free trade area is a grouping of two or more customs territories for which
  the customs duties and other trade restrictions are lifted for an essential part
  of trade between the Member States.[23] It only relates to the free movement
  of goods between the Member States. In respect of third countries there is
  neither a common customs tariff nor a common trade policy.

- A customs union replaces one or more customs territories by one customs
  territory so that customs duties and other trade restrictions between the
  Member States are lifted for substantially all the trade between these states.
  Each Member State applies identical duties and other trade restrictions in
  respect to third states. This entails in practice that besides the internal free
  trade in goods, a common customs tariff and a common trade policy is
  applied to third countries.

---

[21] GATT 1994, Art. XXIV:4.
[22] *ibid.* Art. XXIV:5.
[23] R.S. Imhoof, "Le GATT et les zones de libre-échange" (Geneva, 1979).

In customs unions (but not free trade areas) restrictions on trade in respect of third countries are not allowed to be greater or more restrictive than the individual restrictions applied by the Member States before they entered into the customs union (Article XXIV 5(a)). This means in real terms, *inter alia*, that the common customs tariff may only be equal to or less than the average of the national tariffs before the establishment of the customs union.[24]

3.12   **Applications**   It has been accepted that the E.U. satisfies the description of a customs union.[25] The question of whether certain E.U. provisions (*e.g.* concerning agriculture[26] and the preferential agreements with some third states such as the Mediterranean or ACP countries) are compatible with the GATT crops up regularly.[27]

As regards the European Coal and Steel Community, a special waiver for admission was granted by the contracting states, since this regional union does not apply to "substantially all the trade" between the Member States.[28]

Various regional unions fall within the exception of Article XXIV(5), including:

- the association between the E.U. and the countries of the European Free Trade Association (EFTA)(see paragraph 2.35)[29];

- the association between the United States and Canada to establish a free trade area between both countries[30];

- the free trade zone between the United States, Mexico and Canada (NAFTA) (see paragraph 2.36) [31];

---

[24] For problems on the application of this rule in respect of the E.U., see D. Carreau, T. Flory and P. Juillard, *op.cit.* pp. 127 *et seq.*

[25] Consult, *inter alia*: G. de la Charriére, "L'examen par le GATT du traité de Rome instituant la Communauté économique européenne" (1958) A.F.D.I. 621; M. Hilf, F.G. Jacobs and E.U. Petersmann, *op.cit.* pp.127 *et seq.*

[26] See GATT Oil Seeds Panel Report (1992) BISD 37S/86 http://www.worldtradelaw.net/reports/gattpanels/oilseedsII.pdf.

[27] See in particular: E.U. Petersmann, "The EEC as a GATT member: legal conflicts between GATT law and European community law" in M. Hilf, F.G. Jacobs and E.U. Petersmann, *op.cit.* pp. 23 *et seq.*; I. Nordgren, "The GATT Panels during the Uruguay Round" (1991/4) J.W.T. 57.

[28] GATT, Basic documents and selected instruments (1953) p. 17.

[29] F. Schoneveld, "The E.C. and free trade agreements—stretching the limits of GATT exceptions to non-discriminatory trade?" (1992/5) J.W.T. 59. See, *e.g.* the agreement between the E.C. and Switzerland, in S. Zamora & R.A. Brand, *op.cit.* II, pp. 337 *et seq.* (with explanation by H. Van Houtte); [1972] O.J. L300/191. These various agreements refer expressly to Art. XXIV of the GATT.

[30] See text in S. Zamora and R.A. Brand, *op.cit.* II, pp. 353 *et seq.* See, *inter alia*, S.A. Baker and S.P. Battram, "The Canada-United States free trade agreement" (1989) *International Lawyer* 37; R.M. Bierwagen and V. Heegemann, "Das Freihandelsabkommen zwischen Kanada und den Vereinigten Staaten: Bestandsaufnahme aus europäischer Sicht" (1989)R.I.W. 33; T. Flory, "L'examen par le GATT de l'Accord de libre-échange Etats-Unis-Canada" (1991) A.F.D.I. 700; D. Stevens, "The Canada–US trade agreement: an analysis of its main provisions" (1989) *Revue de Droit des Affaires Internationales* 918, 1022; A. Weber, "Das amerikanisch-kanadische Freihandelsabkommen vom 2. January 1988" (1988) R.I.W. 975.

[31] J. Jackson, "Reflections on the implications of NAFTA for the world trading system" (1992) 30 Colum.J.Transnat.L. 501; F. Abbott, "Integration without institutions: the NAFTA mutation of the E.C. model and the future of the GATT regime" (1992) 40 Am.J. Comp. L. 917. See the Symposium on NAFTA in (1993) 27 *International Lawyer* 589 *et seq.*

- various free trade areas in Central and South America,[32] South East Asia,[33] and in Africa (see paragraphs 2.38 *et seq.*)

An Understanding on the interpretation of Article XXIV determines the procedural and substantive conditions that the regional unions have to satisfy in order to benefit from the exception. Disputes are submitted to the general dispute settlement procedure of the WTO (see paragraphs 3.106 *et seq.*).

The relationship between the MFN principle and free trade areas and customs unions is the subject of Article XXIV of the GATT. Customs unions and free trade areas may not have the effect that new restrictions are created for trade between members of the regional union and third countries).[34] They should be "trade creating, not trade diverting".[35] In 1947, these two forms of regional trade arrangements were viewed as trade-creating instruments, but there were also concerns about their possible trade-distorting effects. Trade liberalisation under the GATT paralleled a process of increasing economic integration among contracting parties. In order to monitor compliance with the requirements of Article XXIV and the Uruguay Round Understanding, the WTO General Council established the Committee on Regional Trade Agreements ("CRTA"),[36] with the mandate of, *inter alia*, examining all RTAs notified to the Council for Trade in Goods ("CTG") under Article XXIV.[37] Nearly all Members of the WTO have notified participation in one or more RTAs. According to the WTO, in the period 1948–1994, the GATT received 124 notifications of RTAs (relating to trade in goods). Since 1995, 100 additional arrangements covering trade in goods or services have been notified.[38]

GATT recognised the beneficial effect of regional trade arrangements for the integration of particularly developing countries into the global trading system, but also reaffirmed "the primacy of the multilateral trading system, which

---

[32] *e.g.* the treaty establishing a common market between Argentina, Brazil, Paraguay and Uruguay (MERCOSUR), March 26, 1991, (1991) 30 I.L.M. 1041, Treaty on Central American Economic Integration between Costa Rica, Guatemala, Honduras, El Salvador and Nicaragua, December 13, 1960 (S. Zamora and R.A. Brand, *op.cit.* II, pp. 525 *et seq.*), the Cartegena Agreement on subregional integration between Bolivia, Colombia, Ecuador, Peru and Venezuela (Andean Pact), May 26, 1969, (1969) 30 I.L.M. 910 substantially modified by the Protocol of Quito, May 11, 1987, (1989) 28 I.L.M. 1165, Treaty of April 7, 1973 on the establishment of a Caribbean Community and a Caribbean Common Market (CARICOM), July 4, 1973, (1973) 12 I.L.M. 1033. See, for a survey on the American and Latin American customs unions or free trade areas in relation to the GATT, I. Bernier, "Le nouveau visage de l'intégration économique en Amérique: vers une régionalisation du GATT?" in *Perspectives Convergentes et Divergentes sur l'Intégration Économique* (Pedone Paris, 1993) p. 123.

[33] An Agreement on the Preferential Tariff (CAPT) Scheme for the Asian Free Trade Area (ACTA), (1992) 31 I.L.M. 513.

[34] Art. XXIV (4). This provision has given rise to a number of disputes between the E.U. and the U.S. See D. Carreau, T. Flory and P. Juillard, *op.cit.*, pp. 127 *et seq.*

[35] For a useful summary, see "Turkey—Restrictions on Imports of Textile and Clothing Products", Panel and Appellate Body Reports (WT/DS34/R) May 31, 1999, paras 2.2–2.9 and 9.97–9.192; see also Madeleine Hosli and Arild Saether (eds), *Free Trade Agreements and Customs Unions: Experiences, Challenges and Constraints* (EIPA, Maastricht, 1997).

[36] WT/L/127; http://www.wto.org/english/tratop_e/region_e/regcom_e.htm.

[37] See "Turkey Textiles", report of the panel, para. 2.7. http://www.worldtradelaw.net/reports/wto panels/turkey-textiles(panel).pdf.

[38] See http://www.wto.org/english/tratop_e/region_e/regfac_e.htm See also *Turkey Textiles,* report of the panel, paras 2.3–2.6.

includes a framework for the development of regional trade agreements, and we renew our commitment to ensure that regional trade agreements are complementary to it and consistent with its rules."[39]

Lowering of customs duties

3.13   **Tariff restrictions (customs duties)**   Countries establish their customs duties product by product. Generally, goods, the importation of which is encouraged, enjoy a favourable customs duty; goods, the importation of which should rather be slowed down, are burdened with a higher duty.

The GATT does not prohibit the imposition of customs duties. It merely states that restrictions only applied to imported goods must be in the form of customs duties and not, for instance, in the form of discriminatory internal taxes (Article III), exorbitant import fees (Artice VIII) or quantitative restrictions (Article XI).

However, the GATT does impose an obligation on the contracting states to negotiate regularly on the reciprocal granting of tariff concessions, *i.e.* on the lowering of customs duties (Article XXVIII *bis*). So far eight negotiation rounds have been held. They are called after a city, a person or a country; Geneva (1947), Annecy (1949), Torquay (1950–1951), Geneva (1955–1956), Dillon Round (1960–1962), Kennedy Round (1963–1967), Tokyo Round (1973–1979),[40] Uruguay Round (1986–1993). A ninth round is widely expected

Earlier rounds were largely restricted to tariff negotiations. Since the Kennedy Round, and particularly since the Tokyo Round, however, the negotiations have also involved various other problems in international trade. These negotiation rounds are therefore called multilateral trade negotiations (MTN).

3.14   **The negotiation rounds**   Two principles govern the negotiation rounds[41]:

(a) Reciprocity (GATT, Article XXVII), which means that a contracting state concedes to other states advantages of the same order as the advantages the state has obtained for itself.[42] This also means that, for instance, after acceding to the GATT, new contracting states have the benefit of advantages already in existence, but must in turn also grant these advantages to the other contracting states.

---

[39] The 1996 Singapore Ministerial Declaration: WT/MIN(96)/DEC, para. 7.

[40] The designations "Tokyo Round" and "Uruguay Round" indicate the increasingly important role of both Japan and the developing countries in the regulation of international trade. See particularly D. Carreau, "Les négociations commerciales multilatérales au sein du GATT: le Tokyo Round" (1980) Cah.Dr.Eur. 145; J.H. Jackson, J.V. Louis and M. Matsuhita, *Implementing the Tokyo Round* (Ann Arbor, Mich., 1984); G.R. Winham, *International Trade and the Tokyo Round* (1986, Princeton).

[41] See, *inter alia*, M. Broszkamp, Meistbegünstigung und Gegenseitigkeit im GATT (Carl Heymanns, Cologne, 1990).

[42] Obviously it is difficult in practice to calculate exactly the various trade concessions. See on this, E. McGovern, *op.cit.* pp. 136–137.

(b) Most favoured nation treatment (GATT, Article I): this principle has as a consequence that every tariff concession granted by one contracting state to another contracting state must unconditionally apply to all other contracting states.

The tariff negotiations are conducted multilaterally.

Negotiating technique Until the Dillon Round there were "product-by-product" negotiations. Each contracting state made up a list of its proposed tariff concessions. These lists were then compared, "weighted"[43] and negotiated. This technique produced few concrete results.   **3.15**

Since the Kennedy Round, a technique of linear tariff reduction has been applied.[44] The negotiations concern first a formula for general tariff reductions that applies to all products (*i.e.* the percentage of reduction and its application in time). After approving the principal formula of tariff reduction, exceptions are negotiated and so-called "negative lists" are drawn up. The result of the global negotiations is then "consolidated" product by product for each contracting state: that state can no longer apply higher customs duties on goods from other contracting states than those agreed during the negotiation round. The consolidated list of customs duties becomes a new protocol to the GATT.[45]

The schedule consists of three parts for each country, *i.e.*:

- customs duties for countries which enjoy most favoured treatment (see paragraph 3.09);

- preferential customs duties for developing countries (see paragraphs 3.49 *et seq.*);

- non-tariff concessions per product (see paragraphs 3.32 *et seq.*).

The schedules are binding. If a contracting state wants to depart from its schedule, the other contracting states must in principle agree unanimously to this. Nonetheless, Article XXVIII provides for a more flexible procedure: tariff changes may also be negotiated directly with the states that are most affected by such change.[46] Furthermore, states may call on the safeguards clauses of Article XIX (massive imports that could cause major injury to local business) for a temporary increase in certain import duties or quantitative restrictions (see paragraph. 3.54).

---

[43] Tariff concessions for a product that is seldom exported and/or for which there is little or no local supply, "weighs" less than a concession for products that are frequently imported and/or for which there are also local suppliers.

[44] G. Curzon, *Multilateral Commercial Diplomacy: the GATT and its Impact on National Commercial Policies and Techniques* (Praeger, New York, 1966).

[45] The tariff negotiations of the Uruguay Round are, for instance, consolidated in the Marrakesh Protocol to the General Agreement on Tariffs and Trade 1994.

[46] The Uruguay Round includes an "Understanding on the Interpretation of Article XXVIII (Modification of GATT schedules)" which establishes new procedures for the negotiation of compensation when tariff bindings are modified or withdrawn, including the creation of a new negotiating right for the country for which the product in question accounts for the highest proportion of its exports.

International rules for customs duties

3.16 **Product classification** There are different kinds of products. Customs clearance therefore requires product classification so that the customs officials are able to determine the specific nature of the goods, in order to establish the customs duties due.

An efficient passage through customs demands, therefore, a common and uniform system for the classification of goods. In this way the same good will be classified identically in each country for customs purposes. The harmonisation of customs classification is in the hands of the World Customs Organisation (WCO), representing 153 customs administrations world-wide, responsible for processing more than 45 per cent of all international trade. [47] The WCO has developed and introduced the Harmonised Commodity Description and Coding System, which is used world-wide as the basis for classifying goods and for the collection of customs revenue.[48] The WCO keeps the classification up to date by issuing "Recommendations".[49]

The "harmonised system" has a list of chapters (ranging from simple to more complex goods) under which all goods can be accommodated. Each chapter is divided into a number of headings; each heading is subdivided into sub-posts. They are all arranged according to the decimal system. The chapters are collated in sections. For example, in Chapter 1 (live animals), heading 01.01 applies to: "live horses, asses, mules"; sub-post 01.01.11 concerns "Pure-bred breeding horses". In Chapter 95, "toys, games and sports requisites", sub-post 95.06 applies to: "Articles and equipment for gymnastics, athletics and other sports or outdoor games, not specified or included elsewhere in Chapter 95". Sub-post 95.06.21 applies to "sail boards".

Some general principles for interpretation of the classification apply:

- The headings of the sections and chapters are only for easy reference; the products must be classified according to the text of the different product descriptions and the general guidelines, as mentioned in an introductory note in each section or chapter.

- A product that is not yet assembled, or is unfinished or incomplete, will be considered as a finished product for the classification when it possesses the intrinsic characteristics of the finished product.

- When a product can be categorised under more than one product description, the most characteristic description is preferred; for composite products or mixtures the description of the good or of the part that gives the product its intrinsic character applies; if neither can be applied, the product description that comes numerically last prevails.

---

[47] In fact the WCO is merely the new name for the Customs Co-operation Council, established in 1952. http://www.wcoomd.org/

[48] *ibid.*

[49] *ibid.*

- Goods which according to the above rules are not covered by any product description, are placed under the description of a product with which they show the most likeness.

Customs value Customs duties are sometimes charged by item, sometimes **3.17** by volume or sometimes by weight. However, they are usually charged on the value of the imported goods (*ad valorem*). This requires that the customs officials determine the value of the goods. Up until 1981 the importer was given very little scope to influence the determination of the customs value. Although Article VII of the GATT excluded valuation on an arbitrary or fictitious basis, it left the customs officials the choice between the real value of the imported goods and the value of similar foreign goods. The value of the imported goods themselves was seldom applied. The duty was usually charged on the basis of the price for which similar foreign goods were bought or offered for sale.[50] Moreover, whereas GATT formally excluded valuation on the basis of the value of national goods, the United States valued some goods on the basis of the price of domestically produced goods with which the imported goods compete (the American Selling Price—ASP).

Customs valuation rules Article VII is the principal provision governing **3.18** the valuation of goods in GATT. Subsequently, the Tokyo Round introduced the so-called Valuation Code, which was signed by the most important trading nations which used its uniform criteria for the determination of the customs value of goods.[51] Many developing countries hesitated to do so, wishing to avoid the restraint of the Code (which excludes overvaluation). Indeed, it was easier for them to charge import duties than income tax. Since customs duties are frequently the principal source of revenue in developing countries, they are often inclined to inflate the customs value of imported goods, which they would no longer be able to do under the Customs Valuation Code. The Uruguay Round built upon this foundation and introduced the WTO Valuation Agreement. This Agreement is essentially the same as the Tokyo Round Valuation Code and applies to the valuation of imported goods for the purpose of levying *ad valorem* duties on such goods. It applies to all WTO Members. Developing countries have been granted a delay in the application of the Agreement.[52]

The WTO Valuation Agreement mandates the WCO to administer the Agreement through its Technical Committee for Customs Valuation. This Committee ensures uniformity in the interpretation and application of the Agreement at a

---

[50] The "selling price on the free market", the criterion of the Brussels Customs Value Convention (1950), generally applied during the 1950s and 1960s.

[51] Agreement on the application of Art. VII of the General Agreement of Tariffs and Trade, *inter alia* [1980] O.J. L71/107. See on the Code, H. Glashoff, "Der 'Kauf von Waren' im neuen Zollwert-System" (1980) R.I.W. 626; S. Sherman, "Reflections on the new customs valuation code" (1980) L. and Pol. Int'l. Bus. 119; S. Sherman & H. Glashoff, *Customs Valuation, Commentary on the GATT Customs Valuation Code* (Kluwer, Deventer, 1988); H. de Pagter and R. van Raan, *The Valuation of Goods for Custom Purposes* (Kluwer, Deventer, 1981).

[52] For more on this, see http://www.wto.org/english/tratop_e/cusval_e/cusval_e.htm. Y. Shin, "Implementation of the WTO Customs Valutation Agreement in Developing Countries—Issues and Recommendations" (1999) 33 J.W.T., No. 1, pp. 125–144.

technical level. It collects information on the application of the Agreement member countries. Moreover, it examines specific technical problems arising from the day-to-day customs valuation systems and suggests appropriate solutions. These suggestions are issued in the form of Advisory Opinions, Commentaries, Case Studies and Studies, which are published in the *Compendium of Customs Valuation*.

3.19   **Transaction value**   The Valuation Agreement has made the "transaction value" the most important criterion for customs valuation. It is now the basis for valuation of more than 90 per cent of world trade.

The transaction value is based on the purchase price for the imported goods, which is the price that is actually paid or is to be paid if the goods are bought "for export to the country of importation". The general application of the transaction value has undoubtedly made customs treatment, which used to vary considerably from country to country, more uniform and predictable.

Goods sold directly from the exporting country to the importing country are without doubt "sold for export to the country of importation". But even when the destination of goods is unclear when they leave the country, *i.e.* when goods are sold "in transit", the sale is qualified as a sale for export.

Customs officials cannot reject a purchase price because it is too low, or lower than for similar transactions. It is also irrelevant whether this price gave the seller some profit. Where necessary, prices that are too low can be penalised as an anti-dumping procedure (see paragraphs 3.69 *et seq.*), but may not as such be discarded as a basis for valuation. Neither are high prices an obstacle for valuation: the customs officials collect the duty on the high purchase price, even though the market price is considerably lower.[53]

3.20   **Purchase price in contract or invoice**   The transaction value is usually evidenced by the price on the invoice.[54] The customs officials thus will ask for the invoice to determine the transaction value for customs clearance. A price invoiced in another currency than that of the country of importation, shall, as a rule, be converted into the local currency against the going exchange rate for the determination of the customs value. However, the customs officials must follow the exchange rate parties have fixed in their sales contract.[55]

---

[53] The French customs have thus collected high customs duties on goods which were invoiced too highly in order to export money from France under the pretext of payment, in defiance of currency regulations; Case 65/79, *Procureur v. R. Chatain* [1980] E.C.R. 1345, [1981] 3 C.M.L.R. 418; Case 54/80, *Procureur v. S. Wilner* [1980] E.C.R. 3673, [1981] 2 C.M.L.R. 444. The court decided that the authorities are not bound by the over-valuation for other than customs reasons. For duties on exorbitant transport costs (*e.g.* air transport instead of transport by sea), see Case 27/70, *Edding v. Hauptzollamt Hamburg* [1970] E.C.R. 1035.

[54] See H. van Houtte, "International sales price as a basis for customs valuation" in P. Sarcevic and P. Volken (ed.), *International Sale of Goods: Dubrovnik Lectures* (Oceana, New York, 1986), p. 365.

[55] It is in this case useful to hand over a copy of the contract of sale to the customs officials as proof of the contractual rate.

The contract of sale is also important to determine the final purchase price when no invoice has been issued yet. The customs officials then rely on the price (revision) provision in the contract. When the outcome of a price formula is not known at the moment of importation, the final valuation must be postponed until a price calculation becomes possible.

Adjustment and splitting up of the purchase price The purchase price **3.21**
often covers a number of performances for which no duty is owed. The Agreement determines how the purchase price must be adjusted for the valuation. Only the adjustments allowed under the Agreement can be made. However, adjustments become easier, or even superfluous, when the invoice sufficiently itemises the individual elements of the purchase price or invoiced separately.

(a) The contract and the invoice may separate the price of, for instance, services, know-how (see paragraphs 6.07 *et seq.*) and technology from the price for the tangible goods. Indeed, the Agreement only aims at valuation of "goods", *i.e.* tangible goods. Intangibles are as such not subject to custom duties; services, know-how, technology, etc. are connected with tangible goods and are a condition for the sale.

(b) The Agreement provides that transport costs after importation may have to be deducted from the transaction value if they are distinguished from the actual price of the goods. Consequently, goods should be invoiced "ex works" and transportation expenses should be split between transportation costs to the border (to be included in the transaction cost) and the costs to transport from the border to the destination—for which no duties are charged.[56]

(c) In time, the building, erecting and maintenance of an industrial installation, along with technical assistance come after the importation of the parts. If these performances are separated from the actual price for the imported goods, they are not subject to customs duties. The invoice therefore should not state an overall price for the sale of the parts and the work done, but rather specify a separate price for the latter.

(d) Evidently taxes due after importation do not increase the transaction value on the day of importation; consequently no duty is due.[57]

(e) The basis for the transaction value is the price actually paid or to be paid. Interest paid on credit which is granted to the buyer under the contract, does not form part of the price paid for the imported goods. The seller sometimes grants a price discount to a buyer who pays on time or in advance (*e.g.* 5 per cent reduction for payment within 30 days). This discount can be considered as the credit costs for later payment. When the goods are paid with deduction of a price discount but before the customs

---

[56] *e.g.* Case 290/84, *Hauptzollamt Schweinfurt v. Mainfrucht* [1985] E.C.R. 3909, [1987] 1 C.M.L.R. 684.
[57] Annex I, Note to Art. 1.3.1.

officials determine their value, this discount has to be deducted from the original purchase price. When, on the contrary, the goods have not yet been paid for before customs officials had to assess their value, then reference to the discount in the contract or the invoice may, nevertheless, justify that the original purchase price is reduced by the expected discount.

(f) When the contract of sale allows for a discount if a specific quantity is purchased, the customs officials must take account of this discount for the valuation, on condition that the buyer can prove that he has satisfied the conditions for this discount. For the sake of convenience the invoice should mention this discount.

3.22 **Other valuation criteria** Even with the earlier mentioned adjustments the purchase price can in some instances not be used as the basis for the determination of the customs value. This is for instance the case when the seller imposes non-geographic restrictions on the use or availability of the goods (*e.g.* resale price maintenance) that substantially affect their value. This also applies to counter-trade where the price is expressed in barter goods and not in money.

The invoiced price may in some cases be rejected when it concerns a sale between connected enterprises.[58] Nevertheless, this price should not be set aside when the importer can show that the value of the goods "very closely resembles" the customs value of identical or similar goods.

Lastly, the invoiced price may also be disregarded when it is an artificial price. The customs officials, therefore, can still examine whether the price determinations in the contract and the invoice are correct.

The customs administrations may request information from importers when they have doubts about the declared value of the imported goods. If despite the information the doubt persists, the administration can establish the value following the other provisions of the Agreement.

If the value cannot be established on the basis of the purchase price of the imported goods themselves then customs officials have to rely on the transaction value of same or similar goods coming from third parties. If these criteria are unsatisfactory, the value must be construed on the resale price of the imported goods, or must be calculated on the basis of the production costs. These valuation methods must be used in a hierarchical order. If none is satisfactory, there still remains a fall-back method.

3.23 **Customs procedures** Uniform rules for customs classification and valuation are insufficient as long as states maintain their own rules for the customs clearing procedures. An important step in the harmonisation and simplification of customs procedures was made by the Convention of Kyoto (1973).[59] The Appendices to

---

[58] Before the Code came into force the customs officials often increased the intra-company sales prices, because they assumed that these prices were kept artificially low in order to consolidate maximum profits at the most suitable location. The Agreement maintains the rule that the sales price between connected companies can be revised.

[59] [1975] O.J. L100/2.

this Convention contain guidelines and recommendations for, *inter alia*, the clearing of goods, temporary storage, origin of the goods (rules of origin), goods in transit and inward and outward processing. States that have endorsed the Convention of Kyoto must adopt at least one Appendix. So far, about 61 states have endorsed the Convention of Kyoto, the E.U. amongst them. The E.U. has accepted more than one Appendix.[60] In 1999 the Convention of Kyoto has been revised in order to include the use of information technology and to engage the private sector in customs clearance. The revised Convention is not yet in force.[61]

Inspection In the Uruguay Round an Agreement on Pre-shipment Inspection **3.24** was drafted. This Agreement allows customs officials to rely for the value and quantity of the goods on the valuations carried out before dispatch, saving further examination at importation. Hence, the packaging does not need to be opened and time is saved at importation.

E.U. customs law The E.U. is a single customs area. As a result of the **3.25** abolition of customs barriers within the E.U., inter-community trade is no longer subject to any customs formalities. However, the fiscal regulation of inter-community trade remains (*e.g.* VAT), and may still require border formalities.

The common customs tariff applies in principle to imports from third countries. It follows the "harmonised system" for classification (see paragraph 3.16). Two customs duties are indicated for each product description: the "conventional import duty" for GATT members and the "autonomous import duty" for non-GATT members. Furthermore, many individual customs duties apply to developing countries to which the E.U. has granted preferences (see paragraph 2.57), under bilateral conventions or under general preferences (see paragraph 2.56). Thus, the customs tariff often depends on the origin of the goods. The E.U. has extensive regulations for the origin of goods and customs treatment.

Customs tariffs in the E.U. make use of the "Single Document" (*Document unique*), a standard form with a number of copies.[62] The same form can be used by the authorities and statistical services in the country of exportation and in the country of destination, by the sender and the receiver. The Single Document is also used for trade with the EFTA countries.

Prohibition of quantitative restrictions

General Article XI of the GATT includes a fundamental prohibition on **3.26** quantitative restrictions: quotas, import and export licences "or other measures having equivalent effect". Therefore, it is not the legal form of the measure but its effect on trade which is important.

---

[60] See Community Customs Code, [1992] O.J. L302.
[61] See http://www.wcoomd.org/.
[62] Regulation 678/85, [1985] O.J. L79/1.

The GATT regulation on quantitative restrictions, however, has a limited effect because of the many exceptions. Article XI allows for the following exceptions to this prohibition:

- temporary export restrictions of foodstuffs or other "essential" products when there is a shortage of such products on the national market;

- import restrictions on agricultural and fishery products when these restrictions are part of a national policy of subsidising agricultural prices (see paragraph 3.57)[63];

- restrictions on basic products which follow from an international agreement on basic products (see paragraph 2.65).

Moreover, Article XIII–1 prohibits any form of discrimination in the establishment or application of import or export restrictions; quantitative restrictions must apply equally to all third countries (thus, not only to the other GATT members).

Furthermore, quantitative restrictions are also permitted on the basis of other exceptions, particularly for the protection of the balance of payments and the currency reserves of contracting states (see paragraph 3.52) and for the protection of domestic industries against serious injury (see paragraph 3.54). Quantitative restrictions are mainly lifted within regional unions or on the basis of other co-operation agreements (*e.g.* OECD, which also liberalises the trade in services).

3.27   **Import licensing procedures**   Countries use import licensing mechanisms for a variety of purposes, including the administration of quotas, tariffs, rate quotas and the like. In general, licensing regimes are not prohibited under the GATT, but, they are not permitted to operate as independent restrictive mechanisms in themselves. On that basis, there is a well-developed case law that while automatic licensing procedures are generally permitted, discretionary licensing procedures are generally prohibited. Even then, however, as the *Korea Beef* panel put it, "where a quota is [legally] in place, the use of a discretionary licensing system need not necessarily result in any additional restriction."[64]

An Agreement on import licensing procedures was concluded at the end of the Tokyo Round (1979). The main purpose of this convention was to simplify the import formalities and to communicate timely relevant information to the other contracting states. The new Agreement on import licensing procedures, concluded during the Uruguay Round, increases transparency and predictability. Amongst other things it requires the contracting states to publish enough information concerning the basis on which licences are granted. Automatic licensing

---

[63] See a further discussion in D. Carreau, T. Flory, and P. Juillard, *op.cit.*, pp. 117 *et seq.*
[64] See Korea Beef, report of the panel, para. 782. http://www.wto.org/english/tratop_e/dispu_e/161r_e.pdf.

procedures are deemed not to have trade restrictive effects when certain conditions are fulfilled.

Textile and clothing   Trade in textile and clothing products (understood in a   **3.28**
wider sense, *i.e.* from fibre to clothing) was governed by special regimes outside
the normal GATT rules. Both bilateral as well as multilateral arrangements have
been used to limit the importation of textiles from developing countries (particularly South East Asia) to the industrialised countries.

The 1974 Multifibre Arrangement (MFA), concluded within the framework of
GATT, offered "a framework for bilateral agreements or unilateral actions that
established quotas limiting imports".[65] This agreement was initially concluded
for a period of four years and has been repeatedly extended with some amendments. The last version, known as MFA IV, was itself extended several times
until 1994 when it was finally taken over by the Uruguay Round Agreement on
Textiles and Clothing.[66]

In its own terms, the MFA aimed at liberalisation of the international trade in
textiles, the increase of textile export from developing countries, the prevention
of imbalances in the market and an "orderly growth" in the textile trade. To
reconcile these conflicting objectives the Arrangement allowed for specific
import restrictions under international supervision.[67]

The MFA confirmed that it was appropriate and consistent with equity to
favour the importation of textiles from developing countries. Nevertheless, most
restrictions affected the importation of cheaper textiles from such countries.

A Textiles Surveillance Body (TSB), established within the framework of
GATT, oversaw observation of the Multifibre Arrangement. It also acted as
mediator in multilateral negotiations or disputes. The TSB could only issue
recommendations to the contracting states.

The Uruguay Round Agreement on Textiles and Clothing (the ATC)   The   **3.29**
Uruguay Round envisaged the formulation of modalities that would permit the
eventual integration of the sector of textile and clothing into GATT".[68] To that
end, the Agreement on Textiles and Clothing (the ATC) was concluded as a

---

[65] See WTO, *Introduction to the WTO: Trading into the Future* (2nd ed., 1999), p. 20.

[66] For the 1986 version see GATT, *Basic Instruments and Selected Documents* (1987), pp. 7 *et seq.*
cf. A. Majmudar, "The Multifibre Agreement (1986–1991): a move towards a liberalised system?"
(1988/2) J.W.T. 109. For more on this, see Jackson, J., W. Davey, and A. Sykes, *Legal Problems
of International Economic Relations: Cases, Materials and Text* (3rd ed., West Publishing Co., St
Paul, Minn., 1995), pp. 1184–1195.

[67] Consult V. Aggarwal, *Liberal Protectionism: The International Politics of International Textile
Trade* (Berkeley, 1985); H. Zheng, *The Legal Structure of International Textile Trade* (New York,
1988); A. Majmudar, *op.cit.*; W.R. Cline, *The Future of World Trade in Textiles* (Washington, D.C.,
1986); F.A. Khavand, "Droit international des textiles et pays en développement" (1987) Rev.gen-
.dr.int.pub. 1241; H.G. Krenzler, "The Multifibre Arrangement as a special regime under GATT",
in M. Hilf, F.G. Jacobs and E.U. Petersmann (eds), *The European Community and GATT, op.cit.*
pp. 141 *et seq.*; N. Blokker, *International Regulation of World Trade in Textiles* (Nijhoff, Dordrecht, 1990); R. Khanna, "Market sharing under Multifibre Arrangement: consequences of non-
tariff barriers in the textiles trade" (1990/1) J.W.T. 71; F. Marrella, "L'organisation mondiale du
commerce et les textiles"(2000) 104 R.G.D.I.P. pp. 659–693.

[68] See preamble to the ATC, para. 1.

transitional instrument intended to phase out the GATT-inconsistent arrangement of the MFA over a period of 10 years.

Article 2 is "the core of the ATC".[69] According to this provision, the reintegration process is carried out on the basis of importing countries' notifications of their respective quantitative restrictions that they maintained under the MFA on the eve of the entry into force of the WTO Agreement in 1995.[70] Any restrictions that had not been duly notified had to be terminated forthwith.[71] No new restrictions in terms of products or Members were to "be introduced except under the provisions of this Agreement or relevant GATT provisions".[72] The restrictions are governed only by the provisions of the ATC. Moreover, the ATC sets a four-stage process leading to their total elimination and the full reintegration of the textile industry into the mainstream rules of the WTO system by 2005.[73] This means that, by the first day of 2005, the ATC will have accomplished its task of reintegrating the textile industry into GATT 1994 and make itself superfluous— hence the ATC itself will cease to exist after the end of 2004. Indeed, the Agreement on Textiles and Clothing is "the only WTO agreement that has self-destruction built in."[74]

The ATC also has a special provision concerning the possible use of a special safeguard measure, here termed a "transitional safeguard". These measures may be taken only if a member determines that a particular product is being imported into its territory in such increased quantities as to cause (or threaten) serious damage to the domestic industry producing like and/or directly competitive products. The ATC stresses that there should be a clear causal link between the increased quantity of imports and the resulting damage or threat thereof. The Agreement also contains an "indicative list" of economic variables that should be considered in the assessment of the adverse effect of these imports on the domestic industry, such as output, productivity, utilisation of capacity, inventories, market share, exports, wages, employment, domestic prices, profits and

---

[69] "Turkey—Restrictions on Imports of Textile and Clothing Products", report of the panel, WT/DS34/R, http://www.worldtradelaw.net/reports/wtopanels/turkey-textiles(panel).pdf of May 31, 1999, para. 9.68.

[70] It is notable that "under the ATC the right to maintain MFA derived quantitative restrictions and the integration process by stages are not related. The provisions of the ATC make clear that the fact that a product has not yet been re-integrated into the general GATT rules does not in any manner imply a right to introduce new import restrictions under Article 2.1 of the ATC on such products. The main benefit for Members resulting from the notification of an integration programme within 6 months of the entry into force of the WTO Agreement, is the use of the special safeguard mechanism under the ATC. There is no relation between the safeguard provisions of the ATC and the right to introduce new quantitative restrictions under Article 2.1 of the ATC.": "Turkey—Restrictions on Imports of Textile and Clothing Products", report of the panel, op.cit., at para. 9.74.

[71] Apparently, only four WTO members notified existing restrictions to the TMB pursuant to Art. 2.1 of the ATC: Canada, the European Communities, Norway and the United States. See Turkey Textiles panel report op.cit. at para. 9.69. This means that only these countries are allowed to maintain GATT-inconsistent restrictions for the duration of the transitional period of ten years provided that the provisions of the ACT are complied with. For an interesting practical application of this provision, see "Turkey Textiles" panel report, op.cit.

[72] See Art. 2.4 of the ATC.

[73] Taking the total volume of a member's 1990 textile imports as the benchmark, the ATC provides that each member must integrate the sector according to the following schedule: 16% on January 1, 1995; 17% on January 1, 1998; 18% on January 1, 2002; and 49% on January 1, 2005.

[74] WTO, Introduction to the WTO: Trading into the Future (2nd ed., 1999), p. 20.

investment.[75] Unlike general safeguard measures, transitional safeguards are applied on a member-by-member basis provided that there is a "sharp and substantial increase in imports . . . from such a Member or Members individually . . . "[76]

In order to supervise implementation of the Agreement, the ATC has also established the Textiles Monitoring Body (TMB), a standing organ composed of a chairman and 10 members appointed by WTO members designated by the Council for Trade in Goods but who act in their personal capacity. The TMB serves as a forum for consultations, reviews measures and deals with disputes at the request of Members, and gives non-binding recommendations reached by consensus. The TMB reports to the Council for Trade in Goods. In cases where the recommendations of the TMB leaves a dispute unresolved, the dispute settlement provisions of GATT 1994 as well as the DSU (see paragraphs 3.106 *et seq.*) remain applicable.

Voluntary export restraints   Besides the Multifibre Arrangement, many   **3.30** so-called voluntary export restrictions (voluntary export restraint agreements, VERs—also called orderly market arrangements, OMAs) were negotiated bilaterally at the instigation of the country of importation. In exceptional circumstances a voluntary export restraint was even granted unilaterally after warnings from the country of importation that it would take retaliatory measures.

The VERs were intended as a means of reducing the export of products from a particular state to one or more other states for an agreed period on a "voluntary" basis. Many such agreements concerned the export of private cars or electronics from Japan to the United States and the E.U. Mainly the markets of the United States and the E.U. were protected by such agreements; the restrictions particularly affected exports from Japan, South Korea, the E.U. and Taiwan.[77]

According to the GATT, certain import restrictions are permitted under the terms set out in Article XIX in the event of a surge of imports that causes or threatens serious injury to relevant domestic producers (see paragraph 3.54). The purpose of many VERs was, however, to by-pass the application of this provision because measures taken pursuant to Article XIX must, in principle, be applied in a non-discriminatory manner, *i.e.* equally to all other contracting states,[78] whereas a voluntary restraint agreement only operates bilaterally. Moreover,

---

[75] See Art. 6, para. 3 of the ATC. See also "United States—Measure Affecting Imports of Woven Wool Shirts and Blouses from India", WT/DS33/R, report of the panel, January 6, 1997. http://www.worldtradelaw.net/reports/wtopanels/us-woolshirts(panel).pdf.

[76] See Art. 6, para. 4 of the ATC.

[77] See, *e.g.* R. Carbaugh and D. Wassink, "Steel voluntary restraint agreements and steel-using industries" (1991/4) J.W.T. 73; T. Flory, "L'accord bilatéral CEE-Japon sur l'automobile" (1991) A.F.D.I. 689; M. Kostecki, "Marketing strategies and voluntary export restraints" J.W.T. 87; M.W. Lochmann, "The Japanese voluntary restraint on automobile exports" (1986) Harv.Int'l.L.J. 99; H.G. Preusse, "Voluntary export restraint—an effective means against a spread of neo-protectionism?" (1991/2) J.W.T. 5.

[78] M.C. Bronckers, "Selective safeguard measures in multilateral trade relations" in *Issues of Protectionism in GATT, European Community and United States Law* (Kluwer Deventer, 1985) p. 81. Similarly, various Panel Reports; see *e.g.* GATT, *Basic Instruments and Selected Documents*, 1981, 126.

VERs were also often enacted when the conditions of Article XIX were not satisfied because it could not, for instance, be proved that there was a causal link between large imports and injury to local producers.

3.31 **Compatibility with GATT** Initially some had argued that VERs were compatible with the GATT.[79] However, in 1988 a GATT Panel (see paragraph 3.09) declared the VERs and the national implementing measures incompatible with the GATT. The Panel, reviewing the arrangement mainly in the light of Article XI(1) of the GATT, which prohibits quantitative restrictions (see paragraph 3.26), concluded that Article XI(1) applies to any measure of a contracting state in respect of export restrictions, "irrespective of the legal status of the measure". Based on this decision, a VER was prohibited when the effects of the VER depend mainly on an intervention by the authorities.

VERs are now prohibited by the new Agreement on Safeguards.[80] This Agreement, drafted during the Uruguay Round, rejects emphatically the use of VERs: "a Member shall not seek, take or maintain any voluntary export restraints, orderly marketing arrangements or any other similar measures on the export or the import side."[81] Any VER in effect at the time of entry into force of the Agreement also had to be brought into conformity with the Agreement or be phased out. Measures maintained in accordance with GATT provisions (other than Article XIX) and Multilateral Trade Agreements in Annex 1A (other than the Safeguards Agreement) are not covered by this prohibition.[82]

Other non-tariff restrictions

3.32 **General** The more contracting states had to reduce their customs duties and were prevented by the GATT from introducing import restrictions, the more they relied on "non-tariff barriers" (NTB), which achieved the same restrictions on international trade but by different means.[83]

Protection of the national market can take many forms. It appears from an inventory made up by the GATT that there are about a thousand different types of distortions of international trade.[84]

The GATT contains a general rule on non-tariff barriers under Article XI. According to this provision, all border measures other than "duties, taxes or other charges" are prohibited. The prohibition applies to all non-tariff measures that

---

[79] *cf.* G. Burdeau, "Les engagements d'autolimitation et l'évolution de commerce international" (1991) A.F.D.I. 748; D. Carreau, T. Flory and P. Juillard, *op.cit.* pp. 261 *et seq.*; G. Fievet, "Les accords d'autolimitation, une nouvelle technique d'accords communautaire" (1983) Rev.Marché-.Comm. 597; J.H. Jackson, "Consistency of export-restraint arrangements with the GATT" (1988) World Ec. 485; Jones, "Voluntary export restraints, political economy, history and the role of GATT" (1989/3) J.W.T. 134; M. Tatsuta, "Voluntary export restraints, implementation and implications" (1985) RabelsZ 328.

[80] WTO Agreement on Safeguards, Art. 11.

[81] *ibid* Art. 11:1(b).

[82] *ibid* Art. 11:1(c).

[83] See D. Carreau, T. Flory and P. Juillard, *op.cit.* pp. 140 *et seq.* A.E. Scaperlanda, *Prospect for Eliminating Non-tariff Distortions* (Sijthoff, Leiden, 1973).

[84] GATT, *Basic Instruments and Selected Documents* (1981), p. 18.

are made effective through "quotas, import or export licences or other measures"—a provision with a quite comprehensive scope. Furthermore, this prohibition applies to barriers affecting both imports as well as exports. There are of course exceptions to this principle, which include those applying agricultural and fisheries products under Article XI:2, the balance-of-payments exceptions under Articles XII and XVIII, and the general exceptions under Article XX.

A number of specific non-tariff barriers have also been the subject of specific agreements (see paragraph 3.03). All but one of these agreements have been included in the WTO Agreement, which applies to all members thereof. The Agreement on Government Procurement (see paragraph 3.34) has, however, continued in the WTO as a "plurilateral" agreement.

State trading enterprises   State trading enterprises with varying degrees of   **3.33** monopolistic or quasi-monopolistic control over the importation and exportation of goods and services have been a common feature of the modern world. Although they were more widely used by the centrally planned economies, they are by no means unknown in the typical free-market economies (see paragraph 2.02).

The "Understanding on the Interpretation of Article XVII", negotiated during the Uruguay Round, has adopted the following working definition for "state trading enterprises":

"Governmental and non-governmental enterprises, including marketing boards, which have been granted exclusive or special rights or privileges, including statutory or constitutional powers, in the exercise of which they influence through their purchases or sales the level or direction of imports or exports."[85]

The presence *per se* of these enterprises does not violate the rules of the system[86]; but their operations could be restrictive to trade and thereby violate the WTO Agreement (GATT Article XVII).[87]

The rules of the GATT therefore apply to the import and export transactions of state trading enterprises. Purchases and sales may only be based on commercial

---

[85] "Understanding on the Interpretation of Article XVII of the General Agreement on Tariffs and Trade 1994", para. 1. http://www.wto.org/english/thewto_e/whatis_e/eol/e/pdf/notstr1.pdf

[86] Art. XVII:1(a) stipulates that if a Member "establishes or maintains a state enterprise, or grants to any enterprise, formally or in effect, exclusive or special privileges, such enterprise shall, in its purchases or sales involving either imports or exports, act in a manner consistent with the general principles of non-discriminatory treatment prescribed in this Agreement for governmental measures affecting imports or exports by private traders." On the applicable GATT rules see, particularly, J.H. Jackson, "State trading and nonmarket economies" in W.F. Ebke and J.J. Norton (eds), *Festschrift in honor of Sir Joseph Gold* (Heidelberg, 1990) pp. 175 *et seq*. For a practical application, see P.D. McKenzie, "China's application to the GATT: State trading and the problem of market access" (1990/5) J.W.T. 133.

[87] See "Korea Beef", report of the panel, WT/DS161/R, WT/DS169/ R of July 31, 2000 http://www.wto.org/english/tratop_e/dispu_e/161r_e.pdf para. 568.

considerations such as price, quality, quantity, availability, marketability and transport. Enterprises of other GATT states must have adequate opportunities to enter into contracts of sale with state enterprises.

State trading enterprises are therefore required to operate in the same way as purely commercial enterprises: all their activities must be based on commercial considerations. Indeed, the general prohibition of non-tariff barriers (GATT Article XI:1) also applies to quantitative restrictions made effective through import monopolies. The terms "import and export restrictions" include restrictions made effective through state trading operations in order "to extend to state trading the rules of the General Agreement governing private trade and to ensure that the contracting parties cannot escape their obligations with respect to private trade by establishing state-trading operations."[88]

Transparency in the operation of state trading enterprises has been the main concern of the Uruguay Round Understanding on the Interpretation of Article XVII. To that end, WTO members are required to notify such enterprises to the Council for Trade in Goods for review by a working party set up for that purpose. Members are further required to "ensure the maximum transparency possible" in their notifications "so as to permit a clear appreciation of the manner of operation of the enterprises notified and the effect of their operations on international trade." The option of counter-notification has been introduced for members that have reason to believe that another member has not adequately met its notification obligation.

Special agreements

3.34   **Government procurement**   Supplies of goods and services to the government usually involve substantial quantities. In order to advance the national economy and sustain employment, in many countries this trade is reserved directly or indirectly for local enterprises. Although such practices are in conflict with the principles of free trade, they are not prohibited by the GATT. Indeed, they are even expressly permitted for purchases by state-owned enterprises (see paragraph 2.03).

3.35   **Government procurement under the WTO**   An Agreement on government procurement was concluded on the margin of the WTO Agreement.[89] It binds only those Members of the WTO that have specifically ratified the Agreement—

---

[88] Note to Arts XI, XII, XIII, XIV and XVIII. See "Japan—Agricultural Products", report of the panel, para. 5.2.2.2; "Canada—Marketing Agencies", report of the panel, (1988) para. 4.24.

[89] A. Reich, "The new GATT agreement of government procurement—the pitfalls of plurilateralism and strict reciprocity" (1997) 31 J.W.T. Issue 2, 125–151; S. Arrowsmith, "Towards a multilateral agreement on transparency in government procurement" (1998) 47 I.C.L.Q. 793–816; C. Bovis, "The European public procurement rules and their interplay with international trade" (1997) 31 J.W.T. Issue 3, 83–91.

currently about 27 states (including the E.U. and the United States).[90] An earlier version of the Agreement was concluded in 1979 during the Tokyo Round. However, the present Agreement has a broader scope. The Agreement applies to statutory provisions as well as to administrative practices for public procurement of goods and services, including construction services. The Agreement applies not only to central government purchases of goods and services for SDR 130,000 (see paragraph 9.26) or more. It also applies to such purchases by local government entities (threshold generally SDR 200,000) and by utilities (threshold generally SDR 400,000). For construction contracts the threshold is generally SDR 5 million. Annexes to the Agreement list the different entities that are subject to its rules. The Agreement only concerns the signatory states. New states may be admitted if they are willing to open their procurement market to a sufficient extent. However, although the Agreement allows for a special and differential treatment of developing countries, no developing countries are as yet party to it. The one hundred-plus WTO members which are not yet bound by the Agreement, are free to pursue protectionist procurement policies, since government purchasing was explicitly made an exception to the GATT obligation of "national treatment". Even states that are party to the Agreement may practise protection against any country or any area of procurement not covered by the Agreement.[91]

Preferential bilateral agreements　The Agreement is not a multilateral **3.36** agreement in the classic sense. It should be rather described as an accumulation of preferential bilateral agreements. Indeed, each contracting state can indicate to which local government entities and public enterprises the Agreement will be applicable. Moreover contracting states can request that the Agreement is only applicable for specific goods or services on the condition of strict reciprocity between the country of procurement and the country of the offeror. Or they can exclude specific countries, or exclude the application of the Agreement in matters that concern, for instance, the protection of national security (supply of weapons, ammunition and other *matériel*), public morality, public health of people, animals and plants, and intellectual property.

Applicable rules　The basic principle of the Agreement is national treatment, **3.37** *i.e.* no discrimination in public procurement on the basis of nationality or country

---

[90] See, *e.g.* S. Arrowsmith, J. Linarelli and D. Wallace, *Regulating Public Procurement, National and International Perspectives* (Kluwer Law International, The Hague, 2000) ; A. Reich, *International Public Procurement Law* (Kluwer Law International, The Hague, 1999). As of August 2001, the following were parties to the agreement: Austria, Belgium, Canada, Denmark, European Communities, Finland, France, Germany, Greece, Hong Kong China, Iceland, Ireland, Israel, Italy, Japan, Korea, Liechtenstein, Luxembourg, Netherlands, Netherlands with respect to Aruba, Norway, Portugal, Singapore, Spain, Sweden, Switzerland, United Kingdom, and United States; negotiating their accession were Bulgaria, Estonia, Jordan, Kyrgyz Republic, Latvia, Panama; and observer governments were Argentina, Australia, Bulgaria, Cameroon, Czech Republic, Chile, Colombia, Croatia, Estonia, Georgia, Jordan, Kyrgyz Republic, Latvia, Lithuania, Malta, Moldova, Mongolia, Oman, Panama, Poland, Slovak Republic, Slovenia, Taiwan and Turkey.
[91] See A. Reich, "The New GATT Agreement on Government Procurement", J.W.T. 1996, 125, at 136.

of origin of goods. However, the procuring state remains entitled to levy import duties on the goods to be imported.

The Agreement also prescribes very detailed tendering procedures, *i.e.* a tendering notice to be published in a previously determined publication inviting suppliers from all Agreement states to bid for the contract on equal terms. Such notice must be published, at least in a summary form, in one of the official languages of the WTO (English, French or Spanish). Technical specifications for the goods to be supplied should as far as possible be based upon international standards, rather than on national standards which may give local producers an unfair advantage (see paragraph 3.47). The Agreement moreover requires that the award procedure for open or restricted tenders for government contracts must comply with the terms of the Agreement; for instance on conditions for qualification of suppliers eligible to bid (no discrimination between domestic and foreign suppliers in technical, commercial and financial qualifications), on time limits for tendering and delivery and on contents of tender documentation. The tender period must be sufficiently long to allow foreign enterprises to participate in the tender procedure. The Agreement also contains rules on the submission, receipt and opening of tenders and the awarding of the contract. The public notice of the award procedure must clearly set out:

(a) the nature and quality of the products;

(b) the award procedure;

(c) the delivery date;

(d) the last date for tendering and the language of the tender;

(e) the government authorities awarding the contract;

(f) the payments terms;

(g) the award criteria (other than price). Even for the restricted award procedure the relevant authorities must approach foreign as well as national suppliers in so far as this is compatible with an efficient award procedure.

Unless the national authorities decide not to award the contract for reasons concerning the public interest, the contract must be awarded to the foreign or national supplier:

(a) who is known to be able to perform the contract; and

(b) who offers the lowest price (or who, if evaluation criteria other than the price are considered, enters the most advantageous tender).

Normally, the national authorities may not insist on a condition for awarding the contract which requires the suppliers to "compensate", for instance, by purchasing a proportion of parts or other material in the country concerned (see paragraph 9.42). If, however, compensation is part of the procurement condition, this has to be made clear and the suppliers of one state should not be given preference over suppliers of another state.

Consultation and disputes An aggrieved supplier is encouraged to enter **3.38** into consultations with the procuring entity. The Agreement requires the states to allow aggrieved companies to challenge the bid procedure in a court or before an independent review body. These procedures should be "non-discriminatory, timely, transparent and effective" and should allow for rapid interim measures to correct breaches of the Agreement or to preserve the commercial opportunities. Thus, not only recommencement of tendering procedures not yet completed, but also termination of a contract already awarded should be possible. As an alternative, compensation to the supplier for the loss or damage suffered may be granted.[92] A breach of the Agreement can also be discussed by the Dispute Settlement Body (see paragraph 9.108).

Each party to the Agreement has to give the Committee on Government Procurement, composed of representatives of the parties to the agreement, statistics on the procurements covered by the Agreement This Committee offers a basis for consultation about the operation of the Agreement.

Other government procurement regulations The Agreement applies **3.39** between states that are parties thereto. Separate regulations, which may implement the Agreement but may also go beyond that, often regulate public procurement in a more specific way. The NAFTA Agreement (see paragraph 2.36), applicable between the United States, Mexico and Canada, for instance, contains in Chapter 10 a complete body of procurement rules.[93] The European Union also has enacted directives on public supplies and on public works, which are applicable for procurements within the E.U. for suppliers from within the E.U.[94] In Central Europe, public procurement is being liberalised by the Central European Free Trade Agreement (CEFTA).[95] Finally, in 1994 UNCITRAL (see paragraph 2.23) has drafted a model law on procurement of goods, construction and services with rules for a fair procurement procedure—as required by the Agreement on Public Procurement—which has now been adopted by a number of countries.[96]

Prohibition of discriminatory internal measures

General Article III of the GATT prohibits the imposition of direct or indirect **3.40** internal taxes or other fiscal charges on imported goods that are higher than those

---

[92] This compensation, however, may be limited to costs for tender preparation and protest, so that no lost profits can be awarded (Art. XX,7 c.l).

[93] Mexico, not being a member to the WTO Agreement, is not bound by its rules.

[94] Directive 97/52, Co-ordination of procedures for the award of public service contracts, public supply contracts and public works contracts ([1997] O.J. L328/1) and Directive 98/4, Co-ordinating the procurement procedures of entities operating in the water, energy, transport an telecommunication sectors.

[95] This Agreement is concluded between the Czech Republic, Hungary, Poland and the Slovak Republic (see S. Arrowsmith, *op.cit.*, p. 221).

[96] *e.g.* in Albania, Kyrgyzstan, Poland and Slovakia.

applied to like national products (national treatment).[97] It prohibits protectionism in the application of internal tax and regulatory measures.[98]

The prohibition on discrimination concerns not only national taxes. Imported goods must also receive the same treatment as local products in respect of all laws, regulations and requirements affecting their internal sale, offering for sale, purchase, transportation, distribution and use.[99] This requirement is violated if (a) imported and domestic products are "like" products; (b) the measure at issue is either a law, regulation, or requirement affecting their internal sale, offering for sale, purchase, transportation, distribution, or use; and (c) the measure affords to imported products a treatment less favourable than that accorded to like domestic products.[1]

3.41   **"Effective equality"**   This provision focuses on the "effective equality of opportunities for imported products" in respect of the application of the measures, and not on their actual trade impacts.[2] The following Appellate Body statements may summarise the core elements of this important provision:

> "Article III obliges Members of the WTO to provide equality of competitive conditions for imported products in relation to domestic products. '[T]he intention of the drafters of the Agreement was clearly to treat the imported products in the same way as the like domestic products once they had been cleared through customs. Otherwise indirect protection could be given'. Moreover, it is irrelevant that 'the trade effects' of the tax differential between imported and domestic products, as reflected in the volumes of imports, are insignificant or even non-existent; Article III protects expectations not of any particular trade volume but rather of the equal competitive relationship between imported and domestic products."[3]

3.42   **"Like products"**   The definition of "like products" has been one of the most controversial issues in the application of Article III. The assessment of "likeness" is a difficult task, involving "an unavoidable element of individual,

---

[97] See E. McGovern, *op.cit.* pp. 189 *et seq.*

[98] See "Japan—Taxes on Alcoholic Beverages", report of the Appellate Body (WT/DS8/AB/R, WT/DS10/AB/R, WT/DS11/AB/R) adopted on November 1, 1996, p. 18:http://www.worldtrade law.net/reports/wtoab/japan-alcohol(ab).pdf.

[99] See Art. III:4 in particular.

[1] See "Korea Beef", report of the Appellate Body, (WT/DS161/R, WT/DS169/R) para. 133. http://www.wto.org/english/tratop_e/dispu_e/161r_e.pdf.

[2] See "United States—Section 337 of the Tariff Act of 1930", Report of the Panel (L/6439–36S/345) adopted on November 7, 1989, para. 5.11; *Korea Beef, loc.cit.*, para. 624; "United States—Taxes on Petroleum and Certain Imported Substances", BISD 34S/136, para. 5.1.9; "Japan—Customs Duties, Taxes and Labelling Practices on Imported Wines and Alcoholic Beverages", BISD 34S/83, para. 5.5(b); "Italian Discrimination against Imported Agricultural Machinery", BISD 7S/60, para. 11; A. Mattoo, "National treatment in the GATS—corner-stone or Pandora's Box" (1997) 31 J.W.T. 107–135.

[3] See "Japan—Taxes on Alcoholic Beverages" report of the Appellate Body (WT/DS8/AB/R, WT/DS10/AB/R, WT/DS11/AB/R) adopted on November 1, 1996, p. 16; http://www.world tradelaw.net/reports/wtoab/japan-alcohol(ab).pdf.

discretionary judgement"[4] to be made on a case-by-case basis. According to the Appellate Body,

> "there can be no one precise and absolute definition of what is 'like'. The concept of 'likeness' is a relative one that evokes the image of an accordion. The accordion of 'likeness' stretches and squeezes in different places as different provisions of the WTO Agreement are applied. The width of the accordion in any one of those places must be determined by the particular provision in which the term 'like' is encountered as well as by the context and the circumstances that prevail in any given case to which that provision may apply."[5]

In actual dispute settlement reports, by far the most widely used approach in the assessment of "likeness" is that developed by the Report of the Working Party on Border Tax Adjustments. As summarised by the Appellate Body in *Asbestos*, this approach employs four general criteria in analysing "likeness":

> "(i) the properties, nature and quality of the products; (ii) the end-uses of the products; (iii) consumers' tastes and habits—more comprehensively termed consumers' perceptions and behaviour—in respect of the products; and (iv) the tariff classification of the products . . . these four criteria comprise four categories of 'characteristics' that the products involved might share: (i) the physical properties of the products; (ii) the extent to which the products are capable of serving the same or similar end-uses; (iii) the extent to which consumers perceive and treat the products as alternative means of performing particular functions in order to satisfy a particular want or demand; and (iv) the international classification of the products for tariff purposes."[6]

The Appellate Body has reiterated that this is not a closed list and that any of these or other relevant evidence should be considered as a whole in resolving the issue of likeness under Article III.[7]

Exceptions to the GATT rules

General exceptions Article XX, one of the most important and most con- **3.43**
troversial provisions of GATT, contains a list of general exceptions to the leading principles of the General Agreement. Article XX enables members, on certain conditions, to take measures (such as import or export bans) that would otherwise

---

[4] *ibid.* at p. 24.
[5] *ibid.* at p. 18.
[6] See "European Communities—Measures Affecting the Prohibition of Asbestos and Asbestos Products" (WT/DS135/R), Panel Report, circulated on September 18, 2000 http://www.world tradelaw.net/reports/wtopanels/ec-asbestos(panel).pdf and Appellate Body report (WT/DS135/AB/R), adopted April 5, 2001 para. 101. http://www.worldtradelaw.net/reports/wtoab/ec-asbestos(ab).pdf.
[7] See also A. Mattoo, "National treatment in the GATS: A cornerstone or a Pandora's Box" (1997) 31 J.W.T. 107–135.

be contrary to basic GATT principles. The conditions, contained in the 10 paragraphs as well as the headnote of Article XX, could be divided into general conditions and specific conditions.

The specific conditions require that measures could be justified under Article XX only if they are:

- necessary to protect public morals, human, animal or plant life or health[8];

- related to the import or export of gold or silver;

- necessary to secure compliance with laws or regulations which are not inconsistent with GATT provisions, such as the protection of patents (see paragraph 6.03) trade marks or copyright, as well as to the prevention of counterfeit practices;

- related to products of prison labour;

- imposed for the protection of national artistic, historical and archaeological treasures;

- related to the conservation of exhaustible natural resources, in so far as the measures are applied equally to local production or consumption;

- undertaken in pursuance of agreements on basic products, in so far as they conform with the criteria adopted by contracting states (see paragraph 2.65);

- temporary export restrictions for products which are indispensable for local industry when the price is held below the world price as part of a governmental stabilisation plan;

- essential to the acquisition or distribution of products in short supply.

The fulfilment of these specific conditions does not in itself ensure full justification under the GATT; the general conditions contained in the chapeau of Article XX need to be satisfied as well. These conditions require that measures may not

---

[8] See discussion below on the Agreement on Sanitary and Phytosanitary Measures.

amount to arbitrary or unjustifiable discrimination or to a disguised restriction of international trade.[9]

Dispute settlement practice has established that Article XX is "a limited and conditional" exception from obligations under other provisions of the General Agreement. Most disputes under Article XX have been concentrated on paragraphs (b), (d) and (g) dealing, respectively, with protection of health, compliance with regulations, and conservation of exhaustible natural resources. Relevant "case law" shows that "(i) Panels examine Article XX only if it has expressly been invoked by a party to the dispute, (ii) Panels have interpreted Article XX narrowly, and (iii) the party invoking Article XX bears the burden of proof."[10] In terms of sequence, as well, the Appellate Body report on *Gasoline* summarised the established practice as follows:

"In order that the justifying protection of Article XX may be extended to it, the measure at issue must not only come under one or another of the particular exceptions—paragraphs (a) to (j)—listed under Article XX; it must also satisfy the requirements imposed by the opening clauses of Article XX. The analysis is, in other words, two-tiered: first, provisional justification by reason of characterization of the measure under [one of the exceptions]; second, further appraisal of the same measure under the introductory clauses of Article XX."[11]

---

[9] J. Klabbers, "Jurisprudence in international trade law—Article XX of GATT" (1992/6) J.W.T. 63; *ibid.*, "Trade protectionism and environmental regulations: the new nontariff barriers" (1990) 11 N.W.J.Int'l.L.&Bus. 47; T.L. McDorman, "The GATT consistency of U.S. fish import embargoes to stop driftnet fishing and save whales, dolphin and turtles" (1991) Geo.Wash.J.Int'l.L. 477; T. Skilton, "GATT and the environment in conflict: the dolphin dispute and the quest for an international conservation strategy" (1993) 26 Cornell Int'l L.J. 455; "Dispute settlement panel report on U.S. restrictions on imports of tuna [1991]" 30 (1991) I.L.M. 1594; S. Thaveechaiyagarn, "The GATT and the cigarette case against Thailand—A Thai perspective" (1990) L.&Pol.Int'lBus. 367; E. Phillips, "World trade and the environment: the cafe case" (1995–96), Mich.J.I.L. 827–863; P. Bentley Q.C., "A re-assessment of Article XX, paragraphs (b) and (g) of GATT 1994 in the light of growing consumer and environmental concern about biotechnology" (2000) 24 Ford I.L.J. 107–131; H.J. Priess and C. Pitschas, "Protection of public health . . . under WTO law" (2000) 24 Ford I.L.J. 519–553; "United States—Prohibition of Imports of Tuna and Tuna Products from Canada", adopted on February 22, 1982, BISD 29S/108; "Canada—Measures Affecting Exports of Unprocessed Herring and Salmon", adopted on March 22, 1988, BISD 35S/98; "Thailand—Restrictions on Importation of and Internal Taxes on Cigarettes", adopted on November 7, 1990, BISD 36S/200; "United States—Restrictions on Imports of Tuna", September 3, 1991, not adopted, BISD 39S/155; "United States—Restrictions on Imports of Tuna", June 16, 1994, not adopted, DS29/R; "United States—Taxes on Automobiles", October 11, 1994, not adopted, DS31/R; "United States—Standards for Reformulated and Conventional Gasoline", reports of the panel (WT/DS2/9): http://www.worldtradelaw.net/reports/wtopanels/us-gasoline(panel).pdf and the Appellate Body (WT/DS2/AB/R) http://www.worldtradelaw.net/reports/wtoab/us-gasoline(ab).pdf adopted on May 20, 1996; "United States—Import Prohibition of Certain Shrimp and Shrimp Products", panel report (WT/DS58/R) and Appellate Body report (WT/DS58/AB/R), adopted November 6, 1998; and "European Communities—Measures Affecting the Prohibition of Asbestos and Asbestos Products" *loc.cit.*

[10] For a useful summary of the GATT/WTO jurisprudence on Art. XX, see "GATT/WTO Dispute Settlement Practice Relating to Article XX, Paragraphs (b), (d) and (g) of GATT: Note by the Secretariat: Revision" (WT/CTE/W/53/Rev.1) October 26, 1998.

[11] *Gasoline*, Appellate Body Report, p. 22: http://www.worldtradelaw.net/reports/wtoab/us-gasoline(ab).pdf.

The general exceptions of Article XX have given birth to such highly complex and distinct agreements as the SPS Agreement (see paragraph 3.44) and the TBT Agreement (see paragraph 3.46).

3.44   **Sanitary and phytosanitary measures**   One of the notable achievements of the Uruguay Round was the conclusion of a separate agreement dealing comprehensively with the use of measures to protect human, animal or plant life or health without undermining the multilateral trading system, called the Agreement on Sanitary and Phytosanitary Measures (the SPS Agreement).[12] A measure qualifies as a "sanitary or phytosanitarymeasure"[13] if it is designed and applied to protect animal or plant life or health against risks arising from: (a) the entry, establishment or spread of pests, diseases, disease-carrying or disease-causing organisms; (b) additives, contaminants, toxins or disease-causing organisms in foods, beverages or feedstuffs; and (c) diseases carried by animals, plants or products thereof, or from the entry, establishment or spread of pests. Basing itself on GATT Article XX(b), the SPS Agreement tries to balance the right of countries to adopt and enforce such measures against the multilateral interest to minimise their negative effects on trade.

Article 2 of the SPS Agreement recognises countries' rights to take sanitary and phytosanitary measures necessary for the protection of human, animal or plant life or health. At the same time, member countries are required to do so "only to the extent necessary" to achieve their legitimate objectives, based on scientific principles and sufficient scientific evidence. However, the Agreement also assigns a conditional role to the so-called precautionary principle under Article 5:7 so that countries would be able to introduce such measures even in the absence of sufficient evidence, but only provisionally and subject to an obligation to promptly seek for additional information and objectively review the measures within a reasonable period of time.[14] At the same time, the SPS Agreement requires that sanitary and phytosanitary measures should not arbitrarily or unjustifiably discriminate between members where identical or similar conditions prevail, including between their own territory and that of other members.[15]

One aim of the SPS Agreement is to further the use of harmonised sanitary and phytosanitary measures between members. Members are thus required to base their sanitary and phytosanitary measures on international standards, guidelines

---

[12] C. Thorn and M. Carlson, "The agreement on the application of sanitary and phytosanitary measures and the agreement on technical barriers to trade" (2000) LawP.I.B. 31, pp. 841–854.

[13] As defined under Annex 1 of the SPS Agreement.

[14] In *Hormones*, the panel observed that "the precautionary principle has been incorporated and given a specific meaning in Article 5.7 of the SPS Agreement" (see "European Communities—Measures Affecting Meat and Meat Products, complaint by the United States" (WT/DS26/R/USA) para. 8.158; and "European Communities—Measures Affecting Meat and Meat Products, complaint by Canada" (WT/DS48/R/CAN) para. 8.161.) The Appellate Body affirmed this view such that "the precautionary principle indeed finds reflection in Article 5.7 of the SPS Agreement." See "European Communities—Measures Affecting Meat and Meat Products" (WT/DS26/AB/R/USA, WT/DS48/AB/R/CAN) adopted February 13, 1998, para. 124. No ruling was made on the issue of whether the precautionary principle has developed into a general principle of (customary) international law.

[15] For an interesting study, see J. Pauwelyn, "The WTO agreement on sanitary and phytosanitary (SPS) measures as applied in the first three disputes: *EC—Hormones; Australia—Salmon; and Japan—Varietals*" [1999] 2 J.Int'l.Econ.L. No. 4.

and recommendations developed by the relevant international organisations, including the Codex Alimentarius Commission, the International Office of Epizootics, and the relevant international and regional organisations operating within the framework of the International Plant Protection Convention.[16] This obligation is further strengthened by the principle that measures which conform to international standards, guidelines or recommendations "shall be deemed to be necessary to protect human, animal or plant life or health, and presumed to be consistent with the relevant provisions of this Agreement and of GATT 1994".[17] Higher standards are allowed if there is a scientific justification for so doing, or if, as a consequence of risk assessment conducted in accordance with Article 5, such a level of protection is found to be necessary.

It is fundamental that sanitary or phytosanitary measures be based on a risk assessment which takes into account available scientific evidence as well as other relevant factors enumerated[18] under Article 5:2. They include relevant processes and production methods; relevant inspection, sampling and testing methods; prevalence of specific diseases or pests; existence of pest- or disease-free areas; relevant ecological and environmental conditions; and quarantine or other treatment. The SPS Agreement requires members to "ensure that measures are not more trade-restrictive than required to achieve their appropriate level of sanitary or phytosanitary protection."[19]

Technical barriers to trade   Importation is often made difficult due to   **3.45** statutory and regulatory provisions in the importing country for, *inter alia*, quality, composition, packaging and control of goods. These provisions generally differ from country to country and could become a barrier to international trade: for instance, products which satisfy the quality demands of the country of exportation, will not be admitted for sale or use in the country of importation if it imposes tighter quality regulations.

The requirements imposed on goods are usually justified either by public interest considerations (mainly protection of public health and safety), or for reasons of standardisation. It may also happen that, under the pretext of objective requirements, measures are taken which are actually intended to hinder the importation of certain foreign products.

While recognising that states are justified in introducing measures to protect public health and safety of people, animals and plants or the environment, provided that these measures are not discriminatory (Artice XX; see paragraph 3.47),[20] the GATT prohibits in principle the introduction of requirements which have the effect of "technical barriers" to import and export. Similarly, states are

---

[16] See preamble to the SPS Agreement, para. 6 and Art. 3.

[17] See Art. 3.2 of the SPS Agreement.

[18] The Appellate Body has ruled in this context that "there is nothing to indicate that the listing of factors that may be taken into account in a risk assessment of Article 5.2 was intended to be a closed list." See "Hormones", report of the Appellate Body, para. 187.

[19] SPS Agreement, Art. 6.

[20] See, on the prohibition on advertising of cigarettes in Thailand as a non-tariff barrier, S. Thaveechaiyagarn, "Cigarette case against Thailand: a Thai perspective" (1990) L.&Pol. Int'l.Bus. 367.

justified in restricting imports and exports for the protection of national security (Article XXI; see paragraph 3.51).

3.46   **The Agreement on Technical Barriers to Trade**   An Agreement on Technical Barriers to Trade was concluded during the Tokyo Round (the GATT standards code) and came into effect on January 1, 1980. [21] During the Uruguay Round this agreement was replaced by a new Agreement on Technical Barriers to Trade (the TBT Agreement), which extended and clarified the previous regime.

The main objective of the TBT Agreement is the harmonisation of national regulations. It distinguishes in this respect between "technical regulations" and "standards":

- "technical regulations" are mandatory requirements of a product or a production process in the area of, *e.g.* quality, performance, safety or dimensions; usually they include also terminology, symbols, testing and test methods, packaging and labelling;

- "standards" are technical specifications approved by a recognised standardising body for repeated or continuous application, compliance with which is not mandatory.

The technical regulations and standards cover not only goods, but may also cover processing and production methods related to the characteristics of the products themselves.

The TBT Agreement follows the principles of GATT Article XX.: In principle, countries are free to introduce the technical standards and regulations they deem necessary to achieve legitimate goals. However, they are required to ensure that such standards and specifications do not create unnecessary obstacles to international trade. Moreover, such standards have to respect the national treatment and MFN principles of the trading system—*i.e.* "products imported from the territory of any Member shall be accorded treatment no less favourable than that accorded to like products of national origin and to like products originating in any other country."[22]

3.47   **Introduction of technical regulations and standards**   Technical Regulations should not be more trade-restrictive than necessary to fulfil a legitimate objective. Three legitimate objectives are mentioned in the Agreement: national security, the prevention of deceptive practices, and the protection of human health or safety, animal or plant life or health, or the environment.[23] In such cases, a national standard should still be based on relevant international standards if any. If that is the case, "it shall be rebuttably presumed not to create an

---

[21] See R.W. Middleton, "The GATT Standards code" (1980) J.W.T. 201; H. van Houtte, "Health and safety regulations in international trade", in *Legal Issues in International Trade* (Nijhoff, 1990) pp. 128 *et seq.* See also G. Foy, "Extension of the GATT Standards code to production processes" (1992/6) J.W.T. 121.

[22] TBT Agreement, Art. 2.1.

[23] *ibid.*, Art. 2.2.

unnecessary obstacle to international trade."[24] In cases where there are no international standards, or where the national standards do not conform therewith, any Member State taking such a measure needs to comply with a number of procedural and substantive obligations, including prior publication of proposed regulations, prior notification of products to be affected, and consideration of the views of other interested parties in the preparation of the final version of such a regulation. The only way to by-pass these quite rigorous requirements is by proving urgency as provided under Article 2.10 of the Agreement, which may not always be easy to demonstrate.

Standards should be adopted in conformity with the Code of good practice for the preparation, adoption and application of standards, an annex of the TBT Agreement and intended for the private sector bodies as well as the public sector. The Code confirms that public and private standardising bodies must observe the fundamental GATT rules, for instance relating to most favoured nation treatment and liberalisation of trade. If a proposed national standard is not compatible with an existing international standard, the other parties must receive advance notice of this standard.

In the adoption of national regulations or standards, account should be taken of the comments made by the members. As soon as such standards have been introduced, Member States must be notified. The new standards can only come into effect after a "reasonable period", in order to enable enterprises to adjust their production processes to the new requirements.

Each Member State must also have an information service to respond to reasonable requests for information from other countries or foreign interested parties.

Conformity examination and certification The examination for confor- **3.48**
mity with technical regulations and standards must treat national and foreign products on the same foot; the examination of foreign products must be reasonably priced; test results have to be communicated so that corrective action may be taken; information about imported products has to remain confidential, etc.

Whenever possible, Member States must recognise the test results and certificates issued by relevant bodies in other Member States, even when the test methods differ from their own. Member States are encouraged to become parties to international certification systems. In states where conformity with technical regulations or standards is examined by local government bodies and non-governmental entities, states must take reasonable measures to ensure that these institutions comply with the provisions of the Code of good practice.

Developing countries As in every instrument annexed to the WTO Agree- **3.49**
ment, the TBT Agreement allows for a special and differential treatment of developing countries.[25] Member States are generally required, if so requested, to be sympathetic to the problems of developing countries and to help them in the preparation, adoption and enforcement of technical regulations as well as in the

---

[24] *ibid.*, Art. 2.5.
[25] See in particular Arts 11 TBT Agreement.

establishment of national standardising bodies. Moreover, developing countries can ask the Committee on Technical Barriers to Trade "to grant specified, time-limited exceptions in whole or in part from obligations under this Agreement."[26]

3.50   **Consultation and disputes**   The Agreement has established a "Committee on Technical Barriers to Trade", composed of Member States' representatives. This Committee functions as a forum for consultation and as a supervisory body.

Disputes have to be settled under the auspices of the Dispute Settlement Body (see paragraph 3.108). In line with the integrated nature of the dispute settlement process under the WTO, the applicable rules for any disputes arising in the context of the TBT Agreement are GATT Articles XXII and XXIII as elaborated and applied by the Dispute Settlement Understanding. Reflecting the specific features of the TBT Agreement, panels may "establish a technical expert group to assist in questions of a technical nature, requiring detailed consideration by experts."[27] (See paragraph 3.108.)

3.51   **Protection of security**   Under Article XXI of the GATT the contracting states are allowed to take measures for the protection of national security, thereby derogating from the fundamental principles of the GATT. These measures may concern trade in nuclear fissionable material, arms, ammunition, implements of war and traffic in other goods and materials to supply a military establishment. Moreover, in time of war or other international crisis, contracting states may take all measures necessary to protect their national security. Furthermore, the contracting states may adopt economic embargoes or other measures, normally contrary to the GATT, when required under UN resolutions.

The contracting states themselves decide whether a trade restriction is justified pursuant to Article XXI. Indeed, GATT Panels prefer not to get involved in such political matters.[28]

The export restrictions, applied by NATO countries within the structure of the "Cocom" (Co-ordinating Committee on Export Controls),[29] were justified on the basis of Article XXI of GATT. The Cocom drew up lists of "security sensitive" products and data, the exportation of which, to Cocom appointed countries, was only permitted if all Member States agreed.[30] Cocom was replaced in 1994 by the "New Forum", a group also including former communist countries to harmonise the national policies for transfer of technology to the third world. [31]

---

[26] TBT Agreement, Art. 12.8.

[27] ibid., Art. 14.2.

[28] See D. Carreau, T. Flory and P. Juillard, op.cit. pp. 134–135.

[29] Sometimes also known as the Co-ordinating Committee for East-West Trade Policy.

[30] On Cocom see, inter alia, C. Taquet, "La Belgique et le Cocom" (1984–85) R.B.D.I. 713; B. Crossfeld and A. Junker, Das Cocom im internationalen Wirtschaft (Mohr, Tübingen, 1991); S. Oeten, "Cocom und das System der Koordinierten Exportkontrollen" (1991) RabelsZ 436.

[31] C. Hoelscher and H.M. Wolffgang, "The Wassenaar-Arrangement between International Trade, Non-Proliferation, and Export Controls", Journal of World Trade, vol. 32, pp. 45–63.

Protection of the balance of payments WTO Member States may introduce **3.52**
import restrictions when this is necessary to safeguard their external financial
position and their balance of payments (Article XII). The GATT requires proportionality between the objective (restoring the equilibrium in the balance of
payments) and the means (import restrictions). Moreover, it imposes restrictions
on the scope and duration of the measures.[32] Developing countries, which often
are affected by balance-of-payments problems, have some flexibility to introduce
import restrictions (Article XVIII): they have a "special and differential treatment in respect of their balance-of-payments measures" (Article XVIII:B).[33]

Addressing balance of payments problems may involve the supervision and
help of the International Monetary Fund (IMF). Indeed the GATT imposes on the
contracting states the duty to confer with the IMF on measures for the protection
of the balance of payments (Article XV[2]).

Originally, restrictions on the quantity or value of imports were considered a
permissible exception to Article XI.[34] However, over time, state practice introduced the use of non-quantitative restrictions such as import surcharges and
import deposit schemes[35] which are generally less restrictive to trade than
quantitative restrictions.[36] This practice was later put on a more stable ground by
a Declaration that contracting parties would "give preference to the measure
which has the least disruptive effect on trade".[37]

The Uruguay Round Understanding on the Balance-of-Payments Provi- **3.53**
sions of GATT 1994 This Understanding also confirmed the commitment of
Member States "to give preference to those measures which have the least
disruptive effect on trade".[38] To that end, the Understanding provides that such
price-based measures (including import surcharges, import deposit requirements
or other equivalent trade measures with an impact on the price of imported
goods) could be applied in excess of bound duty levels found in Member's
Schedules of Concessions. While Member States are required to "seek to avoid"
the imposition of new quantitative restrictions and to use only price-based
measures, in cases where they decide to adopt quantitative restrictions, they

---

[32] F. Roessler, "Selective balance of payments adjustment measures affecting trade: roles of GATT
and IMF" (1975) J.W.T. 627; R. Eglin, "Surveillance of balance of payments measures in the
GATT" (1987) World Ec. 1; I. Frank, "Import quotas, the balance of payments and the GATT"
(1987) World Ec. 307; D. Carreau, T. Flory and P. Juillard, *op.cit.* pp. 119 *et seq.*

[33] See "India—Quantitative Restrictions on Imports of Agricultural, Textile and Industrial Products",
report of the panel, WT/DS90/R, adopted September 22, 1999, para. 5.28.

[34] GATT, Arts XII and XVIII:B.

[35] Import deposit schemes require the importer to deposit a sum of money, corresponding to the whole
or partial value of the imported products, for a certain period in an interest-free bank account in
the country of importation.

[36] On the practice of states prior to 1979, see *GATT Analytical Index: Guide to GATT Law and
Practice* (6th ed. 1995), pp. 362–367.

[37] 1979 Declaration on "Trade Measures Taken for Balance-of-Payments Purposes", GATT, Basic
instruments and selected documents (1980) pp. 205 *et seq.* See also the text in P. Kunig, N. Lau
and W. Meng (eds), *International economic law—Basic documents* (de Gruyter, Berlin, 1993)
pp. 579 *et seq.*

[38] See Uruguay Round Understanding on the Balance-of-Payments Provisions of GATT 1994, para.
2; See also A. Nadal Egea, "Balance-of-payments provisions in the GATT and NAFTA" (1996)
30 J.W.T. 5–24.

"shall provide justification as to the reasons why price-based measures are not an adequate instrument to deal with the balance-of-payments situation."[39]

Moreover, Member States must establish, as soon as possible, a time schedule for the abolition of these import restrictions. The power of surveillance and review of those measures is vested in a Committee on Balance of Payment Restrictions.[40]

3.54   **Safeguard measures against large imports** When a contracting state imports increased quantities of certain products because of unforeseen[41] developments and the effect of obligations incurred by a Member under the General Agreement and when such import causes actual or potential serious injury to local producers, the state may take protective measures such as the temporary suspension of tariff concessions for the relevant products or the introduction of quantitative restrictions (GATT Article XIX, and the WTO Safeguards Agreement).[42] In practice, the tariff concessions are usually suspended.

Safeguard measures should be applied in a non-discriminatory manner.[43] They may be adopted unilaterally by a state; however, that state must give immediate notice of the initiation of an investigation and finding of serious injury, as well as the application of a safeguard measure.[44] This requirement enables other interested Member States to be promptly informed so that they may discuss the measure with the concerned member. If this consultation brings no result the other states, affected by the measure, may retaliate against imports from the state

---

[39] See Uruguay Round Understanding on the Balance-of-Payments Provisions of GATT 1994, para. 3.

[40] For an interesting case involving the division of competence between the Committee on Balance of Payment Restrictions and dispute settlement panels, see "India—Quantitative Restrictions on Imports of Agricultural, Textile and Industrial Products", report of the panel (WT/DS90/R) and report of the Appellate Body, (WT/DS90/AB/R) adopted on September 8, 1999.

[41] The term "unforeseen" has been interpreted to mean something that was not "expected" to follow under the concrete factual circumstances of a case, and not a theoretical one involving an "unforeseeable" development. See "Korea—Definitive Safeguard Measures on Imports of Certain Dairy Products", (complaint by the European Communities), report of the Appellate Body, adopted on January 12, 2000 (WT/DS98/AB/R), para. 124.

[42] Safeguard measures for developing countries are treated separately in Art. XVIII.

[43] E. McGovern, *op.cit.* p. 291 (with further references); D. Carreau, T. Flory and P. Juillard, *op.cit.*, pp. 135 *et seq.*; Bronckers, "The non-discriminatory application of Article XIX: tradition or fiction?" (1981/2) L.I.E.I. 35.

[44] The "Korea Dairy" panel rejected a Korean argument that it satisfied the requirement for an immediate notification because it did so "as soon as practically possible". According to the Panel, "[t]here is no basis in the wording of Article 12.1 to interpret the term 'immediately' to mean 'as soon as practically possible'." The Panel thus found that the 14-day period between Korea's initiation of the investigation and its notification thereof did not respect the requirements for "immediate" notification and was in violation of Article 12.1 of the Agreement on Safeguards. See "Korea—Definitive Safeguard Measure on Imports of Certain Dairy Products", report of the panel, WT/DS98/R, adopted on January 12, 2000, para. 7.134. The "US—Wheat Gluten" panel also found that a delay of 16 days between the initiation of the investigation and the notification thereof does not satisfy the requirement of immediate notification of Art. 12.1(a) of the Safeguards Agreement. See "United States—Definitive Safeguard Measure on Imports of Wheat Gluten from the European Communities", WT/DS166/R, issued July 31, 2000, para. 8.197. This same panel found that a delay of 26 days between the finding of serious injury and the notification thereof does not satisfy the requirement of immediate notification of Art. 12.1(b) of the Safeguards Agreement. See "US—Wheat Gluten", para. 8.199; http://www.worldtradelaw.net/reports/wtopanels/us-wheatgluten(panel).pdf. Appellate body report WT/DS166/AB/R http://www.worldtradelaw-.net/reports/wtoab/us-wheatgluten(ab).pdf.

that introduced the safeguard measures provided that such retaliation is not disapproved by the Council for Trade in Goods.

Agreement on Safeguards The "Agreement on Safeguards" defines in **3.55** more detail the substantive and procedural conditions for the application of Article XIX. All safeguard measures introduced after the entry into force of the WTO Agreement should therefore satisfy the requirements set by both provisions. The only exceptions are the so-called "special safeguard" measures taken on the basis of Article 5 of the Agreement on Agriculture and the "transitional safeguard" measures taken in pursuance of Article 6 of the Agreement on Textiles and Clothing.

In general, a WTO Member State is allowed to apply safeguard measures to a product only if it determines that such a product is being imported into its territory in such increased quantities and under such conditions as "to cause or threaten to cause serious injury to the domestic industry that produces like or directly competitive products".[45] As the WTO Appellate Body emphasised in "Argentina Safeguards", "not just *any* increased quantities of imports will suffice. . . . [T]he increase in imports must have been recent enough, sudden enough, sharp enough, and significant enough, both quantitatively and qualitatively, to cause or threaten to cause 'serious injury'."[46] To demonstrate all this, a serious injury investigation necessarily precedes the application of a safeguard measure. Such investigation should cover an evaluation of:

"all relevant factors of an objective and quantifiable nature having a bearing on the situation of that industry, in particular, the rate and amount of the increase in imports of the product concerned in absolute and relative terms, the share of the domestic market taken by increased imports, changes in the level of sales, production, productivity, capacity utilization, profits and losses, and employment."[47]

This provision has been interpreted by panels and the Appellate Body as providing a minimum list of the economic factors whose consideration is "always relevant and therefore required".[48] In the words of the Appellate Body in "Argentina Safeguards",

"Article 4.2(a) of the Agreement on Safeguards requires a demonstration that the competent authorities evaluated, at a minimum, each of the factors listed in Article 4.2(a) as well as all other factors that are relevant to the situation of the industry concerned."[49]

---

[45] See Art. 2.1 of the Agreement on Safeguards. Art. 4.1(a) of the Agreement on Safeguards defines a "serious injury" as follows: "serious injury shall be understood to mean a significant overall impairment in the position of a domestic industry".

[46] See "Argentina—Safeguard Measures on Imports of Footwear", report of the Appellate Body WT/DS121/AB/R, adopted on January 12, 2000, para. 131.

[47] Agreement on Safeguards, Art. 4.2(a).

[48] See "Korea—Definitive Safeguard Measure on Imports of Certain Dairy Products", report of the panel, WT/DS98/R, adopted on January 12, 2000, para. 7.55.

[49] See "Argentina—Safeguard Measures on Imports of Footwear", report of the Appellate Body, WT/DS121/AB/R, adopted on January 12, 2000, para. 136.

The agreement makes it clear that the "safeguard measures shall be applied to a product being imported irrespective of its source".[50] This means that Article XIX despite earlier contentions by some states can in principle not be used selectively to prevent the importation of products from a particular country. The requirement of non-discriminatory application of safeguard measures applies without exception particularly in the case of safeguard measures taking the form of additional duties. In cases where safeguard measures take the form of quotas, the general principles of non-discriminatory application of quantitative restrictions enshrined under Article XIII of GATT 1994 apply subject to a very carefully and strictly crafted exception under Article 5.2(b) of the Safeguards Agreement. An important condition is that the importing country should be able to demonstrate that imports from certain contracting parties had increased disproportionately in relation to the total increase and that such departure would be justified and equitable to all suppliers.[51]

The agreement also sets time limits on the measures that the parties to the agreement can take. Furthermore, a Safeguards Committee is to be entrusted with the collection of data and consultation when Article XIX is invoked. Disputes involving safeguards measures are subject to the general rules of Articles XXII and XXIII of GATT 1994 as elaborated by the DSU (see paragraphs 3.106 *et seq.*).

3.56   **Waiver**   In exceptional circumstances, a two-thirds majority of the contracting states (or the General Council) may waive some of the GATT obligations for a specific state (Article XXV:5). At least half of the contracting states must take part in the vote on a waiver. Waivers are common in the GATT; for instance, a waiver allowed the European Coal and Steel Community to be considered as a customs union, although it did not satisfy all conditions of Article XXIV(8) (see paragraph 3.11).[52] In addition, the system of general tariff preferences in favour of developing countries (see paragraph 3.49) was originally approved pursuant to Article XXV(5).[53]

The guidelines in respect of the granting of waivers were adopted in 1956[54] but were amended during the Uruguay Round.[55] Extensive consultation, in which the interests of all relevant countries are considered, must take place in advance. A waiver can only be applied for a certain period. There should also be annual reports on the application of waivers and waivers need to be reviewed annually

---

[50] Agreement on Safeguards, Art. 2.2.

[51] In an interesting case between the U.S. and the E.C., an issue arose as to whether the U.S., after including imports from all sources in its investigation of "increased imports" of wheat gluten into its territory and the consequent effects of such imports on its domestic wheat gluten industry, was justified in excluding imports from Canada from the application of the safeguard measure. The panel ruled that "the United States was not justified in departing from the explicit provisions of Articles 2.1 and 4.2 SA by excluding from the application of its safeguard measure imports from Canada after having included such imports for the purposes of reaching its overall finding of serious injury caused by increased imports of the product concerned." See "US—Wheat Gluten", report of the panel, *loc.cit.*, para. 8.182.

[52] GATT, *Basic Instruments and Selected Documents* (1953), p. 85.

[53] *ibid.*, p. 85.

[54] GATT, *Basic Instruments and Selected Documents* (1972), p. 24.

[55] See Understanding on the Interpretation of Article XXV and the Agreement on the WTO.

by the contracting parties. Existing waivers may be extended when they are still justified by "exceptional circumstances".

Agriculture   Both historically as well as today, the multilateral trading sys-   **3.57** tem has treated agricultural products differently from non-agricultural products in many senses. The subsidies provision of GATT Article XVI and Article XI(2)(c) have been the most important areas in which agricultural products have been so subjected to discriminatory treatment. While Article XVI in principle prohibited export subsidies on non-agricultural products, countries have been free to provide unlimited subsidies contingent on the exportation of their agricultural products. The same situation prevailed as regards quantitative restrictions under Article XI(2)(c). GATT, in principle, prohibited the use of quantitative restrictions as means of protection while Article XI(2)(c) explicitly allowed such quantitative restrictions for agricultural products.

A number of real or apparent reasons have been invoked to keep agriculture outside the framework of the basic rules and principles of the system, including food security, preservation of rural community culture, the environment, and a host of other factors. Lately, a new term called "multifunctionality" has been invented to designate all such extraneous issues that are believed to have close relations with agricultural trade liberalisation.

There were also other GATT provisions at hand to keep agricultural products outside the scope of application of specific GATT rules.[56] A waiver (see paragraph 3.56) could have the same effect: the national agricultural policy of the United States, for example, has been exempted from the GATT obligations since 1955 by virtue of waiver.[57]

E.U.–U.S. Differences   There has been for some years a difference of opin-   **3.58** ion on the compatibility of the common agricultural policy of the E.U. with the GATT rules. This agricultural policy was challenged during the Tokyo Round, particularly by the United States, but no decision was then made by the contracting states on this issue.

The issue of the European Common Agricultural Policy was again raised during the Uruguay Round.[58] Differences, particularly between the E.U. and the U.S., forced the postponement of conclusion of the Uruguay Round of negotiations.

For the first time in the history of multilateral trade regulation, the Uruguay Round negotiations have resulted in a specific Agreement on Agriculture, which provides a framework for the long-term reform of agricultural trade over the

---

[56] See examples in E. McGovern, *op.cit.* pp. 334 *et seq.*
[57] GATT, *Basic Instruments and Selected Documents* (1955), p. 32. In March 1990 the GATT Council, after a complaint from the E.C., adopted a Panel decision on the validity of the agricultural restrictions of the U.S. based on the waiver of 1955.
[58] See, *e.g.* L.J. Emmerij, "On agricultural subsidies and the GATT negotiations" (1990) S.E.W. 267; F. Schoneveld, "The European Community Reaction to the 'Illicit' Commercial Trade Practices of Other Countries" (1991/2) J.W.T. 17; D.C. Hathaway, *Agriculture and the GATT: Issues in a New Trade Round* (Washington D.C. 1987).

years to come.[59] The Agreement has taken the most important first steps for the stage-by-stage integration of agriculture into the mainstream rules of the system. However, reflecting the delicate balance of negotiating power between the reformers (led mainly by the so-called Cairns Group countries and the United States), on the one hand, and the conservatives (led by the E.U. and backed by countries like Japan), on the other, the Agreement on Agriculture is a highly technical legal text with several major rules subject to sometimes strange exceptions (such as the "due restraint" clause of Article 13 of the Agriculture Agreement).

In what is often termed a process of "tariffication", all previous quantitative restrictions have been converted into their tariff equivalents and the resulting tariffs are subject to reduction commitments over an implementation period of six years (10 years for developing countries). In an attempt to allay the fears of some developed countries, a special safeguards provision has been included which allows the introduction of additional duties on certain quantitative and price trigger levels and regardless of domestic injury considerations. It goes to the credit of the Agreement on Agriculture that all non-tariffs barriers, including such notorious mechanisms as variable import levies, have been prohibited.

3.59   **Export subsidies**   Export subsidies in general are prohibited under the SCM Agreement. However, the SCM Agreement does not apply to agricultural products, which are subject to the provisions of the Agriculture Agreement. A look at the relevant provisions of the Agriculture Agreement shows that export subsidies are expressly allowed only in the agricultural sector. The Agriculture Agreement puts all export subsidies in either of two categories—listed and non-listed export subsidies. While all listed export subsidies are subject to reduction commitments of a dual nature (quantitative and outlay), the non-listed export subsidies are simply allowed subject only to the condition of non-circumvention of the export subsidies discipline created by the Agreement.

One of the notable achievements of the Uruguay Round has been the breakthrough on the subject of internal measures of support. Such practices as market price support mechanisms and deficiency payments have now been brought under a more or less defined discipline. A classification of all such measures has been introduced on the basis of their trade-distortive impact and the pragmatic need to accommodate the special interests of important trading powers such as the E.U. and the United States. Accordingly, all domestic support measures are divided into three categories: green (permitted), amber (subject to reduction commitments), and blue (permitted on production limitation conditions). The constraining power of the discipline in the short term is almost negligible. The basic innovation in this respect consists in the agreement in principle that domestic support schemes should be decoupled from production decision.

The Agriculture Agreement has established the Committee on Agriculture that reviews implementation of the commitments in agricultural trade. The Committee performs its duty of review on the basis of notifications made by WTO

---

[59] R. Green, "The Uruguay Round Agreement on Agriculture" (2000) 31 L. & Pol. Int'l Business 819–836.

Member States. It also serves as a consultative forum on any matter relevant for the implementation of the reform commitments.[60]

Agriculture is one of two areas (the other being services) where an in-built agenda for further negotiations was agreed during the Uruguay Round negotiations and included in the final agreement. The envisaged negotiations already had commenced in March 2000 and were expected to push the reform process further.[61] The E.U. and many other WTO Member States are currently pushing for the launching of a comprehensive round so that agriculture and services would also be brought into such a round which is believed to allow more room for trade-offs and a more meaningful progress.

PART II: INTERNATIONAL COMPETITION RULES

General   The prohibition or gradual abolition of tariff and non-tariff barriers   **3.60** to trade is, on its own, not sufficient for the full liberalisation of international trade. The world market is also distorted by unfair trade practices from states or enterprises.

When, after the Second World War, plans were made for the regulation of international trade and the foundation of an international trade organisation, there was the clear intention to introduce, besides the regulation of tariff and non-tariff restrictions to trade, also rules for fair trade practices.[62] Article 46 of the Charter of Havana included a fairly extensive regulation on fair trade practices.

However, the Charter never came into force. The GATT, which was initially intended as a provisional regulation until the coming into effect of the Charter, does not include an extensive regulation of unfair trade practices.[63] It contains only rules in respect of dumping (by enterprises) or subsidies (by states). These rules were later further elaborated in additional Codes and separate Agreements.

The basic goal of competition policy is "to promote and maintain healthy inter-firm rivalry in markets, wherever this is viable."[64] Two principal ways of achieving this goal are generally recognised: the use of competition law to address anti-competitive market structures and enterprise practices that impede competition and the use of pro-competitive regulation, and the reduction or elimination of government measures that pose unnecessary obstacles to trade and competition.[65]

---

[60] Agreement on Agriculture, Art. 18.

[61] All documents submitted in the negotiation process are available at http://www.wto.org/english/tratop_e/agric_e/negoti_e.htm.

[62] See, *e.g.* J. L'Huillier, Restrictive business practices (GATT Geneva, 1959) pp. 69–75.

[63] See also A. von Bogdandy, "Eine ordnung für das GATT" (1991) R.I.W. 56.

[64] See WTO Secretariat, *The Fundamental Principles Of Competition Policy: Background Note by the Secretariat,* (WTO doc. WT/WGTCP/W/127), June 7, 1999, para. 16.

[65] *ibid.*

3.61　　**Trade Barriers Regulation**[66]　The Trade Barriers Regulation (TBR)[67] is the second of the E.U.'s Regulations concerning commercial policy.[68] The old concept of "illicit commercial practice", has been replaced with "obstacles to trade", which are defined as "any trade practice adopted or maintained by a third country in respect of which international trade rules establish a right of action".[69] The scope of the TBR has been broadened to apply to services (not involving the movement of persons) as well as goods (pursuant on the Uruguay Round agreements). Intellectual property rights may also be covered, where a violation of international rules has an impact on trade between the E.U. and a third country.

The TBR establishes two procedures:

(a) A procedure aimed at "responding to obstacles to trade that have an effect on the market of a third country, with a view to removing the injury resulting therefrom".[70]

(b) A procedure aimed at "responding to obstacles to trade that have an effect on the market of a third country, with a view to removing the adverse trade effects resulting therefrom".[71]

The more significant of these is the latter, which provides a mechanism for Community firms and industries to act against trade barriers affecting their access to third country markets or the E.U. market, by requesting the Commission to investigate complaints and to seek redress—whether by negotiated bilateral agreement, dispute settlement at the WTO, or retaliatory measures.

3.62　　**UNCTAD Restrictive Business Practices Code**　Within the framework of UNCTAD, attempts have been made to introduce a code of conduct for restrictive

---

[66] M.C.E.J. Bronkers, "Private participation in the enforcement of WTO law: the new E.C. Trade Barriers Regulation" (1996) 32 C.M.L.Rev. 299–318. Consult, *inter alia*, I. van Bael and J.F. Bellis, *Anti-dumping and other Trade Protection Laws of the EEC* (3rd ed., CCH, 1996) pp. 467 *et seq.*

[67] Reg. 3286/94 [1994] O.J. L349/94.

[68] The first Regulation was "on the strengthening of the Common Commercial Policy with regard to Protection against Illicit Commercial Practices" [1984] O.J. L252/1, as amended [1994] O.J. L66, The concept of "illicit commercial practices" was broadly described as "practices in international trade attributable to third countries which are incompatible with international law or generally accepted rules". A practice may, for instance, be incompatible with the GATT rules. See the legal reasoning in the *Fediol* judgment of the Court of Justice, June 22, 1989: Case 70/87 *Fediol* [1989] E.C.R. 1781, [1991] 2 C.M.L.R. 489. For a discussion of the old text see P. Kunig, N. Lay and W. Meng (eds.), *op.cit.* pp. 617 *et seq.*; Arnold and Bronckers, "The EEC new trade policy instrument" (1988/6) J.W.T. 19; D. Carreau, T. Flory and P. Juillard, *op.cit.* pp. 160 *et seq.*; J. Bourgeois and P. Laurent, "Le nouvel instrument de politique commercials: un pas en avant vers l'élimination des obstacles aux échanges internationaux" (1985) Rev. Trim. Dr. Eur. 41.

[69] Reg. 3286/94, Art. 2(1). The international trade rules referred to are considered to be primarily the rules established by the WTO, however, they may also refer to any agreements to which the E.U. is a party.

[70] Reg. 3286/94, Art. 1(a).

[71] *ibid.*, Art. 1(b)

business practices.[72] In April 1980 agreement was reached on a set of multi-laterally agreed equitable principles and rules for the control of restrictive business practices[73] (Restrictive Business Practices Code). This code of conduct is soft law (see paragraph 1.13) and is binding neither on states nor on enterprises. Nevertheless, it puts into words the "equitable principles and rules" to which the states and enterprises must adhere.

One of the principles of the Code is that the restrictive business practices may not put at risk the liberalisation of international trade, and particularly of trade with developing countries.

Enterprises must be urged to observe competition legislation in all countries where they operate and to co-operate with the competent authorities to remove restrictive practices. Except within groups or concerns that form a single economic entity, enterprises may not apply certain specific restrictive practices if these hinder access to markets or unreasonably restrict competition.

The following restrictive practices must, *inter alia*, be banned:

- price fixing for, *inter alia*, imports and exports;

- understandings in respect of public tenders (collusive tendering);

- market or customer allocation arrangements;

- collective sales refusal;

- abuse of a dominant economic position, which can involve:

    — elimination of competitors through below-cost pricing;
    — price discrimination;
    — mergers and acquisitions;
    — restrictions on the importation of goods which have been legitimately marked abroad with a legitimate trade mark.

A "Group of Experts on Restrictive Business Practices" was set up within UNCTAD with responsibility for research, consultation and documentation.

Other international initiatives   At a more regional level, the OECD has **3.63** made several recommendations to its Member States in relation to international co-operation on anti-competitive practices affecting international trade (1995), potential conflicts between trade policies and competition policy (1986), effective action against hard-core cartels (1998), and competition in regulated sectors (1979 and 2001).[74]

---

[72] Consult, *inter alia*, J. Davidow, "The UNCTAD restrictive business practices code" in N. Horn (ed.), *Legal Problems of Codes of Conduct for Multilateral Enterprises* (Kluwer Law & Taxation, Deventer, 1980) pp. 193 *et seq.*

[73] This text was adopted in a resolution of the General Assembly of the UN in December 1980; see the text in P. Kunig, N. Lau and W. Meng (eds), *op. cit.* p. 720; A. Ham, "De UNCTAD Code van 1980 voor de controle op beperkingen van de mededinging" (1992) S.E.W. 6.

[74] See www.oecd.org.

A WTO Working Group on the Interaction between Trade and Competition Policy[75] has held several meetings and covered a wide-range of issues, including the relationship between the objectives, principles, concepts, scope and instruments of trade and competition policy, their relationship to development and economic growth, and the interaction between trade and competition policy in general. According to the WTO Secretariat, about 80 WTO Member States, including some 50 developing and transitional countries, have adopted competition laws which typically provide:

"remedies to deal with a range of anti-competitive practices, including price fixing and other cartel arrangements, abuses of a dominant position or monopolsation, mergers that limit competition, and agreements between suppliers and distributors ('vertical agreements') that foreclose markets to new competitors."[76]

Dumping

3.64 **Basic regulation** Dumping is described in Article VI(1) of the GATT as introducing products of one country into the commerce of another country at less than the normal value of the products.[77]

Dumping is not prohibited by GATT; it is only condemned when it causes material injury to an existing sector of business or hinders considerably the setting up of a new industry in the country of importation. The affected state may then under certain circumstances introduce anti-dumping duties in order to offset or prevent such practices.

Dumping is carried out by enterprises. However, the rules of the GATT are not directed at enterprises, but exclusively at the contracting states, which are responsible for the transposition of the GATT anti-dumping rules into national law.

3.65 **Principles** Article VI of the GATT sets out basic principles on dumping. These principles were given more substance by the Anti-dumping Codes of the Kennedy Round (1967) and the Tokyo Round (1979). The 1979 Code was replaced after the Uruguay Round by the WTO, Agreement on Implementation of Article VI of the General Agreement on Tariffs and Trade 1994 (the Anti-Dumping Agreement). Unlike both the Kennedy and Tokyo Round Codes, the new Anti-Dumping Agreement is binding on all Members of the WTO, because of the package-deal approach adopted in Uruguay Round negotiations. At the

---

[75] See WTO doc. WT/MIN(96)/DEC, December 18, 1996.
[76] For further information on trade and competition policy issues within the WTO, see http://www.wto.org/english/tratop_e/comp_e/comp_e.htm.
[77] D. Palmeter, "A commentary on the WTO Anti-Dumping Code" (1996) 30 J.W.T. 43–69.

substantive level, the basic difference between these two instruments lies in the fact that the latter provides for more detailed procedural requirements.[78]

Description of dumping   A product is deemed to be brought into circulation **3.66** below its "normal value" in the country of importation when the price is lower than the comparable price in the ordinary course of trade for the like[79] product when destined for consumption in the exporting country.[80] If there is no such local price in the country of export,[81] then there is dumping when the import price is lower than either:

(a) either a comparable price of the like product when exported to a relevant third country provided that this price is representative; or

(b) or the cost of production in the country of origin plus a reasonable amount for administrative, selling and any other costs and for profits.[82]

Sometimes goods are not imported directly from the country of origin, but are imported via another country (*e.g.* chemicals manufactured in Canada are sent to a subsidiary in Sweden, from where they are sold in Germany). In this case the price in the country of export (Sweden) is used as the normal price. However, a comparison with the price of the country of origin (Canada, in the above example) is permitted when the goods were merely transshipped through the second country, when the products are not manufactured in the country of export or when there is no comparable price for the products in that country.

The prices must each time be compared at the same level of trade; this is usually the "ex factory" price (see paragraph 4.56) and in respect of sales made at (as nearly as possible) the same time. Due allowance shall be made for differences which affect price comparability, such as differences in conditions and terms of sale, taxation, deeds of trade, quantities and physical characteristics.

The difference between the price at importation and the higher price in the country of origin is called the "dumping margin".

Other conditions   Dumping is only condemned under the GATT when it **3.67** causes material injury to domestic industry, when it causes a threat of such injury or when it causes material retardation of the establishment of a new domestic

---

[78] See D. Palmeter, "A commentary on the WTO Anti-Dumping Code", 4 J.W.T. 30 (1996) at 45; P. C. Rosenthal and R. T. C. Vermylen, "The WTO Antidumping and Subsidies Agreements: Did the United States achieve its objectives during the Uruguay Round?" (2000) 31 L. & Pol. Int'l Business 871–896.

[79] The concept of "like product" is in practice very important because the domestic products that are affected by the dumping are not always identical to the imported product. Not only identical products but also products which are not identical but with similar characteristics to the imported product, are considered to be "like products".

[80] Anti-Dumping Agreement, Art. 2(1).

[81] *e.g.* because the product has not been brought into circulation in this country, or because the product is not the subject of normal "business transactions" (*i.e.* on the market), since the country of origin is a country with a state economy.

[82] The profit cannot be higher than the profit which is normally realised for like products in the country of origin.

industry. This injury must be established on the basis of an objective examination as to the volume of the dumped goods and their effect on the price of like products on the local market, as well as on the local industry of said products. Both criteria are given further definition in the Anti-Dumping Agreement. Only injury caused by dumping itself is considered, not injury that can be attributed to other factors.

The concept of "domestic industry" in the country of importation is explained in the Anti-Dumping Agreement to mean the domestic producers as a whole of the like products, or those whose collective output of the products constitutes a major proportion of the total domestic production of these products.

3.68   **Procedure**   The existence, importance and effects of the alleged dumping must be investigated. The investigation can be initiated upon a written application by or on behalf of the domestic industry that claims to have been affected by the dumped imports. This investigation must concentrate on both the existence of the dumping and of the resulting material injury or threat thereof. Evidence has to be provided that there is both dumping as well as a serious injury to domestic industry, and that there is a causal link between the two. The investigation must in principle be concluded within a year from its start.[83]

Interested parties, particularly foreign exporters, must be heard and given the opportunity to defend themselves. Parties are entitled to have access to all information gathered during the investigation, except when this information is 'by nature confidential' (*i.e.* information the disclosure of which "would be of significant competitive advantage to a competitor or . . . would have a significantly adverse effect upon a person supplying the information") or provided on a confidential basis.[84]

When the competent authorities decide after their investigation that the terms of the Anti-Dumping Agreement have been satisfied, they can take anti-dumping measures (in particular, they may charge anti-dumping duties). They must notify the interested parties of their decision.

3.69   **Anti-dumping duties and price undertakings**   During the investigation, or after having been notified of the result of the investigation, the exporter may offer voluntary price undertakings, in which he can increase his export prices or stop exporting the dumped goods to the relevant territory.[85] The authorities are under no obligation to accept the price undertakings, and no exporter can be compelled

---

[83] In no case may the investigations extend beyond 18 months from the date of initiation. See Art. 5.10 of the Anti-Dumping Agreement.

[84] See Art. 6(5) of the Anti-Dumping Agreement. Examples could include: information on costs, including those of each stage of the production process; information on prices, including both the prices paid by the producer to upstream suppliers, the prices charged to downstream buyers—the names of these customers may also be treated as confidential; information on performance, including profitability of operations, margins on individual products, as well as prospectives for investment and future strategy; certain information supplied in the context of a public interest assessment (*e.g.* company performance forecasts), etc. For a summary of discussions at the WTO on the issue of confidential information, see WTO, *Synthesis of Discussion within the Ad Hoc Group Concerning the Treatment of Confidential Information: Note from the Secretariat* (G/ADP/AHG/W/65, April 16, 1999).

[85] Anti-Dumping Agreement, Art. 8.

to make such undertakings. Price increases conceded in price undertakings should not exceed the dumping margin.[86]

The normal sanction for dumping, however, is the levying of anti-dumping duties. These may not exceed the established dumping margin. They are only levied for so long and in so far as it is necessary to neutralise the dumping that is causing injury. In all events, any anti-dumping duty or price undertaking shall be terminated after five years from its imposition, unless the authorities determine that the expiry of the duty or undertaking would be likely to lead to continuation or recurrence of dumping and injury.[87]

Anti-dumping duties can be levied on imports from developing countries only after other constructive remedies have been explored.[88]

During the dumping investigation the authorities may take provisional measures to prevent injury. These provisional measures can take the form of provisional anti-dumping duties or of a security for estimated anti-dumping duties. The provisional measures can only apply for four (exceptionally six) months.

Consultation and disputes There is within the WTO a "Committee on **3.70** Anti-Dumping Practices", where states confer with each other on any matters relating to the operation of the Agreement, including provisional and definitive anti-dumping measures. The Anti-dumping Agreement requests states to show "sympathetic consideration" for representations made by other Member States with respect to any matter affecting the operation of the Agreement.[89] As in other cases, Member States are required to enter into consultations before the dispute settlement process of the WTO is called into play. In principle, if the consultation phase fails to produce a mutually acceptable solution, Members are allowed to request the establishment of a panel, which is generally governed by the general rules of the Dispute Settlement Understanding, subject of course to any specific provisions of the Anti-Dumping Agreement.[90] In the case of disputes involving anti-dumping measures, however, failure to achieve mutually acceptable solutions does not suffice for Member States to request establishment of a panel; "final action" needs to have been taken by the administering authorities of the importing Member State to levy definitive anti-dumping duties or to accept price undertakings, or, in the case of provisional measures, the measures need to have had a significant impact on the Member State that requested the consultations.[91]

E.U. anti-dumping regulation WTO Member States are entitled to take **3.71** anti-dumping measures in accordance with the relevant provisions of the GATT

---

[86] P. Vander Schueren, "New anti-dumping rules and practice: wide discretion, held on a tight leash?" (1996) 32 C.M.L.Rev. 271–297; K. Adamantopoulos & D. De Notaris, "The future of the WTO and the reform of the Anti-Dumping Agreement: a legal perspective" (2000) 24 Ford I.L.J. U.S. 30–61.

[87] Anti-Dumping Agreement, Art. 11, paras 3 and 5.

[88] Anti-Dumping Agreement, Art. 16.

[89] *ibid.*, Art. 17.2.

[90] For a discussion of the integrated system of dispute settlement under the WTO, see paras 3.106 *et seq.*

[91] Anti-Dumping Agreement, Art. 17.4. See also E.U. Petersmann, "GATT dispute settlement proceedings in the field of antidumping law" (1991) C.M.L.Rev. 69.

and the Anti-dumping Agreement. Within the E.U., the Council of Ministers is, by virtue of Article 113 of the EEC Treaty, responsible for trade policy in respect of third countries and therefore also for the adoption of protective measures against dumped imports from those countries.

The first regulation in this respect dates from April 5, 1968, and has subsequently been modified several times. The current basic anti-dumping regulations,[92] which form the legal basis of anti-dumping investigations in the E.U., entered into force between March 1996 and April 1998. In its internal legislation, the E.U. has gone further than required by the WTO in a number of areas—including the so-called "Community interest test" and the "lesser duty rule". The Community interest test

"corresponds to a public interest clause, and foresees that measures can only be taken if they are not contrary to the overall interest of the Community. This requires an appreciation of all the economic interests involved, including the interests of the domestic industry, users and consumers. The lesser duty rule allows the measures imposed by the Community to be lower than the dumping . . . margin, if such a lower duty rate is sufficient to protect the Community industry adequately."[93]

The E.U. anti-dumping regulation is frequently applied and is the subject of extensive case law of the European Court of Justice.[94] The regulation gives a detailed description of concepts such as "normal value",[95] "export price", "like product", "dumping margin" and the injury caused by dumping, as well as the procedure for the investigation into dumping and the protective measures.

Subsidies

3.72   **General**   The use of subsidies in both domestic as well as export trade as means of benefiting national producers and exporters by a state can have the same effect as dumping by an enterprise: the price on the market is kept artificially low. Under Article VI of GATT, a country that imports subsidised products can levy countervailing duties to offset the effect of subsidies provided by another state. Furthermore, Article XVI provides for consultation when subsidies cause material injury to one or more contracting states.

Article XVI distinguishes between domestic or production subsidies on the one hand, and export subsidies, on the other. In principle, while domestic

---

[92] Reg. 384/96.

[93] See *Report from the Commission Eighteenth Annual Report from the Commission to the European Parliament on the Community's Anti-Dumping and Anti-Subsidy Activities,* (COM(2000) 440 final) July 2000, p. 12.

[94] It has sometimes been commented that the E.U. anti-dumping regulation is used for protectionist purposes: R.M. Bierwagen, *op.cit., passim*; R. Kulms, "Competition, trade policy and competition policy in the EEC: the example of antidumping" (1990) C.M.L.Rev. 285.

[95] See Art. 2(a) and in particular 2(a)7 for determination of "normal value" on imports from non-market economy countries, modified by Reg. 905/98 and 2238/2000.

subsidies have been permitted, export subsidies have been prohibited.[96] These rules were subsequently interpreted and applied during the Tokyo Round in a Subsidies Code that was accepted by a limited number of countries. During the Uruguay Round an Agreement on Subsidies and Countervailing Measures (the SCM Agreement) was concluded as part of the Uruguay Round package replacing the Subsidies Code and binding on all Members of the WTO.

Terms of applications The substantive rules of the SCM Agreement are largely based on those of the Code, but enormous developments have also resulted from the Uruguay Round negotiations on the subject.   **3.73**

For the first time in GATT history, the SCM Agreement has defined the notion of "subsidy". The controversial term has now been given a broad definition. It covers not just direct subsidies but also any form of income or price support that results directly or indirectly in the acquisition of a benefit by the recipient. Article 1 of the SCM Agreement defines it in terms of a public financial contribution conferring a benefit on a recipient. As the Appellate Body pointed out in "Canada Dairy", the "benefit" to the recipient is measured against what would have been otherwise available to the recipient in the market place.[97]

The discipline introduced by the SCM Agreement concerns mainly "specific" subsidies—for the most part, subsidies available only to an enterprise or industry, or to a group of enterprises or industries.

An important feature of the SCM Agreement is the so-called "traffic light approach" adopted to introduce a classification of subsidies. Accordingly, a subsidy may be prohibited (red), actionable (amber), or non-actionable (green); each with a Part devoted to itself.

Prohibited subsidies Export subsidies and the so-called local content subsidies (*i.e.* subsidies contingent upon the use of domestic rather than imported goods) fall in the category of prohibited subsidies. While Article 3 of the SCM Agreement describes export subsidies as subsidies contingent (*de facto* or *de jure*) on export performance, Annex I to the SCM Agreement gives an illustrative list of export subsidies covered by the Code and Agreement. The practices covered by the illustrative list annexed to the SCM Agreement are largely the same as those listed by the Tokyo Round Subsidies Code.   **3.74**

Actionable subsidies This category covers those subsidies which are not prohibited *per se* but against which actions may be taken depending on their "trade effects". According to Article 5, Members are obliged not to use subsidies to cause adverse effects to the interests of other Members.   **3.75**

Non-actionable subsidies These are subsidies which are generally considered to have minimal impact on the flow of international trade on either of two grounds: they are not "specific" to any enterprise or industry or group of enterprises or industries; or they qualify, as a "green" subsidy, for any of three   **3.76**

---

[96] See Article XVI, paras 3 and 4, respectively.
[97] *Canada Dairy,* report of the Appellate Body, para. 87.

specifically designated forms of practices as defined under Article 8 of the SCM Agreement[98] relating to research and development activities, regional development programmes, or schemes to help adaptation to new environmental standards and while they are not *per se* non-actionable,[99] they may not be the subject of unilateral countervailing action.

3.77   **Countervailing measures**   A country that is adversely affected by subsidised imports has two basic alternative remedies—unilateral countervailing measures and the multilateral dispute settlement option.

The imposition of countervailing measures is subject to certain substantive conditions, including:

(a) a countervailing measure could be taken only after investigations are initiated and conducted according to prescribed lines to determine the existence, degree and effect of a subsidy;

(b) countervailing measures are allowed only when the subsidy is determined to have caused, or is capable of causing, material injury to an existing industry, or of delaying significantly the setting up of a new industry;

(c) an investigation could normally be initiated upon a written request made to the authorities by or on behalf of the domestic industry producing the like product which is claimed to have been affected by the subsidised imports[1];

(d) countervailing measures could take the form only of additional duties;

(e) the level of such duties may not exceed the estimated amount of the subsidy granted; and

(f) countervailing duties cannot be applied in a discriminatory manner; they should be applied to all products that have actually received the disputed subsidy, no matter what their origin.

The SCM Agreement provides for an elaborate system of rules governing the investigation procedure to be followed before countervailing measures can be imposed. The investigation must establish, first, that a subsidy is being granted on the specific product under investigation; and, secondly, that it is this subsidy that caused the claimed injury to the relevant domestic industry. To find out whether there is such subsidy, the subsidising country required to give its full co-operation. Each investigation must in principle be concluded within the period of one year.

---

[98] Agreement on Subsidies & Countervailing Measures www.wto.org/english/docs_e/legal_e/24-scm.pdf.

[99] They may be referred, after consultations, to the Committee on Subsidies and Countervailing measures by a WTO member believing that they have suffered "serious adverse effects to the domestic industry of that member, such as to cause damage which would be difficult to repair" (Art. 9.1 SCM).

[1] SCM Agreement, Art. 11. Note also that, under Art. 11.6, there is room for the authorities to initiate an investigation on their own.

Proceedings in respect of subsidies may be suspended or concluded if the country of import accepts undertakings in which either the subsidising country promises to suspend or reduce the subsidies or the exporter agrees to revise his prices in such a way that the negative effect of the subsidy has been removed.

Provisional measures   The importing country can impose provisional meas-   **3.78**
ures during the investigation before final countervailing measures are introduced if a preliminary affirmative decision has been made that a subsidy has been granted and injury has been caused to local industry and the authorities judge that such provisional measures are necessary to prevent further injury from being caused. The provisional measures usually take the form of mandatory deposits or bank guarantees (see paragraph 8.52). If the final countervailing duty is higher than the deposited or guaranteed amount the importing country cannot lay claim to the difference; if on the other hand the duty is lower, the importing country must pay back the extra amount or release the bank guarantee in proportion to that amount.

The duration of a countervailing measure is required to be proportionate to the damage suffered and it may not exceed five years (often called the "sunset clause"), unless it is established that the expiry of the duty would likely lead to recurrence of subsidy and injury. It is the duty of the state implementing the countervailing measures to check regularly whether they are still justified under GATT.

Multilateral remedies   Under the SCM Agreement, the "Committee on   **3.79**
Subsidies and Countervailing Measures" has to be informed of existing subsidy regulations; it may be consulted by any Member State, to which it may give advisory opinions on the nature of any subsidy this Member State proposes or maintains. Disputes involving subsidies have to be submitted to the Dispute Settlement Body and they are largely subject to the rules of the Dispute Settlement Understanding. The SCM Agreement also has what are known as "special or additional rules and procedures" which are intended to reflect the peculiarities of some of the covered agreements while keeping the integrated nature of the dispute settlement system intact.[2] The "special or additional rules and procedures" of the SCM Agreement generally prescribe shorter deadlines on the different stages of the dispute settlement process as defined by the DSU.[3]

The E.U. anti-dumping regulation and subsidies   The rules concerning   **3.80**
dumping are *mutatis mutandis* applicable to subsidies. This applies in particular to determination and calculation of the injury caused, procedure, consultation, investigation, undertakings given by the country of origin or exportation, imposition of provisional or final countervailing duties and possible restitution of collected duties.[4]

---

[2] For more on dispute settlement, see paras 3.106 *et seq.*

[3] See, *e.g.* Art. 4.12 of the SCM Agreement which provides that, in the case of disputes involving prohibited subsidies, "time-periods applicable under the DSU for the conduct of such disputes shall be half the time prescribed therein."

[4] For more on this, see para. 3.71

PART III: TRADE IN SERVICES: THE GATS

The international trade in services

3.81 GATT only concerns trade in goods; it does not cover trade in services, such as the business of banking, insurance, tourism, etc. that represents about 35 per cent of international trade transactions and more than 60 per cent of the GNP of many industrialised countries. The absence of international trade rules for the regulation of trade in services has seriously limited the reach of multilateral trade liberalisation.

One of the success stories of the Uruguay Round negotiations (1986–1993) consisted in the conclusion of a General Agreement on Trade in Services (GATS).[5] The GATS is therefore the services version of GATT and, for the first time in history, extends "internationally-agreed rules and commitments . . . into a huge and still rapidly growing area of international trade."[6]

3.82 **Service definition** By "service" is understood "any service in any sector, except services supplied in the exercise of governmental functions" (Article I(3)(b)).[7] It has been said that this description is too wide and that it therefore makes little sense to liberalise the trade in services in the same way as the trade in goods, because services are more person-related than goods.[8]

With this understanding of the term "services", trade in services is defined to include four modes of supply activities:

(a) the supply of a service from the territory of one Member State into the territory of any other Member State often called "cross-border supply" (*e.g.* telecommunication services);

(b) the supply of a service in the territory of one Member State to the service consumer of any other Member State, called "consumption abroad" (*e.g.* tourism services);

(c) the supply of a service by a service supplier of one Member State, through commercial presence in the territory of any other Member State, called "commercial presence" (*e.g.* establishment of branches of banks and insurance companies in another country);

---

[5] See M. Footer, "GATT and the multilateral regulation of banking services" (1993) 27 *International Lawyer* 343; F. Lazar, "Services and the GATT" (1990/1) J.W.T. 135; P. Nicolaides, *Liberalising Service Trade* (Chatham House, London, 1989); F. Weiss, "The General Agreement on Trade in Services 1994" (1995) 32 C.M.L.Rev. 1177–1225; J. M. Lang, "The First Five Years of the WTO: General Agreement on Trade in Services" (2000) 31 LawP.I.B. 801–810.

[6] See WTO Secretariat, Trade in Services Division, *An Introduction to the GATS* (October 1999).

[7] Sub-para. (c) then defines a "service supplied in the exercise of governmental authority" to mean "any service which is supplied neither on a commercial basis, nor in competition with one or more service suppliers"; A. K. Abu-Akeel, "Definition of trade in services under the GATs: legal implications" (1999) 32 Geo.Wash.J.Int'l.L.Econ 189–210.

[8] M. van Empel, "The visible hand of the invisible trade" (1990/2) L.I.E.I. 26–27, 38–39 ("whereas 'goods', once produced, take on an identity of their own, 'services' are determined by the identity of their producer").

(d) the supply of a service by a service supplier of one Member State, through presence of natural persons of a Member State in the territory of any other Member State, called "presence of natural persons" (*e.g.* consultants or accountants moving to another country to do some work).

The importance of this definition can hardly be over-emphasised. The definition indeed holds the key to understanding the nature of the challenges involved in trying to liberalise trade in services and the solutions currently adopted by the GATS.

General principles: comparison with GATT Like the GATT, the GATS **3.83** also incorporates a number of fundamental principles including the non-discrimination rules of most favoured nation and national treatment as well as the transparent administration of national regulations affecting services trade. However, there are also important differences between these two instruments, and a closer look at some of these principles is crucial at this point.

Most favoured nation treatment GATS Article II embodies the funda- **3.84** mental most favoured nation treatment principle in the following words:

"With respect to any measure covered by this Agreement, each Member shall accord immediately and unconditionally to services and service suppliers of any other Member treatment no less favourable than that it accords to like services and service suppliers of any other country."[9]

However, the GATS MFN principle has been subject to an important exception— that Member States are allowed to maintain a measure inconsistent with this principle "provided that such a measure is listed in, and meets the conditions of, the Annex on Article II Exemptions". As a result of this opening, "more than 70 WTO members made their scheduled services commitments subject to a further list of exemptions from Article II."[10] Like the GATT, the MFN principle of the GATS also allows an exception in the case of regional integration initiatives.[11]

National treatment Like GATT Article III, Article XVII of the GATS also **3.85** enshrines the principle of national treatment. The similarities between them are, however, rather limited. The essence of the national treatment principle in both cases of course remains the protection of foreign products and services (and/or service suppliers) from being discriminated against once they are in the territory of other Member States. But, while this principle applies in GATT as a matter of general rule, the same principle under the GATS applies only as regards what

---

[9] A. K. Abu-Akeel, "The MFN as it applies to service trade—new problems for an old concept" (1999) 33 J.W.T. 103–130.
[10] See WTO Secretariat, Trade in Services Division, *An Introduction to the GATS* (October 1999). The full text of this useful introduction is available at http://www.wto.org/english/tratop_e/serv_e/serv_e.htm.
[11] See Art. V of the GATS. GATS does not make any distinction between customs unions and free trade areas.

each Member State has specifically undertaken in its own schedule. Article XVII of GATS, which is found in Part III of the Agreement on specific commitments, thus provides as follows:

> "In the sectors inscribed in its Schedule, and subject to any conditions and qualifications set out therein, each Member shall accord to services and service suppliers of any other Member, in respect of all measures affecting the supply of services, treatment no less favourable than that it accords to its own like services and service suppliers."

3.86   **Market access**   Article XVI provides that "each Member shall accord services and service suppliers of any other Member treatment no less favourable than that provided for under the terms, limitations and conditions agreed and specified in its Schedule." This is the same as the bindings of GATT Article II. Article XVI further sets out six forms of practices which a Member "shall not maintain or adopt":

   (i) limitations on the number of service suppliers;

  (ii) limitations on the total value of services transactions or assets;

 (iii) limitations on the total number of service operations or the total quantity of service output;

 (iv) limitations on the number of persons that may be employed in a particular sector or by a particular supplier;

  (v) measures that restrict or require supply of the service through specific types of legal entity or joint venture; and

 (vi) percentage limitations on the participation of foreign capital, or limitations on the total value of foreign investment.[12]

3.87   **Transparency**   Another basic principle of the GATS is transparency—making all laws and regulations affecting services trade known to other Member States so that their private sectors can be in a position to take advantage of the market opening effects of the GATS. The GATS thus stipulates that Member States "shall publish promptly and, except in emergency situations, at the latest by the time of their entry into force, all relevant measures of general application which pertain to or affect the operation of this Agreement."[13] Additionally, Member States are also required to "promptly and at least annually inform the Council for Trade in Services of the introduction of any new, or any changes to existing, laws, regulations or administrative guidelines which significantly affect trade in services covered by its specific commitments under this Agreement." Member States establish enquiry points to provide specific relevant information to other Members States upon request.

---

[12] GATS, Art. XVI:2; see also WTO Secretariat, Trade in Services Division, *An Introduction to the GATS* (October 1999).
[13] GATS, Art. III:1.

Other principles   Other major principles of the GATS include progressive   **3.88**
liberalisation through multilateral trade negotiations, as is already the case for the
trade in goods, and greater participation of developing countries in international
trade in services, *inter alia*, through access to technology, distribution channels
and information networks. There are also some provisions on general exceptions
and security exceptions in GATS which are similar to Articles XX and XXI,
respectively, of the GATT (see paragraph 3.43). Indeed, these provisions "are
perhaps the closest of all to their GATT equivalents".

Major missing features   New as the GATS is, it contains a number of   **3.89**
noticeable regulatory gaps. These include emergency safeguards, and subsidies
and countervailing measures, which the Agreement only mentions in the sense of
setting agenda for future negotiations.[14] Article X originally set a three-year
deadline (from entry into force of the Agreement) for the completion of multilateral negotiations on emergency safeguard measures. This deadline was
extended first to December 15, 2000 and then to March 15, 2002. Unlike Article
X on emergency safeguards, Article XV on subsidies does not even set deadlines
for the envisaged negotiations.

Annexes to the GATS   The GATS text contains eight annexes which, in the   **3.90**
words of Article XXIX, form an integral part of the Agreement. They deal with
exemptions from the MFN principle, the movement of natural persons supplying
services under the Agreement, air transport services, financial services, maritime
transport, and telecommunications.

Movement of natural persons   To the disappointment of most developing   **3.91**
countries during the Uruguay Round negotiations, the Annex on the movement
of natural persons is not concerned with immigration and related issues. Indeed
a closer look at this part of the Agreement shows that the Annex was included
only to underline this fact. Paragraph 2 thus stresses that the Agreement "shall
not apply to measures affecting natural persons seeking access to the employment market of a Member, nor shall it apply to measures regarding citizenship,
residence or employment on a permanent basis." The Annex in this respect
simply states the obvious and declares that "Members *may* negotiate specific
commitments applying to the movement of all categories of natural persons
supplying services under the Agreement." (Emphasis supplied.)

Air transport services   Although this Annex starts with a comprehensive-   **3.92**
sounding statement to cover all primary and ancillary measures affecting trade in
air transport services (scheduled as well as non-scheduled), a closer look indicates a different reality. For example, it is provided that "any specific commitment or obligation assumed under this Agreement" shall not reduce or affect "a
Member's obligations under bilateral or multilateral agreements that are in effect
on the date of entry into force of the WTO Agreement." The established principle

---

[14] Y. S. Lee, "Emergency safeguard measures under Article X in GATS—applicability of the
concepts in the WTO Agreement on Safeguards" (1999) 33 J.W.T. pp. 47–60.

of general international law that, in case of inconsistency, the later agreement in time prevails, is thus explicitly excluded. Existing arrangements in international air transport services are largely governed by the 1944 International Air Services Transit Agreement, known as the Chicago Convention. The GATS Annex specifically excludes from its coverage this "complex network of bilateral agreements on air traffic rights",[15] encompassing all traffic rights as well as services directly related to the exercise of traffic rights. The scope of the Annex on Air Transport Services is therefore limited to aircraft repair and maintenance, the selling and marketing of air transport services, and computer reservations.

3.93   **Financial services**   This Annex applies to measures affecting the supply of financial services which is defined to cover all insurance and insurance-related services as well as all banking and other financial services.[16] It does not apply to financial services normally supplied by governmental authorities such as activities conducted by a central bank or monetary authority or by any other public entity in pursuit of monetary or exchange rate policies. Even in the case of covered financial services, Member States are free to take what are called "prudential measures", *e.g.* measures taken for reasons of the protection of investors, depositors, policy-holders etc.

3.94   **Telecommunications**   The telecommunications sector is important both in itself and in the sense of the provision of several other services. This is what is known as the "dual role" of telecommunications—as a distinct sector of economic activity and as the underlying means of transportation for other economic activities. The purpose of the Annex on Telecommunications is therefore to elaborate upon GATS provisions with respect to measures affecting access to and use of public telecommunications transport networks and services. It does not however apply to measures affecting the cable or broadcast distribution of radio or television programming.

The fundamental rule in this respect provides that:

> "Each Member shall ensure that any service supplier of any other Member is accorded access to and use of public telecommunications transport networks and services on reasonable and non-discriminatory terms and conditions, for the supply of a service included in its Schedule."[17]

This is a general obligation applicable to every Member State regardless of their specific commitments. Indeed, this is a necessary corollary of Member States' specific commitments on the supply of other services, as it would be practically impossible to render many other services in the absence of full access to the underlying infrastructure of telecommunication services. The only permissible conditions that could be imposed by Member States for access to and use of public telecommunications transport networks and services are those necessary

---

[15] WTO Secretariat, Trade in Services Division, *An Introduction to the GATS* (October 1999).
[16] An elaborate definition of the different forms of banking (and banking-related) and insurance (and insurance-related) services is included in the Annex.
[17] Annex on Telecommunications, para. 5.

to safeguard the public service responsibilities of suppliers of public telecommunications transport networks and services, to protect the technical integrity of public telecommunications transport networks or services, and to ensure that service suppliers of any other Member State do not supply services unless permitted pursuant to commitments in the Member State's Schedule.

GATS emphasises the importance of international organisations such as the International Telecommunications Union (ITU) and IOS in the development of standards for the global compatibility and interoperability of telecommunication networks and services.

Developing countries and GATS

The GATS also incorporates the principle of special and differential treatment **3.95** for developing countries, both in its general provisions as well as in the annexes. Article XXV provides that technical assistance to developing countries shall be provided at the multilateral level by the Secretariat and shall be decided upon by the Council for Trade in Services. The Annex on telecommunications, for instance, provides that developing countries may "place reasonable conditions on access to and use of public telecommunications transport networks and services necessary to strengthen its domestic telecommunications infrastructure and service capacity and to increase its participation in international trade in telecommunications services".[18]

Institutional features

Within the WTO, the Council for Trade in Services oversees the functioning **3.96** of the GATS.[19] The dispute settlement system which evolved over time in the course of GATT also applies to the resolution of disputes under the GATS. In case of complaints, while Member States are required to "afford adequate opportunity" for consultations at the bilateral level, multilateral consultations through the GATS Council or the DSB are also available at the request of interested Member States.[20] If consultations do not solve a matter, Member States have the option of invoking the dispute settlement provisions of the DSU on both violation as well as non-violation grounds.

The non-violation nullification or impairment of the GATS is expressed as follows:

"If any Member considers that any benefit it could reasonably have expected to accrue to it under a specific commitment of another Member under Part III of this Agreement is being nullified or impaired as a result of the application of any measure which does not conflict with the provisions of this Agreement, it may have recourse to the DSU."[21] (See paragraph 3.108.)

---

[18] *ibid.*, para. 6(g).
[19] GATS, Art. XXIV.
[20] *ibid.*, Art. XXII.
[21] *ibid.*, Art. XXIII.

The future agenda

3.97   The discipline introduced by GATS for the regulation of services trade is still in its infancy. Aware of this situation, GATS made provision for the continuation of negotiations. GATS Article XIX set this agenda as follows:

> "In pursuance of the objectives of this Agreement, Members shall enter into successive rounds of negotiations, beginning not later than five years from the date of entry into force of the WTO Agreement and periodically thereafter, with a view to achieving a progressively higher level of liberalization. Such negotiations shall be directed to the reduction or elimination of the adverse effects on trade in services of measures as a means of providing effective market access. This process shall take place with a view to promoting the interests of all participants on a mutually advantageous basis and to securing an overall balance of rights and obligations."[22]

GATS Article XIX also provides for a kind of differential treatment to developing countries, mainly the LDCs. The first of the negotiations envisaged by this provision has already started pursuant to a General Council decision of February 7–8, 2000.[23]

PART IV: INTELLECTUAL PROPERTY

3.98   **Trade restrictions as a result of intellectual property rights**   One of the important achievements of the Uruguay Round has been the conclusion of a comprehensive agreement on trade-related aspects of intellectual property rights, TRIPs. For many years the industrialised countries complained about the fact that developing countries gave insufficient legal protection to various industrial property rights such as patents, trade marks and service marks, industrial drawings, models and copyrights. Moreover, they considered that the developing countries particularly were treated too softly with regard to trade in counterfeit products (see paragraph 6.34).

For their part, the developing countries were reluctant to grant exclusivity to the owners of intellectual property rights. In their opinion, the enjoyment of exclusive rights by companies from industrialised countries will obstruct the transfer of technology to developing countries. Furthermore, many developing countries believe that for certain essential products (particularly pharmaceuticals), no, or only limited, exclusivity should be granted.[24]

The TRIPs Agreement covers copyright and related rights (such as the rights of performers, producers of sound recordings and broadcasting organisations),

---

[22] *ibid.*, Art. XIX:2.
[23] WTO Press Release, Press/167, February 7, 2000.
[24] Symposium: "Public and private initiatives after TRIPs" 9 (1998) DukeJ.C.I.L., No. 1; C. S. Levy, "Implementing TRIPs—A test of political will" (2000) 31 LawP.I.B. 789–796.

trade marks including service marks, geographical indications including appellations of origin, industrial designs, the layout designs of integrated circuits, and trade secrets.[25]

The TRIPs Agreement has three major features. First, it sets out the minimum standards of protection to be provided by each Member State with respect to each form of intellectual property (*e.g.* copyright protection for the lifetime of the author plus 50 years; after patent protection for a period of 20 years from the filing date; etc.). Secondly, it prescribes certain mandatory domestic procedures and remedies for the enforcement of intellectual property rights which include civil, administrative and criminal procedures and remedies. Thirdly, it applies the stringent dispute settlement rules of the WTO (see paragraph 3.108) to intellectual property issues.[26]

Like GATT as well as the GATS, the TRIPs Agreement enshrines the basic principles of non-discrimination, such as the MFN clause and national treatment.[27] Moreover, parties are required to comply with the substantive provisions of the Berne Convention on copyright and the Paris Patent Convention.

Some of the major forms of intellectual property rights protected by the TRIPS Agreement summarised below.

Copyrights and "neighbouring" rights   Section 1 of Part II of the TRIPs   **3.99**
Agreement is devoted to copyrights and related or neighbouring rights (such as the rights of performers, producers of sound recordings and broadcasting organisations). Article 9 essentially incorporates the Berne Convention (1971) and the Appendix thereto. Consequently the Berne Convention Article 7 obligation to accord copyright protection for the lifetime of the author plus 50 years after his/her death is the standard imported by the TRIPs Agreement.[28] Article 14 of the TRIPs Agreement also protects the rights of performers, producers of phonograms, and broadcasting organisations, with the possibility of preventing the unauthorised recording of their performance on a phonogram as well as the broadcasting by wireless means and the communication to the public of their live performances.

Trade marks   TRIPS defines a trade mark as "any sign, or any combination   **3.100**
of signs, capable of distinguishing the goods or services of one undertaking from those of other undertakings."[29] The unregulated use of a trade mark affects the interests of both companies using those marks as well as members of the public, who might be confused as to what product or service is produced by which company, etc. The TRIPs Agreement in this respect incorporates the provisions of the Paris Convention (1967).

---

[25] For a useful introduction to the TRIPs Agreement, see http://www.wto.org/english/tratop_e/trips_e/trips_e.htm.

[26] T. Einhorn, "The impact of the WTO Agreement on TRIPs (Trade Relted Aspects of Intellectual Property Rights) on E.C. Law: A challenge to regionalism" (1998) C.M.L.Rev. 320.

[27] G.E. Evans, "The principle of national treatment and the international protection of industrial property" (1996) 3 E.I.P.R. 149; see also "Canada—Patent Protection of Pharmaceutical Products", report of the panel, WT/DS114/R, adopted April 7, 2000, para. 7.94.

[28] TRIPs Agreement, Art. 9.

[29] *ibid.*, Art. 15.

Trade mark protection is conferred on registration by the competent authorities. In the interest of transparency and security, Members are required to publish each trade mark "either before it is registered or promptly after it is registered and shall afford a reasonable opportunity for petitions to cancel the registration."[30] Once registered, the owner of a trade mark enjoys the exclusive right to prevent all third parties not having his consent from using it in such manner as would result in a likelihood of confusion. There is a presumption of such a likelihood of confusion in case of the use of an identical sign for identical goods or services.

A seven-year minimum period of protection is accorded for the initial registration as well as for each of the subsequent renewals that may made an indefinite number of times. While Member States are free to determine conditions on the licensing and assignment of trade marks, the owner of a registered trade mark "shall have the right to assign the trademark with or without the transfer of the business to which the trademark belongs."[31]

3.101   **Geographical indications**   Place names and appellations of origin often serve as important symbols of the quality of products. They identify a good as originating in a particular country, or even in a particular region or locality in that country, where a given quality, reputation or other characteristic of the good is essentially attributable to its geographical origin.[32] In this connection, the TRIPs Agreement requires that Member States provide the legal means for interested parties to prevent the use of misleading geographical indications, which constitute unfair competition within the meaning of Article 10*bis* of the Paris Convention (1967).[33]

3.102   **Patents**   Under the TRIPs Agreement, patents must be available for any inventions, whether products or processes, in all fields of technology. The fundamental conditions of patentability are that inventions be "new, involve an inventive step and are capable of industrial application".[34] However, countries are allowed to deny the patenting of specific inventions when necessary to protect public policy or morality.[35] Most importantly, Member States are allowed to exclude from patentability "diagnostic, therapeutic and surgical methods for the treatment of humans or animals" and plants and animals other than microorganisms.[36]

Once granted, a patent confers on its owner exclusive rights, *inter alia*, to prevent third parties from making, using, offering for sale or importing for these purposes such a product, and where the subject matter of a patent is a process, to prevent third parties from using the process or selling or importing for sale the

---

[30] *ibid.*, Art. 15.
[31] *ibid.*, Art. 21.
[32] *ibid.*, Art. 27.
[33] *ibid.*, Art. 22:2, for wines and spirits: Art. 23:1.
[34] *ibid.*, Art. 27:1. A footnote to this provision defines the terms "inventive step" and "capable of industrial application" as being synonymous with the terms "non-obvious" and "useful" respectively.
[35] *ibid.*, Art. 27:2.
[36] *ibid.*, Art. 27:3.

product obtained directly by that process.[37] Furthermore, the holder of a right, who has valid grounds for suspecting that items with counterfeit trade mark or pirated copyright are being imported can request the customs authorities not to release these goods.

Layout designs (topographies) of integrated circuits In protecting layout **3.103** designs of integrated circuits, the TRIPs Agreement relies largely on the Treaty on Intellectual Property in Respect of Integrated Circuits (the IPIC Treaty), which was negotiated in 1989 under the auspices of the WIPO. The exclusive rights include the right of reproduction and the right of importation, sale and other distribution for commercial purposes.

The duration of protection of the exclusive rights of the owner of such a right depends on the type of legal regime applicable in Member States. In cases where Member States require registration as a condition of protection, the minimum term for protection of layout designs shall be a period of 10 years from the date of filing an application for registration or from the first commercial exploitation, wherever in the world it occurs. In cases where Member States do not require registration as a condition for protection, layout designs shall be protected for a term of not less than 10 years from the date of the first commercial exploitation, wherever in the world it occurs.[38] Given that the duration of protection under the IPIC was eight years, the TRIPs Agreement has improved the rights of the beneficiaries.

Protection of undisclosed information Basing itself on the 1967 Paris **3.104** Convention, the TRIPs Agreement also accords protection to what is generally known as undisclosed information, or trade secrets. Companies and individuals are thus allowed to prevent information "lawfully within their control from being disclosed to, acquired by, or used by others without their consent in a manner contrary to honest commercial practices".[39] However, important conditions are attached to this right, including the requirement that the information:

- be secret in the sense that it is not generally known among or readily accessible to persons within the circles that normally deal with the kind of information in question;

- has commercial value because it is secret; and

- has been subject to reasonable steps to keep it secret.

Institutional aspect of the TRIPs Agreement A Council for Trade Related **3.105** Aspects of Intellectual Property Rights supervises compliance with the agreement and institutes consultations mechanisms between the states concerned. The TRIPs Council has established appropriate arrangements for a co-operation with

---

[37] *ibid.*, Art. 28.
[38] *ibid.*, Art. 38.
[39] *ibid.*, Art. 39.

WIPO and its organs. Dispute settlement would take place under the Integrated Dispute Settlement Procedure (see paragraph 3.07).

An important obligation of Member States is to ensure the availability of adequate enforcement procedures under their domestic legal systems, so as to permit effective action against any act of infringement of intellectual property rights. To that end, Members are required to make available to rights holders civil judicial procedures concerning the enforcement of any intellectual property right covered by this Agreement. Criminal sanctions should also be made available "at least in cases of wilful trademark counterfeiting or copyright piracy on a commercial scale" and such sanctions must include imprisonment and/or monetary fines "sufficient to provide a deterrent".[40] As such, national judicial and administrative machinery also play an important institutional role in the enforcement of intellectual property rights.[41]

PART V: THE DISPUTE SETTLEMENT SYSTEM OF THE WTO

3.106   **General**   Dispute settlement stands at the centre of the WTO system. With binding rules for a Member State to enter into consultations, and subsequent disputes procedures involving a panel and an appellate body process, the WTO enjoys one of the most well-developed law enforcement mechanisms under public international law. Indeed, it is believed that the dispute settlement process is believed to be the single most important contribution of the multilateral trading system to general international law.[42]

As pointed out already, the dispute settlement is considered the jewel in the crown. However, this is not the result of an overnight development; it is something that has evolved over nearly half a century of experience and trial and error. When GATT 1947 was first agreed, it had only two provisions on dispute settlement: Article XXII on consultation and Article XXIII on nullification or impairment. Over the years, the detailed dispute settlement procedure grew progressively, to become one of the most sophisticated legal systems.[43]

---

[40] *ibid.*, Art. 61.

[41] *ibid.*, Art. 41.

[42] S. P. Croley, J. H. Jackson, "WTO dispute procedures, standard of review and defence to national governments" (1996) 90 A.J.I.L. 193–213.

[43] For details, see E.U. Petersmann, *The GATT/WTO Dispute Settlement: International Law, International Organisations and Dispute Settlement* (Kluwer, 1997). See also E. Canal-Forgues and R. Ostrihansky, "New developments in the GATT dispute settlement procedures" (1990/2) J.W.T. 67; J. Castel, "The Uruguay Round and the improvements to the GATT dispute settlement rules and procedures" (1989) I.C.L.Q. 434; R. Ostrihansky, "The future of dispute settlement within GATT: conciliation v. adjudication" (1990) Leiden J. of Int. L. 125. How the GATT dispute settlement has become more legalistic is described in E. Canal-Forgues, "L'institution de la Conciliation dans le Cadre du GATT" (Bruylant, Brussels, 1993); P.J. Kuiper, "Het GATT en het Volkenrecht" (1993) 107 Med.Ned.Ver.Int.R. 9–23; E.U. Petersmann, "The settlement system of the World Trade Organisation and the evolution of GATT dispute settlement system since 1948" (1994) 31 C.M.L.Rev. 1157–1244; P.E. Kuruvila, "Developing countries and the GATT/WTO dispute settlement mechanism" (1997) 31 J.W.T. 171–208; M.Clough, "The WTO dispute settlement system—a practitioner perspective" (2000) 24 Ford I.L.J., 252–274; J. Cameron and K.R. Gray, "Principles of international law in the WTO dispute settlement body" (2001) 50 I.C.L.Q. U.K. 248–298.

Standing in WTO dispute settlement proceedings GATT/WTO rules reg- **3.107**
ulate the relationships between states; enterprises are in principle not entitled to
commence legal action on the grounds of the GATT provisions. Yet, enterprises,
and particularly exporters, are served by observance of the trade rules, as any
infringements may cause them serious damage. In such cases, enterprises can
only try to convince their respective governments to lodge a complaint against a
country that affects their interests in a manner contrary to multilateral trade
rules.[44] However, governments always have the discretion (the same as for
diplomatic protection) in deciding whether they lodge such a complaint.

In the E.U., enterprises have the right to petition the E.U. Commission to lodge
such a complaint on their behalf.[45] To this end, the E.U. has issued the Trade
Barriers Regulation that "establishes rights for private parties to complain about
illegal trade practices of third countries, and to request the E.U. authorities to
intervene swiftly and effectively."[46]

An integrated system After the conclusion of the Tokyo Round of trade **3.108**
negotiations, one of the serious problems of the GATT dispute settlement system
was the existence of different dispute settlement rules for the different "Codes".
Since the different systems differed in the manner in which they addressed the
interests of countries, there was a problem of "forum shopping". A Panel
established under one Code would not have the competence to interpret the
provisions of other relevant agreements. Indeed, a complaining state could bring
a dispute before a Panel under one agreement where its position was more
favourable but where the defendant state would be unable to invoke defences
based on another agreement.

To overcome this situation, the Uruguay Round did two things: first, with its
"all-or-nothing" approach, almost all Tokyo Round Codes were replaced by
multilateral agreements, binding on all Member States. This has effectively
overcome the forum-shopping problem that existed previously. All multilateral
agreements, including GATT 1994, the GATS, as well as the TRIPs Agreements,
are now subject to the Dispute Settlement Understanding (DSU). The Dispute
Settlement Body (DSB) administers the day-to-day operation of the dispute
settlement system provided under the DSU. Thus, by bringing all multilateral
agreements under an integrated dispute settlement mechanism, the former situation whereby a Panel composed under one agreement had no competence for the
interpretation of another agreement has ceased to exist.

Secondly, in order to reflect the peculiarities inherent in some agreements, the
DSU has included what are known as "special or additional rules and procedures
of dispute settlement" in several of the constituent instruments. An exhaustive

---

[44] See, *e.g.* R.A. Brand, "Private parties and GATT dispute resolution" (1990/3) J.W.T. 5.
[45] For a list of the various cases under the GATT dispute resolution procedure see M. Hilf, F.G. Jacobs
and E.U. Petersmann, *op.cit.* pp. 353–392; P. Pescatore, W. Davey and A. Lowenfeld, *Handbook
of GATT Dispute Settlement* (loose-leaf, Kluwer, Deventer, 1990).
[46] See M. Bronckers and N. McNelis, "The EU Trade Barriers Regulation Comes of Age", (2001)
W.T. 427. For a summary and periodic updates on the day-to-day operation of the Trade Barriers
Regulation in the E.U., see http://europa.eu.int/comm/trade/policy/traderegul/index_en.htm.

list of these special or additional rules has been provided in Annex 1 to the DSU.

3.109   **Consultation**   Under the DSU, when a state is of the opinion (as a result of its own initiative, or after having been addressed by an enterprise) that another contracting state has breached the provision of a covered agreement, it is required to enter into bilateral or multilateral consultations with that state to come to an amicable settlement. Once consultation request have been made, any bilateral settlement must be consistent with WTO rules. Relevant WTO bodies must also be notified of such an amicable settlement.

Under the DSU, a Member State is generally required to enter into consultations within 30 days of a request for consultations from another Member State. If after 60 days from such request there is no settlement, the complaining state may request the establishment of a Panel (see paragraph 3.110). Where consultations are denied, the complaining state may move directly to request a Panel.

3.110   **Report by a Panel**   The most common procedure after this stage is the composition of a Panel at the request of a complaining state. This complaining state must give a summary of the disputed facts and legal issues in its complaint. There are elaborate rules for instituting a Panel in order to safeguard against its establishment being prevented. Indeed, unlike pre-WTO days, the establishment of a panel is nearly automatic and can be denied only in the unlikely event of a consensus not to do so, including the requesting party itself. This is what is know as the rule of "negative consensus".

A Panel is composed of three (exceptionally five) members, who must be completely independent from the parties in dispute. Panel members are usually expert officials from contracting states or from non-governmental organisations, or senior academics in international trade law. Panel members are nominated by the Secretariat, from an indicative list which it maintains, and given to the parties for approval. Parties have a duty to accept the nominations, unless there are "compelling reasons". If no agreement can be reached on the choice of panellists within 20 days from the Panel's establishment, the Panel members are appointed by the Director General of the WTO.

The terms of reference of the Panel usually run as follows:

"To examine, in the light of the relevant provisions in [name of the covered agreement(s) cited by the parties to the dispute], the matter referred to the DSB by [name of party] in document . . . and to make such findings as will assist the DSB in making the recommendations or in giving the rulings provided for in that/those agreement(s)."

The other Member States must be notified about the establishment and composition of panels. Any Member State with an interest in any dispute has the right to be heard by the Panel as a third-party participant.

Panels are required to make an objective assessment of the matter before them, including an objective assessment of the facts of the case and the applicability of and conformity with the relevant covered agreements.[47] In practice, a form of "jurisdiction" has developed, since the panels often refer to decisions of earlier Panels and to rules of international law regarding the observance of treaties.[48]

Under the new rules a Panel should normally complete its work within six months or, in cases of urgency, within three months of its establishment.

Appellate review   The Uruguay Round, moreover, has introduced an appel-   **3.111** late review of Panel reports by a standing Appellate Body.[49] The Appellate Body is mandated to decide on issues of law or on legal interpretations developed by the Panel. The Appellate Body has no remand authority. Appellate proceedings may not exceed 60 days from the date a party formally notifies its decision to appeal.

Adoption of report   Panel and/or Appellate Body reports become binding   **3.112** instruments only after they have been adopted by the WTO Dispute Settlement Body (DSB). The negative consensus principle also applies to decisions of the DSB. As such, Panel reports may be considered by the DSB for adoption 20 days after they are issued. Within 60 days of their issuance they will be deemed to have been adopted unless the DSB decides by consensus not to adopt the report, or one of the parties notifies the DSB of its intention to appeal. Decisions of the Appellate Body are deemed to be adopted by the DSB within 30 days unless the DSB decides by consensus against its adoption. Thanks to this approach, the former practice of blocking adoption of Panel reports at the initiative of a losing party has been abolished.

Monitoring and follow-up of implementation   The DSB has supervision   **3.113** over the implementation of the accepted report by the losing state, which has a duty to report back on this implementation to the DSB. When immediate implementation is not practicable, the losing Member State is allowed a reasonable period for implementation. If the state does not give effect, then other states can take reprisal measures by suspending equivalent concessions, obligations or advantages. These reprisals can, however, only be taken when negotiations between the parties to agree upon adequate compensation have failed, and when

---

[47] If one or more of the litigating parties are developing countries, the Panel report must mention expressly to what extent account is taken of the preferential treatment of developing countries (see para. 3.73). On the practical effect of a Panel see R. Plank, "An unofficial description on how a GATT Panel works and does not" (1987) J.I.A. 53.

[48] For an interesting reflection on this issue, see D. Palmeter, and P. C. Mavroidis, "The WTO legal system: sources of law" (1998) 92 Am.J.Int'l.L., 400; see also P.J. Kuiper, "Het GATT en het Volkenrecht" (1993) 107 Med.Ned.Ver.Int.R. 15–24; A. Chua, "The precedential effect of WTO Panel and Appellate Body reports" (1998), 11 Lei.J.I.L., pp. 45–61; T. P. Stewart and A. A. Karpel, "Review of the dispute settlement understanding: operation of Panels" (2000) 31 LawP.I.B. 593–656.

[49] A. W. Shoyer and E. M. Solovny, "The process and procedures of litigating at the World Trade Organization: a review of the work of the Appellate Body" (2000) 31 LawP.I.B. 677–698; P.C. Marmoidis, "Remedies in the WTO legal system: between a risk and a hard place" (2000) 11 E.J.I.L. 763–814.

the authorisation of the DSB has been secured. The DSB keeps the implementation of its rulings under regular surveillance until the issue is resolved definitively.

3.114   **Other means of dispute settlement**   Parties to a dispute may also opt for a conciliation or mediation, if necessary with the assistance of another Member State or of the Director General of the WTO. They may also ask for dispute settlement by way of arbitration within the WTO. In such cases, parties which consent to arbitration also undertake to observe the arbitral award. The purpose of arbitration is to come to a compromise rather than to a judgment based on legal rules. It should, therefore, not be confused with traditional commercial arbitration (see paragraph 11.01). Arbitration under the GATT/WTO system is seldom used.

CHAPTER 4

INTERNATIONAL SALES

Importance   The contract of sale is one of the oldest and most used contracts   **4.01**
in international trade. It is also an essential part of other transactions such as
franchising (see paragraph 5.09–5.11), distribution agreements (see paragraph
5.02), building contracts and licence agreements (see paragraph 6.09–6.11). Both
buyer and seller should have a clear perception of their respective rights and
obligations. When entering into a transnational sales contract, parties should thus
know which national law is applicable to the contract. This is not always obvious,
since it is often impossible to predict which court will be seized in the event of
a dispute and since each court has to rely on its own conflict of law rules to
establish the applicable law (see paragraph 1.24). Of course, the competent court
(see paragraph 10.01) and the proper law (see paragraph 1.31) can be indicated
in the sales contract. However, even in the absence of a choice of law or choice
of forum clause, the criteria to find the law applicable to the contract are fairly
universal.

PART I: NATIONAL LAW APPLICABLE TO SALES

Hague Convention   The Convention on the Law Applicable to the Inter-   **4.02**
national Sale of Goods—the "Hague Convention"—is applicable in eight countries.[1] These states have incorporated into their national law the conflict of law
rules of the Hague Convention, which apply irrespective of the legal system to
which they refer.

The Hague Convention applies to the international sale of goods, without
specifying when a sale is "international". However, one thing at least is certain:
the mere choice of a foreign law or a foreign forum does not make a contract
"international" (Article 1). A number of transactions are excluded from the
scope of the Convention: the sale of securities, the sale of registered aircraft or
any sale upon judicial order or by way of execution (Article 1). First of all, the
law chosen by the contracting parties governs the sales contract. This choice
must be expressed or implied with reasonable certainty by the terms of the
contract (Article 2). If the parties have not made an express or implied choice of
law, then, alternatively, the following conflict of law rules apply:

---

[1] Hague Convention of June 15, 1995 (www.hcch.net). This convention is in force in Denmark,
Finland, France, Italy, Niger, Norway, Sweden and Switzerland.

(a) Under normal circumstances the national law of the country where the seller ordinarily resides (at the time of receipt of the order) (Article 3).

(b) If a branch of the seller receives an order, the law of the country where this branch is situated.

(c) If the order is received by the seller or his agent in the country where the buyer habitually resides or has his place of business, the law of the buyer's country.

(d) For a sale at a commodity exchange or an auction, by the law of the country of the exchange or of the place of the auction.

The manner and time to examine purchased goods, and the notifications to be dispatched, are all regulated by the law of the place where the examination takes place (Article 4). That law also applies to the measures to be taken when the goods are refused. Parties may opt for another law, but this choice must be explicit.

The Convention does not cover the capacity of the parties, the formal requirements for a sales contract, the transfer of ownership and the legal effects of the sales contract in respect of third parties (Article 5). These issues are still governed by the domestic conflict of laws rules (see paragraph 1.24).

An amended version of the Convention, the Hague Convention of 1986, did not receive enough ratification to enter into force.[2]

4.03   **European Contracts Convention**   Although the Hague Convention deals specifically with international sales of goods, the more general European Contracts Convention, which has already been discussed (see paragraph 1.29), also applies to the sale of goods. Unlike the Hague Conventions, the European Contracts Convention does not exclude from its scope the sale of registered ships, vessels, hovercraft or aircraft.

In the five E.U. countries which are also party to the Hague Convention, both conventions may be relevant in the determination of the law applicable to an international sale. However, it is generally accepted that the more specific Hague Convention prevails for the law applicable to the international sale of goods.

As the Hague Convention and the European Contract Convention contain rather similar rules, the law applicable will generally be the same, so that a choice between the Conventions tends to be irrelevant. However, where the European Contracts Convention contains specific rules on consumer contracts and on

---

[2] Convention on the Law Applicable to Contracts for the International Sale of Goods, concluded in The Hague on December 22, 1986, (www.hcch.net). See in this context O. Lando, "The 1985 Hague Convention on the law applicable to sales" (1987) RabelsZ 60; Y. Loussouarn, "La Convention de la Haye d'octobre 1985 sur la loi applicable aux contrats de vente internationale de marchandises" (1986) R.C.D.I.P. 271; A. Mebroukine, "Several observations with regard to the 1985 Hague Convention on the law applicable to contracts for the international sale of goods", (1988) I.B.L.J. 45.

mandatory rules, these specific provisions prevail over the more general Hague Convention rules.

National conflict of law rules In countries that are party neither to the **4.04** Hague Convention nor to the European Contracts Convention, the national conflict of laws rules remain applicable to international sales contracts. Some countries have developed specific conflict rules for sales contracts.[3] However, most countries use the conflict of laws rules applicable for contracts in general.[4]

PART II: VIENNA CONVENTION ON THE INTERNATIONAL SALE OF GOODS

Background

Purpose A sales contract may be governed by different national laws **4.05** depending on the court seised and its conflict of laws rules (see paragraph 1.24). This gives little legal certainty to the buyer and the seller. Hence came the fairly early initiatives to develop uniform rules in respect of international sales.

Uniform Laws International Sales (ULIS) (The Hague, 1964) The best **4.06** way to reach a greater homogeneity is the introduction of uniform laws for cross-border sales. UNIDROIT (see paragraph 2.29) has, since 1930, promoted a uniform law for international sales. Thanks to this preparatory work, it finally became possible in 1964 to convene an international conference in The Hague, where the Convention Relating to a Uniform Law on the International Sale of Goods and the Convention Relating to a Uniform Law on the Formation of Contracts for the International Sale of Goods were approved.

The intention was that both these conventions should receive wide recognition. However, this did not happen. Many provisions were too complicated, the scope of application was too wide. The conventions were perceived as western European texts which failed to take into account the specific needs of the socialist and third world countries. They also had a critical reception in the common law countries, where they were seen as being too greatly influenced by German law.[5]

---

[3] *e.g.* the American Uniform Commercial Code. See J. J. White and R. S. Summers, *Uniform Commercial Code* (5th ed., West Group, St. Paul, 2000).

[4] *cf.* Survey by O. Lando in "Contracts" in *International Encyclopedia of Comparative Law*, III, 1976, 125–134.

[5] See N. M. Galston (ed.), *International Sales, The United Nations Convention on Contracts for the International Sale of Goods* (Matthew Bender, New York, 1984) pp. 1–12, 1–13; J. Honnold, "The draft convention on contracts for the international sale of goods; an overview" (1979) Am.J.Comp.L. 225; J. Honnold, *Uniform Law for the International Sales under the 1980 United Nations Convention* (Kluwer, Deventer, 1991) 53–54, with, *inter alia*, references to comments from A. Tunc and the U.S. delegation; J. P. Plantard, "Un nouveau droit uniforme de la vente internationale: La Convention des Nations Unies du 11 avril 1980" (1980) J.D.I. 311.

In the end, only nine countries ratified the ULIS Conventions[6]: five countries subsequently withdrew when they adopted the Convention on the International Sale of Goods.[7] The CISG will eventually replace the ULIS Conventions.

4.07   Convention on the International Sale of Goods (CISG) (Vienna 1980)   Because of the lack of success of the Hague Conventions on international sales a new project was started in 1968. An UNCITRAL study group (see paragraph 2.23) examined the changes necessary to make a uniform law of sale more acceptable. It was decided to draft a single new convention, which would regulate both the formation of an international contract of sale and its substantive rules. A proposal drafted by representatives of 14 countries[8] came to fruition in 1978, ultimately resulting in the United Nations Convention on Contracts for the International Sale of Goods (abbreviated as CISG). This Convention was adopted at an international conference in Vienna in 1980.[9]

The CISG came into force on January 1, 1988. As of mid-2001 the Convention applies in 59 states from different parts of the world and with different economic systems.[10] The list of countries joining is continuously growing. The wider acceptance of the CISG may be explained by the fact that more countries from different regions were involved in its drafting, so that the CISG reconciles the different legal traditions.[11]

---

[6] The nine states that ratified the Conventions are: Belgium, Germany, Gambia, Israel, Italy, Luxemburg, the Netherlands, San Marino and the U.K.

[7] CISG Art. 99. Belgium, Germany, Italy, Luxembourg and the Netherlands renounced the Conventions when they adopted the CISG.

[8] See J. Honnold, *op. cit.*, 54.

[9] 62 states participated in the Conference, including all important trading nations, together with eight international organisations, such as the World Bank, the E.C. and UNIDROIT.

[10] Argentina, Australia, Austria, Belarus, Belgium, Bosnia and Herzegovina, Bulgaria, Burundi, Canada, Chile, China, Croatia, Cuba, Czech Republic, Denmark, Ecuador, Egypt, Estonia, Finland, France, Georgia, Germany, Greece, Guinea, Hungary, Iceland, Iraq, Italy, Kyrgyzstan, Latvia, Lesotho, Lithuania, Luxembourg, Mauritania, Mexico, Moldova, Mongolia, Netherlands, New Zealand, Norway, Peru, Poland, Romania, Russian Federation, Saint Vincent and the Grenadines, Singapore, Slovakia, Slovenia, Spain, Sweden, Switzerland, Syrian Arab Republic, Uganda, Ukraine, U.S., Uruguay, Uzbekistan, Yugoslavia, Zambia. The authentic versions of the Vienna Convention are in Arabic, Chinese, English, French, Russian and Spanish.

Court decisions and arbitration awards concerning CISG can be found at www.uncitral.org, www.un.or.at/uncitral/clout, www.cisg.law.pace.edu, www.jura.uni-freiburg.de and www.jura.uni-sb.de.

See also M. R. Will, *Twenty Years of international sales law under the CISG (The U.N. Convention on contracts for the international sale of goods): international bibliography and case law digest (1980–2000)* (Kluwer, The Hague, 2000); F. Enderlein and D. Maskow, *International Sales Law: United Nations Convention on Contracts for the International Sale of Goods, Convention on the Limitation Period in the International Sale of Goods: Commentary* (Oceana, New York, 1992); K. H. Neumayer, *Emptio-venditio internationales: Convention de Vienne sur la vente internationale de marchandise: mélanges* (Verlag für Recht und Gesellschaft, Basel, 1997); R. Happ, "Anwendbarkeit völkerrechtlicher Auslegungsmethoden auf das UN-Kaufrecht" (1997) 5 R.I.W. 376–380; F. Dierdrich, "Lückenfüllung im Internationalen Einheitsrecht: Möglichkeiten und Grenzen richterlicher Rechtsfortbildung im Wiener Kaufrecht" (1995) 41 R.I.W. 353–364; F. Ferrari, "Burden of proof under the United Nations Convention on contracts for international sale of goods (CISG)" (2000) I.B.L.J. 665–670.

[11] A. Garro, "Reconciliation of legal traditions in the UN Convention on Contracts for the International Sale of Goods" (1989) Int.L. 443.

Sphere of application

Definition of "contract of sale"   The CISG does not give a definition of a   **4.08**
contract of sale. From the obligations the CISG imposes on the buyer and the
seller, one can deduce that a sale contract concerns the delivery and the transfer
of the property of goods for a monetary consideration.[12]

Six forms of sale are excluded from the CISG. The first three exclusions are
based on the nature of the transaction. The so-called consumer contract ("goods
bought for personal, family or household use") is excluded, unless the seller at
any time before, or at the time of the conclusion of the contract, neither knew, nor
ought to have known, that the contract was a consumer contract.[13] The exclusion
of consumer contracts substantially limits the scope of application of the CISG.
Other excluded matters are sales by auction and on execution or otherwise by
authority of law. The nature of the goods is the basis for three further exclusions,
i.e. the sale of securities, the sale of ships and planes and the sale of electricity.

International character   The CISG covers "international sales". A sale is   **4.09**
"international" when the parties have their place of business in different states.[14]
Their respective place of business must appear clearly from the contract, from
any dealings between the parties or from information disclosed by the parties
before or at the conclusion of the contract (Article 1, 2). It is indeed important for
the parties to know in advance that the CISG is applicable.[15] It is thus not
necessary that the sold goods are delivered across a border, or that the offer and
acceptance take place in different countries in order to bring a sale within the
scope of application of the CISG.

Furthermore, in order for the CISG to govern an international sale, one of two
conditions must be fulfilled:

   (i) the states, in which the parties reside, must be party to the CISG[16]; or

---

[12] *cf.* ICC award no. 7153 (1992), (1992) J.D.I. 1005. See, however, on the applicability of CISG on
barter agreements, B. Lurger, "Die Anwendung des Wiener UNCITRAL-Kaufrechtsübereinkom-
mens 1980 auf den internatonalen Tauschvertrag und sonstige Gegenschäfte" (1991) Z.R.V. 415.
See also P. Klima commenting on *OLG München*, September 22, 1995 (Unilex 1997/I; (1996)
R.I.W. 1035–1036). The Court found the CISG to be applicable to determine the existence of an
exclusive distribution agreement. If it did exist, this would lead to the obligation to supply the
buyer with goods, which is the basis for future contracts. Such an obligation does not only provide
the other party with the right to distribute the goods, it also includes the general obligation by the
manufacturer to supply the goods to the other party under certain conditions. This general
obligation to supply goods constitutes the basis for future contracts of sale.
[13] Art. 2(a).
[14] See K. Siehr, "Der internationale Anwendungsbereich des UN-Kaufrechts" (1988) RabelsZ
587.
[15] See J. Honnold, *op. cit.*, p. 76–84.
[16] See F. Farrari commenting on *Rb Amsterdam* October 5, 1994, (1995) N.I.P.R. 317–328. In that
case the parties were from the Netherlands and Germany. At the time of conclusion of the contract,
the CISG was in effect in Germany, but not in the Netherlands. German law was applied and the
Court found that this meant the CISG. In *Oberstes Gerichtshof Austria*, February 12, 1998 (Unilex
database, 1999; (1998) *Österreichische Zeitschrift für Rechtsvergleichung* 158, No. 36(LS)) the
parties were from Austria and the Czech Republic and agreed upon Austrian law. At the time of
conclusion of the contract, the CISG had entered into force in Austria, but not in the Czech
Republic. The Court found that the CISG was applicable.

(ii) the rules of private international law of the court seised lead to the application of the law of a contracting state.[17] In the absence of a choice of law the CISG shall thus generally be applicable when the seller and the buyer have their place of business in different countries and the seller's country is a contracting state (see paragraph 4.07).[18]

4.10   **Exclusions**   The parties may exclude the application of the CISG (Article 6).[19] The CISG can thus be excluded in important standard contracts. The standard contracts of the Federation of Oils, Seeds and Fats Association (FOSFA) and the Grain and Feed Trade Association (GAFTA), for example, determine:

> "The following shall not apply to this contract: (a) the Uniform law on sales . . . ; (b) the United Nations Convention on contracts for the international sale of goods . . . ."

Parties may furthermore accept the CISG in part and derogate from other CISG provisions. Such derogation from the CISG is possible even after a conflict has arisen or when the parties are appearing in court.

Moreover, seller and buyer are bound by any usage to which they have agreed and by any practice which they have established between themselves.[20] Moreover, and unless otherwise agreed, they have implicitly made applicable to their contract any usage of which they knew or ought to have known and which, in international trade, is widely known and regularly observed by parties to contracts in the particular trade.

Finally, the CISG is not applicable to the capacity of the parties, the formal validity of the contract, the transfer of ownership and the legal effects of the contract in respect of third parties. These issues are still governed by some national law, to be found in the conflict of law rules (see paragraph 1.24).[21]

---

[17] See C. M. Bianca and M. J. Bonell (ed.), *Commentary on the International Sales Law, the 1980 Vienna Convention* (Giuffré, Milano, 1987), pp. 27–28 and J. Honnold, *op. cit.* p. 84. Private international law thus continues to play a part under the CISG. See, *e.g.* P. Winship, "Private international law and the UN Sales Convention" (1988) Cornell.Int'l.L.J. 487; see, *inter alia*, on the applicability of CISG because of conflict of law: *OLG Frankfurt*, September 17, 1991, (1991) R.I.W. 950 (also (1991) U.L.Rev. 382); *OLG Koblenz*, September 17, 1993, (1993) R.I.W. 934; *Hof's Hertogenbosch*, February 26, 1992 (1992) N.I.P.R. 374; ICC award no. 7197 (1992), (1993) J.D.I. 1029; ICC award no. 6653, (1993), (1993) J.D.I. 1041.

[18] See for the CISG C. M. Bianca and M. J. Bonell, *op. cit.*, pp. 103, 115.

[19] R. Holthausen, "Vertraglicher Ausschlusz des UN-übereinkommens über internationale Warenkaufverträge" (1989) R.I.W. 513; C. Witz, "L'exclusion de la Convention des Nations Unies sur les contrats de vente internationale de marchandises par la volonté des parties" (1990) D pp. 107–112. In *Oberlandesgericht Hamm*, May 6, 1998 ([1999] *Neue Juristische Wochenschrift-Rechtsprechung Report*, pp. 364–365) the Court held that even if the parties did not agree to exclude the CISG in their contract, they may still so agree during litigation. It also stated that the CISG is clearly excluded if the parties agree on the law of a non-contracting state.

[20] For an analysis of the developments of the usages in international trade see R. M. Goode, "Usage and its reception in transnational commercial law" (1997) 46 I.C.L.Q. 1–36.

[21] See P. Winship, "Private International Law in the UN Sales Convention" (1988) Cornell.Int'l.L.J. 487. Regarding assumption of debt and the applicability of the CISG, see *Oberster Gerichtshof Austria*, April 24, 1997 ((1997) 3 *Forum International* 93–94; Z.R.V. 38, 156 No. 56), and note by Ferrari (1997) 3 *Forum International* 90–93.

The period of time within which legal proceedings based upon the CISG must be commenced is not covered by the CISG. Some 30 states have adopted the UNCITRAL Convention on the Limitation Period in the International Sale of Goods, either in its amended 1980 version or in its original 1974 version.[22] This Convention establishes limitation period of four years as well as detailed rules on its application. In countries which are non-signatories of the Convention, the limitation period is either defined by the proper law of the contract[23] or by the law of the forum.

Reservations The CISG allows signatory states to make some reservations. **4.11** For instance, they may exclude Part II (formation of an international contract of sale) or Part III (substantive rules) of the Convention[24]; federal states may extend the application of the CISG to the whole territory of a federal state or limit it to one or more of its individual states.[25]

A contracting state may also exclude the possibility that the CISG becomes applicable only because the rules of private international law point to the law of a Convention state. States that have made this reservation will only apply the Convention when seller and buyer have their place of business in a Convention state.[26]

Finally, states that require a prescribed form for the formation of a contract of sale may declare Article 11 (which permits oral contracts of sale) not applicable. For instance, some Eastern bloc countries, which imposed strict formal requirements in their legislation for international commercial contracts, have made this reservation.[27] However, this restriction does not mean that the CISG requires a contract in written form as soon as one of the contract parties is established in a state that made the reservation. Only when the conflict of law rules for formal requirements point to the law of a state which has made such reservation, would a written form be required.[28]

---

[22] The parties to the 1980 Convention are: Argentina, Belarus, Cuba, Czech Republic, Egypt, Guinea, Hungary, Mexico, Moldova, Poland, Romania, Slovakia, Slovenia, Uganda, the U.S., Uruguay, and Zambia. The parties to the 1974 Convention are, besides the countries previously named, Bosnia and Herzegovina, Brazil, Bulgaria, Burundi, Costa Rica, Dominican Republic, Ghana, Mongolia, Nicaragua, Norway, Russian Federation, Ukraine and Yugoslavia. The Convention is applicable under the same criteria as the CISG (see para. 4.09).

[23] European Contracts Convention, Art. 10, para. 1, litt. d.

[24] Art. 92, 1. For example, the Scandinavian countries do not apply Part II of the CISG, in order to preserve their own uniform laws regarding the formation of an international sale. Moreover they do not apply the CISG where the parties have their place of business in Scandinavia.

[25] Art. 93. As a logical consequence the concept of "Contracting States" of Art. 1(a) will in that case only refer to those regional entities for which the Convention has been declared applicable (J. Honnold, *op. cit.*, pp. 594–595).

[26] Art. 95. China, Czechoslovakia, Saint Vincent and the Grenadines, Singapore and the U.S. made such a reservation. Germany declared that it would not apply the Convention on the basis of Art. 1(1)b in respect of the states which made this reservation.

[27] CISG Art. 96. This reservation was made by Argentina, Belarus, Chile, China, Estonia, Hungary, Latvia, Lithuania, Ukraine and the USSR.

[28] See moreover *Court Budapest*, March 24, 1992, (1993) IPRax, 263 where "usages" set aside the requirement for a written form.

Formation of the contract

4.12 **General**   The CISG regulates the substantive issues of international sales as well as the formation of the contract of sale. Part II of the Convention defines how and when an international contract of sale comes into existence.[29] This is "when the acceptance of an offer becomes effective in accordance with the provisions of this Convention" (Article 23).[30]

But first it must be established what an offer is and how long it lasts. Subsequently, the question is what constitutes an acceptance and when it becomes effective.

Offer

4.13 **Definition**   An offer is an expression of the offeror's will, addressed to one or more specific persons. A proposal that is not addressed to one or more identified persons is only an offer if this is clearly indicated by the person making the offer (Article 14, 2). The sending of price lists, catalogues and the placing of advertisements and the like are in principle not offers.[31]

Moreover, the offer must be sufficiently definite. This means that it must indicate the goods and expressly or impliedly fix or make provision for determining the quantity and the price (Article 14, 1).

Article 14, which requires an offer to have a fixed price, or at least to have a price fixing provision, seems incompatible with Article 55, which covers contracts without any price provision.[32] Some would say that Article 55 only applies for states that are only bound to Part III, which means that the formation of the contract will be governed by national law[33]; according to others, Article 55 takes precedence over Article 14.[34]

The offer is effective as soon as it has reached the offeree (Article 15, 1). The offeror may still withdraw his offer if the withdrawal reaches the offeree before or at the same time as the offer.[35] After the offer has reached the offeree, but

---

[29] See for the possible exclusion of Part II, para. 4.10.

[30] To be perfectly clear, the drafters endeavoured to establish the moment of conclusion of the contract, for instance, for the transfer of risk (see para. 4.46). Proposals to use Art. 23 also for the location of the place of conclusion of contract were not accepted. See C. M. Bianca and M. J. Bonell, *op. cit.*, p. 200. Art. 23 could also be used outside the scope of the Convention to establish the moment of formation of the contract for, *e.g.* taxation purposes (J. Honnold, *op. cit.*, p. 248).

[31] See C. M. Bianca and M. J. Bonell, *op. cit.*, pp. 142–143; *Hungary Supreme Court* September 25, 1992, (1993) *Zeitschrift für Eur̈opaisches Privatrecht* 79.

[32] F. Adami, "Open price contracts in the United Nations Convention on Contracts for the International Sale of Goods", (1989) I.B.L.J. 103.

[33] N. Galston, *op. cit.*, p. 309 and the other authors mentioned there.

[34] See C. M. Bianca and M. J. Bonel, *op. cit.*, p. 47; J. Honnold, *op. cit.*, p. 201; V. Fortier, "Le prix dans la Convention de Vienne sur la vente internationale de marchandises, les articles 14 et 55", (1990) J.D.I. 381.

[35] The English text speaks of "withdrawal". Although "withdrawal" and "revocation" have the same meaning in ordinary usage, the CISG uses the words for different circumstances: there is "withdrawal" when the offer did not yet reach the offeree; there may be "revocation" after the offer has reached the offeree, See C. M. Bianca and M. J. Bonell, *op. cit.* pp. 147–148.

before the acceptance has been dispatched, the offer may still be revoked, unless it was irrevocable, or could be considered by the offeree to be irrevocable.[36]

The revocation of an offer (Article 16) reflects a compromise between the civil law and common law systems. The revocation as it is found in common law systems remains basically intact. However, if the offer states specifically that it is irrevocable, no revocation is possible. If, on the other hand, the offer stipulates a period for acceptance, it is generally presumed that during this period no revocation is possible.[37]

An offer remains in force during the period indicated in the offer. Nevertheless, the offer is terminated (even when it involves an irrevocable offer) when the offeror receives a rejection (Article 17). If no acceptance period is indicated in the offer, the offer remains in force for a reasonable period. Therefore, due account has to be taken of the circumstances of the transaction, such as the means of communication used by the offeror (Article 18, 2).

Acceptance

Ways of accepting By accepting, the offeree indicates his assent to the offer **4.14** (Article 18, 1).[38] As soon as an indication of assent reaches the offeror, the acceptance becomes effective.[39] Actions of the acceptor, such as dispatch of goods or payment of the price, may indicate an implied acceptance. This may be when the offer expressly allows for this possibility, when the implied acceptance by parties has become customary or when it is in conformity with trade usages (Article 18, 3). The contract then becomes effective at the moment of the implied acceptance.

On the other hand, silence or inactivity in itself generally does not amount to acceptance.[40] However, it is deemed to be an acceptance on the rare occasions

---

[36] If the other party has already returned an acceptance, the revocation has no force of law (Art. 16(1)). The text of Art. 16(1) is rather confusing. The first part of the sentence states: "Until a contract is concluded an offer may be revoked . . . " However, the contract only comes into being at the moment the acceptance reaches the offeror (Art. 23 *juncto* Art. 18(2)). Between the dispatch of the acceptance and the formation of the contract some time can elapse.

[37] For a civil law court the fixing of an acceptance period for the offer means automatic irrevocability. In common law countries it only creates an assumption of irrevocability, which can be confirmed or repudiated by the circumstances or customary practices. The text of Art. 16(2)(a) is a compromise between various amendments. Perhaps these vague phrases will lead to different interpretations. See C. M. Bianca and M. J. Bonel, *op. cit.*, pp. 153–157; K. Sono, "Formaton of contracts" in P. Sarcevic and P. Volken (eds), *International Sale of Goods, Dubrovnik Lectures* (Oceana, New York), pp. 116–117 and J. Honnold, *op. cit.*, p. 208. According to J. E. Murray, "An essay on the formation of contracts and related matters under the United Nations Convention on Contracts for the International Sale of Goods" (1988) *Journal of Law and Commerce*, 25, the civil law interpretation must prevail.

[38] In *OLG Frankfurt*, March 31, 1995 (Unilex 1996/I D.1995–11.1) different types of glass were mentioned in the negotiations for a purchase of glass. The seller then delivered a particular type and demanded payment. The Court held that there was no contrast since there was no acceptance: the parties did not reach agreement as to the type of glass.

[39] On acceptance by fax, see *LG Aachen*, May 14, 1993, (1993) R.I.W. 760.

[40] J. Honnold, *op. cit.*, p. 219. See also *OLG Frankfurt*, July 5, 1995 (Unilex 1996/II D. 1995–17.4); *Cámara Nacional de Apelaciones en lo Comercial (Inta S.A. v. MCS Officina Meccanica SpA)*, October 14, 1993 (Unilex 1995/I D. 1993–24; comment: *El Derecho* 32 (1994) No. 8483, April 25, 1994, 3–7.

when it is obvious from the circumstances that the parties are in agreement, *e.g.* because they had specifically stipulated the implied acceptance or because this is the normal practice in their continuous business relationship.[41]

4.15   **Difference between offer and acceptance**   A reply to an offer may contain additional or different terms or other modifications. The offer sometimes includes or refers to the standard conditions of the offeror. However, the other party accepts this offer with reference to his own standard clauses, which differ from those in the offer. In this way the so-called "battle of forms" between the offeror and offeree arises. A reply with additional or different conditions is not an acceptance but a counter-offer if the changes alter the terms of the offer materially.[42] Any different term in respect of, for instance, price, payment, quality and quantity of the goods, place and time of delivery, liability and dispute settlement is expressly mentioned as a material change in the terms of the offer (Article 19, 3). This summary is not exhaustive; other clauses may also be considered essential for the contract, so that differences between offer and acceptance concerning these clauses may prevent the conclusion of a contract.[43]

One should hereby also take into account the usages of the trade (see paragraph 1.33). For instance, it may happen that an arbitration clause was only introduced in the acceptance and not earlier in the offer. An arbitration clause is in principle an essential clause about which offer and acceptance must be in agreement (Article 19, 3). However, when an arbitration clause is customary for a specific sector, the offeror may become bound by the arbitration clause of the offeree, unless this has been expressly excluded.[44]

The original offeror, who gives effect to the modified counter-offer, is, in all events, bound. His performance can be considered as an implied acceptance of the counter-offer.[45]

It often happens that the reply to the offer includes only insignificant alterations, which do not affect the offer materially. In that event, this reply is presumed to be an acceptance with altered terms. The offeror is then in the

---

[41] See K. Sono, *op. cit.*, pp. 122–123; *Filanto v. Chilewich*, June 15, 1993, 789 Fed. Supp. 1229 (S.D.N.Y. 1992).

[42] Art. 19(1) *juncto* 19(2). See "The UN Convention on Contracts for the International Sale of Goods and the 'battle of forms' " (1989) Fordham Int'l.L.J. 649; J. Honnold, *op. cit.*, pp. 228–239; F. Vergne, "The 'Battle of the Forms' under the 1980 United Nations Conventions on Contracts for the International Sale of Goods" (1985) Am.J.Comp.L. 233. For a critical view of this doctrine, see Maria del Pilar Perales Viscasillas, " 'Battle of the Forms' under the 1980 United Nations Convention on Contracts for the International Sale of Goods: a comparison with section 2–207 UCC and the UNIDROIT Principles" (1998) 10 Pace Int'l L.Rev., 97–155 at n.91; For practical problems caused by this approach, see *Roto-Lith Ltd v. F. P. Barlett & Co.*, 297 F.2d 497 (1st Cir., 1962).

[43] K. Sono, *op. cit.*, p. 125.

[44] See Art. 9; K. Sono, *op. cit.*, p. 127; J. Honnold, *op. cit.*, 233.

[45] Suppose a buyer has required warranties against defects in the product in his offer to buy; the seller excludes in his counter offer any liability. If the seller dispatches the goods and the buyer accepts these, then the contract is concluded under the standard conditions of the seller. See J. E. Murray, *op. cit.*, p. 39. See *ibid.*, pp. 38–44 for a general discussion of this problem, compared to American law.

position to prevent the conclusion of the contract on the basis of these differences.[46] He may even revoke his offer after the acceptor had sent his acceptance, if this acceptance contains slight alterations. However, if the offeror does not object to the changes, the contract is concluded with the changes as introduced by the acceptor (Article 19, 2).[47]

When, in his turn, the offeror confirms the sale afterwards in slightly different terms, new problems may arise.[48]

Time limits In the event the offeror has indicated that his offer has to be   **4.16**
accepted within a given time, an acceptance has normally no effect if it does not reach the offeror within that time. Otherwise, the acceptance has to reach the offeror within a reasonable time (Article 18). For offers by mail, this time starts to run from the date of the post mark. If the offer is made by telephone, fax, e-mail or any other means of direct transmission, the period starts from the moment the offer reaches the offeree. Official holidays are included in the calculation for the acceptance period. If the last day of the acceptance period is an official holiday which prevents the timely delivery of the acceptance at the address of the offeror, the period is extended to the next day of business (Article 20).

In the event that the offeree accepts the offer by post, but his letter takes an unusually long time to reach the offeror, the late acceptance is effective in principle, unless the offeror has made it known to the offeree that he cannot accept the acceptance due to its late arrival.[49]

Modifications in the contract

Four corner clause Parties sometimes stipulate that the contractual rights   **4.17**
and obligations, adopted in the written contract, cannot be modified by an oral agreement or by the parties' conduct: the parties can only derogate from the terms of the written contract in writing. American lawyers call such a provision a "four corner clause": the whole contractual relationship is laid down within the four corners of the written contract. Others speak of a "NOM clause" (no oral modification).

The CISG allows for such a clause in the contract of sale. However, a party may be precluded by his conduct from invoking such a clause when the other party has relied on that conduct (Article 29.2).[50]

---

[46] See J. E. Murray, *op. cit.*, pp. 42–43; however, p. 43, second sentence, should read: "When the acceptance reaches the offeror it is effective . . . ".

[47] Similarly, if the alteration is merely in favour of the other party, it does not require express acceptance: see *Oberster Gerichtshof Austria*, March 20, 1997 (Unilex database 1998; 38 *Zeitschrift für Rechtsvergleichung, Internationales Privatrecht und Europarecht*, 204–207).

[48] M. Esser, "Die letzte Glocke zum Geleit? Kaufmännische Bestätigungsschreiben im internationalen Handel" (1988) Z.R.V. 167; *LG Baden-Baden*, August 14, 1991, (1992) R.I.W. 62.

[49] Art. 21(2). See, for some examples of Art. 21 situations, J. Honnold, *op. cit.*, pp. 242–246.

[50] See R. Hillman, "Article 29(2) of the United Nations Convention on Contracts for the International Sale of Goods: a new effort at clarifying the legal effect of 'no oral modification' clause" (1988) Cornell.Int'l.L.J. 449–466; J. Honnold, *op. cit.*, pp. 280–282. Moreover, see *Court Budapest*, March 24, 1992, (1993) I.P.Rax. 263; LG Hamburg September 26, 1990, (1991) Eu.Z.W. 188.

Obligations and remedies of seller and buyer

4.18 **Overview** Part III of the CISG regulates the substance of the contract of sale, such as the respective rights and obligations of the buyer and the seller. It furthermore deals with the remedies for the seller and the buyer.

4.19 **Fundamental breach of contract** The remedies available depend on whether or not there is a so-called "fundamental breach of contract". A breach of contract is fundamental if the damage it causes to the other party is so substantial that the latter is deprived of what he is entitled to expect under the contract. If, however, the party in breach, or any other reasonable person of the same kind and in the same circumstances, could not have foreseen this result, the breach is not fundamental (Article 25).[51]

A "fundamental breach of contract" thus has two elements:

(1) There has to be a substantial detriment, a somewhat subjective notion, which depends on what the aggrieved party expected from the contract. Yet, this subjectivity is limited because these expectations must appear from the contract.

(2) The result of the breach must be foreseeable. As there is a presumption of foreseeability,[52] it is for the party in breach to prove that neither he nor any reasonable person of the same kind[53] and in the same circumstances[54] could have foreseen the result.[55]

Obligations of the seller[56]

Delivery

4.20 **Definition** The CISG does not give a definition, but only a description of delivery. It is clear from this description that delivery is the physical handover of

---

[51] For a more extensive discussion of the development of Art. 25, see C. M. Bianca and M. J. Bonell, *op. cit.*, pp. 205–209, 215; J. Honnold, *op. cit.*, pp. 253–261.

[52] The burden of proof for the unforeseen lies indeed with the party in breach through the provision "unless the party in breach did not foresee ... " C. M. Bianca and M. J. Bonell, *op. cit.*, p. 216.

[53] Not only must it be examined how a "man with due diligence" must act in a certain sector of trade, but also the socio-economic background in which this party operates, including the language, religion and professional status; see C. M. Bianca and M. J. Bonell, *op. cit.*, p. 219.

[54] This provision refers to all circumstances such as legislation, political situation, climate and also previous contracts and negotiations between parties; C. M. Bianca and M. J. Bonell, *op. cit.*, p. 219.

[55] The CISG does not specify when the result has to be unforeseeable. Conditions which may arise after the conclusion of the contract, such as a declaration by the other party make the detriment foreseeable; see C. M. Bianca and M. J. Bonell, *op. cit.*, pp. 220–221; J. Honnold, *op. cit.*, p. 257.

[56] See J. Ghestin, "The obligations of the seller according to the Vienna Sales Convention" (1988) J.Int'l Bus.L. 5.

goods to the buyer. The conformity of the goods is not an essential part of delivery. Therefore, the conformity of the goods is treated as a separate obligation of the seller.

Place   If nothing has been negotiated with regard to place of delivery,[57] the **4.21** seller must in principle make the goods available at the place where he has his place of business at the time of concluding the contract. If the contract of sale involves carriage of the goods, the goods are delivered when they are handed over to the first carrier for transmission to the buyer.[58] If the object of the sale is a specific item, or a good that must be drawn from a specific stock, or must be manufactured, and at the conclusion of contract the parties were aware of the place where the goods were situated or manufactured, the seller must place the goods at the buyer's disposal at that place (Article 31).

Time   The seller shall deliver on the date agreed or implied by the contract. **4.22** If there is a fixed delivery period the seller has a choice within this period (unless it appears from the circumstances that he can only deliver on a specific day within this period, *e.g.*, in a FOB sale (see paragraph 4.55)).[59]

If nothing is fixed for the delivery date, then the seller shall deliver within a reasonable time, *i.e.* a reasonable period depending on the circumstances (Article 33).

If documents related to goods have to be handed over, the moment, place and the manner of the handover are often specified in the contract. If the seller has handed over the documents before the agreed time, up to that time he may rectify any lack of conformity in the documents, if this does not cause unreasonable inconvenience or costs to the buyer (Article 34).[60]

Conformity of the goods

Concept   The seller shall deliver goods, which conform with the specifica- **4.23** tions in the contract, *i.e.* that are of the quality,[61] quantity[62] and description

---

[57] Terms of contract and declarations by parties may be interpreted in accordance with what "a reasonable person of the same kind . . . in the same circumstances" could deduct from the contract (Art. 8). Parties may also be bound by trade usages or practices since the parties are assumed to have implied them in their contract (Art. 9). J. Honnold, *op. cit.*, pp. 179–180.

[58] See also C. M. Bianca and M. J. Bonell, *op. cit.*, p. 253; J. Honnold, *op. cit.*, pp. 287–289.

[59] See F. Enderlein, "Die Verpflichtung des Verkäufers zur Einhaltung des Lieferzeitraums" (1991) I.P.Rax. 313; see, howwever: *AG Oldenburg*, April 24, 1990, (1991) I.P.Rax. 336.

[60] The buyer can in this case claim damages.

[61] See F. Niggeman, "Error about a substantial quality of the goods and the application of the CISG" (1994) I.B.L.J. 395–415.

[62] In case *OLG Koblenz*, January 31, 1997 (Unilex 1997/I D. 1997–4; OLG Report Koblenz, 1997) the seller delivered fewer blankets than was agreed upon and the Court confirmed that lack of conformity includes lack of both quality and quantity.

required by the contract and are packaged in a manner required by the contract.[63] Moreover, as a general rule, and unless the parties agree otherwise, goods do not conform with the contract if they are unfit for the purpose for which this item is normally intended. If a buyer orders a number of cars, he will usually mean cars suitable for driving, and not wrecks fit for the scrap yard. Yet the buyer could have told the seller that he bought the goods for a particular purpose. If an order for cooling equipment mentions "for our office in Gabon", it may be implied from the contract that the cooling equipment must be of a higher cooling capacity than that needed, say, for an office in Denmark.[64] When the seller has given a sample or a model of the merchandise, the delivered goods only conform to the contract if they have the same qualities as the sample or model (Article 35, 2). The goods must be packaged in the manner customary for such goods or, when there is no such manner, in a manner adequate to preserve and protect the goods (Article 35, 2).

4.24   **Limitation of liability**   If the buyer did not rely, or could not reasonably rely, on the expertise or judgment of the seller, the buyer cannot invoke a lack of conformity. Furthermore, the seller is not liable for a lack of conformity if the buyer knew or ought to have known at the time of concluding the contract that the goods were defective. Similarly, since the buyer could have examined the goods when he concluded the contract, he cannot complain afterwards about obvious defects, which he normally should have noticed earlier.[65] Likewise, when the buyer pays an exceptionally low price he cannot expect the highest quality. These elements must be considered from case to case and in the light of what an average businessman in the same line of business would have done.[66]

---

[63] B. Abderrahmane, "La conformité des marchandises dans la Convention de Vienne" (1989) D.P.C.I. 551. See also A. Veneziano, "Non conformity of goods in international sales. A survey of current caselaw on CISG" (1997) I.B.L.J. 39–65. In OBL Innsbruck, July 1, 1994 (Unilex 1995/II D. 1994–17; comment; Koch, (1998) *Pace Review of Convention on Contracts for International Sale of Goods*, 235–236 n.201) the buyer complained that the daisies that he had bought from the seller did not bloom all summer, but the Court held that he failed to establish that the seller had breached a guarantee or committed a fundamental breach of contract in supplying flowers non-conforming with contract specifications. See also P. Huber, "UN-Kaufrecht und Irrtumsanfechtung: Anwendung nationalen Rechts bei einem Eigenschaftsirrtum des Käufers" (1994) *Zeitschrift für europäisches Privatrecht*, 585–602.

[64] See also J. Honnold, *op. cit.*, p. 302.

[65] See C. M. Bianca and M. J. Bonell, *op. cit.*, p. 279. For the buyer's duty to examine, see para. 4.27. Moreover see *LG Baden-Baden*, August 14, 1991, (1992) R.I.W. 62; *OLG Frankfurt*, April 20, 1994, (1994) R.I.W. 593; ICC award no. 6653 (1993), (1993) J.D.I. 1040; Canton of Ticino April 27, 1992, (1993) R.S.D.I.E. 663.

[66] See C. M. Bianca and M. J. Bonell, *op. cit.*, pp. 275–276. In this context the question can be raised whether the seller is liable when the goods do not comply with the criteria required by the national law of the country of destination (see C. M. Bianca and M. J. Bonell, *op. cit.*, pp. 282–283). This must be examined from case to case. Can it be reasonably expected of the seller to know these national rules? This is certainly the case when the same rules are in force in the country of the seller or when the buyer has indicated the country where the goods are to be delivered and the seller regularly supplies to that country. In the casce of *Pretore della giurisdizione di Locarno Campagna*, April 27, 1992 (Unilex 1994 D. 1992–10; R.S.D.I.E. 1993, 665–667) it was found that where the buyer had resold some of the defective furniture without notifying the seller in time about the resale, the buyer had lost its right to rely on non-conformity of the goods.

Moment for assessment of conformity   The conformity is assessed at the **4.25** time the risk passes even if the lack of conformity becomes apparent only after that time (Article 36, 1).[67] The seller remains liable for any lack of conformity, which only could be discovered after the risk had passed. Indeed, the buyer is generally unable to detect inherent defects when he inspects the goods on delivery (paragraph 4.26).

The conformity is not at stake when the goods are damaged after delivery. However, the seller is also liable for a defect which develops after the risk has passed when this is due to a shortcoming on the part of the seller. For instance, the seller may have given the wrong instructions or dispatched or packaged the goods in an unsuitable manner.[68]

If the seller delivers the goods before the agreed date, he can cure any defects up to the contractual date of delivery (Article 37),[69] as long as this does not result in unreasonable inconvenience[70] or expense[71] for the buyer. The seller can, for instance, deliver the missing part, make up any deficiency in the quantity of the goods, repair a defect in the goods, or replace any non-conforming products.[72]

Examination   Generally the goods must be examined after receipt within as **4.26** short a period as is practicable in the circumstances (Article 38, 1).[73] If the contract includes the carriage of the goods, the examination may be postponed until after the goods arrived at their destination (Article 38, 2). Indeed, the goods may be redirected in transit or reshipped without a reasonable opportunity for the buyer to examine them. When the seller knew, or ought to have known at the conclusion of contract that this could happen,[74] the examination may be deferred until the goods have reached their new destination.[75]

---

[67] In *Tribunal de Commerce de Besançon*, September 9, 1996, the Court found that sweaters that shrank by between 6 and 8 centimetres when washed in accordance with the washing instructions on the labels, lacked conformity, even though this was not discovered upon delivery and the claimant complained later by letter. For further information refer to the Pace University website: http://www.cisg.law.pace.edu.

[68] Art. 36(2). This Article also mentions that if the seller has guaranteed that, for a period of time, the goods remain fit for their ordinary purpose or for some particular purpose or will retain specified qualities, he is liable for that period. This provision is, in fact, superfluous, as such contractual warranties are in all events binding under the convention (C. M. Bianca and M. J. Bonell, *op. cit.*, p. 286).

[69] Art. 52(1) gives the buyer the option to refuse premature delivery. Art. 37 is therefore only applicable when the buyer has not refused the premature delivery or when the seller, according to the contract, could choose the time for delivery within the fixed period (see Art. 33(b)). Art. 37 is not applicable when parties change the time for delivery after conclusion of contract. In that case the seller may only rely on Art. 48 (C. M. Bianca and M. J. Bonnell, *op. cit.*, p. 293).

[70] J. Honnold, *op. cit.*, p. 323.

[71] The term "expense" should not be misunderstood. It is obviously the seller who must compensate for the costs arising from his original mistake, but he cannot request the buyer to advance payment for expenses (see C. M. Bianca and M. J. Bonell, *op. cit.*, p. 293).

[72] The four ways of reparation, summed up in Art. 37, appear to be non-exhaustive because of the purpose of the article.

[73] See J. Honnold, *op. cit.*, pp. 327–330; ICC award no. 5713 (1989), (1990) Y.Com.Arb. 70; *OLG Düsseldorf* January 1, 1993, (1993) I.P.Rax. 412.

[74] The seller must be aware of that possibility because he has to allow for possible future complaints (C. M. Bianca and M. J. Bonell, *op. cit.*, p. 301).

[75] Art. 38(3). A quick reshipment does not give the buyer the opportunity to examine before redispatch. The CISG has therefore opted for a flexible regulation (see J. Honnold, *op. cit.*, pp. 327–328; C. M. Bianca and M. J. Bonell, *op. cit.*, p. 295).

The manner of inspection is not regulated by the CISG, but by the national applicable law. The law of the place of examination will usually apply when the manner of examination is not specified in the contract.[76]

4.27   **Notice of lack of conformity**   The buyer must give notice to the seller of the non-conformity within a reasonable period after he has discovered or ought to have discovered the lack of conformity.[77] This reasonable period runs from the moment the buyer is supposed to have examined the goods.[78] Without notice the buyer loses the right to rely on the lack of conformity (Article 39, 1).[79]

A buyer who did not give notice within a reasonable period, but has a reasonable excuse,[80] may still get a price reduction.[81] He may also claim damages (except for loss of profit) (Article 44).[82] These concessions were admitted under pressure from developing countries[83] for which the effects of late notifica-

---

[76] J. Honnold, *op. cit.*, p. 329; P. Schlechtriem, *op. cit.*, p. 69. The manner of examination is also determined by international commercial practices (C. M. Bianca and M. J. Bonell, *op. cit.*, p. 297).

[77] In *Bundesgerichtshof Germany*, November 3, 1999 (Unilex database, 2000; (2000) *Zeitschrift für Insolvenspraxis* 234; *International Court of Arbitration Bulletin*, Vol. 11/No. 2 (Fall 2000) 17 n.23, 20 n.40) the Court held that in case of defective technical equipment, a description of the symptoms should suffice in order to satisfy the requirements of notice and that a specification of the reasons causing the defect is not required. In *Bundesgerichtshof Germany*, December 4, 1996 (Unilex database, 1998; (1998) *Pace Review of the Convention on Contracts for the International Sale of Goods (CISG)*, 365–372). Art. 39 CISG 1/97; 653–654) the buyer bought a computer printing system that comprised a printer, monitor, calculator and software. After delivery the buyer notified the seller that there was no documentation for the printer and requested him to rectify this non-conformity. The seller then sent documentation for the printer as a single piece of apparatus. The buyer had in fact meant documentation on the whole printing system. The Court found that there was no proper notification since the buyer did not describe the lack of conformity with sufficient specificity so as to avoid any misunderstanding.

[78] The examination is not an obligation for the buyer. However, the buyer cannot complain after a reasonable examination period has expired about defects which he should have detected. *Cf., inter alia*, ICC award no. 5713 (1989), (1990) Y.Com.Arb. 70; *LG München*, July 3, 1989, (1990) I.P.Rax. 316; *Rb. Dordrecht*, November 21, 1990, (1991) N.I.P.R. 159; *OLG Düsseldorf*, January 8, 1993, (1993) I.P.Rax. 412. In *Bundesgerichtshof Germany*, November 3, 1999 (Unilex database, 2000; (2000) *Zeitschrift für Insolvenspraxis* 234; comments: Schlechtriem, Pace University website http://www.cisg.law.pace.edu; Witz, *ICC International Court of Arbitration Bulletin*, Vol. 11/No. 2 (Fall 2000), the buyer had the machine delivered by the seller examined by an expert. The Court found that reasonable notice included a period of two weeks for the expert's examination, followed by a one-month period of time for notification. In *Rb. Zwolle*, March 5, 1997, (1997) N.I.P.R. 230 (282–284) the buyer did not immediately give notice of non-conformity of the fish delivered to him. Because this is a delicate product, the Court held that the delay to give notice caused the buyer to lose his right to damages.

[79] See *HG Zürich*, September 9, 1993 (Unilex 1995/II D. 1993–22; RDAI 1995, 1013). In case *OLG Koblenz*, January 31, 1997 (Unilex 1997/I D. 1997–4; OLG Report Koblenz 1997), the buyer lost his right to rely on lack of conformity, because his notice about the non-conformity was incomplete: he notified the seller that five reels of blankets were missing, but he did not specify of which design. Since blankets of different designs were delivered, the notification did not enable the seller to rectify the non-conformity. See, furthermore, C. B. Andersen, "Reasonable time in Article 39(1) of the CISG—is Article 39(1) truly a uniform provision?" in (1998) *Review of the Convention on Contracts for the International Sale of Goods (CISG)*, 63–176.

[80] When an excuse is considered reasonable is not quite clear. See J. Honnold, *op. cit.*, pp. 338–340.

[81] In accordance with Art. 50.

[82] P. Schlechtriem, *op. cit.*, p. 71.

[83] For the development of Art. 44, see C. M. Bianca and M. J. Bonell, *op. cit.*, pp. 324–326 and J. Honnold, *op. cit.*, p. 338.

tion of non-conformity were too severe. Indeed, it is unusual in many developing countries to make a formal complaint.

The buyer must inform the seller in any event about non-conformity within two years after the goods were actually handed over,[84] unless a longer contractual period of guarantee has been given (Article 39, 2). The buyer generally loses the right to claim for non-conformity on the expiry of this period. However, a seller who knew or ought to have known of non-conformity and did not disclose this to the buyer, cannot assert that the buyer notified him too late.[85]

Rights or claims of third parties

Overview   The seller must deliver the goods free from any right or claim of   **4.28**
a third party (unless the buyer has agreed to take the goods subject to that right or claim) (Article 41).[86] The seller must protect not only against well-founded claims, but also against ill-founded claims.[87] The buyer has to inform the seller within a reasonable period of the existence of any rights or claims of third parties, unless the seller is already aware of them.[88]

There is a special regime for goods subject to intellectual property claims:

- In the event that the parties envisaged at the time of conclusion of the contract that the goods would be resold or otherwise used in a given country, the goods have to be free from any intellectual property claim under the law of that country.

---

[84] Art. 39(2) speaks of "actually handed over". According to C. M. Bianca and M. J. Bonell (*op. cit.*, pp. 305 and 310–311), the term "actually" has no special significance and the period starts to run from the handing over of the goods, probably to the first independent carrier. This can be many months before the first examination opportunity. J. Honnold (*op. cit.*, p. 336), on the contrary, holds, and in our opinion correctly, that by the addition of the term "actually", the physical handover to the buyer is emphasised. Also, the context clearly points to the moment at which the examination duty for the buyer commences.

[85] Art. 40. This article is an expression of the principle of good faith.

[86] The buyer has to be protected against potentially expensive and lengthy lawsuits involving the goods. If he, in accordance with Art. 43, gives notice to the seller of the existence of any claims, the seller must take care of resolving the claims (C. M. Bianca and M. J. Bonell, *op. cit.*, p. 318). The speed and effectiveness with which the seller deals with such claims helps to determine whether there is a fundamental breach of contract (J. Honnold, *op. cit.*, p. 345). In *Oberster Gerichtshof Austria*, February 6, 1996 ((1996) 1 *The International Legal Forum* 140; Unilex 1996/II D. 1996–3.1; comment: Honnold, *Uniform Law for International Sales* (1999) 120–121 (Art. 8(3)), 288 (Art. 41), 454 (Art. 74 (damages, loss of profit)), 500 (Art. 80)) the seller delivered gas subject to the condition that it might not be resold in the Benelux countries. Since this had not been agreed in the contract, the Court found that it was a violation of the seller's obligation to deliver goods free from third party claims. See also C. R. Mainz and G. E. Genève, "Garantie, en cas d'éviction et propriété intellectuelle dans la vente internationale—Encore du fil à retordre dans la vente internationale" (2000) ZeuP 66–92; A. Vida?, "Garantie du vendeur et propriété industrielle: les 'vices juridiques' dans la vente internationale de marchandises (Convention de Vienne)" (1994) 47 Rev.Trim.Dr.Com., 21.

[87] Even ill-founded claims can produce expensive lawsuits for which the buyer should not be responsible (C. M. Bianca and M. J. Bonell, *op. cit.*, p. 318).

[88] Art. 43(1) and (2). A buyer who does not complain within a reasonable period can still get a price reduction and claim damages if he has a reasonable excuse for his failure to give the required notice (Art. 44).

- In any other event, the goods have to be free from intellectual property claims under the law of the country where the buyer has his place of business (Article 42(1)).

However, the seller will not be liable if the buyer knew or ought to have known at the conclusion of contract that the goods were subject to an intellectual property claim. Moreover, if the claims relate to technical drawings or other specifications supplied by the buyer, the seller is not liable (Article 42(2)).

Remedies

4.29 **Overview** If the seller fails to perform any of his obligations the buyer may, depending on the circumstances, resort to a number of remedies. He may invoke general remedies such as a request for specific performance, avoidance of the contract, price reduction or compensation of damages. The buyer may also grant the seller extra time to perform his obligations; if it becomes clear that the seller is not going to fulfil his obligations, the buyer may then suspend or rescind the contract.

4.30 **Request of specific performance** The buyer can claim for specific performance when the court would order a specific performance for a similar contract under its domestic sale law (Article 28).[89] However, specific performance is excluded if the buyer has already invoked other remedies that are inconsistent with specific performance (*e.g.* when the buyer has already declared that the contract is terminated) (Article 46).[90]

If the delivered goods do not conform with the specifications of the contract, the buyer has two remedies. Unless this claim is unreasonable in the circumstances,[91] the buyer may order the repair of the non-conforming goods. Moreover, and only if the non-conformity is a fundamental breach of contract,[92] the buyer may demand delivery of substitute goods. The buyer must declare his choice of remedy at the moment of notice of non-conformity or within a reasonable period thereafter (Article 46).

---

[89] This provision was specifically inserted for the common law systems, where the obligation of "specific performance" has a more exceptional meaning; nevertheless, the civil law judge can also use this provision. See J. Honnold, *op. cit.*, p. 268; A. Kastely, "The right to require performance in international sales: towards an international interpretation of the Vienna Convention" (1988) Wash.L.Rev. 607.

[90] C. M. Bianca and M. J. Bonell, *op. cit.*, p. 335–336. The principle that the parties must first perform their obligations is at odds with the common law notion that a claim for damages is the normal remedy. Under Anglo-American law a demand for specific performance can only be accepted when a claim for damages does not give sufficient protection (J. Honnold, *op. cit.*, p. 269).

[91] *e.g.* the cost of small repairs, which can just as well be carried by the buyer, or in cases where the seller is established abroad (J. Honnold, *op. cit.*, p. 364).

[92] The requirement is that there be a fundamental breach of contract, since it would be unfair to burden the seller with the high cost of replacing the goods and dispatching new goods for a relatively small breach of contract (see J. Honnold, *op. cit.*, p. 364).

There is an element of uncertainty in the claim for reparation or for delivery of substitute goods: when the courts would decide that there was no fundamental breach of contract, no substitute goods had to be delivered and no reparation is due.

Time extension and right to cure The buyer may give the seller an additional period of time of reasonable length for performance of his obligations. The seller must perform these obligations within the extended period. During this additional period the buyer is prevented from using any remedies for breach of contract, unless the seller notifies the buyer that he is unable to perform his obligations within the fixed period (Article 47). However, the buyer is in any case entitled to claim damages for delay in performance.[93]   **4.31**

If no performance has taken place after the expiration of this period, the buyer may terminate the contract as well as claim damages.

The seller may, after the date or period for delivery, remedy his failure to perform his obligations,[94] if this can be done without unreasonable delay and inconvenience to the buyer.[95] He must in any event reimburse the buyer for the expenses incurred (Article 48,1). Moreover, the buyer retains the right to claim damages and to terminate the contract.[96]

Furthermore, the seller may extend the period for performance by requesting the buyer to accept performance within the time indicated in the request (Article 48,2). If the buyer does not refuse acceptance within a reasonable period, he is deemed to have accepted the time extension for performance (Article 48,3).[97]

Avoidance of the contract A contracting party cannot easily be released from a contract.[98] The contract may only be avoided when the seller's failure to perform amounts to a fundamental breach of contract, or when the seller has not delivered within the additional period granted by the buyer (see paragraph 4.31) (Article 49,1).   **4.32**

---

[93] *AG Oldenburg*, April 24, 1990, (1991) I.P.Rax. 336.

[94] Compare this with the right to cure of Art. 37 (see paragraph 4.26). In case *OLG Koblenz*, January 31, 1997 (Unilex 1997/I D. 1997–4; *OLG Report Koblenz* 1997) the buyer rejected, without justification, the seller's offer to deliver new goods to rectify the non-conformity of the quantity of the goods. For this reason the Court found that the breach was not fundamental and the buyer was not entitled to damages, nor to a reduction of the price.

[95] J. Honnold, *op. cit.*, pp. 374–379.

[96] See C. M. Bianca and M. J. Bonell, *op. cit.*, pp. 349–352 on the difficult relationship between the right of the seller to cure and the right of the buyer to terminate the contract.

[97] The buyer cannot use remedies which are inconsistent with the performance by the seller during this time extension. Because a request or notice for an extension may have far-reaching effects, it is only effective when it has been received by the buyer. This provision derogates from the general rule that a person has fulfilled his duty to give notice when he has conveyed his message by the appropriate means (Art. 27). A buyer who objects to the request can rely on Art. 27: if the seller did not receive his notice, because of circumstances outside the buyer's control, the buyer may still maintain his objections (J. Honnold, *op. cit.*, p. 379).

[98] See C. M. Bianca and M. J. Bonell, *op. cit.*, pp. 360–361; *OLG Frankfurt*, January 18, 1994, (1994) R.I.W. 240; *OLG Munchen*, March 2, 1994, (1994) R.I.W. 545; *OLG Frankfurt*, April 20, 1994, (1994) R.I.W. 593; *Bundesgericht Switzerland*, October 28, 1998 (Unilex database, 1999; RSDIE (1999) 179–182)).

The buyer loses his right to avoid the contract if he does not claim avoidance within a reasonable time.[99] This reasonable period runs from the expiration of the additional period of time fixed by the buyer, or after the seller has declared that he is unable to perform his obligations within such an additional period. If the buyer has declared that he will not accept late performance, he must declare the contract avoided within a reasonable time after this statement.

4.33   **Reduction of the price**   The buyer may reduce the sale price of the goods, when the goods do not conform with the specifications of the contract (Article 50).[1] He may even reduce the price already paid. However, no reduction is possible when the buyer has already terminated the contract or has requested the seller to cure the defect.[2] Moreover, no price reduction can be claimed if the seller has cured or offers to cure the defect.

The price reduction will be assessed as of the time of the delivery of the goods[3] by deducting the value of the non-conforming goods from the value the goods should have had according to the specifications.[4]

4.34   **Damages and suspension of performance**   See paragraphs 4.47 and 4.49.

4.35   **Partial or full use of a remedy**   The buyer may only demand specific performance, avoidance, price reduction or damages for that part of the goods that has not been delivered or has not been delivered in conformity with the specifications.[5] If there is a fundamental breach of the contract as a whole, the buyer may declare the whole contract avoided (Article 51(2)).[6]

---

[99] This reasonable period has to be determined as follows. When the seller delivers late, within a reasonable time after the buyer has become aware that delivery has been made; for any other breach, within reasonable time after the buyer has declared that he will not accept performance, after he knew or ought to have known of the breach (Art. 49(2)). Cf. *LG Frankfurt*, September 16, 1991, (1991) R.I.W. 952; *OLG Frankfurt*, September 17, 1991, (1992) EuZW 352. In *OLG Oldenburg*, February 1, 1995 (Unilex database, 1998; comment: Koch, *Pace Review of Convention on Contracts for International Sale of Goods*, (1998), 256 n.265) five weeks was found to be a reasonable time.

[1] For an exhaustive description of this remedy, see A. Muria Tunon, "The actio quanti minoris and sales of goods between Mexico and the U.S.: an analysis of the remedy of reduction of the price in the UN Sales Convention, CISG Article 50 and its civil law antecedents", http://www.cisg.law.pace.edu.

[2] J. Honnold, *op. cit.*, pp. 391–398; *Rb. Rotterdam*, November 21, 1996, (1997) N.I.P.R. No. 223 (275–276).

[3] The price of the time of delivery of the goods is taken into account, as it is difficult to determine the value of the goods at the moment of conclusion of the contract (often the goods do not exist at that time). See C. M. Bianca and M. J. Bonell, *op. cit.*, p. 369. Also *Canton of Ticino*, April 27, 1992, (1993) R.S.D.I.E. 663.

[4] In the *Court of Locarno Campagna*, April 27, 1992 (Unilex 1994 D. 1992–10; R.S.D.I.E. 1993, 665–667; comment: Honnold, *Uniform Law for International Sales* (1999) 274 (Art. 38 (timeliness of examination), 322 (Art. 48), 341 (Art. 50); Behr, 17 J.L.C. (1998) 266–268), the Court rejected the seller's offer to pay for the repair of the defective goods and stated that Article 50 CISG was not intended to provide for restitution of the repair cost but a reduction of the purchase price in the same proportion as the value that the goods actually delivered had at the time of delivery, compared to the value that conforming goods would have had at that time.

[5] Art. 51(1); Cf. *LG Baden-Baden*, August 14, 1991, (1992) R.I.W. 62.

[6] J. Honnold, *op. cit.*, pp. 399–402.

Early delivery and excess quantity   The buyer may refuse delivery of the   **4.36**
goods before the fixed date.[7] An early delivery can indeed be very unwelcome for
the buyer. If, however, the buyer accepts this early delivery, it will be considered
as a correct delivery. This means that the buyer must examine the goods and give
notice about possible defects within a reasonable period, that the buyer must pay
the price and that the risk is transferred to the buyer.

If the seller delivers too much, the buyer may refuse or accept the excess
quantity. When he takes delivery of the excess quantity, he must pay the full price
(Article 52(2)).[8]

Obligations of the buyer[9]

Payment of the price

Overview   The buyer has to pay the price. The obligation to pay covers three   **4.37**
elements: the determination of the price, the place of payment and the moment
of payment. These elements are usually agreed in the contract. However, when
the contract does not cover these details, the supplementary rules of the CISG
apply.

Determination of the price   In principle the contract mentions the price, or   **4.38**
at least the method for price fixing. Nevertheless, if the price is neither fixed nor
implied in the contract,[10] the parties are deemed to have impliedly agreed to the
price generally charged at the time of conclusion of the contract for such goods
sold under comparable circumstances in the trade concerned.

Place   The price must be paid at the seller's place of business, unless the   **4.39**
contract states otherwise.[11] If the seller changes his place of business after the
conclusion of contract, he must bear any increase in the expenses incidental to
the payment caused by this change. For payment against the handing over of
goods or documents, the place of payment is the place where the handing over
takes place.

The buyer must not only fulfil the formalities for payment in the country where
he is established, but also in the country where the payment has to take place. The

---

[7] See C. M. Bianca and M. J. Bonell, *op. cit.*, 380.

[8] J. Honnold, *op. cit.*, p. 404.

[9] See F. Niggeman, "Buyer's obligations under the UN Convention on Contracts for the International Sale of Goods" (1988) I.B.L.J. 27; J. Honnold, *op. cit.*, p. 403; C. M. Bianca and M. J. Bonell, *op. cit.*, Ch. 7.

[10] *e.g.* in the case where there was an earlier contractual relationship between the parties in which a price was fixed or when a party states explicitly that the price cannot be fixed in a specific way (C. M. Bianca and M. J. Bonell, *op. cit.*, p. 408).

[11] Art. 57(1)(a); *Rb. Middelburg*, November 30, 1994. If the seller has several places of business, payment must be made at the place of business with which the contract has the closest connection (Art. 10). J. Honnold, *op. cit.*, pp. 415–418. *Cf.* ICC award no. 7153 (1992), (1992) J.D.I. 1005; *OLG Düsseldorf*, July 2, 1993, (1993) R.I.W. 845; *KG Berlin*, January 24, 1994, (1994) R.I.W. 683.

buyer has to bear the costs for the transfer of the payment. Eventually, he carries the risk if the money gets lost during transfer (Article 57).

4.40   **Time for payment**   If no specific time has been agreed, the buyer must pay the price at the moment the goods or documents are put at his disposal. The seller may make payment a condition for the handing over of the goods or documents (Article 58, 1).

If the contract involves the carriage of goods, the seller may dispatch the goods on condition that the goods, or documents controlling their disposition, will only be handed over against payment of the price (Article 58, 2). Unless the contract states otherwise the buyer is not bound to pay the price until he has had the opportunity to examine the goods (Article 58, 3).[12]

The obligation to pay on time also includes the duty to take (timely) the necessary steps to arrange for such payment.[13]

Taking delivery

4.41   **Overview**   The buyer must do all that can reasonably be expected of him to make delivery possible (Article 60, a). If necessary, he has to inform the seller of the exact place of delivery. The buyer must also take possession of the goods (Article 60, b).

In principle, the risk passes upon the taking of delivery of the goods, especially when the contract does not include carriage of the goods (see paragraph 4.46). If the buyer does not take delivery, he breaches the contract and may become liable for any damage to the goods.[14]

Remedies

4.42   **Overview**   The remedies available to the seller are the same as those available to the buyer: he may require the performance of an obligation, declare the

---

[12] Therefore the buyer must sometimes rely on a commercial inspector for inspection of the goods on loading (J. Honnold, *op. cit.*, p. 423).

[13] *e.g.* the buyer may be obliged by contract to remit a letter of credit or to offer a collateral. See C. M, Bianca and M. J. Bonell, *op. cit.*, p. 396. In *Oberster Gerichtshof Austria*, February 6, 1996, ((1996) 1 *The International Legal Forum* 140; Unilex 1996/II D. 1996–3.1; comment: Honnold, *Uniform Law for International Sales* (1999) 120–121 (Art. 8(3)), 288 (Art. 41), 454 (Art. 74 (damages, loss of profit)), 500 (Art. 80)) the buyer was discarded from his obligation to obtain a letter of credit since the seller did not provide him with the name of the port of origin. The buyer was not obliged to obtain a blank letter of credit. National laws or regulations may require an application for a licence for the transfer of money abroad. See L. Sevon, "Obligations of the buyer under the UN Convention on Contracts for the International Sale of Goods", in P. Sarcevic and P. Volken (eds), *International Sale of Goods* (Oceana, New York, 1986) p. 220. A seller who discovers that the necessary steps were not taken in time by the buyer, can grant an extension (Arts 63(1), *et seq.*) and rescind the contract after the fixed period (Art. 64(1)(b)) (J. Honnold, *op. cit.*, p. 440).

[14] See J. Honnold, *op. cit.*, p. 431. *Cf. LG Aachen*, April 3, 1990, (1990) R.I.W. 491; *LG Aachen*, May 14, 1993 (1993) R.I.W. 760.

contract avoided and claim damages. The seller may grant the buyer an additional period of time to perform his obligations. Just like the buyer, the seller may suspend the performance of his obligations or avoid the contract if it is clear in advance that the buyer will not perform his obligations. Furthermore, if the buyer failed to supply necessary specifications, the seller may fill in these specifications.

Specific performance and extension of time   The seller may require the **4.43** buyer to pay the price and take delivery (Article 62), unless the seller has resorted to other remedies inconsistent with this requirement. For instance, when the seller declares the contract avoided, he may no longer demand performance; if the seller allows the buyer a period of grace, he cannot require instant specific performance.[15]

If the buyer takes delivery, but fails to pay the price, a claim for payment is the obvious remedy. If the buyer moreover refuses to take delivery, a claim for payment will be combined with a claim to take delivery of the goods.[16]

The seller may grant the buyer a reasonable time extension to perform. During that period the seller may not invoke other remedies, unless the buyer gives notice to the seller that he will not perform (Article 63). The seller, however, can always claim damages. After the expiration of the additional period the seller may invoke all other remedies. Lack of performance during the additional period can be a ground to avoid the contract thereafter.[17]

Avoidance of the contract   The seller may declare the contract avoided **4.44** when there is a fundamental breach of contract.[18] Moreover, when the seller has granted the buyer an additional period and the buyer has not paid within that period or taken delivery, the seller may likewise avoid the contract. He may also set aside the contract when the buyer declares that he will not perform his obligations within the fixed period. However, if the buyer has already paid the price, the seller generally loses his right to declare the contract avoided. However, as long as the seller is unaware of a late payment, he can invoke the lack of payment as ground to avoid the contract (Article 64).[19]

Specifications   A contract of sale may provide that the buyer will specify the **4.45** shape, measurements or other features of the goods at a later time. However, a buyer who does not give the required specifications should not be able to block performance. Consequently, the seller may make the specifications himself if the buyer has failed to provide the specifications on the fixed date, or if the buyer

---

[15] In this event there is only a temporary inconsistency and the right to performance is only suspended (C. M. Bianca and M. J. Bonell, *op. cit.*, p. 454).

[16] Art. 28, however, states that a court is not bound to give an order for specific performance if it is not required to do so under its national law for contracts of sale. See para. 4.31.

[17] C. M. Bianca and M. J. Bonell, *op. cit.*, 460; J. Honnold, *op. cit.*, pp. 440–441.

[18] In case *OLG Koblenz*, January 31, 1997 (Unilex 1997/I D. 1997–4; *OLG Report Koblenz* 1997) the question was raised whether violation of an exclusive distribution contract can amount to a fundamental breach. Although in this case the buyer lost his right to avoid the contract, the Court stated, *obiter*, that if proven, such violation can amount to fundamental breach.

[19] J. Honnold, *op. cit.*, pp. 442–446.

fails to respond to the request for specifications from the seller within a reasonable period.[20] A seller who issues the specifications, must communicate these specifications to the buyer and allow him a reasonable time to request different specifications. If the buyer fails to do so, the specifications of the seller are binding (Article 65, 2).

4.46   **Passing of risk**[21]   It is important for both seller and buyer to know when the risk passes: the buyer must pay the price if the goods are lost or damaged after the risk has passed to him (Article 66); he is exempted from payment if the loss or damage is due to an act or omission of the seller or a person acting for him.[22]

Parties may include in the contract a specific clause for the passing of risk or they may indirectly address the issue by referring to an Incoterm (see paragraph 4.55). Otherwise, the supplementary rules of the CISG apply.

Under the CISG, the risk generally passes from the seller to the buyer at the moment of delivery. When the contract calls for the buyer to fetch the goods at the seller's place of business and the buyer does not take over the goods at the agreed time, the risk passes at the time the goods are placed at his disposal.[23] If the buyer has agreed to take over the goods at another place than that place of business, the risk only passes when the buyer is aware that the goods are indeed placed at his disposal at the agreed place of delivery.[24] If the contract relates to generic goods not yet identified, these goods are deemed to be placed at the disposal of the buyer when they are identified.[25]

For a sales contract involving carriage, the following distinction is made:

- If the seller has not agreed to hand over the goods at a specific place, the risk passes to the buyer when the goods are handed over to the first independent carrier.

- If the seller is bound to hand over the goods to the carrier at a specific place, the risk only passes to the buyer when the goods are handed over at that place. Whether the seller brings the goods to that place or whether they are brought there by an independent carrier is a separate issue.[26]

---

[20] C. M. Bianca and M. J. Bonell, *op. cit.*, p. 478; J. Honnold, *op. cit.*, p. 357.

[21] The CISG does not make a distinction, unlike the Hague Convention, between the delivery of goods consistent and inconsistent with the contract. Delivery concerns only the physical handover of the goods. See J. Honnold, *op. cit.*, p. 449.

[22] The fact that the CISG does not explicitly exclude the passing of risk when goods are lost or reduced in value "through a person for whom the seller is liable" (Art. 96, Hague Convention), does not exclude the passing of the risk under the CISG in such a case. The principle that a provision in respect of the seller extends to persons for whom the seller is liable, was considered self-evident in the CISG and was therefore deliberately not adopted in Art. 66 (C. M. Bianca and M. J. Bonell, *op. cit.*, p. 484).

[23] Art. 69(1). J. Honnold, *op. cit.*, p. 472.

[24] Art. 69(2). J. Honnold, *op. cit.*, p. 474.

[25] Art. 69(3).

[26] See B. von Hoffman, "Passing of risk in international sale of goods", in P. Sarcevic and P. Volken (eds), *op. cit.*, pp. 265, 286; for the discussion on the scope of Art. 67(1), see C. M. Bianca and M. J. Bonell, *op. cit.*, pp. 491–493.

The fact that the seller still holds the documents does not prevent the risk passing to the buyer.[27] Furthermore, for sales contracts involving carriage of generic goods, the risk will not pass to the buyer until the goods are clearly identified (Article 67). Thus, the seller cannot allege that the buyer carried the risk for generic goods (*e.g.* grain) lost during transport unless it is clear that it was the part to be delivered to the buyer which was lost.

For the sale of goods during transit the risk passes at the conclusion of the contract. There is one exception to this rule: if the circumstances (the expressed or implied agreement in the contract, a handover of insurance documents by the seller, or other external elements) so indicate, the risk only passes to the buyer when the goods are handed over to the first carrier, who issued the transport documents.[28]

Common provisions for seller and buyer

Anticipatory breaches

Suspension   If it appears after the conclusion of the contract that a party will   **4.47**
be unable to perform a substantial part of his obligations (*e.g.* because of a serious deficiency in his ability to perform or in his creditworthiness), the other party may suspend the performance of his own obligations (Article 71). Thus, a buyer who agreed to pay before delivery may suspend payment if the seller turns out to be insolvent and is unable to deliver. A seller who delivers on credit may suspend the delivery if the buyer will be unable to pay.[29]

Because such a suspension may cause considerable detriment to the other party, the party suspending performance must give immediate notice to the counterparty. If the latter party then provides an adequate guarantee that he will perform, the former party cannot suspend performance.[30]

Avoidance   If it is clear[31] that one of the parties will commit a fundamental   **4.48**
breach of contract prior to the date the other party has to perform their part of the

---

[27] The withholding of documents is often used in international trade to guarantee that the price will be paid (J. Honnold, *op. cit.*, p. 463). Art. 67 confirms the principle that the risk passes when the seller has lost effective control over the goods, even if he has still legal control. P. Schlechtriem, *The UN Convention on Contracts for the International Sale of Goods* (Manzsche, Wier, 1986), p. 88.

[28] Art. 68. See H. Berman and M. Ladd, "Risk of loss or damage in documentary transactions and the Convention on the International Sale of Goods" (1988) Cornell.Int'l.L.J. 423. This solution has as an advantage the fact that the time the damage occurred does not become an issue and that only the buyer can claim compensation.

[29] J. Honnold, *op. cit.*, p. 485; C. M. Bianca and M. J. Bonell, *op. cit.*, pp. 519–520; M. G. Strub, "The codificaiton of the doctrine of anticipatory repudiation in the 1980 Convention on the International Sale of Goods" (1989) *International Trade Law and Practice* 581; M. G. Strub, "CISG: Anticipatory Repudiation Provisions and Developing Countries" (1989) I.C.L.Q. 475. See also *AG Frankfurt*, January 31, 1991, (1991) I.P.Rax. 345.

[30] An ordinary statement is not usually sufficient. Therefore, a seller who cannot produce because of a strike, must demonstrate, for example, through reports of negotiations with the social partners, that the strike is indeed coming to an end (C. M. Bianca and M. J. Bonell, *op. cit.*, 523).

[31] More substantial evidence is required than the evidence required for the suspension of contract. (J. Honnold, *op. cit.*, p. 487).

contract, that other party may declare the contract avoided (Article 72). In general he must give the other party reasonable notice[32] so that the latter can still guarantee his performance.[33]

In the case of delivery by instalments, one party may declare the contract avoided for the future if a breach of contact in respect of one instalment justifies the presumption of a fundamental breach of contract for future instalments. Moreover, he may also declare avoided the part of the contract related to the defective instalment, without rescinding the contract as a whole. Furthermore, in the case where instalments are linked in such a way that the avoidance in respect of one instalment implies that further deliveries become meaningless, the buyer may declare the contract avoided for the deliveries already made, as well as for the subsequent deliveries (Article 73).[34]

Damages

4.49   Overview   As a rule, damages are due when there is:

    (i) a breach of contract;

    (ii) a loss suffered by the other party; and

    (iii) a causal link between the breach of contract and the loss (Article 74).[35]

The amount of damages depends on the size of the loss, including lost profits. However, the damages may not exceed the loss that the party in breach foresaw, or should have foreseen, at the time of the conclusion of contract.[36]

Rather than the actual size of the damage, it is the possible size that must be foreseeable, objectively assessed in the light of the facts the party in breach knew or ought to have known. The relevant amount is what a businessman in that particular trade could normally have foreseen, taking into account the information the contract party had at his disposal.[37] Unpredictable consequential damages do not have to be compensated.

---

[32] This reasonable notice is not required if the other party declares that he will not perform his obligation (Art. 72, 3).

[33] C. M. Bianca and M. J. Bonell, *op. cit.*, p. 530; J. Honnold, *op. cit.*, p. 497.

[34] C. M. Bianca and M. J. Bonell, *op. cit.*, p. 532; J. Honnold, *op. cit.*, p. 500–502.

[35] See E. C. Schneider, "Measuring damages under the CISG: Article 74 of the United Nations Convention on Contracts for the International Sale of Goods" (1997) 9 Pace Int'l L.Rev. 223–237.

[36] The test of foreseeable damage originates from the Anglo-American concept of the "remoteness of damage". Nonetheless, the theory of sufficient cause, *inter alia*, applied in Germany, results in a similar restriction of liability (J. Honnold, *op. cit.*, p. 505). *Cf.* ICC award no. 6281 (1989), (1989) J.D.I. 1114; *L.G. Frankfurt*, September 16, 1991, (1993) R.I.W. 1029. In *Bundesgericht Switzerland*, October 28, 1998 (Unilex database, 1999; (1999) R.S.D.I.E. 179–182) the buyer successfully claimed damages for loss of clientele as a result of delivery of substandard meat by the seller. It found that this was foreseeable since the buyer was a wholesale trader in a sensitive market and had an obligation to carry out.

[37] The contracting partner could have drawn attention to the potential losses in case of a breach of contract. See C. M. Bianca and M. J. Bonell, *op. cit.*, p. 542.

The party claiming damages must take all reasonable measures to mitigate the loss (Article 77) (*e.g.* a quick sale of his perishable goods where appropriate).[38]

If he fails to take such measures, his damages are reduced by the loss he could have avoided. If a party fails to pay the price or any other sum that is in arrears, interest is due besides damages (Article 78). It is up to the courts to decide which national law will determine the interest rate.[39]

Replacement and resale If the buyer, after avoidance of the contract, has **4.50** bought goods in replacement of the non-delivered goods (replacement purchase), he can recover the extra expenses besides general damages.[40]

Likewise, the seller who has resold the goods but received less than he would have received under the original contract, may recover extra damages. Even if no replacement purchase or resale takes place, these damages are due. They reflect the difference between the initial contract price and the market price of the goods at the place of delivery and time of avoidance (Article 76).[41]

Exemptions

Force majeure[42] A party is not liable when his failure to perform is due to **4.51** an impediment beyond his control that renders performance impossible (natural disasters, economic sanctions, wars, etc.).[43] However, this impediment should be unforeseeable at the time of conclusion of contract and could not reasonably have been overcome afterwards. The exemption is only temporary: it applies as long as the impediment lasts and to the extent of its effect. The party who fails to

---

[38] In *OLG Köln*, January 8, 1997 (Unilex 1997/I D. 1997–1) the buyer was forced to contract with a third party to treat its leather goods while he was waiting for the seller to return the tenancy machine after adjustments. The Court held that the buyer was entitled to claim the sum paid to the third party from the seller and that the buyer did not violate his duty to mitigate loss.

[39] The courts considered the following laws applicable for the determination of the interest rate:
— law of place of payment: ICC award no. 7153 (1992), (1992) J.D.I. 1005;
— law of creditor: *LG Stuttgart*, September 5, 1989, (1990) I.P.Rax. (1991) 317; *LG Frankfurt*, September 16, 1991, (1991) R.I.W. 952; *KG Berlin*, January 24, 1994, (1994) R.I.W. 683; *OLG München*, March 2, 1994, (1994) R.I.W. 545; ICC award no. 7197 (1992), (1993) J.D.I. 1028;
— law of place of actual loss: *LG Aachen*, April 3, 1990, (1990) R.I.W. 491;
— proper law of contract: *AG Oldenburg*, April 24, 1990, (1991) I.P.Rax. 336; *LG Hamburg*, September 26, 1990, (1991) I.P.Rax. 400; *Belgian Cass*, November 29, 1990, (1990) *Rechtskundig Weekblad* 1270;
— law of debtor or creditor: *OLG Frankfurt*, June 13, 1991, (1991) R.I.W. 591; *OLG Frankfurt*, April 20, 1994, (1994) R.I.W. 593.
Cf. also: G. Reinhart, "Fälligkeitszinsen und UN-Kaufrecht" (1991) I.P.Rax. 376.

[40] Art. 75. C. M. Bianca and M. J. Bonell, *op. cit.*, p. 554; J. Honnold, *op. cit.*, p. 508.

[41] If, however, the buyer declares the contract avoided after having taken delivery of the goods, the time of the delivery will be applied for the calculation of damages. This provision was introduced to avoid speculation by a buyer (C. M. Bianca and C. M. Bonell, *op. cit.*, p. 556; J. Honnold, *op. cit.*, p. 510).

[42] J. Honnold, *op. cit.*, pp. 529–552.

[43] In *Trubunal de Commerce de Besançon*, September 9, 1996 (Pace University website: http://www.cisg.law.pace.edu), sweaters delivered by the seller shrank. The Court awarded a smaller amount of damages than requested by the buyer because the manufacturing of the textile was beyond the control of the seller.

perform, must give notice to the other party about the impediment and its effect on his ability to perform.

Force majeure excludes a claim for damages. It does not, however, exclude other remedies. Thus, it does not prevent the contract being declared avoided (Article 79).[44]

Avoidance

4.52 **Effects** Avoidance of the contract releases the parties from their contractual obligations. However, it does not affect the specific contractual provisions in respect of the avoidance of contract (*e.g.* compensation because of avoidance). Despite the avoidance, the parties remain bound by the provisions for dispute settlement. Thus, an arbitration clause, for instance, still applies, even if the contract is declared avoided (Article 81).[45]

In addition, a party who has (partially) performed the contract is entitled to restitution of money or goods if the contract is subsequently avoided.[46] If the seller must reimburse the price, he must pay the buyer interest on the contract sum from the date the price was paid (Article 84).

The buyer loses the right to declare the contract avoided if he is unable to restitute the goods in substantially the same condition as they were in on delivery. However, he may still declare the contract avoided if the impossibility of restitution is not due to his fault, if the goods were partially or completely damaged as a result of a normal examination, or if the goods were used in the normal course of business before the lack of conformity was discovered (Article 82).[47]

Preservation of the goods

4.53 **Preservation measures** If the buyer is late in taking delivery of the goods, he bears the risk for their loss or damage. However, a seller in control of the goods must do whatever is reasonable under the circumstances to preserve them, even if this entails extra expenses.[48] The seller is entitled to retain the goods until the buyer has reimbursed him for these costs.

---

[44] See moreover, P. Rathjen, "Exemption from liability of the seller or buyer under Art. 79, 80 CISG" (1999) 45 R.I.W. 561–565; S. H. Jenkins, "Exemption for non-performance: UCC, CISG, UNIDROIT Principles—a comparative assessment" (1998) 72 *Tulane Law Review*, 1925–1929.

[45] See J. Honnold, *op. cit.*, p. 560. This provision is somewhat superfluous in view of the autonomy of the arbitration clause.

[46] If, however, the seller reimbursed the contract price that the buyer paid by cheque that was subsequently dishonoured, restitution is regulated by national law and not by the CISG. See *Oberlandesgericht München*, January 28, 1998 ((2001) *Zeitschrift für die wirtschaftserchtliche Praxis*, 23–24).

[47] See *Bundesgerichtshof Germany*, June 25, 1997 (Unilex database, 1998; [1998] 7 *European Current Law* No. 232 [133]) where the buyer discovered, when using the stainless steel wire delivered to him by the buyer, that it was substandard. The Court held that both parties were aware that the goods had to be processed before any non-conformity could be discovered, and that the buyer was still entitled to avoid the contract.

[48] Art. 85. This can range from covering up the goods, keeping them in cold storage, to more specialised preservation (see J. Honnold, *op. cit.*, p. 576).

A buyer who rejects the delivered goods because of non-conformity, must likewise take all necessary steps reasonable under the circumstances, to preserve the goods. He similarly is then entitled to retain the goods until he has been reimbursed for his reasonable expenses.[49]

A party under an obligation to preserve goods may deposit them in the warehouse of a third party at the expense of the other party to the contract, provided the storage costs are reasonable (Article 87). The goods may be sold if there is unreasonable delay in taking possession, in paying the price or in reimbursing the preservation expenses (Article 88). The other party must be given notice of the intended sale.

Perishable goods, unreasonably expensive to preserve, may be sold in the appropriate manner. The other party must be given reasonable notice of the sale.

A party who is selling the goods for good reason may retain his expenses from the proceeds of the sale, but must refund the balance to the other party (Article 88).

PART III: INCOTERMS 2000

Origin

Supplementary clauses   International contracts of sale often contain stan-   **4.54**
dard abbreviations for place of delivery and/or place and time of passing of the risk, for the transfer of ownership, for the insurance of the transported goods, etc. By adopting such abbreviations, parties include in their contract the detailed rules covered by the abbreviation.

The oldest and most common abbreviations, mainly used for carriage by sea, are FOB (free on board) and CIF (cost, insurance and freight). However, the abbreviations do not always have precisely the same meaning in different ports and centres of trade. An FOB or a CIF sale in Hamburg,[50] Amsterdam,[51] London[52] or Vancouver[53] does not necessarily imply identical obligations.[54] This leaves scope for confusion and conflict in international trade.

---

[49] Art. 86. If the buyer is not yet in possession of the goods, but the goods were dispatched and placed at his disposal at their destination, the buyer must still take possession on behalf of the seller in order to exercise his right to reject, provided the buyer can do so without the payment of the price and without unreasonable inconvenience or expense. The buyer does not have to receive the goods if the seller himself or a person authorised by him to take charge of the goods, is present at the destination.

[50] R. Sieveking, *Die Geschäftsbedingungen des Waren-Vereins der Hamburger Börse* (1979).

[51] R. van Delden, *Overzicht van de Handelskoop* (Kluwer, Deventer, 1983).

[52] D. M. Sassoon and H. O. Merren, *C.I.F. and F.O.B. contracts* (3rd ed., Stevens & Sons, London, 1984). In England these clauses are described by the Institute of Export.

[53] M. Pomerleau and E. Lapointe, "The Canadian contract 'FOB PORT OF EMBARKATION' " (1987) I.B.L.J. 763.

[54] V. Digenopoulos, *Die Abwandlung der CIF-und FOB-Usancen europäischer Seehäfen-Lieferklau- seln im internationalen Handel* (3rd ed., 1971); F. Wooldridge, "The kinds of FOB-contracts" in *Law and International trade—Festschrift C. M. Schmitthoff* (Fischer, Frankfurt, 1973), p. 383.

4.55   **Role of the International Chamber of Commerce**   The International Chamber of Commerce (ICC) (see paragraph 2.43) has attempted to remedy this situation. As early as 1923 it published a survey of all abbreviations in use in a number of countries. Since 1936 the ICC has published the International Commercial Terms (Incoterms). The Incoterms aspire to reflect the common practice in various countries. However, in reality the national usages are so diverse, that it is impossible to give them a common interpretation.[55]

The Incoterms are regularly updated and, if necessary, revised. The original list of Incoterms was later supplemented, notably in 1953, 1967, 1976, 1980, 1990 and most recently in 2000.[56] Only the English text of Incoterms is authentic.

In each amendment, developments in international trade and in the means of transport were taken into account. While initially the Incoterms were focused on the obligations of parties in carriage by sea, the later changes, particularly since 1980, also take other forms of transport into consideration; for example, the so-called multi-modal transport in which more than one means of transport is used.[57] They have also been adapted to the development of the electronic transmission of data.[58]

In consultation with the UN's Economic Commission for Europe (see paragraph 2.22), each Incoterm is abbreviated in three letters. Until 1953 the Incoterms only concerned the following abbreviations, always mentioning the place of destination or delivery of the goods:

- C&F (cost and freight): CFR;

- CIF (cost, insurance and freight): CIF;

- delivered ex quay (duty paid): DEQ;

- delivered ex ship: DES;

- ex works: EXW;

- FAS (free alongside ship): FAS;

- FOB (free on board): FOB;

- carriage paid to . . . : CPT.

Later the following terms were added:

- delivered at frontier: DAF (1967);

---

[55] R. van Delden, *op. cit.*, pp. 19–20; D. M. Sassoon and H. O. Merren, *op. cit.*, pp. 24 *et seq.* and pp. 387 *et seq.*

[56] See *Incoterms 1990*, ICC publication no. 460 (ICC Publishing, Paris); *Incoterms 2000*, ICC Publication no. 560. For a comprehensive overview, see: www.iccwbo.org/incoterms/wallchart.

[57] See also the UN Convention of Geneva of May 24, 1980 on international (or multi-model) transport of goods, text in (1980) *European Transport Law* 487; C. J. Cheng, *Basic Documents on International Trade Law* (Kluwer Law International, 1999).

[58] See J. Ramberg, *Incoterms in the Era of Electronic Data Interchange* (Kluwer, Deventer, 1990). If electronic data interchange is used, it is for instance essential to ensure that the buyer is in the same legal position as if he had received a bill of lading from the seller.

- delivered duty paid: DDP (1967);

- free carrier . . . : FCA (1980);

- carriage and insurance paid to . . . : CIP (1980);

- delivery duty unpaid: DDU (1990).[59]

The Incoterms are not part of international customary law and they must be incorporated in the contractual relationship at least impliedly.

Classification

According to conditions In view of a better understanding and greater **4.56** transparency, the Incoterms were classified in four categories.[60] Every Incoterm lists the obligations of the seller and buyer under 10 headings, where for each heading the seller's side is the mirror image of the buyer's side.[61]

Under the C-terms, the seller must conclude the contract of carriage and pay the carrier, but he is not liable for the risk of loss of the goods, for their damage or for the extra expenses caused by events that occurred after loading and shipping of the goods: CFR (cost and freight), CIF (cost, insurance and freight), CPT (carriage paid to . . .) and CIP (carriage and insurance paid to . . .). To what point (destination) the seller has to pay the transport costs is indicated after each C-term.[62]

Under the D-terms the seller bears all risks and costs connected with the carriage of goods to the place of destination: DAF (delivered at frontier), DES (delivered ex ship), DEQ (delivered ex quay), DDU (delivered duty unpaid) and DDP (delivered duty paid).

The seller is not released from the risk and the costs before the goods have actually reached their destination. The D-terms are divided into two groups: under DAF, DES and DDU the seller delivers the goods without customs clearance, while under DEQ and DDP he must clear the goods.

There is one single E-term, *i.e.* ex works (ex factory, with indication of the named place) (EXW). Under EXW the seller makes the goods available for the buyer at the seller's own business premises (factory, workshop, storage, etc.).

Under the F-terms, the seller is expected to deliver the goods to a carrier appointed by the buyer and paid by the buyer: FCA (free carrier), FAS (free

---

[59] DDU has an important function when the seller is prepared to deliver the goods in the country of destination without customs clearance or payment of duty. DDU is particularly interesting for trade within the E.U.

[60] It would serve no purpose to summarise the various Incoterms, or even the ones most commonly used, in this short contribution. This would only cause confusion, since each Incoterm already has a well thought-out and brief indication of the obligations of the parties. See www.iccwbo.org/incoterms.

[61] If, *e.g.* for the heading "transport arrangements" of a particular Incoterm, heading A.3 states that the seller has to make the transport arrangements for which he must pay, heading B.3 will describe that the buyer has "no obligation" in this respect.

[62] Moreover, the seller is obliged to take out insurance and pay the insurance costs by virtue of CIF and CIP.

alongside ship) and FOB (free on board). In practice, the description of the "carrier" is important. If the buyer instructs the seller to deliver the goods to a person who is not a "carrier" in the normal sense, for instance a shipping agent, the seller is considered to have complied with his obligation to deliver as soon as the goods are in the charge of that person. Therefore, a carrier is not just the enterprise that actually performs the transport, but also the enterprise that contracts to perform or arrange the carriage of goods. In other words, the term "carrier" includes transporters as well as transport contractors. This definition of "carrier" complies with that adopted in the CISG[63] and in the Hamburg Rules on the carriage of goods by sea.[64]

4.57   **According to means of transport**   For any means of transport, including multi-modal transport, the following Incoterms are appropriate:

- FCA: free carrier, named place;
- CPT: carriage paid to named place of destination;
- CIP: carriage and insurance paid to named place of destination;
- DAF: delivered at frontier at named place;
- DDU: delivered duty unpaid at named place of destination;
- DDP: delivered duty paid at named place of destination.

For carriage by sea and inland waterways, the following terms are used:

- FAS: free alongside ship, named port of shipment;
- FCA: free carrier, named place;
- FOB: free on board, named port of shipment;
- CFR: cost and freight, named port of destination;
- CIF: cost, insurance and freight, agreed port of destination;
- DES: delivered ex ship, named port of destination;
- DEQ: delivered ex quay duty paid, named port of destination.

For carriage by rail transport, FCA is often used.

Effects

4.58   **Legal effects**   It is generally assumed that Incoterms are only applicable if the parties have adopted them (at least impliedly) in the contract. In practice, it

---

[63] J. Honnold, "Uniform law and uniform trade terms—two approaches to a common goal", in N. Horn and C. M. Schmitthoff, *op. cit.*, pp. 161 *et seq.*

[64] U.N. Convention on the carriage of goods by sea, Hamburg, March 30, 1978, Art. 1; text in (1978) I.L.M. 608.

is certainly recommended that parties expressly agree to adopt the Incoterms 2000 in their contractual relationship.[65] Court decisions[66] and arbitration awards[67] recognise the contractual nature of the Incoterms' binding force.

For a long time Incoterms enjoyed less acceptance in certain trading nations, such as, for instance, the United States, where Incoterms have only recently been commonly applied.[68] The Uniform Commercial Code refers to the American Foreign Trade Definitions. Therefore the parties' decision to opt for the Incoterms 2000 instead of the UCC provision must be expressed unambiguously in the contract.

Incoterms are supplementary law. Parties may refer to an Incoterm, but still adopt specific changes or additions.

Incoterms and currency reserves Each Incoterm involves different costs **4.59** for the seller or the buyer. Offers for EXW or FOB sales entail a minimum of expenses for the seller since the costs of carriage, insurance, etc., have to be borne by the buyer.

To control their foreign currency, some countries advise or compel enterprises to buy FOB and to sell CIF. In a FOB purchase the importer is usually allowed to pay in his own currency. The same applies for a CIF sale.[69]

Incoterms and the contract of sale Incoterms only concern the modalities **4.60** of delivery and the partition between seller and buyer of the risk of loss of or damage to the goods. These are only a few of the many elements of a sale contract. They have to be combined with other contract provisions and with the law applicable to the contract (see paragraph 4.02). The parties to a sale contract need to specify, for instance, the transfer of property or transfer of title to the goods. If the parties themselves did not provide for these matters in the contract of sale, these elements will be determined by the law applicable to the contract (see paragraphs 4.02–4.03). Incoterms, moreover, do not themselves deal with breach of contract and consequences following from it. Such matters have to be resolved either by specific provisions in the contract of sale or by the applicable law.

PART IV: RETENTION OF TITLE BY THE SELLER

General For the sale of goods (particularly equipment), the contract of sale **4.61** often includes a retention of title clause in which the seller retains ownership of the goods, even though they have been delivered to the buyer, until the buyer has

---

[65] See also the explanation at para. 2.43 on Incoterms 1990: "Merchants wishing to use these rules should now specify that their contracts will be governed by 'Incoterms 1990'".

[66] *e.g.* Belgian *Cass.*, June 27, 1985, (1988) R.C.J.B. 5.

[67] See, *e.g.* ICC award no. 2438 (1975), (1976) J.D.I. 968 and ICC award no. 3894 (1981), (1982) J.D.I. 987.

[68] See, *e.g. Phillips Puerto Rico Core Inc. v. Tradax Petroleum Ltd* 782 F.2d. 314 (2d. Cir., 1985).

[69] See also D. Carreau and P. Juillard, *Droit international économique* (4th ed., L.G.D.J., Paris, 1998), 295–296.

paid the price.[70] The content and effect of retention of title clause are not regulated by the CISG.

Such a clause sometimes gives rise to problems in international contracts of sale, since the respective laws may vary considerably or concerns, for instance[71]:

- the scope of the retention of title clause;

- the effects of retention of title on claims from creditors of the seller and buyer.

In practice, more than one law may be applicable to the retention of title clause in an international contract. The scope of the retention of title clause[72] (see paragraph 4.62) depends in the first instance on the parties' will and is governed ultimately by the proper law of the contract. However, a retention of title clause is more than an ordinary contractual arrangement: the *lex rei sitae, i.e.* the law of the country where the sold goods are located, applies in principle to the ownership affected by the clause. In case of the bankruptcy (insolvency) of the buyer, the law governing the bankruptcy also determines the effects of the retention of title in such cases.[73] This gives all the more reason for the seller to thoroughly investigate the legal effects of a retention of title before including such a clause in an international sales agreement.

4.62   **Scope of the retention of title clause**   It is accepted in most countries that the seller may retain the title to the goods sold until full payment of the price has been made. This applies both in countries where the transfer of property takes place by agreement at the conclusion of the contract of sale (*e.g.* in Belgium and France), as well as in countries (*e.g.* the Netherlands and Germany) where the property is transferred at another moment (*i.e.* at the time of delivery).[74] The reservation of title clause has full effect between seller and buyer. If the buyer does not pay, the seller may reclaim the goods from the buyer since he still owns them. However, depending on the legal system, problems may arise when the seller concurs with other creditors of the buyer (see paragraph 10.39).

Besides the above described common retention of title clause, there are other types of retention of title, which have considerably wider scope, in a number of countries[75]:

---

[70] For research on the practical use of reservation of title clauses in commercial contracts, see J. Spencer, "The commercial realities of reservation of title clauses" (1989) J.B.L. 220.

[71] For a thorough comparative law survey, see T. M. Margellos, *La Protection du Vendeur à Crédit d'Objets Mobiliers Corporels à Travers la Clause de Réserve de Propriété* (L.G.D.J., Paris, 1989).

[72] See Y. Loussouarn, "Les conflits de lois en matière de réserve de propriété" (1982) *Comité français de droit international privé* 91. For a telling example, see *OLG Hamm*, July 13, 1989, (1991) R.I.W. 115.

[73] J. G. Gerard, "L'opposabilité de la clause de réserve de propriété en cas de faillite internationale" (1989) R.B.D.C. 635–644.

[74] See G. Monti, G. Nejman and W. J. Reuter, "The future of reservation of title clauses in the European Community" (1997) I.C.L.Q. 886.

[75] See R. Welter, "Collateral in international trade", in N. Horn (ed.), *The Law of International Trade Finance* (Kluwer Law & Taxation, Deventer, 1989), p. 547.

- The "prolonged" retention of title protects the seller even when the sold goods are resold (proceeds of sale clause) or processed in the manufacturing of other goods (manufacture/aggregation clause). Under a proceeds of sale clause the seller is secured when the purchaser resells the goods and the sub-purchaser acts in good faith. Through the manufacture/aggregation clause the seller keeps title, even when the buyer uses the goods to manufacture other products or to incorporate them into composite products, because the seller obtains—at least partially—the ownership of the resulting product.

- Under the "current account" retention of title clause the transfer of property is not only postponed until the price is paid in full, but also until the buyer has settled all other debts to the seller.[76]

Under a retention of title clause the risk for the goods generally remains with the seller, even when the seller has already delivered the sold goods. Nevertheless, the buyer may contractually agree to take over the risk.

Retention of title and bankruptcy of the buyer   The retention of title is   **4.63** more effective if the seller can also oppose his title against third parties, that is to say, for example, in the event of bankruptcy of the buyer against the other creditors of the buyer.

Until recently, according to Belgian law, the retention of title could not be invoked against other creditors of the buyer in the event of the latter's bankruptcy. In that case the unpaid seller could only claim payment. Presently in Belgium and in other countries,[77] however, the retention of title may be invoked against other creditors of the bankrupt buyer. The impact of a retention of title *vis-à-vis* other creditors of the buyer is covered by a specific statute in France (May 12, 1980).[78] The European Insolvency Regulation (Article 7) (see paragraph 10.35) indicates that retention of title is not automatically affected by the *lex concursus* when the goods were outside the area of the courts where the insolvency was declared.

Harmonisation of laws   Many attempts have been made to harmonise the   **4.64** laws, or at least the private international law rules, in respect of retention of title in international sales. Harmonisation becomes increasingly important in the light of the increase in international trade and also the growth of the European Union

---

[76] In Germany there is also the Konzernvorbehalt: the buyer will only obtain the title of property of the sold good if he pays the seller, but also honours his debts in respect of other entities of the group of which the seller forms a part.

[77] Belgium: Art. 101 Insolvency Act; Germany: Art. 49 Konkursordnung; the Netherlands: see O. K. Brahn, *Fiduciaire Eigendomsoverdracht en Eigendomsvoorbehoud* (Tjeenk, Zwolle, 1978) (including the customary standard clauses in the Netherlands, *op. cit.*, pp. 39–40); U.K.: see G. McCormack, *Reservation of Title* (1st ed., Sweet & Maxwell, London, 1990); C. Kessel, "Eigentumsvoerbehalt und Rezession in Grossbritannien", (1991) R.I.W. 812. See also J. W. Rutgers, *International reservation of title clauses, a study of Dutch, French and German Private International Law in the light of the European law* (TMC Asser Press, The Hague, 1999).

[78] *cf.* C. Klein, "Schutzwirkung des Eigentumsvorbehalts im französischen Insolvenzverfahren" (1991) R.I.W. 809; F. Perochon, *La Réserve de Propriété* (Litec, Paris, 1988). If goods, subject to retention of title, are resold by the buyer, the first seller is entitled to receive the proceeds of this resale: the sold good must still be in its original state.

and the harmonisation of its laws.[79] However, harmonisation in the field of property law is particularly difficult. Another problem is that relationships between different security instruments vary in the national legal systems of states.[80]

For many years the Council of Europe has attempted to introduce common substantive rules through a convention. The Council thought that setting a minimum standard for retention of titles would be sufficient.[81] However, countries such as Austria, Germany and the Netherlands, where there is wider experience of comprehensive clauses, insisted that retention of titles clauses remained unchanged in their jurisdictions. The European Commission has also prepared various drafts for a directive on the external effect of the retention of title. No agreement has been reached. Where the Council's initiative aimed particularly at the substantive unification, the draft directive aimed rather at common conflict of law rules. Both proposals were restricted to the common retention of title clause and until present no solution has been found.

In the United States, Article 9 of the Uniform Commercial Code[82] regulates retention of title clauses and, more generally, security instruments, no matter what they are called or the form they take. It was first introduced in 1962 and subsequently amended in 1972 and 1998–1999. The purpose of Article 9 is to introduce a single "unitary" security device. It creates a registration scheme and introduces one set of basic terms (e.g. "security agreement", "secured party", "debtor", "collateral"[83] and "security interests") to replace different security devices such as pledges and conditional sales.

---

[79] Monti, Nejman, and Reuter, op. cit., 886, 867.

[80] See Monti, Nejman and Reuter, op. cit., pp. 894–896, for the situation in Europe.

[81] Monti, Nejman and Reuter, op. cit., p. 892.

[82] For a comprehensive explanation of Art. 9, see J. J. White and R. S. Summers, Uniform Commercial Code (5th ed., West Group, St. Paul, 2000) pp. 709–919.

[83] "collateral" has been defined as any tangible or intangible asset owned by the debtor in which the debtor grants a security interest to its secured creditor. See op. cit., p. 712.

CHAPTER 5

DISTRIBUTION AGREEMENTS

Importance   Almost all products pass from supplier to final consumer via a   **5.01**
distribution system. The producer often has to set up a distribution network for
the efficient marketing of his products. Indeed, it is usually necessary to sell
through "local" persons. These local salesmen are generally more aware of the
needs and opportunities of the local market and help to create the impression that
the product is familiar and trustworthy. Furthermore, they can give after-sales
service.

Forms of distribution   There are many ways of setting up a distribution   **5.02**
network. A distribution network can consist of distributors *sensu stricto*, agents,
occasional intermediaries and/or sales representatives.[1]

A distributor has been granted by the producer or importer the right to sell in
a particular area. He buys the goods and sells them to customers. His earnings are
the difference between the purchase price and the sales price of the goods.
Distributors provide the producer with an effective distribution system, obviating
the need for the producer to develop every point of sale. Moreover, the distributors can guarantee regular sales.

An agent does not buy the goods in order to sell them on. Instead, he seeks out
customers for a principal and transmits their orders to this principal; if necessary,
he may enter into contracts for his principal. He has no title to the goods he is
offering for sale, and in this he differs from the distributor. The producer
maintains control (*i.e.* over the price) when he markets his products through
agents.

Local agents are often used for sales to the authorities and for distribution in
small markets. In some Arab countries the intervention of a local agent is
compulsory. The authorities there must often be informed about the content of the
agency agreement; they sometimes impose a standard agency contract.[2-3]

---

[1] R. Baldi, *Distributorship, Franchising, Agency: Community and National Laws and Practice in the
EC* (Kluwer, Deventer, 1987); R. Baldi, *Le Droit de la Distribution Commerciale dans l'Europe
Communautaire* (Bruylant, Brussels, 1988); H. King, D. Campbell and L. Lafili (eds) *Distributor-
ship, agency and franchising in an international arena: Europe, the United States, Japan and Latin
America* (Kluwer, Deventer, 1990); G. Bogaert and U. Lohmann (ed.), *Commercial Agency and
Distribution Agreements: Law and Practice in the Member States of the European Community and
the European Free Trade Association* (Graham & Trotman, London, 1993).

[2-3] For Saudi Arabia, Royal Decree No. 11 of 20.2.1382, executed by the Implementation Rules No.
1897 of 24.5.1401 H. See A. Hamid El-Ahdab, *Arbitration with the Arab Countries* (Kluwer,
Deventer, 1990) pp. 613–614.

An occasional intermediary has in principle no obligation to actively and continuously promote business within the territory or towards a group of customers for which he is responsible: he may agree to promote a specific business, or to inform the counterpart about business which may come to his notice, without any continuing obligation to develop the market. Moreover, the activity of an occasional intermediary may be limited to the simple supply of information about a possible business (names of potential customers, indication of a particular deal, etc.), while the commercial agent's activity comprises necessarily the negotiation of contracts on behalf of the principal.

A sales representative is an employee acting in name and on behalf of his company. He works under a contract of employment—this is in contrast to the agent who acts independently in name and on behalf of the principal. The sales representative is specifically protected in many countries by the law, which entitles him to severance pay and customer compensation at the termination of the contract.

Commercial considerations, local laws, exchange regulations, customs and tax considerations determine the type of distribution channels.

Are the goods to be sold directly? Through an independent distributor? Through a local agent? Each choice has its advantages and disadvantages. Distributors and/or agents are, in some countries, protected by law. This could, for instance be a reason for the manufacturer to opt for a distribution system that is not covered by that law.

Distribution patterns may evolve. Often, the manufacturer starts by supplying the market directly. When the market is sufficiently large, he operates through agents and finally, he appoints an independent distributor. The manufacturer may later regret that part of the profits flows to his distributors and so set up his own sale companies, or may revert to direct sales.

The use of sales representatives and occasional intermediaries is less common in international distribution. Therefore, attention will be focused on the distributor (see paragraph 5.03) and the agent (paragraph 5.22).

PART I: DISTRIBUTION AGREEMENTS

5.03   **Legal framework**   Manufacturers generally bring their products on the market through wholesalers; wholesalers usually distribute through retailers. The relationship between manufacturer and wholesaler or between wholesaler and retailer is usually laid down in a distribution agreement which contains a sales concession and a supply and/or purchase agreement.

- A sales concession obliges the supplier to allow the distributor to resell the products to end users for the duration of the contract.

- A purchase agreement obliges the distributor to purchase products from the other party for the duration of the agreement.

- A supply agreement obliges the other party to supply these goods for the duration of the contract.

The distribution agreement gives the framework for the future purchases by the distributor from his supplier (as distinguished from the successive contracts of sale which effect these deliveries). Moreover it specifies how the distributor will cover the market assigned to him.

Distribution agreements are usually covered by the general law of contract. Generally, the agreement does not require a written document in order to make it valid, it being usually sufficient that the mutual agreement of the parties is established. However, it is best that the relationship between parties is documented from the very start in a clear contract. Oral agreements and gentlemen's agreements are doubtful beacons in the event of a dispute.

Private international law   In the European Union, the contractual relation- **5.04** ship between the principal and the distributor is governed by the European Contracts Convention (see paragraph 1.29). If no law is chosen by the parties (Article 3), the contract is governed by the law of the country with which the distribution agreement is most closely connected (Article 4, 1). This is presumed to be the law of the country where the party who has to effect the characteristic performance has his habitual residence (Article 4, 2). For distribution agreements, the distributor effects the characteristic performance; thus the law of the habitual residence of the distributor is usually the proper law of the contract.

However, distribution agreements may also be subject to the mandatory rules of the country where goods are distributed. Indeed, even if a law is chosen, the mandatory rules of the country with which the agreement has close connections may be relevant (Article 7, 1); if the case is brought before a court of this country, its mandatory rules must be applied (Article. 7, 2). Therefore, if, for instance, the agreement has effect on Belgian territory, the Belgian statute on exclusive distributors may govern the termination of the contract (see paragraph 5.07).

Drafting a distribution contract   Parties have great contractual freedom in **5.05** the determination of their reciprocal rights and obligations. In order to make good contracts they have to pay attention to the following factors:

- Who are the parties to the agreement? In some cases more legal entities belong to the same economic group: which legal entity will be responsible for the contractual obligations? Can the contractual obligations be transferred to other entities of the group; to a third party? Does the agreement remain valid if the other party is taken over by a competitor?

- The distribution agreement must clearly define the object of the relationship. For which products is the distribution granted? What about new products? For which territory? Is the distributor the exclusive representative for that area? Is the supplier also allowed to deliver directly?, etc.

  It is, in general, not customary for a distributor to sell way outside his geographic area, *i.e.* his "natural" market. Transport costs and possible double customs duties often make this exercise unappealing. Within the European Union, however, there are no customs duties, and the transport costs are likely to be less. In this situation, sales outside the distribution areas and possible parallel imports into the area of another distributor may become appealing. Through territorial exclusivity the distributor can protect himself against competition from outside. However, for example, within the European Union, this protection must not go too far otherwise it will conflict with the competition rules (see paragraph 5.13).

- Is the distributor allowed to distribute competing products during and after termination of the agreement? It is important to specify whether the distributor will exclusively deal in the products of the supplier or whether he may also distribute competitive, products. It is also important that the distributor does not become a competitor of the supplier after termination of the contract. To avoid this, it is useful to include a non-competition clause to regulate the position after termination of contract. The agreement should, therefore, also regulate the return of the remaining stock, which the distributor is no longer allowed to sell.

- Is the distributor obliged to keep certain commercial or technical information confidential during or after the life of the agreement?

- To what extent is the distributor responsible for the publicity and promotion of the product? Will the manufacturer supply him with brochures and other material for this purpose? How?

- Is the distributor obliged to notify the supplier about any breach of the supplier's intellectual property rights (patents, trademarks, etc.) and defend these rights in law ?

- Under what modalities are the goods to be sold to the distributor (price, place of delivery, place and time of payment, currency of payment)? A purchase price which is too high will drive the distributor out of the market.

  It is recommended that a price list should be attached to the distribution agreement. Moreover, the power of the supplier to increase the price is often limited by contract. In that case the distributor may, for example, have stipulated that the new price list will only be effective after three months or, at least, that it will not affect orders already placed.

- To what extent can annual minimum sales quotas be imposed? Are these quotas only indicative, or are they sanctioned by contract termination ? How will future sales quotas be determined?

- Is a recommended sales price suggested to the distributor? It is contrary to E.U. competition rules and to the laws of many countries to oblige the distributor or resellers to sell the goods for a fixed price; they must have freedom to fix their own sales price. In some countries the distributor is considered to be an agent and is covered by the rules for agencies if he is not free to determine his own price. Although the supplier may want to recommend sales prices, as soon as a recommended price becomes in fact binding, it may infringe competition law (see paragraph 5.13).

- Is the distributor obliged to keep products in stock, to maintain certain quality standards for his staff, to give a certain service? Some products require a large stock, expensive equipment and/or qualified staff. In such a situation the distributor may be obliged to make considerable investments.

- What is the term of the agreement? Distributors understandably hesitate to invest in their business if their distribution rights can be terminated at will by the manufacturer. The supplier on the other hand may not want to be bound for too long. For him it is essential to keep some room to manoeuvre.

The agreement is sometimes concluded for a specific term. However, usually it is entered into for an indefinite time but either party is given the right of terminating the agreement upon a specific date after having given notice of a fixed number of months before that date.

In order to reconcile the interests of both sides the agreement sometimes indicates that it cannot be terminated during an initial period but may be renewed afterwards. The parties may also accept that the agreement will be terminated if specific criteria are not met (*e.g.* sales quota, sales increases, promotion activities). Likewise, the parties may agree that specific conditions (*e.g.* the insolvency of a party, etc.) terminate the contract. The agreement may thus give the manufacturer a wide range of options for dismissing the distributor. These contractual clauses, however, are sometimes void under the law of the distribution area (see paragraph. 5.06).

- Distribution agreements must determine what will happen when the agreement comes to an end. Must compensation be paid for goodwill? Must stock be returned and if so, under what conditions? May the distributor start dealing in competing products?

- What law is applicable to the agreement? It is recommended that the distribution agreement should indicate the law applicable to the agreement. If no choice of law is made, the law of the residence of the distributor is generally applicable (unless there is evidence of a closer connection with another legal system) (see paragraph 5.04). Even though a particular law is applicable to the agreement, local mandatory law may be applicable to specific matters such as, for instance, to the termination of the agreement (see paragraphs 5.06–5.07).

- A choice of forum clause (see paragraph 10.08) or an arbitration clause (paragraph 11.14) may indicate which instance will settle possible disputes concerning the distribution agreement.

Termination of the distribution agreement

5.06   Definite and indefinite term   If the distribution agreement has been entered into for a fixed period, the distributor knows in advance how long the relationship will last and what he can expect. When the end of the contract term comes in sight, he will have adequate time to take appropriate measures; he may liquidate his stocks and reduce his investments, or look for another distributorship.

However, there is a great chance that a fixed-term distributor will not put the same vigour into his efforts near the end of the contract term as a distributor who expects his distributorship to go on for a long time. For that reason, suppliers and distributors often agree to a distributorship for an indefinite period: the distributor will commit himself fully to his distributorship in the hope that the relationship will continue for a very long time.

When a distributorship is granted for an indefinite period in principle the supplier may always terminate such an agreement. In most countries, unfair cancellation of a distributorship agreement gives rise to a right to damages. In some countries the distributor has an additional right to compensation for acquired customers, goodwill, etc. Hereafter, Belgian and German law illustrate how legal systems may protect distributors.

5.07   Belgium   Under the Belgian Act on the termination of Distributorships of July 27, 1961 the distributor for an indefinite period may claim compensation when no reasonable notice of termination has been given, on condition that the termination of contract is not due to a serious breach on the part of the distributor. The distributor may also claim additional compensation for the customers who turn to the supplier or the new distributor after termination of the distribution agreement, for reimbursement for investments made and, for costs incurred for employees dismissed because of the termination of the distribution agreement.

5.08   Germany   Under German law the termination of the distribution agreement is regulated by the agency law (Article 89b HGB) when the distributor is in a situation of economic subordination to the supplier comparable to that of a *Handelsvertreter*. The distributor has a right to compensation for the customers he has made (*Ausgleichsanspruch*). Similarly to Belgian law, this compensation cannot be claimed if the termination of the distributorship is due to a breach of contract by the distributor, but compensation remains due if the supplier's behaviour justifies that the distributor terminates the contract.

PART II: FRANCHISE AGREEMENTS

5.09   Definition   The franchise agreement is a contract in which the franchisor grants an independent franchisee the right to sell goods (*e.g.* clothes, fast food, toys, furniture) or services (*e.g.* software consultancy, hotel accommodation, car hire) under the distinctive sign of the franchisor and to make use of the uniform sales presentation. The franchisee may also avail himself of the know-how of the franchisor and benefit from the franchisor's commercial and technical assistance.

Sometimes the franchisee manufactures the goods which he markets. In that case the franchise agreement is a mere licence for the use of a trademark and a house-style and for the transfer of know-how and technology. These contracts are considered in the next chapter (see paragraphs 6.06 *et seq.* and particularly paragraph 6.12). Generally, however, the franchisee buys some or all products from the franchisor. Such a franchise agreement then is a kind of distribution agreement.

In addition to the investment in the sales outlet, the franchisee usually must also pay "front money" before being admitted to the franchise chain, being allowed to make use of the franchise mark and/or presentation and benefiting from the collective publicity of the franchise chain. In addition, he is obliged to regularly pay a royalty or continuing franchise fee for such use during the term of the contract. Moreover, he also has to pay the franchisor for the goods purchased from the latter.

The franchisee is generally granted a certain exclusivity to sell in his area, often on condition that he fulfils specific conditions (*e.g.* turnover, stocks, purchases).

Franchisors and franchisees may find inspiration for a contract which strikes a fair balance between their respective rights and responsibilities in the ICC Model International Franchising Contract.[4]

In most countries the franchise agreement is an innominate contract, governed by general contract law. However, some countries, including the United States, Canada and Japan, have specific franchise laws.

Termination of the franchise agreement The franchisee is usually **5.10** appointed *intuitu personae*. The agreement, therefore, often includes a clause which terminates the contract if the franchisee goes bankrupt or his business is taken over. Even when this is not stipulated in the agreement, the franchise agreement will normally end under these circumstances.[5] Besides, the law applicable to the termination of distribution agreements is often applied to the termination of franchise agreements (see paragraph 5.06).[6]

Private international law The franchise agreement is generally considered **5.11** to be subject to the law of the country where the franchisor resides, if the franchise agreement does not nominate another law. For it is the franchisor who effects the characteristic performance, which is relevant for the proper law of contract (see paragraph 1.31). However, one may also consider that the franchisee delivers the characteristic performance so that the proper law may be the law of the franchisee.[6a] Of course, the mandatory rules of the country of the franchi-

---

[4] ICC Publication no. 557.

[5] O. J. Marrorati, "Termination of the franchise relationship" (1997) Int'l.Bus.Law. 216

[6] G. Bogaert and U. Lohmann (eds), *Commercial Agency and Distribution Agreements* (Belgium) pp. 96–97 (Denmark) 123, (Germany) 205, (the Netherlands) pp. 328–329, (Norway) 481.

[6a] See, *e.g.* F. Vischer, L. Huber and D. Oser, *Internationales Vertragsrecht* (Stâmpfli Bern, 2000), p. 306; J. M. Leloup, *La Franchise* (Delmas Paris, 2000), p. 375.

see may also be applicable—even though another law is chosen as the proper law of the contract (see paragraph 1.26).

PART III: VERTICAL AGREEMENTS AND OBSERVANCE OF COMPETITION RULES

5.12   **Setting the scene**   Distribution and franchise agreements, as other types of vertical agreements,[7-8] often limit the competition opportunities of the supplier and/or the distributor/franchisee. For example, the supplier may give up the right to appoint other distributors/franchisees or to sell directly the distribution area. The distributor/franchisee may forgo his right to distribute products, which compete with those of the supplier; he may commit himself not to sell outside his area, etc.

However, national competition law may restrict the possibility for parties to limit competition by distribution contract or franchise agreement.[9] Within the E.U., E.C. competition law also imposes some restrictions.[10]

5.13   **E.U. versus national competition rules**   As a result of the coexistence of E.U. and national competition rules, it is important to know whether the Commission or the competent national authorities have jurisdiction in competition cases. As a general rule, Community law takes precedence over national law. This means that national courts have a duty not to apply national law which conflicts with Community law.[11] As a result, behaviour that infringes Community law can never be authorised under national law.[12] Further, Articles 81(1), (2) and Article 82 of the Treaty have direct effect and may be applied by national courts. In respect of Article 81(3), currently only the Commission has the power to grant exemptions from the Provisions of Article 81(1).[13]

Finally, competence over competition matters is divided between the Community and the Member States, depending on whether or not the conduct has an

---

[7-8] Vertical agreements are agreements between undertakings which operate, for purposes of the agreement, at a different level of the production or distribution chain and which relate to the conditions under which the parties may purchase, sell or resell certain goods or services (Art. 2 of Regulation of December 12, 1999: 2790/1999: [1999] O.J. L336/21).

[9] See, for the applicability of the respective national competition laws, L. Idot, "Quelques pistes pour la résolution des conflits de droits de la concurrence en matière de distribution" (1993) D.P.C.I. 214; D. I. Baker, A. N. Campbell and M. J. Reynolds, *Global Forum on Competition and Trade Policy, Harmonisation of International Competition Law Enforcement* (1996).

[10] R. Whish and B. Sufrin, *Competition Law* (3rd ed., Butterworth, London, 1993); D. G. Goyder, *E.C. Competition Law* (3rd ed, Clarendon Press, Oxford, 1998); J. Faull and A. Nikpay, *The E.C. Law of Competition* (University Press, Oxford, 1999); V. Korah, *Cases and Materials on E.C. Competition Law* (Hart, Oxford, 1998); R. Lane, *E.C. Competition Law* (Addison-Wesley, Reading (Mass). 1999); P. Taylor, *E.C. and United Kingdom Competition Law and Compliance: a Practical Guide* (Sweet & Maxwell, London, 1999); M. Furse, *Competition Law of the United Kingdom and E.C.* (Blackstone Press, London, 1999).

[11] Case 6/64, *Costa v. Enel* [1964] E.C.R. 585.

[12] Case 123/83, *BNIC v. Clair* [1985] E.C.R. 391.

[13] Art. 9(1) of Regulation 17/62. Current proposals, from the Commission to the Council, if effected, will result in the national authorities and courts being authorised to grant exemptions under Art. 81(3). Proposal for a Council Regulation "on the implementation of the rules on competition laid down in Articles 81 and 82 of the Treaty". COM (2000) 582 of September 27, 2000.

effect on inter-state trade. If no such effect exists, national law will govern the case. It must be remembered that even where an agreement is confined to one Member State, E.U. competition law will apply if market partitioning will result.[14] If inter-state trade is affected, both Community and national law may be applied; however, the application of national competition law must not impair the effectiveness and uniformity of Community competition rules and the measures taken to enforce them. The Commission issued a notice containing guidelines on the allocation of competence and the co-operation between Community and national authorities,[15] If the proposed reforms are brought to fruition, a network of close co-operation will arise,[16] with cases being allocated informally according to the "best placed authority".[17]

Article 81(1) and (2) E.C. Treaty: prohibition Distribution and franchise   **5.14** agreements are covered by the competition rules of Article 81 E.C. Treaty. This Article declares in section 1:

> "The following shall be prohibited as incompatible with the common market: all agreements between undertakings, decisions by associations of undertakings and concerted practices which may affect trade between Member States and which have as their object or effect the prevention, restriction or distortion of competition within the common market . . . ".

To fall within the prohibition of Article 81, the distribution/franchise agreement has "to affect trade between Member States" and "to prevent, restrict or distort competition within the common market". However, this does not mean that Article 81 only covers distribution agreements between a supplier and a distributor/franchisee who reside in different E.U. countries. Even an agreement between a supplier and a distributor/franchisee in the same country may affect inter-state trade (*e.g.* because this agreement is part of a national distribution network which inhibits imports from abroad).[18] Moreover, it is not necessary for the parties to be established within the E.U., since the prohibition extends to undertakings that affect the market from outside the E.U.[19]

Under Article 81(2), agreements contrary to Article 81(1) are void. Such agreements or, at least, of clauses infringing Article 81(1), cannot be enforced in court.

---

[14] Case C–8/72 *Vereniging van Cementhandelaren v. Commission* [1972] E.C.R. 977; [1973] C.M.L.R. 8179 at 29–30.
[15] Commission Notice on co–operation between national competition authorities and the Commission in handling cases falling within the scope of Arts [81] or [82] of the E.C. Treaty: [1997] O.J. C313/3.
[16] Proposed Regulation Art. 11.
[17] Explanatory Memorandum to the proposed Regulation, under C.1.(a)
[18] Case C–8/72 *Vereniging van Cementhandelaren v. Commission* [1972] E.C.R. 977.
[19] *Sixth Report on Competition Policy* (1976) 34. Cases 89, 104, 114, 116, 117, and 125–129/85, *Woodpulp* [1988] E.C.R. 5193.

If there is a risk that an agreement infringes Article 81(1), the agreement may be notified to the Commission to obtain a negative clearance, which means that the Commission does not consider the agreement in breach of Article 81(1).[20] Historically, as a general rule, failure to notify an agreement to the Commission resulted in significant fines, if the agreement was later found to be in breach of Article 81(1). However, since the entry into force of the new block exemption (see paragraph 5.19), the parties to a vertical agreement are no longer required to notify their agreement from the outset in order to be immune from fines (*cf.* below).[21]

5.15   **De minimis**   The prohibition of Article 81(1) does not apply if the agreement has only limited effect on the market (*e.g.* if the parties only have a small share of the market of the contract product).[22] In its *Notice on Agreements of Minor Importance*, the Commission declared that no Article 81(1) issues are raised by agreements between small and medium-sized enterprises with fewer than 250 employees and a turnover of less than € 40 million. Agreements between larger companies will be regarded *de minimis* if the parties to the agreement are under relevant market share criteria. For vertical agreements, this market share threshold is 10 per cent. However, this does not apply to price-fixing clauses or clauses granting absolute territorial protection: such clauses may infringe Article 81(1) however small the parties' market share.[23]

5.16   **Article 81(3) E.C. Treaty: exemption**   Some restrictions may have a beneficial effect. Article 81(3), therefore, exempts from the competition rules agreements which "contribute to improving the production or distribution of goods or to promoting technical or economic progress, while allowing consumers a fair share of the resulting benefit". This exemption is granted on condition that

---

[20] This Procedure will no longer be available if the competition reforms (see paragraph 5.13) are carried through.

[21] Under the proposed regulation, as there will no longer be a requirement to notify, parties may become subject to fines of up to 10% of annual turnover where they intentionally or negligently infringe Arts 81 or 82. (Art. 22.2 of the proposed Regulation.)

[22] Cases 56/65 *LTM v. MBU* [1996] E.C.R. 235; Case 5/69 *Völk v. Vervaecke* [1969] E.C.R. 302; Case 1/71 *Cadillon v. Höss* [1971] E.C.R. 356.

[23] Commission Notice on agreements of minor importance which do not fall within the meaning of Article 81(1) of the Treaty establishing the European Community: [1997] O.J. C372/13. In May 2001, the Commission published a draft revising *de minimis* notice, inviting interested parties to comment on it (Notice of the Commission relating to the revision of the 1997 notice on agreements of minor importance which do not fall under Article 81(1) of the E.C. Treaty: [2001] O.J. C149/18). According to the Commission's proposal, the market share threshold would be set at 10% for agreements between competitors and 15% for other types of agreement (para. 8). In the case of agreements between both competitors and non-competitors in markets where there are parallel networks of agreements by suppliers or distributors, the market share threshold is reduced to 5% (para. 9). With regard to vertical agreements, the *de minimis* rules would never apply to agreements containing hardcore restrictions of Art. 4 of block exemption Regulation 2790/1999 (*cf.* para. 5.17). Agreements between small and medium-sized enterprises would no longer be caught under the *de minimis* rule, but the commission considers that, based on the case law of the Court of Justice, these agreements rarely affect inter-state trade. These agreements may, of course, always be subject to national competition laws.

competition is not in fact completely eliminated or restricted more than is necessary.

Parties may always request an exemption by notifying their agreement to the Commission.[24] When the Commission is convinced of the beneficial effect of the agreement, it may grant an exemption. Exemptions have been granted for a number of distribution/franchise agreements.[25] However, when a distribution/franchise agreement forbids all sales outside its own market, competition is restricted too much for an exemption to be granted.[26]

Block exemptions Distribution and franchise agreements, like some other   **5.17** agreements, are usually intended to promote proper regulation of the market and have little adverse effect on competition. The benefits that flow from exclusive distribution agreements have been recognised by the ECJ[27] which considered that such agreements would not restrict competition if the appointment enabled a manufacturer to penetrate a new market. A manufacturer may agree not to distribute within the exclusive distributor's territory. Additionally, the exclusive distributors may be restricted from actively selling in another territory; however, passive sales cannot be prohibited, as such a restriction would amount to absolute and thus illegal territorial protection.[28]

In order to avoid individual examination of each and every distribution/franchise (or, more generally, vertical) agreement, the Commission declared that these agreements satisfy the conditions laid down in Article 81(3) of the Treaty if their content conforms to given criteria.

Historically Group exemptions existed in the area of vertical agreements: **5.18** for exclusive distribution,[29] for exclusive purchasing (including beer supply and service station agreements),[30] and for franchising agreements.[31] In addition, a

---

[24] The current system of notification is governed by Regulation 17/62: First Regulation Implementing Articles 81 and 82 of the Treaty [1962] O.J. 204, as last amended by Regulation 1216/99 [1999] O.J. L148/5. See also L.O. Blanko, *E.C. Competition Procedure* (Clarendon Press, Oxford, 1996); R. Whish and B. Sufrin, *Competition Law* (3rd ed. Butterworth, London, 1993) pp. 285–330; D. G. Goyder, *E.C. Competition Law* (3rd ed., Clarendon Press, Oxford, 1998) pp. 256–273; W. P. J. Wils, "Notification, clearance and exemption in European Community competition law: an economic analysis" (1999) 24 E.L.Rev. 139. If the Commission proposals (see para 5.13) are brought about, the notification system will be abolished in favour of a "self-analysis" by the parties to the agreement with the risk of fines where the parties intentionally or negligently infringed Arts 81 or 82 (see para. 5.14).

[25] see, *e.g.* Decision of July 8, 1965, *D.R.U./Blondel* [1965] O.J. L2194; Decision of December 19, 1974, *Duro-Dyne/Eurpair* [1975] O.J. L29/11; Decision of December 19, 1974, *Goodyear Italiana/Euram* [1975] O.J. L38/10; Decision of February 24, 1999, *Whitbread* [1999] O.J. L88/26. With regard to franchising: Decision of July 13, 1987, *Computerland* [1987] O.J. L222/12.

[26] Decision of September 23, 1964, *Consten-Grundig* [1964] O.J. L2545; Cases 56 and 58/64 *Consten-Grundig* [1966] E.C.R. 513.

[27] Case 56/65 *Société Technique Miniére v. Maschinenbau Ulm GmbH* [1966] E.C.R. 235; [1966] C.M.L.R. 357.

[28] Joined Case 56 & 58/64 *Consten and Grundig v. Commission* [1966] E.C.R. 299; [1966] C.M.L.R. 418.

[29] Regulation 1983/83 [1983] O.J. L173/1.

[30] Regulation 1984/93 [1983] O.J. L173/5.

[31] Regulation 4087/88 [1988] O.J. L359/46.

specific regulation was introduced for the exemption of motor vehicle distribution agreements.[32] If an agreement complied with the requirements of the block exemption regulation, it fell automatically outside the scope of the cartel prohibition. No individual exemption had to be requested from the Commission. The regulations concerning these group exemptions contained lists with so-called "white" and "black" clauses. The use of "white" clauses, the permissible restrictive clauses, in a vertical agreement ensured the application of the exemption. The use of "black" clauses rendered the group exemption automatically inapplicable. This black clause approach enabled manufacturers and distributors to frame their agreements so that they fell within the sector-specific rules and did not have to be notified to the Commission. These block exemptions, which were the subject of increasing critique, expired on May 31, 2000.[33]

5.19   **The new block exemption**   Since June 1, 2000, a new general block exemption regulation has replaced the block exemptions concerning distribution (except motor vehicle distribution), purchasing, and franchise agreements.[34] It is accompanied by "guidelines" published by the Commission in order to render its application more transparent.[35] One of the fundamental changes to the block exemptions has been the abolition of the "white" listed clauses. This considerably increases the scope of the parties to create agreements as they see fit, providing always that they do not contain "black" clauses.

The new block exemption applies to vertical agreements in general, such as industrial supply agreements, both exclusive and non-exclusive distribution and

---

[32] Regulation 1475/95 [1995] O.J. L145/25 (formerly Regulation 123/85 [1985] O.J. L15/16). This regulation has been the object of critical evaluation by the Commission: Report on the evaluation of Regulation (E.C.) no. 1475/95 on the application of Article [81](3) of the Treaty to certain categories of motor vehicle distribution and servicing agreements, adopted by the Commission on November 11, 2000: COM (2000) 743 final (not published, but see http://europa.eu.int:comm/ competition/carsector/distribution/evalreg147595/report). For critical comments, see also K. Middleton, "The legal framework for motor vehicle distribution—a new model?"(2001) 22 E.C.L.R. 3; J. M. Thouvenin, "Vers une remise en cause du système de distribution des automobiles en Europ? A propos du rapport de la Commission européenne sur l'évaluation du règlement (CE) n° 1745/95 sur les accords de distribution et de service de vente et d'après-vente de véhicules automobiles" (2001) 447 Rev. Marché Commun et de l'U.E. 240.

[33] J. Nazerali and D. Cowan, "Reforming E.U. Distribution Rules—has the Commission found vertical reality?" (1999) 20 E.C.L.R. 159; V. Korah, "The future of vertical agreements under European Community competition law" (1998) 19 E.C.L.R. 506; A. Kilmisch and B. Krueger, "Decentralised application of European Community competition law: current practice and future prospects" (1999) 24 E.L.Rev. 463; J. Lever and S. Neubauer, "Vertical restraints, their motivation and justification" (2000) 21 E.C.L.R. 7; J. Nazerali and D. Cowan, "Unlocking E.U. Distribution Rules—has the Commission found the right keys?" (2000) 21 E.C.L.R. 50; *ibid*, "Legislative developments: the removal of vertical restraints in E.C. Competition policy", (1998) 4 Colum.J.E.L. 194.

[34] Regulation 2790/1999 [1999] O.J. L336/21. See also J. Bocken, "Verordening 2790/99: de nieuwe groepsvrijstelling voor verticale overeenkomsten" (2000–2001) R.W. 897; J. Ratliff and A. De Matteis, "European Commission adopts block Exemption on vertical restraints" (2000) 28 Int'l.Bus.Law. 206; J. Boyce, "Analysing vertical agreements under the competition rules" (2000) European Counsel 27; I. Igartua, "How will the new vertical restraints regulation affect franchising" (2000) Intern. Bus. Lawyer, 163.

[35] Commission Notice: guidelines on vertical restraints: [2000] O.J. C291/1.

purchasing arrangements, selective distribution agreements, franchise agreements, etc. Its scope has also been broadened to cover not only agreements, but also concerted practices between undertakings,[36] as well as agreements between more than two undertakings. In addition, it covers both final and intermediate goods as well as services. It does not apply to agreements between competing undertakings, except in three situations,[37] nor does it apply to agreements, covered by other block exemption regulations.[38]

The new block exemption can only apply to agreements where the supplier (or, in the case of vertical agreements containing exclusive supply purchase obligations, the buyer) has a market share not exceeding 30 per cent of the relevant market.[39] The definition of the relevant market requires a delimitation of both the relevant product and the relevant geographical market.[40] The 30 per cent market share threshold is calculated on the basis of the market sales value of the contract goods or services and other goods or services sold by the supplier, which are regarded as interchangeable or substitutable by the buyer by reason of the products' characteristics, their prices and their intended use.[41]

Restrictions Irrespective of the market share of the undertakings concerned, **5.20** if a vertical agreement contains one or more of the "hardcore" restrictions listed in Article 4 of Regulation 2790/99, the entire agreement will not benefit from the

---

[36] A concerted practice is a form of coordination between undertakings which, without having reached the stage where an agreement properly so called has been concluded, knowingly substitutes practical cooperation between them for the risks of competition (Case 48/69 *ICI v. Commission* [1972] E.C.R. 619).

[37] The exemption applies to non-reciprocal vertical agreements entered into between competing undertakings if (i) the buyer has a total annual turnover not exceeding € 100 million; (ii) the supplier is a manufacturer and a distributor of goods, while the buyer is a distributor not manufacturing goods competing with the contract goods; or (iii) the supplier is a provider of services at several levels of trade, while the buyer does not provide competing services at the level of trade where it purchases the contract services (see Art. 2(4) of Regulation 2790/1999).

[38] These other regulations concern motor vehicle distribution (Regulation 1475/95 [1995] O.J. L145/25), technology transfer (Regulation 240/96 [1996] O.J. L31/2), specialisation (Regulation 2658/2000 [2000] O.J. L304/3), and research and development (Regulation of 2659/2000 [2000] O.J. L304/7).

[39] Where the 30% threshold is exceeded, the agreement, decision or concerted practice cannot benefit from the block exemption and requires an individual exemption (see para 5.21).

[40] The relevant product market comprises the product in question and all products substitutable for that product. The relevant geographical market is the area in which the goods are subject to homogeneous competitive conditions. For guidance as to how the Commission applies the concepts of relevant product and geographical market in its enforcement of Community competition law, see Commission Notice on the definition of the relevant market for the purposes of Community competition law: [1997] O.J. C372/5. The Commission's interpretation of the relevant market is in any case without prejudice to the interpretation that may be given by the Court of Justice or the Court of First Instance.

[41] Art. 9 (1) of Regulation 2790/99. If no market sales value data are available, recourse may be made to other market information, such as market sales volumes. The market share does not only include the share of the undertaking party to the agreement, but also the share(s) of connected undertakings (Art. 11 of Regulation 2790.99). The market share threshold relevant for the application of the group exemption is relatively flexible in that some increases of market share above the 30% threshold in connection with an originally exempted agreement do not withdraw the benefits of the exemption for certain defined periods of time (Art. 9 (2) of Regulation 2790/99).

group exemption.[42] It is also unlikely to qualify for individual exemption.[43] Such hardcore restrictions are:

(a) restriction of the buyer's ability to determine its sale price, without prejudice to the possibility of the supplier's imposing a maximum sale price or recommending a sale price, provided that they do not amount to a fixed or minimum sale price as a result of pressure from, or incentives offered by, any of the parties;

(b) the restriction of the territory into which, or of the customers to whom, the buyer may sell the contract goods or services, except:

—the restriction of active sales into the exclusive territory or to an exclusive customer group reserved to the supplier or allocated by the supplier to another buyer, where such a restriction does not limit sales by the customers of the buyer;

—the restriction of sales to end users by a buyer operating at the wholesale level of trade;

—the restriction of sales to unauthorised distributors by the members of a selective distribution system; and

—the restriction of the buyer's ability to sell components, supplied for the purposes of incorporation, to customers who would use them to manufacture the same type of goods as those produced by the supplier;

(c) the restriction of active or passive sales to end users by members of a selective distribution system operating at the retail level of trade, without prejudice to the possibility of prohibiting a member of the system from operating out of an unauthorised place of establishment;

(d) the restriction of cross-supplies between distributors within a selective distribution system, including between distributors operating at different levels of trade;

(e) the restriction agreed between a supplier of components and a buyer who incorporates those components, which limits the supplier to selling the components as spare parts to end-users or to repairers or other service providers not entrusted by the buyer with the repair or servicing of its goods.

In addition, the exemption does not apply to certain types of obligations contained in vertical agreements, again irrespective of the market share of the undertakings concerned. These obligations are listed in Article 5 of Regulation 2790/99. Unlike the hardcore restrictions of Article 4, the presence of an Article 5 restraint in a vertical agreement does not withdraw the entire agreement from the scope of the exemption but only the clause in question, insofar as that clause

---

[42] Note that these agreements can also never benefit from the *de minimis* rules (see para. 5.15).
[43] Commission's guidelines on vertical restraints: [2000] O.J. C291/26–28, para. 46.

is severable from the exempted part of the agreement. The Article 5 clauses include:

(a) any direct or indirect non-compete obligation, the duration of which is indefinite or exceeds five years. A non-compete obligation which is tacitly renewable beyond a period of five years is to be deemed to have been concluded for an indefinite duration. However, the time limitation of five years shall not apply where the contract goods or services are sold by the buyer from premises and land owned by the supplier or leased by the supplier from third parties not connected with the buyer, provided that the duration of the non-compete obligation does not exceed the period of occupancy of the premises and land by the buyer;

(b) any direct or indirect obligation causing the buyer, after termination of the agreement, not to manufacture, purchase, sell or resell goods or services, unless such obligation:

— relates to goods or services which compete with the contract goods or services; and
— is limited to the premises and land from which the buyer has operated during the contract period; and
— is indispensable to protect know-how transferred by the supplier to the buyer;

and provided that the duration of such non-compete obligation is limited to a period of one year after termination of the agreement; this obligation is without prejudice to the possibility of imposing a restriction which is unlimited in time on the use and disclosure of know-how which has not entered the public domain;

(c) any direct or indirect obligation causing the members of a selective distribution system not to sell the brands of particular competing suppliers.

The Commission may withdraw the benefit of the group exemption for agreements that fall within the scope of the block exemption but which the Commission nevertheless considers not to fulfil the criteria for exemption under Article 81(3).[44] Significantly, in terms of fines, a withdrawal is only effective from the date of a formal Commission decision and does not have retroactive effect. If the agreement is limited to a particular Member State, which can be considered as a distinct geographic market, that state can also withdraw the benefit of the block exemption.[45] Where parallel networks of similar vertical restraints cover over 50

---

[44] Art. 6 of Regulation 2790/99.
[45] Art. 7 of Regulation 2790/99.

per cent of a market, the Commission has the power to withdraw the benefit of the exemption with respect to such particular market or restraints.[46]

If the proposed reforms (see paragraph 5.13) are adopted, the following paragraph will be of historical interest only.

5.21   **Individual exemptions**   Agreements or obligations that do not automatically qualify for exemption (either because the market share threshold is exceeded or because they contain restraints mentioned in Articles 4 or 5) are not *per se* illegal. They require a full Article 81 analysis, *i.e.* an appreciation of their effects on competition. Factors that will be examined in this regard include, among others, the market position of the supplier, of competitors, and of the buyer, entry barriers, maturity of the market, level of trade, and nature of the product.[47]

If an agreement falls under Article 81(1), it must then be examined whether it can qualify for an individual exemption under Article 81(3), by fulfilling the four cumulative conditions of Article 81(3).[48] With regard to franchise agreements, the more important the transfer of know-how is to the agreement, the more likely the agreement is to qualify for individual exemption.[49]

The new block exemption regulation implies that the parties themselves analyse their agreement under Article 81(1) and 81(3). The Commission's guidelines help the parties with their assessment. In the event that an agreement or practice is later examined by the Commission (*e.g.* because there are strong third party complaints or the agreement is notified at a later stage by the parties as a result of litigation in national courts over the enforceability of a vertical restraint), the Commission has the burden to prove that the agreement falls under Article 81(1); parties can then still demonstrate that an exemption is due under Article 81(3). In the latter case, the Commission may retroactively grant an individual exemption, as of the date the vertical agreement came into force.[50]

PART IV: AGENCY AGREEMENT

Introduction

5.22   **Definition**   The commercial agent is an intermediary who identifies and visits potential customers to negotiate and possibly conclude transactions in the name

---

[46] Art. 8 of Regulation 2790/99.

[47] See the Commission's guidelines on vertical restraints: [2000] O.J. C291/26–28 (paras 121–133).

[48] In order to be exempted under Art. 81(3), the vertical agreement must: (a) contribute to improving production or distribution or to promoting technical or economical progress; (b) allow consumers a fair share of these benefits; (c) not impose on the undertakings concerned vertical restraints which are not indispensable to the attainment of these benefits; and (d) not afford such undertakings the possibility of eliminating competition in respect of a substantial part of the products in question. See also the Commission's guidelines on vertical restraints: [2000] O.J. C291/28 (paras 134–136).

[49] Commission's guidelines on vertical restraints: [2000] O.J. C291/28, paras 119/8 and 200.

[50] Art. 4(2) and 6(2) of Regulation 17/62, as amended by Regulation 1216/99.

and on behalf of his "principal".[51] The commercial agent is independent of his principal (unlike the sales representative who is an employee). Nevertheless, the principal and the customer are directly bound by the transaction concluded by the agent in the name and on behalf of the principal.

Legal framework Some countries like Austria, Germany, Denmark and **5.23** Switzerland have had legislation on agency agreements for many years while other countries such as Belgium, the United Kingdom, Ireland and Luxembourg, had no such specific legislation.

In 1986 the European Community issued a directive for the co-ordination of the laws of the Member States relating to self-employed commercial agents.[52] Following the text of the Directive, its provisions apply to contracts concluded after the date of implementation into national law.[53] The content of the European agency directive will be discussed below.

The International Institute for the Unification of Private Law (UNIDROIT) (see paragraph 2.29) has drafted a Convention to unify the law of agency. This draft was meant to supplement the rules contained in the 1980 Vienna Convention on the International Sale of Goods (see paragraph 4.07). A diplomatic conference held in Geneva in 1983, and attended by delegations from

---

[51] For a more thorough examination of agency agreements see *The ICC Model Commercial Agency Contract* (ICC Publishing, Paris, 1991); G. Bogaert and U. Lohmann, *Commercial Agency and Distribution Agreements: Law and Practice in the Member States of the EC and the EFTA* (Graham & Trotman, London, 1993); P. Crahay, *Guide des Contrats Internationaux d'Agence et de Concession de Vente* (Story-Scientia, Brussels, 1989) p. 368; G. H. L. Fridman, *The Law of Agency* (7th ed., 1996); A. Jausas, *Agency and Distribution Agreements: an International Survey* (Graham & Trotman, London, 1994); B. S. Markesinis and R. J. C. Munday, *An outline of the law of agency* (4th ed., Butterworths, London, 1998); F. M. B. Reynolds, *Bowstead and Reynolds on Agency* (16th ed., Butterworths, London 1996); C. M. Schmitthoff, *The Law and Practice of International Trade* (Stevens & Sons, London, 1990) pp. 278–316; L. S. Sealy and R. J. A. Hooley, *Commercial Law*, Chapter 2, "The law of agency" (2nd ed., Butterworths, London 1999) pp. 87–225; H. Stumpf, *Internationales Handelsvertreterrecht* (Recht und Wirtschaft, Heidelberg, 1986) p. 219; A. de Theux, *Le Statut européen de l'Agent commercial* (FUSL, Brussels, 1992).

[52] Council Directive 86/653 [1986] O.J. L382/17; J. Worthy, "Exporting through commercial agents—the European way" (1990) E.B.L.R. 81.

[53] National implementing measures: Austria: Handelsvertretergesetz 1993; Belgium: Statute du 13.04.1995; Denmark: Lov nr. 272 af 02.05.1990 om handelsagenter og handelsrejsende; Finland: Lag om handelsrepresentanter och försäljare (417/92) 8.05.1992; France: Loi 91–593 of June 25, 1991; further implemented by decree no. 92–506 of June 10, 1992; See also J. M. Le Coup, "La loi du 25 juin 1991 relative aux rapports entre les agents commerciaux et leurs mandants ou le triomphe de l'intérêt commun" (1992) J.C.P. 3557; Germany: Gesetz zur Durchführung der EG-Richtlinie zur Koordinierung des Rechts der Handelsvertreter vom 23.10.1989, Gesetz zur Neuregelung des Kaufmanns-und Firmenrechts und zur Anderung anderer handels-und gesellschaftsrechtlicher Vorschriften (Handelsrechtsreformgezets-HRefG) vom 22.06.1998; Great Britain: the Commercial Agents (Council Directive) Regulations 1993 (S.I. 1993 No. 3053); the Commercial Agents Ordinance, Legal Notice No. 9 of 1994, The Commercial Agents (Council Directive) (Amendment) Regulations 1998 (S.I. 1998 No. 2868); Greece: Presedential Decree No. 219/91 of May 18, 1991; Ireland: E.C. (Commercial Agents Regulations, 1994 and 1997; Italy: Arts 1742–1752 Cod. Civ. Statutory decree of September 10, 1991; Statutory decree of February 15, 1999; Luxembourg: Statute of June 17, 1992 and Statute of June 3, 1994; Netherlands: Commercial Code, Arts. 74–74c, Statute of July 5, 1989; see also H. Urlus, *De Agentuurovereenkomst* (Kluwer, Deventer, 1990); Portugal: Statute no. 178/86 of July 3, 1986; Statute no. 118/93 of April 13, 1993; Spain: Statute 12/1992 of May 27, 1992; Sweden: Lag om handelsagentur 1991.

58 countries, approved a Convention on Agency in the International Sale of Goods.[54] This Convention, however, has not yet entered into force.[55]

Private international law

5.24   What national law governs transnational agency agreements is not governed by a widespread text. The European Directive does not deal with the law applicable to the principal-agent relationship. A 1978 convention on the law applicable to agency of the Hague Conference on Private International Law (see paragraph 2.30) is at present only in force in Argentina, France, the Netherlands and Portugal.[56] In other countries the law applicable to agency contracts must be found by applying the general conflict of law rules.[57] In many European countries this will result in the application of the European Contracts Convention.

Agency gives rise to three different relationships: the contractual relationship between the agent and the principal, the contractual relationship between the agent and a third party and the relationship between the principal and the third party. Each may be governed by a different law.

The relationship between the principal and the agent is governed by the law chosen by the parties in their agency contract; in the absence of a choice of law, the law of the residence of the agent, *i.e.* the party who effects the characteristic performance, applies.[58] This law is to apply to the formation and validity of the agency relationship, the obligations of the parties, the conditions of performance, the consequences of non-performance and the extinction of those obligations.[59]

---

[54] UNIDROIT Convention on Agency in the International Sale of Goods, Geneva January 31–February, 17 , 1983, U.L.Rev., Vol. I–II, Rome, 1983, pp. 161–174; M. J. Bonell, "The 1983 Geneva Convention on Agency in International Sale of Goods" (1984) 32 Am.J.Comp.L. 717–749.

[55] Like the Vienna Convention, the Geneva Convention will enter into force when ratified or acceded by 10 contracting states. So far it has been ratified only by France, Italy, Mexico, the Netherlands and South Africa.

[56] P. Hay and W. Müller-Freienfels, "Agency in the conflict of laws and the 1978 Hague Convention" (1979) Am.J.Comp.L. 1; Chr. A. J. F. M. Hensen, "Het Europees IPR in botsing met Haagse Verdragen, problemen van samenloop", *Eenvorming en Vergelijkend Privaatrecht* (1990), p.199; P. Lagarde, "La Convention de la Haye sur la loi applicable aux contrats d'intermédiaries et à la représentation" (1978) R.C.D.I.P. 31; M. G. Pfeifer, "The Hague Convention on the law applicable to agency" (1978) Am.J.Comp.L. 434; H. L. E. Verhagen, *Agency in International Private Law. The Hague Convention on the Law Applicable to Agency* (Nijhoff, The Hague, 1995).

[57] R. Baldi, *Distributorship, Franchising, Agency* (Kluwer, 1987, Deventer) pp. 137–165; R. Baldi, *Le Droit de la Distribution Commerciale dans l'Europe Communautaire* (Bruylant, Brussels, 1998) pp. 183–221; P. Kindler, "Handelvertreter und Vertragshändlervertrage im IPR" (1987) R.I.W. 660.

[58] Under Art. 6 of the Hague Convention, the law of the state where the agent is primarily to act shall apply if the principal has his business establishment (or if he has none, his habitual residence) in that state. European Contracts Convention, Arts 3 and 4; Hague Convention on the Law applicable to Agency, Arts 5 and 6, 1. A. de Theux, *Le Statut européen de l'Agent commercial* (FUSL, Brussels, 1992) pp. 366–374.

[59] Hague Convention, Art.8.

Moreover, the law of the place of performance shall be taken into consideration to determine the modalities to perform the agency.[60]

There is no general rule to establish the law, which determines whether or not the intervention of the agent has established a contract between the principal and the third party. Under the Hague Convention, Article 11, this issue is governed by the law of the state in which the agent has his business establishment; however, if there are more connecting factors with the country in which the agent has actually operated, the law of that country applies.[61]

Since the European Contracts Convention excludes this particular question from its scope of application, the solution must be found in its general conflict of law rules.[62] Consequently, the law of the habitual residence of the seller, being the party effecting the characteristic performance, applies if no other law is chosen by the parties (see paragraph 1.29).[63]

The relationship between the agent and the third party is governed under the Hague Convention (Article 11) by the law of the country where the agent has operated. Under the European Contracts Convention, Articles 3–4, it is governed by the law of the residence of the agent (*i.e.* the party who is to effect the characteristic performance).

The contents of the E.C. Agency Directive

Ratione personae The Directive applies to self-employed intermediaries[64] **5.25** who have the authority to negotiate the sale or purchase of goods for a principal, or to negotiate and conclude such transactions on behalf of and in the name of the principal.[65]

Estate and land agents as well as agents in the service sector (*e.g.* travel agents and insurance agents) fall outside the scope of the Directive.[66] However, some Member States have extended their agency law also to these agents.[67] Moreover, each Member State may declare the Directive not applicable to persons whose

---

[60] *ibid.*, Art.9.
[61] *e.g.* if this is also the country of residence of the principal or third party.
[62] European Contracts Convention, Art. 1, para. 2(f).
[63] *ibid.*, Art. 4; Hague Sales Convention of June 15, 1955, Art. 3.
[64] The Directive, however, does not give a criterion to determine the independence. The Member States are given a certain margin of discretion. They may put the emphasis on the legal as well as economic independence: A. de Theux, *Le droit de la représentation commerciale. Etude comparative et critique du statut des représentants salariés et des agents commerciau* (Bruylant, Brussels, 1975), paras 9, 30 *et seq.*
[65] The Directive does not make a distinction between an agent whose activities take place in one or more Member States, within or outside the Community.
[66] The following are not considered as commercial agents: a person who, in his capacity as an officer, is empowered to enter into commitments binding on a company or association; a partner who is lawfully authorised to enter into commitments binding on his partners; a receiver, a manager, a liquidator or a trustee in bankruptcy (Art. 1. para. 3).
The Directive shall not apply to (Art. 2. para. 1): commercial agents whose activities are unpaid; commercial agents when they operate on commodity exchanges or in the commodity market.
[67] *e.g.* Belgium.

activities as commercial agents are considered "secondary"[68] (*e.g.* persons who occasionally collect orders for mail order companies from private individuals, or who conduct collective sales at house parties).

Obligations of the agent and the principal

5.26   **Substance**   The agent must look after the interests of the principal. He must act dutifully and in good faith. This includes, in particular, making proper efforts to negotiate and conclude transactions, communicating to his principal all the necessary information available[69] and complying with reasonable instructions given by his principal.[70]

An agent who has been given precise and detailed instructions by his principal may sometimes be considered as a sales representative.

The principal, for his part, must act dutifully and in good faith in his relations with the agent.[71] He must give the agent the necessary documentation relating to the goods concerned, as well as all information necessary for the performance of the agency contract. Furthermore, the principal must inform his agent within a reasonable period of his acceptance, refusal or non-execution of a commercial transaction which the agent has procured for the principal. Finally, it is the principal's duty to pay the agent the agreed remuneration or, if no such agreement exists, a remuneration customary in the agent's place of business or reasonable in view of all aspects of the transaction.

These obligations of the principal and commercial agent are mandatory. Parties are not permitted to derogate from these provisions.[72]

The Directive, however, does not cover the involvement of sub-agents, confidentiality, business secrets, reimbursement of the agent's expenses and the *del credere* provision (*i.e.* the agent accepts liability for the insolvency of the customer). These matters remain governed by the domestic law of the Member State.[73]

Remuneration

5.27   **Methods of remuneration**   The agent may be remunerated by way of a commission, or in another way. Remuneration which varies according to the number or value of the business transactions, is deemed to be a commission.[74]

The agent is entitled to receive a direct commission for any transaction

---

[68] Directive, Art. 2 para. 2. See *e.g.* for Germany, HGB para. 92b.

[69] *e.g.* to inform the principal about the general developments in the sector concerned. For this, the agent needs to be aware of the market conditions, their development, the competition situation and changes in the needs of the customers.

[70] Directive, Art. 3; A. de Theux, *Le Statut européen de l'Agent commercial* (FUSL, Brussels, 1992) p. 25.

[71] Directive, Art. 4; A. de Theux, *op. cit.*, pp. 28–32.

[72] Directive, Art. 5.

[73] In respect of business secrets of the principal: *e.g.* HGB para. 90; in respect of the *del credere* clause: *e.g.* HGB para. 86(b) and Dutch Commercial Code Art. 74(b).

[74] Directive, Art. 6 para. 2.

concluded as a result of his intervention. He is entitled to an indirect commission for any transactions the principal concluded with a customer previously acquired by the agent for a similar transaction. If the agent is either allocated a specific geographical area or a particular group of customers, and the transaction has been entered into with a customer from that area or group, he is also entitled to indirect commission.

The agent is entitled to a commission when the order of his customer has been accepted by the principal (or the agent himself). This commission becomes due as soon as the principal has performed or should have performed his part of the transaction, or when the customer has performed his part of the deal. The commission has also to be paid not later than the last day of the month following the quarter in which the commission became due.

The right to commission can only be lost if the agreement between the customer and the principal will not be performed, but only on the condition that this non-performance is neither due to the principal nor the customer. This provision is mandatory; it cannot be changed by contract to the detriment of the agent. Moreover, the parties cannot stipulate other eventualities in which the commission is lost. The agent is entitled to verify the commission due.

The principal shall inform the agent within a reasonable period about the effect he will give to the transactions submitted by the agent. The principal has to submit to the agent a statement of the commissions due, not later than the last day of the month following the quarter in which these commissions became due. The statement must contain all facts relevant for the calculation of the commissions. The agent may ask the principal for all particulars necessary to verify the amount (*e.g.* an extract from the accounts). The Directive does not grant the agent access to the accounts of the principal; however, the national law of the Member State may grant him this right.[75]

The agent is also entitled to receive a commission for each transaction concluded within a reasonable period[76] after the agency contract's termination, if this transaction resulted mainly from the agent's efforts during the agency period. In the contract, parties may stipulate in advance the period after termination for which such commission will be due.

In the event for the same transaction, a commission would be due to the terminated agent as well as to the new agent, the first agent has priority. Nevertheless, equity may require in specific circumstances the commission to be shared between both agents.

Termination of the agency contract

Contract for a fixed period   A contract for a fixed period is terminated when   **5.28**
this period has expired, unless the period is extended by the parties.[77] In the latter

---

[75] Directive, Art. 12 para. 4. This right is granted under German and Dutch Law, for instance.

[76] This period may be specified in the implementing national agency statute. The period under Belgian agency law, for instance, is 6 months.

[77] The directive does not provide for the unilateral termination of an agency for a fixed period. In that event there is a breach of contract.

event the contract becomes an agreement for an indefinite period, unless the parties have agreed that the contract is extended only for a limited period.

When a contract for a definite fixed term is converted into a contract for an indefinite term it may only be terminated if the required period of notice is observed (see paragraph 5.29). For the calculation of this period the initial duration of the contract for a definite term must also be taken into account.

5.29   **Contract for an indefinite period—notice terms**   Either party may terminate an agency contract for an indefinite period after proper notice.[78] The notice term is a minimum of one month for the first year of the agreement, two months when the agreement enters its second year, and three months for the third and following years. However, under the directive, the implementing agency statute may require a notice term of four months for the fourth year of the contract, of five months for the fifth year, and six months for the sixth and subsequent years.[79] The parties are not allowed to fix a notice term shorter than that required under the applicable statute. If, on the other hand, parties agree on a longer period of notice, the notice term for the principal may not be shorter than the notice term to be observed by the agent. Unless otherwise agreed between the parties, the end of the notice term must coincide with the last day of the calendar month.

The directive does not impose sanctions for non-observance of the legal notice terms. This is for the implementing agency statute to provide. Most legal systems provide for compensation; some may require specific performance.[80]

5.30   **Serious reasons**   The contract may be terminated without prior notice if a party fails to perform all or part of his obligations. Termination without notice is also possible in exceptional circumstances, when it cannot be reasonably expected that a party even temporarily continues performance.[81] The directive does not specify whether the contract should be rescinded by the parties or by the court. Neither does it cover the validity of a termination clause. Again, these modalities are covered by the respective implementation statutes.[82]

5.31   **Indemnity or compensation**   The directive leaves the Member States the choice of: (a) indemnifying the agent after termination of the agency for the customers acquired by that agent[83] or (b) compensating for damage caused by

---

[78] See A. de Theux, *op. cit.*, p. 172.

[79] Directive, Art. 15, para. 3: Denmark, Greece, Italy and Spain have adopted this possibility. German law imposes a minimum notice period of three months during the fourth and fifth year, and of six months if the agreement is older than five years. Dutch law imposes a notice period of four months for the first three years, five months for the fourth to the sixth years, and six months from the sixth year onwards.

[80] A. de Theux, *op. cit.*, p. 171; M. Ilangi, "Termination of commercial agency agreements under Israeli Law" (1995) 17 C.L.B. Int.Bus. 281.

[81] Those reasons do not necessarily depend on the behaviour of the other party.

[82] Directive, Art. 16; A. De. Theux, *op. cit.*, pp. 175–192.

[83] See, *e.g.*, German law and Italian law.

termination.[84] The relevant implementing statutes can also grant both remedies, which are not mutually exclusive.[85]

Indemnity for customers is due if:

(i) the agent has acquired new customers or has significantly increased the volume of business transactions with existing customers;

(ii) the principal continues to benefit substantially from the business with such customers; and

(iii) payment of this indemnity is fair (*e.g.* because the agent lost these customers).

The compensation can at the most be the average annual income produced by the agency. The last five years serve as a basis for the calculation of this average income (unless the agency lasted for a shorter period).

Compensation for termination covers the commission lost by the agent because of the termination. Moreover, the compensation includes the costs and expenses of the agent, incurred at the request of the principal but which can no longer be recovered. The agent must prove the amount of such compensation. Parties cannot agree on this compensation before the contract is terminated. However, no compensation is due if the agency is terminated by the principal because of a breach of contract by the agent which justifies immediate termination. Neither is compensation due if the contract is terminated by the agent, unless such termination is justified by the principal's behaviour or because of the agent's age, infirmity or illness. Furthermore, no compensation is due if the agent, with the consent of the principal, assigns his rights and duties under the agency contract to a third party.

The agent must inform the principal of his intention to claim compensation within a year after termination, otherwise he loses his claim.

The implementing statutes may also provide for compensation if the agreement restricts the agent's possibility to compete (see paragraph 5.32).[86]

Non-competition The principal may prevent the agent from dealing in **5.32** competing products during or after the term of the agency contract. However, this clause is only valid in so far as: (a) it relates to goods covered by the agency contract; (b) it is limited to a specific geographical area and/or to specific customers and (c) it is restricted in time (to a maximum of two years after termination). National provisions may further restrict the validity or applicability of the clause. Moreover, the courts may, if necessary, moderate the impact of the non-competition clause.[87]

---

[84] This seems to be the case in French and U.K. law.
[85] This is the case in *e.g.* Danish, Greek and Spanish law.
[86] *e.g.* under German law in HGB, para. 90(a).
[87] Thus the Dutch courts may annul or moderate the competition clause if the commercial agent is unreasonably disadvantaged by this clause (Commercial Code Art. 74).

Aspects of competition law

5.33   **E.C. Article 81**[88]   Article 81 of the E.C. Treaty does not apply to restrictions imposed on "genuine" agents by their principals, insofar as such restrictions concern contracts negotiated or concluded by the agent on behalf of his principal. The Commission considers as "genuine" agreements where the agent does not bear any or bears only limited financial or commercial risks. Typical restrictions which the Commission considers as being outside the scope of Article 81 include limitations relating to the territory in which or the customers to whom the agent may sell and prices and conditions at which the agent must sell or purchase. If, however, the agent bears substantial risks and carries out an independent economic activity, the agreement will be subject to Article 81 in the same way as other vertical agreements.[89] In its guidelines on vertical restraints, the Commission indicated some situations in which it will generally not consider agents as independent dealers.[90]

Provisions of an agency agreement that concern the relationship between the agent and the principal (rather than restrictions relating to contracts to be negotiated or concluded by the agent), such as exclusive agency or non-compete provisions, are always subject to Article 81 scrutiny, regardless of whether the agent bears significant commercial or financial risks.

If an agency agreement infringes Article 81, it will be void and unenforceable unless it benefits from exemption, either under a group[91] or under an individual exemption.

---

[88] For guidance as to the E.U. Commission's policy towards competition aspects relating to agency agreements, see the Commission's Notice: Guidelines on vertical restraints [2000] O.J. C291/1, paras 12–20 (which replaces the former Notice in respect of exclusive dealing contracts with commercial agents and dealers of December 24, 1962 [1962] O.J. C2921).

[89] Guidelines, *op. cit.*, para. 15. See also Cases 40–48, 50, 54–56, 111, 113 & 114/73, *Cooperative Society Suiker Unie and others v. Commission* [1975] E.C.R. 1663; *Fischer-Price/Quaker Oats Ltd Toyco* [1988] O.J. L49/19; *Aluminium Imports from Eastern Europe* [1985] O.J. L92/1; *European Sugar Industry* [1973] O.J. L140/17; *Pittsburgh Corning Europe* [1972] O.J. L272/35; and Case 311/85 *Flemish Travel Agencies* [1987] E.C.R. 3828. For critical comments on this judgment, see: N. Koch and G. Marenco, "L'article 85 du Traité CEE et les contrats d'agence" (1987) Cah. Dr. Eur., 603 as well as J. Goyder, *E.C. Distribution Law* (Kluwer, Deventer, 1993) pp. 165–178. See also Cases C–266/93 *Bundeskartellamt v. Volkswagen AG and VAG Leasing GmbH* [1995] E.C.R. I–3477.

[90] Guidelines *op. cit.*, para. 16.

[91] The vertical restraints block exemption may apply (see Art. 1(g) of Regulation 2790/1999 [1999] O.J. L336/21) or the motor vehicle distribution block exemption (Regulation 1475/95 [1995] O.J. L145/25).

CHAPTER 6

INTERNATIONAL TRANSFER OF TECHNOLOGY

Technology It is assumed in most countries that economic growth is not **6.01** possible without industrialisation. For this to occur, the acquisition of technology is vital. At present, there is a considerable demand for the transfer of technology in developing countries.

"Technology" is commonly understood as meaning systematic and practical applied technical knowledge which is required or useful for the manufacturing of products, for the application of operating procedures or production processes, or even for the performance of services.

Technology which meets certain criteria (*e.g.* innovation, applicability in industry) has been legally protected by industrial property rights for some time. For instance, by virtue of a patent granted by a national or regional patent office, the patent holder has an exclusive right, restricted in time and territory, to exploit his invention and to prevent its application by others. As early as 1883, the Paris Convention for the international protection of industrial property was agreed. This convention represents the first effort of several countries to adopt a common approach to industrial property (see paragraph 6.04).[1]

Within some technological fields (*e.g.* biotechnology or information technology) there have emerged particular industrial property rights, such as plant variety rights[2] and topographies of semi-conductor products.[3] A number of countries have also implemented protective measures for computer software, based on copyright[4]

---

[1] See G. Tritton, *Intellectual property in Europe* (Sweet & Maxwell, London, 1996), p. 35.

[2] See, *e.g.* the International Convention for the Protection of New Varieties of Plant (Paris) of December 2, 1961; Regulation EC 2100/94 on Community plant variety rights [1994] O.J. L227. For the text of some national statutes, search at the WIPO Collection of Laws for Electronic Access (CLEA) database at http://clea.wipo.international. G. Bergmans, *La Protection des Innovations Biologiques: une Étude de Droit Comparé* (Larcier, Brussels, 1991); F. Dessemontet, *Le Génie Génétique—Biotechnology and Patent Law* (CEDIDAC, Lausanne, 1998); G. Dutfield, *Intellectual Property Rights, Trade and Biodiversity* (Earthscan Publications, London, 2000).

[3] See, *e.g.* section 6 of the TRIPs Agreement; Council Directive 87/54 on the legal protection of original topographies of semi-conductor products [1987] O.J. L24, 36; the U.S. Semi-conductor Chip Protection Act of November 8, 1984 and the Japanese Act concerning the layout of a semi-conductor integrated circuit of May 31, 1985. *Cf., inter alia,* A. Christie, *Integrated Circuits and their Contents: International Protection* (Sweet & Maxwell, London, 1995); F. Gotzen (ed.) *La Protection des Circuits Intégrés: un Nouveau Droit Intellectuel* (Story Scientia, Brussels, 1990).

[4] See, *e.g.* Council Directive 91/250 on the legal protection of computer programs [1991] O.J. L122 and EP and Council Directive 2001/29 on the harmonisation of certain aspects of copyright and related rights in the information society [2001] O.J. L167. See S. Lai, "Substantive issues of copyright protection in a networked environment" (1999) 8 Inf. & Comm. Tech. Law 127; A. Raubenheimer, "Implementation of the EC Software Directive in Germany: special provisions for protection of computer programs" (1996) I.I.C. 609–647; P. Hidalgo, "Copyright protection of computer software in the European Community: current protection and the effect of the adopted

or patent law.[5] Moreover, there is the mainly contractual protection of technology for secret or confidential know-how (see paragraph 6.07).

6.02 **Transfer of technology** Technology can be transferred to third parties through the assignment of the property rights on the technology, or by the granting of a user's licence.

Technology covered by patent has territorial protection. In principle (see paragraph 6.05), a separate patent has to be taken out in each country for one and the same invention and the exclusive right is in each case valid for that particular country. Many patent holders do not wish (or do not have the financial means) to exploit their invention in all countries where they enjoy patent protection. The transfer of property or user's rights in respect of their national patents is, thus, a classic way to exploit the invention. Such a transfer must, however, take place in each country.

Because of the complexity of most technological processes, the traditional ways of transferring technology have undergone an evolution. On the whole, the owner of technology will no longer restrict himself to the transfer of proprietary or user's rights. Moreover, he will often be responsible for the building of ready-made factories which incorporate the technology concerned (so-called turn-key contracts, see paragraph 6.12) and for the training of the technical personnel of the contract partner.

In international contracts for the transfer of technology (particularly in licence agreements) conditions are adopted which may restrict competition. And so it happens frequently that the patent holder (licensor) prohibits the licensee from exporting the products produced under licence to countries in which he exploits his invention or where he has granted licences to other enterprises (see paragraph 6.11). Although this restriction on economic freedom of the licensee is a result of the territorial protection of patents, such contractual provisions may still be in conflict with national or international competition law (see paragraphs 6.13 *et seq.*). Furthermore, in developing countries these restrictions are often experienced as an unjustified restraint of national industrial expansion.

PART I: PROTECTION OF TECHNOLOGY UNDER NATIONAL AND INTERNATIONAL LAW

Patents on inventions

6.03 **National patents and the TRIPs Agreement** The TRIPs Agreement (see paragraph 3.98) requires all WTO states to make patent protection available for

---

directive" (1993) *International Lawyer* 113; T. Gallatin, "The scope of computer protection in the U.S." (1992) *Copyright World* 16; G. Hoffman and B. Dorny, "Recent intellectual property legislation in the United States" (1992) E.I.P.R. 196; J. Berkvens, "Data regulation in copyright law: will the problem of software ever be solved?" (1993) E.I.P.R. 79.

[5] On the furious debate on the patentability of computer software, see *e.g.* D. Attridge, "Challenging claims! Patent computer programs in Europe and the USA" (2001) I.P.Q. 22; M. Lehmann, "Titelschutz für Software" (1998) *Computer und Recht* 2; F. J. Schoniger, "Patentfahigkeit von Software" (1997) *Computer und Recht* 598. See also the Online-Forum on patenting of software-related inventions, at: http://europa.eu.int/comm/internal_market/en/indprop/softforum.htm.

any inventions, whether products or processes, in all fields of technology without discrimination, subject to the normal tests of novelty, inventiveness and industrial applicability.[6] It is also required that patents be available and patent rights enjoyable without discrimination as to the place of invention, and whether products are imported or locally produced.

Patent protection is limited in time (generally 20 years).[7] Once granted, a patent confers on its owner exclusive rights, *inter alia*, to prevent third parties not having its consent from bringing the protected invention into circulation.

Once a patent is granted, it must be published. It is assumed that this publication will contribute to further technological innovation, since it may be expected that the competitors of the patent owner will try to develop something more innovative to catch up with his competitive advantage.

Patents are territorially limited rights. It follows that a patent right has no operation beyond the territory of the state under whose laws it is granted. Another aspect deriving from the territorial nature of patents is the principle of independence: parallel patents lead an "autonomous" life. Accordingly, the scope of protection granted by national patents protecting the same invention in different countries is not necessarily the same and the amendment of a patent in one forum has no effect on parallel patent rights abroad.[8] Yet, the regulation of transnational trade, in general, and the international exploitation of patent rights, in particular, has progressively led to international agreements concerning *inter alia*, the patent granting system and the harmonisation of patent laws.

The Paris Industrial Property Convention   The 1883 Paris Convention for   **6.04**
the Protection of Industrial Property[9-10] (the Paris Industrial Property Convention) is the cornerstone of the international patent granting system. The fundamental principles of "right of priority" and "national treatment" set out by the Convention have been of capital importance to the internationalisation of intellectual property rights over the last century.

On the one hand, the principle of "national treatment" opposes protectionist provisions in national industrial property systems.[11] It requires contracting states to accord nationals of other contracting states the same rights under their domestic industrial property laws as they accord to nationals.

Furthermore, the "right of priority" entitles a patent applicant of a contracting state to a period of 12 months after the initial patent application to apply for

---

[6] On TRIPs and patents, see, *e.g.*, M. C. E. J. Bronckers, "The exhaustion of patent rights under WTO law" (1998) J.W.T. 137; R. H. Marshall, "Patents, antitrust, and the WTO/GATT: using TRIPS as a vehicle for antitrust harmonisation" (1997) Law&Pol.Int.Bus. 597.

[7] See TRIPs Agreement Art. 33 (a minimum of 20 years counted from the filing date of the patent application).

[8] See Paris Convention Art. 4*bis*, (para. 6.04).

[9-10] Paris Convention for the Protection of Industrial Property of March 20, 1883, as revised at Brussels on December 14, 1900, at Washington on June 2, 1911, at The Hague on November 6, 1925, at London on June 2, 1934, at Lisbon on October 31, 1958, and at Stockholm on July 14, 1967, and as amended on October 2, 1979.See full text at http://www.ipr-helpdesk.org.

[11] A. D'amato & D. E. Long, (eds), *International Intellectual Property Law* (Kluwer Law International, London, 1997) 251.

[12] Paris Industrial Property Convention, Art. 4.

protection for the same invention in any other contracting state. Within this one-year period, the application dates back to the earliest application filing date.[12] The main practical advantage to applicants interested in multinational patent protection is this "grace period", which can be used to evaluate the economic viability of the invention and to design the patentability strategy.

The responsibility for the administration of the Paris Convention and of similar conventions (in respect of copyright, trade marks, industrial designs and models, etc.) is that of the World Intellectual Property Organisation (WIPO), established in Geneva.[13]

6.05   **Centralisation of applications**   The Paris Industrial Property Convention does not provide for a centralised procedure to file simultaneous patent applications in several countries. A second category of treaties provides, for that reason, for the international centralisation of patent applications.

The Patent Co-operation Treaty[14] is a world-wide treaty that permits an applicant to file an "international application" at one of several designated national patent offices. The applicant designates the countries for which protection is desired. If the applicant wishes to obtain patent protection in a number of contracting states to the European Patent Convention, the appropriate "route" is a Euro-PCT application, that is, a patent application under the Patent Co-operation Treaty requesting a European patent for all (or a number) of the European states.[15] Although the Patent Co-operation Treaty substantially simplifies the patent *application* process, it does not centralise the patent *granting* phase, which remains the responsibility of the national patent authorities in the designated states (or the European Patent Office, as far as the Euro-PCT application is concerned). Furthermore, the Patent Co-operation Treaty does not modify the requirements of patentability applicable in each of the contracting states.

The limited effects of the Patent Co-operation Treaty stressed the necessity of a more complete and integrated patent system, initially in Europe.

The Convention of Munich of October 5, 1973 on the grant of European patents (European Patent Convention, EPC) introduced a single patent application for all or some of the contracting states, as well as a single examination of the application on the basis of general requirements of patentability. This examination takes place at the European Patent Office in Munich.[16] In each contracting

---

[12] Paris Industrial Property Convention, Art. 4.

[13] WIPO, *Introduction to Intellectual Property. Theory and Practice* (WIPO, Geneva, 1997); P. Geller, "From patchwork to network: strategies from international intellectual property in flux" (1998) Duke J.Comp.&Int.L. 69; C. D. Stith, "International intellectual property rights" (1997) *International Lawyer* 311. See http://www.wipo.org.

[14] Patent Co-operation Treaty (PCT), done at Washington on June 19, 1970, amended on September 28, 1979 and modified on February 3, 1984. See full text at http://www.ipr-helpdesk.org. The Patent Co-operation Treaty procedure is explained in detail, *inter alia*, in: I. Muir, M. Brandi-Dohrn and S. Gruber, *European Patent Law. Law and Procedure under the European Patent Convention and Patent Co-operation Treaty* (University Press, Oxford, 1999); G. Tritton, *Intellectual Property in Europe* (Sweet & Maxwell, London, 1996) 38–49.

[15] G. Tritton, *op. cit.*, 105–111.

[16] This convention is ratified by all E.U. states, Cyprus, Monaco, Liechtenstein, Monaco, Switzerland and Turkey (as of June 2001). See for the text http://www.ipr-helpdesk.org/. *Cf., inter alia*: F. K. Beier, K. Haertel and G. Schricker, *Europäisches Patentübereinkommen—Münchner Gemein-schaftskommentar* (K. Heymanns Verlag, Munich, 1998); I. Muir, M. Brandi-Dohrn and S. Gruber,

state the effect of a European patent so granted is the same as the effect of a national patent by virtue of the existing national laws. The treaty came into force on October 7, 1977.

European Community patent   The introduction of a Community patent **6.06** will add a totally new dimension to the current European patent system. A two-tier patent system will be articulated where Community and national patents (generally issued from a European patent grant) coexist.

Since the creation of the European Community, it was acknowledged that a fully integrated European market requires a patent with unitary and autonomous character, a true Community patent. With this objective in mind, the Community Patent Convention was signed in Luxembourg on December 15, 1975, but it never entered into force.[17] Despite two subsequent conferences in 1985 and 1989 introducing substantial modifications in the legal system set up by the Convention, the Community patent never saw the light of day.

However, the need for a unitary Community patent remained and, in recent years, its introduction became a priority issue in the political agenda of the European Commission.[18] It appears now that the Community patent will be introduced in the form of a Community Regulation.[19]

Once granted, the patent has effect in all the E.U. Member States and is subject to common substantive rules in those countries regarding, for instance, the patentability, the term of the patent, the rights and obligations of the patent owner, the assignment or licensing of the patent.[20]

The European Community patent would grant to the patent owner a single exclusive right for the whole territory of the E.U. This has the following advantages for the patent owner: he only has to file one application (this was already the case under the Munich Convention) and, more importantly, he has to comply with only one common patent regulation. At present, national patents still allow him to partition off markets by taking out a patent for the same invention

---

op. cit., G. Paterson, *The European Patent System* (2nd ed., Sweet & Maxwell, London, 2001); R. Singer and M. Singer, *The European Patent Convention* (Sweet & Maxwell, London, 1995); M. van Empel, *The Granting of European Patents: Introduction to the Convention on the Grant of European Patents, Munich, October 6, 1973* (Sijthof, Leiden, 1975).

[17] Convention for the European Patent for the Common Market (Community Patent Convention), [1976] O.J. L17/1, as modified by the Council Agreement relating to Community patents [1989] O.J. L 401/1.

[18] See European Commission, Promoting innovation through patents. Green Paper on the Community patent and the patent system in Europe, COM(97) 314 final, issued on June 24, 1997 [1997] O.J. EPO, 443 and European Commission, Follow-up to the Green Paper on the Community Patent and the Patent System in Europe, COM(99) 42 final, issued on February 12, 1999, see http://www.ipr-helpdesk.org/.

[19] The European Commission presented a Proposal for a Council Regulation on the Community patent on August 1, 2000 (COM(2000) 412 final).

[20] The Convention on the Community Patent is now embedded in the so-called "1989 Agreement" (Protocol on a possible modification of the conditions for entry into force of the agreement relating to Community patents and the joint declaration, [1989] O.J. L401), which has not entered into force; *cf.* A. Benyamini, "Patent infringement in the European Community" (1993) I.C.C. Studies 7 *et seq.*; M. Burnside, "The Community Patent Convention: is it obsolete in its present form?" (1992) E.I.P.R. 285; J. Neukom "What price the Community patent?" (1992) E.I.P.R. 111–112; C. Wadlow, *Enforcement of Intellectual Property in European and International Law* (Sweet & Maxwell, London, 1998), 213 *et seq.*

in all Member States (so-called "parallel patents": see paragraph 6.11) and by assigning territorially restricted ownership or user's rights.[21] This will no longer be possible with the Community patent, since this patent has territorial effect for the whole area of the Community (just as is the case, for instance, for a patent granted in the United States, which is governed only by federal legislation).

However, the possibility will remain of (and this is different from, for example, the United States) applying for a national patent in one or more countries instead of a Community patent. Nevertheless, territorial and other restrictions on the transfer of proprietary or user rights of national patents remain subject to E.C. competition law (see paragraphs 6.14 *et seq.*).

Know-how

6.07   **Secret technical information**   Know-how is an entirety of technical information which is secret, substantial and identified.[22]

The technical information referred to may be varied in nature: an invention for which no patent has been taken out, to avoid detection by competitors (see paragraph 6.03), technical knowledge essential for the proper exploitation of the patented invention, short-term technical knowledge which gives a lead over competitors but for which the costs of a patent application are too expensive, non-patentable inventions, technical experience, skill, detailed drawings, blue prints, plans, calculations, sometimes also technical assistance, etc.

This information must be secret. The know-how must not be known or easily accessible in its entirety, or in the context and composition of its components. After all, an essential part of the value of know-how exists in the advantage it gives its owner over his competitors. However, "secret" does not mean that each separate component of the know-how must be completely unknown or unavailable outside the enterprise of the owner of the know-how.

Furthermore, the technical information must be essential. This means that it has to be of significance to the production process or to a product or service. The know-how must therefore be useful in the sense that it improves the competitive position of the owner as regards, for instance, access to new markets.

The know-how must be properly identified, *i.e.* described or otherwise established in such a way that it can be verified that it satisfies the criteria of secrecy

---

[21] See, on this issue, P. Demaret, *Patents, Territorial Restrictions and EEC Law: a Legal and Economic Analysis* (IIC-studies, Weinheim, 1978); C. Ebenroth and W. Hübschle, *Gewerbliche Schutzrechte und Marktaufteilung im Binnenmarkt der Europäischer Union* (Verlag Recht & Wirtschaft, Heidelberg, 1994); D. Guy and G. Leigh, *The EEC and Intellectual Property* (Sweet & Maxwell, London, 1981); S. Farr, "Patents in a Single European Market" (1992) Pat. World 27; I. Govaere, *The Use and Abuse of Intellectual Property Rights in European Community Law* (Sweet & Maxwell, 1996, London); R. Myrick, "Will intellectual property on technology still be viable in a unitary market?" (1992) E.I.P.R. 298.

[22] Definition derived from Art. 7 of the Commission Reg. 556/89 on know-how licensing agreements, [1989] O.J. L61/1. *Cf.* also J. M. Deleuze, "Le contrat de transfert de processus technologique, Know-how" (Masson, Paris, 1979); F. Pollaud-Dulian, *Droit de la Propriété Industrielle* (Montchrestien, Paris, 1999) 315 *et seq.*; A. Troller, "The legal protection of know-how-General Report" in H. Cohen-Jehoram (ed.), *The Protection of Know-how in 13 Countries—Reports to the VIIIth International Congress of Comparative Law* (Kluwer, Deventer, 1972) 149 *et seq.*

and substantiality. This condition is particularly important for the transfer of proprietary or user rights in respect of know-how. As long as the owner of know-how keeps his technical knowledge to himself, it is of little importance whether it is circumscribed or otherwise recorded. A description, either in the contract (which is seldom the case) or in a separate confidential document, is obviously necessary for the transfer of ownership or the granting of a licence.

The law does not grant an exclusive right for know-how. In some cases know-how may be protected as a "trade secret" by criminal law or labour contract law, in some cases also by the law on unfair competition.[23] Neither is know-how protected by treaty. In practice, it is for the owner of know-how to protect the secret nature of his technological knowledge by an adequate contractual requirement of confidentiality.[24]

PART II: CONTRACTS FOR THE TRANSFER OF TECHNOLOGY

Transfer of proprietary rights

Contractual provisions Technology, whether or not patented, is transferred **6.08** by contract or invested in a company.[25]

Most patent laws demand certain formal requirements to make the transfer stand up against third party actions.

The transfer of a patent should not be confused with a "sale of an invention". A transfer of a patent implies that only the exclusive right to exploit one or more national (or international: see paragraph 6.06) patents is transferred. In countries where no patent has been transferred, the patent owner remains free either to exploit the patent himself, or to grant a licence in respect of it, or to assign the ownership of the patent to someone else.

Transfer of ownership of know-how actually means that the owner of know-how:

(a) communicates to the transferee all relevant technical information;

(b) agrees not to exploit the know-how in one or more countries, nor to grant a licence for exploitation and nor to transfer the know-how in ownership

---

[23] Comparative law survey of the protection mechanisms of know-how in, for instance, Belgium, Germany, Italy, the Netherlands, Spain, Japan and the U.S. in H. Cohen-Jehoram, *op. cit.*, mainly pp. 157–159.

[24] Suitable contractual provisions in this respect are, for instance in P. Hearn, *International Business Agreements* (Gower, Aldershot, 1987) pp. 158–181; ORGALIME (European federation for the metal industry), *Modèle de Contrat Licence de Fabrication d'un Matériel non breveté* (Brussels, 1987); J. M. Deleuze, *Le Contrat International de Licence de know-how* (4th ed., Paris, 1988); J. Delacollette, *Les Contrats de Commerce Internationaux* (Droit/Economie, Brussels, 1991) pp. 63–66. Consult also M. Fontaine, "Les clauses de confidentialité dans les contrats internationaux" (1991) I.B.L.J. 3.

[25] T. Cottier, P. Widmer and K. Schindler, *Strategic Issues of Industrial Property Management in a Globalizing Economy* (Hart Publishers, Oxford, 1999); J.-M. Mousseron, R. Fabre, J. Raynard & J.-L. Pierre, *Droit du Commerce International, Droit International de l'Entreprise* (Litec, Paris, 2000) 225 *et seq.*; U. Täger & A. von Witzleben (eds), *Strategies for the Protection of Innovation* (Kluwer, Dordrecht, 1991).

to another person. However, although the ownership of know-how is difficult to establish, the transfer of ownership is even more delicate.

The price for the transfer of ownership of a patent or know-how is usually expressed in a fixed sum. The transferee may agree in a contract to pay the transferor during a fixed period a percentage of the turnover, or even of profits realised by the exploitation of the transferred rights, over and above the fixed sum. In practice, the granting of a share in the profits is not recommended. This share is difficult to calculate in relation to one particular product. Furthermore, there is the risk that the contract for transfer of title will be considered as a partnership, which means that the transferor in that case has to share in the losses as well as being jointly liable for the debts of the transferee.

Licensing agreements

6.09   **Exploitation of technology by a third party**   Licensing agreements regarding patents are more common in international trade than the transfer of ownership. Under a licence the owner of an exclusive right (patent, trade mark, copyright) grants a third party, under certain conditions, exemption from the legal prohibition to exploit the right in question. In other words the licensor grants a user right, while remaining owner of the exclusive right.

However, most licensing agreements involve more than a simple exemption of a prohibition. Usually the licensor has an obligation to enable the licensee to actually exploit the patent. This may involve, for instance, the licensor giving the licensee secret or confidential information (know-how) which is not described as such in the patent. Furthermore, the licensor has to guarantee the licensee the "quiet enjoyment" of the patent: if a third party challenges the validity of the patent, the licensor must defend the patent in court; if he has granted an exclusive licence (see paragraph 6.10), he has to take action against anyone who exploits the patent without his permission. Therefore, the obligations of the licensor are comparable with those of a lessor.[26]

Licensing agreements can also concern know-how. In this case, however, there can be no question of a true "licence", in the sense of a dispensation or an exemption from a prohibition, since there exists no exclusive right for know-how. The licensor (owner of the know-how) has a duty to share confidential, essential and appropriately defined technical information with the licensee to enable him to apply the technology in question in industry (see paragraph 6.07). The licensor will protect himself against disclosure of the know-how by the licensee by imposing an obligation of secrecy and adequate penalty clauses. For as soon as the know-how is disclosed, it loses its economic value.

---

[26] J. Delacollette, *op. cit.* 50–57; P. Hearn, *op. cit.* 105–111; V. Zenhäusern, *Der internationale Lizenzvertrag* (Universitätsverlag, Freiburg, 1991), 3–67.

Common clauses   Licensing agreement for patents and/or know-how[27] tradi-   **6.10**
tionally contain clauses for the following issues.[28] Each time the validity of the
clauses has to be checked against the applicable competition law (see paragraphs
6.13 *et seq.*).

(a) The scope of application of the licence:

— Territorial: for which area(s) is the licence granted?

— In substance: is the full right for exploitation granted in the licence,
or is it restricted to specific applications (*e.g.* for only one branch of
industry)? Does the licence include the right to manufacture, to use
(production processes), to sell?

— As to the person: is the licence exclusive (in that case the licensor
may not grant a licence to a third party in that particular area)? Is the
licensee allowed to transfer the rights deriving from the licence to a
third party by way of sub-licence, or to vest them in a company?

(b) The disclosure to the licensee of technical information, which is indispensable for the industrial application of the technology granted in the
licence. It is sometimes stipulated that the licensor will give technical
assistance to the licensee, and that he will train personnel on how to apply
the technology.

(c) The obligation of the licensor to guarantee for instance:

— the validity of the licensed patent (and the effect of invalidity of this
patent on the continuing existence of the licence agreement);

— the secret character of the licensed know-how;

— against potential claims from third parties for the licensed patent of
know-how.

Unless otherwise agreed, the licensor does not guarantee the return on the
industrial application of the licensed technology.

(d) The obligation of the licensor to notify the licensee of improvements and
adaptations to the licensed technology and to extend the licence to these
new developments. It is sometimes agreed that the licensee may not
improve or adapt the technology without permission from the licensor.
When he is allowed to improve or adapt, he usually has to grant the
licensor a licence for the improvements and adaptations.

---

[27] Most often the licensing agreements involve patents as well as know-how, which together form the
technological knowledge for which the user's right is granted (so-called "mixed licensing
agreements").

[28] *cf., inter alia,* T. Bodewig, "Neue Guidelines für Lizenzverträge in den USA", (1997) GRUR
International, 958–971; J.D. Lew, "International licensing contracts" in J.D. Lew and C. Stanbrook
(eds), *International Trade: Law and Practice* (Euromoney Publications, London, 1990) I, pp. 21
et seq.; L. Melville, *Forms and Agreements on Intellectual Property and International Licensing*
(3rd ed., London, 1988) (looseleaf); K. Yelpaade, D. Worley and D. Campbell, *Licensing Agreements: Patents, Know-how, Trade Secrets and Software* (Kluwer, Deventer, 1988). *Cf.* also D. Pfaff
and S. Nagel, *Internationale Rechtsgrundlagen für Lizenzverträge im gewerblichen Rechtsschutz*
(C. H. Beck'sche Verlag, Munich, 1993).

(e) The obligation of the licensee concerning the quality of the products he manufactures under licence. Quality is important for the licensor's reputation. Therefore, the obligation to purchase the necessary raw materials and/or machinery from the licensor to ensure quality is sometimes imposed on the licensee.

(f) The price the licensee has to pay. Generally, this price consists of three elements:

— a fixed lump sum for imparting technological knowledge;
— a royalty which is usually calculated as a (possible decreasing) percentage of the turnover realised by the licensee with products produced under licence[29];
— a guaranteed minimum in royalties per annum, apart from the achieved turnover.

In addition, there are rules stipulated for, for example: the control over the accounts of the licensee for the determination of the royalties due, the payment of taxes which have to be paid by virtue of the licence, the currency in which payment has to take place (see paragraphs 9.04 *et seq.*), etc.

(g) The term of the contract, the conditions of premature termination (*e.g.* if the secret know-how is disclosed other than with the assistance of the licensor), the obligation of secrecy of parties after termination of the contract.

(h) The choice of the applicable law and the proper forum in case of a dispute. There is often an arbitration clause (see paragraphs 11.01 *et seq.*).

(i) Enforceable undertaking of secrecy are stipulated for the pre-contractual negotiations, for the performance of the contract[30] as well as for the period after termination of the contract.

6.11   **Territorial restrictions**   The principle of territorial protection of patents (see paragraph 6.03) has as a result that an owner of a patent can have so-called parallel patents in different countries for one and the same invention. This enables him to partition off and protect national markets from other companies.

If, for instance, company X has parallel patents for the same invention in countries A, B and C, it can decide:

- to exploit its patent in country A;

- to assign the patent to a local enterprise Y in country B;

- to grant an exclusive licence to a local enterprise Z in country C.

---

[29] On possible profit sharing by the licensor in profit of licensee, see para. 6.08.
[30] E. Hondius (ed.), *Precontractual liability—Reports to the XIIIth Congress of the International Academy of Comparative Law* (Kluwer, Deventer, 1991) p. 22.

Since each of the patents has a limited territorial effect the patent owner X may, by reason of his exclusive right, prevent Y from exploiting his patent (*e.g.* selling) in countries A and C. He can impose the same prohibition on Z in countries A and B. Prohibited exploitation in those countries would indeed infringe on the exclusive right of the patent owner X in countries A and C, and on the exclusive right (by assignment) of Y in country B. For the same reasons X is not permitted to export to country B, because this would infringe on the acquired exclusive right of Y.

Though this is the corollary of patent law itself, it still sometimes gives rise to problems. These restrictions can not, for example, be reconciled with the rules for free movement of goods in the E.U. To the European Court of Justice, the free movement of goods "is a fundamental principle forming part of the legal and economic circumstances which must be taken into account by the proprietor of the patent in determining the manner in which his exclusive right will be exercised".[31]

Composite transfer of technology

Franchising and turn-key contracts The transfer of technology is fre- **6.12** quently part of a global package in which rights regarding the exploitation of patented inventions, know-how, trade marks, industrial design rights, etc. are granted. Furthermore, the transfer provides for technical assistance by the owner of the technology, as well as for the training of the personnel of the recipient of the technology. These composite transfers result in two types of contracts: franchise agreements and turn-key agreements.

If the transfer of technology is mainly intended for the marketing of the product, it will be part of a "franchise" agreement. What is usually understood by this is a contractual system of co-operation between independent under-takings, in which one party (the "franchisor") grants the other party (the "fran-chisee") the right in exchange for payment (money or otherwise) and under certain conditions, to manufacture and sell products, as well as the exploitation of the trade mark and a trading method which is identified by the brand name or trade mark. Furthermore, the franchisor will give assistance and various other services to the franchisee (*e.g.* MacDonalds, Yves Rocher)[32] (see paragraph 5.15).

Composite transfer of technology is mainly intended for industrialisation, particularly in developing countries. In this case it is part of an agreement for delivery and assembly of a ready-made industrial plant according to agreed

---

[31] Case 187/80 *Merck v. Stephar* [1981] E.C.R. 2062; [1981] 3 C.M.L.R. 463. Recently repeated by the ECJ *inter alia* in Case C–316/95 *Generics v. Smith Kline & French Laboratories* [1997] E.C.R. I–3929. *Cf.* also W. Allexander, "Intellectual property and the free movement of goods—1996 case law of the European Court of Justice" (1998) I.C.C. 16–27 ; F. K. Beier, "Industrial property and the free movement of goods in the internal European market" (1990) I.I.C. 131–161; J. J. Burst and R. Kovar, *Brevet, Savoir-faire et Droit Communautaire* (Litec, Paris, 1987) pp. 1–20; G. de Ulloa "Licensing contracts and the territoriality clauses: parallel imports" (1991) E.C.L.R. 220 *et seq.*
[32] For the application of competition law to these contracts, see para. 5.19 on Regulation 2790/99.

specifications ("turn-key" agreements),[33] where the buyer wants an industrial plant that operates to a certain production capacity and which satisfies specific criteria. The supplier, therefore, has to guarantee a specific result. He is free in the choice of means to achieve this result. The risk of the project and the operation of the industrial plant is for the supplier.[34] Because of the particular result required, the buyer usually demands that the supplier provides contractual guarantees or a so-called "autonomous guarantee", generally a "performance bond" or a "maintenance bond" (see paragraph 8.55), issued by the supplier's bank. Turn-key agreements are often concluded with states where the authorities act as buyers.

If a client is established in a country with little foreign currency, payment is sometimes made by means of "countertrade" (see paragraphs 9.37 *et seq.*). The specific forms of project financing are also used for the financing of these contracts (see paragraph 8.49).

PART III: TRANSFER OF TECHNOLOGY AND COMPETITION LAW

6.13   **Applicable legislation**   To partition off national markets with parallel patents may in the E.U. infringe on the fundamental rules of free movement of goods (see paragraph 6.11). Furthermore, provisions in licensing agreements may be in conflict with the cartel prohibition of Article 81(1) of the E.C. Treaty. Contractual provisions in breach of this rule are automatically void (Article 81(2)).

Many restrictions may be a direct result of the exclusive right granted to the patent owner in accordance with the law, and are therefore delicate to assess under competition law. The situation for know-how licences is legally less complicated, since the law does not grant the owner of know-how an exclusive right.

Taking into account developments in the case law of the European Court of Justice on licensing agreements, the Commission decided on so-called "block exemptions" for patent licences (1984)[35] and for know-how licences (1988).[36]

---

[33] UN, *Guide on Drawing up Contracts for Large Industrial Works* (New York, 1973); UN Economic Commission for Europe, *General Conditions for the Erection of Plant and Machinery Abroad* (brochure no. 574 D); A. Brabant, *Le Contrat International de Construction* (Bruylant, Brussels, 1981) pp. 85 *et seq.*; L. Costet, "Les contrats de réalisation d'ensemble industriel" (1981) *International Trade Law and Practice* 559; V. Karim, *Les Contrats de Réalisation d'Ensembles Industriels et le Transfert de Technologie* (Blais, Quebec, 1987); G. P. MacDonald and B. B. Palmer, "International construction contracts", in J. D. Lew and C. Stanbrook, *International Trade: Law and Practice* (Euromoney Publications, London, 1990) I. pp. 87 *et seq.*; D. Wallace, *The International Civil Engineering Contract* (London, 1974) (Suppl. 1980).

[34] It is a customary clause that the supplier is obliged to have particular tasks (*e.g.* the building work) performed by local undertakings (the so-called "imposed subcontractors"), but that he remains liable for their work.

[35] Commission Regulation 2349/84 on the application of Art. 85(3) of the Treaty to categories of patent licensing agreements, [1984] O.J. L219/15 as partly amended by the Commission Regulation 151/93 [1993] O.J. L21/8. See W. Ulrich, "Patents and know-how, free trade, interenterprise co-operation and competition within the internal european market" (1993) I.I.C. 435.

[36] Commission Regulation 556/89 on the application of Art. 85(3) of the Treaty to certain categories of know-how licensing agreements, [1989] O.J. L61/1 as partly amended by the Commission Regulation 151/93 [1993] O.J. L21/8. Consult, *inter alia*, V. Korah and W. Rohtnie, *Know-how*

Since 1996, the fragmentary approach has been replaced by a more comprehensive regulation granting a block exemption to "technology transfer agreements".[37] In 2000 two new regulations provided for new block exemptions for various agreements that had been excluded from the Technology Transfer Regulation. Regulations 2658/2000 and 2659/2000 deal, respectively, with specialisation agreements[38] and research and development agreements.[39]

Block exemption for technology transfer agreements

Scope of application In Regulation 240/96 the E.C. Commission sets out a **6.14** detailed regulation for the exemption of patent licensing agreements and agreements for the licensing of know-how. Accordingly, the block exemption applies to pure patent licensing agreements, pure know-how licensing agreements and the so-called "mixed agreements", agreements in which besides a patent licence, a licence for know-how is also granted.

The group exemption applies to agreements between two parties only. The block exemption does not apply to the following agreements[40]:

(a) agreements between members of "patent pools" or know-how pools, although they rarely have only two members;

(b) licensing agreements between competitors which participate in a joint venture, or between one of them and the joint venture, if the relevant agreements concern the joint venture;

(c) agreements under which one party grants the other a patent and/or know-how licence and in exchange the other party grants the first party a patent, trade mark or know-how licence or exclusive sales rights (reciprocal

---

Licensing and EEC Competition Rules: Regulation 556/89 (ESC, Oxford, 1989); S. Poillot Peruzzetto, "Commentaire du Règlement 556/89 relatif aux accords de licence de savoir-faire" (1989) Cah.Dr.Eur. 266; D. Waelbroeck, "Know how licensing and EEC competition rules: a commentary on Regulation 556/89" (1992) *Antitrust Bulletin* 1047; D. Winn, "Commission know-how Regulation 556/89: Innovation and territorial exclusivity, improvements and the quid pro-quo" (1990) E.C.L.R. 131–146; C. Zeyen, "The E.C. block exemption regulation on know-how: practical difficulties and legal uncertainties" (1991) E.C.L.R. 231–236.

[37] Commission Regulation 240/96 on the application of Art. 85(3) of the Treaty to certain categories of technology transfer agreements, [1996] O.J. L31/1. Consult, *inter alia*, H. Goddar, "Recent developments in European intellectual property and licensing regulations" (2000) *Les Nouvelles* 156; T. Prime and D. Booton, *European Intellectual Property Law* (Dartmouth & Ashgate, Aldershot, 2000), esp. at pp. 38 *et seq.*; N. Parr, "Avoiding antitrust pitfalls in drafting and enforcing intellectual property agreements in the European Union" (1997) E.I.P.R. 43; P. Vos and M. Slotboom, "The EC Technology Transfer Regulation—a practitioner's perspective" (1998) *The International Lawyer* 1.

[38] Commission Regulation 2658/2000 on the application of Art. 81(3) of the Treaty to categories of specialisation agreements, [2000] O.J. L304/3.

[39] Commission Regulation 2659/2000 on the application of Art. 81(3) of the Treaty to categories of research and development agreements, [2000] O.J. L304/7. See W. Winzer, "Die Freistellungsverordnung der Kommission über Forschungs- und Entwicklungsvereinbarungen vom 1. Januar 2001" (2001) GRUR Int. 413.

[40] Neither is the Regulation applicable to licence agreements in respect of breeder's rights (Art. 5(4) of Reg. 2349/84) (para. 6.01).

licence), where the parties are competitors in relation for the products in question[41];

(d) licensing agreements containing provisions relating to intellectual property rights except where such agreements are ancillary to the licensing of patents or know-how;

(e) pure sales agreements.

If the Regulation is not applicable to the agreement, an individual exemption must be sought.

6.15   **Structure**   As with its predecessors, the Regulation has the following structure:

(a) the exemption applies to agreements with one or more clearly defined obligations (see paragraph 6.16);

(b) the exemption is not precluded by the presence of any other contractual obligations "which are generally not restrictive of competition" (see paragraph 6.17);

(c) the exemption does not apply if the agreement contains provisions as referred to in paragraph 6.18: this is the "black list" of clauses that are forbidden.

The exemption granted pursuant to the Regulation may be revoked by the Commission if it decides the agreement exempted pursuant to the Regulation nevertheless has "effects" which are incompatible with the provisions of Article 81(3).[42]

6.16   **Exempted clauses**   The block exemption is applicable to agreements which include one or more of the following obligations.[43]

1. An obligation on the licensor not to license other undertakings to exploit the licensed invention in the licensed territory and not to exploit the technology there himself:

   • in the case of a pure patent licensing agreement, to the extent that and for as long as the licensed product is protected by parallel patents of the licensee;

---

[41] It is of no significance that the granting of rights by one party to the other takes place in separate agreements or by intervention of connected undertakings. Moreover, the Regulation applies to reciprocal licences provided the parties are not subject to any territorial restriction within the common market with regard to the manufacture, use or putting on the market of the licensed products or to the use of the licensed or pooled technologies.

[42] Art. 7 gives a number of examples, for instance, the absence of effective competition for relevant products, barriers to parallel trade, etc.

[43] The exemption also applies to agreements which include trade restricting obligations not covered by the Regulation, provided these agreements are notified to the Commission and there is no opposition by the Commission against the exemption within six months (Art. 4).

- in the case of a pure know-how licensing agreement, for a period of 10 years starting from the first putting on the market within the Community by one of the licensees;
- in case of a mixed licensing agreement, for 10 years starting from the first putting on the market within the Community by a licensee, or, if longer, the period available to pure patent licenses, but only in Member States in which the licensed technology is protected by necessary patents.[44]

2. An obligation on the licensee (a) not to exploit the licensed invention in territories within the Community which are reserved for the licensor; (b) not to manufacture or use the licensed invention in territories within the Community which are reserved to other licensees and (c) not to market actively the products in the territories of other licensees:

- in the case of a pure patent licensing agreement, to the extent that and for as long as the licensed product is protected by parallel patents;
- in the case of a pure know-how licensing agreement, for a period of 10 years starting from the first putting on the market within the Community by one of the licensees;
- in the case of a mixed licensing agreement, for 10 years starting from the first putting on the market within the Community by a licensee, or, if longer, the period available to pure patent licenses, but only in Member States in which the licensed technology is protected by necessary patents.

3. An obligation on the licensee not to market even passively (that is, in response of unsolicited orders) the products in the territories of other licensees during a period of five years from the moment any licensee has first put the licensed product on the market in the Community.

4. An obligation on the licensee to use only the licensor's trade mark or the get-up determined by the licensor to distinguish the licensed product, provided that the licensee is not prevented from identifying himself as the manufacturer of the licensed product.

5. An obligation to limit production and sales to what the licensee requires for his own products (provided that he may freely determine the required amount).

For points 4 and 5, the respective obligations are exempted:

- in the case of a pure patent licensing agreement, to the extent and for as long as the licensed product is protected by parallel patents;
- in the case of a pure know-how licensing agreement, during the lifetime of the license for as long as the know-how remains secret and substantial;

---

[44] A patent is necessary if in its absence the realisation of the licensed technology would not be possible or would only be possible to a lesser extent or in more difficult conditions.

- in the case of a mixed licensing agreement, for the longer period available to pure patent or know-how licenses.

6.17   **Provisions not restrictive of competition**   The exemption shall apply notwithstanding the presence, in particular, of any of the following obligations, which are generally not restrictive of competition.[45] The white list of the Regulation, which is not limitative, contains 18 obligations, *inter alia*:

1. an obligation on the licensee not to divulge know-how communicated by the licensor (even after the agreement has expired);

2. an obligation on the licensee not to grant sublicences or assign the licence;

3. an obligation on the licensee to pay a minimum royalty or to produce a minimum quantity of the licensed product or to carry out the minimum number of operations exploiting the licensed invention;

4. an obligation on the licensee not to exploit the patent after termination of the agreement in so far as the patent is still in force or the know-how is still secret;

5. an obligation on the licensee to restrict his exploitation of the licensed invention to one or more technical fields of application covered by the licensed technology patent;

6. an obligation on the licensee to mark the licensed product with an indication of the licensor's name or of the licensed patent;

7. an obligation (a) to inform the licensor of infringements of the patent; (b) to take legal actions against the infringer; and (c) to assist the licensor in any legal action against an infringer;

8. an obligation on the licensee to observe specifications concerning the minimum quality of the licensed product, provided that such specifications are necessary for a technically satisfactory exploitation of the licensed invention, and to allow the licensor to carry out related checks;

9. an obligation on the parties to communicate to one another any experience gained from exploiting the licensed technology and to grant one another a licence in respect of inventions relating to improvements and new applications, provided such communication or licence is non-exclusive;

10. an obligation on the licensee to use his best endeavours to manufacture and market the licensed product.

6.18   **Prohibited clauses**   The black list of the Regulation is limitative. The exemption[46] is not applicable if:

---

[45] These obligations may nevertheless be prohibited by Art. 81(1) "because of particular circumstances". Even then they will nonetheless be exempted (Art. 2(2)).
[46] Also the exemption mentioned in n. 34 above.

1. One party is restricted in the determination of prices, components of prices or discounts for the licensed product.

2. One party is restricted from competing within the Community, with undertakings connected with the other party or with other undertakings in respect of research and development, production, use or distribution of competing products.

3. One or both parties are required:

   (a) to refuse without any objectively justified reason to meet demand from users or resellers in their respective territories who would market products in other territories within the common market;

   (b) to make it difficult for users or resellers to obtain the products from other resellers within the common market, and in particular to exercise industrial or commercial property rights or take measures so as to prevent users or resellers from obtaining outside, or from putting on the market in, the licensed territory products which have been lawfully put on the market within the common market by the patentee or with his consent; or do so as a result of a concerted practice between them. Obligations on the licensor and the licensee hinder parallel imports in the Member States without any objectively justified reason.

4. The parties, which were competing manufacturers before the licence was granted, agree to allocate customers within the same technical field or use of the same product.

5. The parties agree on restrictions regarding the quantities of the licensed product to be manufactured or sold (subject to the explicit permissions by other provisions in the Regulation).

6. The licensee is obliged to assign in whole or in part to the licensor rights to improvements to or new applications of the licensed technology.

7. The licensor is obliged not to license other undertakings even after the period stipulated in Article 1 (see paragraph 6.16), which *de facto* results in a longer territorial protection of the licensee; or one of the parties is obliged for a longer period that stipulated in Article 1 not to exploit the licensed technology in the territory of the other party or of other licensees.

Block exemption for categories of specialisation agreements

New approach   Like Regulation 2790/1999 on Vertical Restraints (see para- **6.19** graph 5.19) and Regulation 2659/2000 on Research and Development Agreements (see paragraph 6.23), Regulation 2658/2000 on Specialisation Agreements moves away from the approach of listing exempted clauses and places more emphasis on a market share test and on specifying the "hardcore" restrictions which are not allowed in the relevant agreements.

6.20   Scope of application   Agreements on specialisation in production are agreements under which two or more undertakings concentrate on the manufacture of certain products or provision of certain services. The block exemption covers:

(1) "unilateral specialisation" agreements between competitors.[47] By such an agreement, one party gives up the manufacture of certain products or provision of certain services in favour of another participant.

(2) "reciprocal specialisation" agreements. By such an agreement, each participant gives up the manufacture of certain products or provision of certain services in favour of another participant.

(3) "joint production" agreements, whereby the participants undertake to jointly manufacture certain products and provide certain services.

The block exemption also applies to specialisation clauses contained in agreements whose primary object is, for instance, the assignment or use of intellectual property rights. It is assumed that the specialisation agreement is necessary for the implementation of such contracts.

In addition, to ensure that the benefits of specialisation will materialise without one party leaving the market downstream of production, unilateral and reciprocal specialisation agreements are covered by the Regulation where they provide for supply and purchase obligations. These obligations may, but do not have to, be of an exclusive nature.

The period of validity of the Regulation has been fixed at 10 years.

6.21   Market share threshold   The block exemption can only apply to agreements where the combined market share of the participating undertakings does not exceed 20 per cent of the relevant market. The definition of the relevant market is based upon the notion of relevant product and the relevant geographical market. The 20 per cent market share threshold is calculated on the basis of the market sales value corresponding to the preceding calendar year.[48]

6.22   Prohibited clauses   Irrespective of the market share of the undertakings concerned, the agreement will not benefit from the block exemption of it contains any of the restrictions listed in Article 5:

(a) the fixing of prices when selling the products to third parties;

(b) the limitation of output or sales;

(c) the allocation of markets or customers.

---

[47] Unilateral specialisation agreements between non-competitors may benefit from the block exemption provided from Regulation 2790/99 (see para. 5.19).

[48] Regulation 2658/2000, Art. 6(1). If no market sales value data are available, recourse may be made to other market information, such as market sales volumes. The market share threshold of 20 per cent is somehow flexible. According to Art. 6(2) of the Regulation, some *a posteriori* increases of market share (that is, when initial market share was not more than 20 per cent but subsequently rises) continue to be exempted for defined periods of time.

On the other hand, the "black list" does not cover:

(a) provisions on the agreed amount of products in the context of unilateral or reciprocal specialisation agreements or the setting of the capacity and production volume in the context of a joint production agreement;

(b) the setting of sales targets and the fixing of prices that a production joint venture charges to its immediate customers.

Block exemption for research and development agreements

Scope of application   A Regulation of the Commission of November 29, **6.23** 2000 exempts certain categories of research and development agreements from the prohibition of Article 81(1) E.C. Treaty.[49] The period of validity of the Regulation is 10 years.

The new block exemption applies to agreements entered into between two or more undertakings which relate to joint research or joint exploitation of products and processes; joint exploitation of the results in prior research or exploitation agreements or joint research and development of products or processes excluding joint exploitation of the results.

Article 3 of Regulation 2659/2000 sets out the conditions for exemption. In the first place, all the parties must have access to the results of the joint research and development for the purposes of further research or exploitation. If, however, the agreement excludes joint exploitation of resuts, each party must be free independently to exploit the results. Secondly, the joint exploitation must relate to results which are protected by intellectual property rights or constitute know-how. Thirdly, it is compulsory that the undertakings charged with manufacture fulfil orders for supplies from all the parties, unless where joint distribution is provided for.

Duration and market share threshold   Two hypotheses are advanced. **6.24** Where the concerned undertakings are not competitors, the exemption lasts for the duration of the research and development. In case of joint exploitation, the exemption continues to apply for seven years as from the first commercialisation within the common market.

In case of competitors, however, the exemption lasts for the duration of the research and development only if, at the time of entering into the agreement, the combined market share of the participating undertakings does not exceed 25 per cent of the relevant market. The definition of the relevant market is based upon the notion of relevant product and the relevant geographical market. The 25 per cent market share threshold is calculated on the basis of the market sales value corresponding to the preceding calendar year.[50]

---

[49] *cf.* n. 39, above.

[50] Regulation 2659/2000, Art. 6(1) If no market sales value data are available, recourse may be made to other market information, such as market sales volumes. The market share threshold of 25 per cent is somehow flexible. According to Art. 6(2) of the Regulation, some *a posteriori* increases of market share (that is, initial market share was not more than 25 per cent and subsequently rises) continue to be exempted for defined periods of time.

Below the 25 per cent market share threshold, the exemption continues beyond the duration of the research and development agreement.

6.25   **Prohibited clauses**   Irrespective of the market share of the undertakings concerned, the agreement will not benefit from the block exemption of it contains any of the restrictions listed in Article 5:

    (a) the restriction for the participating undertakings to carry out research and development independently or in co-operation with third parties in a field unconnected with the field covered by the agreement;

    (b) the prohibition to challenge the validity of intellectual property rights in the common market relating to the research and development, without prejudice to the possibility to provide for termination of the agreement if one of the parties challenges the validity of such intellectual property rights;

    (c) the limitation of output or sales;

    (d) the fixing of prices in contracts with third parties;

    (e) the allocation of customers or the prohibition to make active sales in territories reserved for other parties after the end of seven years from the time the contract products were first commercialised within the common market;

    (f) the prohibition on the making of passive sales in territories reserved for other parties;

    (g) the requirement not to grant licences to third parties where the exploitation of the results of the joint research and development is not provided for or does not take place;

    (h) the limitation as to the acceptance of demand from users or resellers;

    (i) the limitation on making parallel import difficult or impossible.

On the other hand, the "black list" does not cover:

    (a) the setting of production targets where the exploitation of the results includes the joint production of the contract products;

    (b) the setting of sales targets and the fixing of prices charged to immediate customers where the exploitation of the results includes the joint distribution of the contract products.

PART IV: TRANSFER OF TECHNOLOGY TO DEVELOPING COUNTRIES

6.26   **Technological deficit**   Developing countries need technology for industrialisation. In most cases, this technology originates from abroad. The wide technological gap between developed and developing countries may be bridged through the transfer of technology (through investment, licensing or other transfer arrangements).

However, the transfer of technology from industrialised countries to developing countries, can give rise to various problems,[51] for example:

- the amount of royalties may inhibit fast industrialisation and may burden the balance of payment;

- an export prohibition or the obligation on the licensee to purchase certain raw materials and/or machinery from the licensor may affect the cost-effectiveness of the local exploitation;

- usually there are no guarantees that the exploitation of transferred technology will be possible, let alone profitable, or that it is suitable to local needs.

In order to protect national interests, the agreements for the transfer of technology are subjected to control and restrictions in many developing countries. Transfer of technology is also the subject of bilateral (investment) treaties (see paragraphs 7.05 *et seq.*), of multilateral treaties and of codes of conduct (see paragraph 6.32) regarding contracts for the transfer of technology. Above all, it must be underlined that the TRIPs Agreement (see paragraphs 3.98 *et seq.*) provides a global framework for protecting technology development and technology acquisition.

The impact of TRIPs on transfer of technology to developing countries   **6.27** The rationale behind the TRIPs Agreement is that an increased level of protection and enforcement of intellectual property rights should contribute to "the promotion of technological invention and to the transfer and dissemination of technology" (Article 7). As from January 1, 2000, all developing countries are bound by the provisions of the TRIPs Agreement.[52]

Several provisions in TRIPs expressly refer to transfer of technology to developing countries.

---

[51] See, *e.g.* S. Alikhan, *Socio-Economic Benefits of Intellectual Property in Developing Countries* (WIPO, Geneva, 2000); M. Blakeney, *Legal Aspects of the Transfer of Technology to Developing Countries* (ESC, Oxford, 1989); M. Ferrantino, "The effect of intellectual property rights on international trade and investment" (1993) *Weltwirtschaftliches Archiv* 300; T. Frankel, "Knowledge transfer: suggestions for countries on the receiving end" (1995) Boston Univ. I.L.J. 141; U. Kumar, "Benefits of the industrial property system and the African developing countries" (1993) World Comp. 71; K. E. Maskus, "The role of international property rights in encouraging foreign direct investment and technology transfer" (1999) Duke J.Comp.&Int.L. 109; C. A. Primo Braga and C. Fink, "The relationship between intellectual property rights and foreign direct investment" (1999) Duke J.Comp.&Int.L. 163; R.T. Rapp and R.P. Rozek, "Benefits and costs of intellectual property protection in developing countries" (1990/5) J.W.T. 75; A. Subramanian, *Trade-Related Intellectual Property Rights and Asian Developing Countries: an Analytical View* (Asian Development Bank, Manila, 1995); A. Wolff, "Technology transfer to developing countries" (1998) *Comparative Law Yearbook of International Business* 399.

[52] With the exception of the patentability of certain products. Least developed countries can delay the implementation of the Agreement until 2006.

In the patent field, the TRIPs Agreement allows Member States to, *inter alia*, establish compulsory licences on various grounds (Article 31).[53] Compulsory licensing enables countries to compel the owner of a patent to license it to others for social and other policy reasons and accordingly has the effect of limiting the monopoly power of the patent holder.[54]

According to Article 66(2) of TRIPs, developed countries are obliged to provide incentives under their legislation to their own enterprises and institutions for the purpose of promoting and encouraging the transfer of technology to the least developed countries "in order to enable them to create a sound and viable technological base".[55] The Council for TRIPs is responsible for administering and monitoring compliance with the TRIPs Agreement. Types of measures taken include export and investment promotion, export finance and other financial incentives, including tax credits and loans, infrastructure projects and provision of training, and technical information, including technical assistance and expertise.[56]

Competition policy may also be used to promote transfer of technology. Article 40 of the TRIPs Agreement permits applying competition rules to restrictive business practices in voluntary licensing agreements. Yet, except for a number of illustrative examples (such as grant-backs, no challenge clauses, coercive package licensing), the determination of unlawful practices is left to the Member States.[57]

Technology transfer rules beyond TRIPs

National and regional regulations

6.28   **Legislative changes in developing countries**[58]   In the late 1960s and the 1970s, a number of developing countries subjected contracts for the transfer of technology to precautionary control by government institution. The purpose of this legislation was to protect the technology transferee, not only against the

---

[53] In addition to this the Paris Convention (see para. 6.04) authorises the competent national authorities to grant a compulsory patent licence to one or more third parties if the patent owner fails to make sufficient use of his invention during a minimum period (three or four years, depending on the situation) and if he is unable to justify this failure with valid reasons.

[54] S. K. Verma, "The TRIPs Agreement and Development" *in* S. J. Patel, P. Roffe and A. Yusuf, (eds), *International Technology Transfer. The Origins and Aftermath of the United Nations Negotiations on a Draft Code of Conduct* (Kluwer Law International, The Hague, 2001) 332 *et seq.*; E. Durán and C. Michalopoulos, "Intellectual property rights and developing countries in the WTO Millenium Round" (2000) J.I.E.L. 853.

[55] C. M. Correa, "Review of the TRIPs Agreement. Fostering the transfer of technology to developing countries" (2000) J.I.E.L. 853; S. K. Verma, *op. cit.*, 346 *et seq.*

[56] For the Council's Annual Report for 2000, see WTO document under no. IP/C/W/132, available at www.wto.org.

[57] C. M. Correa, "Pro-competitive measures under the TRIPS Agreement to promote technology diffusion in developing countries" (2001) J.W.I.P. 481; H. Ulrich, "Competition, intellectual property rights and transfer of technology" *in* S. J. Patel, P. Roffe and A. Yusuf, *op. cit.*, 363 *et seq.*; C. M. Correa, *op. cit*, 954–955.

[58] P. Gallagher, *Guide to the WTO and Developing Countries* (Kluwer, London, 2000) 52 *et seq.*; A. Omer, "An overview of legislative changes" *in* S. J. Patel, P. Roffe and A. Yusuf, 301 *et seq.*

foreign technology transferor, but also against himself, for he was often insufficiently informed about the existing technology and the procurement conditions thereof on the international markets.[59]

More recently, and especially against the TRIPs background, the focus on "control" of transfer of technology has been abandoned. A number of countries have liberalised the provisions of their technology transfer legislation or have implemented it in a pragmatic way. Accordingly, "negative clauses" (*i.e.* clauses which are in principle prohibited because they restrict the economic autonomy and the profitability of the investment) may be permitted if the contract is evidently advantageous for the country concerned.

Regional unions Special rules for technology transfer contracts are also in   **6.29**
force in regional unions of developing countries.

The Andean Group Countries Common Regime on Foreign Investment and Transfer of Technology of 1996[60] has been revised in order to adopt a more liberal approach towards foreign investment and transfer of technology. In particular, foreign investors have the same rights and obligations as national investors. Member States may now consider foreign contributions, such as trade marks, industrial models and technical know-how as contributions to foreign investment.

The North American Free Trade Agreement (NAFTA) (see paragraph 2.36) leaves to domestic laws the adoption of appropriate measures to prevent or control licensing practices on the basis of intellectual property rights that may affect competition in the relevant market.

International treaties

Investment treaties Numerous bilateral investment treaties (see paragraphs   **6.30**
7.05 *et seq.*) between industrialised countries and developing countries also concern the transfer of technology. The notion of "investment" is usually given a wide definition, and includes, for instance, "rights to industrial property, technical manufacturing processes and technical skills" (see also paragraph 7.06). The investments protection introduced by the treaty is thus also applicable to technical knowledge.

In recent bilateral investment treaties, especially those sponsored by the United States, supervision over the transfer of technology is explicitly provided for.[61]

---

[59] See, for an overview, the first edition of this book.

[60] Agreement of Cartagena of May 26, 1969 between Bolivia, Colombia, Ecuador, Peru and Venezuela; Andean Pact: Decision 344 regarding Common Provisions on Industrial Property (1995) I.L.M. 1635. *Cf.* I. Mogollón-Rojas, "The New Andean Pact Decision No. 486 on the Common Industrial Rights Regime—complying with TRIPS Regulations" (2001) J.W.I.P. 549.

[61] UNCTAD, *International Investment Instruments: A Compendium* (UN Publication, New York, 1996), cited in: P. Roffe and T. Tesfachew, "The Unfinished Agenda" *in* S. J. Patel, P. Roffe and A. Yusuf, *op. cit.*, 398.

Similarly, in the inconclusive attempt to provide a Multilateral Agreement on Investment in the OECD framework (see paragraph 7.44), it had been proposed to prohibit performance requirements related to:

"transfer of technology, a production process or other proprietary knowledge to local persons or enterprises, unless this is enforced by a court or competition authority to remedy violation of competition laws, or this concerns the transfer of intellectual property and is undertaken in a manner consistent with the TRIPs Agreement."

6.31   The Cotonou Agreement   After 1975 the ties between the European Union and a group of African, Caribbean and Pacific (ACP) countries were governed by the regularly adapted and updated Lomé Convention. However, this Convention expired in February 2000. A new 20-year partnership agremeent between the E.U. and a group of 77 ACP countries was signed in June 2000 in Cotonou (Benin) (see paragraph 2.58).

The Cotonou Agreement contains relevant provisions in trade-related areas, such as competition policy or the protection of intellectual property rights (Articles 45 and 46). It must be stressed that a fully WTO-compatible regime is one of the objectives of the Cotonou Agreement. Economic operators should then be more inclined to establish closer relations with their ACP partners, domestic and foreign investment is expected to grow and more know-how and technology will be transferred—all of which will boost ACP countries' competitiveness and ease their smooth and gradual integration into the world economy.

6.32   International "codes of conduct"   There are relatively few international instruments with built-in implementation mechanisms, including financial provisions and monitoring arrangements. Most technology-related provisions at international level are of a "best-efforts" nature.[62]

Here are some illustrations:

* The Guidelines of the OECD concerning multinational companies, which are not legally binding, formulate some general principles for the international transfer of technology:

    — endeavour to ensure that their activities fit satisfactorily into the scientific and technological policies and plans of the countries in which they operate, and contribute to the development of national scientific and technological potential, including, as far as appropriate, the establishment and improvement in host countries of their capacity to innovate;

    — to the fullest extent practicable, adopt in the course of their business activities practices which permit the rapid diffusion of technologies with due regard to the protection of industrial and intellectual property rights;

---

[62] UNCTAD, Expert Meeting on International Arrangements for Transfer of Technology, Geneva, June 27, 2001, documents available at: www.unctad.org.

— to grant licences for the use of industrial property rights or to other-wise transfer technology on reasonable terms and conditions.

● Similarly, the Tripartite Declaration of the International Labour Organisa-tion (ILO) on multinational companies also deals with exploitation of technology in developing countries: investors have to take into account the characteristic features and needs of the host countries and the possibility of contributing to the development of the appropriate technology. Moreover, the technologies should directly or indirectly create jobs in the developing countries.

● The negotiations towards a UN Code of conduct on transnational corpora-tions have so far been unsuccesful.[63]

PART V: INTERNATIONAL RULES IN RESPECT OF "COUNTERFEIT ARTICLES"

Counterfeiting and the TRIPs Agreement Counterfeiting of patented **6.33** inventions and especially trade marks occurs frequently in the international trade of luxury articles, medicines and foodstuffs in particular. This counterfeiting is not only an infringement on the exclusive right of the patent or trade mark owner, but it can also be detrimental (in the case of foodstuffs and medicines, even damaging) to consumers, who are under the impression that they are buying the genuine, reputable article.

Counterfeiting and piracy[64] have grown into an international phenomenon, accounting for between 5 per cent and 7 per cent of world trade. The traditional legal routes against counterfeiting do not usually offer a solution, because the law on industrial property in the countries where these products are manufactured or sold is inadequate or insufficiently enforceable. For this reason, attempts have been made world-wide to introduce the necessary remedies.

During the Tokyo Round of the GATT (see paragraph 3.13), fruitless efforts were made, at the instigation of the industralised countries, to establish a "code of conduct" regarding counterfeiting (Draft Anti-counterfeiting Code, ACC).[65] In the meantime the International Chamber of Commerce (see paragraph 2.30)

---

[63] See J. Faundez, "The code and globalization—contemporary relevance" *in* S. J. Patel, P. Roffe and A. Yusuf, *op. cit.*, 301 *et seq.*; P. Lansing and A. Rosaria, "An analysis of the United Nations proposed code of conduct for transnational corporation" (1991) World Comp. 33.

[64] Piracy refers to the infringement of copyright. According to the TRIPs Agreement, "pirated copyright goods" shall mean any goods which are copies made without the consent of the right holder or person duly authorised by the right holder in the country of production and which are made directly or indirectly from an article where the making of that copy would have constituted an infringement of a copyright or a related right under the law of the country of importation." *Cf.* M. Traphagan, "Software piracy and global competitiveness: Report on global software piracy" (1998) Int'l Rev. of Law, Comp. & Tech. 431.

[65] The draft agreement on measures to discourage the importation of counterfeit goods (GATT Doc. L/8417 (July 31, 1979)). *Cf., inter alia,* T. Cottier, "The prospects for intellectual property in GATT" (1991) C.M.L. Rev. 386 *et seq.*

has established a Counterfeiting Intelligence Bureau in London to detect actual cases of trade in counterfeit products.[66]

The major breakthrough at international level has been the adoption of the TRIPs Agreement (see paragraph 3.98).[67] On the one hand, the improvement of substantive provisions on intellectual property provides an indirect way of combatting counterfeiting. Another way of dealing with counterfeiting within the TRIPs Agreement is the adoption of measures and procedures for enforcing intellectual property rights. In this respect, the TRIPs Agreement urges Member States to introduce adequate sanctions on the infringement of intellectual or industrial property rights (fines, prison sentences, confiscation and destruction of the counterfeit articles and compensation). Furthermore, section 4 in Part III (Enforcement) contains special requirements related to border measures. In order to facilitate the implementation of this part of the TRIPs Agreement, the World Customs Organisation has issued a model law to give national customs authorities powers to prevent cross-border traffic in counterfeit and pirated goods.[68]

These TRIPs provisions include the following rules and principles:

- The contracting states shall adopt legal rules which grant the owner of an exclusive right the power to challenge the release by the national customs authorities of goods of which there is a prima facie suspicion that they are counterfeit products[69]; to avoid abuse, it may be required that the owner of the exclusive right must first deposit a security.

- The customs authorities may suspend the release of the relevant goods for 10 working days, with possibly one extension of another 10 working days; if the owner of an exclusive right has not brought a claim to a competent court within that period, the goods must be released, if they otherwise satisfy the conditions for import or export.

- The owner of an exclusive right shall indemnify the importer or owner of the goods, if it appears that the goods were wrongfully detained by the customs authorities on instigation of the owner of the exclusive right.

- The Member States may also determine that the customs authorities must officially refuse to release goods which are suspected to be counterfeit products.

- Under threat of other, *i.e.* civil, sanctions, the national authorities may order that the counterfeit articles are taken out of trade, or even destroyed if this

---

[66] For the same purpose the Netherlands has founded a "Stichting Namaakbestrijding", the U.K. "the Anti-Counterfeiting Group", France "l'Union des fabricants", Italy "le Comité de lutte anti-contrefaçon" and the U.S. "the International Anti-Counterfeiting Coalition".

[67] R. Mackenzie, "Protecting transnational investment in intellectual property rights: legal issues and risk management strategies" (2000) E.B.L.R. 105; J. Werner, "Trade mark protection and counterfeiting—the Kappa Group experience" (1999) J.W.I.P. 407.

[68] World Customs Organisation, *Model for National Legislation to Give Customs Powers to Implement the Agreement on Trade-related Aspects of Intellectual Property Rights* (WCO, Brussels, 1995), available at: www.wcoomd.org.

[69] By virtue of the *de minimis* rule, the Member States may decide that the regulation does not apply to small quantities of fake articles found in personal luggage of travellers or to small parcels sent by post.

is permitted under the applicable law. When adopting these measures proportionality between the seriousness of the offences and the intended sanction shall be taken into account and the rights of third parties have to be safeguarded.

• Recourse against the decisions of the national authorities should be available.

Combating counterfeiting in the E.U.   The European Union has adopted a   **6.34**
system of border measures to prevent counterfeit or pirated goods from entering of leaving its territory. The first measure was adopted on December 1, 1986.[70] The system was then thoroughly revised by Council Regulations 3295/94[71] and 241/1999.[72]

Under the current regime, the scope of border controls includes not only imports, but also exports and goods in transit.[73] The notion of "counterfeited articles" has been extended to cover, besides "goods wrongfully fitted with brandnames or trademarks", patented products, as well as medicinal and plant protection products which are the subject of supplementary protection certificates.

The Regulation imposes obligations on the national customs authorities. If they suspect certain declared goods to be "fakes" they must refuse to release those goods for free circulation in the E.U. The ECJ has ruled that national legislation impinging on the obligations arising from the Regulation must be set aside.[74] Furthermore, the national governments must take appropriate measures (such as the destruction of the goods) once it is established that counterfeit articles, as defined by the Regulation, are brought into circulation.

---

[70] Regulation 3842/86 for the adoption of measures to prohibit the bringing into free circulation of counterfeit articles, [1986] O.J. L357/1 (erratum: [1987] L33/18). More detailed rules were adopted by the Commission Regulation 3077/87 [1987] O.J. L219/19. For a commentary, see S. Billings, "EEC Council Regulation 3842/86. An effective piracy weapon?" (1988) E.I.P.R. 346–348; An analogous regulation in the U.S. was declared in conflict with the GATT by a Panel; see J. Rogers, "The demise of section 337's GATT legality" (1990) E.I.P.R. 275 et seq.; L. Barons, "Amending section 337 to obtain GATT consistency and retain border protection" (1991) L.&Pol.Int'l.Bus. 289; F. Foster and J. Davidow, "GATT and reform of US Section 337" (1996) *International Lawyer* 97.

[71] Council Reg. 3295/94 on measures to prohibit the release for free circulation, export, re-export or entry for a suspensive procedure of counterfeit and pirated goods [1994] O.J. L341. See A. Clark, "The use of border measures to prevent international trade in counterfeit and pirated goods: implementation and proposed reform of Council Regulation 3295/94" (1998) E.I.P.R. 414; J. Phillips, "Fakin' it" (1999) E.I.P.R. 275–278.

[72] Council Regulation 241/1999 amending Regulation 3295/94 laying down measures to prohibit the release for free circulation, export, re-export or entry for a suspensive procedure of counterfeit and pirated goods [1999] O.J. L27.

[73] The ECJ ruled in the *Polo/Lauren* case that the Regulation is applicable to counterfeited goods imported from a non-Member State and which are temporarily detained in a Member State by the customs authorities in the course of their transit to another non-member: ECJ, April 6, 2000, *The Polo/Lauren Company /Dwidua*, Case C–383/98 [2000] E.C.R. I–2519; [2000] E.I.P.R. N–135.

[74] In the *Adidas* case, the ECJ ruled that a provision of national law requiring the names of consignees of consignments detained by the customs authorities to be kept confidential was incompatible with the provisions of Regulation 3295/94. ECJ, October 14, 1999, *Adidas AG*, Case C–223/98 [1999] E.C.R. I–7081.

In 1998, the European Commission issued a Green Paper on Combating Counterfeiting and Piracy in the Single Market.[75] On the basis of this, the European Commission has adopted a Communication announcing a series of practical measures intended to improve and step up the fight against counterfeiting and piracy in the Single Market. Special emphasis will be put now on the enforcement of anti-counterfeiting and anti-piracy measures *within* the Community, rather than at its common borders. Harmonisation will concern mainly the measures and procedures for searching, seizure and proof, the criteria for calculating damages and the right to information.

PART VI: CONFLICT OF LAW RULES

6.35   **Licensing agreements**   Licensing agreements are contracts in which the right to use intangible property rights is granted to a licensee (see paragraph 6.09). They have contractual and proprietary aspects.

The contractual aspects of a licensing agreement are governed by the proper law of the contract. This law can be identified through the conflict of law rules (as described in paragraph 1.24). It is common for licensing agreements to contain an explicit choice of law, which must be observed. The court may, if necessary, accept an implied choice of law. If, in order to find this law, the "characteristic performance" ought to be found, it appears that this performance is in principle performed by the licensor who grants the user right (not by the licensee, who in most cases only pays royalties). Thus, the licensing agreement is basically governed by the law of the licensor. However, if the licensee takes on a number of other obligations (*e.g.* distribution of goods), the licensee is the producer of the characteristic performance, which means that the licensing agreement is governed by the law of the licensee.[76] The criterion of the "characteristic performance" for licensing agreements may also be rejected. This can be when "it appears from the entirety of circumstances that the agreement has a closer connection with" the state in which the intellectual property rights are concentrated and protected. In many countries it has therefore been accepted that agreements for intellectual property rights are governed by the law of the state that protects those rights.[77]

The proprietary extent of the licensing agreement is, on the contrary, governed by the law by virtue of which the intellectual rights exist, have substance and are protected. Thus, this law determines whether there can in fact be a licence and to

---

[75] COM(98) 569 final, E.C. Green Paper on Combating Counterfeiting and Piracy in the Single Market, October 15, 1998.

[76] See J. J. Fawcett and P. Torremans, *Intellectual Property and Private International Law* (Clarendon Press, Oxford, 1998) 558 *et seq.*; E. Ulmer, *Intellectual Property Rights and the Conflict of Laws* (Kluwer/Commission of the European Communities, Deventer, 1978) pp. 94 *et seq.*; C. Wadlow, *Enforcement of Intellectual Property in European and International Law* (Sweet & Maxwell, London, 1998); C. Wadlow, "Intellectual property and the Rome Contracts Convention" (1997) E.I.P.R. 11; E. V. Zenhäusern, *Der internationale Lizenzvertrag* (Universitätsverlag, Freiburg, 1991) pp. 100 *et seq.*

[77] J. J. Fawcett and P. Torremans, *op. cit.*, 567–570 with further references; V. Zenhäusern, *op. cit.*, 98.

what extent the licensee can institute a claim if third parties infringe on his right.[78]

Assignment   Contracts for transferring the title of patents, trade marks and other intellectual property rights have contractual as well as proprietary effects.   6.36

The contractual effect is determined by the law of the contract chosen by the parties or indicated by the conflict of law rules (see paragraph 6.37).

The proprietary effect is determined by the law of the country in which the intellectual property rights are rooted. That law will establish whether, for example, the partial assignment of an industrial property right is possible.[79] This law will also outline the formalities (*e.g.* registration) necessary to make the assignment stand up against third parties.[80]

---

[78] J. J. Fawcett and P. Torremans, *op. cit.*, 545–546; E. Ulmer, *op. cit.*, 90–91; V. Zenhäusern, *op. cit.*, 88–89.

[79] J. J. Fawcett and P. Torremans, *op. cit.*, 546; E. Ulmer, *op. cit.*, 90–91.

[80] E. Ulmer, *op. cit.*, 88–90. See in general, S. Soltysinski, "Choice of law and choice of forum in transnational transfer of technology transactions" (1986) I. Rec.Cours. 239.

CHAPTER 7

FOREIGN INVESTMENT

Overview Foreign investment plays an important role in rich industrialised **7.01**
countries as well as in poorer developing countries.[1] In less developed countries,
foreign investment has often become an essential engine for economic development. That explains why some specialised international organisations aim at
facilitating foreign investment in developing countries.

Countries may not always like the hold that foreign investors have over them.
In less developed countries, for instance, foreign investors often control a
considerable part of the national economy. Host countries may want to limit or
regulate foreign investments. Foreign investments are indeed a risk as well as a
blessing. Each country therefore needs to articulate a balanced policy to attract
as well as control foreign investments.[2]

PART I: INTERNATIONAL INVESTMENT VEHICLES

Overview Many international organisations put considerable funds at the **7.02**
disposal of developing countries for the financing of development projects. The
origins of the funds differ from organisation to organisation. Generally, only a
small proportion comes from their own capital; more money is raised either from
rich donor countries or on the private capital market.

---

[1] The majority of foreign direct investment, whether from the U.S., the E.U. or Japan, is in the
developed economies of the OECD. Direct investment in OECD countries accounts for over 70%
of Japan's $465 billion in investments, 75% of the U.S.'s $621 billion in investments and over 80%
of the nearly $1 trillion of the E.U.'s investments. Investments in non-OECD countries follow a
vague pattern of specialisation among the three major investors, the U.S., the E.U. and Japan. U.S.
investments are more heavily concentrated in Latin America, accounting for 60% of U.S. investments in non-OECD countries. The E.U. has a higher concentration of investments in Africa (46%)
and Central Europe (34%). Foreign direct investment by OECD countries was $2.1 trillion in 1994
and $3.2 trillion in 1998. For detailed data, see *International Direct Investment Statistics Yearbook*
(OECD, Paris, 1999); www.cnie.org/nle/econ–61.html and www.oecd.org/daf/investment/recent-
trends.htm; S. N. Carlson, "Foreign investment laws and foreign direct investment in developing
countries" (1995) 29 Int.L.577.
[2] See, *e.g.* the World Bank's "Guidelines on the Treatment of Foreign Direct Investment" (1992) 31
I.L.M. 1363 and (1992) 7 I.C.S.I.D. Rev. 2, devoted exclusively to these guidelines; A. H. Qureshi,
"International investment law", in *International Economic Law* (Sweet and Maxwell, London,
1999), pp. 369–391; M. J. Trebilcock, R. Howse, "Trade and investment" in *The Regulation of
International Trade* (2nd ed., Routledge, London and New York, 1998) pp. 335–367; A. R. Parra,
"The scope of new investment laws and international instruments", in R. Pritchard (ed.), *Economic
Development, Foreign Investment and the Law* (Kluwer International, 1996); M. Sornarajah, *The
International Law on Foreign Investment* (Cambridge University Press, 1994).

International financing organisations are not only important for the funds they invest themselves in projects in developing countries (road construction, telecommunication, building of factories, etc.); their investments are also an important incentive to involve private investors in these projects.

When an international financing organisation decides to support a specific project in a developing country, the state or one of the state entities generally has to commission the work. The financing organisation in consultation with the customer then puts the work out to tender for prospective foreign investors. In principle, the most attractive offer is accepted, but sometimes other considerations play a part in the awarding of the contract, such as the nationality of the tenderer. During the execution of the project the financing agency frequently maintains control over the work, often paying the contractor directly.

7.03   **The World Bank**   The World Bank plays a significant role in the financing of projects in developing countries. In fact the World Bank is a combination of five closely associated institutions:

- the International Bank for Reconstruction and Development (IBRD);

- the International Development Association (IDA);

- the International Finance Corporation (IFC);

- the Multilateral Investment Guarantee Agency (MIGA);

- the International Centre for Settlement of Investment Disputes (ICSID).

Established in 1944, the IBRD is the oldest and most important of the five organisations. It grants loans to the governments of developing countries for the financing of specific projects considered useful for the development of the recipient country. Thus, the IBRD finances, for instance, road works, telecommunications, agricultural projects, industrial development, and also education and health projects. Funds come in part from contributions by the Member States of the IBRD; the majority of funds, however, are raised on the capital market. Moneys received from the IBRD must be paid back with interest after a few years. The IBRD frequently funds projects in co-operation with private financial institutions, such as banks.[3] In 2000 the World Bank had $120.1 billion outstanding in loans.[4]

The IDA was founded in 1960 to complement the IBRD. It is solely intended for the poorest developing countries and finances the same kind of projects as the IBRD, but on less stringent conditions. For instance, it charges less or no interest on its loans and it also provides loans for a longer period, usually 50 years, for which the repayment demands only start after 10 years. The IDA gets its working

---

[3] P. Fresle, "Co-financing and mixed credits", in N. Horn (ed.), *The Law of International Trade Finance* (Kluwer Law and Taxation, Deventer, 1989) p. 411; H. Morais, "World bank promotion of private investment flows to developing countries through co-financing and other measures" (1988) I.C.S.I.D. Rev. 1; E. U. Petersmann, "Die Entwickelungsdarlehen und Kofinanzierungen der Weltbank" (1984) ZaÖRV 290 ; J. W. Head, "Evolution of the governing law for loan agreements of the World Bank and other multilateral development banks" (1996) A.J.I.L. 90, pp. 214–234.

[4] World Bank Annual Report (Washington, 2000); World Bank Highlights Fiscal Year 2000 on http://www.worldbank.org/html/extpb/annrep/fiscal.htm.

capital from the IBRD and the richer countries. In 2000 the IDA had $86.6 billion outstanding in credits.[5]

The IFC promotes growth in the developing world by financing private sector investments and providing technical assistance and advice to governments and businesses. In partnership with private investors, the IFC provides both loan and equity finance for business ventures in developing countries. It finances private enterprises in exchange for shares in those enterprises. When the time is right, it disposes of this share participation in order to reinvest the proceeds in other enterprises. In 2000 the IFC had a share capital of $2.3 billion.[6] Since its founding in 1956, the IFC has committed more than $29 billion of its own funds and has arranged $19.2 billion in syndications and underwriting for 2,446 companies in 136 developing countries.

The Multilateral Investment Guarantee Agency helps to encourage foreign investment in developing countries by providing guarantees to foreign investors against loss caused by non-commercial risks. MIGA also provides technical assistance to help countries disseminate information on investment opportunities (see paragraphs 7.45–7.50).

The International Centre for Settlement of Investment Disputes provides facilities for the settlement—by conciliation or arbitration—of investment disputes between foreign investors and their host countries (see paragraphs 7.36–7.44).

Regional development banks Regional development banks are also involved in project financing[7]; for instance, the African Development Bank,[8] the Asian Development Bank,[9] the Inter-American Development Bank.[10] These   **7.04**

---

[5] World Bank Annual Report (Washington, 2000); World Bank Highlights Fiscal Year 2000 on http://www.worldbank.org/html/extpb/annrep/fiscal.htm.

[6] See http://www.ifc.org.

[7] G. Handl, "The legal mandate of multilateral development banks as agents for change towards sustainable development" (1998) 92 Am.J.Int'l. L. 642; Sc.L. Hoffman, *The Law and Business of International Project Finance* (Kluwer Law International, 1998).

[8] The African Development Bank is the premier pan-African development finance institution established in 1964 to foster economic growth and social progress in Africa. The Bank is owned by 77 Member States in Africa, Europe, Asia, and the Americas. It is based in Abidjan, Côte d'Ivoire, West Africa. See more information on www.afdb.org; P. Ofosu-Amaah, I. Vasques, "The role of multilateral institutions in African development" (1999) 30 L.and Pol.Int'l.Bus. 697; H. M. Mule and P. E. English, *The African Development Bank* (Intermediate Technology Public, London, 1996).

[9] The Asian Development Bank, a multilateral development finance institution, was founded in 1966 by 31 governments to promote the social and economic progress of the Asia-Pacific region. It now has 59 Member States—43 within the region and 16 non-regional. The Asian Development Bank gives special attention to the needs of the smaller or less-developed countries and to regional, sub-regional, and national projects and programmes. See more information on www.adb.org; (1966) I.L.M. 262.

[10] The Inter-American Development Bank, the oldest and largest regional multilateral development institution, was established in 1959 to help to accelerate economic and social development in Latin America and the Caribbean. The Bank was created in response to a long-standing desire on the part of the Latin American nations for a development institution that would focus on the pressing problems of the region. The Bank's original membership included 19 Latin American and Caribbean countries and the U.S. Today Bank membership totals 46 nations. Annual lending has grown dramatically from the $294 million in loans approved in 1961 to $5 billion in 2000. For more information see www.Iadb.org; Annual Report (2000, Inter-American Development Bank, Washington D.C.).

banks fund each projects in a particular region. Their capital is in part subscribed by the countries of the region. However, a large part of the capital is brought in by wealthy countries from outside the region. Sometimes the banks allow companies from donor countries to benefit from projects in proportion to their countries' respective contribution ("flow back").

7.05 **European Bank for Reconstruction and Development** Projects in the former Eastern bloc countries may be financed by the European Bank for Reconstruction and Development (EBRD: Banque Européenne de Reconstruction et de Développement—BERD). The E.U., the European Investment Bank and the E.U. Member States have 51 per cent of the votes in this London-based institution; some 46 other countries (not only Eastern bloc countries, but also the United States, Canada, Japan) also participate. The EBRD began its operations in 1991. It borrows money on the capital markets and predominantly finances projects in the private sector through loans or capital participation. The EBRD also supports large infrastructural works. It aims, particularly, at supplementing funding by the other international lending agencies (World Bank, IFC) (see paragraph 7.03). The EBRD operates as a bank: it supports only economically viable projects; it demands repayment with interest; it does not give preferential treatment; its funding of each project is restricted.[11]

7.06 **The E.U.** Development projects in most countries in Africa, the Caribbean or the Pacific (ACP countries) may be financed by the Investment Facility under the Cotonou Agreement (see paragraph 2.58). Also the European Investment Bank grants substantial loans to non-E.U.countries for development projects.[12]

Projects within the E.U. are financed by the E.U. institutions. Thus the European Investment Bank grants loans for new investments and more specifically for regional development projects. It also finances the improvement of public infrastructure, for example, road networks. The European Social Fund finances projects in the economically weaker regions of the E.U.

7.07 **UN organisations** Furthermore, development projects may be funded by the UN or one of its specialised agencies (FAO, WHO, etc.) (see paragraph 2.27). An important source of investment is in this respect the United Nations Development Programme (UNDP) (see paragraph 2.25). The UNDP is financed by voluntary contributions from the Member States and invests annually in thousands of projects.

---

[11] See (1990) 29 I.L.M. 1077; [1990] O.J. C241/1; J. Demoly and G. Kre, "La Banque européenne pour la réconstruction et le développment" (1991) R.A.E. 2, 5; D. Dunnet, "The European Bank for Reconstruction and Development" (1991) C.M.L.R. 571; P. Juillard, "L'accord de Paris du May 29, 1991 portant création de la Banque européenne pour la réconstruction et le développement" (1992) A.F.D.I. 711; I. Shihata, "The Role of the European Bank for Reconstruction and Development in the Promotion and Financing of Investment in Central and Eastern Europe" (1990) I.C.S.I.D. Rev. 207; I. Shihata, *The European Bank for Reconstruction and Development* (Nijhoff, Dordrecht, 1990).

[12] See http://www.cib.org and http://www.cif.org.

In many developing countries the UNDP has a Resident Co-ordinator to supervise all projects that the United Nations or its specialised agencies finance in that country and to give advice on new projects.[13]

PART II: TREATMENT OF FOREIGN INVESTMENTS

Investment law, investment contract and investment treaty

Investment laws A foreign investor generally requires specific guarantees and benefits from the host country before he invests there.[14] Sometimes the host country passes special legislation to attract foreign investors.[15] Through these investment laws the host country offers the foreign investor a more favourable treatment (*e.g.* tax reductions, flexibility in respect óf social legislation and labour laws; more favourable currency regulation for payments abroad, etc.). The host country may confine a liberal investment regime to a designated investment zone.[16]

7.08

The advantages granted to foreign investors go against the principle that local legislation should equally apply to investment by own nationals or by foreigners.[17] Substantial investments generally require the permission from the local authorities of the host country.[18] When the host country is a WTO member, its investment laws must respect the GATT principle of non-discrimination and free trade (see paragraph 3.03). Furthermore, the Agreement on Trade Related Investment Measures (TRIMs), which resulted from the Uruguay Round, specifically requires from an investor from another WTO Member State that he purchases or

---

[13] See www.undp.org.

[14] D. Lamethe, "Les relations entre les gouvernements et les entreprises en matière de grand projets d'investissement" (1998) 125 J.D.I. 45–66 ; P. Juillard, "L'évolution des sources du droit des investissements" (1994) *Collected Courses Hague Academy of International Law*, 250, VI, pp. 9–215; A. Perry, "Effective legal system and foreign direct investment" (2000) 49 I.C.L.Q. 779–799 ; P. Weil, "The state, the foreign investor and international law" (2000) 15 I.C.S.I.C. 401–416.

[15] See *Investment Laws of the World* (Oceana Dobbs Ferry, 10 volumes, 1973) (loose-leaf); R. Pritchard (ed.), *Economic Development, Foreign Investment and the Law* (1996, Kluwer International); S. N. Carlson, "Foreign investment laws and foreign direct investment in developing countries" (1995) 29 IntL. 577.

   Recent foreign investment laws include the following: Cuba: Cuban Investment Act (1995) 35 I.L.M. 331; R. First, "Cuba's changing foreign investment climate" (1996) 9 Transnat.L. 295; Nepal: M. Paudel, "Legal framework for foreign investment in Nepal" (1997) 12 I.C.S.I.D. Rev. 29; Romania: Ch. Costa, "The tie that binds: the story of foreign investment law in Romania" (1999) 4 J.Int'l L.S. 105; Russia: "Law on Protection of the Rights and Interests of Investors" (1999); "New law on protection of investor rights" (1999) I.F.L.R. (No. 7) 53; Uzbekistan: Decree on foreign investments in Uzbekistan (1998); A. Newman, "Investing in Uzbekistan: a rough ride on the silk road" (1999) 30 L.and Pol. Int'l Bus. 553.

[16] D. Carreau and P. Juillard, *Droit International Économique* (LGDJ, Paris, 1998) pp. 473–483.

[17] The World Bank's "Guideline on the treatment of foreign direct investment" (1992) 31 I.L.M. 1363, encourages host countries to establish a favourable treatment for all investors. A specifically favourable legal treatment should only be granted to foreign investors where this is reasonably justified by the circumstances; the third guideline calls for national treatment of foreign investors, provided this treatment is fair and equitable.

[18] The World Bank's "Guidelines on the treatment of foreign investment" ((1992) 31 I.L.M. 1363), second guideline, however, cautions against overregulation and recommends a policy of open admission.

uses products from the host country and restricts his freedom to import and export. Moreover no Member State shall breach the obligation of national treatment (GATT Article III) and the prohibition of quantitative restrictions (GATT Art. XI). Transitional arrangements allow Member States to maintain notified TRIMs for a limited time. A Committee on TRIMs monitors the operation and implementation of the commitments.[19] Breaches of the investment law by the host country can often be submitted to arbitration.[20]

7.09   **Investment contracts**   A host country may change its national investment laws.[21] Such changes risk affecting investments that have already been made. An investor who seeks protection against changes in the law may enter into a formal agreement with the host country in which the host country specifically commits itself to treating the investment as indicated in the agreement.[22]

Such an investment contract, often called an "economic development agreement", establishes, *inter alia*, the modalities of investing, the contribution to long-term economic development of the host country, the repatriation of profits, the reinvestment policy and, possibly, the ownership of the local enterprise.

It is accepted that investment contracts between a state and a private person may be (partially) governed by international law: the binding force of the contract then depends on international law while national law still may be relevant for contract interpretation and implementation.[23] International law is

---

[19] See "Trade related aspects of investment measures", in *The results of the Uruguay Round of Multilateral Trade Negotiations: the Legal Texts* (GATT Secretariat, Geneva, 1994) pp. 163–167; P. Civello, "The TRIMs agreement : a failed attempt at investment liberalization", (1999) 8 Min.J.Gl.Tr. 97; R. Edwards, "Towards a more comprehensive World Trade Organization Agreement on Trade Related Investment Measures" (1997) 33 Stan.J.Int'l.L. 169; T. S. Shenkin, "Trade-Related Investment Measures in bilateral investment treaties and the GATT" (1994) 55 Univ. Pittsb. L.Rev. 541; D. MacDougall and P. Cameron, "Trade in energy and natural resources: Trade-Related Investment Measures—focus on Eastern Europe" (1994) 28 J.W.T. 171; C. T. Ebenoth and D. Grashoff, "Trade-Related Investment Measures (TRIMS)—Osteuropäischer Reformstaaten in der Erweiterungsphase des GATT" (1994) 40 R.I.W. 181; P. Civello, "The TRIMs Agreement: a failed attempt at investment liberalization" (1999) 8 Minn.J.Gl.Tr. 97.

[20] See A. Parra, "Provisions on the settlement of investment disputes in modern investment laws" in "Bilateral investments treaties as multilateral instrument on investment" (1997) 12 I.C.S.I.D. Rev. 287; M. Sornarajah, *The Settlement of Foreign Investment Disputes* (Kluwer, The Hague, 2000).

[21] The expression of a state's right to control investment activities is firmly rooted in the notion of its permanent sovereignty over natural resources located within its territorial boundaries. However, see D. Carreau, T. Flory and P. Juillard, *op. cit.*, pp. 483–501, who argue that the host country may be bound by its investment legislation through international law on the basis of the doctrine of "unilateral acts".

[22] N. Rawding, "Protecting investments under state contracts: some legal and ethical issues" (1995) 11 Arb. Int. 341; P. Bernardini, "The renegotiation of the investment contract" (1998) 13 I.C.S.I.D. Rev. 411.

[23] R. Bentham, "The law of international development contracts" (1989) G.Y.I.L. 418; D. Bettems, *Les Contrats entre Etats et Personnes Privées Étrangères* (Méta-Ed., Le Mont sur Lausanne, 1989); K.H. Boeckstiegel, *Der Staat als Vertragspartner ausländischer Privatunternehmen* (Athenäum, Frankfurt, 1971); C. Curtis, "The legal security of economic development agreements" (1988) Harv.Int'l. L.J. 317; P. Fischer, *Die Internationale Konzession* (Springer, Vienna, 1974); A. Maniruzzaman, "International arbitration and mandatory public law rules in the context of state contracts: an overview" (1990) 3 J.I.A. 53; S. Pogany, "Economic development agreements" (1992) 1 I.C.S.I.D. Rev. 1; G. Sacerdoti, "State contracts and international law: a reappraisal" (1986) I.Y.I.L. 26; P. Y. Tschanz, "Contrats d'Etat et mesures unilatérales de l'etat devant l'arbitre international" (1985) R.C.D.I.P. 47. See also the resolution of the Institut de Droit International on *The Proper Law of the Contract in Agreements between a State and a Foreign Private Person*,

admitted to be relevant because these contracts often have international dimensions.[24] Indeed, one of the parties to such a contract is the state; the other party is often a company with a budget that exceeds the national budget of a developing country. The agreement frequently concerns the exercise of sovereign rights of the state, such as the exploitation of natural resources, tax privileges for the investor and the investor's obligation to build an infrastructure in relationship to his exploitation (roads, harbour, housing, hospital). Moreover, investment contracts regularly contain an explicit stabilisation clause (see paragraph 7.08), which restricts the legislator of the host country to enact law, which would affect the contractual obligations or at least declare that such law will not affect the investment contract. Furthermore, dispute settlement is generally not within the jurisdiction of the host state: investment contracts often provide for arbitration in an international forum.[25]

Subject to international law, the agreement becomes largely immune from the national law of the host country. The host state then cannot unilaterally change the substance of the investment contract through a legislative measure. Investment contracts, governed by international law, therefore, offer far-reaching protection to the foreign investor.

Investment treaties   Finally, investment treaties, which prescribe how the   **7.10** host country must treat foreign investments, can also protect foreign investors.[26] That treatment thus becomes a treaty obligation between the host country and the country of the investor. If the host country breaches such an obligation, it can be

---

Institute of International Law Yearbook (1979) II, 192; A. Von Mehren, "Arbitration between states and foreign enterprises: the significance of the Institute of International Law's, Santiago de Compostela Resolution and Commentary" (1990) I.C.S.I.D. Rev. 54; also the arbitration award in *Texaco-Calasiatic v. Libya* of January 19, 1977 (1978) 17 I.L.M. 1, 13, 32 and (1977) J.D.I. 350, 356; D. Mazzini, "Stable international contracts in emerging markets: an endangered species?" (1999) 15 Bost.I.L.J. 343.

[24] One of the techniques by which foreign private parties have striven to protect their investment, particularly in the field of natural resources exploration and production, consisted in removing their contractual relationship from the reach of the host state's municipal law, the latter being of potential application under one of the most common rules of conflict, the one connecting the contract with the law of the place of its performance. This result was achieved in a first phase of the parties' relations by making the agreement subject to the general principles of law or to principles of law common to the countries of which the parties are nationals or to principles of law common to civilised nations. By this peculiar choice-of-law provision the foreign investor succeeded for a long period of time in denationalising the development agreement by avoiding the application of the municipal law of the host state. The same objective was obtained through the internationalisation of the agreement, by making the same subject to public international law. A. S. Bekoe, "The illusory choice: examining the illusion of "choice" in choice of law provisions: a country study exploring one aspect of foreign investment in the Caribbean" (1999) 42 Harv.-Int'l.L.J 505.

[25] A. Derman, "Nationalisation and the protective arbitration clause" (1988) J.I.A. 131; M. Sornarajah, *The Settlement of Foreign Investment Disputes* (Kluwer, The Hague, 2000). ICSID arbitration (para. 7.32) is a regular option. Once in a while an *ad hoc* arbitration is chosen. See, *e.g.*, *Saudi Arabia v. Aramco* (1958) 27 I.L.R. 117; *B.P. v. Libya* (1974) 53 I.L.R. 297; *Texaco Calasiatic v. Libya* (1978) 17 I.L.M. 1; *Wintershall AG and others v. Quatar* (1989) 27 I.L.M. 795; *Kaiser Bauxite Company v. Government of Jamaica* (1975) 114 I.L.R. 142 (1999); *American Manufacturing and Trading, Inc. v. Republic of Zaire* (1997) 36 I.L.M. 1531; *Fedax N.Y. v. Republic of Venezuela* (1998) 37 I.L.M. 1378.

[26] G. Sacerdoti, "Bilateral treaties and multilateral instruments on investment protection" (1997) Rec.Cours.

held responsible under international law by the investor's state for breach of a treaty and risks to be sanctioned under international law.[27]

Breaches of investment treaties can often be submitted to arbitration.[28]

7.11   **Multilateral Investment Treaties**   In 1995 the OECD members started negotiations on a "Multilateral Agreement on Investment" (MAI) in order to establish a strong and comprehensive legal framework for foreign direct investment among the participating countries. The MAI was intended "to provide a comprehensive framework for investment with high standards of liberalisation and investment protection and with an effective dispute settlement". The negotiations have been unsuccessful as, *inter alia*, the limitations of the agreement on the state's regulatory powers appeared difficult to accept.[29]

However, a few investment arrangements within a broader multilateral treaty of economic co-operation and integration (*e.g.* the North American Free Trade Agreement[30] (see paragraph 7.12), the Common Market for Eastern and Southern Africa,[31] MERCOSUR and the Energy Charter Treaty (see paragraph 7.15) may be relevant for the foreign investor.

7.12   **NAFTA**   NAFTA, in its Chapter 11, requires the NAFTA parties to extend a non-discriminatory treatment to investors and investments of other NAFTA countries. A NAFTA investor who alleges that a NAFTA host government has breached its obligations under Chapter 11 may, at its option have recourse to ICSID arbitration (see paragraph 7.38), to the ICSID Additional Facilities (see

---

[27] M. Sornarajah, "State responsibility and bilateral investment treaties" (1986) J.W.T. 79. See, *e.g.* International Court of Justice, decision of July 20, 1989, *USA v. Italy* (1989) I.C.J. Rep. 108.

[28] See A. Parra, "Provisions on the settlement of investment disputes in modern investment laws" in "Bilateral investments treaties as multilateral instrument on investment" (1997) 12 I.C.S.I.D. Rev. 287; M. Sornarajah, *The Settlement of Foreign Investment Disputes* (Kluwer, The Hague, 2000).

[29] See *Un Accord Multilateral sur l'Investissement: d'un Forum de Négociation à l'Autre*? (Pedone, Paris, 1999); C.Vadcar, "Le Projet d'accord multilatéral sur l'investissement: problématique de l'adhésion des pays du Sud" (1998) 125 J. D. I. Clunet, 9–44; Y. Kodama, "Dispute settlement under the draft Multilateral Agreement on Investment—the quest for an effective investment dispute settlement mechanism and its failure" (1999) 16 J.I.A. 45; P. Muchlinski, "The rise and fall of the multilateral agreement on investment: where now?" (2000) 34 Int.L; M. Daly, "Investment incentives and the Multilateral Agreement on Investment" (1998) 32 J.W.T. 2, 5; R. Geiger, "Towards a Multilateral Agreement on Investment" (1998) 31 Cornell Int'l.L.J. 467; P. Juillard, "MAI: A European view" (1998) 31 Cornell Int'l.L.J. 477; S. Picciotto, "Linkages in international investment regulation: the antinomies of the draft Multilateral Agreement on Investment" (1998) 19 U.Pa.J.Int'l.Ec.L. 731; S. J. Canner, "The Multilateral Agreement on Investment" (1998) 31 Cornell.Int. L.J. 659; M.J. Trebilcock and R. Howse, "The Multilateral Agreement on Investment", in *The Regulation of International Trade* (2nd ed., Routledge, London and New York, 1998) pp. 357–366; "Symposium on Multilateral Agreements and Investment" (1998) 31 Cornell.Int'l. L.J., No. 3; G. Kelley, "Multilateral investment treaties: a balanced approach to multilateral corporations" (2001) 39 Col.J.T.L. 483–531; A. Böhmer, "The struggle for a multilateral agreement on investment" (1998) 41 G.Y.I.L. 267–298.

[30] See, *e.g.* NAFTA Treaty (para. 2.36); S. Ruibin, ed., *NAFTA and Investment* (Kluwer, The Hague, 1995); M. Omalu, *NAFTA and the Energy Charter Treaty: Compliance with, Implementation and Effectiveness of International Investment Agreements* (Kluwer, 1999); J. Lax, "A Chile forecast for accession to NAFTA: a process of economic, legal and environmental harmonisation" (1999) 7 Card. J. Int'l Law, 97.

[31] A. P. Muthrika, "Creating an attractive investment climate in the COMESA Region" (1997) 12 I.C.S.I.D. Review vol. 2, 237.

paragraph 7.43) or to arbitration under the UNCITRAL Arbitration rules (see paragraph 11.21) or to the host country's domestic courts. The first awards have been rendered.[31a]

MERCOSUR   The Cartagena Agreement Commission, in its Decision 291   **7.13** (1991), has opened the MERCOSUR member countries somewhat to investors from other member countries. The Protocols of Colonia and Buenos Aires(1994) introduced reciprocal promotion and protection of investments respectively from member countries and non-member countries.

The Energy Charter Treaty   The Energy Charter Treaty opened for sig-   **7.14** nature in 1994 and is at present in force in 44 countries, including nearly all the countries of Western and Eastern Europe and the former USSR region, Australia and Japan.[32] It creates a legal framework to promote long-term investment and co-operation in the energy sector, including exploration, production, transit and trade, the protection of investments and the transfer of profits.[33] Its objectives are to facilitate energy co-operation between countries formerly divided by the Iron Curtain; to assist Eastern European countries in transition to a market economy and to stimulate their economic recovery; to improve the security of energy supply from Eastern Europe, ensuring its transit through third countries[34]; to maximise the efficiency of production, conversion, transport, distribution and the use of energy; to enhance safety and to minimise environmental problems. The Treaty obliges contracting parties to accord non-discriminatory treatment[35] to investors of other contracting parties as regards new investments.[36] The Energy

---

[31a] See *inter alia* T. Weiler, "The Ethyl Arbitration" (2000) 11 *Am. Rev. Int'l. Arb.* 187; ICSID Additional Facility Arbitral Awards: *Waste Management Inc. v. Mexico* (2000) 15 ICSID Review 214; (2000) 40 I.L.M. 56; *Metalclad Corporation v. Mexico* (2001) 16 ICSID Review 1, but set aside by a decision of the Supreme Court of British Columbia of May 2, 2001, *Mealey's International Arbitration Reports* May 2001.

[32] The U.S. announced that it was not in a position to sign the Treaty. Canada will make a decision after completing consultations with its provisions. See more information and country reports on http://www.encharter.org/English/Country/index.html.

[33] T. W. Wälde, R. Lubbers, *The Energy Charter Treaty: an East-West Gateway for Investment and Trade* (Kluwer International, Boston, 1996); OECD, *The Energy Charter Treaty: a Description of its Provisions* (International Energy Agency, Paris, 1994); R. Babadji, "Le traité sur la Charte européene de l'énergie" (1996) A.F.D.I. 872–893.

[34] R. Liesen, "Transit under the 1994 Energy Charter Treaty" (1999) 17 J.E.N.R.L. 56.

[35] The non-discrimination treatment standard has been understood not to apply to any existing non-conforming measure that is maintained by a contracting party. Furthermore, contracting parties may at any time amend existing discriminatory measures as long as the amendment does not decrease the conformity of the measure. J. Poré, R. de Blauw, *The Energy Charter Treaty: Origins, Aims and Prospects* (Royal Institute of International Affairs, London, 1995) p. 113.

[36] The making of investments is defined as establishing a new investment or acquiring an existing investment. To be considered an investment in the energy sector, the investment must be associated with an economic activity concerning the exploration, extraction, refining, production, storage, land transport, transmission, distribution, trade, marketing or sale of energy raw materials or products. T. W. Wälde and R. Lubbers, *The Energy Charter Treaty: an East-West Gateway for Investment and Trade* (Kluwer International, Boston, 1996) p. 97; F. Poirat, "L'article 26 du traité relatif à la charte de l'énergie: Procédures de règlement de différends et statut des personnes privées" (1998) 1 Rev.gen.dr.int.pub. 45–84.

Charter Treaty provides for stringent procedures to settle disputes between states and foreign investors.[37]

Trade in energy materials and products between signatories shall be governed by the provisions of the GATT and its related instruments (see paragraph 3.03), even if one of them is not a member of the WTO.

7.15   Bilateral investment treaties (BITs)   Most of the investment treaties apply bilaterally, that is to say only between two states.[38] Formally, the bilateral investment treaty (BIT) regulates investments in both directions, *i.e.* when both contracting states either import or export capital. However, the poorer state was often intended to be the capital importing state and the richer state was rather seen as the protecting state. In fact an investor from a "poorer" state finds his investment in the "richer" state protected as well under the BIT.[39]

There are at present more than 1,800 BITs [40] among more than 160 countries.[41] These form an extensive and varied safety net for the protection of transnational investment flows.

Bilateral investment treaties set out in detail the treatment nationals of one contracting state will enjoy in the other contracting state. The investment treaties

---

[37] M. Omalu, *NAFTA and the Energy Charter Treaty: Compliance with, Implementation and Effectiveness of International Investment Agreements* (Kluwer, 1999); T. W. Wälde, "Investment arbitration under the Energy Charter Treaty—from dispute settlement to treaty implementation" (1996) 12 ArbInt. 429–466.

[38] A. T. Guzman, "Explaining the popularity of bilateral investment treaties" (1998) 38 Va.J.Int'l.L. 639; M. I. Khalil, "Treatment of foreign investment in bilateral investment treaties" (1992) 8 I.C.S.I.D. Rev.–FILJ 339; K. J. Vandevelde, "Political economy of a bilateral investment treaty" (1998) 92 Am.J.Int'l.L. 621; B. Kishoiyian, "The utility of bilateral investment treaties in the formulation of customary international law (1994) NW.J.Int'l.L. and Bus. 327; R. Dolzer, *Bilateral investment treaties* (Nijhoff, The Hague, 1995); R. Dolzer and M. Stevens, "Bilateral investment treaties" (1996) 16 N.I.L.R. 103; E. Denza and S. Brooks, "Investment protection treaties: United Kingdom experience" (1987) I.C.L.Q. 908; N. Huu-Tru, "Le réseau suisse d'accords bilatéraux d'encouragement et de protection des investissements" (1988) Rev.Gen.dr.int.pub. 577; J. Karl, "The promotion and protection of German foreign investment abroad" (1996) 11 I.C.S.I.D. Rev.–F.I.L.J. 1; P. Juillard, "Le Réseau français des Conventions bilatérales d'investissement" (1987) D.P.C.I. 9; J. Salacuse, "BIT by BIT: The growth of bilateral investment treaties and their impact on foreign investment in developing countries" (1990) Int.L. 655; K. Vandevelde, "The bilateral investment treaty program of the United States" (1988) Cornell Int'l.L.J. 201; G. Sacerdoti, "Bilateral treaties and multilateral instruments on investment protection" (1997) 269 Rec. Cours. 251.

[39] K. J. Vandervelde, "The political economy of a bilateral investment treaty"(1998) 92, A.J.I.L. 621–641; K. J. Vandevelde, "The economics of bilateral investment treaties" (2000) 41 Harv.I.L.J 469–502; P. Peters, " Exhaustion of local remedies: ignored in most bilateral investment treaties" (1997) 44 N.I.L.R. 233–243.

[40] A. A. Escobar, "Introductory note on bilateral investment treaties recently concluded by Latin American states" (1996) 11 I.C.S.I.D. Rev.–F.I.L.J. 86; The UN Centre on Transnational Corporations counted 1306 BITs as of the end of 1996: ICSID, *Bilateral Investment Treaties 1959–1996* (1997).

[41] See the list and status of investment treaties (signed and brought into force since 1990) in (1997) 36 I.L.M 1404; United Nations Centre on Transnational Corporations, *Bilateral Investment Treaties 1959–1995* (1995, UN) and on the web-page http://www.worldbank.org/icsid/treaties/i–9.htm; http://www.access.gro.gov/congress/cong006.html (Belgium together with Luxembourg has concluded 38 bilateral treaties, Austria 21, Canada 17, China 71, Cuba 9, Denmark 31, France 65, Germany 112, Hong Kong 11, Italy 37, Netherlands 58, Russian Federation 32, Spain 37, the United Kingdom 84 and the United States 37); Bahrain–USA (1999) 39 I.L.M. 252; Jordan–USA (1997) 36 I.L.M. 1498; Japan–Hong Kong (1997) 36 I.L.M. 1423; India–UK (1995) 34 I.L.M. 935; Russian Federation–Sweden (1996) 37 I.L.M. 1506.

contain for the most part similar provisions. The core provisions, which are found in most investment treaties, are described below. Some recent treaties will serve as an illustration.

Protected investment   Investment conventions regulate the various forms of **7.16** investment. Most treaties have a non-exhaustive list of the kind of investments the treaty intends to cover. This is usually a wide definition.

" 'Investments' means all invested or reinvested property and assets and, in particular:

(a) movable and immovable property and other property rights, such as mortgages, securities, real guarantees, usufruct and similar rights;

(b) stocks, shares of capital (*parts sociales*) and any other forms of participation;

(c) debentures, claims or rights to any contractual performance having an economic value;

(d) copyrights,[42] industrial rights, technical procedures, registered trademarks, trade names and goodwill;

(e) concessions to prospect for, exploit and extract natural resources, in so far, at the time of their investment, such property and assets are invested in accordance with the laws of the contracting party in the territory of which the investments is made.

No change in the legal form in which the property and assets were invested or reinvested, will affect their status as 'investments', within the meaning of this Agreement."[43]

Some treaties state specifically that the investment must conform to the national law of the host country.[44] Other treaties require that the investment be in the national interest of the host country.[45] Sometimes the investment has to be part of an approved plan of the host country.[46] Generally there is no freedom to invest, since each offer for investment has to be approved by the host country.[47] Not only the original investment but also any modification in the investment is often protected.[48]

Treatment of the investment   The treaties impose standards for the treat- **7.17** ment of the investment. Virtually no treaty accepts any longer the standard of

---

[42] See C. Primo Braga, "The relationship between intellectual property rights and foreign direct investment" (1998) 9 DukeJ.C.I.L. 163; F. Dubuisson, "Les accords internationaux relatifs à la protection des investissements et le droit d'auteur" (1998) 31 B.T.I.R. 450–484.

[43] BIT U.S.–Jordan, Arts 1 and 2 (1997) 36 I.L.M. 1498; BIT U.K.–India, Art. I (1995) I.L.M. 939; BIT BLEU (Belgian-Luxembourg Economic Union)–China, Art.1,2. (1985) I.L.M. 539.

[44] See, *e.g.* BIT BLEU–China, Art. 1,2; BIT BLEU–USSR, Art. 1,2 (1990) I.L.M. 302; BIT US–Jordan Art. 2 (1997) 36 I.L.M. 1498.

[45] See, *e.g.* BIT BLEU–Rwanda, Art. 1,3; BIT UK–India, Art. III (1995) I.L.M. 939.

[46] See, *e.g.* BIT BLEU–Malaysia, Art. 1,3,e.i.

[47] See M. Salem, *op. cit.*, p. 603.

[48] See, *e.g.* BIT BLEU–Malaysia, Art. 1,3; BIT BLEU– China, Art. 1,2; BIT BLEU–Hungary, Art. 1,1; BIT U.K.–India, Art. I(b) (1995) I.L.M. 939.

national treatment under which foreign investors are treated no better than nationals (see paragraph 1.07).[49] Many investment conventions incorporate a dual standard.

(a) In all events, the treatment must be "proper and equitable". The minimum standard for the observance of property rights and procedural rights thus applies (see paragraph 1.06).[50]

(b) The treatment must also be the same as that of an investor coming from the most favoured nation (see paragraph 3.09). Furthermore, the treatment must be non-discriminatory (see paragraph 3.43).[51] Thus, investors may not only rely on the investment treaty concluded between the host country and their own country, but also on any investment treaty concluded between that host country and a third state, or on a law enacted for the benefit of nationals of the host country.[52]

7.18   **Stabilisation, observance and renegotiation clauses**   Sometimes an investment treaty forbids the host country from introducing legislative or other measures that would negatively affect the investment. The clause then declares that the law applicable to the development agreement is the law of the host state in force at the time of the conclusion of the contract, thus excluding the applicability of any future laws and regulations. The host state thus "freezes" the legislative and administrative framework that existed when the investment was made (stabilisation clause).[53] Later changes in the law or administrative procedures will only apply if they do not interfere with the investment or the return on the investment.

The stabilisation clause may also provide that the agreement takes precedence over any provisions enacted subsequent thereto by way of legislation or administration regulation, if the effect of such provisions is to the investor's prejudice (observance clause).[54]

There is some discussion about the legal scope of such stabilisation clauses. Some hold that a state cannot contract out the essence of its sovereignty, *i.e.* cannot curb its legislative and executive power for the benefit of a foreign

---

[49] See, however BIT Belgium–Tunisia, Art. 1, in which national treatment is the minimum standard.

[50] BIT US–Jordan, Art. 2.4 and 2.5 (1997) 36 I.L.M. 1498.

[51] BIT UK–India, Art. IV (1995) I.L.M. 939.

[52] D. Wallace, "The inevitability of national treatment of foreign direct investment", 31 Cornell Int'l.L.J. (1998), 615 .

[53] W. Peter, "Stabilisation clauses in state contracts" (1998) R.D.A.I. 875–892.

[54] See, *e.g.* BIT BLEU–China, Art. 9; BIT BLEU–Hungary, Art. 41(b) ; BIT BLEU–Indonesia, Art. 5(b); BIT BLEU–Tunisia, Art. 3. Also Kazakhstan, 1997 Model Contract for Oil and Gas (Decree 108 of January 17, 1997), Article 28.2: "Amendments and additions to legislation which cause a deterioration in the status of the Contract adopted after its conclusion shall not be applied to the Contract": Barrows, "Basic oil laws and concession contracts" (1997) *Russia and NIS* (1997) Supp. 25, 1. This result may be reached by conferring to the agreement the force of law, so that its provisions may not be modified by general legislation. This is the pattern followed in Egypt, Qatar and other Middle Eastern countries as well as in countries of the former Soviet Union (such as the Republic of Azerbaijan, where a recent petroleum agreement was made subject as to its effectiveness to "legislation giving this Agreement the full force of law").

244

investor. Others argue that nothing prevents the state from voluntarily ceding sovereignty in respect of certain persons. Such a measure would not be in conflict with the notion of permanent sovereignty over natural wealth and resources (see paragraph 7.29). On the contrary, it could even be considered as an expression of this sovereignty. Besides, a stabilisation clause does not prevent a host state from changing its legislative and administrative practice; it merely states that such changes will not affect those who can rely on the stabilisation clause.[55] Stabilisation clauses have been recognised in several arbitration awards as valid and binding.[56]

Nationalisation in breach of a stabilisation or observance clause is unlawful under international law, although, incidentally, the compensation due under international law in the event of such breach may be specified in the investment agreement.

Doubts concerning the legal effectiveness of stabilisation or observance clauses and the state's desire to preserve its sovereign prerogatives, have brought about the renegotiation clause, particularly in agreements relating to natural resources exploration and exploitation.[57] By this clause the state undertakes to renegotiate in good faith the agreement in the event of supervening circumstances of any kind (including a change in governmental policy), instead of unilaterally altering the terms of the agreement. Failed negotiations may lead to arbitration in order to restore the contractual equilibrium or, in absence of the arbitrator's power to that effect, to determine the destiny of the agreement.

Multilateral investment regimes   Specific multilateral arrangements may **7.19** have an impact on investments. In this context the Trade-Related Investment Measures (TRIMs) (see paragraph 7.08), the World Bank's Guidelines on the Treatment of Foreign Direct Investment (see paragraph 7.01), the OECD Code of Liberalisation of Capital Movements[58] as well as the OECD Declaration on International Investment and Multinational Enterprises[59] should be mentioned.

---

[55] See, *e.g.* P. Mayer, "La neutralisation du pouvoir normatif de l'Etat en matière de contrats d'Etat" (1986) J.D.I. 5; M. Salem, *op. cit.* p. 605; D. Carreau, T. Flory and P. Juillard, *op. cit.* pp. 501–513; E. Paasivirta "Internationalisation and stabilisation of contracts versus state sovereignty" (1989) B.Y.I.L. 315.

[56] See, *e.g.* the arbitration awards in *Aramco v. Saudi Arabia* (1961) A.F.D.I. 300; *Texaco Calasiatic v. Libya* (1978) I.L.M. 1, 16; (1977) J.D.I. 360, (45); *AGIP v. Congo* (ICSID) (1982) I.L.M. 727; *Letco v. Liberia* (1988) J.D.I. 166, 178; I.C.C. award no. 3380 (1980), (1983) Rev.Arb. 14.

[57] See P. Bernardini, "The renegotiation of the investment contract" (1998) 13 I.C.S.I.D. Rev. 411; W. Peter, *Arbitration and Renegotiation of International Investment Agreements* (Kluwer, The Hague, 1995); A. R. Parra, "Provisions on the settlement of investments disputes in modern investment laws, BIT's, and multilateral instruments on investment" (2000) 15 I.C.S.I.D. 287–366.

[58] This code is legally binding on OECD members, although there is no enforcement mechanism. Instead, the code provides a framework of notification, examination, and consultation. It promotes the removal of restrictions on capital movements, including foreign investment and the repatriation of profits. The Code has been improved on various occasions since its adoption in 1961; important recent additions were right of establishment (1986) and cross-border financial services (1992). See more information on http://www.oecd.org/daf/cmis/codes/codes.htm.

[59] The members of the OECD adopted this Declaration on June 21, 1976, and then updated it in 1979, 1984 and 1991. The Declaration is not a legally binding treaty, but a general statement of policy regarding foreign investment. Member countries are expected to accord multinational enterprises national treatment and to assure that this treatment is followed at the sub-national level. The Declaration requires members countries to make incentives or disincentives as transparent as

Moreover, for investments from the E.U. into African, Caribbean and Pacific region countries (ACP countries), the Cotonou Agreement may be relevant. This Partnership Agreement, signed in 2000 in Benin, replaced the Lomé Convention, which had provided the structure for trade and co-operation between the E.U. and the former British, French and Belgian colonies in Africa, the Caribbean and Pacific (see paragraph 3.81).The Cotonou Agreement (see paragraph 2.58) recognised the importance of foreign investments for the economic development of the ACP countries and is an attempt to promote such investments.[60] Indeed, investments will enable ACP countries to become less dependent on the import of a raw material, improve their position on the world market, or make it possible to diversify their industry. The Agreement establishes an investment facility,[61] managed by the European Investment Bank. It functions as a revolving fund and the returns accruing from its operations flow back to the facility. The facility invests in the form of loans, equity and quasi-equity; it also issues guarantees in support of domestic and foreign private investment.[62]

Lastly, the Agreement encourages the E.U. Member States to enter into bilateral economic development agreements with ACP countries and to conclude agreements relating to specific projects of mutual interest.[63]

PART III: PROTECTION AGAINST EXPROPRIATION

Expropriation, nationalisation and confiscation

7.20   **Terms**   States may blame business for inefficient exploitation or for insufficient contribution to the local economy. Foreign investors may be accused of repatriating too much capital instead of reinvesting in the host country. In order to cure these evils the host state then can sometimes expropriate specific enterprises or whole business sectors, *i.e.* assign proprietary rights of a private investor to a public entity.

A distinction can be made between expropriation in its strict sense, nationalisation, confiscation and creeping expropriation:

- Expropriation in its strict sense usually involves individual transfers of ownership. It usually is done for reasons of general interest and should be coupled with compensation, fixed by the executive power and, if necessary, approved by the judiciary.

---

possible so that "their importance and purpose can be ascertained". (See OECD Committee on International Investment and Multinational Enterprises); B. Blanpain, *The OECD Guidelines for Multinational Enterprises and Labour Relations 1982–1984: Experience and Review* (Kluwer, Boston, 1985). See also the texts of the documents on the Internet: http://www.oecd.org/daf/cmis/codes/clcmart.htm.

[60] Art. 75 "Investment promotion"; see text on http://europa.eu.int/comm/developmnt/cotonou/agreement/agr-en34.htm

[61] Art. 76 "Investment finance and support".

[62] Art. 77 "Investment guarantees".

[63] Art. 78 §3 "Investment protection".

- Nationalisation requires the expropriation of a complete sector of the economy (*e.g.* all oil companies, all banks, etc.) and frequently affects the exploitation of natural resources. It is generally carried out in a formal way (*i.e.* through a formal decree) within the framework of the state's economic or social policy.

- Confiscation is the taking of property contrary to the rules of international law. For instance, an expropriation without compensation for the investor is deemed to be a confiscation (however, see paragraph 7.31). (Expropriation intended as a sanction is sometimes also termed confiscation.)

- States can expropriate or nationalise without openly admitting the fact when they charge exceptionally high taxes, or prohibit the repatriation of money, take over the management of a company, etc. As the consequences of these measures are virtually the same as those of an overt expropriation or nationalisation, such measures can be considered to constitute creeping expropriation.[64]

For convenience's sake, the text will continue to use the collective term "expropriation" whether or not it concerns expropriation in its strict sense, nationalisation, confiscation or creeping expropriation.

Expropriation and international law

Human rights

Treaties   The European Convention on Human Rights determines that expro-   **7.21**
priation is only acceptable if done in the general interest and in compliance with
the law and the general principles of international law.[65] The Convention protects
anyone whose property has been expropriated by a state party to the European
Convention.

Other human rights conventions, like the UN Convention on Civil and Political Rights, do not include any provision for expropriation. Perhaps it was too difficult to get world-wide acceptance for a provision that curbs the right of a state to expropriate.

Expropriation law

Overview   The general principles of international law are relevant if the   **7.22**
property of foreigners is expropriated.

---

[64] See, *e.g.* the various manifestations of a creeping expropriation in M. Pellonpää and M. Fitzmaurice, "Taking of property in the practice of the Iran–United States claims tribunal" (1988) N.Y.I.L. 53, 85–101.

[65] European Convention on Human Rights, Protocol I, Art. 1. See B. Stern, "Property rights, expropriation and nationalisation under the European Convention on Human Rights" (1991) D.P.C.I. 394.

International law in respect of expropriation is, however, changing. Traditional views are making way for modern concepts, such as the permanent sovereignty over natural resources. However, the confrontation between the traditional and modern theories creates uncertainty. That explains why states enter into investment treaties to bring some certainty in the protection of investments (see paragraph 7.10).

Traditional view

7.23   **Minimum standard**   According to the international law followed by Western lawyers for decades, the host country must guarantee foreigners and their property a certain minimum standard of protection.[66] For example, the acquired rights of foreigners must be respected, foreign investments must be treated "fairly and equitably" and foreign property cannot be taken arbitrarily.

A state cannot hide behind its own law to violate this minimum standard. The host country that harms a foreign investor or takes his property contrary to the minimum standard, commits an international wrong. The country of the investor may intervene with a demand for reparation (diplomatic protection). This diplomatic protection, however, is only possible after the investor himself has done everything necessary to seek reparation in the host country but without any result (exhaustion of local remedies).[67]

In the early 1900s the minimum standard, as applied in Western countries, was seriously challenged by Latin-American lawyers who wanted to liberate their countries from the hold of foreign investors. The Soviet Union too, with its massive expropriations after 1917, rejected these rules. Many of the socialist and developing countries that resorted to the taking of property after the Second World War likewise demanded the right to determine their own political and social order and to protect their own economic independence, aspirations which were irreconcilable with the minimum standard.

During the period 1930–1970, Western countries maintained that the minimum standard still implied the following:

(a) expropriation can only take place in the general interest;

(b) it shall not be done in a discriminatory way;

(c) it must be coupled with an effective, prompt and appropriate compensation;

(d) it shall take place according to lawful expropriation procedures, which guarantee the expropriated person sufficient legal protection (due process of law).

---

[66] S. K. B. Asante, "International law and foreign investments: a reappraisal" (1988) I.C.L.Q. 590; D. Carreau, T. Flory and P. Juillard, *op.cit.,* pp. 632–634; W. D. Verwey and N. J. Schrijver, "The taking of foreign property under international law: a new legal perspective?" (1984) N.Y.I.L. 3, 6–8.

[67] See B. Stern, "La protection diplomatique des investissements internationaux. De Barcelone Traction à Elettronica Sicula ou les glissements progressifs de l'analyse" (1990) J.D.I. 897.

These criteria were formulated in detail in 1938[68] and were largely confirmed in 1962 by UN Resolution 1803 on permanent sovereignty over natural resources.[69] They were also reiterated by the United States in 1975[70] and by the World Bank Guidelines on the Treatment of Foreign Direct Investment in 1992.[71] The different elements of the traditional criteria for expropriation are addressed below.

General interest Traditional international law suggests that a state may only   **7.24** take property if the general interest requires it to do so. However, there is no consensus on what is covered by "general interest". UN Resolution 1803 (1962) (see paragraph 7.28) declares on this issue that the expropriation must take place "on grounds or reasons of public utility, security, and the national interest which are recognized as overriding purely individual or private interests, both domestic and foreign."

The expropriation thus should not be intended for the promotion of individuals or minority groups.[72] Furthermore, its objectives should be mainly economic and not purely political. The United States, for instance, declared that for those reasons, the expropriations of American property in Cuba was invalid because Cuba described the action as: "A luminous and stimulating example for the sister nations of America and all underdeveloped countries of the world to follow in their struggle to free themselves from the brutal claws of imperialism."[73]

Nevertheless, the expropriating state retains a large margin of appreciation for the determination of whether or not an expropriation was in the general interest.[74]

Prohibition of discrimination The prohibition of discrimination means that   **7.25** foreigners, irrespective of nationality, must receive the same treatment when expropriated as other foreigners and as nationals of the expropriating state. However, a different treatment for different groups of foreigners is not necessarily discriminatory if this distinction can be justified.[75]

Expropriating states may thus spare some foreigners because they are protected by an investment treaty (see paragraph 7.10), without this better treatment

---

[68] See the diplomatic memo of the American Secretary of State C. Hull in relation to the Mexican nationalisations (1938), in H. Steiner and D. Vagts, *Transnational Legal Problems* (Foundation Press, New York, 1986) p. 491.

[69] UN Resolution 1803 (XVII of December 14, 1962), "Nationalisation, expropriation or requisitioning shall be based on grounds or reasons of public utility, security . . . In such cases the owner shall be paid appropriate compensation . . . ".

[70] See U.S. Department of State, Statement on Foreign Investment and Nationalisation of December 30, 1975 (1976) 15 I.L.M. 186. This declaration was a reaction by the American government to the expropriation rules of the Charter of Economic Rights and Duties of States (see para. 7.29).

[71] (1992) 31 I.L.M. 1363, fourth guideline.

[72] W. Verwey and N. Schrijver, *op. cit.*, p. 15.

[73] R. Higgins "Conflict of interests" in *International Law in a Divided World* (Dufour, Chester, 1965) pp. 62–63.

[74] M. Pellonpää and M. Fitzmaurice, *op. cit.*, p. 62, who refer for this point to the decision of the U.S.–Iran Claims Tribunal, concerning Amoco International Finance Corporation. Even the European Commission on Human Rights examines only marginally within the framework of the European Convention on Human Rights whether the expropriation was in the general interest.

[75] W. Verwey and N. Schrijver, *op. cit.*, p. 13; M. Pellonpää and M. Fitzmaurice, *op. cit.*, p. 65. See Permanent Court of International Justice, case of *Oscar Chinn P.C.I.J.*, ser. A/B, Nos 63, 87 in respect of admissible forms of distinction.

being declared arbitrary favouritism.[76] The state may also act in a non-discriminatory manner for reasons of national security when expropriating businesses owned by some nationalities, while similar businesses owned by its own citizens or by citizens of friendly nations are not expropriated.[77]

7.26   **Compensation**   In the nineteenth century proprietary rights enjoyed the fullest protection. The state could only expropriate in the general interest—interpreted strictly—and only if it was linked with full compensation. In the twentieth century the taking of property became more common. Whole sectors of industry were nationalised. Demands for full compensation proved untenable. The Russian nationalisations after the revolution of 1917 and the Mexican and Spanish nationalisations in the years between the two World Wars were of such a scale that the expropriating state could not possibly pay full compensation. Under those circumstances international law had to be satisfied with only demanding an "appropriate" compensation. This compensation, however, had to be paid promptly and effectively. Thus, the United States declared in 1938 that international law requires a prompt, appropriate and effective compensation. Prompt, appropriate and effective compensation was also demanded for the many nationalisations which occured after the Second World War.[78] UN Resolution 1803 of December 14, 1962 states likewise that the expropriating state must pay appropriate compensation. In 1992 the World-Bank Guidelines on the Treatment of Foreign Direct Investment confirmed once again that the compensation must be prompt, appropriate and effective.[79] But when is compensation "prompt, appropriate and effective"?

International law demands a prompt compensation for the taking of property. However, experience has taught that expropriating states often endlessly postpone the payment of compensation.[80] The period within which compensation must be paid is in fact flexible. The state must pay "without undue delay",[81] but this term is determined in the light of the circumstances and particularly the ability of the expropriating state to pay the compensation.[82] The World Bank Guidelines on the Treatment of Foreign Direct Investment allow payment over a period not to exceed five years, to the extent that objective circumstances make immediate payment impractical.

---

[76] W. Verwey and N. Schrijver, *op. cit.*, p. 13.

[77] D. Carreau, P. Juillard and T. Flory, *op. cit.*, p. 663.

[78] *e.g.* in Eastern Europe and China (after the Second World War), Iran (1951), Egypt (1956), Indonesia (1957), Cuba (1961), Algeria (1963), Peru (1968), Bolivia (1969), Chile (1970), Libya (1971), Mauritania (1972), etc.

[79] (1992) 31 I.L.M. 1363, fourth guideline.

[80] In many cases an average period of 16 years has passed between the expropriation and the final settlement: R. Lillich and B. Weston, *International Claims, their Settlement by Lump Sum Agreements* (1975) pp. 210 *et seq.*

[81] W. Verwey and N. Schrijver, *op. cit.*, p. 18. Also OECD Draft Convention on the protection of foreign property, (1967) 6 I.L.M. 124.

[82] W. Verwey and N. Schrijver, *op. cit.*, p. 18.

If the compensation is not paid promptly, interest is in principle due from the moment of the expropriation till the final settlement. An interest rate of between 10 per cent and 12 per cent is generally charged.[83]

The compensation must be effective. This generally implies that the payment has to take place in freely negotiable and exportable currencies. Compensation in government bonds, the revenue of which cannot be exported, is therefore inadequate, though at present the compensation is sometimes paid in commodities.[84]

The compensation must be appropriate. The amount of compensation is determined by many different factors. The size of the compensation depends, of course, on the valuation method.[85] What is the book value of the company? Is compensation related to the market value, which can be very low during a wave of nationalisations? May exorbitant profits, made by the company in previous years at the expense of the host country, be deducted from the compensation? The appropriate compensation can vary enormously, depending on the answers to these questions.[86]

Nowadays, expropriating states generally use the book value as criterion for determining the amount of compensation, as this criterion seems fair: the investors themselves at the time have used the depreciated book value instead of the higher market value, often for tax reasons. Foreign investors on the other hand might prefer to see the fair market value criterion applied.[87]

If necessary, other criteria could also be used. If the market value of the enterprise cannot be established, for instance, because there is no real market value for the shares, the enterprise may be valued as a "going concern", that is as a source for future profits.[88]

---

[83] See: M. Pellonpää and M. Fitzmaurice, *op. cit.*, pp. 169–174. The international panel that may have to decide on the compensation is, nevertheless, free in its determination of the interest rate, taking into account the circumstances.

[84] W. Verwey and N. Schrijver, *op. cit.*, p. 19.

[85] See, *inter alia*, the fourth guideline of the World Bank "Guidelines on the Treatment of Foreign Direct Investments" (1992) 31 I.L.M. 1363 which highlights in detail several different valuation techniques; S. Khalilian "The place of discounted cash-flow in international commercial arbitration" (1991) J.D.I. 31; W. Lieblich, "Determinations by international tribunals of the economic value of expropriated enterprises" (1990) J.I.A. 37; W. Lieblich, "Determining the economic value of expropriated income-producing property in international artitration" (1991) J.I.A. 59; I. Seidl-Hohenveldern, "L'évaluation des dommages dans les arbitrages transnationaux" (1988) A.F.D.I. 7; O. Waelbroeck, "La réparation des atteintes auz investissements étrangers: le discounted cash-flow" (1990) R.B.D.I. 464; J. Westberg, "Compensation in cases of expropriation and nationalization: awards of the Iran–United States claims tribunal" (1990) I.C.S.I.D. Rev. 256.

[86] R. Dolzer, *Eigentum, Enteignung und Entschädigung im geltenden Völkerrecht* (Springer, Berlin, 1985); P. Gann, "Compensation standards for expropriation" (1985) Colum.J.Transnat. L. 615; P. Friedland and E. Wong, "Measuring damages for the deprivation of income—producing assets: I.C.S.I.D. case studies" (1990) I.C.S.I.D. Rev. 400; C. F. Amerasingue, "Issues of compensation of the taking of alien property in the light of recent cases and practice" (1992) I.C.L.Q. 1; R. Wolfrum, "Die Bewertung von internationalen Enteignugsanspreichen unter besonderer Beruchsichtigung der Rechtsprechung des Iran/US Claims Tribunals", *Liber Amicorum I, Seidl-Hohenseldern* (Kluwer, 1998), p. 823.

[87] The market value is described as "the price that a willing buyer would pay to a willing seller in circumstances in which each had good information, each desired to maximise his financial gain, and neither was under duress or threat" (M. Pellonpää and M. Fitzmaurice, *op. cit.*, p. 131).

[88] M. Pellonpää and M. Fitzmaurice, *op. cit.*, pp. 130–166; D. Carreau, P. Juillard and T. Flory, *op. cit.*, pp. 697–705. See World Bank Guidelines, IV, para. 6.

In the case of recent investments it is also possible to be guided by the original cost price of the expropriated investment.[89] If the enterprise has more debts than assets at the time of the expropriation, the liquidation value may be upheld.[90]

The legal context of the expropriation is important too for the determination of the size of the compensation. If the host country honours its obligations under international law—including the payment of appropriate compensation—the expropriation is legitimate under international law and the compensation needs only to be appropriate. But if the host country's expropriation does not comply with international law, the expropriation becomes unlawful and consequently the state must compensate in full (*restitutio in integrum*), *i.e.* not only the loss actually suffered (*damnum emergens*), but also lost future profits (*lucrum cessans*).[91]

In fact, however, a lump sum paid by the expropriating state, to the country of the dispossessed, pursuant to a so-called lump sum agreement, is usually accepted even if this sum is considerably less than the value of the expropriated goods.[92]

7.27   Due process of law   The expropriation must be legally correct. The decision to expropriate and to enforce the expropriation must conform to the laws of the expropriating state. Expropriated investors must have access to domestic courts to question the expropriation and their claim must be treated fairly.

There must be some objective assessment of, *inter alia*, the compensation. The expropriating authorities cannot have the last words on this compensation.[93]

Permanent sovereignty of the host country

7.28   Resolution 1803   In 1962 the General Assembly of the United Nations declared solemnly in its Resolution 1803 that each nation has permanent sovereignty over its natural resources. It thus became recognised that a nation has a permanent right over its oil supplies, harbours, waterways and other natural resources. This permanent sovereignty must be exercised in the interest of the people of that nation:

---

[89] See ICSID arbitration award of August 8, 1980, *Benvenuti v. People's Republic of the Congo* (1982) 22 I.L.M. 740.

[90] M. Pellonpää and M. Fitzmaurice, *op. cit.*, p. 149; see World Bank Guidelines, IV, para. 6.

[91] Permanent Court of International Justice, *Chorzow* (1927) P.C.I.J. Series A, no. 13; D. Bowett, "State contract with aliens: contemporary developments on compensation for termination or breach" (1988) B.Y.I.L. 49; D. Carreau, P. Juillard and T. Flory, *op. cit.*, pp. 703–704; W. Verwey and N. Schrijver, *op. cit.*, p. 19. See, *e.g.* the ICSID decision in *Amco v. Indonesia*, (1991) 30 I.L.M. 173.

[92] R. Lillich, "Lump sum agreements" (1985) *Encyclopedia of International Law*, vol. 8, 367; R. Lillich and B. Weston, "Lump sum agreements: their contribution to the law of international claims" (1988) Am.J.Int'l.L. 69.

[93] Chile was criticised when it allowed the compensation for the nationalised American investments to be estimated by a Chilean official, who had to decide on the basis of Chilean documents and without any other proof (see on these Chilean expropriations, *inter alia*, I. Seidl-Hohenveldern, "Chilean Copper nationalisation cases before German courts" (1975) Am.J.Int'l.L. 110, 115; the Declaration of the U.S. (1971) I.L.M. 1307).

"1. The right of peoples and nations to permanent sovereignty over their natural wealth and resources must be exercised in the interest of their national development and of the well being of the people of the State concerned."

Permanent sovereignty implies that the state may be entitled to expropriate its natural resources, even if it has contracted out its exploitation to foreign investors.

Resolutions of the General Assembly of the UN are not binding as such (see paragraph 1.11). However, as Resolution 1803 on the Permanent Sovereignty was unanimously adopted by the Member States of the UN, it made permanent sovereignty over natural wealth part of international law.[94]

The notion of permanent sovereignty was adopted in several more recent UN Resolutions.[95] The mirror image of permanent sovereignty—namely the right of self-determination—became recognised by the UN Covenants on Civil and Political Rights and on Social, Economic and Cultural Rights. Both Covenants start with an identical article on self-determination:

"All peoples may, for their own ends, freely dispose of their natural wealth and resources without prejudice to any obligations arising out of international economic co-operation, based upon the principle of mutual benefit, and international law." (Article 1(2).)

Permanent sovereignty and the New Economic Order The notion of **7.29** permanent sovereignty was consecrated in the Charter of Economic Rights and Duties of States, a UN Resolution of 1974, which established the so-called "New Economic Order". Article 2(1) of the Resolution reads:

"Every state has and shall freely exercise full permanent sovereignty, including possession, use and disposal, over all its wealth, natural resources and economic activities."[96]

It is clear from this citation that the concept of permanent sovereignty was extended by the Charter: it not only concerns natural wealth, as in Resolution 1803, but "all economic activities".

The Charter had wide support in the 1970s. Although it was not adopted unanimously,[97] its principles, including the permanent sovereignty over economic activities, had been approved by 120 countries. In its time, however, many did not accept the Charter as binding law.[98]

---

[94] See, *e.g.* the arbitration award *Texaco-Calasiatic v. Libya* (1978) I.L.M. 27–31.

[95] W. Verwey and N. Schrijver, *op. cit.*, pp. 27–60.

[96] See J. Castaneda and M. Virally, "La Carte des droits et devoirs économiques des états" (1974) AFDI 31 and 57; S. K. Chatterjee, "The Charter of Economic Rights and Duties of States: an evolution after years" (1991) I.C.L.Q. 669. More generally: M. Bulajic, *Principles of International Development Law* (Nijhoff, Dordrecht, 1986); G. Feuer and H. Cassan, *Droit international de développement* (Dalloz, 1985, Paris).

[97] Six industrialised countries voted against: the U.S., the U.K., West Germany, Belgium, Luxembourg and Denmark. Ten other countries abstained, including Canada, France, Italy, Japan and the Netherlands.

[98] See, *e.g.* for the legal value of the Charter of Economic Rights and Duties, arbitration award *Texaco and Calasiatic v. Libya* (1978) 17 I.L.M. 27 para. 85.

The concept of the New Economic Order and therefore also of "permanent sovereignty" was further elaborated by the International Law Association, a private association of international lawyers (see paragraph 2.45). At its 1986 Seoul Conference, the "Declaration on the Progressive Development of Principles of Public International Law relating to a New International Economic Order" laid down, under paragraph 5.1:

"Permanent sovereignty over natural resources, economic activities and wealth is a principle of international law."[99]

Since then, the New Economic Order and its Charter, which was an exponent of the confrontational politics between the rich and poor of its time, have slipped into oblivion.[1]

7.30   **Influence on the traditional criteria**   The rise of the concept of permanent sovereignty gave the impression that the traditional principles of international law in respect of expropriation had "served their time".

In Resolution 1803 of 1962 the compensation for expropriation still had to be in accordance with international law. Under the UN Covenants (1966) the right of self-determination over natural wealth must still be exercised in accordance with international law.[2] The Charter of Economic Rights and Duties (Article 2,c), however, merely referred to the national law of the host country for the valuation of the compensation.

Traditional international law required that an expropriation be in the general interest. The notion of permanent sovereignty had somewhat eroded this requirement: any claim for control over natural wealth became in the "general interest" of the state.[3] Nowadays the "general interest" thus seems no longer a useful criterion. Only in the case of a serious violation could the general interest still be a relevant condition.[4]

Traditionally, a state was not allowed to expropriate in a discriminatory manner. The Charter, however, considered the property rights of aliens in respect of natural wealth to be precarious: because of its permanent sovereignty, a state could at any time take back these property rights. States were thus not obliged to treat all foreigners equally. Under the Charter investments and expropriations were only subject to national law.

---

[99] *International Law Association, Report of the Sixty-second Conference* (1986) 6. Also, P. Peters, N. Schrijver and P. De Waart, "Responsibility of states in respect of the exercise of permanent sovereignty over natural resources. An analysis of some principles of the Seoul Declaration (1986) by the International Law Association" (1989) N.I.L.R. 285.

[1] See, *e.g.*, T. Waelde, "A Requiem for the 'New Economic Order'. The Rise and Fall of Paradigms in International Economic Law and a Post-Morten with Timeless Significance", in *Liber Amicorum I. Seidl-Hohenveldern* (Kluwer International, 1998), 771– 804.

[2] See: W. Verwey and N. Schrijver, *op. cit.*, p. 49.

[3] Moreover, the requirement of general interest has disappeared from the more recent UN Resolutions. The Charter states, *e.g.* that the host country only has to regulate foreign investments "in accordance with its national objectives and priorities". It is assumed that every expropriation achieves the national objectives.

[4] M. Pellonpää and M. Fitzmaurice, *op. cit.*, p. 63.

Resolution 1803 still required that the compensation should be appropriate. The Charter of Economic Rights and Duties of States (1974) clarified what this entailed:

" . . . appropriate compensation . . . taking into account its relevant laws and regulations and all circumstances that the state considers pertinent."

The amount of this compensation thus depended entirely on the circumstances of the expropriation and the background of the expropriated property. In that event not only the value of the expropriated goods ought to be taken into account, but also the previous actions of the dispossessed, the social and economic necessity of the state and the state's financial ability to pay the compensation.[5] Consequently, under the new principles, only "reasonable" compensation was due for expropriations.[6] This could mean that that no compensation was due, under specific circumstances. In no event should the compensation be so large that it would prevent the state from exercising its permanent right to expropriate.[7]

The requirement of due process of law also received a different meaning under the Charter: in principle, only the legal authorities of the expropriating state were entitled to decide on expropriation in accordance with their national law. Only with the express approval of the host country could other legal bodies, for example, arbitrators or the International Court of Justice, review the expropriation under international law.

However, even at that time is was not generally accepted that the permanent sovereignty affected the traditional criteria of international law to such extent. According to the Seoul Declaration of the International Law Association (see paragraph 7.29), for instance:

"5.5. A State may nationalize, expropriate, exercise eminent domain over or otherwise transfer property or rights in property within its territory and jurisdiction subject to the principal of international law requiring a public purpose and non-discrimination, to appropriate compensation as required by international law, and to any applicable treaty, and without prejudice to legal effects flowing from any contractual undertaking."[8]

Since then, the principles proposed by the Charter have been largely abandoned. The dream of a whole generation of international lawyers was scattered.

Investment treaties

Content   In the afterdays of the New Economic Order there was confusion as 7.31 to the exact content of the general principles of international law with regard to

---

[5] W. Verwey and N. Schrijver, *op. cit.*, p. 20.
[6] See, *e.g. Libyan American Oil Company (Liamco) v. Libya* (1981) 20 I.L.M. 161.
[7] W. Verwey and N. Schrijver, *op. cit.*, p. 20.
[8] *International Law Association, Report of the Sixty-second Conference* (1986) 7. Also P. Peters, N. Schrijver and P. de Waart, "Responsibility of states in respect of the exercise of permanent sovereignty over natural resources. An analysis of some principles of the Seoul Declaration (1986) by the International Law Association" (1989) N.I.L.R. 285.

the protection of investments. The capital exporting countries required respect for certain minimum standards; the poorer, usually capital-importing, countries sometimes argued that permanent sovereignty gave the host country full control over foreign investments (see paragraph 7.29).This uncertainty made foreign financiers and enterprises hesitant to invest capital in developing countries.

To attract capital in spite of the uncertainty, the developing countries grant specific protection to investments through bilateral investment treaties (see paragraph 7.16). They thus restrict their ability to expropriate.[9]

Such investment treaties generally require the three conditions also imposed by traditional international law: first, that the expropriation must be in the general interest; secondly, that it shall not be discriminatory; thirdly, that compensation must be paid (see paragraph 7.24). Moreover, some treaties require a treatment equal to that of other foreign investors and/or of their own nationals (prohibition of discrimination).[10] Practically all treaties stipulate the assessment of compensation for expropriation on the basis of the "real", "actual" or "marketable" value of the investment on the day before the measure to expropriate was taken or published.[11]

7.32   **Effects**   Investment treaties are not affected by the principle of permanent sovereignty over natural resources. The host country cannot rely on this sovereignty for a unilateral withdrawal from an investment treaty.

The great number of investment treaties since 1974 which—despite the Charter—refer to the traditional rules for expropriation, also question the revolutionary principles proclaimed by the majority of nations in the Charter.[12] Perhaps the difference between the Charter and the bilateral investment treaties can be dismissed as a difference between the general rule and the individual exception the poorer countries were forced to make in order to attract investments. Maybe the difference can simply be reduced to a distinction between the "ideal" and "realistic" approaches. If international customary law relies more on actual conduct than on rhetoric, the investment treaties and not the Charter of Economic Rights and Duties reflect represent international law on expropriation.

Effects of expropriation

7.33   **Territorial restriction**   A state can only expropriate on its own territory. The expropriation does not have extraterritorial effect (see paragraph 1.18) and therefore does not affect property situated abroad. The question sometimes arises whether intangible assets (like debts, shares,[13] copyrights, trade marks, patents)

---

[9] A. Guzman, "Why LDCs sign treaties that hurt them : explaining the popularity of bilateral investment treaties" (1998) 38 Va. J. Int'l. L. 639.

[10] See, *e.g.* treaty of BLEU with Hungary (Art. 3).

[11] See, *e.g.* treaty of BLEU with Indonesia (Art. 5); and with Malaysia (Art. 4).

[12] See B. Kishoiyian, "The utility of bilateral investment treaties in the formulation of customary international law" (1994) 14 NW.J.Int'l.L.andBus. 327; W. Verwey and N. Schrijver, *op. cit.*, pp. 60–75.

[13] See, *e.g.* M. Lederer, *Die internationale Enteignung von Mitgliedschaftsrechten* (Lang, Frankfurt, 1989).

were indeed located on the territory of the expropriating state; otherwise the expropriation does not affect them. Ships and their cargoes can only be expropriated if, at the moment of expropriation, they were legally located within the expropriating state.[14]

However, an expropriation may still have indirect effects outside the territory: if a holding company is expropriated in the country where it has its seat, the control over its foreign subsidiaries is also affected.[15]

Recognition Will courts recognise foreign expropriations, for instance, **7.34** when they have to decide on property rights? In principle, they have to assume that the foreign expropriation is valid under the law of the expropriating state, because the courts have no jurisdiction to question the validity of an Act of State of a foreign state.[16] Nevertheless, the court will refuse to recognise a foreign expropriation if it is contrary to the criteria accepted in international law.

PART IV: WORLD BANK MECHANISMS FOR THE PROTECTION OF INVESTMENTS

ICSID arbitration

Objective In the 1960s the traditional rules of international law for expro- **7.35** priation and compensation were under threat (see paragraph 7.29). It did not take long for the effects to be felt: the investment flow to the developing countries threatened to dry up. In 1965 and in order to promote investments the World Bank created the International Centre for Settlement of Investment Disputes (ICSID), a conciliation and arbitration system, to offer a foreign investor protection against the risk of expropriation.

At present, 134 countries are bound by the Washington Convention, which created ICSID.[17]

---

[14] See F. Rigaux and J. Verhoeven, "Nationalisation et relations internationales" (1982) J.T. 489, 491–497; C. Staker, "Public international law and the *lex situs* rule in property conflicts and foreign expropriations" (1987) B.Y.I.L. 151.

[15] See in relation to the effects of the nationalisation of Saint-Gobain in France on the shareholders of Glaceries Saint-Roch in Belgium, Namur Court (1987) 26 I.L.M. 1251. See also G. Burdeau, "La Contribution des nationalisations françaises de 1982 au droit international des nationalisations" (1985) 5 Rev.Gen.dr.int.pub. 25–28.

[16] See on this point R. Ergec, "La doctrine de l'Act of State et la jurisprudence belge" (1984) R.I.D.C. 61–93; C. Flinterman, *De Act of State Doctrine* (TMC Asser Instituut, The Hague, 1981); F. Rigaux, *Droit Public et Droit Privé dans les Relations Internationales* (Pedone, Paris, 1977) pp. 228–251. For the U.S. Supreme Court, March 23, 1964, (*Sabatino*) (1964) Am.J.Int'l.L. 779; see however the so-called Sabatino amendment (1965) I.C.L.Q. 452.

[17] Convention of March 18, 1965. See C. Schreuer, *The ICSID Convention: A Commentary* (Cambridge University Press, 2001); See as well, *inter alia*, C. Schreuer "Commentary on the ICSID Convention" (1996) 11 I.C.S.I.D. Rev. 2–318 and following issues. As of April 2001 the ICSID Convention was adopted by 148 Contracting States (134 of them having also deposited the instrument of the ratification). An updated list of contracting states can be found in the most recent volume of *Yearbook of Commercial Arbitration*.

7.36   **Scope of application**   Both the investor and the host country may bring a dispute to ICSID when the following conditions are satisfied[18]:

(a) The dispute must relate to an investment. The ICSID Convention, however, does not give a definition of "investment". Therefore, the traditional forms of investment as well as the newer transactions, which entail investment of capital, such as a service contract, public works or the transfer of technology, can be submitted to ICSID arbitration.

(b) Both the host state and the state of which the private investor is a subject, must be party to the ICSID Convention. That implies that the investor cannot be of the same nationality as the country in which he invests. Yet, host countries generally require the foreign investor to operate through a local company. In that event, ICSID may still have jurisdiction when the investor and the host country have agreed to consider this company for the purpose of ICSID as a foreign party under the control of a foreign investor.[19]

(c) The investor as well as the host country must have accepted the ICSID jurisdiction. Often, the investor accepts the ICSID jurisdiction in the investment contract concluded with the authorities of the host state (see paragraph 7.09).[20] Investment laws (see paragraph 7.08) moreover sometimes state that investment disputes with foreign investors have to be submitted to ICSID.[21] The host state may also adopt ICSID arbitration in his investment treaty.[22] Most investment treaties include such a clause. If a dispute on investments then arises with a national of a co-signatory of the treaty, the host country remains bound by his commitment. A mere unilateral acceptance of ICSID jurisdiction by the investor will trigger an agreement between the host country and the investor on ICSID-arbitration.[23]

---

[18] See C. Lamm, "Jurisdiction of the International Centre for Settlement of Investment Disputes" (1990) I.C.S.I.D. Rev. 462; C. Schreuer, "Commentary on the ICSID Convention: Article 25" (1996) 11 I.C.S.I.D. 318–492.

[19] See ICSID Convention, Art. 25(2)(b). See *e.g.* ICSID award February 4 and 9, 1988, *SAOBI v. Senegal* (1990) J.D.I. 192; (1992) Y.Com.Arb. 42.

[20] G. Delaume, "How to draft an ICSID Arbitration clause" (1992) I.C.S.I.D. Rev. 168.

[21] 27 national investment laws refer to ICSID. See, *e.g.* ICSID arbitration award December 27, 1985, *Southern Pacific Properties v. Egypt* (1991) Y.Com.Arb. 19.

[22] 286 bilateral investment treaties as well as the NAFTA agreement (see para. 3.12) refer to ICSID. See P. Peters, "Dispute settlement arrangements in investment treaties" (1991) N.Y.I.L. 91; ICSID arbitration, *Amco Asia and others v. Republic of Indonesia* (1984) 23 I.L.M. 351; see also R.G. Dearden, "Arbitration of expropriation disputes between an investor and the state under the North American Free Trade Agreement" (1995) 29 J.W.T. 113–127.

[23] The treaty often states that the host country shall unconditionally accept ICSID arbitration the moment an investor who is a subject of the other treaty party asks for arbitration (see, *e.g.* between BLEU and Indonesia, Art. 10; treaty with Korea, Art. 8). Sometimes the treaty simply refers to the ICSID arbitration rules (see, *e.g.* treaty between BLEU and China, Art. 6 of Protocol (if the investor opts for the ICSID rules)). Occasionally it just leaves a choice between ICSID arbitration or any other arbitration (see, *e.g.* treaty between BLEU and Hungary, Art. 9).

ICSID itself does not settle disputes, it only offers the legal framework for a dispute settlement. This can take the form of a conciliation procedure or arbitration.

Conciliation procedure An investor or contracting state may refer an 　**7.37** investment dispute to a Conciliation Commission. A Conciliation Commission consists of a sole conciliator, or any uneven number of conciliators. They are appointed by the parties and/or the ICSID. Members of the Conciliation Commission are in principle nominated from a panel. Each contracting state may appoint four persons for this panel.

The Conciliation Commission shall hear the arguments and explanations of the parties. It is the duty of the Commission to clarify the issues in dispute and to bring about agreement between the parties on mutually acceptable terms. When agreement is reached, the Commission shall draw up a report recording the agreement accepted by the parties. If the conciliation is unsuccessful, this failure will also be recorded by the Conciliation Commission. The parties may then submit their dispute to arbitrators. Statements of the other party made in a failed conciliation procedure cannot be mentioned in an arbitration procedure.

As yet, very few disputes have been referred to ICSID for conciliation. Perhaps parties hesitate to make use of ICSID conciliation because the outcome is uncertain and depends completely on the goodwill of the parties.

Arbitration Any investor or contracting state may refer a dispute to an 　**7.38** arbitral tribunal under the auspices of ICSID. The tribunal usually consists of three arbitrators, one arbitrator appointed by each party and the third, the chairman, appointed by agreement of the parties. If a party does not appoint an arbitrator (or when the parties disagree about the chairman), ICSID appoints an arbitrator or the chairman instead,[24] usually selected from the pre-established list of ICSID arbitrators.[25] However, persons who are not on the list may also be elected as arbitrator.

The arbitration proceedings are conducted in accordance with the ICSID Convention, and unless the parties have agreed otherwise, the arbitrators must follow the arbitration rules drawn up by ICSID.[26] Procedural question not covered by the ICSID Convention, by the ICSID arbitration rules or by the agreement of the parties, shall be decided by the tribunal.[27]

ICSID arbitration and the applicable law One of the great attractions of 　**7.39** ICSID arbitration is the law ICSID arbitrators have to apply to a dispute.[28]

The arbitrators must in the first place apply the law chosen by the parties. If the parties have opted in the investment contract for international law (see paragraph 7.09), the arbitrators will sanction an expropriation in breach of the

---

[24] ICSID Convention, Arts 38 and 40.
[25] Each contracting party may nominate four persons for this list panel.
[26] ICSID Convention, Art. 44.
[27] *ibid.*, Art. 44.
[28] A. R. Parra, "The role of the ICSID Secretariat in the administration of arbitration proceedings under the ICSID Convention" (1998) 13 ICSID 85–100.

rules of international law, even if the expropriation was in conformity with the national law of the host state.

Very often the contract will, however, indicate that it is governed by the law of the host state. When there is no choice of law, the arbitrators shall impartially apply the national law of the state in which the investment took place (including its conflict of law rules).

National law of the host state is often of little help, since expropriations are usually carried out in conformity with the national law of the host country. For that reason the ICSID Convention (Article 42) requires furthermore that, besides national law, "such rules of international law as may be applicable" have to be applied, too.

ICSID thus offers efficient legal protection against expropriation by the host country. In fact the national law only applies if it satisfies the test of international law.[29] National law that goes contrary to international law or the contract must be ignored by ICSID arbitrators.

7.40 **Remedies against an ICSID award** Another advantage of ICSID arbitration is that the award cannot be set aside by a national court (*e.g.* of the host country). If the arbitration proceedings have had obvious defects, the award can only be annulled by a special *ad hoc* Committee specially constituted by ICSID for this purpose.

The grounds for annulment are rather limited: improper constitution of the arbitral tribunal, manifest excess of powers, corruption of arbiters, serious departure from a fundamental rule of procedure, failure to state the reasons on which the award is based.

Some awards have already been submitted to *ad hoc* Committees for annulment.[30] For instance, an *ad hoc* Committee has annulled an arbitration award because of manifest excess of powers, because the arbitrators had settled the dispute solely on the basis of equity instead of national law, as is required by the ICSID Convention.[31]

If the award is annulled, the parties must submit the dispute to a (newly constituted) ICSID arbitral tribunal. The new tribunal is not bound by the findings of the first arbitrators or the *ad hoc* Committee, but shall examine the dispute once more in full.[32]

7.41 **Exclusive jurisdiction of ICSID arbitrators** Another advantage of ICSID arbitration is its exclusivity. An ICSID arbitration clause excludes the jurisdiction of the national courts. Once ICSID arbitration is chosen, the national courts are

---

[29] See, *e.g.* the ICSID award *Letco v. Liberia* (1987) 26 I.L.M. 647, 658: "The law of the contracting State is recognised as paramount within its own territory, but is nevertheless subjects to the control by international law". In the ICSID award *AAPL v. Sri Lanka* (1991) 30 I.L.M. 577; (1992) Y.Com.Arb. 106, the arbitrators applied the investment treaty directly.

[30] ICSID Convention, Art. 52. See, *e.g. Klöckner v. Cameroon* (1987) J.D.I. 135; *Amco Asia v. Indonesia* (1987) J.D.I. 174; (1986) 25 I.L.M. 1439; *Mine v. New Guinea* (1991) J.D.I. 166; (1991) Y.Com.Arb. 40. See also A. Broches, "Observations on the Finality of ICSID Awards" (1991) I.C.S.I.D. Rev. 321.

[31] *Klöckner v. Cameroon* (1986) Y.Com.Arb. 162.

[32] See, *e.g. Amco v. Indonesia* (1988) 27 I.L.M. 1281, 1284.

no longer competent to hear an investment dispute. They even cannot order attachments or other provisional measures.[33]

An ICSID arbitration clause also excludes diplomatic protection for the investor by his own state against the host state.[34] A dispute between the host state and the state of the investor before the International Court of Justice—as has happened a few times in the past—is therefore excluded.[35] The dispute can only be resolved legally by ICSID arbitration between the host state and the investor himself.

Enforcement of the ICSID arbitral award   The losing party shall abide by **7.42** the award except when the enforcement of the award has been stayed, *e.g.* when annulment of the award is requested (see paragraph 7.41).[36] Each ICSID state recognises the award as binding and guarantees the enforcement within its territory as if the ICSID award were a final judgment of a court of that state.[37] Nevertheless, a state can still avoid enforcement against specific assets, if a court grants it immunity from execution (see paragraph 2.08).[38] However, there may be either courts that do not grant this immunity, or assets which are not immune. Moreover, a host state refusing to enforce an ICSID award risks being out of favour with the World Bank and the international financial world, which undoubtedly has repercussions in the long run.

Additional tasks   ICSID may likewise give assistance not covered by the **7.43** Convention (see paragraph 7.33) (the so-called Additional Facility).[39] ICSID may thus arrange conciliation proceedings or arbitration for an investor who is not a national of an ICSID state or when the dispute does not concern investments. Arbitral awards issued under the Additional Facility may only be enforced under respective national arbitration laws.[40] The ICSID Convention rules on enforcement are not applicable.

ICSID may also initiate fact-finding procedures. These procedures, however, do not benefit from the advantages of ICSID arbitration such as independence from national law and national courts.

MIGA guarantee for investments

Objective   To promote investment in developing countries the World Bank **7.44** also created the Multilateral Investment Guarantee Agency—MIGA. MIGA was

---

[33] C. Brower and R. Goodman, "Provisional measures and the protection of ICSID jurisdictional exclusivity against municipal proceedings" (1990) I.C.S.I.D. Rev. 431.

[34] ICSID Convention, Art. 27.

[35] See, *e.g.* International Court of Justice, *Liechtenstein v. Guatemala re Nottebohm*, I.C.J. Rep. 1959, p. 6; *Belgium v. Spain re Barcelona Traction*, I.C.J. Rep. 1970, p.3.

[36] ICSID Convention, Art. 53.

[37] *ibid.*, Art. 54.

[38] *ibid.*, Art. 55. See, *e.g. Letco v. Liberia*, 650 F.Suppl. (S.D.N.Y. 1986); (1987) 26 I.L.M. 695; French appeal case *Sohbi v. Senegal* (1991) J.D.I. 1005; (1991) 30 I.L.M. 1167.

[39] See "Additional Facility Rules", with introduction by A. Broches in (1979) Y.Com.Arb. 374. For more updated information see http://www.worldbank.org/icsid/facility/facility.htm.

[40] See E. Leahy and D. Orentlicher, "Enforcement of arbitral awards issued by the Additional Facility of the International Centre of Settlement of Investment Disputes" (1989) J.I.A. 15.

founded in 1985 by a multilateral convention and has been operational since 1988.[41]

MIGA promotes foreign investments in developing countries. MIGA carries out research on the investment opportunities and informs the international business community about local investment. More importantly, however, MIGA offers the foreign investor protection against non-commercial risks.

7.45   **Guaranteed investments**   MIGA only covers business people or companies, which respectively are nationals of a state that is a member of MIGA, or are incorporated and have their seat in such a Member State, or are controlled by companies or nationals of Member States (or which are Member State owned).

The MIGA Convention protects many forms of investment. Its main aim, of course, is foreign direct investments, but the Convention is also intended for equity interests, such as shares and for loans made or guaranteed by holders of equity. A financial input is not even required. Assets such as know-how, patents, management contracts, franchising agreements, arrangements for joint ventures or profit sharing and other forms of co-operation may also be covered by MIGA.[42]

In any event, only "new" investments may be guaranteed, *i.e.* investments made after the investor requested a guarantee from MIGA.

The investment must be made in a developing country member of MIGA.[43] In addition, the guarantee may only be granted after the government of the host country has approved the MIGA guarantee.[44]

The guarantee is only issued when MIGA has established that the investment will contribute to the development of the host country. MIGA also limits its own risk. It checks the investment conditions within the host country (correct treatment, legal protection). If necessary, it concludes an agreement with the host country for the treatment and legal protection of the guaranteed investments.[45] MIGA enjoys the most favoured status in such agreements: the host country must concede the same preferences to MIGA as granted to a third party in an investment treaty.[46]

7.46   **Covered risks**   The MIGA Convention covers four important types of non-commercial risks:

---

[41] Convention of October 11, 1985, (1989) 28 I.L.M. 1598; (1987) Y.Com.Arb. 219. In July 1994 it was signed by 166 states and ratified by 154 states. For more information see http://www.miga.org/screens/about/members/members.htm. See also F. I. Shihata, "L'Agence Multilatérale de Garantie des Investissements" (1987) A.F.D.I. 601; J. Touscoz, "L'Agence Multilatérale de Garantie des Investissements" (1987) D.P.C.I. 311; J. Touscoz, "Les opérations de garantie de l'Agence Multilatérale de garantie des Investissements" (1987) J.D.I. 901.

[42] Convention, Art. 12; Operational Regulations, Art. 102–108 (1988) 27 I.L.M. 1227.

[43] *ibid.*, Art. 14 and Annex 2 (cat.2).

[44] *ibid.*, Art. 15.

[45] F. I. Shihata, *op. cit.*, p. 607. Thus, MIGA has entered into investment agreements with, *inter alia*, Bangladesh, Ghana, Hungary and Poland.

[46] Convention, Art. 23 b(ii).

(a) Currency transfer. MIGA may protect the investor against restrictions on the repatriation of funds from the host state. It can protect against restrictions in respect of the local currency or against exchange rates which are lower than those mentioned in the contract of guarantee. MIGA also offers protection when the host country fails to perform the currency transfer within 90 days from the demand or within any other period provided in the contract of guarantee.[47]

(b) Expropriation and similar measures. MIGA guarantees against any legislative or administrative acts or omissions, of the host state which prejudice the investor's rights or interests in an investment. In principle it does not cover non-discriminatory measures adopted in good faith by the host state in the general interest or to regulate the economic activity (e.g. tax or price regulations). However, these activities nevertheless could be covered if they in fact constitute a creeping expropriation (see paragraph 7.21).[48]

(c) Breach of contract. MIGA may cover breach of contract by the host state. This guarantee only comes in effect when the investor has no access to court or arbitration,[49] when no decision is rendered within a reasonable period of time, or when a decision rendered against the host state cannot be enforced.[50]

(d) War and civil disturbance. The Board of Directors may extend the coverage to other non-commercial risks, upon a joint request from the investor and the host country. However, the coverage can under no circumstances be extended to the risk of devaluation or currency depreciation. Neither can it be extended to any action or omission by the host government to which the investor has agreed or for which he is responsible.[51]

In addition MIGA may cover other non-commercial risks upon the joint request of the investor and his host country.

Contract of guarantee MIGA coverage implies a contract of guarantee **7.47** between MIGA and the investor.[52] General conditions of guarantee set out the type of coverage and compensation.

The contract of guarantee specifies the holder of the guarantee, the project invested in, the nature of the investment, the covered risks, the terms of the guarantee and any other arrangements between the investor and the host state. In addition it spells out the rights and obligations of MIGA and the investor. The premium to be paid depends on the coverage. MIGA does not cover the full

---

[47] See "Operational Rules" June 22, 1988, Art. 1.24 (1988) 27 I.L.M. 1227.

[48] Operational Rules, Arts 1.36 and 1.37.

[49] e.g. because there are unreasonable procedural obstacles (Art. 1.44).

[50] e.g. because the decision cannot be enforced within a period of 90 days or within the period fixed in the contract of guarantee (Art. 1.44).

[51] MIGA Convention, Arts 11(b) and (c).

[52] For this reason, in 1989 MIGA drew up a standard contract of guarantee as well as general conditions of guarantee for "equity investments" ("MIGA: Standard contract of guarantee and general conditions of guarantee for equity investments, January 25, 1989" (1989) 28 I.L.M. 1233).

investment. The contract specifies what part (10 per cent or more) remains uninsured. Moreover, MIGA shall only compensate after the investor has exhausted all legal remedies of the host country.[53]

7.48   **Dispute settlement**[54]   The contract of guarantee indicates that any dispute between MIGA and the investor shall be submitted to arbitration (ICSID arbitration (see paragraph 7.39) is usually chosen).[55] The arbitrators have to apply the contract of guarantee, the MIGA Convention, as well as the general principles of law.[56]

Disputes between MIGA Member States on the interpretation and application of the MIGA Convention (*e.g.* the treatment by the host state of a citizen of another country) must be submitted to MIGA's Board of Directors.[57]

Disputes between MIGA and a Member State (*e.g.* on recovery from the host state of a compensation paid by MIGA) are to be settled first by negotiation; if this remains unsuccessful, by conciliation and, if needs be, by arbitration.[58]

7.49   **Conclusion**   MIGA does not compete with the private insurance companies. On the contrary, it intends to be complementary by covering non-commercial risks, while the commercial risks are covered by the private sector. Furthermore, MIGA co-operates with private insurance companies so that the private insurers can improve the MIGA cover and cover other risks.[59]

MIGA contributes to a favourable investment climate. Difficulties and expropriations can be dealt with in all objectivity by MIGA on the basis of established rules. Besides, MIGA is politically neutral: according to the Convention it cannot get involved in the political affairs of the Member States.[60]

In short, MIGA offers the investor and the host country the security necessary to maintain the flow of investment to the developing countries.

---

[53] MIGA Convention, Art. 17.
[54] J. Touscoz, "Le réglement der différents dans la Convention institutant l'Agence Multilatérale de Garantie des Investissements" (1988) Rev.Arb. 629.
[55] Operational Rules, Art. 2.16.
[56] Operational Rules, Art. 2.17.
[57] MIGA Convention, Art. 56.
[58] *ibid.*, Art. 57 and Annex II; Operational Rules, Arts 4.20 *et seq.*
[59] *ibid.*, Art. 21.
[60] *ibid.*, Art. 34.

CHAPTER 8

FINANCE OF INTERNATIONAL TRADE

Overview International trade often requires financing. Each year about **8.01**
$ 700 billion is spent on financing imports and exports. Over the years, banks
have developed abundant credit instruments and facilities.[1] Not all of them can
be discussed within the confines of this textbook; the focus will be on some of
the more common credit and finance instruments.

PART I: DOCUMENTARY CREDITS

General characteristics

Introduction Documentary credit, "the life blood of international com- **8.02**
merce",[2] is the most frequently used method to pay for goods in international
trade.[3]

The buyer (importer) often does not want to pay before he is in possession of
the goods and can examine whether they are in conformity with the contract; the
seller (exporter), from his side, does not want to dispatch the goods as long as he
is not certain that the agreed price will be paid. In an international setting these

---

[1] For current surveys see, *inter alia*, D. B. Cox, *Finance of International Trade* (4th ed., Northwich,
Worcester, 1988); C. M. Chinkin, P. J. Davidson and W. J. Ricquier, *Current Problems of
International Trade Financing* (2nd. ed., Butterworths, Singapore, 1990); K. Pilbeam, *International finance* (Macmillan, Houndmills,1994); E. Clark, M. Levasseur and P. Rousseau, *Inter-
national Finance* (Chapmen & Hall, London, 1993); R. C. Tennekoon, *The Law and Regulation of
International Finance* (Butterworths, 1991); N. Horn (ed.), *The Law of International Trade
Finance* (Kluwer Law & Taxation, Deventer, 1989); F. Wood, *The Law and Practice of International Finance* (Sweet & Maxwell, 1995); C. J. Cheng and C. M. Schmitthoff, *Basic Documents
on International Trade Law* (Nijhoff, Dordrecht, 1999); L. D'Arcy, C. Murray and B. Cleave,
Schmitthoff's Export Trade: the Law and Practice of International Trade (10th ed., Sweet &
Maxwell, London, 2000); J. C. T. Chuah, *Law of International Trade* (Sweet & Maxwell, London,
1998); M. J. Trebilcock and R. Howse, *The Regulation of International Trade* (2nd ed., Routledge,
London, 1999);
[2] *R.D. Harbottle (Mercantile) Ltd. v. National Westminster Bank Ltd* [1978] Q.B.146, 155.
[3] Consult on documentary credit, *inter alia*, L. Maura Costa, *Le Crédit Documentaire. Etude
Comparée* (LGDJ, 1998); G. A. Penn, A. M. Shea and A. Arora, *The Law and Practice of
International Banking* (2nd ed., Sweet & Maxwell, London, 1997); F. Eisemann and R. A. Schütze,
Das Dokumentenakkreditiv im internationalen Handelsverkehr (3rd ed., Recht und Wirtschaft,
Heidelberg, 1989); F. M. Ventris, *Bankers' documentary credits* (3rd ed., Lloyd's of London,
1990); R. Jack, *Documentary credits* (Butterworths, London, 1993); J. F. Dolan, *The Law of Letters
of Credit* (rev. ed., Warren, Gorham & Lamont, Boston, 1996); W. Brooke, *Standby and Commercial Letters of Credit* (2nd ed., 1996); P. Todd, *Bills of Lading and Banker's Documentary Credit*
(3rd ed., Lloyd's of London Press, 1998); B. Kozolchyk, "Letters of credit", *International
Encyclopedia of Comparative Law IX*, (1979) Chap. 5; C. Busto, *ICC Guide to Documentary*

incompatible interests may make international sales rather difficult. Distance, unfamiliarity with each other and different trade practices might create distrust that is difficult to bridge. The system of documentary credits helps to reconcile the seller's and the buyer's interests.

8.03   **Definition**   A documentary credit implies an arrangement in which a bank, acting for and on behalf of the customer (buyer), undertakes to pay the beneficiary (seller) a sum of money (or to accept a bill of exchange drawn by the beneficiary), or to authorise another bank to do so on presentation by the beneficiary of the bill of lading and other specified documents and on condition that all other credit terms are met.[4]

The essence of the documentary credit is the representation of goods by the bill of lading. Possession of the bill of lading thus equals title to the goods, covered by this bill of lading. A transfer of the bill of lading means transfer of the ownership over the goods.

A bank issues a documentary credit at the request of its customer because this method of payment is provided in the underlying agreement[5] (usually a contract of sale of goods). However, documentary credits cover also international construction projects, investments and services.[6]

8.04   **The bank as key player**   The bank of the customer (buyer), which has opened a documentary credit for the beneficiary (seller), is called the *issuing bank*. The personal undertaking of the issuing bank is evidenced by a letter of credit (L/C),[7] which is sent to the beneficiary: the issuing bank shall pay when the

---

Credit Operations for the UCP 500 (ICC, Paris, 1994); International Chamber of Commerce, *ICC Uniform Customs and Practice for Documentary Credits* (ICC, 1994); P. Ellinger, "The law of letters of credit" in N. Horn (ed.), *The Law of International Trade Finance* (Kluwer Law & Taxation, Deventer, 1989); J. Raymond, A. Malek, and D. Quest, *Documentary Credits: the Law and Practice of Documentary Credits including Standby Credits and Demand Guarantees* (Butterworths, London, 2001); N. de Gottrau, *Le Crédit Documentaire et la Fraude: la Fraude du Bénéficiaire, ses Conséquences et les Moyens de Protection du Donneur d'Ordre* (Helbing et Lichtenhahn, Basle, 1999); J. D. Lipton, "Documentary credit law and practice in the global information Age" (1998–99) 2, Fordham.Int'l.L.J. 1972–1990.

[4] Art. 2 of the "Uniform Customs and Practices for Documentary Credits" (UCP) (paras 8.10 *et seq.*): "Any arrangement, however named or described, whereby a bank (the Issuing Bank), acting at the request and on the instructions of a customer (the Applicant) or on its own behalf, (i) is to make a payment to or to the order of a third party (the Beneficiary), or is to accept and pay bills of exchange (draft(s)) drawn by the Beneficiary; or (ii) authorises another bank to effect such payment, or to accept and pay such bills of exchange (draft(s)); or (iii) authorises another bank to negotiate; against stipulated document(s), provided that the terms and conditions of the Credit are complied with."

[5] There are standard recommendations by the banks for application for the issue of documentary credits; see, *e.g.* the forms of Midland Bank, in R. Jack, *op. cit.*, pp. 323 *et seq.*

[6] The "Uniform Customs and Practice for Documentary Credits" (UCP) (see paragraph 8.10) makes the documentary credit applicable to goods as well as "services and/or other performances" (Art. 4), though in this case practice prefers a Standby letter of credit (paras 8.22) or a bank guarantee (paras. 8.52 *et seq.*).

[7] Consult, *inter alia*, P. Ellinger, "The law of letters of credit" in N. Horn (ed.), *The Law of International Trade Finance* (Kluwer Law & Taxation, Deventer, 1989) pp. 203.

documents specified in the L/C (paragraphs 8.12 *et seq.*), are presented on time and in conformity with what the L/C requires.[8]

The issuing bank cannot invoke against the beneficiary any exception from the underlying agreement (*e.g.* the sales contract) or from its credit agreement with its customer.[9]

Since the underlying agreement and the documentary credit are separate, the customer cannot in principle request a court to enjoin the issuing bank from paying because the delivered goods did not conform to the contract (save in case of fraud, paragraph 8.17).[10]

The issuing bank often authorises a bank from the country of the beneficiary (seller, exporter) to examine the specified documents and to negotiate, accept or pay the beneficiary's draft. This latter bank is called the *advising bank*. The advising bank will often be the branch or subsidiary of the issuing bank in the exporter's country. Otherwise, it is a local bank with which the issuing bank has regular business (a "correspondent").

The advising bank has to ascertain with reasonable care the "apparent authenticity" of the credit on which it has to advise. If the advising bank suspects fraud in the letter of credit, it must ask the issuing bank to confirm its authenticity.

The customer is often not satisfied with the undertakings of the foreign issuing bank, but requires from the local advising bank a direct commitment to pay or to accept a bill of exchange. If the advising bank agrees, *i.e.* when it "confirms" the documentary credit, the advising bank becomes the *confirming bank*.[11]

In case of a confirmed documentary credit, the exporting beneficiary has a claim against the issuing bank as well as against the confirming bank. In some countries the issuing bank and the confirming bank are then deemed to be jointly and severally liable.[12]

When the advising bank is a branch of the issuing bank, it is in principle not necessary to have the documentary credit confirmed, since the branch is part of the legal entity of the issuing bank and confirmation by the branch does not result in an additional claim on another bank for the exporter. Still, confirmation by the branch may be useful when the issuing bank may not be able to perform its

---

[8] The ICC publishes standard forms for the issuing and transfer of letters of credit: *The New ICC Standard Documentary Credit Forms*, ICC Publication no. 516. See also R. Jack, *op.cit.*, pp. 313 *et seq.*

[9] M. Van Der Haegen, "The rule on disregarding defences in the irrevocable documentary credit" (1986) I.B.L.J. 703.

[10] Ch. Bontoux, "Saisie-arrêt le crédit documentaire" (1985) Banque (Fr.) 73; L.Gani, *La Saisissabilité des Droits Patrimoniaux en Matière d'Accréditif Documentaire* (Lausanne, 1987); L. Mauro Costa, *op.cit.*, pp. 78–82.

[11] The constructions may be more complicated in practice. The documentary credit is sometimes confirmed by a bank in an important trade centre in the country of the exporter; this confirming bank advises the credit to the exporter through a third bank which is established in the town of the exporter. This third bank may be the bank with which the exporter does his usual business. A special form of confirmation is the so-called "*soft confirmation*". This confirmation is conditional; it is mainly used for documentary credits of beneficiaries established in countries with exchange control (see para. 9.02); P. Jasinski, "Les crédits documentaires dont le paiement ou le remboursement est assuré par des organismes financiers internationaux" (1987) Banque (Fr.) 444.

[12] UCP Art. 9b. According to Belgian and Dutch opinion, however, the beneficiary must first ask the confirming bank for payment; the issuing bank will only be called upon should the confirming bank fail to pay.

obligation to pay as a result of measures by local authorities (particularly restrictions on foreign exchange: see paragraph 9.03).[13]

Confirmation of a documentary credit must be distinguished from the "guarantee of a documentary credit". For instance, an exporter, beneficiary of a documentary credit, may ask his local bank to guarantee the undertaking of the issuing bank, even though the local bank lacks authorisation or was not requested by the issuing bank to confirm the credit.

8.05   **Irrevocable or revocable credit**   Documentary credits are either revocable or irrevocable.[14]

A revocable credit may be amended or cancelled by the issuing bank at any time and without prior notice to the exporting beneficiary.[15] Therefore, a revocable credit is rarely used.[16]

Only an irrevocable credit offers the exporter the necessary guarantee for payment. Only such credit may be the subject of a confirmation by a corresponding bank.[17] However, even an irrevocable credit does not give the beneficiary any claim to payment until the bank accepts the documents as conforming to the terms of the credit; only then will the beneficiary be certain of being paid.

The underlying agreement often requires an irrevocable credit. Moreover, in the absence of an indication to the contrary, the credit is deemed to be irrevocable.[18]

8.06   **Issuing of a documentary credit**   The documentary credit involves various stages.

The exporter (seller) and the importer (buyer) stipulate in the underlying agreement that the payments will take place on the basis of a documentary credit. It is usually agreed that the exporter will only dispatch the merchandise after he has received the letter of credit from the issuing bank.[19]

The importer then requests his bank (the issuing bank) to issue the letter of credit for the benefit of the exporter.[20] This request must clearly specify which documents the exporter has to present. Furthermore, the letter of credit must

---

[13] See S. Zamora, "Recognition of foreign exchange controls in international creditors' rights cases" (1987) Int.L.1055.

[14] Revocation can take place on instigation of the importer or on initiative of the issuing bank.

[15] UCP Art. 8a.

[16] In special cases (*e.g.* when the exporter has confidence in the solvency of the importer) a revocable credit is preferred because this form of credit is less expensive. This is often the case when firms are part of the same concern.

[17] UCP Art. 9b. See also, G. A. Penn, A. M. Shea and A. Arora, *op.cit*, p. 305. Even a confirmed credit does not always offer a sufficient guarantee. Suppose that an exporter is a beneficiary of a confirmed irrevocable documentary credit in the context of a FOB sale (see paragraph 4.56) and that the importer fails to supply a ship. Through the negligence of the importer the exporter is in this case unable to receive payment. This is why exporters are recommended to sell on a CIF basis (see paragraph 4.56).

[18] UCP Art. 6.

[19] Even in the absence of such a clause it is assumed that the letter of credit must reach the exporter before dispatch of the goods.

[20] In practice the client fills in the forms made available by the bank.

mention an expiry date and a place for the presentation of the specified documents.[21]

The issuing bank then sends the letter of credit to the advising bank.

Coming into effect The advising bank examines the prima facie genuine- **8.07**
ness of the letter of credit and informs the exporter of the documentary credit. If
the advising bank is also the confirming bank, it moreover commits itself to pay
the exporter.

The exporter checks whether the credit conditions are in conformity with the
terms and conditions of the underlying agreement and makes sure that he will be
able to satisfy all conditions of the documentary credit (particularly to tender the
documents as requested by the letter of credit).

When the exporter then dispatches the merchandise as provided by the underlying agreement, he receives the required documents from carriers, insurance
companies and the like (see paragraphs 8.12 *et seq.*) and hands them over to the
advising bank. This bank examines whether the documents are in conformity
with the credit conditions. If this is the case, the advising bank pays the exporter
(see paragraph 8.14).[22]

Legal relationships between the parties The legal relationships between **8.08**
the different parties in a documentary credit could be summarised as follows.[23]

(a) The customer and his bank have usually entered into an agreement for the
     issue of a documentary credit,[24] subject to certain conditions and up to a
     contractually fixed "ceiling". The bank generally demands a security from
     the customer, for instance, shipping documents (*e.g.* the bill of lading).
     The bank may, where necessary, retain these documents until the client has
     paid.[25]

(b) The issuing bank signs a letter of credit for the benefit of the seller. In this
     letter of credit the bank undertakes to pay or to accept or negotiate a bill
     of exchange as soon as the documents specified in the underlying agree-
     ment are presented. The letter of credit stipulates an expiry date and a
     place for the presentation of documents for payment (see paragraph 8.12).

---

[21] UCP Art. 42. A letter of credit sometimes contains the condition that the credit will be automatically extended by law for a certain period, unless the bank informs the beneficiary that it does not
wish to renew the credit. In practice this is called an evergreen clause. This clause should not be
confused with a "revolving" credit (see paragraph 8.20). The UCP (Art. 5a, second paragraph)
determines that in order to guard against confusion and misunderstanding, banks should discourage
"any attempt to include excessive detail in the credit".

[22] See, for the different methods of payment, para. 8.16.

[23] For a thorough examination, see G. A. Penn, A. M. Shea and A. Arora, *op.cit.*, pp. 336 *et seq.*

[24] It may also be that a documentary credit is issued without giving credit to the client, *e.g.* because
he already has an account at the bank, on which there is a positive balance sufficient to cover the
amount of the potential credit.

[25] For the relationship between customer and issuing bank, see *inter alia* R. Cranston, *European
Banking Law: the Banker—Customer Relationship* (2nd ed., Lloyd's of London Press, 1999); G.
A. Penn, A. M. Shea and A. Arora, *op.cit.*, pp. 336 *et seq.*; P. Ellinger "Letters of credit" in N.
Horn and C. M. Schmitthoff, *The Transnational Law of International Commercial Transactions*
(Kluwer, Deventer, 1982), pp. 255 *et seq.*

Depending on the applicable law the relationship between the issuing bank and the beneficiary is based either on a contract (*e.g.* the United Kingdom and the United States[26]) or on a unilateral expression of will (*e.g.* Belgium,[27] The Netherlands[28]). The distinction may be important: in the first hypothesis, it must be shown that the beneficiary has accepted the bank's offer. Whenever the beneficiary has complied with the terms of the letter of credit, he can claim payment from the issuing bank.[29]

(c) The relationship between the issuing bank and the advising bank is one of principal and agent. Indeed, the advising bank acts in name and on behalf of the issuing bank.[30] The advising bank, which has paid the beneficiary or has accepted a bill of exchange drawn by the beneficiary in accordance with the mandate, has to be reimbursed by the issuing bank.

(d) As regards the beneficiary, the advising bank merely is an agent of the issuing bank. The beneficiary has thus no claim against the advising bank.

(e) When the advising bank becomes the confirming bank, it is jointly liable with the issuing bank to pay or to accept a bill of exchange towards the beneficiary.

Applicable rules

8.09   Private international law   As most documentary credits involve international transactions, the law applicable to the documentary credit is an important issue.[31] The following principles are relevant:

---

[26] E. P. Ellinger and E. Lomnicka, *Modern Banking Law* (3rd ed., Clarendon, Oxford, 2001); H. C. Gutteridge and M. Megrah, *The Law of Bankers' Commercial Credits* (7th ed., Europa Publications., London, 1984) *op.cit.,* p. 34; G. A. Penn, A. M. Shea and A. Arora, *op.cit.,* p. 295; R. Jack, *op.cit.,* pp. 6, 72 *et seq.*; R. Cranston, *Principles of Banking law* (Clarendon, Oxford, 1997); Uniform Commercial Code, ss. 5–103(1)(a), as well as the commentary on ss. 5–114: "The letter of credit is essentially a contract between the issuer and the beneficiary".

[27] D. de Vos, W. Wilms and J. Leers, *New Belgian Banking Law* (Wiley, Chichester, 1994).

[28] R. van Delden, *Betalingsverkeer (documentair krediet/documenten)* (Kluwer, Deventer, 1990) pp. 67 *et seq.*, particularly pp. 83 *et seq.*. This legal ground is still disputed. Some authors stick to a contractual construction.

[29] For the legal relationship between issuing bank and seller, see *inter alia* G. A. Penn, A. M. Shea and A. Arora, *op.cit.* p. 339; P. Ellinger, "Letters of credit" in N. Horn and C. M. Schmitthoff, *The Transnational Law of International Commercial Transactions*, (Kluwer Law & Taxation, 1982). pp. 262 *et seq.*

[30] Art. 11 of the UCP refers to the obligations of the banks when these correspond by teletransmission (*e.g.* a telefax); H. N. Bennett, "Bank-to-bank reimbursements under documentary credits: the Uniform Rules" (1998) Ll.Mar.&Com.L.Q., 114.

[31] See, *inter alia*, L. Maura Costa, *Le Credit Documentaire—Etude Comparative* (LGDJ, Paris, 1998), pp. 181–213; A. Gozlan, *International Letters of Credit: Resolving Conflict of Law Disputes* (2nd ed., Kluwer Law International, The Hague, 1999); E.A. Caprioli, "Conflicts of laws in documentary credit contracts, a comparative law approach" (1991) IBLJ 905; J.J. Newton, "Choice of law rules and trade finance contracts" (1997) Ll.Marit.&Com.L.Q. 344; J.P. Mattout, *Droit Bancaire International* (Banque, Paris, 1987) pp. 303 *et seq.*; D.R. Stack, "The conflicts of law in international letters of credit" (1984) Va.J.Int'l.L. 171 ; C. von Bar, "Kollisionsrechtliche Aspekte der Vereinbarung und Inanspruchnahme von Dokumentenakkreditive" (1988) Z.H.W. 46. A choice of law and of the court or arbitral tribunal in a letter of credit can be useful; *cf.*, *inter alia*, F. Bonelli, "The Rome Treaty of June 19, 1980 and the Banking Law" (1985) I.B.L.J. 389; G. L.

(a) The law applicable to the documentary credit must be distinguished from the law applicable to the underlying agreement.[32]

(b) The law chosen in the credit agreement will apply to the customer–issuing bank relationship. If no law is chosen, the relationship is, in general, governed by the law of the country where the "most characteristic performance" is performed or where the party who delivers this performance is domiciled (see paragraph 1.30); this is usually the country where the bank issues the credit.

(c) For the relationships between the issuing bank, the advising bank and the beneficiary, it is best to make a choice of law. If no law has been chosen, the law of the country where the credit is realised (*i.e.* the country where the beneficiary presents the documents and receives the payment,[33] generally the country of the advising or confirming bank) applies.

(d) The issuing bank–advising bank relationship is deemed to be governed by the law of the country where the advising bank is established if no law has been chosen. As this law normally also applies to the relationship between the advising bank and the beneficiary, it is convenient that the same legal system applies to the two aspects of the same transaction.

The "Uniform Customs and Practice" (UCP)   Since 1933 the International **8.10** Chamber of Commerce (see paragraph 2.30) has drafted rules for the use of documentary credits in international commerce, the Uniform Customs and Practice for Documentary Credits (UCP). The UCP was revised five times, most recently in 1983 (UCP 400) and then in 1993 (UCP 500). Initially, this private codification received only limited approval, because it did not take into account, for instance, the law and practices of the British Commonwealth, of the United States[34] as well as of the socialist countries. Since 1962, when experts from those countries became more involved with the drafting, the UCP became more widely accepted as a codification of the international practice of documentary credits. At present the UCP is incorporated in general conditions of banking associations and has been adopted by banks in more than 160 countries. The ICC has estimated that some 95 per cent of credits world-wide are issued subject to UCP 500.[35]

Cecchini, "Le operazioni bancarie fra convenzione di Roma e lex mercatoria" in *Studi in memoria di M. Giuliano* (Cedam edit., Padova, 1989) pp. 281 *et seq.*

[32] *Walda Bank v. Arab Bank Plc* [1996] 1 Ll.L.R. 470; *Turkiye Is Bankasi A.S. v. Bank of China* [1993] 1 Lloyd's Rep. 132.

[33] C. M. Schmitthoff, *op.cit.* p. 420. An interesting example is *Offshore International SA v. Banco Central SA* [1976] 2 Ll.L.R. 402, 403; *Bayerische Vereinsbank Aktiengesellschaft v. National Bank of Pakistan* [1997] 1 Ll.L.R. 59; *Seaconsar Far East Ltd v. Bank Markazi Jomhouri Islami Iran* [1997] 2 Ll.L.R.89; aff'd [1999] 1 Ll.L.R. 36.

[34] Where a full chapter of the Uniform Commercial Code (UCC) (Art.5) regulates the documentary credit.

[35] For more information consult J. F. Dolan, "Letters of credit: a comparison of UCP–500 and the new U.S. Article 5" (1995 Revision) (1999) J.B.L. 521; C. Busto, *ICC Guide to Documentary Credit Operations for the UCP 500* (ICC, Paris, 1994); A. Gozlan, *International Letters of Credits: Resolving Conflict of Law Disputes* (2nd ed., Kluwer Law International, 1999); International Chamber of Commerce, *ICC Uniform Customs and Practice for Documentary Credits* (ICC, Paris, 1994);*http://www.iccwbo.org.*

The English text of the UCP is binding. There is also an official French translation (*Règles et Usances Uniformes relatives aux Crédits documentaires*'—RUU).

The 49 articles of the present UCP, UCP 500, provide a practical working aid to bankers, lawyers, importers, exporters, transport companies and insurers.[36] The UCP, phrased in a fairly succinct language, not only reflects existing practice, but also introduces new rules.[37]

The UCP lays down the rules for, *inter alia*, the form of documentary credits, the requirements for the issuing and for the further stages (advising, confirming) of the credit, the obligations and liabilities of the banks, the documents necessary for the documentary credit, the transfer of the documentary credit, etc.

The UCP is not a comprehensive regulation; for instance, it does not clarify whether the customer may obtain an attachment to prevent the bank from paying the beneficiary.[38] This issue has to be determined under the provisions of the applicable law—which often excludes such attachment as it undermines the essence itself of the documentary credit (see paragraph 8.04). The applicable law moreover determines the nature and binding effect of the UCP (customary law, standard clauses, commercial usages, etc.) (see paragraph 8.11).

8.11　**Binding force of the UCP**　Article 1 determines that:

"The Uniform Customs and Practice for documentary credits shall apply to all documentary credits, where they are incorporated into the text of the Credit. They are binding on all parties thereto, unless otherwise expressly stipulated in the Credit."

This means that the parties may expressly exclude some UCP provisions. Opinions vary on the legal nature of the UCP.[39]

- In France the UCP is recognised as customary law. Applicable unless they are expressly excluded by the parties.[40]

---

[36] For the text, see ICC Publication no. 500. See also ICC Publication no. 511: *Documentary Credits: UCP 500 and 400 Compared*; ICC Publication no. 515: *The New ICC Guide to Documentary Credit Operations*; ICC Publication no. 516: *The New Standard Documentary Credit Forms*; J. F. Dolan, "Weakening the letter of credit product: the new uniform customs and practices for documentary credits" (1994) I.B.L.J. 149; J. F. Dolan, "Letters of credit: a comparison of UCP–500 and the new U.S. Article 5" (1995 Revision) J.B.L. (1999) 521; R. P. Buckley, "The 1993 revision of the Uniform Customs and Practice for documentary credits" (1995) 28 Geo.Wash.J.Int'l.L.&Econ. 265–313; E. P. Ellinger, "The Uniform Customs and Practice for documentary credits—the 1993 revision" (1994) Ll.Mar.&Com.L.Q. 377–406; H. N. Bennett, "Stern doctrine and commercial common sense in the law of documentary credits", (1999) Ll.Mar. &Com.L.Q. 507; *http://www.iccwbo.org*.

[37] *cf*. J. Stoufflet, "L'oevre normative de la Chambre de Commerce internationale dans le domaine bancaire" in *Le Droit des Relations Économiques Internationales. Etudes offertes à B. Goldman* (Litec, Paris, 1982) pp. 367–368.

[38] *cf*. L.Gani, *op. cit.*; L. M. Costa, *op .cit.*, pp. 78–82.

[39] See, *inter alia*, E. P. Ellinger, "Letters of credit" in N. Horn and C. M. Schmitthoff *op. cit, international commercial transactions* (Kluwer Law & Taxation, 1982), pp. 251–254.

[40] See J. Stoufflet, "L'oevre normative de la Chambre de Commerce Internationale dans le domaine bancaire" in *Droit des relations économiques internationales. Etudes offertes à Berthold Goldman* (Litec, Paris) p. 361; Cass. Fr., October 14, 1981, (1982) *Dalloz* 301; Cass. Fr., March 14, 1984, (1985) *Dalloz I.R.* 245; J. P. Mattout, *op.cit.* p. 302.

- In Germany, the UCP is considered to be either commercial usages in the sense of *Handelsgesetzbuch* paragraph 346,[41] or standard clauses subject to the specific *Allgemeine Geschäftsbedingungengesetz* (ABG).[42] Indeed, the general banking conditions of German banks include an express reference to the UCP.[43]

- In the Netherlands, the UCP is not recognised as customary law.[44] An express incorporation in the contract as provided in Article 1 UCP is therefore required.[45]

- The incorporation is required in the United Kingdom as well, where the UCP is considered to be standard conditions.[46] In Belgium the UCP is considered customary law by some legal writers, but by the majority of commentators as conditions which the parties have to accept, at least impliedly.

- The "Uniform Commercial Code" (UCC) of the United States contains rules for documentary credits. New York State (where most transactions involving documentary credits are financed) has adapted the UCC provisions to suit the needs of international trade.[47]

In practice there are very few disputes over the legal nature of the UCP, because the UCP is most often explicitly incorporated in the contract and letter of credit. Such express reference to the UCP deserves recommendation.

The documents

General rules The UCP includes some general rules regarding docu- **8.12**
ments.

- The obligations following from the documentary credit are separate from and independent of the underlying agreement. All parties involved in a documentary credit deal with documents, and not with goods, services and/

---

[41] See, *e.g.* J. Zahn, E. Eberding and D. Ehrlich, *Zahlung und Zahlungssicherung in Aussenhandel* (6th ed., de Gruyter, Berlin, 1986) pp. 10 *et seq.*; R. Eberth, "Documentary credits in Germany and England" (1977) J.B.L. 30.

[42] See, *e.g.*, C.W. Canaris, *Bankvertragsrecht* (de Gruyter, Berlin, 1998) pp. 485–486, with further references.

[43] R. Eberth, *op.cit.*, p. 30.

[44] Hoge Raad, March 12, 1982, (1982) N.J. 267; Hoge Raad, October 28, 1983, (1985) N.J. 131; Hoge Raad, April 26, 1985, (1985) N.J. 607.

[45] F. de Rooy, *Documentary Credits, op.cit.* p. 17.

[46] *M. Golodetz & Co. Inc. v. Czarnikov—Rionda Co. Inc.* [1980] 1 W.L.R. 495; *Forestal Mimosa v. Oriental Credit* [1986] 1 W.L.R. 631; *Attock Cement Co. Ltd v. Romanian Bank for Foreign Trade* [1989] 1 All E.R. 1189.

[47] Under the New York law, the UCP will prevail over the UCC, if the parties' intention or the trade usage showed that the documentary credit should be subject to the UCP (NY UCC paras 5–102(4) (McKinney Supp. 1998)); see J. F. Dolan, "Letters of credit: a comparison of UCP–500 and the new U.S. Article 5" (1999) J.B.L. 521; C. White, "The influence of International Practice on the Revision of Article 5 of the UCC", (1995), 16 Nw.J.Int'l.L. & Bus. 189.

or other performances to which the documents may relate (UCP, Article 4).The documentary requirements are interpreted strictly.[48]

(a) All instructions for the issuance of credits and the credits themselves must state precisely the document(s) against which payment, acceptance or negotiation is to be made (UCP, Article 5b).

(b) When documents other than transport documents, insurance documents and commercial invoices (which are as such dealt with by the UCP, Articles 23–38) are called for, the credit should stipulate by whom such documents are to be issued and their wording or data content (UCP, Article 21).

(c) Banks must examine all documents with reasonable care to ascertain whether they appear, on their face, to be in compliance with the terms and conditions of the credit (UCP, Article 13a; see paragraph 8.15).[49] If this condition is satisfied, the banks have no liability for the form, sufficiency, accuracy, genuineness or legal effect of any document(s). Moreover, they have no responsibility for the general and/or particular conditions stipulated in or imposed by the documents. Nor do they have any liability or responsibility for the description, quantity, weight, quality, condition, packaging, delivery, value or existence of the goods represented by any document(s) (UCP, Article 15).[50]

(d) Banks which are utilising the services of another bank to examine documents or give effect to the instructions of the applicant for the credit, do so on behalf of and at the risk of that applicant. They assume no liability if their instructions are not carried out, even if they had taken the initiative for the choice of this other bank (UCP, Article 18).

8.13 **Documents to be submitted** The UCP contains general rules on documents and deals more in detail with the invoice, the transport documents and the insurance documents. These main documents will be briefly explained in the following paragraphs.

(a) The commercial invoice describes, amongst other things, the goods sold, the quantity (number, weight or volume) and the packaging. The invoice should be issued by the beneficiary named in the credit and made out in the name of the customer of the credit. The description of the goods in the

---

[48] *Bundesgerichtshof*, July 2, 1984, (1985) N.J.W. 550; *Glencore International A.G. v. Bank of China* [1996] 1 Ll.L.Rep. 135; H. N. Bennett, "Stern doctrine and commercial common sense in the law of documentary credits ", (1999) Ll.Mar.&Com.L.Q. 507; C. MacMillan, "Strict compliance under U.C.P. 500" 1997 Ll.Mar.&Com.L.Q. 7; *cf.* similar strict requirements for the bills of exchange (see para. 9.27).

[49] Documents on their face inconsistent with one another are not in compliance with the terms and conditions of the credit (Art. 13a, first paragraph *in fine*).

[50] Nor do the banks assume responsibility for the good faith or acts and/or omissions, solvency, performance or standing of the consignors, the carriers, the forwarders, the consignees or the insurers of the goods, or any other person whomsoever.

invoice must correspond with the description in the letter of credit (UCP, Article 37c), which in turn should be in conformity with the underlying agreement.

Sometimes the importer is given a pro forma invoice before the goods are delivered. This document must include the essential details of the underlying agreement. With the pro forma invoice the buyer (importer) can give his bank the necessary instructions for the issue and the determination of the type of credit; with the pro forma invoice, he can also apply for the necessary import, export or foreign currency licences.

(b) A transport document, most often a bill of lading, has to be submitted. The bill of lading (UCP, Article 23) is essential for the operation of documentary credit. It must indicate the name of the carrier and be signed or authenticated by the carrier (or by the captain or by an agent on their behalf). It also must specify the goods that have been loaded on board a named vessel. It also must state the port of loading and the port of discharge. The bill of lading fulfils four functions[51]:

   (i) proof of delivery of the goods to the carrier (or his representative, e.g. the captain or an agent). The carrier may specify in the bill of lading the condition and quantity of the goods of which he has taken possession; if there are no such annotations, it is called a clean bill of lading[52];

   (ii) proof of the contract of carriage and of the obligation to deliver the goods at the place of destination to the legitimate holder of this document;

   (iii) a negotiable instrument which represents the mentioned goods (document of title). The endorsement of a bill of lading makes the goods become the property of the endorsee;

   (iv) title for the holder of the bill of lading to take possession of the goods at the place of destination.

The bank may also accept other transport documents, such as:

   (i) a charter party (UCP, Article 25), i.e. written evidence that freight is made available for the carriage of goods. The charter party is often an additional document to the bill of lading.

---

[51] P. Todd, *Modern Bills of Lading* (2nd ed., Blackwell, Oxford, 1990); P. Todd, *Bills of Lading and Bankers' Documentary Credits* (3rd ed., Lloyd's of London Press, 1998); M. D. Bools, *The Bill of Lading* (1997, London); T. Kian Sing, "Of straight and switch Bills of lading" (1996) Ll.Marit.&Com.L.Q. 416; B. Kozolchyk, "Evolution and present state of the ocean bill of lading from a banking law perspective" (1992) 23 J.Mar.L.&Com. (Ll.Marit.&Com.L.Q.) 161–245; L. Cova-Arria, "Legal obstacles to the implementation of the electronic bill of lading in civil law countries" (1997) 32 Europ.Transp.L. 709; J. S. Mo, "Forwarder's bill and bill of lading", (1997) 5 A.P.L.R. 97; S. G. Wood, "Multinational transportation: an American perspective on carrier liability and bill of lading" (1998) 46 Am.J.Comp.L. (Suppl.) 403; D. Faber, "Electronic bill of lading" (1996) Ll.Marit.&Com.L.Q. 232.

[52] Bills of lading with clauses restricting the condition of packaging, goods and/or delivered quantity are termed: "foul B/L", "unclean B/L", "claused B/L".

(ii) The waybill (UCP, Article 24): written proof of both the contract of carriage and the delivery of the goods in the hands of the carrier responsible for the transport. Unlike the bill of lading, the waybill is made out to a named person, is non-negotiable and does not confer title.

(iii) The multi-modal transport document (UCP, Article 26) covers transports with at least two different modes of transportation (*e.g.* train, ship, aircraft, lorry). It is not generally recognised as a negotiable document of title. In practice, however, multi-modal transport documents often declare themselves to be negotiable and are accepted as such.[53]

(c) The insurance policy or certificate, issued and signed by an insurance company, underwriters or their agents (UCP, Articles 34–36). The term, the risks covered, the insured value, the currency and the type of the insurance cover must conform to the credit granted. The goods are to be insured for at least their CIF value plus 10 per cent.

(d) Moreover, many "secondary" documents may have to be submitted as well, such as:

(i) Storage certificates: important documents when goods to be delivered are stored or deposited with a third party.

(ii) All sorts of declarations and certificates to prove, for example: composition and quality of the goods, health requirements, veterinary requirements, phytosanitary requirements, suitability and cleanliness of the transport means and other statements from experts. Often required are: certificates of origin (for instance, for the granting of import licences and the calculation of import duties), and/or a mate's receipt (evidence of the receipt and shipping of the goods).

The underlying agreement and the letter of credit must be drafted carefully. It is always possible that the buyer may refuse to sign a certificate of delivery, which must be tendered; or that the technical expert appointed by both parties does not fulfil his task, or that the buyer does not appoint an expert.

8.14 **Examination of the documents** Banks must examine the documents within a "reasonable time".[54] The length of the reasonable time depends on, *e.g.* the need for urgency or the complexity and language of the documents, but may not exceed seven banking days following the day of receipt of the documents (UCP, Article 13b).[55]

---

[53] *cf.* M. Rowe, "Bills of exchange and promissory notes—uses and procedures in international trade" in N. Horn, *op.cit.*, pp. 249–250.

[54] P. Ellinger, "Reasonable time for examination of documents" (1985) J.B.L. 406.

[55] *Seaconsar Far East Ltd v. Bank Markazi Jomhouri Islami Iran* (1997) 2 Ll.L.Rep. 89; aff'd (1999) 1 Ll.L.Rep. 36; H. N. Bennett, "Stern doctrine and commercial common sence in the law of documentary credits" (1999) Ll.Mar.&Com.L.Q. 507.

The banks must examine the documents with "reasonable care" (see paragraph 8.16). The bank must take care to ensure, for instance, that:

- the documents are presented within the time fixed in the letter of credit;

- the beneficiary presents all documents stipulated in the letter of credit;

- the presented documents appear on their face to be in compliance with the terms and conditions of the letter of credit;

- the documents are duly signed;

- documents to order are correctly endorsed, *i.e.* to order of the bank;

- the documents do not appear on their face to be inconsistent with one another, which could indicate that they do not all relate to the same documentary credit;

- the demanded sum does not exceed the documentary credit limit;

- the draft is drawn on the right party and that the credit reference is mentioned;

- the insurance is sufficient and in the correct currency;

- the required number of bills of lading have been presented.

"Reasonable care"   The examination must be carried out by the bank with   **8.15**
reasonable care ("de façon professionnelle"). The bank does not need to ascertain whether the contents of the documents truly reflect reality. Nor may the bank get involved with the legal enforceability of the presented documents: even when the documents are legally questionable they may have commercial value to the customer, and "it is not for the bank to reason why".[56]

The duty of care is specified in the UCP. Unless otherwise instructed in the letter of credit, banks will refuse documents indicating the defective condition of the goods and/or the packaging (Article 32). In other words, they will require a clean bill of lading (see paragraph 8.13).[57]

The bank is excused, when it accepts bona fide fake or forged documents, if it could not notice something that should have alerted it. The bank, however, is liable when it accepts a fake document that shows an obvious irregularity, or when it knows at the time of presentation that the documents were drawn up with intent to damage the customer.

---

[56] *Midland Bank Ltd v. Seymour* (1955) 2 Lloyd's Rep. 147; *Golodetz & Co. Inc. v. Czarnikow-Rionda Co. Inc., The Galatia* (1979) 2 Ll.L.Rep. 450; *Kydon Compania Naviera SA v. National Westminster Bank Ltd., The Lena* (1981) 1 Ll.L.Rep. 68.
[57] Well-defined wordings, *e.g.* "clean on board", are not required.

Difficult problems may arise when there is a discrepancy between the instructions of the client and the presented documents. For example, the bank cannot accept a bill of lading that indicates a harbour for shipping different from that in the customer's instructions, even if it appears afterwards that the goods were loaded in the harbour as instructed.[58] In this context the House of Lords is often cited: "There is no room for documents which are almost the same or which will do just as well."[59] The bank thus should insist that the documents comply strictly with the credit requirements (doctrine of strict compliance). However, at present the standard of strict compliance is somewhat softened.[60] Ambiguous documents may still be refused. However the bank does not have to insist on the rigid and meticulous fulfilment of the wording. "Banks should not act like robots but . . . check each case individually and use their judgment."[61] Thus a bank does not have to refuse a document with a printing mistake;[62] nor an insurance policy which covers more risks than was required by the instructions, if this does not result in additional costs for the customer.

In case of doubt, the advising bank accepts the documents on condition of "reserve" and the credit is paid under reserve. It is then for the issuing bank to make a definitive decision on the documents.

When the documents do not conform to the credit, the bank should notify without delay[63] the beneficiary and specify all the discrepancies, so that the beneficiary can still remedy the discrepancies, *e.g.* by adding a missing document and presenting the correct documents on time. It is advisable, therefore, to present the documents to the bank well before the expiry date.

The bank's obligation to examine gives rise to many disputes because of the sheer number and diversity of documents that must be presented.[64]

8.16   **Payment**   The advising/confirming bank may pay at sight (cash payment) on presentation of the documents.

The underlying agreement can also provide for a deferred payment, whereby the bank gives the beneficiary a written irrevocable undertaking to pay at a later date in accordance with the terms of the credit, in exchange for the specified documents. The deferred payment gives the customer the time to resell the goods and to repay the bank from the proceeds of the resale.

Instead of accepting deferred payment, the beneficiary may also draw a bill of exchange on the advising bank, on the issuing bank or on the buyer (*i.e.* the

---

[58] Paris, January 19, 1952 (1952) I *Gazette du Palais* 286.
[59] *Equitable Trust Company of New York v. Dawson Partners Ltd* (1927) 27 Ll.L.Rep. 90.
[60] L. Mauro Costa, *op.cit.*, p. 44–50.
[61] *Opinions (1980–1981) of the ICC Banking Commission*, ICC Publication no. 399, p. 35.
[62] Nevertheless, in the U.S. Case *Beyene v. Irving Trust Co.*, 762F.2d.4 (1985), refusal of a document that refered to a certain "Mohammed Sofan" while the letter of credit indicated "Mohammed Soran"; the court decided that the bank did not have to pay.
[63] In all events not later than within seven banking days (UCP Art. 13 (b)).
[64] In the case *Bankers Trust Co. v. State Bank of India* (August 8, 1990), summarised in (1991) J.B.L. 174–175, 900 documents had to be presented.

drawee).[65] When the drawee accepts the bill of exchange, he confirms his commitment to pay on the maturity of the bill of exchange. The bill of exchange can be transferred to third parties or can be negotiated (see paragraph 9.28).

The beneficiary may also negotiate a bill of exchange already drawn on the buyer or the issuing bank. The beneficiary then receives payment of the bill of exchange (subject to deduction of discount and commission) from the advising/confirming bank.

The advising/confirming bank then dispatches the documents to the issuing bank, which reimburses the advising/confirming bank as has been agreed.[66] Banks, which regularly act for each other as issuing and/or advising bank, set off their mutual debts by way of a current account.[67-68]

The issuing bank then hands over the documents to the customer and debits his account.[69] The documents (*e.g.* the bill of lading) give the customer title to the goods, and he can obtain their delivery.

Exception of fraud   The documentary credit is autonomous, *i.e.* it operates   **8.17**
separately from the underlying agreement (UCP, Article 3). Consequently, disputes between buyer and seller under the underlying agreement do not affect the operation of the documentary credit.

There is only one exception to that rule, the exception of fraud.[70] When fraud (especially by the beneficiary) has been established, the (issuing and/or confirming) bank must refuse to honour the credit, even though all the documents were correctly presented. A bank which knowingly accepts a forged document and pays, is liable.

A mere allegation of fraud is insufficient.[71] The customer has to actually prove it. In an English case, a buyer, who had received worthless packages, applied to

---

[65] The letter of credit to the beneficiary then contains the following clause: "We hereby engage with the drawers and/or bona fide holders that drafts drawn and negotiated in conformity with the terms of this credit will be duly honoured on presentation and that drafts accepted within the terms of this credit will be duly honoured at maturity."

[66] If the beneficiary satisfies all conditions of the credit the bank has to pay, even if it knows that the customer is unable to repay the bank, *e.g.* as a result of bankruptcy.

[67-68] For the different forms of set-off in documentary credit, see *inter alia* Ph. Wood, *English and International Set-off* (Sweet & Maxwell, London, 1989), pp. 626 *et seq.*: D. Petkovic, "Set-off and letters of credit" (August 1989) I.F.L.R. 29. For set-off between the issuing bank and the beneficiary, see, *e.g. Hong Kong & Shanghai Banking Corporation v. Kloeckner & Co AG*, summarised in (1990) J.B.L. 60–61.

[69] If the currency of account (para. 9.04) of the credit is a foreign currency, the customer has to bear the exchange difference. He may nevertheless cover this risk; see para. 9.21.

[70] See, *inter alia*, L. Mauro Costa, *op. cit.*, 1 p. 105–120 ; P. Ellinger, "Fraud in documentary credit transactions" (1981) J.B.L. 258; S. Epschtein, "Le crédit documentaire et la fraude" (1978) Banque (Fr.) 587; C. Martin, "Documentary credit, fraud and the 1983 amendment of the regulations and usances (R.U.U.)" (1985) I.B.L.J. 371; J. P. Mattout, *op.cit.* pp. 354 *et seq.*; C. M. Schmitthoff, *Export Trade*, (10th ed., Sweet and Maxwell, London, 2000) paras 11.042–11.043.

[71] In practice, it is difficult to prove fraud: the documents are deemed to be conforming, and usually the client only receives the goods after the bank has paid.

the court for an order to prevent payment by the bank. His request was unsuccessful, because the buyer could not actually prove the fraud.[72] Courts in other countries (Canada, France, Italy, the United States[73] and Switzerland, for instance) are less demanding: prima facie evidence of fraud is sufficient.

It is not required that the beneficiary actually knew of the fraud.[74]

Special forms of documentary credit

8.18   **Transferable documentary credit**   A letter of credit, the basis of the common documentary credit, is not negotiable. When the seller (*e.g.* a broker or trader) in his turn has purchased the goods, it may be useful for him to pass on to the initial seller the credit he received from his customer.

The beneficiary may assign (irrevocably) the benefit of the credit to a third person (UCP, Article 49). This assignment is allowed, even if the credit does not mention that it is transferable.

Under UCP Article 48, the beneficiary (first beneficiary) may also transfer the right and at least certain of the duties arising under the credit to another person, usually his supplier (second beneficiary).[75] The second beneficiary then steps into the shoes of the first beneficiary. He will obtain payment provided that the conditions of the original credit are complied with. This is only possible, *i.e.* the documentary credit is only "transferable", if it is expressly accepted as such by the customer and the issuing bank and in the manner consented to by them. Moreover, the transferring bank may still refuse to transfer the credit, except to the extent and in the manner expressly consented to by such bank.

Unless otherwise stated in the credit, a transferable credit can be transferred only once. If the intermediary has to purchase goods from more than one supplier, transfer of fractions of the credit may be useful. In that event, a part of a transferable credit (not exceeding in the aggregate the amount of the credit) can be transferred separately, on condition that credit transfer for partial shipments/drawings is not excluded under the original letter of credit.

The credit can only be transferred on the terms and conditions specified in the original letter of credit. However:

---

[72] *Discount Records Ltd v. Barclays Bank Ltd* (1975) 1 W.L.R. 315. In this judgment the judge asserted: "I would be slow to interfere with banker's irrevocable credits, and not least in the sphere of international banking, unless a sufficiently grave cause is shown; for interventions by the Court that are too ready or too frequent might gravely impair the reliance which, quite properly, is placed on such credits." This consideration is characteristic of the English doctrine of strict compliance in respect of documentary credits; more on this in, *inter alia*, C. M. Schmitthoff, *op.cit.*, pp. 406 *et seq.*

[73] P. Ellinger, "The law of letters of credit" *op.cit.* pp. 222–223.

[74] L. Mauro Costa, *op .cit.*, p. 114–120 ; also *United City Merchants (Investments) Ltd. v. Royal Bank of Canada* (1983) 1 A.C. 168, HL. In this case, the fraud was committed by the carrier, who had hidden on the bill of lading the fact that dispatch had taken place after the agreed date.

[75] The same merchandise may be sold or resold by different intermediaries, e.g. during transit (especially by endorsement of a bill of lading: see para. 8.13) before it is sold to the ultimate buyer.

(a) The name of the first beneficiary can be substituted for that of his customer.[76] The amount of the credit, the unit prices stated therein, the expiry date, the last day for presentation of documents and the period for shipment may be reduced to reflect differences between successive transactions.

(b) The first beneficiary may substitute his own invoice(s) for those of the second beneficiary(ies), if the amounts do not exceed the original amount stipulated in the credit.

(c) The transferable documentary credit remains in the currency of account (see paragraph 9.04) stipulated in the letter of credit of the issuing bank.

Back-to-back credit   A beneficiary of a documentary credit may be unable   **8.19**
to transfer the documentary credit because the latter is not transferable; he also may not want to transfer it because he wants to avoid the client knowing the initial price of the goods. The beneficiary may, in that case, request a new documentary credit to be issued for the benefit of his supplier (back-to-back credit). The back-to-back credit is an autonomous documentary credit, which is based on an already issued documentary credit. The UCP does not provide specific rules for back-to-back credits.

The original credit has to be distinguished from the back-to-back credit issued on the instruction of the first beneficiary (generally by another bank). The back-to-back credit is legally autonomous from the original credit.

However, payment under the original credit depends on payment under the back-to-back credit. Indeed, the original credit, will only be paid if the second bank has submitted to the issuing bank of the initial credit, documents which comply with the first letter of credit. The second bank submits these documents in order to be reimbursed by the first bank for what it has paid under the back-to-back credit. The original credit is thus used as "security" for the back-to-back credit. The second bank often requests even that the bill of lading under the original credit is made to its order. The original credit and the second credit are thus placed "back-to-back" ("crédits adossés").

When the terms of the back-to-back credit are not in compliance with those of the original credit, or when the stipulated documents are not identical, the second bank takes a risk as the original credit is no (complete) cover. For instance, when the back-to-back credit is has a different money of account (see paragraphs 9.04 *et seq.*) than the original credit, the first beneficiary assumes the exchange risk.

"Revolving" credit   When parties are in a long-term supply relationship   **8.20**
(*e.g.* a distribution agreement) the buyer may solicit from his bank a "revolving" credit to a fixed limit for the benefit of the seller. Each payment by the buyer is

---

[76] The intermediary often would not like the supplier to know the identity of his customer (importer). However if the original credit specifically requires that the name of the customer appears in any document other than the invoice, such requirement must be fulfilled: UPC Art. 48(h).

then credited to the current account of the seller so that new credit can be drawn in favour of the seller up to the stipulated ceiling and within the fixed term.

For example, a "revolving" credit is used for a term of one year, for the benefit of the exporter "x", to the amount of $10 million. When bills of exchange are drawn on the importer on the basis of the credit, the right of the importer to draw on his credit is temporarily reduced by the amount of the drafts. When the bills of exchange have been paid, an amount corresponding with those payments and up to an upper limit of $10 million will again become available to the importer.[77] In other words, credit becomes available to the importer the full extent of the credit limit after repayment, and during the term of the credit. A revolving credit saves costs, since there is no need to renew the credit continuously. However, it has its restrictions by agreement, such as the number of renewals or the total sum of the renewals. The UCP does not provide specific rules for "revolving" credits.

8.21   **"Red clause" credit**   A "red[ink] clause" (anticipatory documentary credit) is a special clause in which the advising or confirming bank is authorised to pay an advance (either advance payment or anticipatory drawn) to the beneficiary before the documents are presented. The advance payment must enable the suppliers to finance their own purchases in advance. Often advance payment is made upon submission of a document showing where the goods are, *e.g.* a storage document.[78] The "red clause" is not subject to any particular regulation in the UCP.

8.22   **The standby letter of credit**[79]   A standby letter of credit is in fact a bank guarantee (see paragraph 8.52) in the form of a letter of credit, which guarantees the beneficiary the payment of compensation when the other party to the under-lying agreement has not performed its obligations.[80] The standby letter is usually issued on the instructions from the supplier (*e.g.* a seller or a contractor).

The guarantor (issuing bank) has to pay after presentation of documents showing that the beneficiary is entitled to payment, for instance, because of default by the guaranteed debtor. Documents, which prove such default are, *e.g.* an arbitral award, a statement by an expert, a reservation in a certificate of delivery or a written refusal to grant such a certificate. The documents required to prove a default of the debtor must be explicitly specified in the letter of credit.

---

[77] See, *Nordskog & Co. v. National Bank* (1922) 10 Ll.L.Rep. 652: "A revolving credit is one for a certain sum which automatically is renewed by putting on at the bottom that which is taken off at the top".

[78] G. A. Penn, A. M. Shea and A. Arora, *op.cit.* p. 305 ; Schmitthoff, *op.cit.*, para. 11–032.

[79] R. Jack, *The Law and Practice of Documentary Credits Including Standby Credits and Demand Guarantees* (Butterworths, London, 1993); B. Kozolchyk, "The financial standby letters of credit" (1995) I.B.L.J. 405–435.

[80] "Guarantees are usually taken to provide a second pocket to pay if the first should be empty", E.B. Ellinger and E. Lomnicka, *Modern Banking Law* (4th ed., Oxford, 2001) p. 529.

Standby letters of credit are now widely used in commercial transactions throughout the world.[81] The payments backed by standby letters of credit now exceed the amount covered by documentary letters of credit. However, until recently there have been no specific guidelines for standby letters of credit; one could only rely upon the ICC's Uniform Customs and Practice for Documentary Credits (UCP 500) (see paragraph 8.10) with only a limited relevance for standby letters. At present, the International Standby Practices (ISP 98) is of more use.[82]

The "International Standby Practices" (ISP 98)[83]   The ISP, which provide   **8.23** specific rules for standby letters of credit and independent guarantees (see paragraph 8.52), were adopted in 1998 by the International Chamber of Commerce and entered into effect on January 1, 1999. The rules of ISP 98 simplify the drafting of standby letters of credit and address frequently encountered problems.

ISP 98 must be incorporated into a standby letter of credit by express reference. Rules less appropriate for the specific case can be altered by the standby itself.

ISP 98 states expressly (rule 1.06d) that a standby letter is documentary credit: the obligation of the issuer to pay depends on the presentation of required documents, which have to be examined on their face. The issuer bears no liability for performance or breach of any underlying transaction (rule 1.08a).

A standby letter is irrevocable and binding from the time that it is issued.

ISP 98 offers a clear and comprehensive set of rules that give more certainty. Written exclusively for standby letters of credit, ISP 98 reduces the cost and time of drafting and avoids many disputes and unnecessary litigation. It is intended to

---

[81] Standby letters of credit originated in the U.S., and came about because of prohibitions on national banking associations from issuing bonds by way of guarantees. Japanese banks have a similar prohibition in relation to the issuing of guarantees. Until recently, outside the U.S., standby letters of credit were used mostly in transactions with an American or Japanese connections. In 1997, more than $450 billion in standbys were held by non-U.S. banks in the U.S. market alone. Standby credits have featured in *Hong Kong and Shanghai Banking Corp. v. Kloekner & Co. AG* (1989) 2 Ll.L.Rep. 323 ; *Paclantic Financing Co. Inc v. Moscow Narodny Bank Ltd* [1984] 1 W.L.R. 930; *Border National Bank v. American National Bank* 282 F. 73 (5th Circ., 1922); R. Eberth, "Der Standby letter of credit im Recht der Vereinigten Staaten von America" (1981) Z.V.g.L.R.Wiss. 29. The standby letter is defined as follows by the U.S. Federal Reserve Board: "[a documentary credit] which represents an obligation to the beneficiary on the part of the issuer (1) to pay money borrowed by, or advanced to, or for the account of the account party, or (2) to make payment on account of any evidence of indebtedness undertaken by the account party or (3) to make payment on account of any default by the account party in the performance on an obligation". (See C. Del Busto, "Are standby letters of credit a viable alternative to documentary credits?" (1991) J.I.B.L. 72.)

[82] ICC Publication No 590. ISP98 has been drafted by the ICP Working Group and is the result of a five-year project led by the Institute of International Banking Law & Practice. Were standby letters of credit subject to both the ISP98 and the UCP500, then the ISP98 would prevail in the event of any conflict. ; G. Affaki, "How do ISP standby rules fit in with other uniform rules?"(1999) *Documentary Credits Insight*, 1.

[83] L. Bernnet, "ICC: International Standby Practices—ISP98" (1999) BankingL.J. 4; J. E. Byrne, J. G. Barnes, *The Official Commentary on the International Standby Practices* (ICC Publication, Paris, 1998); M. C. Guinot, " Rules and international practices in relation to standby: ISP98" (2000) RDAI, 271–279.

be compatible with the United Nations Convention on Independent Guarantees and Standby Letters of Credit (see paragraph 8.20).

8.24   United Nations Convention on Independent Guarantees and Standby Letters of Credit[84]   On December 11, 1995, UNCITRAL adopted the Convention on Independent Guarantees and Standby Letters of Credit.[85] This Convention entered into force on January 1, 2000 in a few countries.[86] It is part of the ratifying state's legislative system, with no need for specific contractual incorporation in the instrument it purports to cover. The UNCITRAL Convention contains mainly optional rules that apply to the extent they are not set-aside in the contract. A possible exception might be the Articles 19 and 20, respectively dealing with fraud and provisional court measures.

PART II: COMMERCIAL CREDITS

8.25   Outline   "Long-term" credit concerns credits from five to 20 years after delivery of the goods. "Medium-term" financing usually covers two to five years. "Short-term" credits cover transactions in which the financing does not exceed two years.

Medium-and long-term financing have increased considerably in recent years, especially because of the growing export of machines, ready-made plants and other capital goods. Their construction and assembly require much time and investment; moreover, importers are in general only in a position to pay when the delivered equipment is up and running. Consequently they often require long payment terms.

Most international transactions , however, do not require medium- or long-term financing:

- most capital goods are exported to enterprises in other industrialized countries, which do not need extensive credit facilities from their supplier;

- export of capital goods to developing countries is often financed by project financing (see paragraph 8.49), where the foreign purchases are often paid for by grants or other financial methods within the framework of the development co-operation;

- export of capital goods to countries with insufficient foreign currency reserves is often "paid" for through some form of counter-trade (see

---

[84] E. E. Bergsten, "A new regime for international independent guarantees and standby letters of credit: the UNCITRAL Draft Convention on Guaranty Letters" (1993) 27 Int.L. 859–879; F. de Ly, "The UN Convention on Independent Guarantees and Stand-by Letters of Credit" (1999) 33 IntL. 831–846; N. Horn, "Die UN-Konvention über unabbüngige Garantien: ein Beitrag zur lex mercatoria", (1997) RIW p. 717.

[85] 35 I.L.M. 735 (1996); UNGA Document, A/CN./9/431, 4 July 1996. Text of the Convention and Introductory note by J. E. Byrne and H. Burman.

[86] The Convention was ratified by Equador, Salvador, Kuwait, Panama, Tunisia, and signed by Belarus and the U.S.

paragraph 9.37), which is less suitable for the traditional export financing;

- a considerable part of export consists of consumer goods, which can only be covered by short term financing; indeed, a rule of thumb in credit matters is that the financing term should not exceed the life span of the financed merchandise.

Institutions, that assist the business community in their respective countries, have developed specific formula of export financing. Moreover the Multilateral Investment Guarantee Agency (MIGA), an international institution, assists business from different countries in their export activities (see paragraph 7.44).

Export insurance

Institutions Various institutions insure import, export and foreign invest- **8.26** ment risks, mostly without actually financing the transactions.[87] The most important export insurance institutions[88] in a number of countries are[89]:

Australia:	Export Finance and Insurance Corporation (EFIC);
Austria:	Oesterreichische Kontrollbank AG (OeKB);
Belgium:	Nationale Delcrederedienst (NDD)—Office National de Ducroire (OND);
Canada:	Export Development Corporation (EDC);
Czech Republic:	Republic Export Guarantees Development Corporation (EGAP);
Denmark:	Eksport Kredit Fonden (EKF);
Finland:	Finnvera oyj (Finnvera);
France:	Compagnie Française d'Assurance pour le Commerce Extérieur (COFACE);

---

[87] On international credit risk management, consult B. W. Clarke (ed.), *Handbook of International Credit Management* (Gower, Aldershot, 1989); S. M. Basu and H. L. Rolfes, *Strategic Credit Management*, (Wiley, New York, 1995).

[88] Consult the following websites for more information also ut: Australia (EFIC) *http://www.efic.gov.au/*; Austria (OeKB) *http://www.oekb.co.at/*; Belgium (NDD—OND) *http://www.ducroire.be*; Canada (EDC) *http://www.edc.ca./*; Czech Republic (EGAP) *http://www.egap.cz/*; Denmark (EKF) *http://www.ekf.dk/*; Finland (Finnvera) *http://www.finnvera.fi/*; France (COFACE) *http://coface.fr/*; Germany (HERMES) *http://www.hermes-kredit.com/*; Greece (ECIO) *http://www.oaep.gr*; Italy (SACE) *http://www.isace.it*; Japan (EID/MITI) *http://www.eid.miti.go.jp*; Netherlands (NCM) *http://ncmgroup.com/*; New Zeland (EXGO) *http://www.state.co.nz/*; Norway (GIEK) *http://www.giek.no*; Portugal (COSEC) *http://www.cosec.pt/*; Spain (CESCE) *http://www.cesce.es/*; Sweden (EKN) *http://www.ekn.se/*; Switzerland (ERG) *http://www.swiss-erg.com/*; United Kingdom (ECGD) *http://www.ecgd.gov.uk*; United States (Exim Bank) *http://www.exim.gov/*.

[89] For a complete survey, see OECD, *The Export Credit Financing Systems in OECD Members and Non-members* (OECD, Paris, 1995); See also webpage *http://www.oecd.org/ech/act/xcred/ecas.htm*.

Germany:	HermesKreditversicherungs-Aktiengesellschaft (HERMES);
Greece:	Export Credit Insurance Organisation (ECIO);
Italy:	Instituto per i ServiziAssicuranzione del Credito all'E-sportazione (SACE);
Japan:	Nippon Export and Investment Insurance (NEXI— formerly EID/MITI);
Netherlands:	Nederlandsche Credietverzekering Maatschappij NV (NCM);
New Zealand:	EXGO;
Norway:	The Norwegian Guarantee Institute for Export Credits (GIEK);
Portugal:	Companhia de Seguro de Creditos, SA (COSEC);
Spain:	Compañia Española de Seguros de Crédito a la Exporta-cion, SA (CESCE);
Sweden:	Exportkreditnämnden (EKN);
Switzerland:	Gesellschaftstelle für Exportrisikogarantie (ERG);
United Kingdom:	Export Credits Guarantee Department (ECGD);
United States:	The Export–Import Bank (EXIMBANK).

8.27   Insured risk   The public or private institutions which are specifically concerned with export insurance usually cover the following risks:

(a) commercial risks: rescission or cancellation of contract, suspension of performance, non-payment because of insolvency or default of the debtor;

(b) political and related risks, war, natural disasters, measures by foreign public authorities and all other extraneous events which constitute *force majeure* for the insured or debtor[90];

(c) financial risks: transfer risk (risk that foreign currency will not be available to meet the repayment obligations).

8.28   Country-risk assessment   Insurance institutions have usually established a premium rating and a ceiling for each importing country. They have fixed a total sum for commitments that at any given moment may be vested in respect of the

---

[90] *e.g.* the withdrawal of an import licence or a licence for a bill of exchange, or a trade embargo, or compulsory insurance for goods which were previously imported freely, or prohibition on the transfer of foreign exchange of amounts which were paid in the local currency.

credit insurance for transactions with a particular country and enterprises established in that country.

This rating for the premium (category) is fixed on the basis of a number of criteria that determine the so-called "country-risk".[91] These criteria are grouped under a number of headings: public debt and the public debt/public income ratio; payment record; economic growth; impact of economic policy; political environment. Each heading is given a rating ("part score") for the risk assessment. The assessment for short-term credit risks differs from that for medium-and long-term credit risks.

A premium agreement has been reached between the OECD countries. Country classification and minimum "benchmark" criteria (best of public buyers' risk) have been fixed for risk.[92]

Fault by the insured   If the loss is (partly) due to a fault of the insured or a   **8.29**
person for whom he is liable, then no compensation has to be paid. For instance, compensation is often excluded in case of:

(a) technical or financial mistakes in the elaboration and performance of contractual obligations;

(b) careless exposure to the risk of non-transferability of payments or credits in foreign currencies[93];

(c) acceptance of contract conditions which differ from international practice and which exorbitantly limit the rights of the insured.[94]

The special conditions of the insurance policy often specify when no cover is granted because of fault by the insured.

Export financing

Financing   Public and private institutions have also become involved in the   **8.30**
actual export financing, in order to facilitate export. Their financing can take the form of a direct supplier's credit or buyer's credit. Moreover, public institutions are often refinancing credits issued by banks (for instance, through the re-discounting of negotiable instruments). Furthermore, public institutions may

---

[91] cf., inter alia, B. Marois, Le risque-Pays (P.U.F., Paris, 1990); H. Belcsak, "Country risk assessment" in B.W. Clarke (ed.) Handbook of International Credit Management, op.cit. pp. 68 et seq.; J. Calverley, Country Risk Analysis (2nd ed., Butterworths, London, 1990); J. Madura, International Financial Management (West Publishing Company, St.Paul (Minn.), 1989) pp. 479 et seq.

[92] See www.oecd.org/ech/act (premium agreement or, Knaepen package).

[93] e.g. the fact that local funds, kept on deposit in the country of the debtor, are not proportional to the time schedule or size of the works to be carried out in that country.

[94] e.g. a penalty clause, an annulment clause or a force majeure clause which give abnormal effects to the covered risks; acceptance of a dubious judicial or arbitral jurisdiction.

grant interest subsidies to reduce the credit costs. However, several countries have accepted the OECD guidelines and their national institutions have given effect to these guidelines.[95]

8.31   **The OECD "consensus"**   Export financing institutions in the OECD countries take into account the "OECD consensus". This consensus refers to the Arrangement on Guidelines for officially supported export credits which has been adopted by the OECD countries.[96] This Arrangement provides guidelines on officially supported export credits outside the E.U. with a repayment term of two or more years and relating to the sale of goods and/or services, or to leases equivalent to such sales. The use of soft credits is strictly limited to the poorer countries.

Guidelines are fixed on:

(a) Downpayment: purchasers must, without official support, make down payments equal to a minimum of 15 per cent of the export contract value.

(b) Credit length: the repayment terms for export credits are determined according to the level of prosperity of the countries of destination. Countries are classified under two categories, based on World Bank thresholds: those that are graduated by the IBRD (GNP per capita above $5,445 based on 1997 data) are in Category 1; Category 2 consists of all other countries. The maximum repayment terms are five years (eight and a half after prior notification) for Category 1 countries, and 10 years for Category 2 countries (except that the maximum repayment term for conventional power plant is 12 years or in case of project financing).

(c) Premium Agreement.

(d) Interest rates: a minimum rate has to be respected (commercial interest reference rates—CIRE).

---

[95] For a good survey, see, *inter alia*, OECD, *The export credit financing systems in OECD members and non-members, op. cit.*; H. Loubergé, P. Maurer and H.B. Dowell, *The Financing and Insurance of Export Credit* (Association de Genève, Genève, 1988); M. Stephens, *The Changing Role of Export Credit Agencies*, (IMF, Washington D.C. 1999); H. Meyer-Giesor and H. Louberge, *Problems and Perspectives of the Credit Insurance* (Association de Genève, Genève, 1988); M. C. Kuhn, *Officially Supported Export Credits: Recent Developments and Prospects* (IMF, Washington D.C., 1999); J. E. Ray, *Managing Official Export Credits: the Quest for a Global Regime* (Institute for International Economics, Washington D.C., 1995).

[96] For the text, see OECD, *The Export Credit Financing Systems . . . , op.cit.*, pp. 263 *et seq.*; for a good overview of the establishment and impact of the OECD consensus, see D. J. Blair, *Trade Negotiations in the OECD. Structures, Institutions and States* (Kegan Paul International, London, 1993) pp. 42–108; see also, J. E. Ray, "The OECD" 'Consensus' on export credits" in *The Marcus Wallenberg papers on International Finance* (Int.LawInst., Washington D.C., 1989) Vol. 2; OECD, *Arrangements on guidelines for officially supported export credits* (OECD, Paris, 1992); see also webpage http://www.oecd.org/ech.htm and http://www.berneunion.org.uk.

Institutions of export finance[97]   8.32

Australia	Export Finance and Insurance Corporation (EFIC—direct lending);
Austria	Oesterreichische Kontrollbank AG (OeKB—refinancing);
Belgium	Finexpo (Comité de soutient financier aux exportations);
Canada	Export Development Corporation (EDC—direct lending);
Czech Republic	Czech Export Bank (CEB—direct lending);
Denmark	Eksport Kredit Fonden (EKF—state financing);
Finland	FIDE Ltd (FIDE);
France	Direction des Relations Economiques Extérieures Ministère de l'économie (DREE);
Germany	Kreditanstalt für Wiederaufbau (KfW);
Italy	SIMEST Spa;
Japan	Japan Bank for International Co-operation (JBIC);
Netherlands	Ministry of Economic Affairs, Hoofdafdeling Export en Exportbeleid financieringsaangelegenheden;
Norway	A/S Eksportfinans;
Portugal	Banco de Fomento e Exterior (BFE—no official institution);
Spain	Banco Exterior de España (BEE);
Sweden	AB Svensk Exportkredit (SEK);
Switzerland	Official export credit not available;
United Kingdom	No official institution;
United States	The Export–Import Bank (EXIMBANK—direct lending).

Supplier's and buyer's credit

Overview   The buyer may obtain export credit in two ways: 8.33

- from the seller himself, whether or not assisted by the bank (supplier's credit);

---

[97] For information about the institutions, search on the Internet: Czech Republic (CEB) *http://www.ceb.cz/eng/maineng.htm*; Finland (FIDE) *http://wwww.fide.fi/*; France (DREE) *http://www.commerce-exterieur.gouv.fr/sommaire.htm*; Japan (JBIC) *http://www.jbic.go.kr/*; see also n. 87 above.

- directly from the bank (buyer's credit).

In most international transactions the seller is required to offer potential buyers an adequate financing package with more favourable conditions than those of his competitors. The execution of an international sales contract depends often on the condition precedent of adequate financing.

Putting together financial packages is usually a fairly complicated affair. Sufficient attention should be given, for instance, to validity and enforceability of the different obligations under the relevant applicable laws.[98] Banks therefore often request a so-called "legal opinion" from specialised law firms in the respective countries.[99]

8.34   **Supplier's credit**[1]   A supplier's credit is a medium- or long-term credit with a fixed interest rate, issued by a bank to an exporter (seller, supplier). Supplier's credits are usually issued with the co-operation of a commercial bank[2] and a national export finance institution.

This credit consists of the seller discounting six-monthly bills of exchange made out and accepted by the buyer to the order of the seller. The seller's bank pays with the reservation of a good outcome; it then will recover the amount paid from the seller when the buyer fails to honour the bill of exchange on the expiry date (see paragraph 9.28). The seller cannot invoke the buyer's default to refuse payment to his bank. The seller's bank can also open a credit line for the seller by discounting the negotiable instruments submitted by the seller.

For a supplier's credit, the sales contract should, *inter alia*, provide for:

(a) the form of negotiable instruments (promissory notes to order of the seller issued by the buyer; bills of exchange drawn by the seller on the buyer and accepted by the latter);

(b) the date of maturity of each instrument;

(c) the manner of delivery by the seller of the negotiable instruments (*e.g.* through a documentary credit issued by the buyer's bank for the benefit of the seller: see paragraph 8.02);

(d) the obligation for the buyer to pay on time.

8.35   **Buyer's credit**[3]   Under a buyer's credit, the seller's bank provides the buyer or his bank with the funds to pay the exporter at once for the purchase of equipment.[4] For the seller, a buyer's credit does not require an administrative follow-up (as is the case with the supplier's credit).

---

[98] *cf.* G. van Hecke, "Crédits bancaires internationaux et conflits de lois" (1977) D.P.C.I. 497.

[99] *cf.* M. Gruson (ed.), *Legal Opinions in International Transactions* (2nd ed., London, 1989).

[1] J. P. Mattout *op.cit.* pp. 130 *et seq.*

[2] As regards the special obligations of banks for supplier's credit, see J. Hoffmann, *Verhaltensp-flichten der Banken und Kreditversicherungsunternehmen-Zur Situation des Kaufpreisschuldners beim Lieferantenkredit* Heidelberg, 1991).

[3] J. P. Mattout *op.cit.* pp. 125 *et seq.*

[4] See C. Gavalda and J. Stoufflet *op.cit.*, pp. 281–282.

The buyer undertakes to reimburse the credit to the seller's bank without any possibility of invoking exceptions from the underlying sales contract.

Buyer's credits are generally used only for transactions that involve large sums, because otherwise its costs would be too high.

Secured lending

Security interests A company sometimes obtains credit or a loan because it has granted its creditor a security interest.[5] This security increases the debtor's incentive to repay the debt. Such security facilitates the credit. Moreover, the security may also secure compensation in the event of default by the debtor. In the event of the debtor's insolvency, some securities are enforceable against the debtor's insolvency administrator, depending also on the relevant insolvency laws (see paragraph 10.38). For the borrower the granting of security interests are advantageous too: the more he is able to use the value inherent in its assets as collateral for a credit, the greater is the likelihood of lowering the credit cost. **8.36**

In some countries, a creditor is only able to obtain a security right in assets that are owned by the debtor at the time of the creation of the security right. Other countries allow to secure credit by assets that continually turn over, such as receivables and inventory of raw materials, unfinished products or finished products. Some legal systems give a broad freedom in the description of assets that may be given as security (*e.g.* revolving inventory); other systems require that the security is actually itemised. Some legal systems require "dispossession" of the debtor for some securities; others allow that the debtor retains possession and can continue to use the assets given as security. These systems usually have a public notice filing system to publicise the security right. The enforcement of security rights varies also from legal system to system and from security to security: sometimes enforcement is speedy and without excessive costs; sometimes this is not the case.

A common security in international sales, is the retention of title in the goods sold (see paragraph 4.61). However, pledges, hpothecs, transfers of title or trusts may be other forms.

Applicable law The contractual aspects of the agreement by which security is granted, is governed by the proper law of contract (see paragraph 1.29). The proprietary aspects of the security rights are, as a general rule, governed by the law of the place where the asset, given as security, is located. Some countries, however, like the United States, follow an alternative approach based on a distinction between the issues, which arise between the immediate parties to a transaction (and where they can chose the applicable law) and the issues which involve third parties (which are governed by the law of the place the assets are located).[6] **8.37**

---

[5] See, *e.g.* B. Coutenier, "Mechanisms of international receivables-backed financing, aspects of international and comparative law" (1999) 3 I.B.L.J., 295–332.
[6] See *e.g.* Uniform Commercial Code, Art. 9.

When the pledged asset is removed to another state, as a rule the laws of the prior and new location will govern successively. The initial validity of the security is governed by the law of the original location of the asset, while the law of the subsequent location of the asset determines the impact of that new location on the security.

PART III: PARTICULAR FINANCING TECHNIQUES

International factoring

8.38   **Overview**   Factoring (in France, often called *affacturage*) is a credit insurance and financing technique in which an enterprise assigns its receivables, *i.e.* money that the company is owed through invoices, etc., to a factoring company (the factor) on the basis of a factoring agreement.[7] Factoring is used increasingly in international trade,[8] particularly in Western Europe.[9]

Sometimes the factoring company has to pay the receivables if the account debtor has not paid after the date of maturity. Most often, however, the parties agree that the factoring company will make advance payments on these receivables before the date of maturity. In that event the factoring is not only a credit insurance but also a financing technique. Moreover, because of the advance payments, the exchange risk (see paragraph 9.08) is transferred from the exporter to the factor.

Factoring usually involves a number of services from the factoring company, such as accounts receivable bookkeeping and analysis, actual collection of the receivables and dunning procedures. Those services allow the seller to concentrate on his actual business, namely the selling and marketing of his products.

Factoring usually requires a master agreement in which the factor undertakes, for the term of the contract, to take over from the seller all receivables[10] up to a certain limit for each account debtor (80 to 85 per cent of the invoiced amount) and up to the ceiling of the global credit line. The factor most often deducts his fee from the amount to be paid for the assigned debts.

8.39   **Specific issues**   The master agreement between the seller and the factor determines whether and under what conditions the factor has recourse against the seller for non-performance by or insolvency of the buyer. If the master agreement

---

[7] W. C. Philbrick, "The use of factoring in international commercial transactions and the need for legal uniformity as applied to factoring transactions between the United States and Japan" (1994) 99 Com.L.J., 141–156; A. Sinay-Cytermann, "Les conflits de loi concernant l'opposabilité des transferts de créance" (1992) 81 R.C.D.I.P. 35–60; D. Girsberger, "Defenses of the account debtor in international factoring" (1992) 40 Am.J.Comp.L., 472 *et seq.*; U. Brink, K.F. Hagenmuller, H.J. Sommer, *Factoring: Handbuch des nationalen und internationalen factoring* (3 Auflage, Fritz Knapp Verlag, Frankfurt, 1997).

[8] See F. R. Salinger, Factoring law and practice (2nd ed., Sweet & Maxwell, London, 1995) pp. 115 *et seq.*; J. Beuving, *Factoring* (Nijmegen, 1996).

[9] Also, *e.g.* Brazil, South Korea, Singapore, Malaysia, Hong Kong and Kuwait are often considered for export factoring.

[10] Factoring usually concerns short-term receivables for a term of 90 to 120 days.

excludes the right to recourse (so-called "no recourse" or "true factoring") only the factor bears the credit risk.

If, on the other hand, the factor has the right to recourse (so-called "spurious factoring"), he can recover the unpaid debts of the buyer from the seller. It is doubtful whether one can still speak of an assignment of an account receivable in this case. Although recourse is always possible in respect of negotiable instruments (bills of exchange), no recourse should be possible when receivables, not represented in a negotiable instrument, are assigned.

It has been suggested that spurious factoring should be reclassified as a mere opening of a credit facility for the benefit of the seller.[11] The factor would then not become owner of the account receivable. The various legal systems have different views on this issue. The legal nature and the transfer of the receivables to the factor thus have to be examined in the light of the applicable law.[12]

Even if the master agreement does not provide for a genuine recourse against the seller when the buyer fails to pay on the expiry date, it may give the factor such recourse when the seller knew, or ought to have known, that the buyer was already insolvent at the time of the assignment of the debt.

Furthermore, the master agreement sometimes grants the factor recourse against the seller when the non-payment of the buyer is exclusively the result of a breach of contract by the seller, for instance, in case of non-conformity of the delivered goods. This exceptional recourse must be drafted carefully. The clause could require the presentation of certain documents by the buyer (such as are required for the demand of a standby credit (see paragraph 8.22) or a documentary guarantee (see paragraph 8.02)).

The factor may also exercise recourse against the seller when the assigned receivables have disappeared, for instance through a set-off between seller and buyer.

The factor usually does not assume political risk (see paragraph 8.27) or transfer risks in case the buyer's country imposes exchange controls. The seller should therefore still keep a credit insurance.

The factor undertakes to buy all receivables from the seller for the duration of the master agreement, generally up to an agreed ceiling Sometimes, specific ceilings for each debtor are fixed, too. The master agreement, moreover, often gives the factor the discretion to refuse doubtful receivables. The factor who then takes over doubtful receivables, often reserves the right of recourse against the seller.

In traditional international factoring (so-called indirect factoring), four parties participate: the seller (exporter), the export factor, the import factor and the buyer (importer): the export factor, who is perhaps unfamiliar with the law in the importer's country and with the buyer's creditworthiness assigns the receivables

---

[11] See, *e.g.* H. U. Jäger, "Export factoring and forfaiting" in N. Horn (ed.), *The Law of International Trade Finance* (Kluwer Law & Taxation, 1989) pp. 291 *et seq.*
[12] It is assumed that the law governing the factoring contract is normally that of the country where the factor carries on business, except for the case where a choice of law clause has been expressed in the factoring agreement.

to a factor in the importer's country (refactoring). The export and import factors are often part of an international network of factor companies[13] covered by an international factoring agreement.

The growing familiarity with international factoring means that more and more only one factor is involved (so called direct factoring): the exporter appoints only one factor, either in his own country or in the importer's country.

The legal formalities for the assignment of receivables and the conditions for the debtor to be bound by this assignment vary considerably from one legal system to another.[14] The national law applicable to these issues should be carefully examined.

8.40 **International self regulation** International factoring groups, such as Factor Chain International (FCI) or Heller Factoring,[15] have agreed on common rules for factoring transactions. These rules often assume four-party factoring and provide for an arbitration procedure for disputes between the import factor and the export factor. Under these rules, the import factor only covers the credit risk of the importer when he has approved the specific accounts receivable. Unless the import factor gives his approval, he does not assume any risk but merely collects the receivable on behalf of the export factor (see paragrpah 8.35).

8.41 **Convention on International Factoring** In 1988 a Convention on International Factoring was concluded in Ottawa within the framework of UNIDROIT.[16] The Convention entered into force on May 1, 1995 and now applies in six countries.[17]

---

[13] *e.g.* Heller, Factor Chain International, International Factors.

[14] See, *e.g.* R. Welter, "Collateral in international trade" in N. Horn (ed.), *op.cit.* pp. 537–545; H.U. Jäger, *op.cit.* pp. 291–294.

[15] See on the Internet: http://company.occ.com/heller/; http://www.dansk.factoring.com/; http://www.cfa.com; http://www.factoring.org/; http://www.factors-chain.com.

[16] UNIDROIT Convention on International Factoring, text in (1988) I.L.M. 922 *et seq.* See, *inter alia*, N. Horn (ed.), *op.cit.*; F. R. Salinger, *op.cit.*, pp. 279 *et seq. Cf., inter alia*, R. M. Goode, "Conclusions of the leasing and factoring conventions" (1988) J.B.L. 510; J. R. Itturriagagoitia, "Acte final de la conférence diplomatique pour l'adoption des projets de conventions d'Unidroit sur l'affacturage international et sur le crédit-bail international, tenue à Ottawa le 28 mai 1988" (1988) I.B.L.J. 1802; E. Rebman, "Das Unidroit-Übereinkommen über das internationale Factoring" (1989) RabelsZ 599; M. R. Alexander, "Towards unification and predictability: the International Factoring Convention" (1989) Colum.J.Transnat.L 353.; J. Basedow, "Internationales factoring zwischen kollisionsrecht und Unidroit-Konvention", ZeuP (1997), 615 *et seq.*; U. Brink," New German legislation opens door to ratification of Unidroit Factoring Convention" (1998) 4 U.L.Rev., 770–775; F. Ferrari," The international sphere of application of the 1988 Ottawa Convention on International Factoring" (1997) 31 Int.L., 41–63; F. Ferrari, "General principles and international uniform commercial law conventions: a study of the 1980 Vienna Sales Convention and the 1988 UNIDROIT Conventions on International Factoring and Leasing and the UNIDROIT Principles" (1998–1999) Europ.J.L.Rev., 1.

[17] At February 7, 2001, the Convention had entered into force between France, Germany, Italy, Nigeria, Hungary, Latvia; moreover it had been signed by Belgium, Czechoslovakia, Finland, Ghana, Guinea, Morocco, Philippines, the U.S.A, the UK and the United Republic of Tanzania.

The Convention applies whenever the receivables assigned arise from a contract of sale of goods between a supplier and a debtor with places of business in different states and:

- those states and the state in which the factor has its place of business are contracting states; or

- both the contract of sale of goods and the factoring contract are governed by the law of a contracting state (Article 2, 1).[18]

Three- as well as four-party factoring are covered by the Convention (Article 11).

The parties to the factoring agreement or, under certain conditions, the parties to the contract of sale of goods, can exclude the application of the Convention (Article 3). However, the buyer cannot exclude factoring. Indeed, the assignment of a receivable by the supplier to the factor shall be effective notwithstanding any agreement between the supplier and the debtor prohibiting such assignment (Article 6).[19]

The buyer has to accept the assignment of the receivable if:

- he does not have knowledge of any other person's superior right to payment; and

- notice in writing of the assignment is given by the supplier or by the factor with the supplier's authority. The notice must identify the receivables assigned and the factor to whom, or for whose account, the debtor is required to make payment (Article 8). Furthermore, the notice must relate to receivables arising under a contract of sale of goods made at or before the time the notice is given.

The debtor may set up against the factor all defences arising under the contract of sale of goods of which the debtor could have availed himself against the supplier. The debtor may also invoke against the factor any right of set-off with claims against the supplier (Article 9). However, non-performance or defective or late performance of the sales contract does not by itself entitle the debtor to recover what has been paid to the factor, although the debtor can recover that sum from the supplier. The debtor will nevertheless be entitled to recover that sum from the factor, if the factor has not yet paid the supplier, or if the factor made such payment at a time when it knew of the supplier's non-performance or defective or late performance (Article 10).

---

[18] This provision is intended to bring the Convention into line with the Vienna Convention (1980) on the international sale of goods (see paras 4.05 *et seq.*); C. M. Schmitthoff, *op.cit.* p. 458.

[19] The contracting states may make a reservation in respect of this provision according to Art. 18 of the Convention. For example, France has made a reservation on Arts 6(2) and 18.

The Convention does not cover the possibility of a recourse of the factor against the supplier. This must be resolved under the applicable law[20].

UNCITRAL has prepared a Convention on the Assignment of Receivables in International Trade, which completes the legal framework. The draft Convention contains elaborate conflict-of-laws rules.

Forfeiting

8.42   **Overview**   Forefeiting (also: forfeit discount, forfeit agreement), like factoring, requires the assignment of a receivable to a specialised financial institution, the forfeiter. In forfeiting the receivable is usually incorporated in a bill of exchange (or in a promissory note) and the assignment takes place by discounting. Forfeiting also differs from factoring in that it is usually an agreement based on a single underlying transaction: the forfeiter has no duty to accept other discounted negotiable instruments.[21]

8.43   **Specific issues**

(a) Forfeiting usually requires a bill of exchange drawn by the exporter and accepted by the importer (or a promissory note issued by the importer in favor of the exporter). The exporter requests his bank or a specialised forfeiting company to discount this bill of exchange. The forfeiter waives any right to recourse against the exporter in the event of non-payment by the importer (non-recourse basis; see paragraph 8.44). This explains the terms "a forfeit" and "forfeiting".

(b) Forfeiting is used particularly in relation to machinery with payments spread over a period of two to five years. After the delivery, the importer may for instance effect payment by issuing 10 negotiable instruments with a six-monthly expiry date for a period of five years.

Forfeiting usually concerns substantial amounts and covers a longer period than factoring. When importers are located in countries with currency restrictions, the forfeiter may only receive "payment" by means of counter-trade (see paragraphs 9.37 *et seq.*). Forfeiting transfers the exchange risk from the supplier to the forfeiter.

---

[20] Factoring contracts are generally subject to the law of the country where the party effecting the characteristic performance has its principal place of business, that is the law of the factor. See F. Ferrari, "The international sphere of application of the 1988 Ottawa Convention on International Factoring" I.B.L.J. (1999) 895; M. Torsello, "The relationship between the parties to the factoring contract according to the 1988 UNIDROIT Convention on International Factoring" (2000) R.D.A.I. 43–59; J. C. Papeians de Morchoven, "UNIDROIT Convention on International Factoring and its implementation in French law and in Belgian law" (1996) R.D.A.I., 835; J. Basedow, "Internationales factoring zwischen Kollisionsrecht und Unidroit-konvention" (1997) Zeup 5, 615–642; F. Ferrari, "The international sphere of application of the 1988 Ottawa Convention on International Factoring" (1999) I.B.L.J., 895–916.

[21] On forfeiting see C. M. Schmitthoff, *op.cit.* pp. 460 et seq.; I. Guild and R. Harris, *Forfeiting* (Cambridge, 1985); H. U. Jäger," Export factoring and forfeiting" in N. Horn (ed.), *The Law of International Trade Finance* (Kluwer Law & Taxation, 1989) pp. 277 *et seq.*

(c) The exporter and the importer have usually agreed in their contract that the negotiable instrument in lieu of payment will be offered for forfeiting. The exporter therefore already should have the approval of the forfeiter who is to discount the instrument and the importer should have the guarantee of the bank, which, for instance, will guarantee the forfeiting transaction.[22]

(d) The rights and duties of the parties involved in a forfeiting are limited to the particular transaction. There is no master agreement as is the case for factoring (see paragraph 8.38).

(e) Forfeiting has to comply with the law applicable to the discounting of a negotiable instrument or to the assignment of a receivable (*e.g.* concerning the validity and opposability *vis-à-vis* the debtor).

Exclusion of recourse   Under Article 9 of the Geneva Convention on Bills   **8.44** of Exchange (see paragraph 9.31), the drawer of a bill of exchange guarantees both acceptance and payment. (He may exclude the obligation to guarantee the acceptance, but an exclusion of payment by the drawer is considered void.) The forfeiter thus keeps a recourse against the exporter (drawer) if bills of exchange are governed by the Geneva Convention.(When forfeiting covers a promissory note (see paragrpah 9.27), Article 9 of the Convention would not be applicable).

In order to exclude his right of recourse against the exporter, the forfeiter may give a personal undertaking that he will not exercise his right of recourse. This waiver only binds the forfeiter and not any subsequent holders of the bill of exchange.

International leasing

Overview   International leasing (also cross-border leasing) is used more and   **8.45** more in international transactions,[23] *inter alia* for the financing of aircrafts,[24] ships and the like.[25]

---

[22] The guarantee can be as follows: "Notice in writing of any default on the part of the said [acceptor/ promissor] is to be given to us and forthwith upon receipt of such notice payment shall be made by us of all sums then due from us under this guarantee."

[23] S. Amembal, "Emerging lease markets", (1996) W.L.Y. 16; S. A. D. Hall, "Legal features of cross-border transactions" in T. M. Clark (ed.) *Leasing Finance* (2nd ed. 1990), 97; S. S. Gao, *International Leasing: its Financial and Accounting Applications* (Rotterdam, 1995); M. Martinek, "Moderne vertragstypen", vol. 1, Leasing und Factoring, (1995) *Zeitschrift fur das gesamte Handelsrecht und Wirtschaftsrecht* 230, 513; M. Meyer-Reim, V. Streu, "Wirtschaftliche, rechtliche und steuerliche Aspecte des Exportleasing", (1998) 44 RIW 226; F. Graf von Westphalen, "Leasing in export transactions" in N. Horn (ed.), *The Law of International Trade Finance* (Kluwer Law & Taxation, 1989) pp. 327 *et seq.*; C. M. Schmitthoff, *op.cit.* pp. 463 *et seq.*; D. M. Colucci, "Is leasing the key to European Projects", (1999) I.F.L.R. 18; I. Voulgaris, "Le crédit-bail (leasing) et les institutions analogues en droit international privé" (1996) *Rec.Cours.* 259, p. 319; PriceWaterhouseCoopers Leasing Team, *Tolley's International Leasing* (Tolley, Croydon, 2000); E. de Bodt, *Le lesing financier: aspects économiques et juridiques* (De Boeck, Bruxelles, 1996); J. J. van Hees, *Leasing* (Tjeenk Willink Zwolle, Katholieke Universiteit Nijmegen, 1997);

[24] See, *inter alia*, the specific *Airfinance Journal.*

[25] See, *e.g.* G. Ysern, *Ship Leasing* (London, 1989); I. Davies, *Equipment and Motor Vehicle Leasing and Hiring: Law and Practice* (Sweet & Maxwell, London, 1997).

Financial leasing (finance leasing)[26] supposes a supplier who sells equipment to a financial institution (lessor) who then leases this equipment to the user (lessee). Actually the equipment is bought in accordance with instructions from the lessee. This equipment remains property of the lessor but may be used by the lessee against periodic rent payments that reflect the depreciation in value.[27] At the termination of the contract the lessee often has the option to purchase the goods for their residual book value. During the contract the goods serve as a security for the lessor who remains the actual owner (retention of title; see paragraphs 4.61 *et seq.*).

The legal relationships between supplier, lessor and lessee, their reciprocal rights and obligations, as well as the legal, accounting and tax treatment of leasing, vary from country to country.[28] These divergences have to be considered in case of international leasing. UNIDROIT is now embarked on drafting a model law on leasing that responds to the needs of developing countries and countries in economic transition, currently engaged in the reform of their leasing law.[29]

There are usually four parties in international leasing. Besides the lessor, the lessee and the supplier, a bank may be called upon for the financing of part of the purchase price (leveraged leasing). In this event the lessor pays 20 to 50 per cent of the purchase with his own means, the balance being paid by way of an investment credit issued by a bank to the lessor. The bank also requires a security in this case. In most cases the claims from the lessor against the lessee are assigned to the bank. Where possible under the applicable law the lessor passes the title to the leased good as security to the bank.

As with factoring, there are also international groups (so-called "clubs") of leasing companies, for instance: Leaseclub, Multilease, International Financial and Leasing Association.[30]

8.46   **Legal questions in international leasing**   There are particular problems in international leasing.

---

[26] Besides finance leasing there is also operational leasing and leasing of real estate: these are not discussed here as they seldom occur in international trade.

[27] A distinction must be made between full pay-out leasing, where the totality of the payments covers the value of the goods increased with the compensation for the lessor, and non-full pay-out leasing where the totality of payments does not cover the value of the goods and where their residual value at the termination of the contract can still be substantive. Non-full payout leasing is mainly used for expensive equipment for which an active second-hand market exists.

[28] H. Kronke, "Finanzierungsleasing in rechtsvergleichender Sicht" (1990) AcP 383. See also T. Shilling, "Some European decisions on non-possesory security rights in private international law" (1985) I.C.L.Q. 87; G. Khairallah, *Les Sûretés Mobilières en Droit International Privé* (Economica, Paris, 1984).

[29] UNIDROIT is at present preparing an International Convention on International Interests in Mobile Equipment. This Convention embraces not only classic security interests but also what is increasingly recognised as their functional equivalent, namely the lessor's interest under a leasing agreement. More information on internet: http://www.unidroit.org/english/workprogramme/main.htm.

[30] See *e.g.* information on the internet: http://multilease.ch/index.taf; http://www.deutsche-leasing.de; http://www.inrealty.com/ss/leasing.html; http://www.bworks.com/funding/assoc.htm;http://associations.cfol.com/patent-leasing.html.

(a) Under the OECD consensus, official export credit and insurance agencies should not cover the transaction if the importer (*i.e.* the lessee) has not paid a 15 per cent advance (see paragraph 8.29). However, in some countries the leasing contract risks being re-qualified as a sales contract if such advance payment is made.

(b) Retention of title usually offers the lessor an adequate security in domestic lease contracts. In international leasing, when the equipment is used by a foreign lessee, the question arises whether the law of the place where the equipment is used (*lex rei sitae*) affects the retention of title and to what extent this retention of title has to be recognised by other creditors of the lessee, for instance in cases of bankruptcy. For this reason a bank guarantee (see paragraphs 8.52 *et seq.*) is often required as a security for international leasing.

International conventions on leasing   A Convention on International Finan-   **8.47**
cial Leasing was, together with the Factoring Convention (see paragraph 8.41), agreed in 1988 in Ottawa under the auspices of UNIDROIT.[31] The convention already applies in some eight countries when the lessor and the lessee have their places of business in different states and:

- those states and the state in which the supplier has its place of business are contracting states; or

- both the supply agreement and the leasing agreement are governed by the law of a contracting state (Article 3).

The scope of the Convention is limited to the civil and commercial law aspects of leasing. It does not cover tax problems, although these, in practice, have a considerable influence on the decision whether or not to finance the acquisition of equipment by leasing.[32]

The financial leasing transactions that the convention covers imply that:

- the lessee specifies the equipment and selects the supplier without relying primarily on the skill and judgment of the lessor;

---

[31] It entered into force between France, Italy, Nigeria, Hungary, Panama, Latvia, Russia, Belarus and Uzbekistan. Moreover, it is also signed by nine states (Belgium, Czechoslovakia, Finland, Ghana, Guinea, Morocco, Philippines, the U.S. of America, United Republic of Tanzania). For the text, see UNIDROIT website: http://www.unidroit.org/english/conventions/c-leas.htm; also in (1988) I.L.M. pp. 931 *et seq.*, N. Horn (ed.), *op.cit.* pp. 685 *et seq.*; (1988) U.L.Rev. pp. 134–161. *cf., inter alia*, M. Stanford, "Explanatory report on the draft Convention on international financial leasing" (1987) U.L.Rev. pp. 168–365; R.C.C. Cuming, "Model rules for lease financing: a possible complement to the UNIDROIT convention on international Financial leasing" (1998) in *Uniform Law Studies in Memory of Malcolm Evans*, U.L.R., 371–384; J. R. Itturriagagoitia, *op.cit.* p. 1082; J. Poczobut, "Internationales Finanzierungsleasing: das Unidroit-projekt" (1987) RabelsZ 681; R. M. Goode, "Conclusion of the leasing and factoring conventions" (1988) J.B.L. 347.

[32] The Convention does not cover the sale and lease-back construction which is often used in practice. *Cf.* H. Waling, "Leaseback of intangibles" (Sept. 1994) I.F.L.R. 44.

- the equipment is acquired by the lessor in connection with a leasing agreement which, to the knowledge of the supplier, either has been made or is to be made between the lessor and the lessee; and

- the rentals payable under the leasing agreement are calculated so as to take into account the amortization of the whole or a substantial part of the equipment.

It is irrelevant whether or not the lessee has a purchase option for the equipment (Article 1).

The application of the Convention can be excluded only if each of the parties to the supply agreement[33] and each of the parties to the leasing agreement[34] agree to exclude it (Article 5).

8.48   **Uniform rules**   The Convention includes fairly detailed uniform rules in respect of the rights and duties of the parties, and specifies that the lessor's property right in the equipment shall be valid against the lessee's trustee in bankruptcy[35] and against creditors, including creditors who have obtained an attachment or execution (Article 7).

The lessor is, in principle, not liable *vis-à-vis* the lessee in respect of the equipment (unless the lessee has suffered loss as the result of its reliance on the lessor's skill and judgment and of the lessor's intervention in the selection of the supplier or the specifications of the equipment) (Article 8, 1a). Moreover, the lessor will not, in its capacity as lessor, incur any liability *vis-à-vis* third parties for injury or damage caused by the equipment (Article 8, 1b), for it is usually the lessee who has selected the equipment while the lessor only provides the financing thereof.

Where the equipment is not delivered, is delivered late or fails to conform to the supply agreement, the lessee may reject the equipment or terminate the leasing agreement, but the lessor also has the right to remedy its failure to tender equipment in conformity with the supply agreement (Article 12).

The lessee must take proper care of the equipment, use it in a reasonable manner and keep it in the condition in which it was delivered (Article 9, 1). When the leasing agreement comes to an end, the lessee must return the equipment to the lessor in the condition specified above, unless he exercises his right to buy, or holds the equipment on lease for a further period, (Article 9, 2).

In the event of default by the lessee, the lessor may recover accrued unpaid rentals, together with interest and damages. Where the lessee's default is substantial, then the lessor may also claim immediate payment of the future rentals

---

[33] *i.e.* the transaction whereby the lessor, on the specifications of the lessee, enters into an agreement with the supplier under which he acquires the equipment (Art. 1, 1a).

[34] *i.e.* the transaction under which the lessor enters into an agreement with the lessee, granting to the latter the right to use the equipment in return for the payment of rentals (Art. 1, 1b).

[35] "Trustee in bankruptcy" refers to a liquidator, administrator or other person appointed to administer the lessee's estate for the benefit of the general body of creditors.

where the leasing agreement so provides, or he may terminate the leasing agreement and recover possession of the equipment (Article 13).

A significant provision is that the lessor, who transfers his rights in the equipment or under the leasing agreement, is not relieved of any of his duties under the leasing agreement (Article 14, 1). He remains contractually liable in respect of the lessee. On the other hand, the lessee may transfer the right to use the equipment or any other rights under the leasing agreement only with the consent of the lessor and subject to the rights of third parties (Article 14, 1b).

The duties of the supplier to the lessor under the supply agreement are also owed to the lessee, as if the latter were a party to that agreement and as if the equipment were to be supplied directly to the lessee. However the supplier cannot be liable to both the lessor and the lessee in respect of the same damage. Moreover, the lessee is not entitled to terminate or rescind the supply agreement without the consent of the lessor (Article 10).

Project financing

Formulae   The various constructions of project finance (project financing) **8.49** concern very large and expensive projects (construction of nuclear plants, tunnels, mining projects, etc.)[36] and have to cope with, *inter alia*, the following risks[37]:

(a) the risk of non-completion of the industrial installation;

(b) the exploitation risk, *e.g.* the availability of the necessary raw materials and qualified personnel;

(c) the market risk, the question whether the manufactured product will be in demand;

(d) the actual credit risk;

(e) the exchange risk, particularly when the money of account (see paragraph 9.04) of the purchase agreement differs from the currency in which the loan is issued;

---

[36] G.-D. Vinter, *Project Finance: a Legal Guide* (Sweet & Maxwell, London, 1998); Ph. Wood, *Project Finance, Subordinated Debt and State Loans* (Sweet & Maxwell, London, 1995); H. Harries," The contract law of project financing" in N. Horn (ed.), *The Law of International Trade Finance* (Kluwer Law & Taxation, 1989) pp. 345 *et seq.*; T. Donaldson, *Project Finance* (Butterworths, London, 1991); S. L. Hoffman, *The Law and Business of International Project Finance* (Kluwer Law International, 1998); *Project Finance: an International Legal Guide*, (A special supplement to I.F.L.R., Euromoney Publ., 1993); S. L. Hoffman, *The Law and Business of International Project Finance* (Kluwer Law International, Dordrecht, 1998);
[37] H. Harries, *op.cit.* pp. 348 *et seq.*; D. Khairallah, "Overview of IFC project financing" in J. J. Norton (ed.), *op.cit.*, chap. 31; P. Megens, "Construction risk and project finance—risk allocation as viewed by contractors and financiers", (1997) 14, I.C.L.R. 5.

(f) the political risks (see paragraph 8.25): for instance, expropriation, withdrawal of import or export licences, exchange restrictions in respect of repayments to lenders.

The creditworthiness of the borrower and the securities he provides are generally of less importance than the guaranteed output by the financed equipment. In order to calculate the risks project finance is often preceded by a feasibility study to investigate whether the output of the project will cover operation costs, repayments of the credits and dividends on the share capital.

However, the lender is sometimes also secured, at least for part of the credit, by a guarantee from an international institution, or from the state where the project is realised.[38]

A special form of project financing is the "build operate transfer" (BOT) formula, mainly used in connection with important public utility investments, such as power stations,[39] hydro-electric power stations, harbors, airports, tunnels, telecommunications. Under this arrangment, foreign suppliers participate in the share capital of the company entrusted with the exploitation of that particular project, at least for an initial period. The consortium of suppliers thus will initially exploit the project and, after a contractually agreed period, hand it over to the local authorities. BOTs are generally only used for profitable projects in stable, industrialised countries.[40]

Financing of sizeable industrial projects in developing countries usually takes place in co-operation with the World Bank (see paragraph 7.03) or a regional development bank under "co-financing" with private credit institutions (see paragraphs 8.25 *et seq.*).[41]

8.50   **Realisation of the financing**   Projects are often so enormous and risks so high that the contract is awarded to a syndicate of suppliers who have formed a joint venture or a joint subsidiary (project company). When a project company is

---

[38] J. M. Stephenson Jr., *op.cit.* Chap. 32.

[39] S. Peppiatt, "Introduction to power station project financing", (1995) Int'l.Tax.&Bus.Law. 13, 46.

[40] See, *e.g.* J. Delmon, *BOO and BOT Projects: A Commercial and Contractual Guide* (Sweet & Maxwell, London, 1999); J. D. Appiah, "Infrastructure projects: BOT projects developed country structuring" (1991) Int'l.Bus.Law. 206 *et seq*. H. E. Kroeger, T. Kautz, "Treaties may offer route to financing BOT projects in Turkey" (1998) 17 I.F.L.R. 26; S. W. Stein, "Constructions financing and BOT projects" (1995) 23 Int'l.Bus.law., 173; J.A. Huse, "Use of the FIDIC Orange Book in the context of a BOT projects", (1996) 13, I.C.L.R. 434; B. de Cazalet, "Construction contracts in the framework of BOT projects (build, operate, transfer)" (1998) I.B.L.J., 405–416; J. M. Loucle, "Big infrastructure projects: the build, operate, transfer (BOT) aproach" (1997) I.B.L.J., 945–965; L. Vandamme, "To time, to budget, to specification: attributing pre-operational risks in BOT project finance structures" (1999) I.B.L.J., 875–893.

[41] For a good survey on industrial projects in developing countries see, *inter alia*, P. A. Ahmed, *Project Finance in Developing Countries* (Int'l Fin. Corporation, Washington, 1999 DC); A. Goswami, "India: risk profiles in project financing", (1997) 25 Int'l.Bus.Law. 46; R. McCormick, "Project finance in Central and Eastern Europe" (1998) 26 Int'l.Bus.Law. 310; M. N. Khan, "Designing an Islamic model for project finance" (1997) 16, I.F.L.R. 13; J. Cook, "Infrastructure project finance in Latin America", (1996) 24 Int'l.Bus.Law. 260.

established, its financing is organised by way of various contractual constructions,[42] often a consortium of banks. Project financing often also makes use of
various forms of credit, such as buyer's credits (see paragraph 8.33), international leasing (paragraphs 8.45 *et seq.*)[43], etc. In brief, project financing is not
a specific form of credit, but a construction to solve a specific financing problem.

Project financing often makes use of one of the following three structures, each
with an increasing degree of complexity[44]:

(1) A bank consortium issues credit to the project company. This credit is
guaranteed by a security provided by, or on behalf of, the sponsor of the
project. This is, for instance, the state concerned or international institution involved (*e.g.* the World Bank). This structure is used particularly
for projects in developing countries. The role of international organisations in project financing has been mentioned elsewhere (see paragraph
7.02).

(2) The above described bank credit is generally linked with a long-term
unconditional commitment from the supplier or from a third party to
purchase[45] the products manufactured (e.g. oil, minerals, machinery,
etc.)[46] or services rendered (*e.g.* use of a pipeline, a motorway or an
international hotel).[47] In some cases (*e.g.* for ships), formal rent or
leasing contracts (see paragraphs 8.41 *et seq.*) are negotiated. Purchase
commitments are often a condition precedent for the financing. They are
generally assigned to the bank consortium (lender), while the performance of the commitments are sometimes guaranteed by, or on behalf of,
the sponsor of the project.

(3) In a more complicated setting, the bank consortium sets up a specific
finance company (financing vehicle)[48] in order to advance payment on
the purchase price of the products to be produced by the industrial
installation. The goods produced are then delivered to the finance company for resale to companies that have a long-term purchase agreement
with the finance company. The finance company sometimes receives a

---

[42] If the project is executed by a consortium without legal personality (*e.g.* a temporary association),
the same legal problems arise in essence; only they are more complicated because each participant
in the temporary association is also personally liable.

[43] D. M. Colucci, "Is leasing the key to European projects?" (1999) I.F.L.R.

[44] Ph. Wood, *op.cit.* pp. 315 *et seq.*

[45] This unconditional purchase undertaking is, in practice, sometimes replaced by a guarantee from
the sponsor that a minimum quantity will be sold. The sponsor is then liable for the unsold
part.

[46] A classic example is that of an electricity company that wants to build a nuclear power station
without having to include the liabilities on its balance sheet. It sets up a subsidiary, the project
company, and it undertakes to buy all electricity from the project company. The claims from the
project company against the parent company are assigned to the credit institutions.

[47] See, *e.g.* H. A. Grigera Naon, "Legal aspects of international project financing: the case of the oil
and gas business in Argentina" in N. Horn (ed.), *op.cit.*, pp. 361 *et seq.*

[48] The setting-up of such a vehicle is necessary because the bank's charter usually does not allow
banks to buy and sell goods. Moreover, the incorporation of an intermediary entity may be
advantageous for tax reasons.

security from, or on behalf of, the sponsor of the project for the under-taking by the project company to deliver the manufactured goods in accordance with the contract to the finance company. The rights and the security derived from these purchase agreements are assigned to the bank consortium. Where there is no sponsor or guarantor, the bank consortium has to be satisfied with the purchase commitments from future buyers.

The "Eurotunnel", for instance, was financed through project financing. The project company is "Eurotunnel", a common subsidiary of Eurotunnel SA (France) and Eurotunnel Plc (England). There was no specific sponsor for this project. The Eurotunnel companies have, however, concluded long-term con-tracts with the national railway companies (SNCF and British Rail) for the use of the tunnel. The cash-flow generated by these contracts had primarily to serve for the repayment of the credit.

8.51   Contracts for project financing   The various contractual components of project financing have to be carefully negotiated and drafted.[49] The following contracts and contractual clauses in particular may be crucial:

(a) The bank consortium and the sponsor of the project (state, international organisation, multinational enterprise) enter into a completion guarantee agreement. Under this contract the sponsor guarantees that the project will be completed and the industrial installation will be operational within the agreed time.[50] If necessary the sponsor may have to give a bank guarantee (see paragraphs 8.52 *et seq.*). Furthermore, it is usually agreed that the sponsor acquires shares in the project company.

(b) The sponsor must generally give a cost overrun undertaking, *i.e.* an undertaking that the sponsor will finance or cover any overspending of the contract price.

(c) The unconditional purchase commitment from the future customers often take the form of a 'take-or-pay contract: the party who has contracted to buy must pay the agreed amount, even if he does not wish to receive the produced goods or services. (The contract thus resembles a guarantee: see paragraphs 8.52 *et seq.*)

---

[49] *cf.*, *inter alia*, H. Harries, *op.cit.* (for the often difficult private international law problems: pp. 352–353); C. T. Ebenroth, "Das Vertragsrecht der internationalen Konsortialkredite und Projektfi-nanzierungen" (1986) JZ 731; L. C. Hinsch and N. Horn, *Das Vertragsrecht der internationalen Konsortialkredite und Projektfinanzierungen* (de Gruyter, Berlin, 1985).

[50] The legal relationship between the sponsor and the builders of the industrial installation is determined by the turn key contract. See, *e.g.*, B. de Cazalet, "conditions of contracts for design—build and turnkey" (1996) I.B.L.J., 279; P. Le Goff, "A new standard for international turnkey contracts: the FIDIC silver book" (2000) I.B.L.J., 151–158; B. de Cazalet and R. Reece, "The new FIDIC Yellow Book, The new conditions of contracts for plant and design-build" (2000) I.B.L.J., 815–828.

(d) The sponsor sometimes undertakes to assume the rights and duties of the bank consortium in respect of the provided credit when the project or repayment is not realised.

(e) "Covenants" may cover the use of resources, the monitoring of the construction, the production, purchase and supply commitments, securities, the obligations of the "sponsor", etc. They may also waive immunity of jurisdiction when a contracting party is a state or a state entity (see paragraph 2.06).

PART IV: INDEPENDENT GUARANTEES

Description and characteristics

Description Bank guarantees are frequently used in international trade.[51] **8.52** Credits granted to buyers by exporters (or their banks) often need to be guaranteed by a solvent bank in case the buyer would not pay[52]. Contractual performance likewise often is secured by a guarantee. For instance, a state that commissions an important public work from a foreign contractor may insist on a bank guarantee in case the performance is not satisfactory (performance bonds; see paragraph 8.55). A foreign importer who has to issue a documentary credit for the benefit of the exporter may request in his turn from the exporter's bank an independent guarantee for the conformity or quality of the delivered goods or works.[53]

The guaranteeing bank is not obliged to perform the contract himself. It only has to compensate when the principal debtor defaults on the contract. If the undertaking of the debtor relates to the payment of a sum of money, the compensation to be paid by the guaranteeing bank will be that sum of money, possibly increased with deferred interest or penalties. If the debtor had to perform

---

[51] See F. Graf von Westphalen, *Die Bankgarantie im internationalen Handelsverkehr* (2nd ed., Recht und Wirtschaft, Heidelberg, 1990); N. Horn and E. Wijmeersch, "Bank guarantees, standby letters of credit and performance bonds in international trade" in N. Horn (ed.), *op.cit.*, pp. 455 *et seq.*; H. J. Pabbruwe, *Bankgarantie* (3e verm. dr., Kluwer, Deventer, 1998); J. Stoufflet, "La garantie bancaire à première demande" (1987) J.D.I. 265; J. P. Mattout, *Droit Bancaire International* (2e ed., Revue Banque, Paris, 1996); G. A. Penn, A. M. Shea and A. Arora, *The Law and Practice of International Banking* (2nd ed., Sweet & Maxwell, London, 1997); C. M. Schmitthoff, *Export Trade* (10th ed., Stevens & Sons, London, 1997); R.I. Bertrams, *Bank Guarantees in International Trade* (2nd ed., ICC Publishing, Kluwer, The Hague, 1996); A. Pierce, *Demand Guarantees in International Trade* (Sweet & Maxwell, London, 1993); G. Affaki, "Les sûretés dans le négoce international" (2000) 3, J.D.I. 647–708; R. Goode, "Security in cross-border transactions" (1998), 33 Tex.Int'l.L.J. 47–52.
[52] "Guarantees are usually taken to provide a second pocket to pay if the first should be empty", E. B. Ellinger and E. Lomnicka, *Modern Banking Law* (2nd ed., Oxford, 1994) p. 529; C. M. Schmitthoff, *op.cit.* p. 450; see also paras 8.19 and 8.20 on the UNCITRAL Convention on independent guarantees and standby letters of credit and ISP 98.
[53] See *Gulf Bank v. Mitsubishi Heavy Industries* (1994) 2 Ll.L.R. 145.

certain services or works (*e.g.* the construction of a motorway), and he defaults, as determined, say, in a judgment, an arbitral award or an expert report, the guaranteeing bank may either have to compensate the actual damage or pay a lump sum, fixed at the time the guarantee was issued. The guarantee of a fixed sum is most common.

8.53   **Independent character**   Guarantees sometimes depend on an underlying contract: no performance is due under the guarantee if no performance is due under the underlying contract, *e.g.* because the contract is invalid or frustrated.

In international trade, however, guarantees are generally "autonomous", *i.e.* independent of:

- the underlying contract between, *e.g.*, exporter and importer;

- the contract between the client (*i.e.* the debtor) and the bank which issues the guarantee.

The guarantor is bound to honour his guarantee. As a rule, he cannot raise defences that emanate from underlying contract. Nor can he refuse to honour the guarantee because the contract with his client is null and void, or because his client has insufficient credit. The terms and conditions of the undertakings of the guarantor are exclusively determined by the contents of the guarantee.

The bank guarantee is thus not an accessory to the underlying contract, like a suretyship ("caution"). The guarantor who pays the creditor, settles his own debt, while the surety takes on the debt of the principal debtor. Consequently there is no need to challenge the debtor of an underlying contract first before claiming from the guarantor. It is of little importance that the bank guarantee is either called "suretyship" in the underlying contract or even that the contract refers to the legal provisions for suretyship. Courts examine the guarantee on its merits and are not bound by the label and wording used.

8.54   **Terminology**   There is no uniform terminology for bank guarantees. For instance, what is called a "bank guarantee" in England is in every aspect comparable with a suretyship.[54] What is elsewhere called a bank guarantee is often effected in England by way of an "indemnity" (a separate undertaking by the bank to pay the creditor)[55] or, particularly in international trade, by way of a "performance bond" (in which the bank must pay the beneficiary unconditionally on first demand, sometimes after presentation of the stipulated documents[56] (see paragraph 8.55)).

---

[54] See W. Berensmann, *Bürgschaft und Garantievertrag im englischen Recht* (Berlin, 1988).

[55] M. Hapgood, N. Levy, *Paget's Law of Banking* (11th ed., Butterworths, London, 1996). See also R. M. Goode, *Legal Problems of Credit and Security* (Sweet & Maxwell, London, 1988).

[56] M. Hapgood, *op.cit.* pp. 652 *et seq.*

Banks in the United States[57] are not allowed to issue guarantees. Bank guarantees are in this country replaced by standby letters of credit with the creditor as beneficiary (see paragraph 8.18).

Furthermore, the frequently used expression "guarantee on first demand" is not quite accurate. The notion "on first demand" refers primarily to the burden of proof: the issuing bank must pay first before it can challenge the existence of the debt or take an action in respect of the debt (*"pay first, argue later"*). Besides, bank guarantees are not the only undertakings "on first demand"; suretyship also can be "on first demand". Therefore the expression "independent guarantees" is preferred.[58]

Examples of independent guarantees   8.55

(a) The tender guarantee (*bid bond, garantie de soumission*) protects the instigator of a public call to tender. It covers the risk that the bidder awarded with the contract does ultimately not conclude the contract or provide the required performance bond. This guarantee normally ranges from one to 5 per cent of the tender value.

(b) The performance guarantee (*performance bond, garantie de bonne exécution*) serves as a security for correct performance of a contract. The amount of this guarantee is usually determined as a fixed percentage of the agreed contract price.

(c) The advance payment (or repayment) guarantee (*down payment guarantee, repayment bond, garantie de restitution d'acompte*) covers the risk that the contractor fails to repay the received downpayment which he has to reimburse if he ultimately fails to complete the contract (usually from 5 to 30 per cent of the contract value; see paragraph 8.29).

(d) The maintenance (or warranty) guarantee (*maintenance bond, garantie d'entretien*) secures the supplier's undertaking for maintenance of the equipment.

(e) The payment guarantee (*garantie de paiement*), granted to the supplier, guarantees payment by the buyer.

(f) The bill of lading guarantee (*garantie pour connaissement*) is given by the importer to allow for the immediate delivery of the goods mentioned in a bill of lading (see paragraph 8.14) which has not yet been delivered or got lost.

(g) The retention guarantee (*retention money bond*) secures repayment of the retention moneys the employer has released, if defects are later found or if the contractor fails to complete the contract.

---

[57] See, *e.g.* Lord, "The no-guarantee rule and the standby letter of credit" (1979) Banking.L.J. 46; G. A. Penn, A. M. Shea and A. Arora, *op.cit.* p. 287.

[58] See also F. Graf von Westphalen, *Die Bankgarantie im internationalen Handelsverkehr, op.cit.* pp. 48 *et seq.*

8.56   **Applicable law**[59]   The guarantee is governed by the law chosen by the parties. If no choice of law has been expressed, then the guarantee will be governed by the law of the country where the party rendering the characteristic performance has its place of business.

In international banking transactions, it is generally assumed that the bank is rendering the characteristic performance. Therefore, the law of the country where the bank is established will be applicable.[60] But, if in a specific case the guarantee has closer connections with the country of the principal debtor/beneficiary, the latter country might prevail over the country where the bank is located, at least in the countries which adopted the Rome Convention.[61] (See paragraph 1.29.)

The relationship between the first (instructing) and the second (correspondent) bank (see paragraph 8.60) is governed by the law of the place of business of the instructing party.[62] This solution has the advantage that the contractual relationship between beneficiary and guarantor and the inter-banking relationship are governed by the same rules. Some legal writers, however, propose the application of the law of the country where the second bank is established. The second bank is indeed charged with the issuance and execution of the guarantee.

National law, however, is of less significance for independent guarantees. Most rules on independent guarantees have been developed on the international scene, away from domestic concepts and rules.[63]

Applicable rules

8.57   **The Uniform Rules for Contract Guarantees**   In 1978, the International Chamber of Commerce issued the Uniform Rules for Contract Guarantees (URCG)[64] which only allow for the demand of a guarantee after the beneficiary has presented certain documents (*e.g.* a court order, an arbitral award[65] or a written confirmation from the principal). In many cases, the requirement for the

---

[59] *cf.* M. Pelichet, "Bank guarantees and conflict of laws" (1990) I.B.L.J. 335; J. J. Newton, "Choice of law rules and trade finance contracts" (1997) Ll.Mar.&Com.L.Q. 344; O. Elwan, "La loi applicable à la garantie bancaire à la première demande" (1998) 275 *Rec.Cours.* 9.

[60] J. P. Mattout, *Droit Bancaire International, op.cit.* p. 46; F. Bonelli," La Convention de Rome du 19 juin 1980 et la loi applicable aux opérations bancaires" (1985) I.B.L.J. 389 *et seq.*

[61] *cf.* Art. 4(5) Rome Convention; M. Pelichet, "Bank guarantees and conflict of laws" (1990) I.B.L.J. 335, 347–348.

[62] Uniform rules, Art. 27.

[63] See R. F. Bertrams, *op.cit.* See also L. Gorton, "Draft UNCITRAL Convention on Independent Guarantees" (1996) 1, Ll.Mar.&Com.L.Q., 42–49; A. Berg, "Draft UNCITRAL Convention on Independent Guarantees" (1996) 1, Ll.Mar.&Com.L.Q. 49–57; J. Stoufflet, "La Convention des Nations Unies sur les garanties independantes et les lettres de credit stand-by" (1995) 50, R.D.B.B. 50, 132–139; P. de Ly, "The United Nations Convention on Independent Guarantees and Stand-by Letters of Credit" (1999) 33, Int.L. 831–846.

[64] *Règles Uniformes pour les Garanties Contractuelles*, ICC brochure no. 325 (1978). For the text N. Horn & C. M. Schmitthoff (eds), *The Transnational Law of International Commercial Transactions* (Kluwer, Deventer, 1982) pp. 415.

[65] *cf.* B. Leurent, "Bank Guarantees and Arbitration" (1990) I.B.L.J. 401; B. Hanotiau, "Arbitration and bank guarantees", (1999) 16 J.I.A. 15,

beneficiary to produce reliable proof of default created enormous delays in payment, to the extent that the guarantee entirely failed to serve its purpose.

The Rules have been seldom used as parties were reluctant to bind themselves to heavy formalities and banks did not wish to get involved in disputes concerning commercial contracts.

The Uniform Rules for Demand Guarantees In order to avoid these **8.58** difficulties the ICC Uniform Rules for Demand Guarantees (URDG)[66] were adopted in 1991.

At present the URDG have not yet gained wide acceptance, as countries, organisations and individual companies which represent the beneficiary's side of guarantees, and especially the banking community, hesitate to adopt the Rules. The URDG are nevertheless worth studying as they spell out and contain many basic principles on independent guarantees. They only apply to:

" . . . any guarantee, bond or other payment undertaking, however named or described, by a bank, insurance company or other body or person ('the Guarantor') given in writing for the payment of money on presentation in conformity with the terms of the undertaking of a written demand for payment and such other document(s) as may be specified in the Guarantee, such undertaking being given) at the request or on the instructions and under the liability of a party ('the Principal'); or ii) at the request or on the instructions and under the liability of a bank, insurance company or any other body or person ('the Instructing Party') acting on the instructions of a Principal to another party ('the Beneficiary')." (Article 2(a).)[67]

The scope of the URDG is thus confined to guarantees in writing given for the account of a third party (as opposed to the issuer's own account) and providing for payment against a written demand[68] and other specified documents.[69] Except to the extent that it is expressly excluded by the terms of the guarantee (Article 20(c)), any written demand for payment must be supported by the beneficiary's written statement of breach (Article 20(a)). The purpose of this rule is to

---

[66] ICC Publication no. 458 (April, 1992). See R. Goode, *Guide to the ICC Uniform Rules for Demand Guarantees* (ICC Publication no. 510, Paris, 1992); A. Pierce, *Demand Guarantees in International Trade* (Sweet & Maxwell, London, 1993); M. Vasseur, "The New Rules of the International Chamber of Commerce for 'guarantees on demand' " (1992) I.B.L.J. 239 *et seq.*; T. de Galard, "Les nouvelles règles uniformes de la Chambre de Commerce Internationale relatives aux garanties sur demande" (1993) I.B.L.J. 759 *et seq.* The success of the URDG depends ultimately on the extent to which the international business community is prepared to adopt them in practice. According to the ICC adherence list banks in Australia, Denmark, Sweden and United Kingdom adhere collectively to the URDG, while a great number of banks in China, South Africa and Switzerland do so individually. More information on http://www.iccwbo.org/.

[67] The Uniform Rules also apply to counter-guarantees as defined by Art. 2(c).

[68] The expression "writing" includes an authenticated tele-transmission or tested electronic data interchange message equivalent thereto (Art. 2(d)).

[69] R. Goode, *Guide to the ICC Uniform Rules for Demand Guarantee, op.cit.* p. 9. The majority of demand guarantees currently impose no additional documentary requirements (R. Goode, *op.cit.* p. 21).

discourage unfair calling whilst preserving the speed and simplicity of remedy in market practice.[70]

The rules concern independent guarantees. Guarantees of only subordinate and accessory obligations, fall outside the scope of the rules (Article 2(b)).[71] Unless otherwise stated in the guarantee, a beneficiary cannot assign his right to make a demand, although nothing prevents him from assigning the proceeds from a demand presented by him or on his behalf (Article 4).

All guarantees and counter-guarantees are irrevocable unless otherwise indicated (Article 5).

When a demand is made, the guarantor has to examine the demand and all documents specified under the guarantee within a reasonable time and with reasonable care (Articles 9 and 10). He must without delay inform the principal or his instructing party (Article 17). Should the guarantor refuse the demand, he must immediately give notice of his decision to the beneficiary (Article 10(b)).

The guarantor is liable to the beneficiary only in accordance with the terms specified in the guarantee and any amendments thereto, and up to an amount not exceeding that stated therein (Article 16).

Unless otherwise provided in the guarantee, its governing law and exclusive jurisdiction shall be that of the country of the place of business of the guarantor, or, if the guarantor has more than one place of business, that of the country of the branch that issued the guarantee (Article 27 and 28) (see also paragraph 8.57).[72]

8.59   **The Uniform Rules for Contract Bonds**   In each type of guarantee there are at least three parties involved: the guarantor, the principal and the beneficiary. In international contracts there is also an intermediary bank, the so-called instructing party. The guarantor, the party issuing the guarantee, is often the bank; however, guarantees can also be issued by insurance companies and other institutions. The Uniform Rules for Demand Guarantees did not take into account the particular needs of the insurers, because they do not pay much attention to the principal's capacity to perform the contract, but look basically only at the economic solvency of the assured or principal. Moreover, even though insurance companies issue bonds for the purpose of guaranteeing the contract, such bonds are actually insurance contracts, so the risk covered by them is precisely the

---

[70] R. Goode, *Guide to the ICC Uniform Rules for Demand Guarantees, op.cit.* pp. 21, 92.
[71] M. Vasseur, "The New Rules of the International Chamber of Commerce for 'Guarantees on Demand'" *op.cit.* pp. 244 *et seq.*
[72] Arts 27 and 28 are of course subordinate to the rules of law which override contractual provisions and, more particularly, to any overriding provisions of the 1980 EEC Convention on the Law Applicable to Contractual Obligations (see para. 1.29) and Regulation 44/2001 on jurisdiction and the recognition and enforcement of judgments in civil and commercial matters (see para. 10.02), when it is applicable; see R. Goode, *Guide to the ICC Uniform Rules for Demand Guarantees, op.cit.* pp. 35, 115 *et seq.*; M. Vasseur, "The new rules of the International Chamber of Commerce for 'Guarantees on Demand'" *op.cit.* pp. 285 *et seq.*

default. With the support of the main insurance associations, the ICC adopted in 1993 the Uniform Rules for Contract Bonds (URCB).[73]

According to Article 1(a), the URCB apply to any bond that states that the Rules so apply, or that otherwise incorporates them by reference. The URCB formulate a bond that has accessory nature,[74] which has the following consequences:

(a) the guarantor will only be obliged to meet a claim if the principal defaults[75];

(b) the liability of the guarantor depends directly on that of the principal in the contract;

(c) if the guarantor refuses to satisfy a well-founded claim, it will be obliged, except if agreed to the contrary, to satisfy both the interest accrued since the claim was made and the costs of the trial since the guarantor received formal demand for payment from the beneficiary;

(d) if so provided, the guarantor may, in the case of default by the principal, perform the obligation that the latter failed to perform, instead of making monetary compensation for the loss.

The URCB do not cover documentary requirements or the problem of unfair calling.

The applicable law is the law of the country chosen by the parties to govern the operation of the bond.[76] If the parties have not expressly made the bond subject to a particular law, the law that governs the underlying contract applies. If the parties have not stated anything to the contrary, the bond and the contract guaranteed are thus governed by the same law, thus avoiding two different legal systems being applied.

The Uniform Rules for Contract Bonds provide a greater cover of the contract or of the guaranteed obligations than do the demand guarantees,[77] and also a convenient balance between the interests of the contracting parties, without forgetting the need for efficiency, speed, and the satisfaction of the rights of the beneficiary.

---

[73] ICC Publication no. 524 (April 1993). See J.C. de los Ríos, "The new ICC Regulations on contract bonds", (1996) 30 Int.L., 1; P. Simler, "Les regles uniformes de la Chambre de Commerce Internationale (CCI) pour les contract bonds" (1997) 74, R.D.I.D.C. 122.

[74] The accessory nature means that the bond is closely linked to the contract under guarantee and that the liability of the guarantor likewise will be so related, but this liability cannot exceed the liability that the principal has in the contract.

[75] Thus, the bond devised by the URCB clearly differs from demand guarantees where the guarantor must pay the amount of the indemnity on the mere request of the beneficiary and without making any kind of investigation on whether default by the principal of the guarantee has taken place.

[76] This provision follows the view that the contractual guarantees are included within the framework of contractual relationships in which the parties may freely elect the law applicable to them. See, inter alia, M. Pelichet, "Garanties bancaires et contflits de lois" (1990) J.I.B.L. 338.

[77] In demand guarantees, given their greater risk for guarantors, the amount of the cover constitutes a very small percentage of the obligation or obligation guaranteed. However, in accessory guarantees, which have almost no risk of improper claims, the guarantor can offer a much greater cover (from 30% upwards).

Rights and duties of the parties

8.60   **The relationship between bank and principal debtor**   The issuing bank has a mandate from the principal debtor.[78] When the bank pays, it does so in its own name but on behalf of the principal debtor. This constitutes the basis for the duty of reimbursement by the principal debtor.[79]

The bank has a special duty of care when the guarantee is issued. It must explain the risk of an independent guarantee to inexperienced principal debtors. The text of a guarantee is, however, not usually drafted by the issuing bank, but presented *ne varietur* by or on behalf of the beneficiary. The bank should notify the principal debtor, where possible in writing, of its objections to the proposed text. However, in the end the principal debtor decides.

Also, when the guarantee is called by the beneficiary the bank must exercise a duty of care. With the information available, the bank must ascertain with reasonable care whether there are defenses against the calling of the guarantee.[80] The bank must adhere strictly to the terms stipulated in the guarantee: for instance, beyond the expiry date it should not honour a guarantee. It must also notify the principal debtor as soon as the guarantee is called[81] in order to enable the principal debtor, if necessary, to take legal action to stop or prevent payment (see paragraphs 8.62 *et seq.*).

When the expiry date of the guarantee is nearing, beneficiaries sometimes give the issuing bank the choice to extend the validity period of the guarantee or to pay.[82] The bank usually agrees to extend when the request was not manifestly unfair (see paragraph 8.65). However, the bank may extend the guarantee period only with the consent of the principal debtor.[83]

8.61   **The underlying agreement**   The issuing bank is usually not a party to the contract (the principal or underlying agreement) between the principal debtor and the beneficiary.

The issuing bank cannot rely on the underlying agreement to refuse payment of an independent guarantee. Even when it is convinced that the principal debtor has not defaulted on the contract or has not committed any other breach of contract, the bank must pay the beneficiary (see, however, paragraph 8.62). In that event, the principal debtor has to recover the whole amount (paid by the bank

---

[78] The guarantee for considerable amounts is sometimes issued by a syndicate of banks (syndicated bond facilities); see Z. Kronfol, "The syndication of risk in unconditional bonds" (1984) J.B.L. 13.

[79] The principal debtor no longer has an obligation in respect of the bank when the bank makes a mistake and, for instance, pays the beneficiary after it became aware that he had clearly abused his right (see para. 8.66); Cass.Fr., February 6, 1990, (1990) Dalloz 467.

[80] N. Horn and E. Wijmeersch, "Bank guarantees, standby letters of credit and performance bonds in international trade" in N. Horn (ed.), *op.cit.*, pp. 469, 485.

[81] F. Graf von Westphalen, *op.cit.*, pp. 353 *et seq.* Otherwise H. J. Pabbruwe, *op.cit.*, pp. 17–19, except when the guarantor receives a communication to extend or pay (pp. 21 *et seq.*). Uniform Rules for Demand Guarantees, Art. 17 ICC.

[82] On "extend and pay" see, *inter alia*, H. J. Pabbruwe, *op.cit.*, pp. 21–22; see also the observations on Art. 26 in R. Goode, *Guide to the ICC Uniform Rules for Demand*, *op.cit.*, pp. 109–114.

[83] The caller of the guarantee sometimes requests to "hold at our disposal". This can lead to problems if the principal debtor was debited without the crediting of the beneficiary.

and debited to his account) from the beneficiary in a legal action on the underlying agreement.

First (instructing) and second (correspondent) bank   The beneficiary is often not satisfied with a guarantee issued by a foreign bank and demands a guarantee from a bank in its own country.[84] In this event the bank of the principal debtor requests a bank in the country of the beneficiary to issue an independent guarantee for the beneficiary. In this construction the former bank is called the "first" or "instructing bank", while the latter bank is called the "second" or "correspondent bank". Unless otherwise stipulated in the guarantee, the second bank has only an undertaking in respect of the beneficiary. The second bank will only accept to pay if it obtains an undertaking for reimbursement from the instructing bank.[85] The instructing bank so becomes the "counter-guarantor".

The second bank has to pay on first demand when called by the beneficiary in writing. In fact, however, the second bank informs the first bank immediately after the call to ensure that the latter in turn will honor the counter-guarantee and to learn from the first bank any legal objection that can be raised against the demand.

8.62

Unfair calls and stop-payment orders

Procedure   When confronted with an unfair call on the independent guarantee, the principal debtor may apply for an injunction to block payment by the bank. The assessment by the court of such application is delicate.[86] On the one hand the principal debtor has a legitimate interest that no payment is made; but on the other hand, the independent and unconditional nature of the guarantee should not be denied.[87]

Courts are generally very reluctant to interfere with the independent nature of the guarantee and forbid payment only in exceptional cases. In most countries a stop-payment order is only granted when the demand is "manifestly unfair". The unfairness must be "blatantly obvious";[88] it must *"crever les yeux".*[89]

The banks must ascertain the unfairness independently and on the basis of objective facts. They can not base their appraisal only on documents received from the principal debtor.

8.63

---

[84] At first glance this legal situation could be compared with that of a "confirming bank" in a documentary credit (see para. 8.04). However, this analogy is misleading because, unless otherwise agreed in the guarantee, the beneficiary has no claim against the first bank which took the initiative for the guarantee.

[85] See an example of "counter-indemnity" in G. A. Penn, A. M. Shea and A. Arora, *op.cit.*, pp. 280–281.

[86] N. Horn and E. Wijmeersch, "Bank guarantees, standby letters of credit and performance bonds in international trade" in N. Horn (ed.), *op.cit.*, pp. 510 *et seq.*; F. Graf von Westphalen, *op.cit., pp.* 259 *et seq.*

[87] Sometimes an arbitral tribunal or court must decide on the legitimacy of the demand; see, *e.g.* ICC arbitration no. 5639 (1987); no. 5721 (1990), (1990) J.D.I. 1020; see, *inter alia*, B. Hanotiau, "Arbitration and bank guarantees" (1999) 16, J.I.A. 15; *Themehelp Ltd v. West and Others* [1995] 5 T.L.R. 247.

[88] H. J. Pabbruwe, *Bankgarantie* (Kluwer, Deventer, 1988), p. 25.

[89] M. Vasseur, in "Garantie indépendante", *op.cit.*, no. 120.

Four grounds (listed below) may be invoked to obtain a stop-payment order.[90]

8.64   **Non-compliance with the terms of the guarantee**   The demand must meet the terms of the guarantee. The guarantor is not held to pay if the conditions agreed are not fulfilled. Therefore a call before the commencement date or after the expiry date, or by someone not entitled to request payment is ineffective.

If the guarantee depends on the submission of specific documents, these documents have to be presented to the guarantor.

It is generally not accepted that set-off with counterclaims against the beneficiary justifies non-payment of the guarantee.[91]

8.65   **Invalidity of the underlying contract**   As a rule, the underlying contract cannot relieve the guarantor from his duty to guarantee. The guarantee, for instance, is not affected when the underlying contract is void. However, in exceptional cases this principle may be set aside, when, for instance, the underlying contract is contrary to international public policy, *e.g.* because it relates to drug trafficking.

It also has been argued that the guarantor is no longer bound when the court has pronounced the underlying contract dissolved or null and void.[92] Even if this view is not followed, one may argue that a subsequent call on the guarantee is evidently fraudulent, while the beneficiary had actual knowledge of the dissolution or avoidance.[93]

8.66   **Manifest fraud**   The bank is not entitled to pay when it is aware of manifest fraud by the beneficiary.[94] As the guarantor should not be concerned with the underlying contract, the fraud must indeed be "manifest". There is, for instance, manifest fraud when the beneficiary calls a performance bond although he has formally accepted the works.[95] There is also manifest fraud when the beneficiary demands the guarantee although he is aware that the underlying contract in null and void (see paragraph 8.68),[96] or when he himself has seriously defaulted.

In the United States "evil intent" is required: that is the case when the guarantee is called, although it is established that the principal debtor has strictly adhered to the underlying contract.[97] English courts, on the other hand, rather adhere to the independent character of the guarantee and the strict compliance of

---

[90] *cf.* also F. Graf von Westphalen, *op.cit.*, pp. 174 *et seq.*, as well as (1990) I.B.L.J. survey of jurisprudence by M. Vasseur (France, p. 357), M. Elland-Goldsmith (England, p. 421) and D. Lechien (England, p. 437).

[91] R. F. Bertrams, *Bank Guarantees in International Trade* (2nd ed., Kluwer, 1996), p. 249.

[92] According to an arbitral award the demand is unlawful if the commercial contract has been terminated; in this case the guarantee has lost its cause ("ICC arbitration no. 5721 (1990)" (1990) J.D.I. 1020).

[93] N. Horn and E. Wijmeersch, "Bank guarantees, standby letters of credit and performance bonds in international trade" in N. Horn (ed.), *op.cit.*, p. 490.

[94] *cf.* fraud in documentary credit (see para. 8.17).

[95] Cass.Fr., June 10, 1986, (1987) Dalloz 17.

[96] See for other examples of fraudulent calling, H. J. Pabbruwe, *op.cit.*, pp. 25 *et seq.*

[97] N. Horn and E. Wijmeersch, *op.cit.*, pp. 486–487; G. A. Penn, A. M. Shea and A. Arora, *op.cit.*, pp. 277–280.

its terms; they are very reluctant to grant stop-payment orders because of fraud.

Abuse of law   The bank is not entitled to pay when the beneficiary commits   **8.67**
a manifest "abuse of law".[98] This is, for instance, the case when the beneficiary demands the guarantee, either with the intent to cause damage, or without the normal care of a reasonable person.

It has, for instance, been decided that there was manifest abuse of law when, for political reasons, Iranian enterprises systematically called guarantees issued by American banks, while they did not do so for guarantees issued by Swedish enterprises under the same underlying contract.[99] Or when a second bank,[1] ordered by a court not to pay the beneficiary, nevertheless requested payment from the first bank. Or if the demand was made for reasons that had nothing to do with the underlying contract, for instance, because the beneficiary needed certain foreign currency.[2] Or if the beneficiary demands the guarantee with the clear intention of putting the principal debtor under pressure to change the underlying contract or to review the price.

Guarantor and counter-guarantor in the event of unfair demand   The   **8.68**
following problems arise in the relationship between the guarantor and the counter-guarantor in the event of an unfair call.

(a) If the principal debtor is of the opinion that the demand is manifestly unfair, he usually seeks a stop-payment order against the first bank before the court in his own country. However, the second bank remains bound to pay the beneficiary, even though it knows that it cannot invoke the counter-guarantee and claim payment from the first bank, because of the court injunction there.

   If the second bank gets involved in the action for a stop-payment order in the courts of the country of the first bank, problems with regard to the eventual enforcement in the country of the beneficiary may arise This problem could be avoided by directly requesting a stop-payment order in the country of the second bank.

(b) Independent guarantees often require that the guarantee is paid "notwithstanding any court decision prohibiting payment". However, it is doubtful whether a counter-guarantor, *i.e.* a first bank, can refuse to give effect to a final judgment of his own national court. Moreover, the second bank may have to obey a stop-payment order from a foreign or its own court.

---

[98] In Switzerland and the Netherlands a stop-payment order was *e.g.* imposed on the bank in the event of abuse of law when it is clear that the principal debtor had strictly observed his obligations under the underlying contract. *Cour de Justice Geneva*, September 12, 1985, (1985) S.J. 616; *Pres. Leeuwarden court*, October 6, 1986, (1986) Kort geding 476.

[99] *Pres. Brussels court*, April 8, 1982, (1982) Dalloz 504.

[1] *Cour de Justice Geneva*, September 12, 1985, cited (1985) S.J. 616.

[2] N. Horn and E. Wijmeersch, "Bank guarantees, standby letters of credit and performance bonds in international trade" in N. Horn (ed.), *The Law of International Trade Finance, op.cit.*, p. 507.

(c) If it can be shown that the second bank is aware of the beneficiary's unfair demand of the guarantee, the first bank does not have to honour the counter-guarantee. As in the case of fraud in documentary credit, the counter-guarantee is no longer independent if there is deceitful collusion between the beneficiary and the second bank (see paragraph 8.65).[3]

---

[3] See, *e.g.* Cass.Fr., December 11, 1985, (1986) J.C.P. no. 20.593.

CHAPTER 9

INTERNATIONAL PAYMENT

Overview   International trade usually entails international transfers of funds.   **9.01**
The rules regarding international payments are therefore an important part of
international trade law.[1]

PART I: PROBLEMS OF MONETARY LAW

Exchange control

Exchange restrictions   Some countries[2] have very flexible exchange regula-   **9.02**
tions for capital transfers and for current transactions. Other countries still
maintain exchange restrictions[3] for the protection of their currency.[4] The restrictions do not only apply to payments for the purpose of transferring capital, but
also to payments in connection with the so-called "current transactions" (*e.g.*
foreign trade and other current business, including services). Many countries
have kept exchange formalities for statistical purposes so that they still have the
legal framework to reimpose exchange controls in times of crisis.

Article VIII, section 2 (a) of the IMF Agreement forbids a Member State to
impose restrictions on payments and transfers for current transactions without the
prior approval of the IMF. This provision has been adopted by the countries of

---

[1] See, *inter alia*, R. Cranston, *Principles of Banking Law* (Clarendon Press, Oxford, 1997); G.C.
Heinrich, "Funds transfers, payments, and payment systems: international initiatives towards legal
harmonisation" (1994) 28 *International Lawyer* 787–824; G. Penn, A. Shea and A. Arora, *The Law
and Practice of International Banking* (2nd ed., Sweet & Maxwell, London, 1997); G. Radicati di
Brozolo, "International payments and conflicts of laws" (2000) 48 A.J.C.L. 307–326; P. Volken,
P. Sarcevic (eds), *International contracts and payments* (Graham & Trotman/Martinus Nijhoff,
1991); M. Vasseur, "Les tranferts internationaux de fonds: la loi type des Nations Unies sur les
virements internationaux. Les cartes de débit" (1993) 2 RecCours 117–405.
[2] *e.g.* Bahrain, Hong Kong, Panama, Singapore, Vanuatu, etc.
[3] "The guiding principle in ascertaining whether a measure is a restriction on payments and transfers
for current transactions . . . is whether it involves a direct governmental limitation to the availability or use of exchange as such."(IMF Annual Report, 1960, pp. 29–30); see on IMF and its
members http://www.imf.org/external/np/sec/memdir/members.htm.
[4] B. A. Simmons, "Money and the law: why comply with the public international law of money?"
(2000) 25 YaleJ.Int.Law, 323–362 ; W.F. Ebke, *Internationales Devisenrecht* (Recht und Wirtschaft, Heidelberg, 1990); Ph. Wood, *Law and Practice of International Finance* (Sweet &
Maxwell, 1981) Chap. 5.; H. Siebert, *Improving the World's Financial Architecture: the Role of the
IMF* (Institut für Welwirtschaft, Kiel, 1999).

which the national currency is most often used for international payment transactions (the so-called "Article VIII countries" (see paragraph 9.03)).[5]

9.03   **Foreign exchange control**   Countries which have adopted Article VIII of the IMF Agreement[6] moreover have to take into account the exchange controls imposed by other IMF Member States:

> "Exchange contracts which involve the currency of any member and which are contrary to the exchange control regulations of that member maintained or imposed consistently with this Agreement shall be unenforceable in the territories of any member."[7]

Practically all the components of this provision raise problems of interpretation[8]:

> "Exchange contracts"   This term has led to two different interpretations:
>
> — According to English case law, "exchange contract" must be interpreted as a currency transaction in the restrictive sense, *i.e.* "a monetary deal in currencies",[9] "a contract to exchange the currency of one country for the currency of another".[10] This view is shared by the

---

[5] There are 183 members of the IMF and among them 150 countries adopted provisions of the Art. VIII s.2 of the IMF Agreement. The following IMF members have not accepted the obligations of Article VIII: Afghanistan, Albania, Angola, Azerbaijan, Belarus, Bhutan, Bosnia and Herzegovina, Burundi, Cambodia, Cape Verde, Colombia, Congo, Egypt, Eritrea, Ethiopia, Iran, Iraq, Laos, Liberia, Libya, Maldives, Mozambique, Myanmar, Nigeria, Sao Tomé and Principe, Somalia, Sudan, Syria, Tajikistan, Turkmenistan, Uzbekistan, Vietnam, Federal Republic of Yugoslavia, Zambia. Moreover, countries that adhered to the transitional arrangements of Art. XIV, are not bound by Art. VIII 2(a). More information about the IMF and its members can be found on http://www.imf.org/external/about.htm.

[6] Whether or not they are availing themselves of the transitional arrangements of Art. XIV.

[7] Art. VIII 2(b) of the Articles of Agreement.

[8] See J.J. Gold, "The IMF's Article VII, Section 2(b) and scrupulosity", in *Yearbook of International Financial & Economic Law,* gen. ed. J.J. Norton (Kluwer, 1996); P. Balfour, "Extraterritorial recognition of exchange control regulations—The English viewpoint" in N. Horn (ed.), *The Law of International Trade Finance* (Kluwer, Deventer, 1989) pp. 125 *et seq.*; K. Bohlhoff and A. Baumanns, "Extraterritorial recognition of exchange control regulations—A German viewpoint" in N. Horn (ed.), *op.cit,* pp. 107 *et seq.*; Dicey and Morris, *The Conflict of Laws* (13th ed., Sweet & Maxwell, London, 2000), pp. 1612–1622; F. Gianviti, "Réflexions sur l'article VIII section 2 (b) des statuts du Fonds Monétaire International" (1973) R.C.D.I.P. 471, 629; A.T. Marks, "Exchange control regulations within the meaning of the Bretton Woods Agreement: a comparison of judicial interpretation in the United States and Europe" (1990) 8 Int.Tax&Bus.Law, 104; J. Gold, "IMF: some effects on private parties and private transactions" in J.J. Norton (ed.), *Prospects for International Lending and Reschedulings* (Bender, New York, 1988); *ibid.,* "Art. VIII, s. 2(b) of the IMF Articles in its international setting" in N. Horn (ed.), *op.cit.,* pp. 65 *et seq.*; T.S. Link, "Article VIII, Section 2(b) of the IMF Articles—The current United States practice and outlook" in N. Horn (ed.), *op.cit.* pp. 143 *et seq.*; F.A. Mann, *The Legal Aspect of Money* (5th ed., Clarendon, Oxford, 1992) pp. 372 *et seq.*; G.A. Penn, A.M. Shea and A. Arora, *op.cit.,* pp. 75 *et seq.*

[9] See also C.M. Schmitthoff, *Export trade* (10th ed., Sweet and Maxwell, London, 2000) pp. 438–439 (with further references to case law); *contra*: F.A. Mann, *op.cit.* pp. 378–381. The English interpretation is disapproved of in many countries. The decision in *Re Wilson, Smithett & Cope v. Terruzzi,* for example, was not granted enforcement in Italy: *Corte di cassazione,* December 13, 1984, (1986) Riv.dir.int.civ.&proc. 148.

[10] In *Re United Railways of Havana v. Regla Warehouses Ltd* (1961) A.C. 1007.

United States courts, and other common law countries share the restrictive view taken by the English courts.[11]

— A less restrictive view that was also held by the drafters of the IMF Agreement at the Bretton Woods conference,[12] is taken by the majority of the other jurisdictions.[13] They do not limit the notion of "exchange contract" to "a contract to exchange currencies", but also include any agreement that would affect the exchange resources of another IMF Member State: " . . . contracts under which payments or transfers are to be made, whatever else must be rendered or done under the terms of the contract."[14]

Under the less restrictive view, the following are to be considered as "exchange contracts": a purchase[15] or subscription of shares in a foreign company, a loan agreement, a credit agreement, deposits, a sale of goods and a contract for services. A bill of exchange in U.S. dollars accepted by a Norwegian company as a security for a credit granted to a German company was also considered an "exchange contract".[16] However, countertrade agreements, where payments are not made in currency (see paragraph 9.42), do not fall under this definition.[17]

The restrictive interpretation, adopted in the United Kingdom and the United States is more favourable to creditors. They will push for the law and jurisdiction of such a country. Indeed, courts of these countries will not excuse a defaulting borrower under Article VIII 2(b) for non-payment because the contract violated foreign exchange restrictions—especially when their own law governs the contract.[18]

---

[11] See W.T. Burke, "Enforcement of foreign exchange control regulations in domestic courts" (1976) Am.J.Int'l.L. 101; T.M. Asser, "Foreign exchange contracts and the applicability of Article 2 of the UCC" (1996) 113 Banking.L.J. 578; R.W. Edwards, op.cit., p. 485; T.W. Link, "Article VIII, Section 2(b) of the IMF Articles—The current United States practice and outlook", in N. Horn (ed.) op.cit. pp. 143 et seq.; J.S. William, "Enforcement of foreign exchange control regulations in domestic courts" (1976) Am.J.Int'l.L. 101.

[12] J. Gold "Article VIII, Section 2(b) of the IMF in its International Setting" in N. Horn (ed.), op.cit., 65–106; F.A. Mann, op.cit., pp. 380–381.

[13] See, inter alia: French and German case law in F.A. Mann, op.cit.; German case law in (1989) R.I.W. 987; Luxembourg: Tribunal de Luxembourg, February 1, 1956, (1957) Pasicrisie Luxembourgeoise 36; Belgium: F. Rigaux, "L'exécution en Belgique d'un contrat de change prohibé par la loi d'un autre Etat" (1988) Ann. Dr. Liège 72. See also G. Delaume, "De l'élimination des conflits de lois en matière monétaire réalisée par les statuts du FMI et de ses limites" (1954) J.D.I. 332. In England the question remains open whether Art. VIII 2(b) is a conflict of law rule (in which case the English courts apply the private international law of the forum) or a substantive law rule (in which case the IMF provisions must be interpreted according to the lex contractus): P. Balfour, op.cit., 127; J. Gold and P.R. Lachman, "The Articles of Agreement of the IMF and the exchange control regulations of Member States" (1962) J.D.I. 666.

[14] J. Gold, in N. Horn, op.cit. p. 87.

[15] Paris, June 20, 1961, (1962) J.D.I. 718.

[16] Bundesgerichtshof, April 27, 1970, (1970) NJW 1507.

[17] J. Gold, op.cit.; R. Derham, "Set-off and netting of foreign exchange contracts in the litigation of a foundation of a counterparty", (1991) J.B.L. 463.

[18] See also W.F. Ebke, "Article VII Section 2(b), international monetary co-operation, and the courts", in Festschrift in honor of Sir Joseph Gold (Recht und Wirtschaft, Heidelberg, 1990) pp. 73–80; (1989) Int'l Lawyer 677. A consequence thereof is that "the parties to international loan agreements hardly ever choose German law as governing their contractual relationship, even

"Which involve the currency of any member" This phrase usually receives a wide interpretation[19]; it is sufficient that exchange resources or the balance of payment of a Member State can be indirectly affected.[20] The law of the state whose resources are affected and not so much the law of the currency actually used (*lex monetae*), should determine whether its currency is involved.[21]

"Contrary to the exchange control regulations" This condition refers to the national regulations on capital transfers and/or current transactions, in so far as they protect the country's exchange resources. Mere trade-policy regulations (tariffs, trade restrictions, etc.) do not seem to fall under this definition.[22]

"Maintained or imposed consistently with this Agreement" The IMF has to approve of the foreign exchange control regulation. Exchange restrictions for "current transactions" are in principle incompatible with the IMF Articles of Agreement, at least for the "Article VIII countries" (see paragraph 9.02) and thus cannot be imposed or maintained under the Agreement. They may nevertheless be imposed under certain conditions.[23] Consequently it has been argued that capital transfer contracts fall outside the scope of Article VIII 2(b).[24]

---

though Germany is a major international lender" (*op.cit.*, 77). See also C.T. Ebenroth, "Internationale Kreditverträge unter Anwendung von Art. VIII Abschnitt 2(b) IWF-Abkommens" (1991) R.I.W. 617; W.F. Ebke, "Der Internationale Währungsfonds und das internationale Devisenrecht" (1991) R.I.W. 1; U. Ehricke, "Die Funktion des Artikel VIII Abschnitt 2 (b) des IWF-Vertrages in der internationalen Schuldenkrise" (1991) R.I.W. 365 *et seq.*; G.A. Penn, A.M. Shea and A. Arora, *op.cit.*, 77; U. Unteregge, *Ausländisches Devisenrecht und internationale Kreditverträge* (Heidelberg, 1991).

[19] This wider view, however, is not unanimously accepted. See, *e.g.* arbitral award of March 23, 1981, (1983) J.T. 727.

[20] G. van Hecke, "Currency" no. 18 in *International Encyclopedia of Comparative Law*.

[21] The *lex patrimonii*, F.A. Mann, *op.cit.* p. 390; see also Paris, June 20, 1961, 1962 J.D.I. 718.

[22] F.A. Mann, *op.cit.*, p. 388; J. Gold in N. Horn (ed.), *op.cit.*, pp. 88–89.

[23] Exchange restrictions may be imposed according to the IMF in the four following cases: (i) controls of international capital movements (Art. VI–3: restrictions are allowed without prior approval of the Fund in so far as payments for current transactions are not affected); (ii) approval of the Fund (Art. VIII–2(a)); (iii) declaration of the Fund on the scarcity of a certain currency (Art. VII–3(b)); (iv) during the transitional period after becoming a member of the IMF (Art. XIV–2). It is not always clear what Art. VIII 2(b) means by "current transactions". Art. XXX (d) of the IMF Articles of Agreement defines such transactions as follows:
" . . . payments which are not for the purpose of transferring capital, and includes without limitation:
   (1) all payments due in connection with foreign trade, other current business, including services, and normal short-term banking and credit facilities;
   (2) payments due as interest on loans and as net income from other investments;
   (3) payments of moderate amount for amortisation of loans or for depreciation of direct investments; and
   (4) moderate remittances for family living expenses."

[24] D. Carreau and P. Juillard, *Droit International Économique* (4rd ed., LGDJ, Paris, 1998) p. 354. *Contra*: F.A. Mann, *op.cit.*, p. 376; *Bundesgerichtshof*, February 21, 1976, (1977) *Wertpapiermitteilungen* 332; Paris, May 14, 1970, (1974) R.C.D.I.P. 486; J. Gold in N. Horn (ed.), *op.cit.*, pp. 77–81; R.W. Edwards, "International monetary collaboration", *op.cit.*, p. 480.

"Exchange contracts . . . shall be unenforceable"   Divergent views exist as to the significance of the "unenforceability":

— In some cases, it has been held that the contract exists and remains valid, but can only be enforced in court if the defendant does not raise Article VIII 2(b) as a defence.[25]

— The leading authors hold, however, that the courts must, on their own motion, invoke Article VIII 2(b) and refuse to give effect to the contract. On their own motion they thus have to reject a claim for compensation for non-performance or an application for specific performance[26] Even when the contract has already been performed in part, the remainder of the performance will be unenforceable.[27]

The consequences of the "unenforceability" are in any case determined by the *lex contractus*.[28]

If the exchange control regulation is imposed by a country that is not a member of the IMF,[29] the impact of its breach will have to be determined under the proper

---

[25] Dicey and Morris, *op.cit.*, p. 1620; K. Bölhoff and A. Baumanns, *op.cit.*, p. 119. Regarding the arbitrability of disputes under Art. VIII 2(b) see O. Sandrock, "Are disputes over the application of Article VIII Section 2(b) of the IMF Treaty arbitrable?", in *Festschrift in Honor of Sir Joseph Gold* (Recht und Wirtschaft, Heidelberg, 1990) pp. 351 *et seq.*; see para. 11.08.

[26] J. Gold in N. Horn (ed.), *op.cit.*, pp. 90–91; F.A. Mann, *op.cit.*, p. 39; G. van Hecke, "Currency", no. 18, in *International Encyclopedia of Comparative Law* (Mohr, Tübingen, 1972). Executive Board Decision of the IMF of June 10, 1949, see S. Zamora and R.A. Brand, *Basic Documents of International Economic Law* (CCH, Chicago, 1990) I, pp. 415 *et seq.*; J. Gold in N. Horn (ed.), *op.cit.*, pp. 105–106. It is questioned whether such decisions of the Executive Board are binding for the courts: F.A. Mann, *op.cit.*, p. 377.

[27] J. Gold in N. Horn (ed.), *op.cit.*, p. 90. The contract is "unenforceable by the courts and nothing more"; see *United City Merchants v. Royal Bank of Canada* (1983) 1 A.C. 168, 189, cited in Dicey and Morris, *op.cit.*, p. 1620. The French Cour de Cassation speaks in this respect of the "inefficacité du contrat"; Cass. Fr., March 7, 1972, (1973) R.C.D.I.P. 768; Cass. Fr., June 18, 1969, (1970) R.C.D.I.P. 465. See also P. Drakidis, "Du caractère non exécutoire de certains 'contrats de change' d'après les statuts du Fonds Monétaire International" (1970) R.C.D.I.P. 363; F. Gianviti, "Le contrôle des changes étranger devant le juge national" (1980) R.C.D.I.P. 479, 659. In Germany, for instance, the Bundesgerichtshof has held that Art. VIII 2(b) is a procedural rule that has a threshold function; if the contract is contrary to a foreign exchange control, the court will simply dismiss any legal action as if it would, for example, decline its jurisdiction *ratione loci*; the court will not examine the merits of the case: W. Ebke, "Article VIII, Section 2(b) of the IMF Articles of Agreement and international capital transfers. Perspectives from the German Supreme Court" (1994) *International Lawyer* 761. See the various court decisions cited in F.A. Mann, *op.cit.* pp. 398–399; see also K. Böhlhoff and A. Baumanns in N. Horn (ed.), *op.cit.*, pp. 107 *et seq.*; W.F. Ebke, *op.cit.* pp. 81–82; B. Kohl, "Zur Anwendbarkeit von Art. VIII Abschnitt 2(b) des Abkommens von Bretton Woods" (1986) Iprax 285.

[28] D. Gränicher, *Die kollisionsrechtliche Anknüpfung ausländischer Devisenmasznahmen* (Basel & Frankfurt a.M., 1984); T.M. Asser, "Foreign exchange contracts and the applicability of Article 2 of the UCC" (1996) 113 Banking.L.J. 578; B. Crawford, "The legal foundations of netting agreements for foreign exchange contracts" (1993) 22 Can.Bus.L.J. 163; F.A. Mann, "The private international law of exchange control under the IMF Agreement" (1953) I.C.L.Q. 97; G. van Hecke, "Currency", *op.cit.* p. 18. According to the Executive Board of the IMF a national judge may not refuse to give effect to Art. VIII 2(b) on the ground that the violated exchange control regulation is not contrary to the public policy of the forum or that the law of the country that imposed the regulations is not the proper law of the contract; *Bundesgerichtshof*, March 11, 1970, (1970) N.J.W. 1002; *Oberlandesgericht Dusseldorf*, February 16, 1983, (1984) R.I.W. 397. See also J. Gold in N. Horn (ed.), *op.cit.*, p. 90.

[29] Art. VIII 2(b) is only applicable between members of the IMF: G. van Hecke, "Currency", *op.cit.*, p. 18.

law of the contract. In order to avoid the impact of Article VIII 2(b), transactions are sometimes localised in one of the few countries that have not yet become a member of the IMF or adopted Article VIII. However, it has been argued that Article VIII 2(b) is a rule of international customary law and part of international public policy.[30] On this ground, even non-IMF members may sanction breaches of foreign currency regulations.

Money of account and money of payment

9.04   **Definition**   The fact that the price in a contract is expressed in a specific currency does not necessarily imply that payment will be made in this currency. A distinction has to be made between the money of account (*monnaie de compte, Schuldwährung*) and the money of payment (*monnaie de paiement, Zahlungs-währung*).[31]

- The money of account is the currency the contract uses to measure the value of the price. In the event this currency depreciates or devaluates between the signing of the contract and the agreed payment date, the monetary obligation remains in principle the same (principle of nominalism), although the economic value of the price is diminished.[32]

- The money of payment is the currency in which the payment is effected.

When, for example, an international sale is concluded for a price of $1,000,000, this currency is considered as the money of account, so that payment may eventually be made in another currency.

One should select a stable currency of account, *i.e.* either a strong currency or a monetary unit of account (*e.g.* Special Drawing Rights (SDR) (see paragraph 9.26)) However, exporters usually prefer their own national currency as currency of account. In fact, the choice of the currency of account often depends on the bargaining power of the contracting parties and their need for foreign currencies.

---

[30] F. Rigaux, *op.cit.*, p. 71; G. van Hecke, "Currency", *op.cit.*, pp. 16–17. For the question whether in this case Art. VIII 2(b) is a rule of international customary law and is part of the international public policy of the forum, see I. Seidl-Hohenveldern, "Article VIII Section 2(b) of the IMF Articles of Agreement and public policy", in *Festschrift in Honor of Sir Joseph Gold, op.cit.* pp. 379 *et seq.*

[31] F. Arend, *Zahlungsverbindlichkeiten in fremder Währung* (Bern & Frankfurt a/M., 1989); R.M. Goode, *Payment Obligations in Commercial and Financial Transactions* (Sweet & Maxwell, London, 1983); N. Horn (ed.) *Monetäre Probleme in internationalen Handels- und Kapitalverkehr* (1976); N. Horn, "Payment and financing arrangements in international trade", in N. Horn (ed.), *The Law of International Trade Finance* (Kluwer, Deventer, 1989) pp. 9 *et seq.*; E. Krispis, "Money in private international law" (1967) 120 I.Rec.Cours. 191–311; F.A. Mann, *op.cit.*, pp. 205 *et seq.*; M. Niyonzima, *La Clause de Monnaie Étrangère* (Maklu, Antwerpen, 1991); C.M. Schmitthoff, *Export Trade* (10th ed., London, 2000) pp. 224 *et seq.*; G. van Hecke, "Conversion de la monnaie de compte en monnaie de paiement" (1979) Rev.Banque 61; *ibid.*, "Currency", *op.cit.* Vol. III, Ch. 36, pp. 15 *et seq.*; *ibid.*, "Crédits bancaires internationaux et conflits de lois" (1977) D.P.C.I. 321.

[32] This problem is to be governed by the *lex monetae*: R.M. Goode, *op.cit.*, p. 126; G. van Hecke, "Crédits bancaires internationaux" *op.cit.*, p. 322.

Different currency of account and currency of payment Very often, the **9.05** currency of account becomes also the currency of payment because the country of the place of payment allows payments in foreign currency. This is the case in most industrialised countries.

There may, however, be situations where the currency of payment differs from the currency of account:

1. The country of the place of payment may have exchange controls (see paragraph 9.02) that prohibit payment in foreign currencies.

2. The debtor may prefer to pay in the local currency of the place of payment (*i.e.* usually his own country). Such payment in local currency can generally not be refused under the law of the place of payment (the so-called local payment rule).[33] Payment in local currency can only be excluded by contract if such exclusion is valid under the local law.[34]

3. If the debtor does not pay in due time and proceedings must be commenced before the court, the local law may provide that the courts can only award judgments expressed in the currency of the forum. The court will then order the debtor to make payment of the equivalent of the currency of account in the local currency.[35] Many jurisdictions (*e.g.* United Kingdom, United States, Germany, Belgium) have abandoned this rule.[36]

However, the creditor cannot refuse payment in the currency of account.[37] When the currency of account depreciates, the debtor often opts for payment in the currency of account.

Conversion The issue of conversion arises when the currency of account is **9.06** not the currency of actual payment. Since the value of currencies fluctuates in

---

[33] H. Batiffol and P. Lagarde, *Droit International Privé* (LGDJ, Paris, 1983) Vol. II, p. 613; J. Dach, *op.cit.*, p. 156; R.M. Goode, *op.cit.*, p. 130; F.A. Mann, *op.cit.*, pp. 308 *et seq.*; K. Schmidt, *Geldrecht. Geld, Zins und Währung im deutschen Recht* (Berlin, 1983) 331 (with reference to BGB para. 244); G. van Hecke, *Emprunts internationaux, op.cit.*, p. 170. If the contract does not determine the place of payment, that place is determined by the proper law of the contract.

[34] F.A. Mann, *op.cit.*, p. 324.

[35] In the event of an order to pay in a currency other than the currency of account, some international contracts provide for a currency indemnity clause; for a sample, see G.A. Penn, A.M. Shea and A. Arora, *op.cit.*, p. 427. For a general survey, see M.M.Cohen, *Foreign Currency Judgments* [1996] Lloyd's Marit.&Com.L.Q. 323; S. Stern, "The courts and foreign currency obligations" [1995] Lloyd's Marit.&Com.L.Q. 494; N. Freedman, "Judgements in foreign currency—when to convert?" (Sept. 1984) I.F.L.R. 22. The author concludes as follows: " . . . the only way to achieve consistency with respect to currency conversion is to include a conversion rule as a contractual provision".

[36] See, for the U.K. *Ispahani v. Bank Melli Iran* [1998] Lloyd's Rep. Bank. 133; *Camdex International Ltd v. Bank of Zambia* [1997] C.L.C. 714; *Miliangos v. George Frank (Textiles) Ltd* [1976] A.C. 143 and further comments in Dicey and Morris, *op.cit.*, pp. 1612–1622; R.M. Goode, *op.cit.*, pp. 135 *et seq.* See for the U.S.: New York, C. Beal, "Foreign currency judgements: a new option for United States courts" (1998) U.Pa.J.Int'lEcon.L. 101; *Mitsui v. Oceantrawl Corp.* 906 F. Supp. 202 (1995); A.M.C. 558 (SDNY 1996); *Comptex v. La Bow* 783 F. 333, 337 (2d Cir.(1986)). See for Germany K. Schmidt, *op.cit.*, p. 367.

[37] G. van Hecke, "Conversion de la monnaie de compte en monnaie de paiement", *op.cit.*, p. 62; J.P. Mattout, *Droit Bancaire International* (2e éd., Paris, 1996).

time and place, the exact conversion date and place become important with regard to the proper rate of exchange.

In the contract, the parties may indicate the exchange rate to be applied (*e.g.* US$100,000 (currency of account) to be paid in euros (currency of payment) at the rate of exchange of the foreign exchange market in Brussels). The contract may also provide for a fixed rate of exchange (*e.g.* US$100,000 to be paid in euros at a fixed par of € 0.95 to US$1). When the contract does not fix an exchange rate, the courts will effect the conversion according to the proper law of the contract (see paragraph 1.31)[38] or according to their own law.

9.07   **Conversion date and place**   As regards the date with reference to which the rate of exchange is to be ascertained,[39] a number of countries (*e.g.* Belgium, Germany, the Netherlands, Austria) have adopted the "payment date" rule, *i.e.* the moment on which the creditor is actually in possession of the sum of money. For the creditor, this is a favourable solution[40] when the currency of payment depreciates in respect of the currency of account, but not in the event of a currency of account depreciation. In the latter case, the creditor will not receive the economic value he would have obtained if he were paid on the date of maturity. The debtor bears the exchange rate risk from the date the payment is due until the date the payment is made.

Some countries (*e.g.* Switzerland[41] and Italy[42]) have therefore adopted the "breach date" rule: the conversion date is the date of maturity of the debt. This arrangement favours the creditor when the currency of account depreciates in respect of the currency of payment after payment was due: the debtor will not retard payment because of the depreciation of the money of account. Conversely, the rule does not favour the creditor when the currency of payment depreciates after the date of maturity; the creditor has to bear the exchange rate risk from the date of maturity until the date of payment.[43]

The United Kingdom, which traditionally applied the breach date rule, has now adopted the payment date rule.[44] Outside proceedings, it means the rate at

---

[38] S.P. Dwyer, "Conversion of foreign money: contractual damages", in J.R. Lacey (ed.), *The Law and Policy of International Business: Selected Issues* (University Press of America, 1991).

[39] Approach of the *lex mercatoria*: "Conversion of the money of account into a different money of payment has to be made according to the exchange rate prevailing at the time when payment is due. If the debtor is in arrears, the creditor may require payment either at the rate when payment is due or at the rate of the time of actual payment": K.P. Berger, *The Creeping Codification of the Lex Mercatoria* (Kluwer, 1999).

[40] About the pros and cons of the various conversion methods, see G. van Hecke, "Conversion de la monnaie de compte en monnaie de paiement", *op.cit.*

[41] *Code des obligations*, Art. 84.

[42] *Codice civile*, Art. 1278.

[43] R. Birk, "Aufrechnung bei Fremdwährungsforderungen und internationales Privatrecht" (1969) *Aussenwirtschaftsdienst des Betriebs-Beraters* 12; *ibid.*, "Die Umrechnungsbefugnis bei Fremdwährungsforderungen im internationalen Privatrecht" (1973) *Ausenwirtschaftsdienst des Betriebs-Beraters* 425.

[44] *Miliangos v. George Frank (Textiles) Ltd* (1976) A.C. 443 cited; F.A. Mann, *op.cit.*, pp. 354 *et seq.*

the date of actual payment; in proceedings it means the date of enforceability of the judgment,[45] unless some other date is proposed by statute.[46]

In the United States, in case of court proceedings the conversion date is the date of judgment.[47] However, the Third Restatement on Foreign Relations[48] has favoured a flexible approach, applying the appropriate conversion rule, which best compensates the plaintiff without granting either party a windfall. This requires analysis of the facts and figures of each case. This approach makes it difficult to foresee which conversion rate will be applicable.[49]

It is generally admitted that a creditor, who is not paid by his debtor at the due date, is entitled to claim damages for the actual loss incurred because of the depreciation.[50]

As the rates of exchange frequently differ from place to place, it is important to determine the place of conversion. If this place is not fixed by the parties, the rate of exchange at the place of payment should prevail.[51]

PART II: PROTECTION AGAINST EXCHANGE RATE RISKS

Overview   Transborder payments usually involve the currency of a country   **9.08**
foreign to at least one party to the transaction. In some fields of trade, parties expect more profits from the currency speculation than from the supplied product itself. However, most often, parties want to protect themselves against exchange rate fluctuations.

Three specific techniques are often used:

(a) maintenance of value clauses;

(b) hedging transactions;

(c) exchange rate insurance.

---

[45] R.M. Goode, *op.cit.*, p. 137.

[46] Dicey and Morris, *op.cit.*, pp. 1612 *et seq.*

[47] F.A. Mann, *op.cit.* pp. 319–320 and 347–351. *Cf.* Restatement Second, Conflicts of Law, s.144.

[48] Third Restatement on Foreign Relations §823 (1987).

[49] In order to avoid the unfairness of the breach date and judgment date rules when the forum currency declines in relation to the currency of the obligation, some courts have awarded a separate sum to compensate for damages equal to the decline in value between the breach date and the judgment date. See *BV Bureau Wijsmuller v. United States* 633 F. 2D 202 (2D Cir. 1980). This method insures adequate compensation for the plaintiff regardless of the rule applied. R.A. Brand, "Exchange loss damages and the Uniform Foreign Money Claims" (1992) 23 Law&Pol'y Int'l Bus.Law 111.

[50] R.M. Goode, *op.cit.*, pp. 143–144. See Belgian Cass. September 4, 1975, Pasicrisie (1976) I 16; Italian Cass. March 29, 1938, (1939) J.D.I. 182; Switzerland I.F.L.R. Sept. 1984, pp. 43–44. *Cf.* also Art. 75(4) of the Convention on International Bills of Exchange and Promissory Notes (para. 9.31). It has been held that this right to compensation would also apply by virtue of the 1980 Vienna Convention on Contracts to the International Sale of Goods (para. 4.08): H. Asam and P. Kindler, "Ersatz des Zins—und Geldentwertungsschadens nach dem Wiener Kaufrechtsübereinkommen vom 11.4.1980 bei deutsch-italienischen Kaufverträgen" (1989) R.I.W. 841.

[51] F.A. Mann, *op.cit.*, p. 319.

Maintenance of value clauses

9.09   Introduction   Long-term contracts (*e.g.* purchase of aircraft, construction works, etc.) often contain maintenance of value clauses.[52] Such clauses relate the value of the currency of account to a specific index or to the value of a specific currency (index clause, currency clause). If this relationship is (substantially) changed at the date of maturity or at the time of actual payment, *e.g.* because of inflation or depreciation of the currency of account, the agreed sum of money will have to be adapted. The parties may also agree to renegotiate the contract, when the fluctuation exceeds the agreed margin.[53]

Maintenance of value clauses must be incorporated into the contract. Their validity and enforceability are in principle determined by the proper law of the contract.[54]

9.10   Gold and gold value clauses   Some traditional clauses, such as gold clauses (in which gold is the currency of payment) and gold value clauses (in which gold is used only as a standard of value while payment is effectuated in the currency of payment) have now become obsolete. Gold is no longer important in expressing the value of a currency. Moreover, the fluctuation of the gold price prevents it from functioning any longer as a stable standard of value. In international treaties, the gold and gold value clauses that were once frequently used,[55] are now systematically being replaced by references to the SDR (see paragraph 9.26) as the standard of value.[56]

9.11   Foreign currency clauses   A clause can provide that foreign currency will be used as the currency of account (*e.g.* euro, Swiss franc or U.S. dollar) in which the agreed sum of money must actually be paid. However, it may be that foreign

---

[52] See mainly W. Braun, *Vertragliche Geldwertsicherung im grenzüberschreitenden Wirtschaftsverkehr* (Berlin, 1982); W. Durkes (ed.), *Wertsicherungsklauseln* (9th ed., Recht und Wirtschaft, Heidelberg, 1982); H.J. Hahn, "Value clauses and international monetary law" (1979) G.Y.I.L. 53; International Chamber of Commerce, *Exchange Risks in International Contracts* (Paris, 1987); K. Schmidt, *op.cit.*, pp. 180 *et seq.*; C.M. Schmitthoff, "Legal aspects of monetary problems in export transactions", in N. Horn (ed.), *Monetäre Probleme im internationalen Handel und Kapitalverkehr* (Baden Baden, 1975) pp. 73 *et seq.*

[53] N. Horn, "Standard clauses on contract adaptation in international commerce", in N. Horn (ed.), *Adaptation and Renegotiation of Contracts in International Trade and Finance* (Kluwer Law & Taxation, Deventer, 1985) 126.

[54] G. van Hecke, "Crédits bancaires internationaux", *op.cit.*, p. 322; K. Schmidt, *op.cit.*, pp. 198 *et seq.*; F.A. Mann, *op.cit.*, pp. 271 *et seq.* Apart from any special legislation, the principle of nominalism as such does not invalidate maintenance of value clauses. In some countries, nominalism has been introduced by statute. Art. 1895 of the French and Belgian Civil Code, for example, expressly recognises nominalism for loans, but it is generally admitted that this provision does not constitute a mandatory rule; F.A. Mann, *op.cit.*, p. 169.

[55] See T. Treves, "Conventions de droit privé uniforme et clauses-or" (1976) Riv.dir.int.civ.&proc. For the conversion problems in this respect, see R.S. Rendell, "International treaties: effect of price of gold" (June 1984) I.F.L.R. 37–38; P. Nicholas, "La conversion du 'Franc' des conventions internationales de droit privé maritime" (1981) Dr.Mar.Fr. 285.

[56] J. Gold, *Legal and Institutional Aspects of the International Monetary System* (IMF, Washington, 1984) II, pp. 592 *et seq.* See also UNCITRAL Provisions on unit of account and adjustment of liability in international transport and liability conventions (July 1982) in C.J. Cheng, *Basic Documents on International Trade Law* (3rd ed., Kluwer, 1999) pp. 641 *et seq.*

exchange restrictions at the place of payment prohibit payment in foreign currency (see paragraph 9.02).

If the currency of account will not be also the currency of payment, the clauses should also specify the date and place for the conversion rate (see paragraph 9.07).

Currency option clauses Currency option clauses express the debt in two or   **9.12**
more currencies of account or currencies of payment. At the date of maturity, one of the parties will have the option of choosing between the stipulated currencies.[57]

An alternative form of the currency option clause is the composite currency clause, in which the money of account or the money of payment is expressed in the SDR. At the date of payment, the currency unit may then be "decomposed" into one or more of the constituent currencies, at the option of one of the parties.

Index clauses Index clauses linked to price or other standards of value are   **9.13**
widely used in domestic transactions to protect against any depreciation of the domestic currency's purchasing power.[58] They are, however, rare in international transactions, where no common index is available.[59]

Sometimes developing countries wish to link their sales prices to the price evolution in industrialised countries. UNCITRAL has made efforts in this respect to establish a proper international index clause.[60]

Revision clauses In long-term contracts, parties can agree to review the   **9.14**
contractual terms, and in particular the monetary obligations, in specific circumstances[61] (cost increase, hardship, etc.). Adaptation, revision or escalation[62] clauses may thus allow a fresh assessment or a periodical revision of the price.

Hedging transactions

Intra-concern hedging In order to reduce the exchange rate risk, companies   **9.15**
may try to reach a balance between income and expenditure in a specific foreign currency (matching). However, in practice a perfect balance is hardly ever found.

---

[57] See mainly Ph. K. Irani, "Multi-currency clauses and conflict of laws issues", in K. Kheng Lian (ed.) *Current Developments in International Banking and Corporate Financial Operations* (Butterworths, London, 1989) pp. 76 *et seq.*, with model clauses, *op.cit.*, pp. 92 *et seq.*

[58] F.A. Mann, *op.cit.* p. 146.

[59] C.M. Schmitthoff, *op.cit.*

[60] (1981) UNCITRAL Yearbook 70; J. Gold, *op.cit.*, II, 139.

[61] F.A. Mann, *op.cit.*, p. 144; N. Horn, "Payment and financing arrangements in international trade", *op.cit.*, p. 11.

[62] In practice, escalation and rise and fall clauses are frequently used. For example: "Unless firm prices and charges are expressly agreed upon, the Seller shall be entitled to increase the agreed prices and charges by the same amount by which the prices and charges, including the cost of labour and other production costs, to be paid or borne by the Seller have been increased between the date of the quotation and the date of delivery."

Monetary cross-claims in foreign currency are set off so that the exchange risk only affects the excess. To this end, set-off arrangements may be made by which the parties eventually receive the net balance (netting).[63]

Within company groups the exchange rate risk is often passed to a specialised subsidiary, *e.g.* a re-invoicing company or a currency management centre.[64]

9.16   **Forward exchange contracts**   A creditor of an amount in foreign currency may conclude a forward exchange contract (forex). The creditor sells to the bank a corresponding amount of the foreign currency at a forward exchange rate, irrespective of the spot rate of the foreign currency at the date of maturity. Consequently, at the day of payment, the creditor receives the previously fixed amount of domestic currency.[65] If the debtor wants to hedge against the exchange risk, he may conversely in advance buy the amount of foreign currency he has to pay.

The advantage of forward exchange contracts is that subsequent changes in the rate of exchange no longer affect the transaction. However, the spot rate of exchange at the date of maturity may be more appealing than the agreed forward rate. This handicap can be resolved by means of a break forward contract: under such an agreement, the customer can terminate the forward exchange contract if a previously agreed rate of exchange (the break rate) is attained.

Forward exchange markets exist for most currencies commonly used in international trade.

9.17   **Cross-currency swaps**[66]   Currency swap agreements are mainly used for long-term transactions involving considerable sums of money.

In a currency swap agreement, two parties decide to exchange sums of one particular currency for sums of another currency over a certain period at an agreed interest rate. The operation can be analysed as an exchange by the parties of the cost of their respective debts, expressed in different currencies.[67]

For example: A is creditor of a sum of $x at July 1, and wants to book these receivables in euros. B is creditor of a sum of €y at July 1, and wants to book these receivables in dollars. A and B decide to make a swap of their respective receivables. A becomes a future creditor (on July 1) in euros, B becomes a future creditor in dollars. In the hypothesis that $x equals €y, the exchange risk no

---

[63] See, *e.g.* S. Borenstein, "Netting", in B. Antl, *Management of Currency Risk, op.cit.* pp. 231 *et seq.*; Ph. Wood, "Netting agreements in organized and private markets", in D.A. Kingsford-Smith (ed.) *Current Developments in Banking and Finance* (Sweet & Maxwell, London, 1989) pp. 1 *et seq.*; Bank For International Settlements, *Report on Netting Systems* (Basle, 1989).

[64] See F.W. Meierjohann, "The issue of organisational structure", in B. Antl, *op.cit.*, pp. 119 *et seq.*; *ibid.*, "Multi-currency management centres", *op. cit.* pp. 215 *et seq.*

[65] D.B. Cox, *Finance of International Trade* (4th ed., Northwich, Worcester, 1988) pp. 9–19; N. Douch, *op.cit.* pp. 391 *et seq.* For a detailed study, S. Das, "Forward foreign exchange contracts", in B. Antl, *op.cit.* pp. 245 *et seq.*

[66] See P. Goris, *The Legal Aspects of Swaps* (Graham & Trotman/Martinus Nijhoff, 1994); S. de Covny, *Swaps* (Woodhead-Faulkner, Cambridge, 1991); S.R. Henderson and J.A.M. Price, *Currency and Interest Rate Swaps* (2nd ed., Butterworth, London, 1988); C.R. Beidleman, *Interest Rate Swaps* (Irwin Burr Ridge, 1991); H. Popper, *International Capital Mobility: Direct Evidence from Long-term Currency Swaps* (Washington D.C., 1990); R.G. Brown, *Foreign Currency Options* (Butterworth, London, 1989).

[67] International Chamber of Commerce, *Exchange Risks in International Contracts, op.cit.*, p. 16.

longer exists and the respective currencies are delivered at the due date. In practice, however, receivables to be swapped are generally due on different dates and are not of equivalent value. The swap transaction then has to be adjusted (*e.g.* with additional compensation) to take into account these differences in due dates and value. The exchange risk will only remain for the part of the receivables not covered by the swap.

There are specific markets for parties who envisage swap transactions.

Foreign currency accounts   Companies which regularly effect and receive payments in the same foreign currencies, may use foreign currency accounts. To that end, a separate account is opened for each foreign currency. The exchange rate risk is limited through the set-off between incoming and outgoing. The balance may then be converted into the domestic currency of the company at the most favourable time, *i.e.* at the most favourable exchange rate. **9.18**

Foreign currency loans and deposits   A creditor may also enter into a foreign currency loan to hedge against the exchange rate risk. The foreign currency borrowed is immediately converted into domestic currency and passed on to the account of the creditor. The loan is to be reimbursed with the foreign currency which the creditor will receive from his debtor at the date of payment. **9.19**

The debit interest the loan entails is counterbalanced by the credit interest the creditor receives on the amount in domestic currency. A currency loan is attractive when the difference in interest rates between the currency loans is rather small.

Conversely, a debtor may also limit the exchange rate risk by exchanging a currency deposit for a foreign currency loan.

Currency futures and currency options   A currency future is a contract whereby parties agree to buy or sell a given currency at a fixed price at a specified future date. **9.20**

A currency option is a contract that gives one party, in the course of a specified agreed period, the right (but does not oblige him) to buy (call option) or sell (put option) a given amount of currency at a fixed price (exercise or strike price), in consideration of the payment of a premium (usually 2 to 3 per cent of the amount of the option).[68] The holder of the option has the right to decide not to exercise his option.

Unlike currency options, currency futures contain undertakings that the parties have to perform.

Futures and options can be negotiated on specialised markets for a limited number of currencies.[69]

---

[68] International Chamber of Commerce, *Exchange Risks in International Contracts op.cit.* p. 18; M.D. Fitzgerald, "Currency options", in B. Antl, *Management of Currency Risk, op.cit.* pp. 301 *et seq.* The so-called American option must be exercised within a determined period, while the so-called European option must be exercised at a fixed date.

[69] See R.G. Brown, *Foreign Currency Options* (Butterworths, London, 1989); A. Buckley, *op.cit.*, pp. 183 *et seq.*; B.L. Carroll, *Financial Futures Trading* (London, 1989).

Exchange rate insurance

9.21 **Export credit insurance** Export credit insurance (see paragraph 8.26) also allows exporters to hedge against exchange rate risks. However, to the extent that an exchange rate risk is closely connected with a "political risk" (see paragraph 8.27), private export insurance companies usually refuse to cover such risk. In most industrialised countries, insurance cover for exchange rate risks is therefore provided by public agencies.

PART III: PAYMENT IN EURO AND SDR

The Euro

9.22 On January 1, 1999, the euro[70] became the official currency of 11 of the 15 Member States of the European Union[71] with a fixed conversion rate against their national currencies.[72] Since then the value of the euro against the other currencies, including those of the four Member States staying out of the euro zone, has fluctuated according to market conditions.

The introduction of the euro was expected to bring numerous benefits. For example, the single currency would reduce transaction costs for intra-E.U. trading. Prices, it was hoped, would fall significantly as a result of increased competition and price comparability in euro countries. Market transparency and lower costs of business investments should facilitate transnational investments. The euro is also expected to yield geopolitical benefits: Europe will at last have monetary and financial influence commensurate with its economic significance, and European policy will become more influential. However, there still is

---

[70] G. Bekerman and M. Saint-Mark, *L'euro* (PUF, Paris, 1999); C. Bamfort, "The change to a Single Currency", C.A.E. Godbart, "The transition to EMU" and H. Wittelsberger, "Legal aspects of the change over to a Single Currency", in *European Economic and Monetary Union : The Institutional Framework* (Kluwer, 1997) pp. 5–37; C. Bamfort, "The change to a single currency: legal problems and solutions" (1996) Butt. J. Int'l. Banking & Fin. l. ; N. O'Neill, "Cross-border payment arrangements for the euro" (1998) 4 Butt. J. Int'l. Banking & Fin. L.; F. Riolo, "EU: Legal Framework of the Euro" (1999) 4 Bank. L.J. 8; J.M.Sorel, "L'Euro vu de l'exterieur: une monnaie entre puissance et incertitudes" (2000) 1 J.D.I. 7–33.

[71] Austria, Belgium, Finland, France, Germany, Ireland, Italy, Luxembourg, the Netherlands, Portugal and Spain. The 12th member, Greece, joined the euro on January 1, 2001 (Council Regulation 1478/2000 [2000] O.J. L167/19).

[72] 1 euro =

40.3399	BEF - LUF	7.66 %
1.95583	DEM	34.38 %
166.386	ESP	5.40 %
6.55957	FRF	17.47 %
0.787564	IEP	4.72 %
1936.27	ITL	12.94 %
2.20371	NGL	10.53 %
13.7603	ATS	2.38 %
200.482	PTE	1.30 %
5.94573	FIM	3.22 %

(Weights of 11 constituent currencies of the euro) Council Regulation 2866/98 [1998] O.J. L359/1 on the conversation rates between the euro and the currencies of the Member States adopting the euro. All rates took the form of six significant figures expressing the value of one euro in the various national currencies. All six figures must be used in all calculations: this is crucial to the principle of total equivalence.

a risk that growth and inflation rates differ from one euro country to another. Inflation and budget imbalances have to be kept in check by co-ordination of economic policies and the common monetary policy. Prudent fiscal and monetary policies should keep interest rates on the euro and prices within the euro countries relatively low and stable.

Of course the transition to a single currency will bring with it a few drawbacks[73]: the rules on conversion and rounding off, designed to guarantee fair conversions, make for complex calculations. "Euro clauses", used to convert national currency into euro, must comply with Community regulations.

The historical and legal background of the euro The history of the euro,   **9.23** linked to that of the European Monetary Union (EMU), goes back to 1968, when a blueprint for the stage-by-stage realisation of economic and monetary union was set out. In 1979 the European Monetary System (EMS) was established: bilateral rates were fixed between all currencies in the system and had to fluctuate within pre-set margins. At the centre of the EMS was the ECU, a basket currency made up of fixed percentages of the participating national currencies. In 1992 the Maastricht Treaty introduced a legal basis for the EMU and the single currency.

In 1995 the European Council decided that the new currency would be known as the "euro" and set firm dates for the transition period (January 1, 1999 to December 31, 2001) and the final period (January 1, 2002 to July 1, 2002 at the latest).

In the transition period there was a total equivalence between the euro unit and the national currency units, with fixed conversion rates. The subdivisions of the national currencies were maintained. In the final period, which started on January 1, 2002, euro notes and coins were brought into circulation.

Continuity of contracts The principle of continuity of contracts[74] forbade   **9.24** contracting parties from altering or terminating contracts because of the introduction of the euro. Agreement to make payment in an old national currency became an obligation to make payment in its equivalent euro amount.[75]

However, a contract could be renegotiated or terminated if it contained a valid clause to that effect.[76]

---

[73] See P. Temperton, (ed.), *The Euro* (John Wiley & Sons, 1997); D. Miles, *The Ostrich and the EMU: Policy Choices Facing the United Kingdom* (London, 1997); K. Jones, "The euro—ready or not: trading implications of the new common currency" (1999) 22 Fordham Int'l. L. J. 786 ; M. Dassesse, "The new legal environment of the euro zone: a potential minefield ahead?" (1998) 5 Butt. J. Int'l. Banking & Fin.L.

[74] Art. 16 of the Regulation 1103/97 on certain provisions relating to the introduction of the euro of June 17, 1997; [1997] O.J. L162/1.

[75] H. Freis, "Continuity of contracts after the introduction of the euro: the United States response to European economic and monetary union" (1998) 53 Bus. Law 701; M. Gruson, "The introduction of the euro and its implications for obligations denominated in currencies replaced by the euro" (1997) 21 Fordham, Int'l L. J. 65; J.S. Tamburini-Kender and E. Putman, " L'euro et le droit des contrats" (1998) R.I.D.E. 313–324.

[76] Abuses of such clause are sanctionable under the Council Directive 93/13 on unfair clauses ([1993] O.J. 95/29).

9.25   **The role of the European Central Bank**   The European Central Bank (ECB) plays an important role in relation to the euro. The ECB (with its seat in Frankfurt), in conjunction with the national central banks (NCBs) of the E.U. Member States, form the European System of Central Banks (ESCB). The NCBs of the E.U. Member States which do not participate in the euro area are members of the ESCB with a special status: they are still allowed to conduct their respective national monetary policies and do not take part in the decision-making regarding the single monetary policy for the euro area and the implementation of such decisions.

The primary objective of the ESCB is to maintain price stability. It supports the general economic policies of the European Union and acts in accordance with the principles of an open market economy. The basic tasks to be carried out by the ESCB are :

- to define and implement the monetary policy of the European Union;

- to conduct foreign exchange operations;

- to hold and manage the official foreign reserves of the Members States; and

- to promote the smooth operation of payment systems.

The European Central Bank, assisted by the NCBs, collects the necessary statistical information either from the competent national authorities or directly from economic agents.

The ECB may impose fines and periodic penalty payments on undertakings that fail to fulfil an obligation arising from ECB regulations or decisions.

Special Drawing Rights

9.26   **SDRs and IMF**   Special Drawing Rights (SDRs), the reference value for determining transactions with the IMF, were created in 1969 by the International Monetary Fund (IMF) with the main purpose of introducing new international liquidity and monetary reserves.[77] Indeed, at that time the lack of sufficient traditional monetary reserves (mainly currencies) made it difficult for several central banks to deliver the required foreign currencies for international payment transactions.[78]

---

[77] Articles of Agreement of the IMF, First Amendment (1969). See J. Carter Murphy, "International moneys: official and private" in *Festschrift in Honor of Sir Joseph Gold* (Recht und Wirtschaft, Heidelberg, 1990), pp. 237 *et seq.*

[78] The prolonged deficit in the balance of payments of the U.S. was mainly responsible for the first major reform of the international monetary system, the invention of special drawing rights. Members of the IMF were worried about the accumulation of the U.S. dollars in their reserves, or the accumulation of them without an exchange guarantee, but they were also worried that elimination or reduction of the U.S. deficit would retard the growth of monetary reserves. On the role of the SDR in international trade, see J. Gold, "Aspects of the IMF's activities in relation to international trade", in J.J. Norton (ed.), *World Trade and Trade Finance* (Bender, New York, 1985) pp. 1 *et seq.*

The SDR is a composite currency, *i.e.* a basket consisting of the following four most-traded convertible currencies: U.S. dollar: 45 per cent, euro: 29 per cent, yen: 15 per cent, pound sterling: 11 per cent. The value of the SDR can be found on the web.[79]

SDRs have replaced the monetary gold as money of payment between the IMF and participating members.[80] SDRs are also being used as a unit of account. They are often used as such in treaties. For agreements between private parties, however, they do not seem to be very popular, although they are a unit of account which refers in a balanced way to the important world currencies.[81]

PART IV: BILLS OF EXCHANGE AND PROMISSORY NOTES

Function in international trade

Characteristics   The history of international trade is closely linked to bills of **9.27** exchange and promissory notes. As early as the twelfth century, money-changers in Northern Italy were exchanging money into foreign currency for their clients, importers who purchased goods abroad.[82] Exposed to the risk of robbery and other perils when taking the currency to fairs,[83] the traders were happy for money-changers to take care of the money transfer: the client would pay the amount in local currency and obtain a receipt promising that the equivalent amount would be refunded in foreign currency abroad. Although there may have been earlier forms of such transactions in the Arab world of finance, these receipts are commonly regarded as the first promissory notes. Later, instead of taking the money to the place of destination, the money-changer had a foreign colleague pay the required amount in his local currency.[84]

A bill of exchange (or draft) is an unconditional order requiring payment at a fixed future time, of a certain sum in money to the bearer of the draft or to the order of a specified person. The order to pay usually emanates from a creditor (seller, exporter), who is called the *drawer*. The order is addressed to the debtor (buyer, importer), who is called the *drawee*. The drawee becomes the *acceptor* when he expressly confirms in writing on the draft that he will pay. The order is usually given to a third party but can also be given to the drawer (in which case the bill of exchange may be treated as a promissory note).

The payee, the beneficiary of the bill, can easily transfer the obligations stipulated in the bill by way of endorsement of the bill to a third party, called the

---

[79] See www.imf.org.

[80] R.W. Edwards, *op.cit.*, pp. 207 *et seq.*

[81] F.A. Mann, *op.cit.*, p. 500.

[82] R. Welter, "Bills of exchange in international trade", in P. Volken, *International Contracts and Payments* (Graham & Trotman, 1991); J.S. Rogers, *The Early History of Law of Bills and Notes: a Study of the Origins of Anglo-American Commercial Law* (Cambridge University Press, Cambridge, 1996).

[83] M. Rowe, "Bills of exchange and promissory notes—uses and procedures in international trade", in N. Horn (ed.), *The Law of International Trade Finance* (Kluwer International Deventer, 1989), p. 243.

[84] G. Ripert, and R. Roblot, *Traité de Droit Commercial* (16th ed., Paris, 2000) vol. 2, at para. 1916.

endorsee. (The bill can, for instance, be endorsed to the bank to be discounted.) The endorsee so becomes a holder of the bill, and can in turn endorse it. The possibility of successive endorsements is unlimited.

A *promissory note* is an unconditional promise to pay at a fixed future time a certain sum in money to the bearer of the note or to the order of a specified person. The promissory note is to be distinguished from the bill of exchange because it contains a direct promise of payment by the person who signs it, where a bill of exchange is an order to pay. A promissory note does not involve a drawee. However, by emitting the promissory note, the maker assumes the same obligations as a drawee who has accepted a bill of exchange.

The bill of exchange and the promissory note are negotiable instruments that exist independently of the underlying transaction that gave rise to the instrument. They are "autonomous" or "abstract" instruments, independent from the commercial deal, so that any defence arising from the underlying agreement (*e.g.* non-performance of the seller) cannot be raised by the debtor under the bill of exchange or promissory note against the bona fide holder thereof.

Both the bill of exchange and the promissory note are subject to strict formal requirements (the so-called *rigueur cambiaire*) since the unconditional payment order or promise appears directly from the instrument itself. As long as the legal forms are respected, bills of exchange and promissory notes contain secure commitments.

In international trade, bills of exchange are often used in payment and financing constructions. In international sales, bills of exchange sometimes are drawn in duplicate: one document accompanies the goods sold and may get lost or destroyed during transportation; the second document is forwarded to the collecting bank. If both documents are adequately drafted, payment of one document discharges the whole bill.

Promissory notes play a less important role in international trade.

Different systems

9.28   **Diversity of rules**   The law of bills of exchange and promissory notes is not the same in the two main legal systems of the world:

- Some (mostly civil law) countries have implemented in their national law the Geneva Uniform Law relating to Bills of Exchange and Promissory Notes.[85] This Uniform Law, mainly based on French and German law, is

---

[85] The national laws of most European countries are largely based on the three so-called Geneva Conventions of 1930. After preliminary work effected by the two Conferences of the Hague in 1910 and 1912, the draft of the League of Nations was completed at the Geneva Conference in 1930. Three conventions were signed there: 1. the Convention providing a uniform law for bills of exchange and promissory notes; 2. the Convention for the settlement of certain conflicts of laws in connection with bills of exchange and promissory notes, and 3. the Convention on the stamp laws in connection with bills of exchange and promissory notes. Austria, Belgium, Denmark, Finland, France, Germany, Greece, Hungary, Italy, Luxembourg, Monaco, the Netherlands, Norway, Poland, the Soviet Union, Sweden, Switzerland, Brazil, Japan ratified all three Conventions and adopted the text of the Uniform Law as national law.

accepted in the countries of the European Continent (including central and eastern Europe),[86] in some Asian countries,[87] and in Brazil and Australia.

- The common law countries have generally adopted a system that goes back to the U.K. Bills of Exchange Act 1882 and to the United States Uniform Negotiable Instruments Act 1896. This system applies in the United Kingdom, most countries of the Commonwealth, the United States, in some South American countries and in Oceania.[88]

Both systems contain divergent substantive rules on essential issues. Moreover, the interpretation by the national courts of the said "uniform" rules is sometimes very different. The co-existence of two major systems is very inconvenient in a matter where formalities are highly important as they govern the validity of the instrument and its legal effects. Moreover, a bill of exchange can be subject to different national laws. For example, it can be drawn by a company in the United States, accepted by an importer in England and avalized (see paragraph 9.29) by the mother company of the importer in Germany while it is payable at a bank in Switzerland and endorsed before its maturity to a company in Poland. Each succeeding stage is in principle governed by the local law.

Essential differences   There are some essential differences between the   **9.29**
"Geneva system" and the common law system.

(a) Cutting off of claims and defences. In the Geneva system, the lawful holder of the negotiable instrument is in principle protected against rights and defences the debtor invokes on the basis of the underlying agreement.

  The common law system makes a distinction between a "normal" lawful holder and a holder "in due course":

  — a "normal holder" is open to a wide variety of defences and claims and is less protected than the lawful holder under the Geneva system;
  — a holder "in due course" is a holder who is without knowledge of any claim to, or defence upon, the instrument by the debtor or by a third person, and who therefore has special protection.

(b) Endorsement by an agent without authority. Under the Geneva system, an endorsement made by an unauthorised agent (without the consent of his

---

[86] Some countries did not ratify the Geneva Conventions, but their law is nearly identical to the Geneva Uniform Law. (See *e.g.* the former East European countries: Slovakia, Czech Republic, Albania, Bulgaria, Bosnia, Croatia, Serbia, Macedonia, Slovenia, Estonia, Latvia, Lithuania, Moldova, Ukraine, Belarus).

[87] *e.g.* the People's Republic of China, Indonesia, Japan, Jordan, South Korea, Lebanon, Mongolia, Oman, Saudi Arabia, Syria, Taiwan, Thailand, Yemen.

[88] The legislation of New Zealand, Fiji, Tonga, Hong Kong, India, Malaysia, Pakistan, the Philippines, Singapore, and Sri Lanka is nearly identical to the British Bills of Exchange Act 1882.

principal) has no effect on the title of the lawful holder of an instrument with an uninterrupted series of endorsements (Uniform Law, Article 16). The principal, who may have a course of action outside the negotiable instrument against the unauthorised agent, bears the loss and will have to pay the bona fide holder.

The common law system applies the maxim "know your endorser". An endorsement made by someone without authority does not confer rights upon the transferee or even qualify him as a holder.

(c) Effects of guarantee or aval. The Geneva Uniform Law has created a specific concept of guarantee, called the *aval*. The giver of an aval is bound in the same way as the person for whom the aval is given. If an aval does not specify for whom it is given, it is deemed to be given for the drawer. The rights and liabilities of the giver of the aval are governed solely by the law of bills of exchange. The liability of the giver of an aval is not accessory (contrary to a surety): the giver of an aval remains liable even if the guaranteed undertaking is null and void (provided, however, that the bill of exchange and the aval are formally valid) or if the person whose liability is guaranteed doesn't exist (*e.g.* the drawer of a fictitious bill). The Geneva concept of aval, which is rather formalistic, has proved its effectiveness, for example, in connection with forfeiting (see paragraph 8.42).

In the common law system, the guarantee relating to negotiable instruments is governed by the general principles of surety. This means that the guarantor of a negotiable instrument may raise against the normal holder any defences drawn from the law of surety. He may, for instance, assert that the underlying undertaking has been amended without the consent of the guarantor and to such an extent that the liabilities of the latter have been increased.

9.30 **International bills of exchange and exchange risks** International transactions entail exchange risks. Drawers often try to protect themselves against such risks by inserting maintenance of value clauses. These clauses, however, may make the amount due no longer "certain in money" so that they may invalidate the bill. Therefore, instead of a maintenance of value clause the bill of exchange should be drawn in a stable currency (see paragraph 9.26). The drawer of a bill of exchange can also impose the currency in which actual payment must be made.[89] If no currency of payment has been specified and if the amount due is mentioned in a currency other than the one of the place of payment, the debtor may also pay in the currency of the place of payment (local payment rule), converted on the day the bill is payable. If he defaults, the holder of the bill of exchange may request payment in local currency, at the exchange rate either of

---

[89] See Geneva Convention providing a Uniform Law for Bills of Exchange and Promissory Notes, June 7, 1930, Art. 41.

the day the bill is payable or of the day of payment. The drawer may also specify a fixed conversion rate in the bill of exchange[90] (see paragraphs 9.05 et seq.).

UNCITRAL Convention

In order to overcome the difficulties to which the different legal systems give **9.31** rise, UNCITRAL, after 17 years of extensive preparation and negotiation, adopted a Convention on International Bills of Exchange and Promissory Notes in 1987, which tries to combine both systems as fully as possible. This Convention was approved and opened for signature on December 9, 1988. However, the Convention has not yet come into force.[91]

The Convention only covers instruments that are expected to circulate internationally, i.e. between at least two nations, one of which is a contracting state, provided that either the place where the bill is drawn or the place of payment is situated in a contracting state. Moreover, the Convention will apply only to international negotiable instruments that bear in both their heading and their text the words "International Bill of Exchange (UNCITRAL Convention)" or "International Promissory Note (UNCITRAL Convention)" (Article 1).

The Convention addresses questions relating to the transfer of an international bill of exchange and promissory note and covers the rights and liabilities of parties to, and of holders of such instrument. It also addresses the presentation of such instrument, its non-acceptance or non-payment, and the conditions precedent to parties' rights of recourse. Moreover it deals with the discharge of liability, with lost bills and promissory notes and with time bars.

The UNCITRAL Convention contains a number of new provisions of practical importance for international trade.[92]

For instance, the Geneva Uniform Law allows the drawer to stipulate the charging of interest only if the instrument is "payable at sight or at a fixed period after sight". This rule led to the impractical method of drawing a separate bill for the interest. The UNCITRAL Convention (Article 7) allows the charging of interest on all kinds of bills and notes. Moreover, the interest to be paid may have a variable rate (Article 8). The UNCITRAL Convention also contains useful rules to reduce exchange rate risks.

It is too early to say that the Convention—notwithstanding its numerous attractive and novel features—has not been successful. However, the process of acceptance and ratification of this Convention so far has been very slow.

---

[90] The UNCITRAL Convention (see para. 9.31) reduces exchange rate risks by allowing instruments to be drawn in a unit of account which is established by an intergovernmental institution, or by agreement between two or more states (e.g. the euro (see para 9.22) and the SDR (see para. 9.26)). As a general rule, an instrument must be paid in the currency in which the sum payable is expressed (unit of account). The drawer may, however, specify in the instrument the currency of payment. If no rate of exchange is indicated in the instrument, the amount to be paid must be calculated according to the rate of exchange on the date of maturity. When no payment was made at the date of maturity and the currency depreciated afterwards, the holder can claim damages (Arts 75 and 76).

[91] The Convention enters into force after ratification by 10 countries. At the time of writing, only Guinea and Mexico had ratified it.

[92] Herrmann, G., "International bills of exchange and promissory notes: legal problems and disparities overcome by new United Nations Convention", in Horn, N. (ed.), *The Law of International Trade Finance* (Deventer, 1989), p. 259.

PART V: INTERNATIONAL PAYMENT ARRANGEMENTS

General overview

9.32   **Modes of payment**   Payment of course involves more risks in international than in domestic transactions because of the distance and lack of acquaintance between the parties. Specific arrangements have therefore to be made (see paragraph 9.02).

Only exceptionally do parties stipulate "cash with order" (CWO): for instance, when the creditor has doubts about the creditworthiness of his debtor.[93] For important international transactions, however, an advance payment is usually required. Payment "cash on delivery" or "cash against documents" (CAD) is accepted for minor transactions if the exporter is not acquainted with the financial status of his debtor. Very often, however, payment facilities (credit) are granted.

"Payment on open account" is particularly suitable if the parties are acquainted with each other and the creditor has no doubts about the solvency and the willingness of his debtor to pay. The exporter will send the goods and the financial and commercial documents to the buyer who is invited to pay on an agreed date. The buyer has the possibility to examine the goods before payment. If the goods do not conform, he will refuse payment. Most transactions within the E.U. countries are settled by payment on open account.

The use of bills of exchange is very popular in international trade. This mode of payment is dealt with in Part IV of this chapter.

Collection arrangements

9.33   **General**   Under a collection agreement, a bank from the country of the importer collects, as the agent of the bank of the exporter, the money from the importer, either in cash or by accepting a bill of exchange.[94] The collecting bank has to present to the importer certain financial (and commercial) documents related to the goods stipulated in the export contract (see paragraph 9.35).[95] The parties involved in the collection are:

(a) the principal, *i.e.* the exporter who must be paid;

(b) the remitting bank, which receives from the principal the documents, on which basis the payment can be demanded;

---

[93] CWO may be difficult when the exchange control regulation forbids payment without prior remittance of the transportation documents of the goods.

[94] See B. Clarke, "An outline of settlement methods", in B.W. Clarke (ed.), *op.cit.* pp. 195 *et seq.*; J.P. Lardinois, "Documentary collections", in B.W. Clarke, *op.cit.*, pp. 230 *et seq.*; E. Schinnerer, "Collection by banks and its documents", in N. Horn (ed.), *op.cit.*, pp. 187 *et seq.*; G. Sinclair, "Terms and conditions for international trade", in B.W. Clarke (ed.), *op.cit.*, pp. 161 *et seq.*

[95] N. Horn, "Payment and financing arrangements in international trade", *op.cit.*, p. 15.

(c) the collecting bank in the country of the importer, which acts as the agent of the remitting bank;

(d) the presenting bank, usually the bank of the importer, which proceeds to the collection upon presentation of the stipulated documents;

(e) the importer, who possibly becomes the drawee-acceptor in the event a bill of exchange has been issued.

Methods of collection   The following methods of documentary collection **9.34** are most commonly used:

(a) Documents against payment (D/P)   The documents of title are delivered to the buyer only on actual payment in cash, on the acceptance of a sight bill. The documents of title allow the buyer to request the delivery of the goods.

(b) Cash against documents (CAD)   The documents are delivered on actual cash payment.

(c) Documents against acceptance (D/A)   The documents are delivered against acceptance by the buyer of a bill of exchange, payable at an agreed maturity date. The accepted bill of exchange may be sent to the country of the exporter to be discounted (Documents against acceptance and return, D/AR).

It is advisable to provide for an aval in the event that the buyer is unable to pay at the date of maturity (D/A plus aval by . . .). Common law countries also use documents against acceptance and trust receipt (DA/TR), whereby the buyer holds the goods only provisionally for the account of the seller or the collecting bank.

(d) D/P in local currency   This method is often used when the buyer is established in a country with few reserve assets or strict exchange control regulations limiting payment in foreign currency. The buyer will pay in the local currency instead of in the currency of account. If the buyer is contractually not entitled to pay in local currency, he will have to bear the exchange rate risk until the exporter has obtained full payment in the money of account.[96]

(e) Documents against signature of a promissory note   This method is similar to the D/A and can be chosen when, for example, promissory notes are exempted from the stamp-duties which are levied on bills of exchange.

(f) Documents against receipt   The buyer delivers a (non-negotiable) receipt in exchange for the documents, while the payment is usually made on open account (see paragraph 9.32). This method is only suitable when the exporter does not doubt the solvency and willingness to pay of his debtor.

---

[96] J.P. Lardinois, *op.cit.*, p. 235.

A similar method is to be found under the documents against written undertaking to pay at due date.

(g) Documents against payment subsequent to acceptance of a time draft   The documents of title, as well as the accepted bill of exchange, are deposited at the presenting or collecting bank. They are delivered to the buyer after payment of the bill of exchange.

9.35   **Uniform Rules for Collections**   In 1956, the International Chamber of Commerce (see paragraph 2.30) adopted the Uniform Rules for Collections. These were last revised in 1995.[97] Collection is defined as follows:

"Collection means the handling by banks of documents as defined in sub-Article 2(b), in accordance with instructions received, in order to:

(i) obtain payment and/or acceptance, or

(ii) deliver documents against payment and/or against acceptance, or

(iii) deliver documents on other terms and conditions."

The documents referred to are:

"(a) 'financial documents', *i.e.* bills of exchange, promissory notes, cheques, or other similar instruments used for obtaining the payment of money;

(b) 'commercial documents', *i.e.* invoices, transport documents, documents of title or other similar documents, or any other documents whatsoever, not being financial documents."

The Uniform Rules further distinguish two types of collection arrangements:

(a) a clean collection, *i.e.* a collection of financial documents not accompanied by commercial documents; and

(b) a documentary collection, *i.e.* a collection of financial documents accompanied by commercial documents or of commercial documents only.

The Uniform Rules also provide how the collection must be realised: presentation of the documents; payment in local or foreign currency; form of protest; advice to the remitting bank,[98] charges and interests. They impose particular duties of care on the intervening banks.

---

[97] *ICC Uniform Rules for collections*, ICC brochure no. 522 (ICC Publications, 1995, Paris). See, *inter alia*, B. Clark, *The Law of Bank Deposits, Collections, and Credit Cards* (Warren, Gorham & Lamont, 1995); J. Bond, *The Complete Book of Collection Letters, Telephone Scripts, and Faxes* (New York, McGraw-Hill, 1994); J.K. Gatenby (ed.), *Recovery of Money* (8th ed., Longman, London, 1993); D.S. Coale, "What now? The future of international collection collections" (1999) 34 Tex.Int'l.L.J. 327; R.G. Ballen, J.P. Savage, and N.O. Littlefield, (1993) "Negotiable instruments, bank deposits and collections, and other payment systems" (1993) 48 Bus.Law. 1583.

[98] The advice of non-payment must immediately be communicated; see case law in R.W. Rendell, "United States—bank's duty on collection" (1987) I.F.L.R. (March) 40–41.

Model law on international credit transfers

UNCITRAL Model Law In 1992 UNCITRAL (see paragraph 2.23) **9.36** adopted a model law on international credit transfers.[99] The Model Law was prepared in response to a major change in the means by which international fund transfers are made. Payment orders are increasingly sent by electronic means rather than on paper.

The model law applies to credit transfers between a sending bank and a receiving bank from different states (Article 1, 1). Branches and separate offices of a bank are considered as separate banks (Article 1, 3). The model law covers paper transfers as well as electronic transfers of funds.

For the model law, a "credit transfer" is a series of operations to place funds at the disposal of a beneficiary (Article 2, a). Such credit transfer starts with the originator's payment order[1] and is completed when the beneficiary's bank accepts the payment order to place the funds at the disposal of the beneficiary (Articles 19 and 10, 1).

The parties involved in the transfer are:

(a) the sender (including the originator and any sending bank), who issues a payment order (Article 2, e);

(b) the receiving bank, which receives a payment order (Article 2, f);

(c) the intermediary bank, which is any receiving bank other than the originator's or the beneficiary's bank (Article 2, g).

The rights and obligations of parties to a credit transfer are elaborated in the model law. They may also be specified by agreement, unless otherwise provided in the model law (Article 4).[2] The credit transfer is governed by the law chosen by the parties; in the absence of agreement, the law of the state of the receiving bank will apply.[3]

---

[99] For the text, see Doc. UNCITRAL, ref. V. 93–91299 February 1994–3,000, United Nations, 1994. See also U.N. Schneider, "The uniform rules of international credit transfers under the UNCITRAL Model Law", in W. Hadding and U.N. Schneider (eds), *Legal Issues in International Credit Transfers* (Berlin, 1993), pp. 451–474; C. Felsenfield, "The compatibility of the UNCITRAL Model Law on International Credit Transfers with Article 4A of the UCC" (1992) 60 Fordham L. Rev. 53–75; G.C. Heinrich, "UNCITRAL—International credit transfers" (1992) 11 Int'l Banking and Fin. L. 78–79; G.C. Heinrich, "Funds transfers, payments and payments systems—international initiatives towards legal harmonisation" (1994) 28 Int. Lawyer 787–824; D. Bentley, "A payments law for the world: UNCITRAL Model Law on International Credit Transfers", in R.C. Effros (ed.), *Payment systems of the world* (New York, 1994); S.J. Karagorgiou, "Developments on the law of international credit transfers" (1994) 12 Int'lBank.&Fin.L. 119; B. Geva, "UNCITRAL Model Law on International Credit Transfers", in *ibid., The Law of Electronic Funds Transfers* (New York, 1992).

[1] A "payment order" is the unconditional instruction, by a sender to a receiving bank, to place at the disposal of a beneficiary a fixed or determinable amount of money (also in euros or SDRs), if the receiving bank is to be reimbursed by the sender and the instruction does not provide that payment is to be made at the request of the beneficiary (Art. 2(b)).

[2] Examples are to be found in Arts 5.3, 14.2 and 17.

[3] See Art. Y. Conflict of laws, as suggested by the U.N. Commission, in Doc. UNCITRAL, ref. V.93–91299 February 1994–3,000, United Nations, 1994, p. 1.

A receiving bank that is not the beneficiary's bank has to pay interest to the latter if the credit transfer is not completed in due time (Article 17). The beneficiary's bank is liable to its customer, in accordance with the law governing their relationship, if it doesn't place the funds at the latter's disposal within the time required (Articles 10, 1 and 17, 6). The liability of one bank to another bank as set out in the model law, may be specified by agreement or by a bank's standard terms. However, a bank may not reduce its liability to an originator or beneficiary that is not a bank (Article 17, 7).

The model law further provides that payments can be made by way of a multilateral or bilateral set-off system in which the banks participate (Article 6, b, iv).

The Cross-Border Payments Directive of the Council of the European Union,[4] that reflects principles of the UNCITRAL Model Law on international credit transfers, imposes specific requirements on financial institutions that conduct cross-border credit transfers on behalf of clients.[5] The Directive is clearly aimed at improving the efficiency of cross-border transfer of funds.[6]

PART VI: COUNTER-TRADE

9.37 **Introduction** Counter-trade (also called compensatory trade) consists of commercial transactions that, by virtue of a contract, are paid for in part or in whole in the form of delivery of goods (or, exceptionally, of services).[7]

---

[4] Directive 97/5/EC on cross-border transfers [1997] O.J. L043/25. Member States had to implement this directive by August 14, 1999. See also, M. Vasseur, "Les principaux articles de la CNUDCI sur les virements internationaux et leur influence sur les travaux de la Commission de Bruxelles concernant les paiements transfrontaliéres" (1993) J.I.B.L. 155–207; L. Bojer, "International credit transfers: the proposed E.C. Directive compared with the UNCITRAL Model Law" (1995) 10 J.I.B.L. 223–228.

[5] The Directive lays down three major requirements. First, the institution is required to inform its customers, both actual and potential, of the conditions for cross-border credit transfers (Art. 3). Secondly, the institution must, at customer's request, give a specific undertaking as to the time that the transfer will take, the charges that are payable and the exchange rate used (Article 5). Finally, where the sender's institution does not execute the transfer as required, Article 8 obliges it to refund to the customer the original amount plus any charges imposed and also pay him interest at the prevailing rate.

[6] See also, G. Walker, W. Blair and others, *Banking and Financial Services Regulation* (Butterworths, London, 1998).

[7] On counter-trade consult, *inter alia*, UNCITRAL *Legal Guide on International Counter-trade Transactions* (United Nations Publications, New York, 1993); J.C. Nobles and J. Lang, "The UNCITRAL legal guide on international counter-trade transactions: the foundation of a new era in counter-trade?" (1996) 30 Int.law. 739; C.G. Alexandrides and B.L. Bowers, *Counter-trade: Practices, Strategies and Tactics* (Wiley, New York, 1987); D. Carreau, T. Flory and P. Juillard, *Droit International Économique* (4th ed., L.G.D.J., Paris, 1998) pp. 253 *et seq.*; M. Fontaine, "Aspects juridiques des contrats de compensation" (1980) D.P.C.I. 181; D. Francis, *The Counter-trade Handbook* (Woodhead-Faulkner, Cambridge, 1987); J. Groothaert, "Financial co-operation and counter-trade", in M. Maresceau (ed.), *The Political and Legal Framework of Trade Relations between the European Community and Eastern Europe* (Nijhoff, Dordrecht, 1989) pp. 221 *et seq.*; S. Martin, *The Economics of Offsets: Defence Procurement and Counter-trade* (Harwood Academic Publ., The Netherlands, 1996); C.M. Korth (ed.), *International Counter-trade* (Quorum, New York, 1987; D. Marin and M. Schnitzer, *Tying Trade Flows: a Theory of Counter-trade* (Centre for Economic Policy Research, London, 1994); L.E. Mercado, "Quelques réflexions sur la commerce international de compensation" (2000) 2 R.I.D.E. 219–245 ; L. Moatti, "Countertrade in international commercial exchanges" (1995) I.B.L.J. 3–29; B.D. Townsend, *The Financing of*

Counter-trade may be defined as:

"a composite transaction in which one party supplies goods, services, technology or other economic value to the second party, and, in return, the first party
purchases from the second party an agreed amount of goods, services, technology or other economic value"[8]

A distinctive feature of these transactions is the existence of a link between the
supply contracts: the conclusion of the supply contracts in one direction is
conditioned upon the conclusion of the supply contracts in the other direction.

Some developing countries use counter-trade for the exchange of agricultural
surplus against equipment, oil, etc. Counter-trade has gained considerable popularity: more than one hundred countries have made regulations in this area,[9] and
about 15 to 20 per cent of world trade is deemed to take place by counter-trade.
A number of reasons explain this success.[10] Many countries have insufficient
hard currency or lack credit facilities to pay their imports.[11] Other countries want
to promote their own export through the counter-trade technique: through
counter-trade they can sell certain products which they could not, or only with
difficulty, have exported otherwise.[12]

"Payment" In legal terms, "payment" does not necessarily imply a transfer   **9.38**
of money. When the seller is "paid" in goods,[13] these goods are, in general, not
part of the seller's ordinary business. So the seller wants to resell them immediately in exchange for money. This will often be done through a trader, an
intermediary (broker or agent) who is specialised in this type of transaction.[14]

The exporter may also assign his rights under the counter-trade agreement to
a third party more familiar with the trade of these goods. This possibility to
assign may be recognised in the counter-trade agreement.

Counter-trade (Butterworth, London, 1986); M. Salem, "Les substituts aux transactions monét-
aires: le troc et les opérations apparentées", in Ph. Kahn (ed.), Droit et Monnaie: Etats et Espace
Monétaire International (Litec, Paris, 1988) pp. 507 et seq.; Schmitthoff's Export trade (10th ed.,
Sweet and Maxwell, London, 2000) pp. 240–248; A.B. Sta Maria, "Counter-trade", in N. Horn
(ed.), The Law of International Trade Finance (Kluwer Law & Taxation, Deventer, 1989) pp. 39
et seq.; B.D. Townsend, The Financing of Counter-trade (Butterworths, London, 1986).

[8] UNCITRAL Legal Guide on International Counter-trade Transactions (United Nations Publications., New York, 1993).

[9] Schmitthoff, op.cit., p. 241; C.G. Alexandrides and B.L. Bowers, op.cit., pp. 119 et seq.; D. Francis,
op.cit. pp. 160 et seq.

[10] See UNCTAD, Echanges Compensés doc. TD/B/C.7.82 of August 28, 1986.

[11] Certain countries, which have difficulty in repaying their foreign debt, have tried for some years
to "pay" through counter-trade (so-called debts for goods swaps).

[12] e.g. because of the protectionism by, for instance, the E.C. and the U.S., New Zealand had difficulty
in exporting lamb. Therefore, lamb was sold to Iran in exchange for oil.

[13] On "payment" in counter-trade, see, inter alia, M. Woiczik, "La compensation dans les échanges
internationaux: une approche de la fonction de paiement" (1990) R.I.D.E. 139; B.D. Townsend,
The financing of counter-trade (Butterworths, London, 1986).

[14] For the different types of traders, see S. Harris, "Counter-trade", in B.W. Clarke (ed.), Handbook
of International Credit Management (Gower, Aldershot, 1989) pp. 303–307. The function of the
trader is sometimes taken over by banks. For a list of traders in the U.S., see C.G. Alexandrides
& B.L. Bowers, op.cit., pp. 78 et seq., pp. 217 et seq.

In a deferred counter-purchase (see paragraph 9.45), one party may fear that the other party will be unable to perform. The other party can then pay a deposit in an escrow account at a bank where the money remains blocked until this other party has performed its undertakings.

The exporter may also take goods in advance from the importer (reverse counter-trade) and pay for them in foreign currency in the blocked escrow account.[15] This money will later be used for the financing of purchases by the importer.[16]

Examples of "counter-trade" contracts

9.39 **Barter** Barter is a contract where the parties give each other one good in exchange for another.[17] There are two kinds of barter:

(a) in true barter, goods are given in exchange for others without a determination of their economic value; this type is rarely used in international trade;

(b) valued barter is based upon the economic value of the exchanged goods.

Barter must be distinguished from reciprocal contracts of sale: the latter suppose two separate agreements (see below), while barter requires one single contract.

9.40 **Reciprocal contracts of sale** Reciprocal contracts of sale are the most common form of counter-trade. An exporter sells goods to an importer and simultaneously enters into another contract whereby he or another person undertakes to buy from the importer or another person goods that are produced in the importer's country. There are thus two parallel commercial contracts: the export sale and the counter-purchase.

Both sales contracts often provide for payment of the same sum. The amounts are thus set off (set-off trade).

A possible balance is to be paid with other goods or in a convertible currency. In the latter situation the value of import and export between the parties is often recorded on a settlement account and the balance must be paid in convertible currency on agreed expiry dates.

Some countries require the counter-purchase by the exporter to exceed the value of the export sale (counter-trade ratio).

---

[15] *cf., inter alia*, F. Dierckx, "Use of the 'Escrow Account' purchase operations" (1985) I.B.L.J. 821; C. Witz, "Les divers comptes bancaires dans les opérations de compensation internationale", Banque (Fr.), (Suppl. June (1988) 484 (Banque et droit)) pp. 18 *et seq.*

[16] D. Francis, *op.cit.*, pp. 75–82.

[17] In European countries (including the U.K.) a legal distinction is made between a contract of sale and an exchange contract. In the U.S., s.2–304(1) of the Uniform Commercial Code states that in a contract of sale, "the price can be made payable in money or otherwise".

The contracts are not always executed simultaneously: the counter-trade agreement (see paragraph 9.44) may provide that the exporter will buy goods as "payment" a few months or even years afterwards (deferred counter-purchase).

There are two types of reciprocal contracts of sale:

(a) The contracts can be made interdependent, in the sense that the importer only enters into a purchase contract with the exporter under the condition that the exporter enters into a counter-purchase contract. Consequently if one of the contracts is not performed, the other contract has neither to be performed (as if the parties had entered into one single contract).

(b) Parties can also enter into a counter-trade agreement, which regulates the transactions between the parties (see paragraph 9.45). Export sales and counter-purchases are in this case negotiated within the framework of the counter-trade agreement, without any formal link or reference in one contract to the other. Non-performance of one contract is sanctioned under the counter-trade agreement. This counter-trade agreement should therefore provide for sanctions (*e.g.* a penalty clause)[18] in the event of default by one of the parties.

Buy-back contracts   Buy-back contracts stipulate that the exporter shall be   **9.41** paid with products manufactured by the industrial plant he is constructing for the importer. These goods are best resold through a manufacturer in an industrialised country; this presupposes that the products are of sufficient quality for circulation under that manufacturer's own name.

In case of buy-back contracts, the exporter often finds himself in the unusual situation that he is paid with products that not only fall outside his normal business, but that moreover compete with the products of his other customers.

Buy-back contracts frequently contain a "preference clause" obliging the buyer not to ask a higher price for the products sold to the exporter than he would ask from other most-favoured customers under comparable conditions.[19]

Buy-back arrangements are mostly long-term contracts. This means that the exporter has no financing until the buy-back operation. These contracts therefore usually go hand in hand with a medium-term export credit (see paragraph 8.25).

Offset arrangements   In an offset arrangement, the exporter has to incorpo-   **9.42** rate in his delivered equipment specific parts manufactured in the country of

---

[18] See, for the problems this may cause, K. Hober, "Counter-trade: negotiating the terms" (1987) I.F.L.R. (March) 28; (April) 17.

[19] *e.g.*: "For the supplies in accordance with Clause [. . .] of this agreement the [exporter] will pay [the supplier], unless otherwise agreed, the lowest f.o.b. price charged under comparable conditions to any customer of [the supplier], except if supplied to a company on the attached list."

importation; or the exporter must establish a local company for the manufacturing of the parts; or he must use services from the importing country. Offset arrangements are frequently used for military equipment or aircraft.

Besides this direct offset there is also "indirect offset", where the exporter undertakes to acquire products and services in the importing country that have no connection with the delivered equipment.

9.43 **Bilateral clearing arrangements** A bilateral clearing arrangement is used mainly in counter-trade between developing countries and/or command-economy countries.

The two states open a joint current account in the national currency of one of them (the so-called "clearing currency") for their mutual counter-trade transactions. They fix an exchange rate for their currencies that applies to this account. The balance due to the state creditor by the state debtor must be paid on the agreed expiry date in a convertible currency in settlement of the counter-trade transactions.

Organisation of counter-trade

9.44 **The "counter-trade agreement"** Counter-trade is usually organised by the parties or government institutions within the framework of a basic agreement, the counter-trade (or framework) agreement. This agreement sets out the general provisions that apply to the coming counter-trade transactions between the parties, or—in the event the agreement is concluded between government institutions—between all exporters and importers of the relevant countries.[20]

Counter-trade agreements usually provide for the following matters.

(a) Indication of the goods suitable for counter-trade. It is important for the exporter that there is a market for the goods in which he will be paid but which he cannot use.

(b) Valuation of the goods to be given as payment, whereby it is important to specify whether the agreed "price" is FOB or CIF.

(c) Since the goods or services, delivered in return, are not always a full compensation, the balance is usually paid in foreign currency. This is done through a clearing account (see paragraph 9.43).

---

[20] See, *e.g.* G.C. Branton, "Limitations on counter-trade agreements" in J.D. Lew and C. Stanbrook, *International Trade: Law and Practice* (Euromoney Publications, London, 1990) pp. 191 *et seq.*; C. Guyot, "Counter-trade: recent legal developments and comparative study" (1986) I.B.L.J. 759; K. Hober, *op.cit.*, p. 17; C.M. Schmitthoff, *op.cit.*, pp. 247 *et seq.*; UNCITRAL, "Draft outline of the possible content and structure of a legal guide on drawing up international counter-trade contracts" (Report of the Secretary General (1989), ref. A/CN 9/322); the Economic Commission for Europe of the UN published a Guide on drawing up international counter-trade contracts in 1990; see also D. Francis, *op.cit.*, pp. 61–66.

(d) It is important for the exporter to be entitled to assign his rights and duties to a third party.[21]

(e) Many counter-trade agreements restrict the right of the exporter to sell goods received as payment, to certain countries.

(f) Many counter-trade transactions, particularly the reciprocal contracts of sale, require a security (usually in the form of an escrow account (see paragraph 9.43) or a bank guarantee from a bank of the country of importation).[22]

(g) The clauses, common in international contracts of sale, should also be part of the counter-trade contracts (*e.g.* clauses on applicable law and jurisdiction).

Counter-trade and the GATT   Article XI(1) of the GATT prohibits quanti-   **9.45**
tative restrictions on import and export (see paragraph 3.26). A national regulation that imposes the use of counter-trade techniques for the import of goods is contrary to this provision, because the import of goods is made dependent on export.[23]

It has been argued, however, that Article XI(1) of the GATT does not apply to all aspects of international trade with developing countries, so that counter-trade obligations imposed by developing countries may be compatible with the GATT. Moreover, Article XI(1) of the GATT allows for import restrictions, for instance, in order to correct the deficit of the balance of payments (see paragraph 3.46).

State imposed counter-trade is, however, often difficult to reconcile with the objective of the GATT, which is to regulate world trade on a multilateral rather than a bilateral basis (as is the case with counter-trade) (see paragraph 3.02).[24]

The Government Procurement Agreement (Article XVI) forbids the contracting states to seek or consider offsets, including counter-trade, in the awarding of contracts (see paragraph 3.37).[25]

---

[21] For instance, the following clause is common: "The [exporter] shall not assign or transfer to a third party all or part of the benefits or obligations of this Agreement without the written consent of [government institution of the country of importation], and such consent if given shall not relieve the [exporter] from any liabilities or obligations under this Agreement. The assignments shall be in the form annexed hereto as Schedule [...]."

[22] For an example, see K. Hober, *op.cit.* p. 18.

[23] F. Roessler, "Counter-trade and the GATT legal system" (1985) Journal of World Trade Law 604; L.H. Liebman, "GATT and counter-trade requirements" (1984) Journal of World Trade Law 252; M.R. Czinkota, "The role of counter-trade in future GATT deliberations" in C.M. Korth (ed.), *op.cit.*, pp. 169–177.

[24] (1985) GATT, *Basic Instruments and Selected Documents* 62; see also D. Carreau, T. Flory and P. Juillard, *op.cit.*, pp. 259–260.

[25] An exception may be made for developing nations.

CHAPTER 10

INTERNATIONAL PROCEDURE

PART I: DOMESTIC PROCEDURAL LAW AND INTERNATIONAL RULES

Key issues   As trade becomes more international, cross-border trade disputes **10.01** also are on the increase. Increasingly, courts are called upon to resolve disputes with a foreign party.

The first question is whether the court has jurisdiction over the case. Each country has its own rules on jurisdiction.[1] These rules often differ from country to country. In the United States, for instance, the courts have jurisdiction not only over a defendant established there but also over a foreign person or company regularly doing business in the United States. United States courts sometimes even exercise jurisdiction over foreigners who may be served with a writ in the United States while on an occasional business visit there.[2] European courts often use more rigid standards to decide on their jurisdiction (see paragraphs 10.06 *et seq.*).

Courts of more than one country may declare themselves simultaneously competent to give judgment in a dispute, so that the same claim can be the subject of proceedings in different countries (*lis pendens*).

In most countries the legislator does not recognise the international *lis pendens* as a ground for lack of competence. The courts sometimes avoid giving judgment when the case is already pending in a foreign court and the judgment of that court will probably be recognised in their jurisdiction.[3] This is, for instance, the case in France,[4] Germany,[5] the Netherlands[6] and Switzerland.[7] In a few legal systems, such as the English,[8] *lis pendens* is a more general exception for court jurisdiction.

---

[1] See, in general, W. W. Park, *International Forum Selection* (Kluwer, The Hague, 1995); J. J. Fawcett, *Declining Jurisdiction in Private International Law* (Clarendon Press, Oxford, 1995).

[2] The existence of this ground for jurisdiction was confirmed in *Burnham v. Superior Court of California.*, 495 U.S. 604, 110 S.Ct.2105, 109 L.Ed.2d 631 (1990). See also G. Born, *International Civil Litigation in United States Courts* (Kluwer, Deventer, 1996); S. Weber Waller, "A unified theory of transnational procedure" (1993) 26 Cornell Int'l.L.J. 101, 103–108.

[3] L. Palsson, "The institute of 'lis pendens' in International Civil Procedure" (1970) *Scandinavian Studies in Law* 59.

[4] B. Audit, *Droit International Privé* (Economica, Paris, 1997) p. 330.

[5] G. Kegel, *Internationales Privatrecht* (Beck, Munich, 1995) p. 836.

[6] L. Strikwerda, *Inleiding tot het Nederlands IPR* (Wolters-Noordhoff, Groningen, 1995) p. 252.

[7] Loi Fédérale d'organisation judiciaire, Art. 9.

[8] L. Collins (ed.), *Dicey and Morris on the Conflict of Laws* (Sweet & Maxwell, London, 2000) p. 400. See also *The Abidit Dover* (1984) A.C. 398, 411–412; *MacShannon v. Rockware Glass Ltd*

Some treaties on jurisdiction avoid *lis pendens* by granting jurisdiction to only one court. Any other court, seised of the case, has to declare itself devoid of jurisdiction. Examples of such treaties are the Lugano Convention (see paragraph 10.03) and bilateral conventions on jurisdiction (see paragraph 10.04). Later possibly also the (future) Hague Convention on Jurisdiction and Foreign Judgments in Civil and Commercial Matters (see paragraph 10.05) will serve this purpose. The Brussels I Regulation (see paragraph 10.02) has the same effect.

Lis pendens may result in conflicting judgments. Clear rules on jurisdiction and *lis pendens* are therefore required.

The summons of a foreign party gives rise to specific legal questions, since a summons or writ is basically an administrative act that cannot be instituted outside national boundaries. The delivery of a summons or writ abroad is only possible with the permission and co-operation of the local administration. International rules are therefore needed for the service abroad of a writ and other judicial documents (see paragraph 10.19).

Each court conducts its legal proceedings according to its national procedural law. However, foreign substantive law must sometimes be applied to a dispute and, if needs be, the court may have to inquire into the substantive rules of this foreign law (see paragraph 10.24), gather evidence, or organise a hearing in another country. There are treaties to organise this international procedural co-operation (see paragraph 10.25).

Finally, judgments passed in one country sometimes need to be recognised or enforced in another country. Recognition and enforcement of foreign judgments is often regulated by treaties (see paragraphs 10.27 *et seq.*).

These questions have to be answered in the light of the procedural law of the court seized. Attempts to draft common procedural principles, did not yet succeed.[9]

10.02 **Jurisdiction and Enforcement Regulation in the European Union** The Brussels Convention of September 27, 1968 on jurisdiction and the recognition and enforcement of foreign judgments has been of great importance for legal practitioners from within, but also outside the European Union.[10] The Conven-

---

[1978] A.C. 795; *Australian Commercial Research and Development Ltd v. ANZ McCaughan Merchant Bank Ltd* [1989] 3 All E.R. 65.

[9] See, *e.g.*, 33 Tex Int'l. L.J. (1998) with a critique on the Draft Transnational Rules of Civil Procedure by G. Born (p. 387) and R. Weintraub (p. 413).

[10] A. Dashwood, R. Hacon and R. White, *A Guide to the Civil Jurisdiction and Judgment Convention* (Kluwer, Deventer, 1987); H. Duintjer-Tebbens, T. Kennedy and C. Kohler (eds), *Civil Jurisdiction and Judgments in Europe* (Butterworths, London, 1992); P. Gothot and D. Holleaux, *La Convention de Bruxelles du 27 Septembre 1968* (Jupiter, Paris, 1985); P. Kaye (ed.), *European Case Law on the Judgments Convention* (John Wiley and Son, Chichester, 1998); P. Kaye, *Law of the European Judgments Convention* (Barry Rose Law Publishers, Chichester, 1999); J. Kropholler, *Europäisches Zivilprozessrecht. Kommentar zum EuGVÜ* (Recht und Wirtschaft, Heidelberg, 1998); H. Gaudemet-Tallon, *Les Conventions de Bruxelles et de Lugano* (Montchrestien, Paris, 1996); N. Watté and A. Nuyts, *Les Arrêts de la Cour de Justice sur L'interpretation de la Convention de Bruxelles* (Kluwer, Diegem, 1998); M. Bogdon (ed.), *The Brussels Jurisdiction and Enforcement Convention/ an E.C. Case book* (Kluwer, The Hague, 1996); H. Born, M. Fallon and J.-L.Van Boxstael, *Droit Judiciare International: Cronique de Jurisprudence* 1991–1998 (Larcier, Brusells, 2001).

tion is now replaced by a Regulation, effective as of March 2002.[11] This Regulation is in force in all the countries of the European Union, with the exception of Denmark (*i.e.* Austria, Belgium, Finland, France, Germany, Greece, Ireland, Italy, Luxembourg, the Netherlands, Portugal, Spain, Sweden, the United Kingdom). Recital 22 of the Regulation states that the Brussels Convention will cover the relations between Denmark and the other Member States bound by the Regulation. The Regulation is called the Brussels I Regulation (to distinguish it from the Brussels II Regulation on jurisdiction and enforcement in divorce and other family matters, unrelated to international trade).

The purpose of the Brussels I Regulation, like the previous Brussels Convention, is threefold. It regulates the jurisdiction of the courts of the Member States, introduces a simplified procedure for the recognition and enforcement of judgments and arranges for the recognition of authentic documents from another Member State.

The Brussels I Regulation only applies to "civil or commercial matters".[12] The nature of the judicial institution that decides the dispute is of no relevance. Not only a civil court or a commercial court but also a labour court or a criminal court (when seised in a civil action) may decide on civil and commercial matters.[13]

Particular matters are excluded from the scope of application of the Regulation (Article 1). For example, the Regulation does not apply to bankruptcies or similar proceedings.[14] (They have their own rules—including a European Regulation—see paragraph 10.29). Likewise, arbitration is also excluded from the scope of the Regulation and is covered by specific Conventions (see paragraph 11.44).[15]

It is important that the courts of the Member States all apply an identical interpretation of the Regulation. The European Court of Justice plays an important role in this instance. Courts of E.U. Member States that decide in last instance, may refer preliminary questions to the European Court of Justice for an interpretation of the Regulation. The judgments of the Court are binding not only

---

[11]The full title of the Regulation is Council Regulation 44/2001 on jurisdiction and the recognition and enforcement of judgments in civil and commercial matters ([2001] O.J. L012).

[12] For instance, the Court of Justice has decided that the Brussels Convention was not applicable to a dispute between a private person and a public entity acting pursuant to its administrative authority (see Case 29/76 *L.T.U. v. Eurocontrol* [1976] E.C.R. 1541, [1977] 1 C.M.L.R. 88; Case 814/79 *Netherlands State v. Rüffer* [1980] E.C.R. 3807, [1981] 3 C.M.L.R. 293). The Brussels Convention was, on the other hand, applicable to a claim for compensation against a teacher of a public school, even if there was a social security claim under administrative law (Case C–172/91 *Sonntag v. Waidmann* [1993] E.C.R. 1963, [1993] I.L.Pr. 466).

[13] Even if a court would not have jurisdicton in a civil matter under the Brussels Convention (now Regulation), but it was seised in criminal proceedings according to national rules and the case then develops a civil dimension, jurisdiction will be allowed. See *Krombach v. Bamberski* [2000] E.C.R. I–1935, annotation H. Muir Watt (2000) R.C.D.I.P., 481.

[14] Case 133/78 *Gourdain v. Nadler* [1979] E.C.R. 733, [1979] 3 C.M.L.R. 180.

[15] Case C–190/89 *Marc Rich v. Impianti* [1991] E.C.R. 3855; [1991] I.L.Pr. 524, which declares the Brussels Convention also not applicable to the appointment of an arbitrator by the court, even if the validity of the arbitration clause is disputed. See, however, Case C–391/95 *Van Uden Maritime BV, Trading as Van Uden Africa Line v. Kommanditgesellschaft in Firma Deco-Line and Another* [1999] I.L.Pr 73, where the Court of Justice declared that the exclusion of arbitration does not extend to provisional measures under Art. 24, as these measures are not ancillary, but parallel to the arbitration process; annotation by E. Peel, "The Brussels Convention" in (1998) 18 Y.E.L. 693; J. Normand, (1999) RCDIP, 340. See also D.T.Hascher, "Recognition and enforcement of arbitration awards and the Brussels Convention" (1996) Arb.Int. 233.

on the judge who referred the preliminary question, but also on any other court of a Member State before which the same question may subsequently arise. The interpretation by the European Court of the Regulation and, *mutatis mutandis*, of the previous Brussels Convention, is therefore very important for a proper understanding of the Regulation. The decisions of the Court of Justice can be found on the web.[16]

10.03 **Lugano Convention** The Lugano Convention was concluded in 1988 in Lugano between the then E.C. Member States and the EFTA countries.[17] It is at present (*i.e.* at the end of 2001) in force in the 15 Member States of the European Community,[18] the EFTA states (*i.e.* Iceland, Liechtenstein, Norway and Switzerland), as well as in Poland.[19] Eventually the Lugano Convention is to become a waiting room for candidate Member States of the European Union.

Just like the Brussels Convention (which was its main source of inspiration), the Lugano Convention promotes the free movement of judgments between the contracting states (so long as the question falls outside the scope of the Brussels I Regulation). However, the Lugano Convention does not benefit from the same guarantee of a uniform interpretation as the Brussels I Regulation, since the European Court of Justice does not have jurisdiction to interpret the Lugano Convention. Because of the great importance of a uniform interpretation of two semi-identical jurisdiction instruments, the Lugano states promised to take account of each other's interpretation of the Lugano Convention as well as of the Brussels Convention (now Regulation).[20]

10.04 **Other international treaties** Many other multilateral and bilateral treaties are concerned with procedural matters.

---

[16] www.europa.eu.int.

[17] Convention on Jurisdiction and the Enforcement of Judgments in Civil and Commercial Matters, signed in Lugano on September 16, 1988, [1988] O.J. L319/9; P. Jenard and G. Möller, "Report on the Lugano Convention" [1990] O.J. C189/57.

[18] Austria, Belgium, Denmark, Finland, France, Germany, Greece, Ireland, Italy, Luxembourg, the Netherlands, Portugal, Spain, Sweden, the United Kingdom.

[19] See Y. Donzallaz, *La Convention de Lugano* (Stæmpfli Editions SA Berne, 1996); G. Droz, "La Convention de Lugano parallèle à la Convention de Bruxelles concernant la compétence judiciaire et l'exécution des décisions en matière civile et commerciale" (1989) R.C.D.I.P. 1; G. Droz, "Problèmes provoqués par l'imbrication des Conventions de Bruxelles (1968), de Lugano (1988) et de San Sebastian (1989)" in *Etudes de Droit International en l'Honneur de P. Lalive* (Helbing and Lichtenhahn, Basle, 1993) p. 21; J. Kropholler, *Europäisches Zivilprocessrecht* (Verlag Recht und Wirtschaft, Heidelberg, 1998); H. Linke, "EG-Gerichtsstands– und Vollstreckungsübereinkommen" (1991) RIW Beilage 5 zu Heft 12; J. Minor, "The Lugano Convention: some problems of interpretation" [1990] C.M.L.Rev. 507; L. Pellis, "Het parallelverdrag (EVEX): geen reden tot euro-forie" (1989) NJB 78; P. Volken, "Das EG/EFTA Parallel-Ubereinkommen über die gerichtliche Zuständigkeit und die Vollstreckung gerichtlicher Entscheidungen in Zivil und Handelssachen" (1987) A.S.D.I. 97.

[20] Protocol 2 of the Lugano Convention. To this end, a Standing Committee composed of representatives of each signatory and acceding state was set up. They meet and exchange views on the functioning of the Convention, in particular the case law that developed under the Brussels Convention See A. Nuyts, "La compétence en matière de contrat de travail" in R. Fentiman, A. Nuyts, H. Tagaras and N. Watté, *L'Éspace Judiciaire Européen en Matières Civile et Commerciale/ The European Judicial Area in Civil and Commercial Matters* (Bruylant, Brussels, 1999) p. 31; H. Gaudemet-Tallon, *Les Conventions de Bruxelles et de Lugano* (Montchrestien, Paris, 1996) pp. 324–327.

The parties to the Brussel I Regulation and/or the Lugano Convention are, for instance, bound by a number of bilateral conventions in respect of matters or countries not covered by these texts Convention. Most of these conventions only concern the recognition and enforcement of foreign judgments.

There are also some multilateral conventions regulating specific matters, such as international transport (see paragraph 1.32). These specific conventions supersede the Brussels I Regulation[21] and the Lugano Convention.[22] There are, in addition, important texts for service abroad (see paragraph 10.19), jurisdictional immunity (see paragraph 2.06), co-operation in respect of evidence (see paragraph 10.25), etc.

Regional areas, like MERCOSUR (see paragraph 2.37), have their own conventions on jurisdictional matters.[23]

A Worldwide Hague Convention?   The Hague Conference on Private Inter-   **10.05** national Law has initiated negotiation of a world-wide Convention on Jurisdiction and Foreign Judgments in Civil and Commercial Matters.[24] Negotiations appeared, however, difficult and the fate of the project remains unclear.[25]

The Convention was intended to apply to civil and commercial matters, but not to arbitration and proceedings related thereto, nor to admiralty or maritime matters (Article 1).

The working of the Convention would be similar to that of the Brussels and Lugano Conventions, with provisions on jurisdiction (Chapter II) as well as on recognition and enforcement of foreign judgments (Chapter III). The underlying idea was that if the rules on jurisdiction are similar in the states parties, recognition of judgments based on these rules of jurisdiction should be easily agreed upon.

PART II: INTERNATIONAL JURISDICTION

Under the Brussels I Regulation and Lugano convention

Introduction   The jurisdiction rules of the Brussels I Regulation, which are   **10.06** to a large extent similar to the Lugano Convention, will serve as an illustration of how the international jurisdiction of a court is determined.

---

[21] Regulation, Art. 67.

[22] Lugano Convention, Art. 57.

[23] See Protocol of Buenos Aires on international jurisdiction in disputes relating to contracts, (1997) 34 I.L.M. 1263; H. Pabst, "Das Internationale Zivilprozessrecht des Mercosur" (1999) IPRax 76.

[24] This Draft Convention was drawn up and adopted by a special commission on October 30, 1999.The current version of the text of the future Convention can be found at the website of the Hague Conference: http://www.hcch.net.

[25] See the reports by Catherine Kessedjian, found at the website of the Hague Conference: http://www.hcch.net; A. Bucher, "Vers une convention mondiale sur la compétence et les jugements étrangers" (2000) S.J. 77; Volume XXIV in *Brooklyn Journal of International Law* (Brooklyn Law School, New York, 1998).

10.07   **Exclusive jurisdiction** Some actions may, because of the nature of the
subject matter or their special link with a territory, be brought only to a particular
court (Article 22).[26] Parties have no choice in the matter. If they bring an action
in another court, that court shall declare of its own motion that it has no
jurisdiction (Article 25).[27] The exclusive jurisdiction rules apply "regardless of
domicile" and even when the defendant and/or the plaintiff have no domicile in
the territory of a contracting state. Which actions give rise to exclusive jurisdiction must be strictly interpreted. The following courts shall have exclusive
jurisdiction, regardless of domicile.

1. (a) In proceedings that have as their object rights *in rem* in immovable
property or tenancies of immovable property, the courts of the contracting state in which the property is situated (Article 22.1).[28] This does not
include the tenancy of business premises or a mixed contract.[29] Nor
does it apply to the remuneration for the use of a house after the
annulment of the transfer of property.[30] A claim for compensation for
not cleaning a holiday house rented in another country for a short
period falls under this provision, even if the plaintiff is an agent
subrogated in the rights of the owner.[31]

(b) However, in proceedings that have as their object tenancies of immovable property concluded for temporary private use for a maximum
period of six consecutive months, the courts of the contracting state in
which the defendant is domiciled shall also have jurisdiction, provided
that the tenant is a natural person and both parties are domiciled in the
same contracting state.[32]

2. In proceedings which have as their object the validity of the constitution,
the nullity or the dissolution of companies or other legal persons or
associations of natural or legal persons, or the decisions of their organs,
the courts of the Member State in which the company, legal person or
association has its seat (Article 22.2).[33] The seat of a legal person is
determined by the private international law of the court seised.

---

[26] Also Lugano Convention, Art. 16.
[27] Also Lugano Convention, Art. 19.
[28] Also Lugano Convention, Art. 16. 1. For immovable property situated in the different states: Case
158/87, *Scherrens v. Maenhout* [1988] E.C.R. 3791; Case C–294/92, *Webb v. Webb* [1994] E.C.R.
I–1717. An action to state that a person holds an immovable property as a "trustee" is not an action
in rem.
[29] Case 73/77 *Sanders v. Van der Putte* [1977] E.C.R. 2383; Case C–280/90 *Hacker v. Europrelais*
[1992] E.C.R. 1111; [1978] 1 C.M.L.R. 331. Nor does it apply to the remuneration for the use of
a house after the annulment of the transfer of property: Case 292/93 *Lieber v. Göbel* [1994] E.C.R.
I–2535.
[30] Case C–292/93 *Lieber v. Göbel* [1994] E.C.R. I–2535.
[31] Case C–38/98 *Dansommer v. Andreas Götz* [2000] E.C.R. I–0393, annotation H. Muir Watt (2000)
R.C.D.I.P. 264.
[32] The Lugano Convention (Art. 16) requires that neither party be domiciled in the state in which the
property is situated.
[33] See also Lugano Convention, Art. 16.2.

3. In proceedings about the validity of entries in public registers, the courts of the Member State in which the register is kept (Article 22.3).[34]

4. In proceedings concerned with the registration or validity of patents, trade marks, designs, or other similar rights required to be deposited or registered, the courts of the Member State in which the deposit or registration has been applied for, has taken place or is under the terms of an international convention deemed to have taken place (Article 22.4).[35] Without prejudice to the powers of the European Patent Office,[36] the courts of each Member State have sole jurisdiction over the registration and validity of a European patent granted by that state.

5. In proceedings concerned with the enforcement of judgments, the courts of the Member State in which the judgment has been or is to be enforced (Article 22.5).[37]

Jurisdiction clause   Parties may agree that a court in a Member State is to   **10.08**
have jurisdiction for the settlement of their disputes. For this purpose they include a jurisdiction clause in their contract.

Under Article 23,[38] when at least one party is domiciled in a contracting state,[39] parties may confer jurisdiction on a court of a Member State. This court is then the only court with jurisdiction for their dispute unless the parties have otherwise agreed. That court would also have jurisdiction to determine whether the contract containing the jurisdictional clause is valid or void.[40]

The chosen court does not need to have a real connection with either the parties or the transaction. All other courts of contracting states which could have jurisdiction pursuant to Articles 2 and 5 (see paragraphs. 10.09–10.10) must decline jurisdiction. However, the jurisdiction clause does not affect the exclusive jurisdiction provisions (see paragraph 10.07). The jurisdiction clause, however, overrules the national law for exclusive jurisdiction. Parties may therefore, for instance, validly nominate a non-Belgian court for the settlement of a dispute over the termination of an exclusive distribution agreement and thus deprive the Belgian court of jurisdiction over this dispute, despite the Belgian 1961 Exclusive Distributorship Act, which grants Belgian courts exclusive jurisdiction.

Article 23 requires two conditions for a jurisdiction clause:

(a) it must be clear that the parties agreed that a court shall have jurisdiction;

---

[34] *ibid.*, Art 16.3.

[35] Also *ibid.*, Art. 16.4. See Case 288/82 *Duijnstee v. Gederbauer* [1983] E.C.R. 3663, [1985] 1 C.M.L.R. 220.

[36] See the Convention on the grant of European patents signed at Munich on October 5, 1973.

[37] Also Lugano Convention, Art. 16.5.

[38] *ibid.*, Art. 17.

[39] It is not necessary that the defendant is domiciled in a contracting state.

[40] Case C–269/95, *Francesco Benincasa v. Dentalkit Srl* [1997] E.C.R. I–3767; annotation P. Volken (1998) R.S.D.I.E. 113.

(b) this agreement must be in writing, evidenced in writing or in a form customary in international trade.

"Such an agreement conferring jurisdiction shall be either:

(a) in writing or evidenced in writing[41] or;
(b) in a form which accords with practices which the parties have established between themselves, or;
(c) in international trade or commerce, in a form which accords with a usage of which the parties are or ought to have been aware and which in such trade or commerce is widely known to, and regularly observed by, parties to contracts of the type involved in the particular trade or commerce concerned.[42]

A clear jurisdiction clause in a written contract signed by both parties obviously satisfies the requirements. However, in many cases the jurisdiction clause is not transparent but must be construed.

It may, for instance, be sufficient that parties agreed orally on jurisdiction what was later confirmed in writing by one of the parties and to which the other party raised no objection.[43] Even a jurisdiction clause in a written contract that was not formally renewed after expiration may satisfy the requirements of Article 23 if the parties continue trading with each other, particularly if one of the parties confirms in writing that the previous contractual provisions remain in force and this was not disputed by the other party.[44]

More stringent rules apply to general conditions.[45] If a jurisdiction clause is only contained in the general conditions of a contract it will only be effective if the actual contract explicitly refers to these general conditions.[46] Jurisdiction clauses in general conditions that are not known to the other party at the conclusion of the contract and are only mentioned at some later time, *e.g.* on invoices, are not valid.[47] The jurisdiction clause should always be drawn up in a language that parties understand.[48] General conditions that are accepted by both

---

[41] Art. 23.2 of the Regulation determines that any communication by electronic means that provides a durable record of the agreement shall be deemed to be in writing.

[42] Art. 23. Until 2007 a person domiciled in Luxembourg is only bound by a jurisdiction clause which that person has expressly and explicitly accepted by signing the exclusive jurisdiction clause (Art. 63). Thus hypotheses (b) and (c) are not in force in Luxembourg. For an application, see Case 784/79 *Porta-Leasing v. Prestige* [1980] E.C.R. 1517, [1981] 1 C.M.L.R. 135. In *Mainschiffahrts-Genossenschaft Eg (MSG) v. Les Gravières Rhénanes SARL* [1997] E.C.R. I–0911 the Court said that one needs to look at the specific branch to establish a usage, and not to International Trade in general. Publicity is not a requirement for establishing the existence of a usage in a particular trade: Case C–159/97, *Transporti Castelletti Spedizione SpA v. Hugo Trumpy SpA* [1999] E.C.R. I–1597; annotation by H. Gaudemet-Tallon (2000) R.C.D.I.P. 559.

[43] Case 221/84 *Berghoefer v. ASA*: [1985] E.C.R. 2699; (1986) 1 C.M.L.R. 13; Case C–106/95, *Mainschiffahrts-Genossenschaft Eg (MSG) v. Les Gravières Rhénanes SARL* [1997] E.C.R. I–0911, above.

[44] Case 313/85 *Iveco Fiat v. Van Hool* [1986] E.C.R. 3337; [1988] 1 C.M.L.R. 57.

[45] M. J. Schmidt, "Kann schweigen auf eine Gerichtsstandsklausel in AGB einen Gerichtsstand nach Art. 17 EuGVÜ/LuganoÜ begründen?" (1992) R.I.W. 173.

[46] Case 24/76 *Colzani v. Rüwa* [1976] E.C.R. 1831; [1977] 1 C.M.L.R. 345.

[47] See Cour d'appel de Paris, October 15, 1997, Dalloz Sirey (1997) I.R. 239–240.

[48] However, see C. Kohler, "Gerichtsstandsklauseln in fremdsprachigen AGB" (1991) IPRax 299.

parties in earlier transactions may also apply in later similar transactions between the same parties.[49]

A jurisdiction clause in the articles of association of a limited company for the settlement of disputes between shareholders and the company is valid if the articles of association are deposited in a place accessible to shareholders or published in a public register.[50]

A jurisdiction clause may only benefit one party or give one party a wider choice than the other party.[51] A jurisdiction clause may thus leave the seller the choice whether to sue the buyer in his own courts or in the courts of the buyer, while it limits the buyer to the courts of the seller. Parties may also agree that each party has to be sued in the courts of his own domicile.[52]

Furthermore, a jurisdiction clause may affect third parties succeeding in the contractual rights and obligations of one of the parties.[53]

A person summoned before a court not competent under the rules stated above, must immediately (*in limine litis*) challenge the jurisdiction of that court. When the defendant enters an appearance on the merits of the case, he is deemed to have submitted to the jurisdiction of the court and can no longer challenge its jurisdiction (Article 24).[54] For practical reasons the defendant may first challenge the jurisdiction of the court, but subsequently enter a defence on the merits of the case.[55]

General jurisdiction: country of the defendant If there is no exclusive **10.09**
jurisdiction and no valid jurisdiction clause, persons (natural or legal) domiciled in an E.U. Member State may be sued in the courts of that state (Article 2).[56]

The domicile of a natural person is determined by the domestic law of the state where he has his domicile (Article 59).[57]

The domicile of a company is determined by its statutory seat, central administration, or principal place of business. In the United Kingdom and in Ireland, "statutory seat" means the registered office, place of incorporation, or place

---

[49] Case 25/76 *Segoura v. Bonakdarian* [1976] E.C.R. 1851, [1977] 1 C.M.L.R. 361.

[50] Case C–214/89 *Powell Duffryn v. Petereit* [1992] E.C.R. 174.

[51] Case 22/85 *Anterist v. Crédit Lyonnais* [1986] E.C.R. 1951; [1991] 2 C.M.L.R. 461; In Case 23/78 *Meeth v Glacetal* [1978] E.C.R. 2133 the parties agreed that the court of the defendant's seat would have jurisdiction. This clause was held by the European Court of Justice to be valid.

[52] Case 23/78 *Meeth v. Glacetal* [1978] E.C.R. 2133; [1979] 1 C.M.L.R. 5201.

[53] *Inter alia*, Case 201/82 *Gerling v. Italian Treasury* [1983] E.C.R. 2503; [1984] 3 C.M.L.R. 638: the third party beneficiary of insurance contract may invoke the jurisdiction clause in the contract between the insurer and insured; Case 71/83 *Tilly Russ v. Nova and Goeminne* [1984] E.C.R. 2417; [1984] 3 C.M.L.R. 499: as regards the relationship between the carrier and a third party holding the bill of lading, the conditions laid down by Art. 17 of the Convention (now Regulation, Art. 23) are satisfied if the jurisdiction clause has been adjudged valid as between the carrier and the shipper and if, by virtue of the relevant national law, the third party, upon acquiring the bill of lading, succeeded to the shipper's rights and obligations. If the third party did not succeed in the rights of one of the parties, it must be ascertained whether he accepted the jurisdiction clause to determine whether it is applicable to him: Case C–387/98 *Coreck Maritime GmbH v. Handelsveen BV and Others* [2000] E.C.R. I–9337.

[54] Also Art. 18 Lugano Convention. See Case 150/80 *Elefanten Schuh v. Jacqmain* [1981] E.C.R. 1671, [1982] 3 C.M.L.R. 1. See also *Tatry v. Maciej Rataj* [1994] E.C.R. I–5439, ECJ.

[55] *ibid.*, Case 27/81 *Rohr v. Ossberger* [1981] E.C.R. 2431.

[56] Also Lugano Convention, Art. 2.

[57] *ibid.*, Art. 52.

under the law of which the formation took place. The domicile of a trust is determined by the rules of private international law of the Member State where the action is brought (Article 60).

Claims instituted by the same plaintiff against a number of defendants may be brought in the place where any one of them is domiciled, if the connection between the claims is such that, if dealt with separately, they could lead to conflicting judgments (Article 6.1).[58]

10.10   **Special jurisdiction**   As an alternative to suing a defendant domiciled in one contracting state in the court of his domicile, in some specific cases he may be sued in the courts of another contracting state.[59]

(a) In respect of contractual obligations, the court of the place of performance of the obligation forming the basis of the legal proceedings has jurisdiction (Article 5.1).[60]

If the parties to a sales or service contract agreed in their contract on the place of performance, Article 5.1(b) governs the situation. In the case of the sale of goods, the courts of the place where delivery should take place, according to the contract, has jurisdiction. In the case of the provision of services, the courts of the place where the services should be provided, according to the contract, has jurisdiction.[61]

When the place of performance is not stated in the contract, it is determined by the proper law of the contract (see paragraph 1.29). The court thus has first to apply its own conflict of law rules for the determination of the proper law (see paragraph 1.24).[62]

If the action involves several autonomous obligations originating from the same contract (*e.g.* discharge of the contract and damages), a court that has jurisdiction over one obligation, cannot assume jurisdiction over the other. In such a case, a claimant would have to bring two separate

---

[58] *ibid.*, Art. 6.1, See Case 189/87 *Kalfelis v. Schroeder* [1988] E.C.R. 5565.

[59] See, in general, K. Hertz, *Jurisdiction in Contract and Tort under the Brussels Convention* (Jurist-og Økonomforbundets Forlag, Copenhagen, 1998).

[60] Also Lugano Convention, Art. 5.1. See Case 14/76 *De Bloos v. Bouyer* [1976] E.C.R. 1497, [1977]; 1 C.M.L.R. 60: the Brussels Convention was amended on the accession of the U.K., Denmark and Ireland in accordance with the *De Bloos* judgment. Even if the existence of the contract is in dispute, the jurisdiction of the court may be invoked by virtue of Art. 5.1: Case 38/81 *Effer v. Kantner* [1982] E.C.R. 825. However, a claim for a defective good by the third buyer against the producer is not a "contractual obligation": Case C–261/91 *Handte v. Société Traitements Mécano-chimiques* [1992] E.C.R. I–3967.

[61] A clause for the determination of the place of performance is not the same as a jurisdiction clause in respect of the formal requirements of Art. 23; the former points indirectly to a competent court: Case 56/79 *Zelger v. Salinitri* [1980] E.C.R. 89, [1980] 2 C.M.L.R. 635. Under the Brussels Convention, it was found that if the clause in the contract determining the place of performance is fictive and merely to grant a specific court jurisdiction, it has no effect: Case C–106/95, *Main-schiffahrts-Genossenschaft eG (MSG) v. Les Gravières Rhénanes Sarl* [1997] E.C.R. I–0911, annotations H. Gaudet-Tallon (1997) R.C.D.I.P. 572, P. Volken (1998) R.S.D.I.E. 120, A. Huet (1997) J.D.I. 631, T. Hartley (1997) E.L.Rev. 362, P. Wautelet (1997) Colum.J.Eur.L. 465.

[62] Case 12/76 *Tessili v. Dunlop* [1976] E.C.R. 1473, [1977] 1 C.M.L.R. 26; Case 288/92: *Custom Made Commercial Ltd v. Stawa Metalbau GmbH* [1994] E.C.R. I–2913.

actions.[63] However, if the court decides that there is one main obligation and the other obligations are only secondary, the fate of the secondary obligations depends on the main obligation.[64]

(b) The court of the place where the harmful event occurred is competent to hear an action for matters relating to tort (Article 5.3).[65] The place of the tort, delict or quasi-delict may be the place where the harmful event took place[66] or where the damage occurred.[67] Where a bill of lading was issued, but another party in fact carried the goods an action against the actual carrier would not be based on contract (Article 5.1), but on tort, delict or quasi-delict (Article 5.3).[68]

(c) Disputes arising out of the operations of a branch, agency or other establishment may be brought to the court of the place where the branch, agency or other establishment is located (Article 5.5).[69] Besides disputes over the actual internal operations of the branch, exploitation disputes also include disputes concerning contractual and non-contractual obligations arising from the activities of the branch.[70] Moreover, "branch" should not be interpreted in a narrow sense. Although it does not cover independent entities representing a foreign company,[71] a subsidiary acting for the parent company is covered.[72]

---

[63] See Case 14/76 *De Bloos v. Bouyer* [1976] E.C.R. 1497, [1977]; Case C–420/97, *Leathertex Divisione Sintertici SpA v. Bodetex BVBA* [1999] E.C.R. I–6747, annotation H. Gaudemet-Tallon [2000] R.C.D.I.P. 76. In this case an agent claimed commission as well as compensation in lieu of notice for the termination of the agency agreement. The European Court of Justice found that these obligations of equal rank, which were to be performed in different countries, could not be claimed before one judge.

[64] Case 266/85 *Shenavai v. Kreischer* [1987] E.C.R. 239; [1987] 3 C.M.L.R. 782.

[65] Also Lugano Convention, Art. 5.3. A claim by reason of "tort" includes any action in law which is intended to question the liability in tort of the defendant and which has no connection with a "contractual obligation". Consequently, the court with jurisdiction based on tort does not have jurisdiction to take cognizance of those elements of the claim that have another basis: Case 189/87 *Kalfelis v. Bank Schroeder* [1988] E.C.R. 5565.

[66] Only direct damages are considered; Art. 5.3 does not apply to damages resulting from the damage suffered by another entity, *e.g.* a daughter company: Case 220/88 *Dumez v. Hessische Landesbank* [1990] E.C.R. I–0049.

[67] Case 21/76 *Bier v. Mines de Potasse* [1976] E.C.R. 1735, [1977] 1 C.M.L.R. 284. The courts of a contracting state in which economic loss was suffered following an initial harmful act in another contracting state, do not have jurisdiction: Case C–364/93 *Marinari v. Lloyds Bank* [1995] E.C.R. I–2719; [1995] I.L.Pr. 737, annotation T. Hartley (1996) E.L.Rev. 162. The place of the harmful event cannot be the place where the harm was merely discovered: Case C–51/97 *Réunion Européenne SA v. Spliethoff's Bevrachtingskantoor BV* [1998] E.C.R. I–6511, [1999] I.L.Pr. 205; annotation E. Peel, (1998) 18 Y.E.L. 700.

[68] See Case C–51/97 *Réunion Européenne SA and others v. Spliethoff's Bevrachtingskantoor BV and the Master of the vessel Alblasgracht V002* [1998] E.C.R. I–6511.

[69] This does not presuppose that the undertakings giving rise to the dispute, entered into by a branch in the name of its parent body, are to be performed in the Contracting State in which the branch is established: Case C–439/93, *Lloyd's Register of Shipping v. Société Campenon Bernard* [1995] E.C.R. I–0961; annotation T. Hartley [1996] E.L.Rev. 162. See also N. E. Enonchony "Service of Process in England on overseas companies and Article 5(5) of the Brussels Convention" (1999) I.C.L.Q. 21.

[70] Case 33/78 *Somafer v. Saar-Ferngas* [1978] E.C.R. 2183; [1979] 1 C.M.L.R. 490.

[71] Case 14/76 *De Bloos v. Bouyer* [1976] E.C.R. 1497; Case 139/80, *Blanckaert v. Trost*: [1981] E.C.R. 819; [1982] 2 C.M.L.R. 1.

[72] Case 218/86 *Schotte v. Parfums Rotschild* [1987] E.C.R. 4916.

(d) An action on a warranty or guarantee, any other third party proceedings or a counter-claim may be brought before the court seised of the original proceedings (Article 6.2 and 6.3).[73] The court already seised of an action by the purchaser for warranty under a sales agreement, therefore, may also take cognisance of an action in third party proceedings and an action on a warranty brought by the reseller against the original seller. However, the Brussels I Regulation imposes no jurisdictional limits on set-offs raised as defense to a claim. Set-off may always be raised as a defence if it is permitted under national law.[74]

(e) Special jurisdiction rules apply to insurance disputes (Articles 8–14)[75]; consumer contract disputes (Articles 15–17)[76]; and individual contracts of employment (Articles 18–21). An employer domiciled in a Member State may be sued in the courts of the place where he is domiciled. Alternatively, he may be sued in the place where the employee habitually carries out his work or, if he does not habitually carry out his work in any one country, in the place where the business that engaged him is situated.[77]

For the payment of architects' fees the Court of Justice has rejected the exception of employment contracts and opted for the general rule. Therefore, the court of the place of payment of the fee has jurisdiction, not the place of performance of the service.[78]

10.11   **Lis pendens**   As explained above, many courts may have jurisdiction so that the plaintiff may sue in the court of his choice. The court first seised of the action

---

[73] See also Arts 6.2 and 6.3, Lugano Convention. Moreover Case C–365/88 *Kongress Agentur Hagen v. Zeehaghe* [1990] E.C.R. I–1845, [1991] I.L.Pr. 3.

[74] Case C–341/93 *Danvaern Production v. Scuhfabriken Otterbeek* [1995] E.C.R. I–2053, [1995] I.L.Pr. 649, annotation T. Hartley, (1995) E.L.Rev. 166.

[75] Also Lugano Convention, Arts 7–12.

[76] Also *ibid.*, Arts 7–12. In Case C–269/95 *Francesco Benincasa v. Dantalkit Srl* [1997] E.C.R. I–3767 the Court stated that a person who concluded a contract with the view of becoming a trader in the future cannot be considered a consumer.

[77] See also Lugano Convention, Art. 5.1. Case 133/81 *Ivenel v. Schwab* [1982] E.C.R. 1891, [1983] 1 C.M.L.R. 538. If the work has been carried out outside the territory of the Member States, Art. 5.1 of the Brussels Convention (the predecessor of Arts 18–21) was found not to be applicable; the competent court should in that case be determined by the domicile of the defendant by virtue of Brussels Convention, Art. 2 (also Regulation, Art. 2): Case 32/88 *Six Constructions v. Humbert* [1989] E.C.R. 341; [1990] I.L.Pr. 206. If the work has been carried out in different Member States, the court of the place where the obligation of the employee principally has to be performed, is competent: Case C–125/92 *Mulox v. Hendrick Geels* [1993] E.C.R. 4075. In Case C–383/95 *Petrus Wilhelmus Rutten v. Cross Medical Ltd* [1997] E.C.R. I–0057, the Court stated that the place where the employee habitually carries out his work, in the sense of Art 5.1., Brussels Convention, is where the employee established the effective centre of his working activities. For the precise determination of this place, regard is taken to the fact that the employee spends most of his working time in a contracting state where he has an office from which he organises his activities for the account of his employer and to which he returns after each business trip abroad; annotations P. Volken (1998) R.S.D.I.E. 101, J. M. Bischoff (1997) J.D.I. 635, H. Gaudemet-Tallon (1997) R.C.D.I.P. 341, T. Hartley (1997) E.L.Rev. 364.

[78] Case 266/85 *Shevanai v. Kreischner* [1987] E.C.R. 239, [1987] 3 C.M.L.R. 782.

is the only court that may decide on the merits. If the same cause of action[79] involving the same parties[80] is later brought in a court of another Member State, that court must decline jurisdiction (unless that court has exclusive jurisdiction—see paragraph 10.07). It shall stay its proceedings until such time as the jurisdiction of the court first seised is established. In that case, it shall of its own motion decline jurisdiction in favour of that court (Article 27).[81] Accordingly, there can only be one court in the contracting states that can give a judgment.[82]

Two alternatives solve the question when the court is seised (Article 30): a court is deemed to be seised either when the document instituting the proceedings is lodged with the court (provided that the plaintiff did not fail to take the required steps to ensure service on the defendant), or when the document is received by the authority responsible for service[83] (if the document has to be served before being lodged with the court).

Related actions   It is possible that proceedings which, although not involv-   **10.12** ing identical actions and same parties, are nevertheless related are pending with different courts. For instance, a customer sues a building contractor for defective construction in one court, while the contractor sues his subcontractor for these defects in another court.[84] In such circumstances there is a risk of conflicting judgments (*e.g.* in one set of proceedings the claim for damages is upheld and in another the claim is rejected as unfounded). To avoid conflicting judgments, the last court seised may stay its proceedings until the first court has passed judgment. This court may also simply refer the case to the first court (Article 28).[85]

Provisional measures   In many countries the courts have extensive powers   **10.13** to order provisional measures in summary proceedings, such as the appointment of experts, protective seizure or an interim arrangement for the relationship

---

[79] A claim for performance of the contract and a claim for termination of the contract have the same cause of action. See Case 144/86 *Gubisch Maschinenfabrik v. Palumbo* [1987] E.C.R. 4861; (1988) R.C.D.I.P. 370, annotation H. Gaudemet-Tallon, (1988) J.D.I. 537, annotation A. Huet; H. Schack, "Rechtshängigkeit in England und Art. 21 EuGVÜ" (1991) IPRax 270. A claim for damage and an action to obtain a declaratory order that damage should not be paid on the same facts, have the same cause of action: Case 406/92 *The owners of the cargo lately laden on board the ship "Tatry" v. the owners of the ship "Maciej Rataj"* [1994] E.C.R. I–5439. This would, however, fall under the provision on related actions (Brussels I Regulation Art. 8).

[80] It is irrelevant where the parties have their domicile: Case C–351/89 *Overseas Union Insurance v. New Hampshire Insurance Company* [1991] E.C.R. I–3317; [1991] I.L.Pr. 495. In Case 406/92 *The owners of the cargo lately laden on board the ship "Tatry" v. the owners of the ship "Maciej Rataj"*: [1994] E.C.R. I–5439 the European Court of Justice found that where the cause of action is the same and some of the parties are the same, the second court has to decline jurisdiction only to the extent that the parties are the same. Also see Case C–351/96 *Drouot Assurances SA v. Consolidated Metallurgical Industries (CMI Industrial Sites), Protea Insurance and Groupement d'Intérêt Economique (GIE) Réunion Européenne* [1998] E.C.R. I–3075; [1998] I.L.Pr. 485 about "same party" in marine insurance.

[81] Also Lugano Convention, Art. 21.

[82] For the relation between the provisions on lis pendens, related actions and Arts 21/22 and 57, see Case C–406/92 *The owners of the cargo lately laden on the ship "Tatry" v. The owners of the ship "Maciej Rataj"* [1994] E.C.R. I–5439; annotation T. Hartley (1995) E.L.Rev. 409.

[83] This authority is determined by the Service Regulation (see para. 10.21).

[84] *e.g.* because of a jurisdiction clause.

[85] Also Lugano Convention, Art. 22.

between the parties. Article 31 provides that any court seised may order these provisional and protective measures—even if another court has jurisdiction for the substance of the dispute.[86] However, the measures should be truly provisional (*e.g.* a bank guarantee to cover money provisionally paid). Moreover, a court should only grant such measures when they may be effected within its territory (*e.g.* because of assets present).[87]

In theory, the protective measures do not affect the substance of the case, as they are ordered before justice is done.[88] In fact provisional measures often have an important influence on the settlement. A protective seizure of goods or an interlocutory injunction, combined with a considerable penalty in case of infringement, is often sufficient for a party to abandon any further defence on the merits of the case. The jurisdiction rules of the Brussels I Regulation may thus be somewhat frustrated by the provisional measures.[89]

The United States[90]

10.14 **Basis of jurisdiction** In the U.S. courts, jurisdiction generally requires some contact between the parties and the state, either regarding the person or a property. Another requirement for jurisdiction is notice to the counter-party.[91]

10.15 **Jurisdiction over persons (in personam)** A court has jurisdiction over a person when that person's affiliation with the forum state is established.[92] Jurisdiction *in personam* may be vested on the basis of domicile (*i.e.* not necessarily presence at the time of the proceedings),[93] on nationality and citizenship,[94] or on the consent to such jurisdiction.[95] When a non-resident starts an

---

[86] Also *ibid.*, Art. 24. See L. Collins, "Provisional and protective measures in international litigation" (1992) 234 Rec.Cours III 9; H. Hanisch, "Internationale Arrestzuständigkeit und EuGVÜ" (1991) IPRax 215. See also Case C–99/96 *Hans-Hermann Mietz v. Intership Yachting Sneek BV* [1999] E.C.R. I–2277 for an example where the court ordered provisional measures, but where it would have had (even though it was not expressly stated in its judgment) normal jurisdiction.

[87] See Case C–391/95 *Van Uden v. Deco Line* [1998] E.C.R. I–7091.

[88] See Case C–261/90 *Reichert and Kockler v. Dresdner Bank* [1992] E.C.R. I–2149 [1992] I.L.Pr. 404, which emphasises that the provisional measures must have a protective character. An example of such protective measure is the English Mareva injunction, in which the court restrains the debtor from removing or disposing assets from its territory for the purpose of frustrating the enforcement of a future judgment. Recently, Mareva injunctions were granted affecting assets abroad (*Republic of Haiti v. Duvalier* [1990] 1 Q.B. 202, CA; *Derby and Co. Ltd v. Weldon* [1990] Ch. 48, 65, CA).

[89] *cf.* G. Maher and D. J. Roger, "Provisional and protective remedies: The British experience of the Brussels Convention" (1999) I.C.L.Q. 302.

[90] For a discussion on U.S. jurisdictional rules, see P. Hay, R. J. Waintraub and J. Borchers, *Conflict of Laws Cases and Materials* (11th ed., Foundation Press, New York, 2000), pp. 35–157.

[91] P. Hay, R. J. Waintraub and P. J. Borchers, *Conflict of Laws Cases and Materials* (11th ed., Foundation Press, New York, 2000), p. 37.

[92] *Milliken v. Meyer*, 311 U.S. 457 (1940).

[93] *Skiriotes v. Florida*, 313 U.S. 69 (1941).

[94] Restatement Second, Conflict of Laws (para. 31).

[95] Restatement Second, Conflict of Laws (para. 32); *National Equipment Rental v. Szukhent* 375 U.S. 311, 84 S.Ct. 411, 11 L.Ed.2d 354 (1964).

action in a forum, that forum also has jurisdiction to hear a counterclaim against him.[96]

Jurisdiction can also reach further. In 1819 the Supreme Court of Massachusetts ruled that the mere service of a writ by arresting the defendant's body was sufficient to establish jurisdiction. None of the parties were domiciled in Massachusetts and the contract between them had no connection with Massachusetts.[97] Under the broad rules of jurisdiction, if service of a process occurs while a person is on a short business visit in a particular state, this is sufficient to establish jurisdiction. It is required that there be a "minimum contact" with the forum state. However, in *International Shoe*, physical presence was said to be sufficient to fulfil this requirement.[98] After this case, many states introduced "long arm statutes", which allowed for the widest possible jurisdiction while still constitutional. The U.S. Supreme Court has stated that among the most firmly established principles of personal jurisdiction in American tradition is that the courts of a state have jurisdiction over non-residents who are physically present in the state.[99]

A U.S. court will also assume jurisdiction on the basis that the defendant has been involved in commercial activities in the state where the court is situated. These commercial activities should not necessarily be related to the subject matter of the action.[1] This is a further application of the minimum contact rule.

These grounds for jurisdiction are not always well received in foreign countries and are often excluded in treaties.

Contest of jurisdiction A party may contest jurisdiction when appearing in a court at the start of the proceedings. In this instance a court may not exercise jurisdiction over the person.[2] Such appearance for the sole purpose of contesting jurisdiction is called special appearance in some states. Alternatively jurisdiction may be contested collaterally. This means that the defendant does not appear in the proceedings. He allows judgment to be given against him. When enforcement is sought in another state, he contests the jurisdiction of the first court. **10.16**

Jurisdiction over property (*in rem*) When a court lacks personal jurisdiction over the defendant, it is still possible that things (objects) may form a basis for jurisdiction.[3] When a proceeding is aimed at interests of all persons in the same thing, it is *in rem*. If the property in the state is not the subject matter of the **10.17**

---

[96] *Adam v. Saenger* 303 U.S. 59, 67–68 (1938).

[97] See *Barrell v. Benjamin* 15 Mass. 354 (1819).

[98] *International Shoe Co. v. Washington* 326 U.S. 310, 90 L.Ed. 95, 66 S.Ct. 154 (1945). The physical presence of a legal person is determined by the conduction of activities.

[99] See *Burnham v. Superior Court of California* 495 U.S. 604, 110 S.Ct. 2105, 109 L.Ed.2d 631 (1990).

[1] See *Penkins v. Benguet Consolidated Mining Co.* 342 U.S. 437 (1952).

[2] Restatement, Second, Conflict of Laws (para. 81).

[3] P. Hay, R. J. Waintraub and P. J. Borchers, *Conflict of Laws Cases and Materials* (11th ed., Foundation Press, New York, 2000), p. 120.

litigation, jurisdiction *in rem* cannot be based thereon.[4] A good example of *in rem* jurisdiction can be found in the case *Heathmount A.E. Corp. v. Technodome.com and Destinationtechnodome.com*,[5] where a Canadian corporation sued two domain names because the court lacked personal jurisdiction over the person who registered these names in bad faith. The Canadian corporation was satisfied with jurisdiction in rem since it did not seek damages, but only an order returning the domain names to it.

10.18 **Limitations to jurisdiction** In certain situations a court will refrain from exercising its jurisdiction.[6] This may happen in the following cases:

(a) The parties agreed that a specific forum would have jurisdiction. These agreements are usually given effect by courts except when it would be "unfair or unreasonable".[7] The exercise by a court of jurisdiction granted in such agreement is called "prorogation". If the action is brought before another court, such court may refrain from exercising jurisdiction. This is called "derogation".[8]

(b) If a defendant was lured into the jurisdiction of a court by fraud, this court may decline jurisdiction.[9]

(c) Another basis for declining existent jurisdiction is *forum non conveniens*. This literally means that the addressed forum is not the appropriate one. This basis for declining jurisdiction is necessary to balance the broad choice of fora a plaintiff has in the United States.[10]

(d) Where an action is brought before a court and subsequently before another, in federal practice the "first filed rule" applies. This entails that all the issues be joined in the first forum. Regarding state law, different rules apply in the different states. In some states a court may dismiss an action. This is, however, discretionary. A court may also, where the action has been brought in another court, apply the *forum non conveniens* doctrine to decline jurisdiction.[11]

---

[4] *Shaffer v. Heitner* 433 U.S. 186, 53 L.Ed.2d 683, 97 S.Ct. 2569 (1977).
[5] Judgment of July 24, 2000, U.S. District Court for the Eastern District of Virginia, Alexandria Division.
[6] P. Hay, R. J. Waintraub and P. J. Borchers, *op. cit.*, p. 158.
[7] Restatement, Second, Conflict of laws (para. 80).
[8] P. Hay, R. J. Waintraub, P. J. Borchers, *op. cit.*, p. 158.
[9] This happened, for instance, in *Telizzi v. Brodie*, 38 A.D.2d 762, 329 N.Y.S. 2d 589 (1972), where the defendants were invited to a theatre performance and told that they would receive questionaires after the performance. They were then served with process in order to establish jurisdiction. The Supreme Court found that this service was invalid and that jurisdiction should be declined. See also P. Hay, R. J. Waintraub and P. J. Borchers, *op. cit.*, pp. 170–172.
[10] P. Hay, R. J. Waintraub and P. J. Borchers, *op. cit.*, p. 172. The doctrine of *forum non conveniens* was accepted by the Supreme Court in 1947: *Gulf Oil Corp. v. Gilbert* 330 U.S. 501, 67 S.Ct. 839, 91 L.Ed.1055 (1947).
[11] P. Hay, R. J. Waintraub and P. J. Borchers, *op. cit.*, pp. 184–185.

PART III: ADMINISTRATION OF JUSTICE

Service abroad

Service abroad of judicial documents   Various bilateral and multilateral **10.19** treaties determine how service abroad has to be effected. These treaties generally provide for a uniform simplified system for service in the contracting states.

In the E.U. there is a Regulation governing service in another Member State (see paragraph 10.21).[12] An important multilateral convention is the Hague Convention of November 15, 1965 on the service abroad of judicial and extra-judicial documents in civil or commercial matters.[13]

The Hague Convention   Apart from the fact that the Convention is applica- **10.20** ble exclusively to civil and commercial matters,[14] two further conditions have to be fulfilled for the Hague Convention to be applicable:

(a) the address of the addressee must be known; and

(b) the service of a writ must take place from one contracting state into another contracting state.[15]

When the conditions are satisfied, service is effected by intervention of a central authority appointed by each of the contracting states.[16] The central authority of

---

[12] Council Regulation 1348/2000 on the service in the Member States of judicial and extra-judicial documents in civil or commercial matters, [2000] O.J. L160, 37.

[13] cf. *Practical Handbook on the Operation of the Hague Convention of November 15, 1965 on the service abroad of judicial and extra-judicial documents in civil or commercial matters* (Maklu, Antwerp, 1992) (loose-leaf); K. B. Reisenfeld, "Service of United States process abroad: A practical guide to service under the Hague Service Convention and the federal rules of civil procedure" (1990) IntL 55; Special Commission report on the operation of the Hague Service Convention (1989) I.L.M. 1558. The Convention of 1965 improves the Hague Convention of March 1, 1954 in respect of civil procedure, replacing in its turn the Hague Convention of July 17, 1905 on civil procedure.

[14] Art. 1 of the Convention. For the service in criminal and fiscal matters see the European Convention on mutual judicial assistance in criminal matters as well as a number of bilateral treaties.

[15] The contracting states are: Antigua and Barbuda, Aruba, Bahamas, Barbados, Belarus, Belgium, Botswana, Bulgaria, Canada, China, Cyprus, the Czech Republic, Denmark, Egypt, Estonia, Finland, France, Germany, Greece, Hong Kong, Ireland, Israel, Italy, Japan, Korea, Latvia, Luxembourg, Malawi, Macao, the Netherlands, Norway, Pakistan, Poland, Portugal, the Seychelles, Slovakia, Spain, Turkey, the U.K. (including Bermuda, the Falkland Islands, Fiji, Gibraltar), the U.S. (including Guam, American Virgin Islands and Puerto Rico), Sweden, Switzerland, Venezuela.

[16] These are, for instance, for: Belgium: Department of Justice; Canada: Central Authorities of provinces, which differ from each other; China: Bureau of International Judicial Assistance; Denmark: Department of Justice; France: Department of Justice; Germany: local authorities of the federal states; Greece: Department of Foreign Affairs; Italy: Clerk of the Court of Appeal of Rome; Japan: Department of Foreign Affairs; Luxembourg: Advocat General of the High Court; the Netherlands: Public Prosecutor of the Appeal Court of The Hague; Portugal: Department of Justice; Spain: Department of Justice; U.K.: Department of Foreign Affairs; U.S.: Office of International Judicial Assistance. The intervention by a central authority is a great improvement in comparison with the Convention of March 1, 1954, which provided for consular intervention. The consul was instructed through the Department of Foreign Affairs to hand over the documents to an authority appointed by the foreign state. As the consular handover can be a time-consuming affair, it occurred more than once that judgment was passed on a foreign defendant by default before the writ was served on him.

the applicant or his process server shall instruct the central authority of the addressee to effect the service.[17] The Hague Convention also provides for a number of alternative methods, such as direct service by mail[18] and service through a process server (Article 10).[19] The Hague Convention includes a specific protection for the addressee in the event that he does not appear or a judgment by default is passed against him: the court may suspend its judgment or the defendant may be given a new term for making an appearance.

10.21   **E.U. Regulation on Service**[20]   This Regulation entered into force on May 31, 2001 in all the Member States except Denmark. It governs the service of judicial documents from one Member Sate in another Member State of the E.U. Each Member State has a transmitting and a receiving agency (Article 20). The transmitting agency of one state sends the documents to the receiving agency of another state. The receiving agency then acknowledges receipt and serves the document on the individual in question (Articles 4 and 6). The documents are exempt from any legalisation in the Member State where it is received (Article 4). The documents need to be in the official language of the Member State where it is to be served. If there is more than one official language, the document should be in the language of the region where it is to be served (Article 4). If the document is not in the appropriate language, the addressee may refuse to accept it (Article 8). The standard form to be used for the transmission of the documents is annexed to the Regulation. This procedure may also be used for the transmission of extra-judicial documents.

The Regulation also permits other forms of service (Articles 12–15).

10.22   **Serving documents in the absence of a treaty**   When service of a document is not governed by treaty or E.U. Regulation, the domestic law of the forum state applies.

The following system is followed in France, Luxembourg, the Netherlands, Italy and Belgium: if the domicile of the foreign addressee is known, the applicant must use an official process server. This public official sends a registered letter to the foreign domicile or residence of the person for service. It is the act of depositing the document at the post office that effects the service, no matter when the document actually reaches the addressee. A German court, on the other hand, may in principle not pass judgment before official evidence has been submitted that the writ was actually served on the addressee personally.[21]

---

[17] Arts 3–6.

[18] L. A. Leo, "The interplay between domestic rules permitting service abroad by mail and the Hague Convention on service: proposing an amendment to the federal rules of civil procedure" (1989) Cornell Int'l.L.J. 335.

[19] Bulgaria, China, the Czech Republic, Germany, Egypt, Korea, Norway, Poland, Slovakia, Switzerland and Turkey have objected to all alternative methods. Some other countries have more limited reservations.

[20] Council Regulation 1348/2000 on the service in the Member States of judicial and extra-judicial documents in civil or commercial matters, [2000] O.J. L160 , p. 37.

[21] This system has implications for international treaties concluded with Germany. *cf.* the reservation made in respect of the Hague Convention of 1965 and the non-applicability of Art. IV of the Protocol annexed to the Brussels Convention.

Cautio judicatum solvi

In the absence of treaty provisions to the contrary, the defendant may in several **10.23** countries request a foreign plaintiff (or a third party on his behalf) to give security for the costs and possible damages resulting from his court action.[22] This requirement has been waived in many treaties.[23]

Proof of foreign law

National court and foreign law There are two approaches for the court in **10.24** relation to foreign law.[24]

The first approach, followed *inter alia* in the Anglo-American legal system, is to consider foreign law as a question of fact that must be proven by the parties. The court is not supposed to know the foreign law or to apply it *ex officio*.

The English courts require that foreign law be proven as a fact by expert evidence or by other means.[25] If the parties do not succeed in providing proof, the court shall apply English law.[26] In the United States, the foreign law should be determined by the trial judge and not by the jury.[27] It is unclear whether the court should refuse the action or apply American law when the parties cannot prove the foreign law.[28]

This approach is in contrast to countries such as Austria, Belgium, France,[29] Germany,[30] Italy and Switzerland[31] that apply the rule *iura curia novit* to foreign

---

[22] For the relevance of the *cautio iudicatum solvi* to arbitration, see O. Sandrock, "The *cautio iudicatum solvi* in arbitration proceedings" (1997) 2 J.I.A. 17. See also the case of the French Court of Cassation, March 16, 1999 (2000) R.C.D.I.P. 223 where a *cautio iudicatum solvi* of £25,000 was found to be an obstruction to justice.

[23] *Inter alia*, the Hague Convention of March 1, 1954 on civil procedure (Art. 17) and the Convention on Establishment of March 13, 1955 (Art. 9). The Convention of 1954 was in respect of *the cautio iudicatum solvi* replaced by the Convention of October 25, 1980 on international access to justice. The *cautio iudicatum solvi* is also abolished in many bilateral friendship and trade conventions (see para. 1.02). See also J. Soek, "Recent developments in the field of *Cautio Iudicatum Solvi*, cost free access and free legal assistance" (1981) N.I.L.R. 284.

[24] See T. C. Hartley, "Pleading and proof of foreign law: the major European systems compared" (1996) 45 I.C.L.Q. 271 ; I. Zajtay, "The application of foreign law" in (1971) *International Encyclopedia of Comparative Law* III, Chap. 14.

[25] See J. O'Brien, *Smith's Conflict of Laws* (Cavendish Publishing Limited, London, 1999) pp. 145–146; where necessary, expert witnesses may be cross-examined.

[26] L. Collins (ed.), *Dicey and Morris on the Conflict of Laws* (Sweet & Maxwell, London, 2000) p. 221; R. Fentiman, "Foreign law in English courts" (1992) L.Q.R. 142.

[27] P. Hay, R. J. Weintraub, P. J. Borchers (eds), *op. cit.*, p. 402.

[28] Federal Rules of Civil Procedure, rule 44.1; S.L. Sass, "Foreign law in federal courts" (1981) Am.J.Comp.L. 97–118. See the case *Tidewater Oil Co. v. Waller*, 302 F.2d 638 (10th Cir. 1962) where the court set out three alternative courses that have been followed where foreign law was not proven: (1) dismissed the claim, (2) applied the law of the forum, (3) indulged in certain presumptions as to the foreign law and applied it accordingly.

[29] B. Audit, *Droit International Privé* (Economica, Paris, 1997) pp. 224 *et seq.*; D. Bureau, "L'application d'office de la loi étrangère" (1990) J.D.I. 317–364; S. Hantel, "Anwendung ausländischen Rechts vor Französichen Gerichten" (1991) RabelsZ. 143–151; A. Ponsard, "L'office du juge et l'application du droit étranger" (1990) R.C.D.I.P. 607–619.

[30] P. Mankowski, "Arrest—Einstweilige Verfügung und die Anwendung ausländischen Recht" (1990) IPRax 372–378.

[31] Loi fédérale d'organisation judiciaire, Art. 16.

law. In these countries the court is supposed to know and apply the foreign law *ex officio*. The courts, however, may invite the parties to submit evidence on the content of foreign law.[32]

Courts of the contracting states may use the London Convention on Information on Foreign Law for information on law from other contracting states.[32] Under this Convention each contracting state has a "sending" and a "receiving" authority: the sending authority transmits the legal inquiries from a court of that country to the receiving authority of another contracting state who shall reply as soon as possible. In practice this Convention is used very little.

In Belgium, France, Italy and Spain, for instance the traditional means of proving foreign law is the written expert opinion, also known as *Certificat de Coutûme*, drawn up by legal practitioners from the relevant country. In Germany a written opinion (*Gutachten*) is required from a university research institute (*e.g.* the Max Planck Institut).

Evidence

10.25 The rules of evidence allocate the burden of proof. Furthermore, they determine the strength and the forms of written evidence, witness testimony, presumptions and hearsay evidence. They outline how witnesses are to be interviewed (*e.g.* by cross-examination by the other party as in the United States; by interrogation by the court, as on the European continent).

In the United States, documentary evidence is often requested by the claimant in a specific discovery procedure that precedes the actual lawsuit. The extent of this pre-trial discovery can often be so wide that its only purpose is to obtain possession of previously unknown incriminating documents from the defendant (so-called "fishing expeditions").[33]

The extraterritorial discovery orders (see paragraph 1.19) from *e.g.* an American court are generally not well received abroad.[34] A statute may prevent own nationals from complying with such orders (the so-called "blocking statutes").[35]

---

[32] European Convention on Information on Foreign Law, London, June 7, 1968. This convention applies between Albania, Austria, Azerbaijan, Belarus, Belgium, Cyprus, Costa Rica, Czech Republic, Denmark, Estonia, Finland, France, Georgia, Germany, Greece, Hungary, Iceland, Italy, Latvia, Liechtenstein, Lithuania, Luxembourg, Malta, the Netherlands, Norway, Poland, Portugal, Romania, Russia, Slovakia, Slovenia, Spain, Sweden, Switzerland, Turkey, Ukraine and the U.K. See B. J. Rodger, J. van Doorn, "Proof of Foreign Law : The Impact of the London Convention" (1997) 46 I.C.L.Q. 151.

[33] G. Born, *International Civil Litigation in United States Courts* (Kluwer, Deventer, 1996) pp. 847–852.

[34] D. Gerber, "Extraterritorial discovery and the conflict of procedural systems: Germany and the United States" (1986) Am.J.Comp.L. 784; H. V. von Hülsen, "Gebrauch und Missbrauch US-Amerikanischer 'pre-trial discovery' und die internationale Rechtshilfe" (1982) RIW 225–235. See also Roggenbuck "U.S.-amerikanischen Discovery im deutchen Zivilprozeß?" (1997) IPRax 76.

[35] *e.g.* for Great Britain: "British protection of Trading Interest Act" (1982) I.L.M. 834; L. Collins (ed.), *Dicey and Morris on the Conflict of Laws* (Sweet & Maxwell, London, 2000) p. 565; for France: Statute 80–538 (1980); see also G. Born, *op.cit*, pp. 850–852.

Or a foreign court may prohibit compliance with this order.[36] It can even prevent a party from instituting a discovery procedure in an American court (the so-called "anti-suit injunction").[37]

Each court applies its own law of evidence. This may occasionally lead to problems in proceedings with foreign dimensions.[38]

Courts in continental Europe often rely on court appointed experts to establish the facts of a case and give an appraisal of the technical aspects of a dispute.

The courts in Anglo-American countries do not as a rule appoint experts to give evidence, but each of the parties gives evidence through an expert witness of its own choice.

In international trade disputes, the facts are sometimes established by independent surveillance organisations at the request of one party (amongst others, Société de Surveillance (SGS) (Geneva); Cargo Superintendents Ltd (London); Superintendence Co. (New York)). These organisations have the advantage of independence and great expertise. Although they are often given the task of determining the facts by one party, their reports may—particularly when there are no conflicting reports—have the same strength of evidence as a court appointed expert.

A court may sometimes be forced to obtain evidence abroad. It may order that witnesses who are residing abroad be heard under oath at their place of residence; it may find it necessary that a foreign location is visited or that documents which can only be removed with great difficulty, are examined locally. As the court has only territorial competence, it then has to authorise a foreign authority (*e.g.* consul or local court) to hear evidence, to visit the location or to examine the documents. However, this rogatory commission can only operate with permission from the local authority.[39] Rogatory commissions are in practice only issued within the framework of bilateral and multilateral treaties.

An important multilateral treaty in this respect is the Hague Convention on the Taking of Evidence Abroad, 1970.[40] Under the Convention, a rogatory commission from a contracting state can be issued to a central authority of another contracting state. Evidence can also be gathered by a consular official or a specially appointed commissioner.[41]

---

[36] *British Airways Board v. Laker Airways Ltd* [1985] A.C. 58, HL; *Midland Bank v. Laker Airways Ltd* [1986] Q.B. 689, CA; *Re Westinghouse Electric Corpn Uranium Contract* [1978] Litigation M.D.L. Docket No. 235 A.C. 547/654; L. Collins (ed.), *Dicey and Morris on the Conflict of Laws* (Sweet & Maxwell, London, 2000) pp. 206–212 and 402–405.

[37] *cf.* W. Kennet, "Les injonctions anti-suit" and H. van Houtte, "À Propos des injonctions anti-suit et d'autre torpilles pour couler des action étrangères" in M. T. Caupain and G. De Leval, *L'éficacité de la justice civile en europe* (Larcier, Brussels, 2000) pp. 133 and 147

[38] D. Coester-Waltjen, *Internationales Beweisrecht* (Gremer, Ebelsbach, 1983).

[39] C. Gavalda, "Les commissions rogatoires internationales en matière civile et commerciale" (1964) R.C.D.I.P. 15.

[40] Convention of March 18, 1970 on the Taking of Evidence abroad in Civil or Commercial Matters. The contracting states are Argentina, Australia, Barbados, Bulgaria, China, Cyprus, Czech Republic, Denmark, Estonia, Finland, France, Germany, Hong Kong, Israel, Italy, Latvia, Lithuania, Luxembourg, Macao, Mexico, Monaco, the Netherlands, Norway, Poland, Portugal, Russia, Singapore, Slovakia, Slovenia, South Africa, Spain, Sri Lanka, Sweden, Switzerland, Turkey, Ukraine, the U.K., the U.S. and Venezuela.

[41] The first method is of European origin, whilst the second is used in the U.S.

Most contracting states of the Evidence Convention—with the exception of the United States—have made the reservation that a contracting state is not required to co-operate with a pre-trial discovery of documents.[42] Some of the states set conditions to their co-operation with pre-trial discovery, for example that the documents should be clearly enumerated in the request or should be easily identifiable.[43] However, the United States Supreme Court has decided that the national rules of evidence providing for a pre-trial discovery may still be applied in certain circumstances, even though they depart from the Evidence Convention.[44]

In the European Union the obtaining of evidence from another Member State is simplified and accelerated by the Regulation on co-operation between the courts of the Member States in the taking of evidence in civil or commercial matters.[45] The Regulation entered into force on July 1, 2001 in all Member States of the E.U. except Denmark. It will apply from January 1, 2004.[46] The basic working of the Convention is that a court of one Member State, the "requesting court" send a request for the taking of evidence directly to a court in another Member State, the "requested court". The requested court then has to deal with the request and respond within a certain time. The Regulation provides standard forms by which such requests and responses should be made. Each Member State also has to appoint a central body responsible for supplying information to courts, helping with difficulties that might arise from requests and forwarding requests which should have been made to a different court.

Claims in foreign currency

10.26 Can an action before the court be expressed in a currency different from the one of the forum country, for instance, when the contract price is expressed in a different currency unit? Can the court order payment in a foreign currency? These questions are important when the forum currency depreciates quicker than the foreign currency.

In many jurisdictions (*e.g.* Austria, Belgium, England, Germany, Italy, Norway and Switzerland), the courts have competence to order payment in foreign currency (see paragraph 9.05).[47]

---

[42] Art. 23.

[43] China, France, Mexico, Estonia and Venezuela.

[44] *Aerospatiale v. U.S. District Court for the Southern District of Iowa 482 U.S.*, 107 Supreme Court 2542, 96 L.Ed.2d 461 (1987). R. Beckmann, "Das Haager Beweisübereinkommen und seine Bedeutung für die Pre-Trial Discovery" (1990) IPRax 201; R. D. Roth, "Five years after Aérospatiale: Rethinking discovery abroad in civil and commercial litigation under the Hague Evidence Convention and the federal rules of civil procedure" (1992) U.Pa.J.Int'l.L.Bus.L. 425–471.

[45] Council Regulation 1206/2001 [2001] O.J. L174.

[46] However, Arts 19, 21 and 22 have been applicable since July 1, 2001. These three articles deal with the implementation of the Regulation.

[47] See, *e.g. Miliangos v. Frank (Textiles) Ltd* [1976] A.C. 443; M. Niyonzima, *La Clause de Monnaie Étrangère dans les Contrats Internationaux* (Bruylant, Brussels, 1991), pp. 202–209. Arbitrators can also give an award in a currency different from that of the seat of the arbitral tribunal; the award is usually expressed in the currency of the contract price unless otherwise agreed by the parties. See, *e.g.* ICC 2103, (1974) J.D.I. 903–904.

PART IV: ENFORCEMENT OF FOREIGN JUDGMENTS

General It often makes sense to sue in the country where the defendant has **10.27** assets, since the judgment can then be enforced without additional proceedings. Nevertheless, it may be necessary to enforce a judgment in another state than where it was rendered.

Each legal system has its own enforcement rules for foreign judgments.[48] In the Member States of the European Union (with the exception of Denmark), the recognition and enforcement of judgments are governed by the Brussels I Regulation; when Denmark is involved, by the Brussels Convention (see paragraph 10.28).[49] The Lugano Convention also covers recognition and enforcement of judgments (see paragraph 10.28). The Hague Convention on the Recognition and Enforcement of Foreign Judgments in Civil and Commercial Matters was not widely accepted and is only in force in Cyprus, the Netherlands and Portugal.[50] A world-wide Convention on Jurisdiction and Foreign Judgments is still in the making (see paragraph 10.05).[51]

Brussels I Regulation and Lugano Convention The purpose of the Brus- **10.28** sels I Regulation and Lugano Convention is "a free movement of judgments"[52] for judgments covered. These texts make enforcement relatively simple.

An E.U. or Lugano Convention court that must recognise or enforce a judgment from a Member/contracting State may not review the substance of the case.[53] It has to accept the foreign judgment as being correct.

---

[48] For a general comparative survey see, *inter alia*, D. Campbell, *International Execution against Judgment Debtors* (Sweet & Maxwell, London, 1993) with reports on, *inter alia*, Argentina, Belgium, Brazil, Canada, Cayman Islands, Denmark, England and Wales, Finland, France, Germany, Hong Kong, India, Ireland, Israel, Italy, Japan, Kenya, Korea, Liechtenstein, Luxembourg, Malta, the Netherlands, New Zealand, Nigeria, Northern Ireland, Norway, Portugal, South Africa, Spain, Sweden, Switzerland and the U.S. See more specifically Y. Quitin, "La reconnaissance et l'exécution des jugements étrangers en droit américain" (1985) R.C.D.I.P. 433; G. Ginsburgs, *The Soviet Union and International Co-operation in Legal Matters* (Nijhoff, Dordrecht, 1991) pp. 226 *et seq.*; T. Hosoi, "Recognition and enforcement of foreign judgments in Japan" (1992) C.L.Y.I.B. 107; A. Sistilli, "Italy: enforcement of foreign judgments" (1996) Int'l.Bus.Law. 542. See also the Draft Agreement between the European Communities and the Government of the United States of America on application of positive comity principles in the enforcement of their competition laws, 1997.

[49] See, in general, W. Kennett, *The Enforcement of Judgments in Europe* (Oxford University Press, Oxford, 2000); P. Kaye (ed.); *Methods of Execution of Orders and Judgments in Europe* (John Wiley and Sons, Chichester, 1996); G. Walter and S. P. Baumgartner (eds), *Recognition and Enforcement of Foreign Judgments Outside the Scope of the Brussels and Lugano Conventions* (Kluwer, The Hague, 2000).

[50] Hague Convention on the Recognition and Enforcement of Foreign Judgments in Civil and Commercial Matters of February 1, 1971. Text in *Recueil des Conventions (1951–1988)*. See C. Fragistas, "Rapport explicatif" (1966) *Actes et documents de la Session Extraordinaire* 358.

[51] See also J.-J. Forner Delaygua, *Hacia un Convenio Mundial de "Exequatur"* (Bosch, Barcelona, 1999).

[52] *cf.* Case C–267/97 *Éric Coursier v. Fortis Bank SA, Martine Coursier, née Bellami* [1999] E.C.R. I–2543, para. 25.

[53] Brussels I Regulation, Art. 36; Lugano Convention, Art. 29.

The enforcement is sought by means of a unilateral application of any interested party of an enforceable[54] judgment.[55] The applicant must give an address for service of process within the jurisdiction of the court applied to.[56] A copy of the judgment which satisfies the conditions necessary to establish its authenticity shall be produced with the unilateral application for enforcement.[57]

Under the Brussels I Regulation, the enforcement order has to be granted *ex parte* and immediately on the completion of certain formalities (Articles 41 and 53). Only on appeal and in a contradictory debate can enforcement be refused on a limited number of grounds (those specified in Articles 34 and 35). Under Article 34 of the Lugano Convention, the judge may check *ex officio* in an *ex parte* procedure whether enforcement should be refused because the foreign judgment does not satisfy some specific criteria (contained in Articles 27 and 28).[58]

The following are grounds for refusal of recognition and enforcement (under the Regulation only on appeal, while also in first instance under the Lugano Convention):

(a) if it is contrary to public policy of the state in which recognition is sought[59];

(b) when the judgment was given in default, if the defendant was not served

---

[54] The judgment must only be formally enforceable in the state of its origin, and the executability in that state is irrelevant: in Case C–267/97 *Éric Coursier v. Fortis Bank SA, Martine Coursier, née Bellami* [1999] E.C.R. I–2543 the debtor has become insolvent, but the judgment was still declared enforceable.

[55] Brussels I Regulation, Art. 38; Lugano Convention, Art. 31. The Brussels I Regulation (Annex II) and Lugano Convention (Art. 32). For instance, in Belgium it is the Court of First Instance; in Germany, the presiding judge of a chamber of the "Landgericht"; in France, the presiding judge of the *Tribunal de grande instance*; in Italy, the *Corte d'Appello*; in Ireland the High Court; in the Netherlands, the presiding judge of the *Arrondissementsrechtbank*; in Spain the *Juzgado di Primera Instanza* and in England and Wales to the High Court of Justice.

[56] Brussels I Regulation, Art. 40; Lugano Convention, Art. 33. See Case 198/85 *Carron v. Germany* [1986] E.C.R. 2437, with annotations by A. Huet in (1987) J.D.I. 476 and H. Gaudemet-Tallon in (1987) R.C.D.I.P. 148.

[57] Brussels I Regulation, Art. 53; Lugano Convention, Arts. 46–47. Annex V of the Regulation contains a standard form to accompany the foreign judgment when recognition is sought. A court may accept an equivalent document, or dispense with the production of this form if it has sufficient information.

[58] For a general discussion of these criteria see *e.g.* P. Kaye, *Law of the European Judgments Convention* (Barry Rose Law Publishers, Chichester, 1999), pp. 3504 *et seq.*; J. Kropholler, *Europäisches Zivilprozessrecht* (Verlag Recht und Wirtschaft, Heidelberg, 1998), p. 316.

[59] Brussels I Regulation, Art. 34.1; Lugano Convention, Art. 27.1.

with the document instituting proceedings in sufficient time and in such a way to enable him to arrange for his defence, unless the defendant failed to commence proceedings when it was possible to do so[60];

(c) if it is irreconcilable with a judgment given in a dispute by the same parties in the Member State in which recognition is sought[61];

(d) if it is irreconcilable with an earlier judgment given in another state involving the same cause of action and the same parties, provided that the earlier judgment fulfils the conditions necessary for its recognition in the addressed state[62];

(e) if the judgment conflicts with the jurisdiction rules in respect of insurance, consumer contracts or exclusive jurisdiction (see paragraphs 10.07 and 10.10).[63]

The party against whom enforcement is sought has a right of appeal against the decision. The appellant must appeal within one month of service of the enforcement order.[64] If no appeal is made within this term the enforcement order becomes irreversible.[65] The term of one month for appealing shall be extended to two months if the party against whom enforcement is sought, is not domiciled in the country of the enforcement order.[66] The judgement given on the appeal may be contested.[67] If an appeal is made against the recognition of a judgment, the court to which the appeal is made may stay the proceedings if an ordinary appeal has been lodged against the judgment in the state of origin.[68] However, if the appeal is once again contested, the court before which this contestation takes place, may not make an order on the staying of the proceedings.[69]

---

[60] Brussels I Regulation, Art. 34.2; Lugano Convention, Art. 27.2. See Case 166/80 *Klomps v. Michel* [1981] E.C.R. 1593; [1983] 1 C.M.L.R. 252; (1981) R.C.D.I.P. 726; Case 228/81 *Pendy v. Pluspunkt* [1982] E.C.R. 2723; [1983] 1 C.M.L.R. 665; Case 49/84; *Debaecker v. Bouwman* [1985] E.C.R. 1779, [1986] 2 C.M.L.R. 400; Case 305/88 *Lancray v. Peters and Sickert* [1990] E.C.R. I–2725, annotation by H. Tagaras (1990) Cah.Dr.Eur. 709; Case C–123/91 *Minalmet v. Brandeis* [1992] E.C.R. 5661. See Case C–78/95 *Bernardus Hendrikman and Maria Feyen v. Magenta Druck and Verlag GmbH* [1996] E.C.R. I–4943 where there was not proper service, but despite this, a defence was entered, but without the authority of the defendants. The Court of Justice held that a court can refuse to recognise the judgment because the defendants were quite powerless to defend themselves; annotations P. Volken (1998) R.S.D.I.E. 133, A. Huet (1997) J.D.I. 621.
[61] Brussels I Convention, Art. 34.3; Lugano Convention, Art. 27.3. In Case C–414/92 *Solo Kleinmotoren v. Boch* [1994] E.C.R. I–2237, the court ruled that an enforceable settlement reached before a court of the state in which negotiation is sought in order to put an end to a pending order, is not a "judgment given in dispute between the same parties in the state in which negotiation is sought".
[62] Brussels I Convention, Art. 34.4; Lugano Convention, Art. 27.5.
[63] Brussels I Regulation, Art. 35; Lugano Convention, Art. 28.
[64] Brussels I Regulation, Art. 43.5; Lugano Convention, Art. 36.
[65] See Case 145/86, *Hoffman v. Krieg* [1988] E.C.R. 645 for the situation where the judgment seises to be enforceble for reasons outside the Convention (now Regulation).
[66] Brussels I Regulation, Art. 43.5; Lugano Convention, Art. 36.
[67] Brussels I Regulation, Art. 44 and Annex IV; Lugano Convention, Art. 37. See, for a definition of "ordinary appeal", Case 43/77 *Industrial Diamond Supplies v. Luigi Riva* [1977] E.C.R. 2175; [1978] 1 C.M.L.R. 349, with annotation by H. Gaudemet-Tallon in (1979) R.C.D.I.P. 433.
[68] Brussels I Regulation, Art. 46; Lugano Convention, Art. 38.
[69] Case C–432/93 *Société d'Informatique Service Réalisation Organisation (SISRO) v. Ampersand Software BV* [1995] E.C.R. I–2269; [1995] I.L.Pr. 713, annotation T. Hartley (1996) E.L.Rev. 169.

The court may reserve judgment if an ordinary remedy (*e.g.* appeal) has been instituted against a decision, the substance of which is the basis for the procedure for recognition in the state where the decision was given, or if the term for appeal has not yet expired.[70]

PART V: INTERNATIONAL INSOLVENCY AND BANKRUPTCY LAW

Introduction

10.29   **Bankruptcy and other forms of insolvency**   A business may become insolvent whenever it is no longer able to meet its payment obligations and has exhausted its credit facilities.

Most legal systems have rules to liquidate insolvent companies whereby creditors are prevented from taking off with what remains of the assets of the business and whereby a third person (*e.g.* bankruptcy administrator, liquidator or receiver) is entrusted with the fair distribution of the assets between the creditors (of which some have legal priority).[71]

As an alternative, the insolvent debtor may be allowed to try to overcome the financial crisis and resume commerce. Such "composition" proceedings, usually carried out under the supervision of a court, seek to reach an agreement between the debtor and its creditors about relief that should allow the debtor to reorganise and restore its business.

Each legal system has its own insolvency and bankruptcy rules. There are different philosophical approaches to insolvency. Some legal systems place more emphasis on the creditors and want to ensure that they loose as little as possible and recover as much as possible as quickly as possible. It is therefore easy to wind up a business. Other systems are more concerned about the recovery of the insolvent business, which may even have to be restructured.[72] Only when this proves unsuccessful will the business be wound up for the benefit of the creditors. The modern tendency is towards rescue: in the old Belgian system, for instance, this alternative existed, but was barely used. After the reforms of 1997, the *Concordat Judiciaire* became much more important. In the Danish Bankruptcy Act (1986) two of the five chapters deal with what is called compulsory compensation and debt rescheduling.[73] The classical French term *droit des faillites* have recently been replaced by the term *droit des entreprises en difficulté*.[74]

---

[70] Case 258/83, *Brennero v. Wendel*, [1984] E.C.R. 3971; [1986] 2 C.M.L.R. 59; Case C–183/90, *Van Dalfsen v. Van Loon and Berendsen* [1991] E.C.R. 4743.

[71] See R. K. Rasmussen, "A new approach to transnational insolvencies"(1997) *Michigan Journal of International Law* 1.

[72] See Cork Report (Report of the Review Committee on Insolvency and Practice (1982) Cmnd. 8558) (U.K.), which distinguishes three different interested groups: the bankrupt person or entity, the creditors and society. For a summary of the report see F. Tolmie, *Introduction to Corporate and Personal Insolvency Law* (Sweet & Maxwell, London, 1998), p. 4.

[73] *cf.* L. L. Petersen and N. Ørgaard, *Danish Insolvency Law—A Survey* (Jurist– og Økonomforbundets Forlag, Copenhagen, 1996).

[74] C. Saint-Alary-Houin, *Droit des entreprises en difficulté* (Montchrestien, Paris, 1996) p. 1.

Nevertheless, all legal instruments dealing with this matter have two elements in common:

1. the control over the assets of an insolvent business is transferred to a third person;

2. claims against the insolvent business cannot be dealt with individually, but must be dealt with collectively by the receiver or liquidator of the insolvent estate.[75]

In this text, the term "bankruptcy" will be used to indicate the various bankruptcy and insolvency procedures.

Under Belgian bankruptcy law, a receiver under supervision of a court draws up, administers and shares out the assets to the rightful parties. The option of a judicial arrangement exists if the majority of creditors agree to give the business a reprieve and to reduce their claims.[76]

In French law the traditional bankruptcy has made way for more modern methods which primarily have as their objective to put the business in order instead of paying the creditors first. Through the *loi relative au redressement et à la liquidation judiciaire des entreprises*, individual claims from creditors are suspended while the *Administrateur* appointed by the court must decide whether to continue, sell or dissolve the business.[77]

English law distinguishes between the insolvency of a natural person and of a legal person. A natural person can be declared bankrupt by means of the Insolvency Act 1986. A bankrupt company has to be wound up. A liquidator is responsible for the distribution of the assets. As an alternative to winding up, other routes are a voluntary arrangement with creditors, an administrative order from a court to appoint an administrator to manage the affairs, business and property of the company, or the appointment of a receiver.[78]

In the United States, besides bankruptcy, Chapter 11 of the Bankruptcy Act entails the reorganisation of the business while in the meantime the third party claims are suspended.[79]

---

[75] See, "Solving the insoluble—A legal guide to insolvency regulations around the world" (1990) I.F.L.R. 1–60. *cf.* P. R. Wood *Principles of International Insolvency* (Sweet & Maxwell, London, 1995), p. 2, where he distinguishes three essential features of bankruptcy.

[76] *cf.* the Belgium Bankruptcy Act of 1997 as incorporated in the Commercial Code (Book III) and the Judicial Accord Act of 1997.

[77] *cf.* Act of June 10, 1994; *cf.* C. Saint-Alary-Houin, *op. cit.*; I.B.L.J. 313; G. Endreo, French report in "Solving the insoluble—A legal guide to insolvency regulations around the world" (1990) I.F.L.R. 20–28.

[78] *cf.* U.K. Insolvency Acts of 1986 and of 1994 (as well as the supplementary Insolvency Rules); Companies Act of 1989; I. Fletcher, *The Law of Insolvency* (Sweet & Maxwell, London, 1996); F. Tolmie, *Introduction to Corporate and Personal Insolvency Law* (Sweet & Maxwell, London, 1998).

[79] *cf.* U.S. Bankruptcy Reform Act of 1978 (Bankruptcy Code), amended by the Bankruptcy Reform Act of 1994. See, *e.g.* D. G. Epstein, *Bankruptcy and Other Debtor-Creditor Laws* (West Publishing Co., St. Paul 1995) pp. 331 *et seq*; I.B.L.J. 237; H. Miller, M. Jacob and J. Liu, United States Report, in "Solving the insoluble—A legal guide to insolvency regulations around the world" (1990) I.F.L.R. 50–60.

It is not easy to understand the legal constructions for insolvency or bank-ruptcy as applied in different countries and to assess the legal effects of foreign bankruptcy proceedings.[80] An UNCITRAL model-law on cross-border insolvency has had no widespread acceptance.[81]

10.30 **Procedural and substantive law** Bankruptcy requires proceedings: court proceedings to grant and sanction a judicial arrangement; court proceedings to declare a person bankrupt and to appoint a receiver; proceedings against debtors and third parties to assemble the bankrupt's assets; proceedings to assess credi-tors' claims and to allocate payments.

Moreover, bankruptcy law also implies substantive rules that affect the exist-ing legal relationships of the bankrupt. They determine how the bankrupt hands over control over his assets to the receiver. They establish the extent to which the contractual debts of the bankrupt can be collected and the validity of agreements concluded in the so-called "suspect period" preceding the bankruptcy. They outline whether a bankrupt can be deprived of some of his political or social rights or whether he may be deprived of his freedom. They determine whether the bankruptcy extends to the assets of the spouse if the bankrupt is a natural person, or to the assets of the shareholders or directors, if the bankrupt is a company.

10.31 **Domiciliary and cross-border proceedings** The bankruptcy remains in many cases domiciliary: the bankrupt, the assets, the creditors and debtors are all part of the same national legal system. Only one court, that of the place where the company or entrepreneur is domiciled, has jurisdiction to declare the entrepre-neur bankrupt, to appoint a receiver and wind up the enterprise. Usually the same local law regulates the impact of bankruptcy on contracts, property, matrimonial property, legal capacity, etc.

A bankruptcy is cross-border when not all the relevant elements (bankrupt and his assets, creditors, debtors, etc.) are located within the same legal system. Most large bankruptcies inevitably have creditors, debtors or some assets abroad, but with trade becoming more international, even in smaller bankruptcies the receiver is often confronted with a foreign creditor or must challenge a foreign debtor or request the seizure of foreign assets.[82]

---

[80] See, *e.g.* in respect the comparison of an American "Chapter 11 procedure" with a German bankruptcy: BGH January 11, 1990, (1991) IPRax 183 and A. Flessner, "Zusammenhänge zwischen Konkurs, Arrest und internationaler Zuständigkeit" (1991) IPRax 162. Moreover, see the highly criticised judgment of the Antwerp court ordering sequestration, September 10, 1984 ((1985) *European Transport Law* 248) that laid down that an English "receivership and liquida-tion" does not prevent a sequestration in Belgium because the company was not in "bankruptcy" (as this is only possible for natural persons). An indication of equivalent constructions for insolvency within the E.U. can be found in Attachment A to the Insolvency Regulation (see para. 10.35).

[81] See J. Berends, "The UNCITRAL Model Law on Cross-Border Insolvency: a comprehensive overview" (1998) Tulane J. Int'l and Comp. L. 309.

[82] See A. Martin-Serf, "La faillite internationale : une réalité pressante, un enchevêtrement juridique croissant" (1995) 122 J.D.I. 31.

Territorial or universal approach   In a bankruptcy with cross-border ele-   **10.32**
ments, one could arrange for a separate bankruptcy in every country where assets
are located, with a local receiver, local creditors and local distribution of assets.
Thus, several bankruptcy laws—each with their own territorial application—
could apply to one bankrupt business. However, not all creditors would be treated
equally. Moreover, there would be a risk of contradictory decisions and of more
expenses and complications.[83] Furthermore, separate bankruptcy proceedings
hinder the restructuring of the insolvent business.[84]

It is therefore better if only one court and one receiver are competent to wind
up the transnational bankruptcy, with one pool of assets, one list of liabilities and
one distribution of the assets—no matter in what country the assets or creditors
are located.[85] Universal bankruptcy, however, can only be realised under two
conditions:

(a) the court that declares a business bankrupt must give the bankruptcy
    universal effect;

(b) this universal effect must be recognised in all countries where debtors,
    creditors or asserts are located.

Specific issues of cross-border bankruptcies

Introduction   In certain legal systems, a judicial order for liquidation will be   **10.33**
applicable internationally. It depends on the universal or territorial approach in
other legal systems whether such an order will have effect in those systems,
whether the powers of the receiver are recognised abroad and whether the rules
on the respect of contracts or securities, on an extension of the bankruptcy to
spouse, partners or directors and the like also have effects abroad.

In some cases the administration and recognition of trans-border bankruptcies
is regulated in a bilateral treaty[86] or a multilateral treaty.[87] In other cases the
relevant foreign law must be consulted.

---

[83] See, for instance the Dutch case of *Pres. Rb Amsterdam*, November 9, 1995, (1996) N.I.P.R. no.
432, where it was decided that the bankruptcy of a company from the Ivory Coast could be ignored
in the Netherlands and a ship belonging to the company might be sold off.

[84] J. A. Pastor Ridruejo, "La faillite en droit international privé" (1971) 133 Rec.Cours II, 169.

[85] See P. Trunk., *Internationales Insolvenzrecht. Systematische Darstellung des deutschen Rechts mit
rechtsvergleichender Bezügen* (Mohr Siebeck, Tübingen, 1998), pp. 34–45.

[86] See, *e.g.* the conventions between France and Switzerland (1869), between Belgium and France
(1899), between Belgium and the Netherlands (1925), between France and Italy (1930), between
Belgium and the United Kingdom (1934), between France and Monaco (1950), between the
Netherlands and Germany (1962), between Belgium and Austria (1969), between France and
Austria (1979), and between Germany and Austria (1979).

[87] See, *e.g.* the Nordic Bankruptcy Convention (1933) between Denmark, Finland, Iceland, Norway
and Sweden, the Montevideo Treaty (1889) between Argentina, Bolivia, Colombia and Peru and
the Bustamante Code (1928) between Bolivia, Brazil, Costa Rica, Cuba, Chile, Ecuador, El
Salvador, Guatemala, Haiti, Honduras, Nicaragua, Panama, Peru, Dominican Republic and Venezuela.

Jurisdiction

10.34 **General**   As already stated, there is a fundamental difference between the universal and the territorial vision on bankruptcy. According to the first view, the bankruptcy need only be declared by one court for the bankruptcy to extend to the full estate of the bankrupt, no matter where the assets are situated. The territorial doctrine, on the other hand, gives each country where assets of the bankrupt are located, jurisdiction to organise local bankruptcy proceedings. The territorial approach results in the institution of parallel proceedings in the respective countries where assets are located. Sometimes foreign proceedings are recognised on a pragmatic basis.[88]

10.35 **Jurisdiction rules of the E.U. Regulation**   Between the Member States of the European Union (except Denmark), jurisdiction in bankruptcy matters is governed by the Regulation on Insolvency Proceedings.[89] The Regulation applies to all insolvency procedures, and to natural as well as legal persons. However, it does not cover insurance or finance undertakings (Article 1).

Under the Regulation, an insolvency procedure can be instituted in the centre where the most important interests of the debtor are situated (Article 3). This court applies its own law (Article 4). Such main insolvency has universal effect. A secondary insolvency procedure can be brought in another Member State that has jurisdiction concerning the assets on its territory, without affecting the main procedure (Article 27).

10.36 **Council of Europe Convention**   The European Convention on Certain International Aspects of Bankruptcy (1990), patronised by the Council of Europe, aims to affect more countries than those of the E.U., but is not yet in force.[90]

The Convention works in much the same way as the E.U. Regulation. It assumes that the government of the country where the insolvent party has the "centre of his main interests" has jurisdiction to make arrangements for the bankruptcy. The liquidator in a bankruptcy has extensive powers in any of the contracting states where the assets of the bankrupt are situated, without the need for recognition of his authority by the local court. However, he must act in accordance with the local laws and regulations. Another contracting state may arrange for a "secondary bankruptcy" without investigation by a local authority whether the conditions for bankruptcy are satisfied: the main bankruptcy organised in the first country is a sufficient basis. The secondary bankruptcy is governed by the local law.

---

[88] See, *e.g.*, J. Smith, "Approaching universality: the role of comity in international bankruptcy proceedings litigated in America" (1999) 17 Boston Univ. Int'l L.J. 367; E. Flaschen and R. Silverman, "Cross-border insolvency co-operation protocols" (1998) 33 Texas Int'l L.J. 587.

[89] Council Regulation 1346/2000 on insolvency proceedings, [2000] O.J. L160. The Regulation enters into force on May 31, 2002.

[90] European Convention on certain international aspects of bankruptcy, signed at Istanbul, June 5, 1990 (1991) I.L.M. 165, European Treaty Series no. 136 ed. July 1990. The Convention will enter into force after three ratifications (Art. 34). It has been signed by Belgium, Cyprus, France, Germany, Greece, Italy, Luxembourg and Turkey, but ratified only by Cyprus.

Comparative law survey   Historically, Belgium, Luxembourg and Denmark   **10.37**
have adhered to the doctrine of universality. Austria, the Netherlands, France,
Italy, Sweden, Finland, Norway, the United Kingdom, the United States, Japan,
Argentina, Mexico have always applied a more territorial approach to bankruptcy.[91]

Bankruptcy is, as a rule, territorial in the United States. The courts administer
a territorial bankruptcy with the local assets for the benefit of American creditors.
However, American courts may entrust the bankruptcy to a foreign administrator.[92]

Applicable law

Lex concursus   The court adjudicating on a bankruptcy follows the bank-   **10.38**
ruptcy provisions of its domestic law. This *lex concursus* defines the procedural
aspects of the administration of the bankruptcy and supplies the substantive rules
for bankruptcy as well. Indeed, procedural and substantive law are intertwined in
bankruptcy (see paragraph 10.30).

The *lex concursus* determines who may be declared bankrupt; it regulates the
conditions for bankruptcy and the presentation of a petition for bankruptcy; it
outlines the organisation of the bankruptcy (including publicity, appointment of
administrator or official receiver, court supervision, nature, size and effects of
dispossession, and composition of the assets), and it regulates the administration
of the bankrupt estate. The receiver may, even in a foreign country, only take
protective measures in accordance with the *lex concursus*. And even in another
country, the receiver can only sell assets if he has a formal authorisation as
required by the *lex concursus*.

The *lex concursus* determines the effect of the bankruptcy on current agreements. It generally applies to the option of refusing to accept contracts concluded
in the suspect period and to the possibility of initiating the *actio pauliana*. The
listing of assets and liabilities, the liquidation as well as the extension of the
bankruptcy to company directors are all covered by the *lex concursus*. It is also
this law that determines whether matrimonial property benefits granted by the
bankrupt to his spouse, a retention of title, preferences or mortgages have to be
respected by the estate of the bankrupt. Likewise, the *lex concursus* decides on
a possible set-off between two different claims. And lastly, the *lex concursus*

---

[91] *cf.* L. Idot, "Perspectives communautaires du droit des 'faillites' " (1991) G. P. 283; P. R. Wood, *Principles of International Insolvency* (Sweet & Maxwell, London, 1995), pp. 264–270.
[92] *cf.* U.S. Bankruptcy Code, s. 304. See C. Kim and J. Smith, "International Insolvencies: An English-American Comparison", *op.cit.* 1; K. Nadelmann, "The Bankruptcy Reform Act and conflict of laws: trial-and-error" (1988) Harv.Int'l.L.Rev. 27; M. Lebow and R. Tait, "International effects of bankruptcy in American law" (1989) I.B.L.J. 257; W. Dahl, "USA: Bankruptcy under Chapter 11" (1992) I.B.L.J. 555; E. F. Scoles and P. Hay, *Conflict of Laws* (West Publishing, St Paul, 1992), p. 940.

regulates the winding-up, the judicial control over and ratification of the bankruptcy proceedings and the effects of the bankruptcy for the creditors.[93]

The E.U. Regulation contains only a few basic rules on applicable law: the bankruptcy proceedings are governed by the law of the Member State where the proceedings are instituted (Article 4); secondary proceedings are governed by the law of the Member State where the secondary proceedings are opened (Article 28); the possibility of set-off is governed by the law applicable to the claim to be set off (Article 6); the rights and obligations of parties to payment systems and financial markets are governed by the law of the Member State applicable to that system or market (Article 9); the law of the Member State applicable to an employment contract determines the effect of insolvency on such contract (Article 10).

10.39   **Other laws**   The law governing the contract (*lex contractus*) remains in principle relevant for the validity, termination, breach and content of the contract (subject to corrections from the *lex concursus*).[94]

The effect of bankruptcy on assets and receivables is determined not only by the *lex contractus* but also by the law of the place where the goods are situated (*lex rei sitae*). The status of secured claims is often delicate in international bankruptcies. The question of whether a claim is secured is answered by the law governing the claim. The *lex rei sitae* describes the requirements for a preferential claim or mortgage (goods, registration, publicity, priority, status of privilege).[95] Finally, the preferential claim and mortgage must be acceptable under the *lex concursus*. According to the principle *locus regit actum*, protective actions (*e.g.* seals on the door, inventory) and management (*e.g.* recovery of debts, sale of perishable goods, etc.) have to be carried out in conformity to the requirements of the country where these actions occur. Assets must be sold respecting the law of the country where these assets are located (*lex rei sitae*).

The impact of a retention of title may be influenced by three legal systems: the *lex contractus* decides whether the parties can contractually defer the transfer of title; the effect on third parties is determined by the *lex rei sitae*; the *lex concursus* decides to what extent a retention of title must be recognised in the winding-up of the estate.[96]

---

[93] See for the scope of application of the *lex concursus, inter alia,* M. Trochu, *Conflits de lois et conflits de juridictions* (Sirey, Paris, 1967), pp. 97 *et seq.*; J. A. Pastor Ridruejo, "La faillite en droit international privé" (1971) II Rec.Cours 187; L. Collins (ed.), *Dicey and Morris on the Conflict of Laws* (Sweet & Maxwell, London, 2000) pp. 1172–1181; G. van Hecke, "Company bankruptcy and similar proceedings in Belgian private international law" in C. Voskuil (ed.), *op.cit.*, pp. 83–87; P. Mayer, *Droit International Privé* (Montchrestien, Paris, 1998), para. 665; P.R. Wood, *Law and Practice of International Finance: Principles of International Insolvency* (Sweet & Maxwell, London, 1995) pp. 10–29 and 85 *et seq.*

[94] *cf.* O. Lando, "Private international law: contracts" in (1976) *International Encyclopedia of Comparative Law*, pp. 93 *et seq.*; see also Art. 10 of the European Convention on the Law Applicable to Contractual Obligations, [1980] O.J. L266/4 and supplementary report of M. Guiliano and P. Lagarde, [1980] O.J. C182/32.

[95] See, *e.g.* G. Venturini, "Private international law: property" in *International Encyclopedia of Comparative Law*, (1976), p. 9; G. Khairallah, *Les sûretés mobilières en droit international privé* (Economica, Paris, 1984), p. 295.

[96] See G. Venturini, *op. cit.*, pp. 8–9; Y. Loussouarn, "Les conflits de lois en matière de réserve de propriété" (1982) *Comité Français de Droit International Privé* 91, and more specifically C. Klein,

Recognition of bankruptcy adjudications and actions by the receiver

General If the bankruptcy covers goods located in different countries **10.40** the receiver may be required to carry out his task in another country. However, the legal system of the second country has to decide whether it will recognise a foreign bankruptcy and the subsequent actions of the receiver.

E.U. Regulation on Insolvency Proceedings Attempts to create a coherent **10.41** system of recognition and enforcement of insolvency procedures within the European Union have for a long time been unsuccessful.[97] The Brussels I Regulation (and Lugano Convention) on jurisdiction and enforcement of judgments (see paragraph 10.02), for instance, do not apply to "bankruptcy, winding-up arrangements, compositions and analogous proceedings".[98] These matters were excluded because of their specific characteristics and the great diversity between the national bankruptcy laws.[99] Even proceedings which follow directly from a bankruptcy (*e.g.* in relation to personal liability of the directors of the bankrupt company) are not covered.[1]

Under the Regulation a decision to open an insolvency procedure, taken by a court that has jurisdiction under Article 3, will be recognised by other Member States from the time that it becomes effective in the state where the proceedings were opened (Article 16). The recognition gives the same effect to the decision as it has in the original State (Article 17). The liquidator may request that the judgment to be published or to be registered in the public registers of the other Member States (Articles 21–22). Judgments by the court where the proceedings

---

"Schutzwirkung des Eigentumsvorbehalts in französischen Insolvenzverfahren" (1991) R.I.W. 809.

[97] The convention on insolvency proceedings concluded on November 23, 1995, was not ratified by all Member States within the time limit and it could not enter into force. See, however, S. Poillot-Peruzzetto, "Le créancier et la faillite européenne" (1997) 124 J.D.I. 757; I. Fletcher, "The European Union Convention on Insolvency Proceedings: choice of law provisions" (1998) 33 Texas Int'l L.J. 119.

[98] Several Member States have all sorts of semi-bankruptcy procedures. "Bankruptcy, proceedings relating to the winding-up of insolvent companies or other legal persons, judicial arrangements, compositions and other analogues proceedings" in the sense of the Brussels I Regulation and Lugano Conventions are: "those proceedings which, depending on the system of law involved, are based on the suspension of payments, the insolvency of the debtor or his inability to raise credit, and which involve the judicial authorities for the purpose either of compulsory and collective liquidation of the assets or simply of supervision". *cf* P. Jenard, "Report on the convention on jurisdiction and the enforcement of judgments in civil and commercial matters" [1979] O.J. C59/11.

[99] Brussels I Regulation and Lugano Convention, Art. 1; Case 133/78 *Gourdain v. Nadler* [1979] E.C.R. 743.

[1] For the distinction between proceedings that flow directly and those that flow indirectly from bankruptcy see Case 133/78 *Gourdain v. Nadler* [1979] E.C.R. 743; T. Hartley, "Scope of the Convention: bankruptcy, winding-up and analogous proceedings" (1979) E.L.Rev. 482. In Case C–267/97 *Coursier v. Fortis Bank SA, Jur* [1999] E.C.R. I–2543 the Court of Justice stated that where a judgment has been given and rights accrued before insolvency, recognition and enforcement of that judgment against an insolvent debtor, will be governed by the Brussels Convention (now Regulation) since this is not a matter relating to in solvency and therefore not excluded from the scope of that Convention (Regulation).

were started and that concern the conduct and closure of insolvency proceedings, may also be recognised without further formalities (Article 25). However, if the recognition of such proceedings or related judgments would be contrary to the public policy of a state, recognition may be refused (Article 26).

Moreover, a recognition does not preclude secondary proceedings in a state where the insolvency is recognised.

10.42   Comparative law survey   The E.U. Regulation regulates the recognition of insolvency proceedings in the E.U. In cases outside the scope of the Regulation and in the absence of a treaty (see paragraph 10.33), each country has to apply its own rules on recognition.[2]

In France, recognition of a foreign declaration of bankruptcy prevents a new (French) bankruptcy being declared for the assets situated in France. The foreign receiver may take all necessary measures of control and management in France. However, he may only take enforcement measures in so far as the foreign bankruptcy is declared enforceable. However, it is unclear for what acts the receiver needs an enforcement order.[3]

Previously in Germany a foreign bankruptcy did not affect the distribution of assets situated in Germany; a special German bankruptcy had to be declared in that event. In 1985, however, the Bundesgerichtshof recognised the universality of a foreign bankruptcy in respect of assets in Germany. Three cumulative conditions must be fulfilled for recognition: (i) the foreign definition of bankruptcy must be fairly similar to the German definition; (ii) the foreign court must have international jurisdiction; and (iii) the declaration of bankruptcy must not be contrary to German public policy.[4]

However, as soon as the bankrupt has a branch or office in Germany, a local bankruptcy again becomes an option and the recognition of the foreign bankruptcy and the receiver is again jeopardised (see paragraph 10.39). This approach was confirmed in the *Insolvenzordnung*.[5]

In the United Kingdom the receiver of a foreign bankruptcy of an individual has the same competence as a domestic receiver.[6] In the case of an insolvent

---

[2] M. Lebow and R. Tait, "International effects of bankruptcy in American law" (1989) I.B.L.J. 257; G. Grasmann, "Effects nationaux d'une procédure d'exécution collective étrangère" (1990) R.C.D.I.P. 421; A. Bottiau, "Aspects internationaux de la faillite en droit americain" (1992) J.D.I. 89; *cf.* P. R. Wood, *Law and Practice of International Finance: Principles of International Insolvency* (Sweet & Maxwell, London, 1995), pp. 242 *et seq.*

[3] S. Vaisse, "The international effects of bankruptcy under French law"(1989) I.B.L.J. 349; B. Audit, *Droit international privé* (Economica, Paris, 1997), p. 632.

[4] *Bundesgerichthof*, July 11, 1985, (1985) N.J.W. 2897; G. Lorcher, "Effects en Allemagne d'un procédure de faillite étrangère" (1991) I.B.L.J. 855; *cf.* T. M. Bos, *Grensoverschrijdend Faillissementsrecht in Europees Perspectief* (Kluwer, Amsterdam, 2000), p. 143.

[5] See, *e.g.* A. "Flessner, Internationales Insolvenzrecht in Deutschland noch der Reform" (1997) IPRax 2; C. G. Paulus, "The new German Insolvency Code" (1998) 33 Texas Int'l L.J. 141.

[6] *cf.* L. Collins (ed.), *Dicey and Morris on the Conflict of Laws* (Sweet & Maxwell, London, 2000), pp. 1184–1186: "An assignment of a bankrupt's property to the representative of his creditors under the bankruptcy law of any other foreign country whose courts have jurisdiction over him . . . is, or operates as, an assignment of the movables of the bankrupt situate in England."

foreign company, the powers of the foreign receiver under the applicable foreign law are almost automatically recognised.[7]

A bankruptcy decision and a receiver from a country where the bankrupt had its main seat are recognised in Belgium, at least when the adjudication in bankruptcy satisfies the general criteria for recognition. The foreign receiver may then administer the bankruptcy in Belgium, take conservatory measures and initiate legal actions against the debtors of the bankrupt. However, if he wants to apply sanctions he must turn to the Belgian courts for an enforcement order.[8]

---

[7] *cf.* M. Elland-Goldsmit, "English Insolvency Law: International Aspects" (1989) I.B.L.J. 207 *et seq.*; F. Tolmie; *Introduction to Corporate and Personal Insolvency Law* (Sweet & Maxwell, London, 1998), pp. 416–417.

[8] *cf.* Art. 570 of the *Code Judiciaire*; *cf.* G. van Hecke, "Company bankruptcy and similar proceedings in Belgian private international law" in C. Voskuil (ed.), *op.cit.*, p. 86; F. Rigaux and M. Fallon, *Droit International Privé* (Larcier, Brussels, 1993) II, p. 494; T. M. Bos, *op.cit.*, p. 141.

CHAPTER 11

INTERNATIONAL COMMERCIAL ARBITRATION

PART I: GENERAL CHARACTERISTICS

ADR and arbitration Business people who wish to avoid submitting their   **11.01**
disputes to a court may prefer to have recourse to arbitration, or other alternative
dispute resolution (ADR) methods.

The most important approach within ADR is mediation, *i.e.* the formula
whereby a mediator discusses the dispute with both parties together and/or with
each of the parties separately in order to bring them to a settlement. However, the
parties have to accept the settlement of their free will. The mediator cannot
impose binding views; he is rather a "midwife" who tries to find a solution that
is acceptable to both parties.

Mediation does not require an institutional framework.[1] However, most media-
tions are carried out within the framework of a mediation institution and pursuant
to the mediation rules of that institution. Many arbitration institutions (see
paragraphs 11.16–11.17 have their own mediation rules.[2] This chapter will not
discuss mediation, as this is a quite informal process. Instead it will focus on
arbitration.

Contracting parties often agree that any possible disputes that arise concerning
a contract will be settled through arbitration—sometimes as the sole method to
solve dispute, sometimes as a fallback position when mediation has not succeeded.

This chapter aims to give some understanding of the basic structure and
organisation of arbitration. It does not discuss the complex issues that are
sometimes raised in arbitration, the solution of which differs from country to
country.[3]

---

[1] See, *e.g.*, H. Brown and A. Marriott, *ADR Principles and Practice* (Sweet & Maxwell, London, 1999).

[2] See *e.g.* the LCIA—mediation rules: www.lcia-arbitration.com; Guide to ICC ADR: www.iccwbo. com. The mediation rules of various national arbitration institutions (see para 11.16) can also be found on their website.

[3] Reports on the national arbitration law of many countries can be found in *e.g.* A. J. van den Berg (ed.), *International Handbook on Commercial Arbitration* (Kluwer, Deventer) (loose-leaf). See also, for instance, for Belgium M. Huys and G. Keutgen, *L'Arbitrage en Droit Belge et International* (Bruylant, Brussels, 1981); M. Storme and B. Demeulenaere, *International Commercial Arbitration in Belgium* (Kluwer, Deventer, 1989). For England, Sutton, Kendall and Gill, *Russell on Arbitration*, (21st ed., Sweet & Maxwell, London, 1997); for France, E. Gaillard (ed.), *Fouchard Gaillard Goldman on International Commercial Arbitration* (Kluwer, The Hague, 1999); for Switzerland, A. Bucher and P. Y. Tschanz, *International Arbitration in Switzerland* (Helbing, Basle, 1988); P. Lalive, J. F. Poudret and C. Reymond, *Le Droit de l'Arbitrage Interne et International en Suisse* (Payot, Lausanne, 1989); for the U.S., M. Domke and G. Wilner, *Domke*

11.02   **Basis: agreement and the law**   Arbitration has both a contractual and a judicial dimension.[4]

On the one hand, arbitration is based on the agreement between parties to submit a dispute for settlement to private persons instead of to a court and to be bound by the award.[5] Moreover, it implies an agreement between the parties and the arbitrator whereby the arbitrator agrees to settle the dispute.[6] No arbitration is possible without such agreement.

On the other hand the arbitrator exercises a judicial task and arbitration is part of procedural law. Arbitration is based on arbitration law laying down the rules for the arbitration procedure and the legal effects of the award. Arbitration is under the control of a court, which resolves problems during the arbitral proceedings and enforces a correct award or annuls an incorrect award.

The arbitration proceedings are in principle subjected to the law of the country where the arbitration is to take place (the so-called "seat") (see paragraph 11.22). It is the court of the seat of arbitration that directs and controls the arbitration.[7] Arbitration laws differ from country to country.

In 1985 UNCITRAL (see paragraph 2.23) drafted a model law to bring more uniformity between the different arbitration laws.[8] States may adopt this model law, even with some changes. Some states have already done so.[9]

---

on Commercial Arbitration (Callaghan, Wilmotte, 1984) (loose-leaf); for Africa, Ph. Fouchard e.a., *L'OHADA et les perspectives de l'arbitrage en Afrique* (Bruylant, Brussels, 2000); for Arab countries, A. El Ahdab, *Arbitration with the Arab Countries* (Kluwer, Deventer, 1992); general, R. David, *Arbitration in International Trade* (1985); A. Redfern and M. Hunter, *Law and Practice of International Commercial Arbitration* (3rd ed., Sweet & Maxwell, London, 1999); M. Rubino-Sammartano, *International Arbitration Law* (Kluwer, Deventer, 1990); P. Schlosser, *Das Recht der internationalen privaten Schiedsgerichtsbarkeit* (2nd ed., Mohr, Tübingen, 1989).

[4] See on the contractual and/or judicial nature of arbitration, *inter alia*, Ch. Jarrosson, *La Notion de l'Arbitrage* (LGDJ, Paris, 1987); A. Kassis, *Problèmes de Base de l'Arbitrage, Part I: Arbitrage Juridictionnel et Arbitrage Contractuel* (LGDJ, Paris, 1987); J. Rubellin-Devichi, *L'Arbitrage. Nature Juridique, Droit Interne et Droit International Privé* (LGDJ, Paris, 1965).

[5] When an "arbitration" is imposed by the authorities, it is not arbitration in the sense intended here.

[6] See K. Lionnet, "The arbitrator's contract,"(2000) 15 Arb.Int. 161–169.

[7] See R. Goode, "The role of the lex loci arbitri in international commercial arbitration" (2001) 17 Arb.Int. 15–39. Nevertheless, some legal systems accept that arbitration proceedings may be subject to a different procedural law than that of the seat of arbitration (see New York Convention, Art. I, 1; European Convention on International Commercial Arbitration (1961), Art. IX). The courts of the applicable procedural law are in that case competent. The award will have the "nationality" of the country whose procedural law is applicable. In reality this means that for those legal systems the arbitration may have its "seat" in the country of the procedural law that has been applied.

[8] See, *inter alia*, A. Broches, *Commentary on the UNCITRAL Model Law on International Commercial Arbitration* (Kluwer, Deventer, 1990); H. Holtzman and J. Neuhaus, *A Guide to the UNCITRAL Model Law on International Commercial Arbitration* (Kluwer, Deventer, 1989); P. Sarcevic (ed.), *Essays on International Commercial Arbitration* (Graham & Trotman, London, 1989).

[9] *Inter alia*, Australia, Bahrain, Bermuda, Bulgaria, Canada, Cyprus, Egypt, Germany, Greece, Guatemala, Hong Kong, Hungary, India, Iran, Ireland, Kenya, Korea (South), Lithuania, Macau, Madagascar, Malta, Mexico, New Zealand, Nigeria, Peru, Russia, Scotland, Singapore, Sri Lanka, Tunisia, Ukraine and Zimbabwe. Some states within the U.S. (California, Connecticut, Oregon, Texas), have also adopted the Model Law. Other states have been inspired to a considerable extent by the UNCITRAL model law when they drafted their own arbitration statute (*e.g.* the Netherlands and Nigeria). See P. Sanders, "Unity and diversity in the adoption of the Model Law" (1995) 11 Arb.Int. 1–37.

International commercial arbitration and national arbitration laws A **11.03** distinction is usually made between national and international arbitration.[10] For national arbitration, all elements (parties, dispute, place of arbitration, arbitrators) are located within a single legal system. National arbitration is thus governed by only one law. In the case of international arbitration, elements are connected to different legal systems. As soon as arbitration is international—and this is the case in international trade—several arbitration laws may be relevant. Which law is then applicable to the arbitration agreement, to the procedure and to the substance of the dispute?

Arbitration governed by public international law is not subject to a national law and national court, even when it concerns commercial disputes.[11] ICSID arbitration proceedings concerning investment disputes between a private investor and a state pursuant to the Washington Convention is therefore outside the scope of national arbitration laws (see paragraph 7.38).

However, when the commercial arbitration proceedings are not governed by public international law, they are subject to a national arbitration law.[12]

PART II: THE AGREEMENT TO SUBMIT TO ARBITRATION

Legal framework

Arbitration clause and submission to arbitration Parties may agree to **11.04** submit existing disputes to arbitration. This agreement on existing disputes is called submission to arbitration. However, a person who fears being in the wrong is unlikely to submit the dispute to arbitration, for it is in his advantage to postpone the settlement for as long as possible.

In most cases, however, parties have agreed to arbitration at an earlier stage when no dispute has yet arisen, for instance in an arbitration clause in an agreement. The arbitration clause is generally included in a contract signed by both parties. Sometimes an exchange of letters, telexes or telefaxes will suffice. It is also possible that the arbitration clause is included in the general conditions added to the offer or acceptance of one of the parties and to which the other party did not object.[13] Even an arbitration clause in a draft agreement or offer that was

---

[10] Some arbitration laws, such as the French and the English, attach specific legal implications to the international character of the arbitration. Some arbitration statutes—or treaties—are sometimes only applicable to "international" arbitration (cf. Switzerland PIL statute, Chap. 12; UNCITRAL model law; European Convention on International Commercial Arbitration (1961) (see para. 11.42). Each of these texts defines when arbitration is sufficiently "international" for the text to apply. See H. van Houtte, "International arbitration and national adjudication", *Hague-Zagreb Essays on the Law of International Trade*, no. 4 (Nijhoff, Dordrecht, 1983), p. 321.

[11] See P. Lalive, "Contrats entre états ou entreprises étatiques et personnes privées" (1983) 181 Rec.Cours 9.

[12] However, see J. Paulsson, "Arbitration unbound: award detached from the law of its country of origin" (1981) I.C.L.Q. 358; J. Paulsson, "Delocalisation of international commercial arbitration: when and why it matters" (1983) I.C.L.Q. 53; T. Rensmann, "Anational arbitral awards" (1998) 2 J.I.A. 37.

[13] See, however High Court, The Hague, February 17, 1984 (1985) Y.Comm.Arb. 485 (general conditions only used in previous transactions). Boucobza, "La clause compromissoire par référence" (1998) Rev. Arb. 495; V. van Houtte, "Consent to arbitration through agreement to printed contracts" (2000) 16 Arb. Int. 1; B. Oppetit, "La clause d'arbitrage par référence" (1990) Rev.Arb. 551.

never formally accepted may be binding if the parties actually performed the transaction.[14] Once an arbitration clause binds parties to submit a dispute to arbitration, they are bound by it.

Arbitration laws make little distinction between an arbitration clause and a submission to arbitration. The distinction is, however, sometimes maintained. Belgian law, for instance, does not allow an arbitration clause for the submission to arbitration of disputes over the termination of a distribution agreement, where the arbitrators would not apply the Act of 1961, but does accept an arbitration agreement once the dispute has arisen (see paragraph 5.07).

Validity of the agreement

Contractual validity

11.05   **General**   Different arbitration laws have their own requirements for the validity of an arbitration agreement. The Belgian arbitration law, for instance, like many other arbitration laws, requires that the arbitration agreement gives equal rights to the parties in the appointment of arbitrators (*Code Judiciaire*, Art. 1678, 1): an arbitration clause which favours one party in the nomination of the arbitrators is invalid. This requirement of equality may invalidate an arbitration clause that nominates the arbitration body of an industrial organisation of which only one of the parties is a member.

11.06   **Applicable law for validity**   The validity of the arbitration agreement is in the first instance determined by the proper law of this agreement. The validity of the arbitration clause thus depends primarily on the proper law of the contract that contains this arbitration clause (see paragraph 1.29 *et.seq.*).

However, it may be that one party claims that the contract containing the arbitration clause is invalid for a reason unrelated to the arbitration clause. The arbitration clause is then protected against the (alleged) invalidity of the agreement as a whole: the nullity of the contract does not necessarily result in the invalidity of the arbitration clause (the so-called "autonomy" of the arbitration clause).[15]

The arbitration clause itself may also be governed by another law than the proper law of the contract,[16] for instance by the law applicable to the arbitral proceedings.[17] It even may be that arbitrators, who want to uphold an arbitration

---

[14] See the Vienna Convention on the International Sale of Goods, Art. 18.3 (see para. 4.14); *Filanto v. Chilewich* 789 F.Supp. 1229 (S.D.N.Y. 1992); Rotterdam court, June 26, 1970 (1976) Y.Comm.Arb. 195; Paris, March 25, 1983 (1984) Rev.Arb. 363.

[15] See, for instance UNCITRAL Model Law, Art. 16, 1; Belgian *Code Judiciaire*, Art. 1697, para. 2; Swiss PIL statute, Art. 178, 3; London Court of International Arbitration rules, Art. 14, 1; as well as Cass. Fr., December 6, 1988 (1989) Rev.Arb. 641, with annotation by B. Goldman, where the arbitration clause was not affected by the allegation that there had not been an agreement on the contract containing this clause.

[16] See, *e.g.* Cass. Fr., May 7, 1963 (1964) J.D.I. 82 and July 4, 1972 (1977) J.D.I. 843.

[17] See, *e.g.* Swiss PIL statute, Art. 178, 2; New York Convention (1958), Art. V, 1(a) and European Convention on International Commercial Arbitration (1961), Art. IX, (a); ICC no. 1507 (1974) J.D.I. 913; ICC no. 4392 (1983) J.D.I. 907; Bulgaria: award 52/65, (1976) Y.Comm.Arb. 123; Swiss Trib.Fed., March 17, 1975 (1976) J.D.I. 729, with critical note Lalive.

clause, do not assess the validity of the arbitration clause on the basis of the proper law of the contract or of the law that would govern the arbitration proceedings, but on the basis of the general principles of law and good faith.[18]

The validity of a submission to arbitration is , in principle, governed by the law of the seat of arbitration, unless the parties have stipulated another law.[19]

Competence If a party challenges the validity of the arbitration clause or **11.07** submission to arbitration, the arbitrators themselves usually decide on this validity—and therefore on their own competence (*cf.* the German term: *Kompetenz-Kompetenz*).[20]

If the arbitrators assume jurisdiction and render an award, but the court declares the arbitration agreement afterwards invalid, the court will consider the award invalid (see paragraph 11.37) and refuse its enforcement (see paragraph 11.39).[21]

Arbitrability

Arbitrable disputes Arbitration, *i.e.* settlement by a third person, is only **11.08** possible for disputes that the parties can also settle themselves. Disputes over rights for which the parties cannot contract are outside the scope of arbitration.[22]

Furthermore, the laws of some states impose more specific restrictions. There are, for instance, restrictions on arbitration for disputes concerning intellectual property rights,[23] stock exchange transactions, anti-trust law,[24] labour law.[25]

---

[18] See, *e.g.* ICC no. 5065, (1987) J.D.I. 1039; Paris, October 21, 1983, (1984) Rev.Arb. 98. See more generally A. Foustoucos, "Conditions required for the validity of an arbitration agreement" (1988) J.I.A. 4–113.

[19] See the criteria for applicable law of the New York Convention (Art. V, 1(a)) (see para. 11.41) and the European Convention (Art. IX, 1(a)) (see para. 11.42): "The arbitration agreement shall be valid pursuant the law to which the parties have submitted it or, in the absence of choice, pursuant the law of the country where the award was made."

[20] European Convention, Art. V; UNCITRAL rules Art. 21. See, however ICC rules, 8.3 which gives this competence at first instance also in part to the International Court of Arbitration. See P. Mayer, "L'autonomie de l'arbitre international dans l'appréciation de sa propre compétence" (1989) 217 Rec.Cours V 323; J. A. Rosen, "Arbitration under private international law: the doctrines of separability and compétence de la compétence" (1994) 17 Fordham.I.L.J. 599.

[21] New York Convention (1958), Art. V, 1(a). Thus, a Belgian Appeal Court ordered that a Swiss arbitration award for the termination of a distribution agreement could not be enforced, as the jurisdiction of the arbitrators depended on an arbitration clause which was invalid by virtue of the Belgian Act of June 27, 1961 (para. 5.13, Cass., June 28, 1979 (1979) J.T. 625).

[22] See, *inter alia*, K. H. Boeckstiegel, "Public policy and arbitrability" in *Comparative Arbitration Practice and Public Policy in Arbitration ICCA Series* no. 3 (Kluwer, Deventer, 1987) p. 177.

[23] M. Blessing, "Arbitrability of intellectual property disputes" (1996) Arb.Int. 191.

[24] W. Brown and S. Houck, "Arbitrating international antitrust disputes" (1990) J.I.A. 1–77; Ch. Kaplan, "Arbitrability of commercial disputes involving competition law" (1988) D.P.C.I. 403; J. H. Moitry, "Arbitrage international et droit de la concurrence: vers un ordre public de la lex mercatoria?" (1989) Rev.Arb. 3; D. Rahmann, "Arbitrability of antitrust issues" (1990) C.L.Y.L.I.B. 97; A. Stille, *Die Schiedsfähigkeit internationaler Kartellrechtsstreitigkeiten im Recht der USA* (Berlin, 1989); Chr. Wolf, "Zwischen Schiedsverfahrensfreiheit und notwendiger Staatlicher Kontrolle" (1993) RabelsZ 643, 648–660 (concerning German competition law).

[25] M. Rubino-Sammartano, *op.cit.*, pp. 101–114; P. Schlosser, *op. cit.*, pp. 224–237.

Before opting for arbitration it is advisable to investigate the arbitrability of the dispute under the relevant law (see paragraph 11.09).

Arbitrators may decide issues that involve the E.U. rules on competition (E.C. Articles 81 and 82—see paragraphs 5.13–5.21). Arbitrators may take into account Articles 81, 1 and 2 E.C. when necessary for the settlement of the main issue, for instance, when a party demands the performance of a contract and the defendant relies on nullity pursuant to Article 81, 2 E.C. In that case the arbitrators must of course correctly interpret and apply the E.U. competition rules.[26]

11.09   **Applicable law**   What law determines in a transnational arbitration whether a dispute is arbitrable?[27]

It is generally accepted that the arbitrability depends in the first place on the law applicable to the arbitration agreement. In case of an arbitration clause, the arbitrability is thus governed by the proper law of the contract of which this clause is a part.

Others, however, contend that each court must examine under its own law whether a dispute is arbitrable. Only if the dispute is arbitrable according to the law of the forum shall the court recognise the validity of the arbitration clause and decline jurisdiction.[28] It is clear that the second approach may lead to parallel court and arbitration proceedings.[29]

It was mentioned earlier that, under Belgian law, an exclusive distribution agreement cannot contain a valid arbitration clause for the termination of this agreement (see paragraph 11.04). However, according to the first opinion the arbitration clause is valid if the proper law of the contract is not Belgian law; according to the second opinion the Belgian court shall never recognize the arbitration clause and can always—despite the arbitration clause—assume jurisdiction. In the last situation it remains questionable to what extent the Belgian judgment can be enforced abroad, especially when an arbitral award has been rendered in the same case.[30]

Capacity of parties

11.10   **Capacity**   Arbitration law excludes some parties from arbitration. The law of many Arab countries, for instance, imposes restrictions on the ability of the state, state institutions or state companies to accept arbitration clauses. Often, special

---

[26] See W. Abdelgawad, *Arbitrage et Droit de la Concurrence* (LGDJ, Paris, 2001); D. Hahn, *L'Arbitrage Commercial International en Suisse Face aux Règles de Concurrence de la CEE* (George, Geneva, 1983).

[27] See B. Hanotiau, "The law applicable to issues of arbitrability" (1998) J.I.B.L. 755.

[28] These authors rely, *inter alia*, on the European Convention on International Commercial Arbitration, Art. VI, para. 2.

[29] H. van Houtte, "May court judgments that disregard arbitration clauses and awards be enforced under the Brussels and Lugano Conventions?" (1997) 13 Arb.Int. 85–92; J. P. Beraudo, "The arbitration exception of the Brussels and Lugano Conventions", (2001) J.I.A. 13–26.

[30] For the first approach, see, *inter alia*, H. van Houtte, "L'arbitrabilité de la résiliation des concessions de vente exclusive", *Mélanges R. Van Der Elst* (Nemesis, Brussels, 1986) p. 821; for the second approach, see, *inter alia*, A. Nuyts, "La loi belge du 27 juillet 1961 relative à la résiliation unilatérale des concessions de vente exclusive à durée indéterminée et les conventions d'arbitrage" (1993) J.T. 349.

permission is required.[31] Similar restrictions also apply in certain European countries[32]: for instance, in principle the French authorities may not submit to purely domestic arbitration, but only to international arbitration.

Many legal systems also impose restrictions on referral to arbitrators by the receiver in a bankruptcy. Often this may only occur with the permission of the court that is in charge of the winding-up.[33]

Applicable law   In Europe it is generally accepted that the capacity of a party   **11.11**
to submit to arbitration is determined by the domestic law of this party. In England and the United States, on the contrary, it is deemed that the capacity is governed by the law applicable to the agreement.[34]

Arbitrators in international arbitrations sometimes set aside a potential incapacity of a state entity because of good faith: if this entity has agreed to arbitration, it is bound by its word.[35] However, when the award must be enforced against the state entity in a country where it is considered unable to submit to arbitration, enforcement may be denied.[36]

Effect

Incompetent court   Courts have no jurisdiction over a dispute when there is   **11.12**
a valid arbitration clause or submission to arbitration: the dispute can only be submitted to arbitrators. However, this lack of jurisdiction must be invoked in the court at the start of the court proceedings (*in limine litis*). If a party enters a defence without having invoked the incompetence of the court, he is, in principle, presumed to have relinquished the arbitration clause.

Provisional and protective measures   Nevertheless, an arbitration clause   **11.13**
does not prevent an application to the court for provisional measures.[37] This is

---

[31] Such permission is often required in Arab countries, particularly for submission to arbitration by a public entity. See, *inter alia*, A. El-Ahdab, *Arbitration with the Arab countries* (Kluwer, Deventer, 1990); S. Saleh, *Commercial arbitration in the Arab Middle East* (Graham, London, 1984).

[32] See, *e.g.* Union internationale des Avocats, *L'intervention de l'État ou d'une Firme Étatique dans l'Arbitrage Commercial International* (Story—Scientia, Brussels, 1992).

[33] Ph. Fouchard, "Arbitrage et faillite" (1998) Rev.Arb. 471; B. Hanotiau, "The law applicable by the arbitrator in the event of bankruptcy of one of the parties to the proceedings" (1996) JIBL 29; F. Mantilla-Serano, "International arbitration and insolvency proceedings", (1995) Arb.Int. 51.

[34] See B. Hanotiau, "The law applicable to issues of arbitrability"(1998) J.I.B.L. 755

[35] See, *inter alia*, Swiss PIL Act, Art. 178; ICC Award no. 4361 *Framatome v. Atomic Energy Organization of Iran* (1986) J.D.I. 1106; J. Ragnwaldh, "A state's plea to decline arbitration—the inapplicability of the internal law of the state" (1998) J.I.B.L. 17.

[36] New York Convention (1958), Art. V, I.a. See P. Schlosser, *op. cit.*, pp. 239–240, 248–249.

[37] See S. Besson, *Arbitrage International et Mesures Provisoires* (Schulthess, Zurich, 1998); C. Brower and W. Tupman, "Court-ordered provisional measures under the New York Convention" (1986) A.J.I.L. 24; C. Goldman, "Provisional measures in international arbitration" (1993) J.I.B.L. 3; Chr. Hausmaninger, "The ICC Rules for a pre-arbitral referee procedure: a step towards solving the problem of provisional relief in international commercial arbitration?" (1992) 7 I.C.S.I.D. Rev. 82; P. Ouakrat, "Arbitration and provisional measures" (1988) D.P.C.I. 239; F. Ramoz-Mendez, "Arbitrage international et mesures conservatoires" (1985) Rev.Arb. 51; W. Semple, "The UNCITRAL Model Law and provisional measures in international commercial arbitration" (1993) J.I.B.L. 765.

often very useful. Indeed, a court injunction may be obtained within days (sometimes even within 24 hours), whilst an arbitral award inevitably takes more time. Furthermore, provisional measures of a local court are often more effective than an arbitral decision made far from the place where it has to be implemented. Besides, a decision by a court in summary proceedings can be enforced virtually straight away, whilst the arbitral award still requires enforcement proceedings before a court. Finally, there are some measures which can only be taken by a court, and not by arbitrators.

The court that is imposing provisional measures must of course respect its own procedural rules. In many legal systems a court can only take provisional measures when the urgency and the interests of the parties so require and when these measures do not affect the substance of the settlement.

An arbitration clause or an arbitration procedure likewise do not prevent a party from getting conservatory measures, such as an attachment, if the court's procedural conditions are fulfilled.[38]

PART III: DRAFTING OF AN ARBITRATION CLAUSE

11.14   **Introduction**   The arbitration clause is not only the basis for arbitration. It often gives it shape as well. An arbitration clause must therefore be carefully structured and worded.[39] Unfortunately, the arbitration clause seldom gets the attention it deserves; one sees many poorly drafted, or sometimes even incomprehensible clauses. For instance, a clause stipulating "dispute resolution by the International Chamber of Commerce in Paris" is unclear: the International Chamber of Commerce provides for the settlement of disputes by arbitration as well as by mediation; moreover does this clause only imply that the ICC is established in Paris, or does it more specifically state that the seat of arbitration has to be in Paris?

Some arbitration clauses stipulate that the parties must first attempt to settle the dispute amicably, before resorting to arbitration (see paragraph 11.01). In this event parties have to use their best endeavours to try to settle the dispute before one can start arbitration.

The following specific elements should preferably be included in an arbitration clause:

Definition of disputes

11.15   **Importance**   It is essential to define the task of the arbitrators. The arbitration clause must clearly determine the disputes covered by the jurisdiction of the

---

[38] L. Ebb, "Flight of assets from the jurisdiction 'in the twinkling of a telex': pre–and post-award conservatory relief in international commercial arbitration" (1990) J.I.A. 1–9.

[39] See, *inter alia*, M. Ball, "Structuring the arbitration in advance—the arbitration clause in an international development contract" in J. Lew, *Contemporary Problems in International Arbitration* (CCLS, London, 1986), p. 297; S. Bond, "How to draft an arbitration clause" (1989) J.I.A. 2–65; L. Marville and H. Scalbert, "Les clauses compromissoires pathologiques" (1988) Rev.Arb. 117; M. H. Maleville, "Pathological arbitration clauses" (2000) J.I.B.L. 61; B. Davis, "Pathological clauses: Frédéric Eisemann's still vital criteria" (1990) Arb.Int. 4.

arbitrators. Arbitration clauses are in principle interpreted strictly by the courts as they are an exception to ordinary jurisdiction. A wide definition of the disputes that have to be submitted to arbitration is therefore advisable.

Whoever submits to arbitration "disputes which arise during the performance of a contract", may have excluded disputes on other issues such as contract interpretation, nullity and non-performance.

Arbitral institution or ad hoc arbitration

Arbitral institutions[40]

International arbitration institutions There are international arbitration **11.16** bodies exclusively in existence for the settlement of international commercial disputes.

The most well-known international arbitration institution is the International Chamber of Commerce (ICC) *(Chambre de Commerce Internationale*, CCI) (see paragraph 2.43).[41] The ICC, with its seat in Paris, has, for more than half a century, built up its expertise and reputation in international arbitration. Because of its international—or rather a national—character it is easily accepted by parties. For that reason many international commercial disputes are submitted for settlement by arbitration under the arbitration rules of the International Chamber of Commerce and organised and supervised by its Court of Arbitration.[42] The Court of Arbitration of the International Chamber of Commerce shall, if necessary, appoint arbitrators or the president of the arbitral tribunal. The arbitrators have to abide by the ICC arbitration rules. This specifically requires, amongst other things, the establishment of the framework for the settlement at the start of the proceedings in Terms of Reference/*Acte de Mission*, which should be signed by the parties.[43] The Court of Arbitration also examines the formal validity of the arbitral award. Parties pay the fees of the arbitrators and the administrative costs in advance directly to the Court of Arbitration.[44]

About 400 arbitration proceedings are instituted annually under the ICC Rules. A third of these cases concern disputes about the sale of goods and distribution;

---

[40] See, *inter alia*, W. Melis, "Function and responsibility of arbitral institutions" (1991) 13 C.L.Y.I.B. 107; B. Vigrass, "The role of institutions in arbitration" in R. Bernstein, *Handbook of Arbitration Practice* (Sweet & Maxwell, London, 1992), pp. 461 *et seq*.

[41] 38 Cours Albert 1er, 75008 Paris (tel. +1 49 53 28 28); *www.iccwbo.org*. See, *inter alia*, J. Arnaldez, "Les institutions d'arbitrage en France—Un centre international: La CCI" (1990) Rev.Arb. 249; S. Bond, "How to draft an ICC Arbitration Clause" (1992) 7 I.C.S.I.D. Rev. 153; L. Craig, W. Park and J. Paulsson, *Annotated Guide to the 1998 ICC Arbitration Rules* (Oceana Publications, 1998); A. Kassis, *Réflexions sur le Règlement d'Arbitrage de la Chambre de Commerce Internationale, les Déviations de l'Arbitrage Institutionnel* (LGDJ, Paris, 1988) and less extensively, A. Kassis, "The questionable validity of arbitration and awards under the Rules of the ICC" (1989) J.I.A. 2–79.

[42] M. Philippe-Gazon, "Role of the ICC International Court of Arbitration" (1997) J.I.B.L. 443; R. J. Graving, "The ICC International Court of Arbitration: meeting the challenges?"(2000) 15 I.C.S.I.D. Rev. 417–453.

[43] See L'Acte de Mission sous le Règlement d'Arbitrage de la CCI—ICC Paris; J. Goldsmith, "How to draft Terms of Reference" (1987) Arb.Int. 298.

[44] See Arbitration Rules App. III: Schedule of Arbitration Costs.

one fifth concern the transfer of technology and one tenth building disputes. About half of the parties are western European businesses; one tenth of the parties are established in Africa or South East Asia.

The London Court of International Arbitration (LCIA) is an alternative international arbitration institution for transnational commercial arbitration.[45]

The World Intellectual Property Organisation is also willing to act as an arbitration institution for the settlement of disputes with regard to intellectual property rights.[46] It has specific arbitration rules for domain name disputes.

11.17 **National arbitral institutions** Parties that see no benefit in an arbitration organised by an international arbitration institution may commit the settlement of a transnational conflict to a national arbitral institution of the country of one of the parties, or of a third country. Arbitration set up by such a national institution may, for instance, be cheaper than that organised by an international arbitral institution.

The CEPANI (Centre pour l'Etude et la Pratique de l'Arbitrage National et International)[47] is the Belgian arbitration institution. CEPANI arbitration may be conducted in French, Dutch, English, German or some other chosen language. In about 40 per cent of CEPINA arbitrations one or more parties are foreign. The average time of a CEPINA arbitration procedure is 13 months. The amount in dispute is on average €500,000. The average cost of the arbitration procedure is €5,000.

Other countries also have national arbitration institutions for the settlement of international commercial disputes: for instance, there is the AAA (American Arbitration Association),[48] Cietac (China International Economic and Trade Arbitration Commission),[49] the Japan Commercial Arbitration Association,[50] the Kuala Lumpur Regional Centre for Arbitration,[51] and the Singapore International Arbitration Centre.[52] In Europe there is, for instance the Chamber of National and International Arbitration of Milan,[53] the Nederlands Arbitrage Instituut,[54] the Arbitration Institute of the Stockholm Chamber of Commerce,[55] the Chamber of

---

[45] The LCIA is located at International Dispute Resolution Centre, 8 Breams Building, Chancery Lane, London EC4A 1HP, tel. +44 020 74 05 8008; website: www.lcia-arbitration.org.

[46] See website: www.arbiter.wipo.int. Moreover R. H. Smit, "General commentary on the WIPO Arbitration Rules" (1998) 9 AmR.I.A. 3–44.

[47] CEPANI is located at 1000–Brussels, Rue des Sols 8 (tel. 02 515 08 59) See website: www. cepani.be.

[48] 140 West 51st Street, New York, N.Y. 10020 (tel. +212 484 400); www.adr.org. See, *inter alia*, P. Friedland, "Arbitration under the AAA's International Rules" (1990) Arb.Int. 301; F. Joly, "Le réglement d'arbitrage international de l'Association américaine d'arbitrage" (1993) Rev.Arb. 401.

[49] www.arbitration.org.cn.

[50] www.jcaa.or.jp.

[51] www.klrca.org.

[52] www.siac.org.sg.

[53] www.mi.camcom.it.

[54] Schouwburgplein 30, Rotterdam, P.B. 22105, 3003 DC Rotterdam (Tel. 10 400 82 00); www. nai-nl.org.

[55] www.chamber.se.

Commerce and Industry of Geneva,[56] the Zuricher Handelskammer,[57] the German Deutsche Institut für Schiedsgerichtsbarkeit,[58] and the International Arbitration Centre of the Austrian Federal Economic Chamber.[59]

Commodity arbitration institutions Important institutions for commodity arbitrations are: the London-based Grain and Feed Association (GAFTA), Federation of Oils, Seeds and Fats Associations (FOSFA) and London Rice Brokers Associations (LRBA); the New York-based American Fat and Oils Association (AFOA) and the Washington-based North American Export Grain Association (NAEGA).[60]   **11.18**

Advantages There are advantages in opting for an arbitration institution, since the arbitration will be conducted in accordance with the institution's rules, and in the light of the institution's vast experience. National arbitration laws accept that parties may refer to the rules of an arbitration institution.   **11.19**

The institution may appoint, remove and replace arbitrators if necessary. It may also resolve procedural problems. The institution furthermore makes sure that the arbitration procedure runs smoothly; its expert staff can advise parties and arbitrators on the conduct of the arbitration procedure. The institution also imposes deadlines for the making of an award.

Some arbitration institutions act as intermediaries for the transmission of documents and communications between parties and arbitrators: briefs must be sent to the secretariat of the institution for further distribution. Arrangements on the hearings are also often made through this secretariat. The involvement of other institutions is more limited. They are not a necessary link for communications between arbitrators and parties and are often less involved in making arrangements for hearings. Nevertheless, a copy of each communication between arbitrators and parties must generally be sent for information to the institution.

Ad hoc arbitration

Implications Of course, parties who opt for arbitration may decide not to make use of an arbitration institution—even for important disputes. They may be concerned about the administrative costs institutions charge. However, the down side is that they will not enjoy the assistance and control that an arbitration institution can give.   **11.20**

---

[56] www.ccig.ch.
[57] www.zurichcci.ch.
[58] www.dis-arb.de
[59] www.wk.or.at.
[60] See, *inter alia*, B. Chapman, "FOSFA international arbitration" (1986) Arb.Int. 323; J. Covo, "Commodities, arbitrations and equitable considerations" (1993) Arb.Int. 57; D. Johnson, "Commodity trade arbitration", in R. Bernstein, *Handbook of Arbitration Practice* (Sweet & Maxwell, London, 1993), p. 257; R. van Delden, "English Commodity Arbitration: a foreigner looking around in London", in *The Art of Arbitration* (Kluwer, Deventer, 1982), p. 95.

In such an event parties themselves have to organise an ad hoc arbitration. This presumes that they—or the arbitrators later—set their own rules for their arbitration proceedings.[61] However, to draw up detailed rules in an arbitration clause is not only laborious but in fact unfeasible, because the nature of the dispute is as yet unknown; yet once a conflict has arisen, it often becomes difficult for parties to agree on procedural rules. Parties should therefore only state some general guidelines in the arbitration clause. Arbitrators can always fill in the details later. Moreover, most modern arbitration laws contain sufficient supplementary rules, so that sometimes an arbitration clause containing no more than the place of arbitration will do. The local arbitration law shall then determine the procedure of the ad hoc arbitration.

Ad hoc arbitration does not have the facility of an institution for the appointment of arbitrators and—wherever needed—for assistance in the arbitration proceedings. As a result, ad hoc arbitration is only useful when the local court can assume to a large extent the function of an arbitration institution.

UNCITRAL Rules

11.21   **Overview** The parties may alternatively submit their arbitration to the UNCITRAL arbitration rules.[62] These arbitration rules, drawn up within UNCITRAL (see paragraph 2.23) by arbitration experts from all over the world, offer a compromise between institutional and ad hoc arbitration.

They are a modern set of rules that are suitable for commercial arbitration involving businesses from all parts of the world. The regulation includes very detailed rules and offers thus a solution for many procedural problems. Moreover, parties may nominate the person or institution responsible for the appointment of their arbitrators (the so-called appointing authority). The appointing authority shall, where necessary, appoint or replace the arbitrator, though it does not further administer the arbitration. The costs for the intervention of the appointing authority are considerably less than those for the supervision of the full arbitration procedure by an arbitration institution.

Seat of arbitration

11.22   **Choice** When parties decide for ad hoc, UNCITRAL or ICC arbitration, they must indicate the seat of the arbitration. It is best to do this in the arbitration clause.

---

[61] It is not recommended to use the rules of an arbitration institution but not to accept its administration and costs. In fact, too many rules in institutional arbitration refer to the intervention of the institution, so that the rules without the administration may easily lead to difficulties. (See ICC nos. 3383 and 2878 (1982) Y.Com.Arb. 119.)

[62] I. Dore, *Arbitration and Conciliation under the UNCITRAL Rules* (Nijhoff, Dordrecht, 1986); P. Fouchard, "Le règlement d'arbitrage de la C.N.U.D.C.I." (1979) J.D.I. 816; P. Jenard, "Le règlement d'arbitrage de la Commission des Nations Unies pour le Droit Commercial International" (1977) R.D.I.D.C. 201; J. van Hof, *Commentary on the UNCITRAL Arbitration Rules. The Application by the Iran–U.S. Claims Tribunal* (Kluwer, Deventer, 1991).

If parties opt for a national arbitration institution but did not indicate the seat of arbitration, in principle the arbitration takes place in the city where the institution has its seat.

The seat of arbitration must be carefully selected.[63] Obviously, only a town or country with the necessary infrastructure (conference rooms, interpreters, etc.) and where a meeting can be conveniently organised, will come into consideration. The arbitration can be organised in the place where the arbitration institution or an arbitrator is established, where the available evidence is located, etc. It is often not a good idea to hold arbitration hearings in the country of one of the parties—the "home" party would have a psychological advantage over the "away" party. Moreover, during the hearings, the "home" party would be able to take advantage of all services (secretariat, researchers, library), while the "away" party would have to manage with more limited resources. "Equality of arms" requires that both parties are able to act under the same circumstances; arbitration on neutral territory is therefore sometimes the best solution.

The selection of the seat of arbitration does not oblige the arbitrators to operate only in that place. Unless parties object, arbitrators may meet, hear witnesses, experts and parties, visit locations, etc., in any place they see fit. They are not even required to deliberate in the seat of the arbitration (they can also meet elsewhere or confer with each other by telephone or letter). However, the arbitrators must always state formally that the award is made at the seat of the arbitration.[64]

Legal considerations   The "seat" of arbitration is more a legal than a factual **11.23** concept. It is essential that arbitration has its seat in a country with a suitable legal system for the supervision of an arbitration procedure, since it is the proper law of the seat of arbitration that determines the validity and the effects of the arbitration agreement, the appointment of arbitrators, the basic requirements for the arbitration procedure and the binding effect of the arbitration award. It is the court of the "seat" that is competent to intervene, whenever necessary, in an arbitration procedure. Moreover, a claim to set aside the award, or declare it null and void, will be judged by the court of the seat in accordance with its local arbitration law. Arbitration must therefore have its seat in a country with a law and forum most appropriate for the particular arbitration.

The choice of the seat of arbitration imposes upon the arbitration and the award the arbitration law of the seat. Before selecting a seat for the arbitration, one should therefore thoroughly examine the arbitration law of that place. Furthermore, the seat of arbitration should be so selected that enforcement of the award is made easy. If enforcement in one of the many contracting states of the New York Convention (see paragraph 11.41) is envisaged, it makes sense to locate the seat of arbitration in another contracting state. If the award must be enforced in one of the states party to the European Convention on International Commercial Arbitration (see paragraph 11.42), the seat should preferably be in

---

[63] See, *inter alia*, K. Iwasaki, "Selection of situs: criteria and priorities" (1986) Arb.Int. 57; M. Storme and F. De Ly, (eds), *The Place of Arbitration* (Mys & Breesch, Ghent, 1993).
[64] See UNCITRAL rules, Art. 16, 4. T. Rensmann, "Wo ergehen Schiedssprüche nach dem New Yorker Übereinkommen? (Hiscox v. Outwaite)" (1991) R.I.W. 911.

another state party to this Convention.[65] If the award is likely to have to be enforced in a state that is not party to the New York Convention or European Convention, the seat of arbitration should be in a country that has a bilateral enforcement treaty with this state.

Other elements

11.24   **Number of arbitrators**   It is better not to nominate the arbitrators in the arbitration clause, because it may be that the persons named are later not prepared, or are unable, to be involved as arbitrators. Moreover, one cannot appoint in an arbitration clause the best-qualified arbitrator for a possible dispute when the nature of such a dispute is still unknown.

It makes sense, however, for the parties to determine in the arbitration clause the number of arbitrators to be appointed. It is customary to submit a dispute to one or three arbitrators, depending on the size of the claim. In many countries arbitration supposes an odd number of arbitrators. In England, on the other hand, the parties may explicitly agree to submit the dispute to two arbitrators; if they cannot agree, a third person, or "umpire", is appointed to take over the settlement.

A tribunal with three arbitrators has its advantages: the tribunal will, for instance, reach a balanced decision; the dialogue between the chairman and the party-appointed arbitrators will help the tribunal understand the argumentation of each party.

However, when only small amounts are at stake, the parties may well consider arbitration by a sole arbitrator. A single arbitrator obviously reduces the costs of arbitration and speeds up the settlement—particularly in international arbitration, where it may be difficult to get together the three arbitrators.[66] In about 40 per cent of the ICC arbitrations one arbitrator adjudicates, and about 75 per cent of CEPANI arbitrations are entrusted to one single arbitrator.

Arbitration rules[67] and laws[68] sometimes require three arbitrators when the parties have not agreed otherwise.

11.25   **Choice of language**   Parties may also decide on the language in which the arbitration is to be conducted, as there is no specific requirement that the official

---

[65] Under the European Convention, enforcement cannot be refused when the arbitrators failed to observe the procedural rules of the domestic arbitration law of the seat in so far as observance was not stipulated by the parties or imposed by the European Convention. Furthermore, the nullity of an award in one contracting state does not in itself prevent enforcement in another state, party to the European Convention.

[66] See, *e.g.* M. Rubino-Sammartano, *op. cit.* pp. 508–509, who proposes arbitration in the first instance by one arbitrator, with the possibility of an appeal—provided a security is supplied—to three arbitrators.

[67] See, *inter alia*, UNCITRAL rules, Art. 5. See, however, AAA rules, Art. 17, LCIA rules, Art. 3, 2, N.A.I. rules, Art. 12, which leave it to the institution to nominate one or three arbitrators. I.C.C. Rules Art. 8, para. 3 provides for the appointment of one arbitrator unless the parties agree otherwise.

[68] *e.g.* Belgian *Code Judiciaire*, Art. 1681, 3; UNCITRAL Model Law, Art. 10, 2. The Dutch Code of Civil Procedure (Art. 1026) leaves the court free to appoint one or three arbitrators.

language of the seat must be used. Several arbitration rules[69] specifically allow the parties to choose the language for arbitration. If no language is chosen, the arbitration generally will be conducted in the language of the contract containing the arbitration clause.

The language of the arbitration is in principle used in all written and oral submissions by the parties and for the wording of the award. Written evidence may be submitted in the original language when both parties and arbitrators understand this language. Invoices and computer print-outs which are intelligible need not be translated. If the arbitrators deem it necessary, they can at any time demand that the documents are translated.

It is best to adopt a single language for the arbitration. However, this is sometimes impossible—for instance, either because the parties are unable to agree on a common language, or because the procedure according to the law of the seat must be conducted in the local language, with which not all parties or arbitrators are familiar. In these cases the arbitration procedure must be multi-lingual, with all the expense of translation and interpreters, and the loss of time this entails. If all parties have a passive knowledge of the other party's language they may agree that each party will use their own language.

The law applicable to the dispute Parties can choose the proper law of the contract (see paragraphs 1.29–1.30). The arbitrators shall then apply the law chosen by the parties. Some arbitration rules[70] and arbitration laws[71] affirm this. The parties have much freedom to choose the applicable law in international commercial arbitration.[72] For instance they may insist that the arbitrators shall decide according to "the general principles of law" (*principes généraux de droit*),[73] according to "legal principles generally known to the parties", etc. In doing so they probably intend to refer to the *lex mercatoria*,[74] a non-national legal system that—according to some—governs international commercial trans-actions (see paragraph 1.33).

11.26

Such reference in our opinion creates some risks. Although recent research has specified the scope of a few principles of the *lex mercatoria*, the *lex mercatoria*

---

[69] *e.g.* I.C.C. Rules Art. 16; CEPANI rules, Art. 22; UNCITRAL rules, Art. 17; N.A.I. rules, Art. 40.

[70] *e.g.* ICC rules, Art. 17; UNCITRAL rules, Art. 33, 1; N.A.I. rules, Art. 46.

[71] Swiss PIL statute, Art. 187; Dutch Code of Civil Procedure, Art. 1054, 2; European Convention on International Arbitration (1961), Art. VII, 1.

[72] O. Lando, "The law applicable to the merits of the dispute" (1986) Arb.Int. 104; J. Lew, *Applicable Law in International Commercial Arbitration* (Oceana, New York, 1978); J. Chr. Pommier, "La résolution du conflit de lois en matière contractuelle en présence d'une élection de droit: le rôle de l'arbitre" (1992) J.D.I. 5.

[73] Ph. Kahn, "Les principes généraux du droit devant les arbitres du commerce international" (1989) J.D.I. 305; M. Rubino-Sammartano, "Le 'tronc commun' des lois nationales en présence" (1987) Rev.Arb. 133.

[74] G. Huphreys, "The Lex Mercatoria in international arbitration: some differences in the Anglo-French point of view" (1992) I.B.L.J. 849; P. Lagarde, "Le choix de la lex mercatoria par l'arbitre" (1990) Rev.Arb. 663; K. H. Boeckstiegel (ed.), *Rechtsforbildung durch internationale Schiedsger-ichtbarkeit* (Heymans, Cologne, 1989); F. Dasser, *Internationale Schiedsgerichte und Lex Merca-toria* (Schulthess, Zurich, 1989); J. Paulsson, "La lex mercatoria dans l'arbitrage CCI" (1990) Rev.Arb. 55; D. Rivkin, "Enforceability of arbitral awards based on the lex mercatoria" (1993) Arb.Int. 67.

still appears too vague, unclear and limited to offer a satisfactory guideline for arbitrators. Anyone opting for the *lex mercatoria* should be anxious about the free hand he leaves the arbitrators in the interpretation of the norms attributed to this *lex mercatoria*.

When no law is chosen by the parties, the arbitrators have to find the applicable law on their own.[75]

By way of exception, regardless the applicable law, other rules may be applicable on aspects not governed by the proper law of the contract. Moreover mandatory rules and public policy considerations may cross the proper law of the contract.[76]

Standard clauses

11.27   **Examples**   If the drafters of a contract do not have the necessary expertise, they would do better to incorporate one of the available ready-made arbitration clauses.[77] These clauses are mostly drafted by an arbitration institution and refer to the services of this institution. Below are reproduced the arbitration clauses recommended by ICC and UNCITRAL for submission of disputes to arbitration by the respective institutions. The text of these clauses is given in more than one language, as this could be useful in practice.

The arbitration clause of the ICC reads in English:
"All disputes arising out of or in connection with the present contract shall be finally settled under the Rules of Arbitration of the International Chamber of Commerce by one or more arbitrators appointed in accordance with the said Rules."
This clause is also available in other languages.[78]

The UNCITRAL arbitration clause reads in English:

---

[75] *e.g.* Y. Derains, "Jurisprudence of international commercial arbitration concerning the determination of the proper law of contract" (1996) I.B.L.J. 514–530; B. Wortmann, "Choice of law by arbitrators: the applicable conflict of laws system" (1998) 14 Arb.Int. 97–113.

[76] See H. Moitry, "Arbitrage international et droit de la concurrence: vers un ordre public de la lex mercatoria?" (1989) Rev.Arb. 3; Y. Derains, "Public policy and the law applicable to the dispute in international arbitration" and P. Lalive, "Transnational (or truly international) public policy and international arbitration" in *Comparative Arbitration Practice and Public Policy in Arbitration* (Kluwer, Deventer, 1987) pp. 227 and 257; P. Mayer, "Mandatory rules of law in international arbitration" (1986) Arb.Int. 274; J. Schiffer, "Sonderanknüpfung ausländischen 'öffentlichen' Rechts durch Richterrecht in der Internationale Handelsschiedsgerichtsbarkeit" (1991) IPRax 84; H. van Houtte, "La loi applicable à l'arbitrage commercial international" (1980) R.I.D.C. 285, 293–300; M. Blessing, "Mandatory rules of law versus party autonomy in international arbitration" (1997) 4 J.Int.Arb. 23; V. Schnyder, "Anwendung ausländischer Eingriffsnormen durch Schiedsgerichte", (1995) 59 RabelsZ 293–308.

[77] S. Bond, "How to draft an ICC Arbitration Clause" (1992) 7 I.C.S.I.D. Rev. 153; G. Delaume, "How to draft an I.C.S.I.D. Arbitration Clause" (1992) 7 I.C.S.I.D. Rev. 168; M. Hoellering, "How to draft an AAA Arbitration Clause" (1992) 7 I.C.S.I.D. Rev. 141.

[78] See the French, German, Arabic, Dutch, Greek, Japanese, Polish, Turkish, Russian, Vietnamese, Spanish, Bulgarian, Italian and Hungarian versions in the introductory pages of the Rules and at www.iccwbo.org.

"Any dispute, controversy or claim arising out of or relating to this contract, or the breach, termination or invalidity thereof, shall be settled by arbitration in accordance with the UNCITRAL Arbitration Rules as at present in force.

Note—Parties may wish to consider adding:

    (a) the appointing authority shall be . . . (name of institution or person);
    (b) the number of arbitrators shall be . . . (one or three);
    (c) the place of arbitration shall be . . . (town or country);
    (d) the language(s) to be used in the arbitral proceedings shall be . . . "

There is, amongst other versions, a French text of this clause.[79]

PART IV: ARBITRATION PROCEDURE[80]

Appointment of arbitrators

Procedure An arbitration tribunal generally consists of three arbitrators. **11.28**
Each of the parties appoints an arbitrator. A third arbitrator is then appointed either by the already appointed arbitrators or by a nominated arbitration institution. The nominated arbitration institution is also competent to appoint an arbitrator if one of the parties refuses to co-operate.

When only one arbitrator has to be appointed but the parties cannot agree, the arbitrator must be appointed by the nominated arbitration institution,[81] or—in the absence of one—by a court.

Choice Lawyers (*e.g.* solicitors, barristers, company lawyers, academics) or **11.29**
experts (*e.g.* engineers, software specialists, building experts) can be appointed as arbitrators.

It is often useful that the two arbitrators appointed by the parties are technical experts and that a lawyer presides over the arbitration; in this case, the two arbitrators provide the arbitration tribunal with technical expertise; the chairman makes sure that the arbitration proceedings are conducted correctly.

---

[79] "Tout litige, controverse ou réclamation né du présent contrat ou se rapportant au présent contrat ou à une contravention au présent contrat, à sa résolution ou à sa nullité, sera tranché par voie d'arbitrage conformément au Règlement d'arbitrage de la CNUDCI actuellement en vigueur.
Note—Les parties voudront peut-être ajouter les indications suivantes:
    (a) L'autorité de nomination sera . . . (nom de la personne ou de l'institution);
    (b) Le nombre d'arbitres est fixé à . . . (un ou trois);
    (c) Le lieu de l'arbitrage sera . . . (ville ou pays);
    (d) La langue (les langues) à utiliser pour la procédure d'arbitrage sera (seront) . . . ."
[80] See H. Holtzmann and G. Bernini, "Comparative arbitration practice" in *Comparative Arbitration Practice and Public Policy in Arbitration* (ICCA Congress series no. 3, Kluwer, Deventer, 1987) pp. 19 *et seq.*
[81] See ICC rules, Art. 9; UNCITRAL rules, Art. 6, 2; CEPANI rules, Art. 18, 2.

More specific considerations for the appointment of an arbitrator relate, for example, to his reputation, openness, ability to judge, nationality, professional experience, availability, etc.[82]

11.30   **Independence and impartiality of arbitrator**   The arbitrator appointed by one party is not an agent of that party: he must have an independent and impartial view.[83] If this independence and impartiality may be questioned the arbitrator must refuse or hand back the appointment. Obviously the same applies for the presiding arbitrator. Arbitrators must, in any event, inform the parties of all instances, such as conflict of interests, financial ties, professional relationships, etc., that could jeopardise their independence and impartiality.

Arbitration laws determine how arbitrators who have not the necessary independence and impartiality should be challenged and replaced.[84] In ad hoc arbitrations the courts decide on the disqualification and replacement of the arbitrators. In institutional arbitration this disqualification and replacement is carried out by the arbitration institution itself.

The courts may set aside an award made by arbitrators who afterwards prove not to have been independent and impartial.

Arrangements at the start of the arbitration proceedings[85]

Options

11.31   Parties have a wide range of options for the setting up of arbitration proceedings.[86] If they don't make full use of these options, they forfeit one of the most attractive and useful advantages of arbitration.

---

[82] See *e.g.* A. de Fina, "The party appointed arbitrator in international arbitrations—role and selection"(1999) 15 Arb.Int. 381–392.

[83] See, *inter alia*, M. Bedjaoui, "The arbitrator: one man—three roles" (1988) J.I.A. 1; S. Bond, "The selection of ICC arbitrators and the requirement of independence" (1988) Arb.Int. 300; R. Coulson, "An American critique of the IBA's ethics for international arbitrators" (1987) J.I.A. 2–103; M. Smith, "Impartiality and the party-appointed arbitrator" (1990) Arb.Int. 320; D. Bishop and L. Reed, "Practical guidelines for interviewing, selecting and challenging party appointed arbitrators in international commercial arbitration"(1998) 14 Arb.Int. 395–429..

[84] G. Aguilar Alvarez, "The challenge of Arbitrators" (1990) Arb.Int. 203; W. Tupman, "Challenge and disqualification of arbitrators in international commercial arbitration" (1989) I.C.L.Q. 26.

[85] See *e.g.* J. Sekolec, "UNCITRAL notes on organizing arbitral proceedings" (1997) 22 Y.Com.Arb. 448–475; Ph. Fouchard, "Aide-Mémoire de la CNUDCI sur l'organisation des procédures arbitrales" (1998) Rev.Arb. 273–277.

[86] Many arbitration rules state explicitly that the parties remain free to determine their own procedural rules. Although they include detailed procedural rules they are only applicable if the parties have not agreed otherwise. Other arbitration rules, on the contrary, leave little room for the will of parties. Thus, the UNCITRAL arbitration rules (Art. 15) state that the arbitrators—and not the parties—shall decide on the procedure. The CEPANI rules and AAA arbitration rules on their part include detailed provisions for the arbitration procedure. Parties who submitted to such detailed rules have in theory no freedom to draw up their own procedural rules. In practice, however, arbitrators are prepared—despite the provisions in the rules—to comply with the procedural wishes of the parties.

Agenda of arbitration Parties and arbitrators may prepare together the   **11.32**
agenda of the arbitration proceedings.

They should not merely fix the various dates for each stage in the settlement
procedure. They should also specify what should happen at each stage. If the
planning is realistic it will be a useful instruction sheet and timetable for the
parties, their lawyers and the arbitrators.

Procedural rules Parties, their lawyers and arbitrators must organise the   **11.33**
best procedure for the dispute. For instance, they can establish the manner in
which parties will present their pleadings. This is particularly useful in transnational arbitrations where the parties come from different legal backgrounds.

Indeed, in some legal systems the pleadings are rather extensive, while in
others they are more concise. In some countries the lawyers particularly empha-
sise the facts, while in other countries the legal arguments get more attention and
the facts are treated rather poorly.

The parties are free to decide how they will present their documents. Parties
could for instance agree to arrange the documents in chronological or topical
order. Headed binders seem more practical than folders with loose documents.

Arbitrators are often buried under mountains of documents, which are not all
relevant. In transnational arbitrations the parties and arbitrators often carry boxes
full of files, backwards and forwards. All these papers must be studied carefully.
This all means time, fees, copying and postage costs. It saves time and money if
the parties agree to present a common set of documents. Reference to and
working with one common set of documents is always easier for both parties and
arbitrators.

Parties may decide that there is no need for the arrangement of a hearing by
the arbitrators, but that the arbitrators must decide on the basis of documents
only. "Documents only" arbitration can be attractive in some cases. The absence
of hearings and pleadings make it easier for the parties to defend themselves
without the assistance of lawyers, thus saving time and money. In transnational
arbitrations in particular, where the parties and arbitrators live far apart and
where it is difficult to arrange meetings, the hearings and pleadings can be very
time-consuming. Besides, "documents only" arbitration is not necessarily detrimental to the party that failed to present an important argument in the pleadings
because the arbitrator ought to ask for clarification on the points which are still
unclear after the initial examination of the documents, or which require further
legal arguments.

Parties may allow the chairman of the arbitral tribunal to take urgent provisional measures, to hear experts or witnesses and to settle procedural questions
on his own without consultation with his fellow arbitrators.

An administrative secretary to assist the arbitrators may also be appointed by
the parties. This secretary takes care of administrative matters, organises hearings, keeps minutes of meetings and looks after the budget for the arbitration,
thus often reducing the administrative burden of the chairman. Particularly in ad
hoc arbitration—*i.e.* arbitration not organised by an arbitration institution—such
a secretary can prove to be of great help. However, it is incorrect to entrust the

secretary with the decision-making as the arbitrators themselves must decide the dispute.[87]

In arbitration between a Continental European and an American party, questions may arise as to discovery of documents and presentation of witness evidence.[88] Should one party be allowed to ask the other party to submit all the documents—even those that are harmful to the latter's arguments? Must witnesses be examined "à l'américaine", with cross-examination of the parties, or "à la française", with questions from the arbitrators? European lawyers and parties often shudder at the thought of cross-examination by an experienced American lawyer; Americans are generally not satisfied with polite soft questions from European arbitrators. Perhaps an early agreement between the parties can create some clarity on the ways to proceed and outline a compromise. Parties and arbitrators should envisage to adopt the Rules on the Taking of Evidence in International Commercial Arbitration (1999), published by the International Bar Association: these rules try to strike the balance between the U.S. and European approaches to evidence.[89]

11.34　**Restriction of the discussion**　The parties may agree that the arbitrators settle the various aspects of the dispute in a series of consecutive awards. This means that the parties do not have to argue the whole case straightaway, but that they can concentrate on the relevant parts—which again saves time and money. Moreover, after each interim award, it becomes easier for the parties to come to a settlement.

Arbitration law and arbitration procedure

11.35　**General**　In so far as the parties have not decided on procedural issues and have not chosen arbitration rules, the law of the place of arbitration (see paragraph 11.22) provides the procedural rules. Moreover, this arbitration law often includes mandatory procedural provisions from which the parties and arbitrators shall not deviate.[90]

If, however, arbitration takes place in one of the contracting states of the European Convention on International Commercial Arbitration, between parties established in one of these contracting states, the procedural provisions of the

---

[87] Under the ICC rules the arbitrators should ask the Court of Arbitration for permission on the appointment of such a secretary, as the arbitration rules do not provide for this function.

[88] See, *e.g.* W. Morgan, "Discovery in arbitration" (1986) J.I.A. 3–9; P. Griffin, "Recent trends in the conduct of international arbitration—discovery procedures and witness hearings" (2000) J.I.A. 19; T. H. Webster, "Obtaining documents from adverse parties in international arbitration"(2001) 50 I.C.L.Q. 345–385.

[89] See *www.ibanet.org*. Moreover M. Bühler and C. Dorgan, "Witness testimony pursuant to the 1999 IBA rules of evidence" (2000) J.I.A. 3–30.

[90] See S. Schwebel and S. Lahne, "Public policy and arbitral procedure" in *Comparative Arbitration Practice and Public Policy in Arbitration* (ICCA Series no. 3, Kluwer, Deventer, 1987), p. 205.

European Convention apply.[91] In all events, however, the arbitrators will have to supplement the few procedural principles provided by the arbitration law (or the European Convention) with their own rules.

The court of the seat of arbitration can intervene in the arbitration when something goes wrong.[92] The arbitration law of the forum provides for the manner in which this intervention has to take place.

Right to a fair trial It is essential in arbitration that every party be entitled **11.36** to due process and a fair trial.[93] The proceedings should be contradictory, whereby the arbitrators communicate to both parties together. Moreover the parties must submit to each other the documents they submit to the arbitrators. When the arbitrators rely on their own information, they must disclose to both parties this information.[94]

However, it is possible for the parties to agree that the arbitrator investigates matters in their absence. The parties may even allow the arbitrators to examine confidential documents of one party that have not been seen by the other party.

A breach of the fundamental rule of the right to a fair trial will result in the award being set aside by the court of the country where the seat of arbitration is located, and in a refusal by the authorities abroad to enforce the award.

Procedure It is common for the parties to agree on the type of evidence they **11.37** will have to submit in the arbitration proceedings. If nothing has been agreed by the parties the arbitrators will determine what evidence constitutes sufficient proof.[95]

The arbitrators can order an expert assessment, a local visit or a personal appearance. They are entitled to hear parties or witnesses and to order the parties in arbitration to submit documents. If witnesses do not appear, or refuse to swear the oath, or if a document ordered by the arbitrator is not submitted, the state court can assist the arbitrator in getting hold of the necessary evidence when the arbitration law of the seat provides for the court's intervention.

---

[91] As of February 1994, this Convention applies to arbitration between Austria, Belarus, Belgium, Bosnia-Herzegovina, Bulgaria, Burkina Faso, Croatia, Cuba, Czech Republic, Denmark, Finland, France, Germany, Hungary, Italy, Luxembourg, Macedonia, Poland, Romania, Russian Federation, Slovakia, Slovenia, Spain, Turkey, Ukraine, Yugoslavia. However, Art. IV, 2 does not apply to arbitrations between parties established in Austria, Belgium, Denmark, France, Germany, Italy and Spain (Paris Agreement of December 17, 1962). See V. Cram-Martos, "The United Nations Economic Commission for Europe and the 1961 Convention on International Commercial Arbitration" (2001) J.I.A. 137.

[92] See W. Park, "Judicial controls in the arbitral process" (1989) Arb.Int. 230; H. van Houtte, "Le juge et l'arbitre, Le rôle du juge pendant la procédure arbitrale" (1993) R.D.I.D.C. 28.

[93] See also C. Jarrosson, "L'arbitrage et la Convention européenne des droits de l'homme" (1989) Rev.Arb. 573; J. H. Moitry, "Right to a fair trial and the European Convention on Human Rights" (1989) J.I.A. 2–115.

[94] C. Reymond, "Des connaisances personnelles de l'arbitre à son information privilégiée" (1991) Rev.Arb. 3.

[95] See, *e.g.* A. Philip, "The standards and burden of proof in international arbitration" (1994) 10 Arb.Int. 317–363.

If one of the parties does not co-operate, without legitimate reasons, the arbitrator has jurisdiction to make an award by default.

11.38   **Award**   The arbitrators are required to make their award within a reasonably short period. The parties can even impose a time limit on the arbitrators. For institutional arbitration, the arbitration rules often set a time limit. However, time limits are frequently extended.[96] Sometimes, when neither the parties nor the arbitration rules have imposed a time frame, the arbitration law of the seat of arbitration fixes a time period to render the award. If this term has expired without an award being made, the arbitration law will decide whether the arbitrators still retain jurisdiction and whether an award made after expiration of the term is valid.

The arbitrators render their award collectively.[97] Their deliberations are secret.

The arbitration law of the seat prescribes what statements an award must contain.[98] In most jurisdictions the award needs to be reasoned; but under English and American arbitration law reasoning is not essential for the award's validity.[99]

PART V: RECOGNITION OR NULLITY

11.39   **Overview**   It seldom happens that the losing party refuses to honour the award. If its refusal is unfounded the award can be enforced by court order. Moreover, if the losing party has well-founded legal objections, the award may be challenged.

The purpose of arbitration is to resolve a dispute definitively and quickly. In principle, therefore, an award is not open for an appeal on the merits. Only if the parties have explicitly provided for an appeal, may the award be reconsidered on the merits by an appellate arbitral tribunal. Parties virtually never agree to an appellate arbitration procedure; as a matter of fact most arbitration rules state that the arbitration award is definite.

Challenge of the arbitral award

11.40   **Procedure**   Proceedings to challenge an award can only be brought before the court of the seat. In many legal systems the challenge of the award implies an application for the annulment or setting aside of the award.

---

[96] There is no appeal to the courts against the decision of an arbitration institution to extend the term: Belgian Cassation, December 8, 1988, (1989) R.B.D.C. 935 annotation H. van Houtte.

[97] The principle that all arbitrators must deliberate may prevent in some countries, such as Belgium, an award by two arbitrators and an "umpire", as is customary in England. See also more generally J. M. Vulliemin, *Jugement et Sentence Arbitrale: Étude de Droit International Privé et de Droit Comparé* (Chabloz, Tolochenaz, 1987).

[98] Under Belgian law, for example, the award must state the names and addresses of parties and arbitrators; short explanation of the legal position of the parties in relation to the facts and the legal requirements, date and place of the arbitration award, signatures of the arbitrators. Absence of signatures results in nullity. (Code Judiciaire, Art. 1704 para. 2, h.)

[99] J. Bingham, "Reasons and reasons for reasons" (1988) Arb.Int. 141; J. L. Devolvé, "Essai sur la motivation des sentences arbitrales" (1989) Rev.Arb. 149.

The scope for challenging an award is generally limited. Grounds for challenge include, for instance, an invalid arbitration agreement, violation of the rights of the defence, an *ultra petita* award of the arbitrators (*i.e.* the arbitrators awarded more than was asked for), or an award that is contrary to public order.

Under most arbitration laws the award cannot be challenged merely because the arbitrators made the wrong analysis of the facts or incorrectly applied the law (the substantive control over the arbitral award is then only restricted to the public policy test).[1]

The specific grounds for challenge, the time limits for challenge and other procedural details must be carefully examined in the relevant legal system.

Exclusion of annulment proceedings Some countries have restricted even   **11.41**
further the scope for challenging an international commercial award. In Switzerland, Belgium and Sweden the parties may agree in advance to exclude any possibility of annulment, if none of the parties is a domestic entity.[2]

Enforcement

Voluntary execution Parties are bound by the arbitral award (unless the   **11.42**
award has been annulled). Many arbitration rules state this explicitly. Most often the losing party honours the arbitral award voluntarily. There is frequently social and commercial pressure from the commercial sector to abide by the arbitration award: an enterprise known for defaulting on arbitral awards looses credibility. However, whenever necessary, the arbitral award can be enforced through a court order. The arbitration award can also be the basis to attach the assets of the reluctant party.

Enforcement in the country of the seat An award may sometimes have to   **11.43**
be enforced in the country of origin, *i.e.* in the country where the seat of arbitration is. The award then needs to receive leave of the court to be enforced or to be ratified by the court for enforcement (*exequatur*). Through the *exequatur* the court grants the arbitral award the same status as a judicial decision: the arbitral award can be enforced in the same way as a court order. The court will only grant an *exequatur* or grant leave for enforcement after examining the arbitral procedure and the award. This examination is in most countries rather basic; in some countries it is more thorough.

In international commercial arbitration, the seat is usually in a neutral place, that is to say in a country different from that of the parties. In that case, probably there will be no assets from the losing party in the country of the seat of arbitration so that the award has to be enforced elsewhere, *e.g.* in the country where the losing party is established.

---

[1] In Belgium, for instance, an award "ex aequo et bono" made by arbitrators without competence hereto could be annulled because the arbitrators exceeded their jurisdiction (see para. 11.10).
[2] Swiss PIL statute, Art. 192; *Code judiciaire belge*, Art. 1717, para 4; Swedish Arbitration Act 1999, Art. 51.

11.44   **Enforcement outside the seat of arbitration—New York Convention**   Enforcement of an award in another country than that of the seat is generally regulated by international treaties.

The most important treaty in this respect is the New York Convention (1958) on the Enforcement of Foreign Arbitral Awards, in force between about 130 states.[3] Some of these countries apply the Convention only when the award is made in a state that is also a signatory to the Convention; other states apply the Convention to the enforcement of any foreign award, no matter where the award was made.

The New York Convention considerably facilitates the enforcement of the award. Anyone seeking enforcement only needs to submit the arbitration agreement and the award. It is for the defendant to show that the award cannot be confirmed by the court. Reasons for refusal to confirm can be: incapacity of a party (see paragraph 11.10), invalidity of the arbitration agreement (see paragraph 11.05), defective information on the appointment of arbitrators and the start of the proceedings (see paragraph 11.33), non-arbitrability of the dispute according to the law applicable to the arbitration agreement, or according to the law of the seat (see paragraph 11.08). The award may never decide more than that which has been agreed in the arbitration agreement (see paragraph 11.37). What the parties have agreed on concerning the appointment of arbitrators and the arbitration procedure must have been respected. Furthermore, the court may refuse to confirm an award if the dispute is not arbitrable according to the law of the forum. Confirmation of the award can also be denied if the award is contrary to public policy.[4]

The New York Convention does not require a double *exequatur*: the award does not need an *exequatur* from a court in the country of the seat before an *exequatur* in the country of enforcement can be obtained. As a matter of logic,

---

[3] Parties to the New York Convention, as of July 1, 1994 were: Albania*,Algeria*, American Samoa*, Antigua and Barbuda*, Argentina*, Armenia*,Australia, Austria, Azerbaijan, Bahrain*, Bangladesh, Barbados, Belarus*, Belgium*, Belize*, Benin, Bermuda*, Bolivia, Bosnia-Herzegovina, Botswana*, Brunei*, Bulgaria*, Burkina Faso, Cambodia, Cameroon, Canada, Canton Islands*, Cayman Islands*, Central African Republic*, Chile, China*, Colombia, Comoro Islands*, Costa Rica, Côte d'Ivoire, Croatia*, Cuba*, Cyprus*, Czech Republic*, Denmark*, Djibouti, Dominica, Ecuador*, Egypt, El Salvador, Estonia, Finland, France*, Georgia, Germany*, Ghana, Gibraltar*, Greece*, Guatamala*, Guinea, Haiti, Holy See*, Hong Kong*, Honduras, Hungary*, India*, Indonesia*, Ireland*, Israel, Italy, Japan*, Jordan, Kazakhstan, Kenya, Korea*, Kuwait*, Kyrgyztan, Laos, Latvia, Lebanon*, Lesotho, Luxembourg*, Macedonia, Madagascar*, Malaysia*, Mali, Malta, Mauritania, Mauritius*, Mexico, Moldova*, Monaco*, Mongolia*,Morocco*, Mozambique*, Nepal*, the Netherlands*, New Zealand*, Niger, Nigeria*, Norway*, Oman, Pakistan, Panama, Paraguay, Peru, Philippines*, Poland*, Portugal, Puerto Rico*, Romania*, Russian Federation*, Saint Vincent and the Grenadines*, San Marino, Saudi Arabia, Senegal, Singapore*, Slovak Republic, Slovenia*, South Africa, Spain, Sri Lanka, Surinam*, Sweden, Switzerland*, Syria, Tanzania*, Thailand, Trinidad and Tobago*, Tunisia*, Turkey*, Uganda*, Ukraine*, Uruguay, U.S.*, U.K.*, Uzbekistan, Venezuela*, Vietnam*,Yugoslavia* and Zimbabwe.
See for an excellent , although outdated commentary on this Convention, A. J. van den Berg, *The New York Arbitration Convention of 1958* (Kluwer, Deventer, 1981). Recent jurisprudence in this respect can be found in Y.Com.Arb. The asterisked countries restrict the operation of the Convention contracting states.
[4] Chr. Kuner, "The public policy exception to the enforcement of foreign arbitral awards in the United States and West Germany under the New York Convention" (1990) J.I.A. 4–71.

if the award has been set aside in the country of the seat (see paragraph 11.37), the award should not receive an *exequatur* elsewhere; however, it is possible under the New York Convention to enforce an award that has been set aside in its country of origin.[5]

Other conventions The European Convention on International Commercial **11.45** Arbitration (1961) simplifies the enforcement of arbitration awards between about 20 countries.[6] An award made in one of these countries may be enforced in another contracting state, sometimes even if it has been annulled in the country of origin.[7]

The Inter-American Convention on International Commercial Arbitration ("the Panama Convention") provides for the reciprocal enforcement of awards on the American continent.[8]

Some bilateral treaties may be relevant for enforcement, either because there is no applicable multilateral convention, or because the bilateral treaty is more favourable. The criteria for enforcement are in many bilateral conventions less detailed than in the New York or European Conventions. These bilateral treaties, however, often require a double *exequatur* for enforcement, *i.e.* an *exequatur* order in the country of origin and an *exequatur* order in the country where the award must be enforced.

Domestic law When no enforcement convention applies, a title for enforce- **11.46** ment has to be sought under the domestic law. Moreover, national law may be useful in countries where the arbitration statute is less stringent than the New York Convention.[9]

PART VI: ADVANTAGES AND DISADVANTAGES OF ARBITRATION

Advantages

Informal settlement The arbitration proceedings are less formal than court **11.47** proceedings. The procedural rules are often established in agreement between the parties (see paragraph 11.02). Arbitrators and lawyers do not wear gowns. Parties' counsel does not plead from the bench like barristers in court; on the

---

[5] See, *e.g.*, Ph. Fouchard, "La portée internationale de l'annulation de la sentence dans son pays d'origine"(1997) Rev.Arb. pp. 329; D. H. Freyer, "Finality and enforceability of foreign arbitral awards: from the double exequatur to the enforcement of annulled awards"(1998) I.C.S.I.D. Rev. 101–123; E. Gaillard, "L'exécution des sentences annulées dans leur pays d'origine" (1998) 125 J.D.I. 645–674; *ibid.* "The enforcement of awards set aside in the country of origin" (1999) 14 I.C.S.I.D. Rev. 16–45.
[6] See para. 10.32.
[7] See European Convention, Art. IX.
[8] For the text of the convention, see (1975) 14 I.L.M. 336. Chile, Columbia, Costa Rica, Ecuador, El Salvador, Guatemala, Honduras, Mexico, Panama, Paraguay, Peru, Uruguay, Venezuela and the U.S. have ratified the Convention. Some but not all of these states are also party to the New York Convention: see A. J. van den Berg, "The New York Convention 1958 and Panama Convention 1975; redundancy or compatibility?" (1989) Arb.Int. 214.
[9] New York Convention, Art. VII.

contrary, arbitrators, lawyers and parties often sit around one big conference table. In court, it is the lawyers who speak in the formal pleadings; in arbitration, statements from counsel and even from parties themselves alternate with discussions with the tribunal. The arbitrators make all efforts to maintain an informal climate.

The informal atmosphere enhances the chance of an amicable settlement. After the parties have put across their arguments and documents, there is a better understanding of each other's legal position, what may lead to a settlement of their dispute. The parties may then request the arbitrators to make an agreed arbitral award along the lines of their amicable settlement.

11.48   **Speedy settlement**   Court proceedings may take a long time. It may take months—sometimes years—before a case can be brought before a court. A hearing is generally more quickly arranged in arbitration proceedings. If the arbitrators make it clear to the parties that they understand the essence of the dispute the parties don't need to repeat their arguments but can direct their attention specifically to the points which are still unclear to the arbitrators, thus saving time and money. The informal atmosphere of arbitration moreover allows the arbitrators and the parties to discuss the case more freely so that the possibilities of a settlement can be better explored.

Although on occasion some time may be lost in the appointment of arbitrators when the opposing party does not appoint its arbitrator, this lack of co-operation does not greatly delay the proceedings. The arbitrator will then be appointed by a court or an arbitration institution (see paragraph 11.28).

In arbitration there is furthermore no risk that the losing party will file an appeal and thus delay the enforcement of the decision. In principle, arbitration only has one instance, so that no time can be lost in appeal procedures

11.49   **Settlement by experts**   The courts usually have sufficient general expertise to settle commercial disputes. However, some disputes require extensive technical knowledge. It is impossible for a judge who has to adjudicate all kinds of disputes to be an all-round technical expert. The judge may of course consider the appointment of an expert, though the intervention of the expert takes time and adds to the costs. It can therefore be better to give the expert the task of adjudicating the dispute directly, *i.e.* appoint him as an arbitrator sufficiently familiar with the technical and commercial background of the dispute so that no further expert will be needed.

Disputes are sometimes rooted in a particular environment. They can therefore only be solved in the light of the practices of that environment, with which judges may be less familiar. This is why traders ask colleagues with knowledge of the same sector to settle their disputes.

11.50   **Confidential settlement**   Court proceedings are public. This publicity of the court is not always convenient: a competitor may draw confidential information from the court room; newspapers may give the dispute unnecessary publicity, etc. Businessmen who desire a confidential settlement may opt for arbitration because, in principle, arbitration is not public: only the parties and their advisers have access to the meetings, the arbitrators are bound to secrecy and the award can only be published with the consent of the parties.[10]

The confidentiality of arbitration, however, is under threat when the arbitral award is later discussed in court in annulment or enforcement proceedings. The dispute and the award then become public (though this risk is not as great as it seems since barely ever is arbitration followed by a judicial procedure). However, discussion in court is restricted to some—usually procedural—aspects of the arbitration and the merits of the case are generally not at issue.

International settlement　Arbitration is often the only way to settle an **11.51** international commercial dispute. Each of the parties may refuse to submit to the jurisdiction of a court in the country of the other party, for fear of being at a disadvantage. Arbitration in a third country offers the solution.

The parties can indicate the law the arbitrators have to apply to the dispute. This can be the law of one of them, or the law of a third state. The experienced international lawyers who generally are chosen as arbitrators, have generally the capacity to find out the relevant rules.

It is said that arbitrators in international arbitration are not bound by a specific legal system, but that they may base their findings also on "equity", "general principles of law", or *lex mercatoria* (see paragraph 11.26). However, this terminology can leave the arbitrators a large degree of discretion. It therefore seems better for parties to submit an international commercial contract to a specific national legal system. As the arbitrators must then, in principle, apply that law (see paragraph 11.26), a great source of uncertainty is avoided.

The arbitration proceedings need not be conducted in the language of the seat. They can be held in any language chosen by the parties. The proceedings may even be conducted in more than one language, if necessary with the assistance of simultaneous translation.

Enforcement abroad　An award, on the other hand, is generally easier to **11.52** enforce abroad than a court decision: The New York Convention on the recognition and enforcement of foreign arbitration awards (1958) facilitates enforcement in some 130 countries (see paragraph 11.44). Additionally, the European Convention on International Commercial Arbitration, applicable between 20 countries, and bilateral conventions, may make enforcement even easier (see paragraph 11.45).

When no convention applies, the enforcement of a foreign court decision may be cumbersome. Some countries request that the whole case is argued again before the court of enforcement.

Disadvantages

Costs　Court procedures are likely to cost less than arbitration. Judges are in **11.53** the employment of the State; their decisions are a public service. Parties do not

---

[10] See H. Bagner, "Confidentiality—a fundamental principle of international commercial arbitration" (2001) J.A.I. 243–249.

have to pay the judges. The costs of judicial proceedings are limited to the summons, the listing of the case, court fees and registration taxes.

Arbitration is usually more expensive since parties generally have to pay the arbitrators for their services. They can be paid on a time basis, *i.e.* for the time spent (the general rule in Anglo-American arbitration). They also can be compensated on the basis of the amount in dispute (more common in ICC arbitration).[11]

Yet, the relatively higher costs of arbitration proceedings are partly compensated by the speed and informal character of the proceedings, which—in turn—reduce the lawyers' fees. Moreover, the parties can defend their case without a lawyer.[12] Arbitration costs are further reduced by the opportunity for an amicable settlement and the appointment of expert arbitrators.[13] Finally, unlike for judicial decisions, registration costs are often not required for arbitration awards.

11.54   **Judicial confirmation**   Arbitration only works efficiently when the arbitrators actually solve a dispute. Arbitration awards are generally executed voluntarily.[14] However, there is always a risk that a losing party refuses to abide or applies for nullity of the arbitral award so that a court procedure must decide on the enforcement or the annulment of the award. Generally, however, enforcement or annulment proceedings have a limited scope; courts only examine the award and the proceedings to a limited extent (see paragraph 11.37). Consequently judicial annulment or enforcement proceedings do not greatly hinder arbitration.

11.55   **Arbitration only binds parties**   The basis for arbitration is an agreement between parties; the award does not bind third parties.

However, parties, who are not party to the original arbitration clause, may be bound by the arbitration clause (for instance, as a result of a third party clause, assignment of the agreement or take-over of the business of the original party).[15] Thus, the holder of a bill of lading, for instance, may be bound by an arbitration clause, signed by the sender and the carrier.[16] It is also conceivable that enterprises in a group are bound by an arbitration clause signed by one company of the group when these enterprises have given effect to the contract containing the

---

[11] Parties therefore should not exaggerate their claim in ICC arbitration and thereby avoid excessive fees for the arbitrators. For small disputes the cost of arbitration is nevertheless relatively expensive. To reduce costs small claims should not be submitted to three arbitrators.

[12] It is usually better that the arguments are presented by lawyers who maintain a certain distance and objectivity in relation to their client. However, in arbitration by professional bodies (see paragraph 11.18), parties sometimes defend their own case without the assistance of legal counsel.

[13] See P. Karrer, "Arbitration saves!" (1986) J.I.A. 1–35; K. Wilson, "Saving costs in international arbitration" (1990) Arb.Int. 151.

[14] According to reports, 90% of ICC awards are honoured by the losing party without any problems: P. Neill, "Confidentiality in Arbitration"(1996) 12 Arb.Int. 287–317.

[15] See P. Delebecque, "La transmission de la clause compromissoire" (1991) Rev.Arb. 19; D. Girsberger and C. Hausmahinger, "Assignment of rights and agreements to arbitrate" (1992) Arb.Int. 121; J. L. Goutal, "Stipulation pour autrui et arbitrage" (1987) Rev.Arb. 139; J. L. Goutal, "L'arbitrage et le tiers—le droit des contrats" (1988) Rev.Arb. 439.

[16] J. L. Goutal, "La clause compromissoire dans les connaissements" (1996) Rev.Arb. 605.

clause.[17] Moreover, third parties (*inter alia*, banks, export insurance companies) may be contractually bound to recognise the arbitration award against their client as a matter that influences their contractual obligations. In this scenario the third party will often participate in the arbitration behind the scenes, since their money will be ultimately affected.[18]

Requests for third party intervention or for consolidation of related arbitration proceedings can only be entertained if all parties agreed to multi-party arbitration.[19]

In order to allow consolidation, parties to related contracts should include the same arbitration clause in which all parties agree to submit to the same arbitration proceedings and in which the appointment of the arbitrators is left to the same arbitration institution. In a multi-party arbitration between the owner, the contractor and the subcontractor, the same award will then bind owner as well as main contractor and subcontractor, thereby avoiding conflicting decisions.[20]

---

[17] See A. Chapelle, "L'arbitrage et les tiers—le droit des personnes morales" (1988) Rev.Arb. 475; D. Cohen, "Arbitrage et groupe de contrats", (1997) Rev.Arb. 471; S. Jarvin, "La validité de la clause arbitrale *vis-à-vis* de tiers non signataires—examen de la doctrine de groupe de sociétés dans l'arbitrage CCI"(1995) I.B.L.J. 729–737.

[18] See B. Chambreuil, "Arbitrage international et garanties bancaires" (1991) Rev.Arb. 33; B. Hanotiau, "Arbitration and bank guarantees" (1999) 2 J.I.A. 15–24.

[19] See, *inter alia*, M. Bartels, "Multi-party arbitration clauses" (1985) J.I.A. 2–61; J. Chiu, "Consolidation of arbitral proceedings and international commercial arbitration" (1990) J.I.A. 2–53; J. L. Devolvé, "La clause d'arbitrage multipartite" (1988) Rev.Arb. 501; I. Dore, *Theory and Practice of Multi-party Commercial Arbitration with Special Reference to the UNCITRAL Framework* (Graham, London, 1990); A. Kassis, "Multi-party arbitration and consolidation clauses" (1988) 14 D.P.C.I. 221; T. Laugier, "Multi-party arbitration and national laws" (1989) I.B.L.J. 985; J. Rubellin-Devichi, "De l'effectivité de la clause compromissoire en cas de pluralité de défendeurs ou d'appel en garantie" (1981) Rev.Arb. 29; D. Thompson, "The same tribunal for different arbitrations" (1987) J.I.A. 2–111; J. van Compernolle, "L'arbitrage multipartite", in *L'Arbitrage- Travaux offerts au professeur A. Fettweis* (Story-Scientia, Brussels, 1989) 81; H. van Houtte, "The rights of defence in multi-party arbitration" (1989) I.C.L.R. 395; *ibid.*, *Multiparty Arbitration* (ICC, Paris, 1991); V. Veeder, "Multi-party disputes: consolidation under English law" (1986) Arb.Int. 310.

[20] See M. Dubisson, "Arbitration in subcontracts for international projects" (1984) 3 J.I.A. 197.

INDEX